Education Law
Text, Cases and Materials

D0863455

Education Law
Text, Cases and Materials

Anne Ruff LLB, LLM, CERT ED (TECH)

Barrister-at-Law
Principal Lecturer in Law, Law Academic Group,
Middlesex University

Butterworths
LexisNexis™

Members of the LexisNexis Group worldwide

United Kingdom	LexisNexis Butterworths Tolley, a Division of Reed Elsevier (UK) Ltd, Halsbury House, 35 Chancery Lane, LONDON, WC2A 1EL, and 4 Hill Street, EDINBURGH EH2 3JZ
Argentina	LexisNexis Argentina, BUENOS AIRES
Australia	LexisNexis Butterworths, CHATSWOOD, New South Wales
Austria	LexisNexis Verlag ARD Orac GmbH & Co KG, VIENNA
Canada	LexisNexis Butterworths, MARKHAM, Ontario
Chile	LexisNexis Chile Ltda, SANTIAGO DE CHILE
Czech Republic	Nakladatelství Orac sro, PRAGUE
France	Editions du Juris-Classeur SA, PARIS
Hong Kong	LexisNexis Butterworths, HONG KONG
Hungary	HVG-Orac, BUDAPEST
India	LexisNexis Butterworths, NEW DELHI
Ireland	Butterworths (Ireland) Ltd, DUBLIN
Italy	Giuffrè Editore, MILAN
Malaysia	Malayan Law Journal Sdn Bhd, KUALA LUMPUR
New Zealand	Butterworths of New Zealand, WELLINGTON
Poland	Wydawnictwo Prawnicze LexisNexis, WARSAW
Singapore	LexisNexis Butterworths, SINGAPORE
South Africa	Butterworths SA, DURBAN
Switzerland	Stämpfli Verlag AG, BERNE
USA	LexisNexis, DAYTON, Ohio

© Reed Elsevier (UK) Ltd 2002

All rights reserved. No part of this publication may be reproduced in any material form (including photocopying or storing it in any medium by electronic means and whether or not transiently or incidentally to some other use of this publication) without the written permission of the copyright owner except in accordance with the provisions of the Copyright, Designs and Patents Act 1988 or under the terms of a licence issued by the Copyright Licensing Agency Ltd, 90 Tottenham Court Road, London, England W1P 0LP. Applications for the copyright owner's written permission to reproduce any part of this publication should be addressed to the publisher.

Warning: The doing of an unauthorised act in relation to a copyright work may result in both a civil claim for damages and criminal prosecution.

Crown copyright material is reproduced with the permission of the Controller of HMSO and the Queen's Printer for Scotland. Any European material in this work which has been reproduced from EUR-lex, the official European Communities legislation website, is European Communities copyright.

A CIP Catalogue record for this book is available from the British Library.

ISBN 0 406 92407 4

Printed and bound in Great Britain by Hobbs the Printers Ltd, Totton, Hampshire

Visit Butterworths LexisNexis *direct* at www.butterworths.com

Preface

Education law has become a topical and dynamic subject, and is likely to remain so for the foreseeable future. It is particularly well suited for the undergraduate and postgraduate law curriculum. Education law cuts across traditional teaching boundaries, and is influenced by work in other academic disciplines. It draws upon its roots in administrative law, yet elements of the law of tort, child law, discrimination law, and human rights legislation are of crucial importance. The values that underpin education law are derived from international as well as domestic law.

Education law is a specialist area of law for practitioners. It is of particular relevance to parents, pupils, students, school governors, teachers, and local education authorities. There has been a dramatic increase in education legislation and litigation by parents and students in the last 20 years, which reflects the influence of consumerism and human rights on this area of law. Parents and students, and to a lesser degree pupils, have acquired more effective legal rights and remedies.

This book examines education law from the perspective of the parent, pupil or student. It is written primarily for law students, but I hope that it may also prove useful for education students who study law as part of their degree programme or teacher training course.

The aim of this book is three-fold. First, the book attempts to enable students to understand how education law operates in practice by demonstrating the relationship between primary and secondary legislation, government guidance and case law, and by illustrating how different areas of English law, including human rights law, relate to each other in this context. Second, the book attempts to encourage students to analyse and question the law as well as to undertake further independent research into legal and educational issues. Third, the book identifies and examines current issues in education law, and on occasion compares the position in other legal systems.

The legal position in England and Wales has been covered, although with devolution there are an increasing number of differences between England and Wales, the most important of which have been noted. I have endeavoured to state the law as it stood at the end of December 2001, and have included brief references to the Education Bill currently before Parliament.

This book would not have been written without the inspiration, support, patience and forbearance of many people; to them all much thanks. I would particularly like to express my gratitude to Nigel Giffin, Professor Malcolm Leder, and Professor Neville Harris, as well as colleagues at Middlesex University and ACE (Advisory Centre for Education), together with the editorial staff at Butterworths, and last but by no means least my husband Chris, and my three sons Oliver, Nicholas and Simon.

Anne Ruff

January 2002

Acknowledgments

Extracts from the following publications have been reproduced in this book. The author and publisher would like to thank those from whom copyright permission has been sought.

Jordan Publishing Ltd:

Various reports from Education Law Reports
Various reports from Family law
Bijsterveld, Sophie van and Mouwen, Kees: ' The Hybrid University as a Concept for the Future' (2001) Education Law Journal 26
Birtwistle, Tim: 'Should Multiple Systems for Academic Appeals Remain? The Role of the Visitor' (2000) Education Law Journal 135
Blair, Anne: 'Home-School Agreements: A Legislative Framework for Soft Control of Parents' (2001) Education Law Journal 79
Hamilton, Carolyn and Watt, B: 'A discrimination education collective worship in schools' (1996) Child and Family Law Quarterly (1)
Harris, Neville: 'Special Educational Needs and Access to Justice' (1997)
Hussain, Amjad and Boardman, John: 'Governance in Further Education A Road to Failure paved with Good Intentions' (2000) Education Law Journal 60
Lewis Brooke, Tom: 'The Future of Partial Selection: Issues Raised by R v Downes ex p Wandsworth London Borough Council (2000) Education Law Journal 159
Lowe, Nigel and Murch, Mervyn: 'Children's participation in the family justice system-translating principles into practice' (2001) 13 (2) Child and Family Law Quarterly 137

Times Publishing Company:

Various reports from The Times Law Reports

Sweet & Maxwell:

Various reports from Local Government Law Reports
Various reports from the Crown Office Digest
Various reports from the European Human Rights Reports
Current Law: CO/2469/96 1996
Black-Branch, Dr Jonathon L: 'Equality, non-discrimination and the right to special education: from international law to the Human Rights Act' (2000) EHRLR
Bradley, Anthony: 'Scope for Review: The Convention Right to Education and the Human Rights Act 1998' (1999) EHRLR 395
Fortin, Jane: 'Rights brought home for children' (1999) 62 Modern Law Review 350
Harris, Neville; 'Law and Education: Regulation, Consumerism and the Education System' (1993)
Lonbay, Julian: 'Education and the Law: The Community Context' (1989) 14 European Law Review 363

The Audit Commission:

Trading Places – The Supply and Allocation of School Places, the Audit Commission (1996)

Utrecht:

Coomans, Fons: ' Identifying Violations of the Right to Education, ' Ch 6 The Maastricht Guidelines on Violations of Economic, Social and Cultural Rights (Proceedings of the Workshop of Experts 22-26 January 1997, ed Theo C van Boven, Cees Flintermann and Ingrid Westendorp) (1998)

Pearson Professional Limited:

Rabinowicz, Widdrington and Nicholas; 'Education: Law and Practice' (1996)

Kluwer Academic Publishers:

Harris, Neville: 'The Three 'Rs' – Rights, Remedies and Regulation' XX(1) (1998) The Liverpool Law Review 7
Meredith, Paul: 'The Fall and Rise of Local Education Authorities' XX(1) (1998) Liverpool Law Review 41

Carfax Publishing Limited:

Berman et al: 'Educational Negligence' (2001) 13 (1) Education and the Law

Blair, Ann: 'Rights, duties, and resources: the case of special educational needs' (2000) 12 (3) Education and the Law 1777

Bradney, A: 'Christian Worship' (1996) 8 (2) Education and the Law

Davis, Martin: 'Students, Academic Institutions and Contracts – a ticking time bomb (2001) 13 (1) Education and the Law 9

Furniss, Clare: 'Bullying in Schools: it's not a crime-is it? (2000) 12 (1) Education and the Law

Greenwold, Jonathon: 'Lawyers in the Classroom: the new law of educational negligence' (2000) 12 (4) Education and the Law 245

Hocking, Stephen: 'Further Education, learning difficulties and the law' (1997) 9 (1) Education and the Law 13

Johnson, Jane: 'The Learning and Skills Act 2000: impact and change for further education' (2000) 12 (4) Education and the Law 259

Kaye, Tim: 'Academic Judgement, the university Visitor and the Human Rights Act 1998 (1999) 11 (3) Education and the Law 165

Kaye, Tim: 'Admissions to school: efficiency versus parental choice?' (1998) 10 Education and the Law 19

Khan: 'Canadian Education Authorities Duty to Make Reasonable Accommodation for Religious Belief' (1997) Education and the Law

Meredith, Paul: ' Editorial Comment: the child's right to education' (2001) 13 (1) Education and the Law 5

Meredith, Paul: 'The Contracting out of LEA functions and the implications for democracy and accountability' (2000) 12 (1) Education and the Law 5

Palfreyman, David: 'The HEI-student legal relationship, with special reference to the USA experience' (1999) 11 (1) Education and the Law 5

Rains, Robert E. 'A Primer on special education law in the United States – Part 3: remedies for misdiagnosis or misplacement of special education students' (1998) 10 (4) Education and the law

Robinson, Anthony: 'European Community nationals and their right to receive education in the member state of their choice' (1998) 10 (2-3) Education and the Law

Ruff, Anne: 'Admission appeals in 1999: the impact of the 1998 Regulations and *R v Birmingham City Council ex parte M* 1998' (1999) 11 Education and the Law 77

Russo and Mawdsley: 'Update on Conflicting 1st Amendment' (2000) Education and the Law

Stewart, Douglas J and Russo, Charles J: 'A comparative analysis of funding non-government schools in Australia and the United States' (2001) 13 (1) Education and the Law 29

Handelshøjskolens Forlong:

Neilsen, Ruth and Szyszczak, Erica: 'The Social Dimension of the EU' (1997)

Lord Chancellors Department:

Leggatt, Sir Andrew: 'Tribunals for ?Users One System, One Service, ' Report of the Review of Tribunals March 2001

Routledge Limited:

Hopkins, N: 'Education and the children of migrant workers: once a child always a child', Journal of Social Welfare and Family Law 114

RoutledgeFalmer (A Member of the Taylor & Francis Group):

Harris, Neville and Eden, Karen: 'Challenges to School Exclusion' (2000)

Incorporated Council of Law Reporting:

Various reports from Weekly Law Reports
Various reports from Queens Bench
Various reports from Appeal Cases

Superintendent of Documents, US Government Printing Office:

Various reports from the United States Reports

Department for Education and Skills:

Bullying – don't suffer in silence – an anti-bullying pack for schools DFEE non-statutory guidance 62/2000
DES Circular 1/89 (Education Reform Act 1988: Local Arrangements for the Consideration of Complaints).
DFE Circular 1/94 (Religious Education and Collective Worship)
DFEE Circular 10/98) Section 550A of the Education Act 1996: the use of force to control or restrain pupils)

DFEE Circular 10/99 (Social inclusion: pupil support)
DFEE Circular 6/97 (careers, Education and Guidance in Further Education Colleges)
DFEE Circular 9/99 (Organisation of School Places)
DFEE Guidance 00116/2000 (Sex and Relationships Education)
DFEE Press Notice 2000/0291
Framework for the Organisation of Schools – Technical Consultation Paper
Quinquennial Review of the Special Educational Needs Tribunal (SENT) (August 2000)
SENT Annual Report 99/00
SFR 20/2001: Permanent exclusions from schools and exclusions appeals England
SFR 27/2001: Admission appeals for maintained Primary and Secondary Schools in England 1999/00

Centre for Educational Research, London School of Economics and Political Science, Clare Market Papers no 9):

Pennell, Hazel and West, Anne: 'Changing Schools' admissions policies in inner London in 1995

Middlesex University:

Ruff, Anne with Dorn, Andrew: 'Parental perceptions of the school admissions appeal process in the London borough of Haringey, Summer 1999' (2000)

Advisory Centre for Education (ACE) Ltd:

Sallis, Joan 'Making Nonsense of Parental Choice' ACE Bulletin 83 (June 1998)

The Children's Society:

Hayden, Carol and Dunne, Simon: 'Outside looking in: children's and families' experiences of exclusion from school (2001)

QCA Publications:

Analysis of SACRE Reports SCAA RE/97/836

SLS Legal Publications (NI):

Lundy, Laura: 'Education Law, Policy and Practice in Northern Ireland' (2000)

Local Government Ombudsman:

Local Government Ombudsman Annual Report 1999/2000)
Report on an Investigation into Complaint No 99/C/2819
Report on an Investigation into Complaint No 00/A/09964
Report on an Investigation into Complaint No 00/B/03593
Report on an Investigation into Complaint No 00/C/05614
Report on an Investigation into Complaint No 98/C/5219
Report on an Investigation into Complaint No 99/A/01723
Report on an Investigation into Complaint No 99/B/00959
Report on an Investigation into Complaint No 99/B/4658
Report on an Investigation into Complaint No 99/C/1864
Report on an Investigation into Complaint No 99/C/4255
Report on an Investigation into Complaint No 99/B/04029 and 00/B/17234

Contents

Preface   v
Acknowledgments   vii
Table of statutes   xvii
Table of cases   xxvii

CHAPTER 1

Introduction   1

1.   Background   2
2.   The legal context   31
3.   Equal opportunities   37
4.   The Human Rights Act 1998   43

CHAPTER 2

Organisation of education (nursery, primary, secondary, further and higher)   59

1.   Introduction   59
2.   Nursery education and childcare   62
3.   Schools   64
4.   Management of maintained schools   74
5.   School organisation in a local education authority   105
6.   Further education and sixth form colleges   120
7.   Higher education   132

Chapter 3

School admissions 153

1. Introduction 153
2. Local education authorities' duties 154
3. Admissions arrangements 171
4. Rights of parents 212
5. Duties of parents 252
6. Alternatives to parental preference 258

Chapter 4

School discipline and exclusions 261

1. Introduction 261
2. School discipline 262
3. Detention 276
4. Corporal punishment and physical force 277
5. Exclusions and reinstatement 285

Chapter 5

Special educational needs 315

1. Introduction 315
2. Definitions 318
3. Role of the LEA 328
4. Role of the governing body 341
5. Identification and assessment of special educational needs 345
6. Statement of SEN 351
7. Appeals and reviews 365
8. The future of SENT 368
9. Young adults with special needs 373
10. Disabled pupils and young persons 379
11. Disability Discrimination Act 1995 380
12. Tortious liability of LEA for failure to diagnose and/or remedy child's special educational needs 388
13. Human rights 401

Chapter 6

The school curriculum 407

1. Introduction 407
2. The basic curriculum 408

3. The national curriculum 414
4. Assessment arrangements 418
5. Charging 427
6. Religion in schools 439
7. Sex and relationship education 467
8. Careers education and guidance 475
9. Religious and philosophical values in the school curriculum 479
10. Complaints about the curriculum 481

CHAPTER 7

The quality of educational provision 487

1. Maintained schools 488
2. Local education authorities 519
3. Further education 521
4. Higher education 524
5. Common law liability 526
6. Tort of negligence 526
7. Breach of contract 533

CHAPTER 8

Complaints procedures 535

1. Maintained schools 536
2. Further education institutions 572
3. Universities 573

Index 613

Table of statutes

References on the right hand side of the column are to page numbers.
Those page numbers in **bold** indicate where an Act is set out in part or in full.

PAGE

Children Act 1989 . 25, 32, 63, 74, 315, 325,
    337, 351, 366, ... 369
s 1(2) 27
  2(9) 273
  3(1) 273
  (5) **273**
  17 .... 63, 319, 337, 339
    (1) 32, **337**
    (2) **338**
    (8) **338**
    (10) **64**, **338**
    (11) **338**
  18 339
    (1) 64
      (a) **63**
      (b) **64**
    (2) 64
    (4) 63
    (5) 74
    (6) **74**
  19 64
  20 339
  23(3) 24
  36 32
  324 366
  Sch 2
     para 3 351
        8 339
  Sch 3 32
  Sch 13
     para 10 24
Chronically Sick and Disabled Persons Act
  1970 13
s 2(1) 13, 327

PAGE

Consumer Credit Act 1974
s 16(5)(b) 151
Criminal Justice and Court Service Act 2000
s 72 255
Data Protection Act 1998
  Sch 11 502
Deregulation and Contracting Out
  Act 1994 23
Disability Discrimination Act
  1995 .... 37, 39, 42, 226, 315,
           318, 320, 323, 325,
       328, 360, 380, 381, 382
s 1, 2 .... **323**
  28A 42, 161, **383**
    (1) **383**
    (2) 342, **383**
    (4), (6) **384**
  28B **42, 43**
    (1) **384**
    (2)-(8) **385**
  28C 42, **43**
    (1) 384, **386**
    (2), (4), (8) **386**
  28D 382
    (2), (9) **382**
  28F 384
  28I(3), (4) **387**
  28K 228, **387**
  28L **387**
  28Q(2) 323
  28R 42, **384**
  28S 42, 43, **385**
    (6) 43, **385**
    (7) 385, **386**

PAGE

Disability Discrimination Act
  1995—*contd*
  s 28T 42, 43, 386
    28U 384
    28V 387
      (1) **387**
      (2), (3), (5) **388**
    28W 386, 388
    29, 30 381
    31B 383
      (1), (8) **383**
    55 384
    Sch 1 .... **323**
      para 1, 2 .... **323**
        3-6, 8 .... **324**
    Sch 3 387
    Sch 4A
      para 1 384
    Sch 4B 384
    Sch 4C 384
Disabled Persons (Services, Consultation and
  Representation) Act 1986
  s 5 ....379, 380
    6 380
Education Act 1944 .... 3, 4, 5, 6, 7,
          8, 24, 25, 115, 330,
          346, 394, 432
  s 7 ....201, 202
    (1) 3
    8 .... 156, 158, 162, 165,
          201, 202, 393, 545
    (2)(c) 393
    17(5) 116
    33, 34 393
    39 437
      (2)(c) 433, 438
      (5) 435, 436
    55 433
      (1) 433, 436, 437
    68 .... 485, 538, 540, 541, 544, 546
    76 ....158, 159
    99 ... 156, 485, 538, 539, 543, 544, 546
    (1) 543
    114(1D) **24**
Education Act 1962 394
  s 1-3 145
Education Act 1980 .... 6, 12, 24, 115,
          166, 328, 394, 441
  s 6 .... 115, 201, 207, 212, 438
    (1) 203
    (2) 201, 203
    (3) 201, 203, 208, 212
      (a) 208, 235
      (b) 208
    (5) 200, 201, 202, 203
      (a) 204
    (6) 206, 209

PAGE

Education Act 1980—*contd*
  s 8 203
    12 115
    31 259
    33(1) 212
Education Act 1981 ..... 12, 315, 391, 392,
          394, 397
  s 1 320
    (3) 320
    2 402
    4 393
    (2) 374
    5 393
    7 393
    (1), (2) 373
Education Act 1993 ....12, 24, 25, 30,
          118, 315, 320, 336,
          339, 365, 401, 505
  s 156(2)(a) 320
    161 343
    (1)(a) 343
    164(3) 334
    166 .... 335, 336, 337
    168 332
    (2)(b) 320
    (5) 336
      (a)(i) 344
    184(1) 118
    218 518
    298 327
    (7) 326
    305(3) 25
    Sch 10 332
      para 3(3)(b) 332
Education Act 1994 12
  s 18A **525**
    20 141
    (1), (2) **141**
    (3), (4) **142**
    21 .... **141**
    22 141
    (1) **142**
    (2) **142**
    (d) 143
      (i), (ii) 143
    (9) 143
Education Act 1996 ....12, 32, 59, 66,
          109, 229, 315, 317,
          325, 337, 349, 360,
          407, 442, 513
  s 1(1) 3
    (4) 322
    2 121
    (1)(a) **59**
    (b) **60**
    (2), (2A), (2B) **60**
    (3) 61, **121**

PAGE

Education Act 1996—*contd*
s 2(4)-(7) 122
4(1) 64
5(3) 67
6(1) 69
7 .... **252**
8(2) 65
(3) **66**
(4) 66
9 .... 130, 158, **159**, 160, 330, 331
10 .... **16**
11 .... **16**
(2) 17
12 .... **19**
13 .... **20**
(1) 513, 514
13A **20**, 513, 517
(1), (2) **513**
14 .... 155, 162, 165
(1) **105**, **155**
(2) **155**
(3), (6) **105**, **155**
(7) **155**
16(6) 419
19 .... 304, 325, 333, 339
(1) **65**, **325**
(2), (3) **65**
(6) **325**
298 326
Pt IV (ss 312-349) 358
s 312 .... 318, 321, 359, 376
(1) 315, **318**
(2) **318**
(3) 319
(4) **318**, 321, 363
(5) 319, 349, 373, 375, 376
313(2), (3) 364
315(1), (2) **328**
316 .... 328, 329, 330, 331
(1) **329**, 330, 331
(2) **329**, 331
(3), (4) **329**
316A 328, 330
317 .... 341, 380
(1) **341**
(2), (4) **342**
(6) 343, **380**
317A 342
(1) **342**
(2), (3) **343**
319 .... 322, 333
(1), (2) **333**
320 333
(1) **333**
(3) **333**, 334
(4) **334**
321 345

PAGE

Education Act 1996—*contd*
s 321(1)-(3) **345**
322 .... 335, 336
(1)-(3) **335**
323 .... 346, 349, 352
(1) **346**
(2), (6) **347**
324 .... 321, 322, 331, 353
(1) 352, 363
(2) **353**
(3) **353**
(a), (b) 356
(4) **353**, 364
(a) 322
(b) 363
(4A) **353**
(5) **353**, 363
(b) 363
(6) **353**
325 .... 352, 366, 368
(1), (2) **352**
(3) **368**
326 .... 359, 366
(1) 364
(3) 367
(4) 364
328 .... 365, 366
329 .... 349, 366
(1), (2) **349**
329A 350
(1), (2), (7) **350**
(8) **350**, 366
(11), (12) **350**
332A 340
(1), (3) **340**
332B 340, 371
(1)-(3), (5), (6) **340**
333-336 366
336A 341
(1), (2) **341**
337 365
(1) 69
342 .... 69, 330
347, 348 365
Pt V (ss 350-410) 408
s 351 .... 408, 480
(1) **408**
(6), (7) 467
352 .... 409, 442
(1) **409**
(a) 442
(c) **467**
(2), (3) **409**
353 .... **416**
354 416
(8) **417**
355 415

PAGE

Education Act 1996—*contd*

s 356 ....414, 415
  (1) **414**
  (2) **414**, 416
  (3) **414**
  (5), (6) 418
  (9) **417**, 469
357 ....415, 430
  (1) **415**
362 ....421, 424
  (1)-(3) **424**
  (4) **425**
363 ....421, 425
364 421
  (a), (b) **421**
365 421
  (1) **422**
  (2), (3) **423**
366 421
367 ....421, 424
  (2)-(4) **424**
368 415
375(2), (3) **443**
398 440
  (a), (b) **440**
400 409
402 420
  (1), (2) **420**
  (3) **421**
403 .... 409, **467**, 469
  (1), (1A) 467
404(1) **468**
405 .... **473**
406 ....409, 480
  (1), (2) **480**
407 481
  (1) **481**
408(2) **409**
409 .... 410, 424, 481
  (1), (2) **481**
  (3), (4) **482**
411 ....167, 169, 230, 237, 330, 331
  (1) 169, 170
    (a) 167, 168, 170
    (b) 168, 169, 170
  (2) 169
    (a) 234
  (3) 169, 170
413 206
423, 429 226
434 264
437 253
  (1) **253**
443 253
  (1) **253**
444 .... 253, 254, 432
  (1) **253**

PAGE

Education Act 1996—*contd*

s 444(3) **254**
  (4) **254**, 255, **432**
  (5) 254, 255, **432**
  (6) 254, **255**
  (8) **255**
450 427
  (1), (2) **427**
451 427
  (1)-(4) **427**
452 428
  (1)-(5) **428**
  (6) **429**
453, 454 428
455 429
  (1)-(3) **429**
456 429
  (4)-(6) **430**
457 430
  (4) **430**
460(2) **431**
482 69
  (3)(a) 69
Pt IX, Ch I (ss 495-541) 16
s 495 538
496 .... 482, 517, 519, 538,
             545, 546, 547
  (1), (2) **538**
497 .... 156, 308, 482, 517,
        519, 542, 545, 546, 547
  (1)-(3) **542**
497A **17, 18**, 517, 519, 520
  (1), (2) **547**
  (3), (4) **520**, **547**
  (7) **547**
497B 17, 18, 548
500-506 118
509 ....432, 433
  (1) **432**, 435, 438
    (b)-(d) 431
  (2) **432**
  (3) **438**
  (4) **432**
509A 431
518 .... 129, 130, 131
  (1), (2) **129**
527A 274, 275
  (1)-(7) **275**
528(1), (2) **381**
537 ....496, 497
  (1)-(3), (5) **497**
537A 496
  (1), (2), (7), (9) **500**
538-541 496
547 80
548 ....282, 283
  (1)-(4) **283**

PAGE

Education Act 1996—*contd*
s 548(5) **283**, 284
550A 261, 284, 285
  (1)-(3) **284**
550B 276, 277
  (1) **276**
  (2)-(4) **277**
551 73
560 425
573(4), (5) 179
579 .... 290, 376
  (1) **61**, **290**
Sch 1 65
Sch 26 351
  para 4, 5 .... **351**
Sch 27 .... 331, 352, 353,
                        355, 365
  para 3 .... 331, **360**
    (3) **360**, 361
  11 366
    (5) 366
Sch 33 226
  para 14 570
Education Act 1997 .... 12, 255, 262,
                        274, 475, 519
s 4 284
9 274
11 223
13 255
15-18 419
19 492
  (1), (2) **492**
21, 22 410
23 410
  (1), (2) **410**
  (3), (4) **411**
24 412
  (1), (2) **412**
25 413
26 .... **379**, 414
  (1) **414**
    (c) 414
  (2) **414**
  (6) **379**
    (b) 379
38 519
  (1) 519
  (2)-(4) **519**
39, 41 520
43 477
  (1), (2) **475**
  (3) **476**
  (4) 538
44 .... 476, 477
  (1), (3) 477
45 .... 477, 478
  (1) **477**

PAGE

Education (No 2) Act 1986 .... 12, 407
s 43(1) **139**, 140, 141
  (2) **139**
  (3), (4) **140**
47 280
Education Reform Act 1988 ... 12, 201, 407,
                        408, 414, 415,
                        423, 450, 451,
                        456, 482
s 15 571
18 422
105(2) 572
124 133
  (1), (2) **133**
125 574
  (1) **133**, **574**
  (2) **133**
  (3) **134**, **574**
    (b) 134
  (4) **134**, **574**
    (a) 134
125A 133
202, 206 576
219 538
Sch 6
  para 1-3 .... **132**
Education (Schools) Act 1992 . 12, 505, 509
s 16 .... 497, 498
Education (Scotland) Act 1980
s 48A 280
Education (Student Loans) Act 1990
s 1 150
Education (Student Loans) Act 1996 12
Sch 33
  para 11A(1)(a) 15
Education (Student Loans) Act 1998 12
Further and Higher Education Act
          1992 .... 12, 125, 375
s 1 125
2, 4 376
7 125
9 521
15 122
  (4) 122
16 122
18 127
  (1) **123**
19(1)-(4) **123**
20 .... 124, 572
21, 22 124
22 122
62 139
65 139
  (3) 524
  (3A) 139
66 139
68 .... 139, 524

PAGE

Further and Higher Education Act
  1992—*contd*
s 70 .... 139, 524
  (1)-(3) **524**
76 133
77 .... 133, 136
  (1), (3), (4) **136**
81 .... 139, 524, 608
91(3), (5) 38
Sch 4 572
  para 1, 10-12 572
Health and Safety at Work etc Act 1974 . 31
Human Rights Act 1998 ....1, 2, 29, 31, 41,
              43, 47, 52, 55, 73,
              96, 161, 226, 398, 403,
              404, 408, 466, **479**,
              535, 536, 580, 587, 607
s 6 .... 55, 606
  (1) 606
  (3)(a) 606
33(2) 399
35(5) 399
Learning and Skills Act 2000 ... 12, 60, 120,
              121, 128, 412,
              467, 521
s 2, 3 .... 125, **126**, 377
4 .... 125, **126**
5 .... **127**, 377
6 381
  (3)(f) 378
  (4) **381**
  (6) 382
7 127
9(1), (2) **521**
13 .... **377**
  (1)-(6) **377**
25 573
41 377
52 522
53(1) 522
    (a)-(e) **522**
54(1), (3) **522**
55(2)(a) **523**
  (4) **521**
58 523
60 .... 509, 523
  (1) **523**
62 523
  (4)(a) 523, **524**
64, 65 523
69(1) 523
71 523
96 .... 411, 413
  (1), (2) **413**
  (5) 411
  (6), (7) **411**
97 413

PAGE

Learning and Skills Act 2000—*contd*
s 97(1), (2) **413**
98-100, 103 412
104, 105 129
110(1) 60
111 122
130 69
140 .... **378**
  (1)-(5) **378**
146 127
148(4) 469
Local Authority Social Services
  Act 1970
s 7 15
  (1) 13, **14**
7A 14
Local Government Act 1974 548
s 25 549
26 551
  (1) **548**
  (6) **550**, 551
    (c) 552
  (10) 550
31(3) 552
Sch 5 .... 550, 552
  para 5(2) 549, **552**
Local Government Act 1986
s 2A(1) 469
Local Government Act 1999
s 15 18
Local Government Finance Act 1992 90
National Assistance Act 1948
s 29(1) 379
Police and Criminal Evidence Act 1984
s 76(2) 293
Protection of Children Act 1999 ..... 31, 91
Race Relations Act 1976 .... 37, 39, 96,
              149, 150, 183,
              199, 208, 226
s 1 .... **39, 40**
  (1)(a) 148
    (b) 40, 147, 148
      (i), (ii) 147, 148
  3(1) 150
Pt III (ss 17-27) 40
s 17 .... 40, 144, 161
18 .... 40, 150, 161, 212
  (1) **212**, 213
18A 40
19 .... 40, 161
19B 40
33 143
  (1) **143**, 144
35, 37, 38 41
57 41
  (3) **148**
71 .... **41**

PAGE

Race Relations (Amendment) Act
    2000 ....40, 41, 161
School Standards and Framework Act
    1998 .... 8, 12, 18, 20, 62, 67,
                    80, 96, 105, 106, 172,
                    177, 312, 407, 481,
                    513, 546, 549
s 1 .... **196**
    (1)-(3), (5) **196**
    (6) 195, **196**
6 ....**20, 21**, 514
    (1), (2), (6) **514**
    (7) 21
7 .... 20, 21
8 17
9 19
10 119
    (1) **119**, **517**
    (2)-(4) **119**
11 120
12 .... **120**
    (1) **120**, **517**
    (2) **120**
14 515
    (1)-(3) **515**
15 .... 515, 516, 517
    (1) 515, **516**
    (2) **516**
    (4) 515, **516**
    (5) **516**
    (6) 515, **516**
17 88
18 518
19 518
    (2), (5) 443
20 68
    (6) 68
21(1)-(3) 68
22 .... 68, 69, 83, 83
    (3), (4) **83**
    (5) **84**
23 75
24 106
    (3) **106**
25 .... 108, 183
26 .... 107, 108
    (2)-(5) **107**
    (6)(e) **108**
27 107
28(1) **110**
    (2) **111**
    (3) 113
    (4) 67
    (6) **111**, 113
    (11) 110
29 114
    (1)(b) 114

PAGE

School Standards and Framework Act
    1998—*contd*
s 30 116
    (1), (2) **116**
    (3) **117**
    (4), (5) 117
    (7), (8) **117**
    (10)-(13) 117
31 117
    (4) 117
32(1) 117
33(1)(c) 114
34 119
35 .... 69, 110
36 75
    (1) 112
37 75
    (3) **75**
38 491
    (1), (2) 74, **77**
39 ....537, 549
    (1) **77**, **537**
40 79
41 .... **73**
42 ....78, 496
    (1) **78**
43(1), (2) **78**
45 .... **84**
46(1) **85**
    (2) 84, **85**
47 .... **85**
    (1), (2) **85**
48 84
49 .... **87**
    (1), (5) **87**
50(1), (2) **87**
    (3)-(7) **87**
51 .... **88**
52 84
54 91
    (6) **94**
55 93
58 94
    (2)-(6) **94**
    (7) 95
59(1)-(4) 95
60 96
    (4), (6) **96**
61 263
    (1) **78**, **263**
    (2) **79**, 263
    (3) **79**
    (4) **264**, 271
        (b) 265
    (5), (6) 264
    (7) **264**
62 .... **273**

PAGE

School Standards and Framework Act
   1998—*contd*
s 62(1), (2) **273**
   (3), (4) **274**
63 .... 79, 263, 494
   (1), (2) **494**
   (3) **495**
   (4) 263
64 289
   (1)-(4) **289**
65 .... 289, 295
   (1), (2) **295**
   (3)-(5) **296**, 297
66 .... 289, 296
   (1), (2) **296**, 297
   (5), (7) **296**
67 .... 289, 302
   (1)-(4) **302**
68 .... 286, 289
69 .... 439, 442
   (1) **442**
   (2)-(4) **439**
70 446
   (1)-(3) **446**
   (7) 439
71 .... 446, 453
   (1), (3), (4) **453**
84 171
86 .... 166, 167, 207, 212
   (1) **166**, 200, **212**
    (b) 170
   (2) **167, 200**, 203, 217
   (3) 203, 217, 220
    (a) **217**, 231
    (b) 207, **217**
    (c) **217**, 218, 221
   (8) 200, 203
    (a) 200
87 .... 217, 223, 304
   (1)-(4) **223**
   (6) **224**
88 171
89 .... 173, 175
   (1) **173**
   (2) **173**, 178
   (3) **173**
   (4) 174
    (a), (b) 174
   (5), (6) **174**
   (7) 175
   (9) 173
90 .... 173, 176, 183
   (1) **176,** 178
   (2) 176
   (3) 176
    (b) 183
   (4)-(6) **176**

PAGE

School Standards and Framework Act
   1998—*contd*
s 90(7) **176**, 183
   (8) **176**
91 .... 172, 173, 206
   (2), (3) 172
92 192
   (1)-(5) **192**
93 .... **195**
   (1)-(3) **195**
94 225
   (1), (2), (5), (6) **225**
95 224
   (1), (2) 242
96 224
   (1), (2) **224**
97 224
   (3) 224
99(1), (2) **184**, 221
   (3) **184**
   (4) **188**, 221
   (5) **188**
100 .... **178, 185**
101 .... 111, **185**
   (1) 111, **185**
   (2) **185**
   (3) 111
   (5) **185**
102 188
   (1), (2) **188**
   (3) 185, **188**
   (4), (5) **189**
103 .... 178, 179, 189
   (2) 179
104 .... 69, 190
   (1) **189**
   (2) **190**
105 190
106 190
   (1), (3) 190
107, 108 191
109 111
   (2) 111
110 255
   (1) **255**
   (2)-(6) 256
111 256
   (4) **256**
   (5), (6) **257**
112 425
117(1) 62
118 .... **62**
   (1)(b) 62
120, 122 63
124 431
127 21
129 129

PAGE

School Standards and Framework Act
  1998—*contd*
  s 131(1) 282
  140 496
  Sch 2 68
  Sch 3 83
    Pt I 69
    Pt II 68, 83
    Pt III 68, 69
  Sch 4 106
  Sch 5 108
  Sch 6
    Pt I 113
      para 2(1)-(3) **113**
           3(4) **114**
           (5), (6) 114
           (7) **114**
  Sch 7 119
  Sch 8 .... 68, 69, 110, 112
  Sch 9 75
    Pt II 77
      para 9(3) **77**
  Sch 12 75
  Sch 13 79
  Sch 14 84
  Sch 16 .... 91, 92
      para 1(3) **92**
           7(1) **92**
           12(1), (2) **92**
           15(1) **92**
           20(1), (3) **93**
           21(1) **93**
  Sch 17 93
      para 8 .... **93**
  Sch 18 .... 289, 301
      para 2(1)-(8) **301**
  Sch 19 442
      para 2 .... **442, 443**
           3 .... **443**
           4 .... **444**
           (2), (3) **444**
           5 .... **442**
  Sch 20 446
      para 2 .... **446**
           3 .... **447**
           (2), (3) 448
           4 448
           5 451
  Sch 23 195
  Sch 24 .... 226, 228, 243
    Pt I
      para 1 .... **226, 227**
           11 .... **228**
           12 .... **239**, 243
               (a) 239, 240, 241
               (b) 240, 241
           15 243

PAGE

School Standards and Framework Act
  1998—*contd*
  Sch 25 ....228, 242
      para 2 227
           3(2) 242
           7, 8 .... **242**
  Sch 26 63
  Sch 30
      para 152 496
Schools Inspections Act 1996 ...... 12, 505
  s 2 506
    (1)-(3) **506**
    (4), (5) **507**
    (6) 506, **507**
    3 507
    (1)-(5) **507**
    7 508
    (3) **508**
    10 ....507, 508
    (1), (5) **509**
    (8) 505
    11 511
    12 509
    13 511
    (1) 510
    (2)-(7), (9) **511**
    14 511
    15 ....509, 511
    16 ....510, 512
    17 512
    (1) **512**
    18, 19 512
    20 .... 510, 511, 512
    21, 22 ....511, 512
    23-25 505
    31 518
    42A 510
  Sch 3 ....**508**, 509
      para 6 .... **509**
Sex Discrimination Act 1975 .... 37, 41, 54,
                          183, 199, 226
  s 1 .... **37**, 164
    (1)(a) 37, 39, 451
      (b) 37, 38, 39
    2 .... 39, 164
    4 37
  Pt III (ss 22-36) 37
  s 22 ... 37, **38**, 39, 40, 161, **162**, 164, 165
    (c) 38
    23 .... 39, 161, 162, 164, 165
    (1) **162**
    23A 39
    24(1) 38
    25 .... 39, 161, 162, 164
    (1) **162**
    (2), (4), (6) **163**
    25A 39

PAGE

Sex Discrimination Act 1975—*contd*
s 26 .... 39, 161
  47, 48 39
  66 .... 39, 161
    (3) 164
Sexual Offences Act 1956
s 5, 6 471
  28 .... 470, 471
Special Educational Needs and Disability
    Act 2001 ...... 12, 31, 42, 225, 315,
                317, 318, 323, 328,
        339, 340, 342, 371, 380, 382
s 1 328
  3 341
  6 .... 366, 376
  7 342
  8 350
  9 353
  10 365
  12, 13 42
  20 228
  25 323
  27, 28 42
  31 386
  Sch 1 365

PAGE

Standards in Scotland's Schools, etc Act
    2000 .... **28**
s 1 .... **28**
  2 .... **28**
    (1), (2) **28**
Supreme Court Act 1981
s 31(6) 551
Supreme Court of Judicature Act 1873 .. 575
Teaching and Higher Education Act
    1998 .... 12, 136, 145, 147
s 22 .... 146, 150, 151
    (1) **146, 150**
    (2), (9) **151**
  39 136
    (1)-(3), (5), (6) **137**
Trade Union and Labour Relations
    Act 1974
s 13 157
Trade Union and Labour Relations
    (Consolidation) Act 1992
s 219 .... **418**
  244 .... 309, 418
Tribunals and Inquires Act 1992 245
s 10(1) 569
  11 570
Unfair Contract Terms Act 1977 ... 526, 533

Table of cases

Page numbers printed in **bold** type indicate where the facts of a case are set out.

PAGE

A

Anderton v Clwyd County Council [1999] Fam Law 188, [1999] ELR 1, CA; revsd [2001]
2 AC 619, [2000] 4 All ER 504, [2000] 3 WLR 776, [2000] 3 FCR 102, [2000] ELR
499, 56 BMLR 1, 144 Sol Jo LB 241, HL 270, 396, 399
Anyanwu v South Bank Student Union (Commission for Racial Equality intervening) [2001]
UKHL 14, [2001] 2 All ER 353, [2001] 1 WLR 638, [2001] ICR 391, [2001] IRLR 305,
[2001] 21 LS Gaz R 39, [2001] NLJR 501 .... **143**
Arrowsmith v United Kingdom (Application 7050/75)19 DR 5 (1980), E Com HR 457
Associated Provincial Picture Houses Ltd v Wednesbury Corpn [1948] 1 KB 223, [1947]
2 All ER 680, 112 JP 55, 45 LGR 635, [1948] LJR 190, 92 Sol Jo 26, 177 LT 641,
63 TLR 623, CA 115, 160, 539, 577

B

B (a minor) (special needs education), Re [1997] 1 FCR 69, 34 BMLR 1, sub nom
R v Oxfordshire County Council, ex p B [1997] ELR 90, CA **374**
B v Harrow London Borough Council. See B v Special Educational Needs Tribunal
B v Isle of Wight Council [1997] ELR 279 .... **320, 357**
B v London Borough of Harrow and Special Educational Needs Tribunal. See B v Special
Educational Needs Tribunal
B v Special Educational Needs Tribunal [1998] 3 FCR 231, [1999] LGR 144, [1998] 17
LS Gaz R 32, 142 Sol Jo LB 134, [1998] Ed CR 176, sub nom B v London Borough of
Harrow and Special Educational Needs Tribunal [1998] ELR 351, sub nom B v London
Borough of Harrow 42 BMLR 88, CA; on appeal sub nom B v Harrow London Borough
Council [2000] 1 All ER 876, [2000] 1 WLR 223, [2000] 3 FCR 1, [2000] ELR 109,
[2000] 06 LS Gaz R 34, 114 Sol Jo LB 83, HL 234, 362
Barkway v South Wales Transport Co Ltd [1950] AC 185, [1950] 1 All ER 392, 114 JP
172, 94 Sol Jo 128, 66 (pt 1) TLR 597, HL 98
Barrett v Enfield London Borough Council [2001] 2 AC 550, [1999] 3 All ER 193, [1999]
3 WLR 79, [1999] 2 FCR 434, [1999] 2 FLR 426, [1999] Fam Law 622, 49 BMLR 1,
[1999] PIQR P 272, HL 527
Bath and North East Somerset District Council v Warman [1999] ELR 81, [1999] Ed CR
517 .... **253**
Bazley v Curry (1999) 174 DLR (4th) 45 .... 101, 102
Belgian Linguistic Case (No 2) (1968) 1 EHRR 252, E Ct HR **49**, 348

PAGE

Belilos v Switzerland (1988) 10 EHRR 466, E Ct HR 587
Birkdale District Electric Supply Co Ltd v Southport Corpn [1926] AC 355, [1926] All ER
    Rep Ext 714, 95 LJ Ch 587, 90 JP 77, 24 LGR 157, 134 LT 673, 42 TLR 303, HL ... 157
Birmingham City Council v Equal Opportunities Commission [1989] AC 1155, [1989] 2
    WLR 520, 87 LGR 557, [1989] IRLR 173, 133 Sol Jo 322, [1989] 15 LS Gaz R 36,
    [1989] NLJR 292, sub nom Equal Opportunities Commission v Birmingham City
    Council [1989] 1 All ER 769, HL **163**, 451
Board of Education v Rice [1911] AC 179, [1911-13] All ER Rep 36, 80 LJKB 796,
    75 JP 393, 9 LGR 652, 55 Sol Jo 440, 104 LT 689, 27 TLR 378, HL 2, **538**
Bolam v Friern Hospital Management Committee [1957] 2 All ER 118, [1957] 1 WLR
    582, 101 Sol Jo 357, 1 BMLR 1 .... 391, 529
Bradford-Smart v West Sussex County Council [2001] ELR 138, [2000] 48 LS Gaz R 37;
    affd [2002] NLJR 142, CA **269**, 271
Breen v Amalgamated Engineering Union [1971] 2 QB 175, [1971] 1 All ER 1148,
    [1971] 2 WLR 742, 115 Sol Jo 203, CA 539
Bromley London Borough Council v Special Educational Needs Tribunal [1999] 3 All
    ER 587, [1999] ELR 260, CA **321**, **358**
Brown v Board of Education of Topeka 347 US 483 (US SC, 1954) 39
Brown v Secretary of State for Scotland: 197/86 [1988] ECR 3205, [1988] 3 CMLR
    403, 1989 SLT 402, ECJ 36

C

C v Buckinghamshire County Council and Special Educational Needs Tribunal [1999] ELR
    179 .... **361**
Calvin v Carr [1980] AC 574, [1979] 2 All ER 440, [1979] 2 WLR 755, 123 Sol Jo 112,
    PC 292
Campbell and Cosans v United Kingdom (1982) 4 EHRR 293, E Ct HR: 49, **278**, 283, 403, 479
Caparo Industries plc v Dickman [1990] 2 AC 605, [1990] 1 All ER 568, [1990] 2 WLR
    358, [1990] BCLC 273, [1990] BCC 164, 134 Sol Jo 494, [1990] 12 LS Gaz R 42,
    [1990] NLJR 248, HL 397
Carmarthenshire County Council v Lewis [1955] AC 549, [1955] 1 All ER 565, [1955]
    2 WLR 517, 119 JP 230, 53 LGR 230, 99 Sol Jo 167, HL 98, 99
Casagrande v Landeshauptstadt München: 9/74 [1974] ECR 773, [1974] 2 CMLR 423, ECJ: 34
Casson v University of Aston in Birmingham [1983] 1 All ER 88 .... 576, **596**
Choudhury v Governors of Bishop Challoner Roman Catholic Comprehensive School. See
    R v Governors of Bishop Challoner Roman Catholic Comprehensive Girls' School,
    ex p Choudhury
Christmas v Hampshire County Council [1995] 2 AC 633, [1995] 3 WLR 152, [1995]
    3 FCR 337, [1995] 2 FLR 276, [1995] Fam Law 537, [1995] ELR 404, 160 LG Rev
    103, 26 BMLR 15, HL 346, **388**
Christmas v Hampshire County Council [1998] ELR 1 .... **394**
Clark v University of Lincolnshire and Humberside [2000] 3 All ER 752, [2000] 1 WLR
    1988, [2000] ELR 345, [2000] NLJR 616, 144 Sol Jo LB 220, [2000] Ed CR 553,
    CA 29, 580, 596, **601**
Costello-Roberts v United Kingdom (1993) 19 EHRR 112, [1994] 1 FCR 65, [1994]
    ELR 1,   E Ct HR **280**
Cotton v Trafford Borough Council (6 October 2000, unreported) 268, 269
Council of Civil Service Unions v Minister for the Civil Service [1985] AC 374, [1984]
    3 All ER 935, [1984] 3 WLR 1174, [1985] ICR 14, [1985] LRC (Const) 948, 128
    Sol Jo 837, [1985] LS Gaz R 437, sub nom R v Secretary of State for Foreign and
    Commonwealth Affairs, ex p Council of Civil Service Unions [1985] IRLR 28, HL   ... 115
Cumings v Birkenhead Corpn [1972] Ch 12, [1971] 2 All ER 881, [1971] 2 WLR 1458,
    135 JP 422, 69 LGR 444, 115 Sol Jo 365, CA **160**, 209, **539**, 543

D

Debell, Sevket and Teh v London Borough of Bromley (12 November 1984, unreported) 38

PAGE

Devon County Council v George [1989] AC 573, [1988] 3 WLR 1386, 153 JP 375, [1989] 1
FLR 146, [1989] Fam Law 149, 87 LGR 413, [1989] 4 LS Gaz R 41, sub nom George v
Devon County Council [1988] 3 All ER 1002, HL **436**
Donoghue v Copiague Union 407 NYS 2d 874 (NY SC App Div, 1978) 530

E

E (a minor) v Dorset County Council [1995] 2 AC 633, [1995] 3 All ER 353, [1995]
3 WLR 152, [1995] 3 FCR 337, [1995] 2 FLR 276, [1995] Fam Law 537, [1995] ELR
404, 160 LG Rev 103, 26 BMLR 15, HL 346, **388**
Equal Opportunities Commission v Birmingham City Council. See Birmingham City
Council v Equal Opportunities Commission
Essex County Council v Rogers [1987] AC 66, [1986] 3 WLR 689, 151 JP 32, sub nom
Rogers v Essex County Council [1986] 3 All ER 321, [1987] 1 FLR 411, [1987]
Fam Law 155, 85 LGR 15, 130 Sol Jo 785, [1986] LS Gaz R 3508, [1986] NLJ Rep
1013, HL **435**
Evans v Monmouthshire County Council and the Governing Body of St Mary's Junior School,
Caldicott (14 June 2001, unreported) 285

F

Fairpo v Humberside County Council [1997] 1 All ER 183, [1997] 3 FCR 181, [1997] 1 FLR
339, [1997] ELR 12 .... **24**, 366
Forbes v Ealing London Borough (30 September 1999, unreported) 331

G

G (a minor), Re [2000] 4 All ER 504. See G (a minor) v Bromley London Borough
Council [2001] 2 AC 619
G (a minor) v Bromley London Borough Council [2001] 2 AC 619, [2000] 3 WLR 776,
[2000] 3 FCR 102, [2000] ELR 499, 144 Sol Jo LB 241, sub nom Re G (a minor)
[2000] 4 All ER 504, 56 BMLR 1, HL 270, 396
G v Wakefield City Metropolitan District Council (1998) 96 LGR 69, sub nom R v Wakefield
Metropolitan District Council, ex p G [1998] 2 FCR 597 358
George v Devon County Council. See Devon County Council v George
Gill v El Vino Co Ltd [1983] QB 425, [1983] 1 All ER 398, [1983] 2 WLR 155, [1983]
IRLR 206, 126 Sol Jo 769, CA 164
Gillick v West Norfolk and Wisbech Area Health Authority [1984] QB 581, [1984] 1 All
ER 365, [1983] 3 WLR 859, 147 JP 888, [1984] FLR 249, [1984] Fam Law 207, 127
Sol Jo 696, [1983] LS Gaz R 2678, 133 NLJ 888; on appeal [1986] AC 112, [1985]
1 All ER 533, [1985] 2 WLR 413, [1985] FLR 736, [1985] Fam Law 165, 129 Sol Jo
47, [1985] LS Gaz R 762, [1985] NLJ Rep 81, CA; revsd [1986] AC 112, [1985] 3 All
ER 402, [1985] 3 WLR 830, [1986] 1 FLR 224, 2 BMLR 11, [1986] Crim LR 113,
129 Sol Jo 738, [1985] LS Gaz R 3551, [1985] NLJ Rep 1055, HL **469**
Glynn v Keele University [1971] 2 All ER 89, [1971] 1 WLR 487, 115 Sol Jo 173 ... **592, 595**
Gold v Essex County Council [1942] 2 KB 293, [1942] 2 All ER 237, 112 LJKB 1, 106
JP 242, 40 LGR 249, 86 Sol Jo 295, 167 LT 166, 58 TLR 357, CA 391
Gould v Regina (East) School Division (1997) WWR 117 530
Gower v London Borough of Bromley [1999] ELR 356, CA 270, **527**
Guardian of the Poor of Gateshead Union v Durham County Council [1918] 1 Ch 146,
87 LJ Ch 113, 82 JP 53, 16 LGR 33, 62 Sol Jo 86, 117 LT 796, 34 TLR 65, CA 543

H

H v Kent County Council and Special Educational Needs Tribunal [2000] ELR 660 ... **347**, 570
Hanuman v United Kingdom [2000] ELR 685, E Ct HR 47, **604**
Haringey London Borough Council v Special Educational Needs Tribunal [1996] CLY
2486 .... **332**

PAGE

Henderson v Henry E Jenkins & Sons and Evans [1970] AC 282, [1969] 3 All ER 756,
    [1969] 3 WLR 732, [1970] RTR 70, [1969] 2 Lloyd's Rep 603, 113 Sol Jo 856, HL ... 99
Hereford and Worcester County Council v Lane [1999] 1 FCR 356, [1998] ELR 319, CA .. **364**
Herring v Templeman [1973] 2 All ER 581, 137 JP 514, 71 LGR 295, 117 Sol Jo 223; affd
    [1973] 3 All ER 569, 72 LGR 162, 117 Sol Jo 793, CA 539, 542, 575, **584**, 602
Hinchley v Rankin [1961] 1 All ER 692, [1961] 1 WLR 421, 125 JP 293, 59 LGR 190,
    105 Sol Jo 158, DC 252
Hines v Birkbeck College [1986] Ch 524, [1985] 3 All ER 156, [1986] 2 WLR 97,
    130 Sol Jo 71; affd [1987] Ch 457n, [1987] 3 All ER 1040n, [1987] 3 WLR 1133n,
    131 Sol Jo 1485, [1987] LS Gaz R 3336, CA 602
Hoffman v Board of Education of New York 49 NY 2d 119 (NY CA, 1979) 530
Holtom v Barnet London Borough Council [1999] ELR 255, CA 345, **346**
Holub and Holub v Secretary of State for the Home Department. See R (on the application
    of Holub) v Secretary of State for the Home Department
Hornsby v Greece (1997) 24 EHRR 250, [1998] ELR 365, E Ct HR 54
Hunter v Board of Education 439 A 2d 582 (Md CA, 1982) 530

I

Ireland v United Kingdom (1978) 2 EHRR 25, E Ct HR 278

J

J v North Lincolnshire County Council. See Jenney (a minor) v North Lincolnshire County
    Council
Jacobi v Griffiths (1999) 174 DLR (4th) 71 .... 101, 102
Jarvis v Hampshire County Council [2001] 2 AC 619, [2000] 4 All ER 504, [2000]
    3 WLR 776, [2000] 3 FCR 102, [2000] ELR 499, 56 BMLR 1, 144 Sol Jo LB 241,
    HL 270, 396
Jenkins v Kingsgate (Clothing Productions) Ltd [1981] 1 WLR 1485, [1980] 1 CMLR 81,
    [1981] ICR 715, [1980] IRLR 6, 125 Sol Jo 587, EAT 164
Jenney (a minor) v North Lincolnshire County Council [2000] LGR 269, sub nom J v North
    Lincolnshire County Council [2000] ELR 245, [2000] PIQR P 84, CA **98**
Jeremiah v Ministry of Defence. See Ministry of Defence v Jeremiah
Johnston v Ireland (1986) 9 EHRR 203, E Ct HR 458

K

Keating v Bromley London Borough Council [1995] 2 AC 633, [1995] 3 WLR 152, [1995]
    3 FCR 337, [1995] 2 FLR 276, [1995] Fam Law 537, [1995] ELR 404, 160 LG Rev
    103, 26 BMLR 15, HL 346, **388**
Kjeldsen, Busk Madsen and Pedersen v Denmark (1976) 1 EHRR 711, E Ct HR **473**, 479
Kokkinakis v Greece (1993) 17 EHRR 397, E Ct HR 479

L

L v Clarke and Somerset County Council [1998] ELR 129 .... **356**
L v Worcestershire County Council and Hughes [2000] ELR 674, CA **330**, 332, 362
Lair v University of Hanover: 39/86 [1988] ECR 3161, [1989] 3 CMLR 545, ECJ 36
Laker Airways Ltd v Department of Trade [1977] QB 643, [1977] 2 All ER 182, [1977] 2
    WLR 234, 121 Sol Jo 52, CA 14
Lamb's Chapel v Center Morches Union Free School District 508 US 384 (1993) **463**
Landesamt für Ausbildungsförderung Nordrhein-Westfalen v Gaal (Oberbundesanwalt beim
    Bundesverwaltungsgericht intervening): C-7/94 [1995] All ER (EC) 653, [1995]
    ECR I-1031, [1995] 3 CMLR 17, ECJ 35
Lee v Secretary of State for Education and Science (1967) 66 LGR 211, 111 Sol Jo 756 116
Lister v Hesley Hall Ltd [2001] UKHL 22, [2001] 2 All ER 769, [2001] 2 WLR 1311,
    [2001] ICR 665, [2001] IRLR 472, [2001] 2 FCR 97, [2001] 2 FLR 307, [2001] Fam Law
    595, [2001] NLJR 728, 145 Sol Jo LB 126, HL 99, **100**, 103, 273

PAGE

M

M v London Guildhall University [1998] ELR 149, CA 600
M (a minor) v Newham London Borough Council [1995] 2 AC 633, [1995] 3 All ER 353,
    [1995] 3 WLR 152, [1995] 3 FCR 337, [1995] 2 FLR 276, [1995] Fam Law 537,
    [1995] ELR 404, 160 LG Rev 103, 26 BMLR 15, HL 346, **388**
McGonnell v United Kingdom (Application 28488/95) (2000) 30 EHRR 289, E Ct HR 587
Mandla v Dowell Lee [1983] 2 AC 548, [1983] 1 All ER 1062, [1983] 2 WLR 620,
    [1983] ICR 385, [1983] IRLR 209, 127 Sol Jo 242, HL 40, 147
Mansell v Griffin [1908] 1 KB 160, 98 LT 51; on appeal [1908] 1 KB 947, 77 LJKB 676,
    72 JP 179, 6 LGR 548, 52 Sol Jo 376, 99 LT 132, 24 TLR 431, CA **276**
Matteucci v Communauté Française de Belgique: 235/87 [1988] ECR 5589, [1989] 1 CMLR
    357, ECJ 36
Meade v London Borough of Haringey [1979] 2 All ER 1016, [1979] 1 WLR 637, [1979]
    ICR 494, 77 LGR 577, 123 Sol Jo 216, CA **156**, 542, **543**
Ministry of Defence v Jeremiah [1980] QB 87, [1979] 3 All ER 833, [1979] 3 WLR 857,
    [1980] ICR 13, 123 Sol Jo 735, sub nom Jeremiah v Ministry of Defence [1979] IRLR
    436, CA 164
Moran v University College Salford (No 2) [1994] ELR 187, CA 597, **598**

N

Nabadda v Westminster City Council [2000] ICR 951, [2000] ELR 489, [2000] 08 LS Gaz
    R 35, CA **149**
Nash v Chelsea College of Art and Design (2001) Times, 25 July 579, **580**
National Union of Teachers v St Mary's Church of England (Aided) Junior School (Governing
    Body) [1997] ICR 334, [1997] IRLR 242, [1997] ELR 169, CA 75
Norrie v Senate of the University of Auckland [1984] 1 NZLR 129, NZ CA 602
Nwabudike (a minor) v Southwark London Borough [1997] ELR 35, 140 Sol Jo LB 128 ..... **97**

O

Orphanos v Queen Mary College [1985] AC 761, [1985] 2 All ER 233, [1985] 2 WLR 703,
    [1986] 2 CMLR 73, [1985] IRLR 349, 129 Sol Jo 284, [1985] LS Gaz R 1787,
    HL 41, 42, **147**
Oxfordshire County Council v B (2001) unreported, CA 363

P

P v National Association of Schoolmasters/Union of Women Teachers [2001] EWCA
    Civ 652, [2001] ELR 607 309
P v Swansea City and County (2000) Times, 1 December 356, 364
Padfield v Minister of Agriculture, Fisheries and Food [1968] AC 997, [1968] 1 All
    ER 694, [1968] 2 WLR 924, 112 Sol Jo 171, HL 157, 539
Page v Hull University Visitor. See R v Lord President of the Privy Council, ex p Page
Patel v Edwards [1978] 1 WLR 1488, 122 Sol Jo 791 602
Patel v University of Bradford Senate [1978] 3 All ER 841, [1978] 1 WLR 1488, 122
    Sol Jo 791; affd [1979] 2 All ER 582, [1979] 1 WLR 1066, 123 Sol Jo 436, CA . 577, 602
Phelps v Hillingdon London Borogh Council [1998] ELR 38 396
Phelps v Hillingdon London Borough Council [1999] 1 All ER 421, [1999] 1 WLR 500,
    [1999] 1 FCR 440, [1998] ELR 587, 46 BMLR 100, [1998] NLJR 1710, 143 Sol Jo
    LB 11, CA; on appeal [2001] 2 AC 619, [2000] 4 All ER 504, [2000] 3 WLR 776,
    [2000] 3 FCR 102, [2000] ELR 499, 56 BMLR 1, [2000] NLJR 1198, 144 Sol Jo
    LB 241, HL 103, 270, **396**, 527, **528**, **530**
Pyx Granite Co Ltd v Ministry of Housing and Local Government [1960] AC 260, [1959]
    3 All ER 1, [1959] 3 WLR 346, 123 JP 429, 58 LGR 1, 10 P & CR 319, 103 Sol Jo
    633, HL 544

PAGE
R

R v Appeal Committee of Brighouse School, ex p G and B [1997] ELR 39, [1996]
COD 125 .... **233**, 250
R v Aston University Senate, ex p Roffey [1969] 2 QB 538, [1969] 2 WLR 1418, 113
Sol Jo 308, sub nom R v Senate of the University of Aston, ex p Roffey [1969] 2 All
ER 964, 133 JP 463 .... 575, **583**, 595
R v Bacon's City Technology College (Governors), ex p W [1998] ELR 488, [1998]
Ed CR 236 300
R v Beatrix Potter School, ex p K [1997] ELR 468 .... **210**, 250
R v Birmingham City Council, ex p Equal Opportunities Commission (No 2) [1993] 1 FCR
753, [1993] Fam Law 338, 91 LGR 14, [1994] ELR 282, CA **165**
R v Birmingham City Council, ex p Youngson [2001] LGR 218 .... **130**
R v Birmingham City Council Education Appeals Committee, ex p B [1999] ELR 305,
sub nom R v Birmingham City Council, ex p M (1998) Times, 13 October **236**, **243**,
245, **569**
R v Blackpool Borough Council Education Committee, ex p Taylor [1999] ELR 237 . 233, **234**
R v Bradford Metropolitan District Council, ex p Parkinson [1997] 2 FCR 67, [1997]
ELR 204 376
R v Brent and Harrow Health Authority, ex p London Borough of Harrow [1997] 3 FCR 765,
[1997] ELR 187, 34 BMLR 9 .... 335, **337**, 356
R v Brent London Borough and Vassie, ex p AF [2000] ELR 550 .... **332**
R v Brent London Borough Council, ex p F [1999] ELR 32, [1999] COD 38 .... 545, **546**
R v Brent London Borough Council, ex p Gunning (1985) 84 LGR 168 .... 113, **115**, 118
R v Buckinghamshire County Council, ex p Milton Keynes Borough Council (1996) 9
Admin LR 159 .... **110**
R v Cambridge University, ex p Beg [1999] ELR 404 .... **586**, 604
R v Camden London Borough and Hampstead School Governors, ex p H [1996] ELR 360,
CA **300**
R v Carmarthenshire County Council, ex p White [2001] ELR 172 435
R v Chelsea College of Art and Design, ex p Nash [2000] ELR 686 579
R v Cheshire County Council, ex p C [1998] ELR 66 .... **334**, 361
R (on the application of Wirral Metropolitan Borough Council) v Chief Schools Adjudicator
[2001] ELR 574 183
R v Cleveland County Council, ex p Commission for Racial Equality [1993] 1 FCR 597,
91 LGR 139, [1994] ELR 44, CA 40, 161, **212**
R v Comr for Local Administration, ex p Croydon London Borough Council [1989] 1 All
ER 1033, sub nom R v Comr for Local Administration for the Croydon District, ex p
Croydon London Borough Council 87 LGR 221, sub nom R v Local Ombudsman, ex p
London Borough of Croydon [1989] Fam Law 187, [1989] COD 226 ..... 231, **232**, 251,
550, 556
R v Comr for Local Administration, ex p H (a minor) [1999] ELR 314, CA 551
R v Comr for Local Administration, ex p S [1999] ELR 102 .... **567**, 571
R v Committee of the Lords of the Judicial Committee of the Privy Council acting for the
Visitor of the University of London, ex p Vijayatunga [1988] QB 322, [1987] 2 WLR
106, 132 Sol Jo 52, [1988] 1 LS Gaz R 36, sub nom R v University of London, ex p
Vijayatunga [1987] 3 All ER 204; affd sub nom R v HM the Queen in Council, ex p
Vijayatunga [1990] 2 QB 444, [1989] 3 WLR 13, 133 Sol Jo 818, [1989] 28 LS Gaz
R 40, sub nom R v University of London Visitor, ex p Vijayatunga [1989] 2 All ER 843,
CA **578**, 579, **581**
R v Cranfield University Senate, ex p Bashir [1999] ELR 317, CA 581
R v Dorset County Council and Further Education Funding Council, ex p Goddard [1995] ELR
109 .... **373**
R v Downes, ex p Wandsworth London Borough Council [2000] ELR 425 177
R v Dyfed County Council, ex p S (minors) [1995] 1 FCR 113, [1994] ELR 320; affd
[1995] 1 FCR 113, [1995] ELR 98, 138 Sol Jo LB 194, CA 433
R v East Sussex County Council, ex p D [1991] COD 374 .... 433, **438**
R v East Sussex County Council, ex p Tandy [1998] AC 714, [1998] 2 All ER 769, [1998]
2 WLR 884, [1998] 2 FCR 221, 96 LGR 497, [1998] ELR 251, [1998] 24 LS Gaz R 33,
[1998] NLJR 781, 142 Sol Jo LB 179, HL **325**, 333, 339, 514

PAGE

R v Education Appeal Committee of Leicestershire County Council, ex p Tarmohamed [1997]
ELR 48, [1996] COD 286 ....**238**

R v Essex County Council, ex p C [1994] 1 FCR 343, [1994] Fam Law 128, 92 LGR 46,
[1994] ELR 54, [1993] COD 398; affd [1994] 1 FCR 773, 93 LGR 10, CA 433

R v Essex County Council, ex p EB [1997] ELR 327 ....**437**

R v Essex County Council, ex p Jacobs [1997] ELR 190 ....**234**

R v Evans (18 May 2001, unreported) 285

R v Exclusion Appeal Panel of Bristol City Council, ex p Governing Body of Fairfield High
School (3 November 2000, unreported) 304

R v Fernhill Manor School, ex p A [1993] 1 FLR 620, [1993] Fam Law 202, [1994] ELR 67,
[1992] COD 446 571

R v Further Education Funding Council, ex p Parkinson [1997] 2 FCR 67, [1997] ELR
204 376

R v Gloucestershire County Council, ex p Barry [1996] 4 All ER 421, 36 BMLR 69, [1996]
33 LS Gaz R 25, 140 Sol Jo LB 177, 1 CCL Rep 19, CA; affd [1997] AC 584, [1997]
2 All ER 1, [1997] 2 WLR 459, 36 BMLR 69, [1997] NLJR 453, 141 Sol Jo LB 91,
9 Admin LR 209, 1 CCL Rep 40, HL 327, 344

R (on the application of C) v Governing Body of Cardinal Newman High School [2001]
EWHC Admin 229, [2001] ELR 359 .... **47**, 238

R (on the application of C) v Governors of B School [2001] ELR 285 .... **306**, 307

R v Governors of Bishop Challoner Roman Catholic Comprehensive Girls' School, ex p
Choudhury [1992] 2 AC 182, [1992] 3 WLR 99, [1992] 2 FCR 507, [1992] 2 FLR
444, [1993] Fam Law 23, 90 LGR 445, [1992] 27 LS Gaz R 36, sub nom Choudhury v
Governors of Bishop Challoner Roman Catholic Comprehensive School [1992] 3 All
ER 277, HL 206, **207**, 220

R v Governors of Buss Foundation Camden School for Girls, ex p Lukasiewicz [1991] COD
98 .... 160, **161**, 186, 480

R v Governors of Dunraven School, ex p B [2000] LGR 494, sub nom R v Headteacher and
Independent Appeal Committee of Dunraven School, ex p B [2000] ELR 156, [2000]
04 LS Gaz R 32, 144 Sol Jo LB 51, CA **292**, **298**, 301, 303

R v Governors of La Sainte Union Convent School, ex p T [1996] ELR 98 210

R v Governors of St Gregory's Roman Catholic Aided High School, ex p Roberts (1995)
Times, 27 January 301

R v Governors of W School and T Education Authority (Borough Council), ex p H [2001]
ELR 192 .... 307, **308**

R v Greenwich London Borough Council, ex p Governors of John Ball Primary School
(1989) 88 LGR 589, [1990] Fam Law 469, CA **200**

R v Haberdashers' Aske's Hatcham College Trust (Governors), ex p T [1995] ELR 350 ....**571**

R v Hackney London Borough, ex p GC [1996] ELR 142, CA 365

R v Hampshire Education Authority, ex p J (1985) 84 LGR 547 .... **320**, 321, 356, 357

R v Harrow London Borough Council, ex p M [1997] 3 FCR 761, [1997] ELR 62: 335, **336**, 356

R v Hasmonean High School (Governors), ex p N and E [1994] ELR 343, CA **218**

R (on the application of B) v Head Teacher of Alperton Community School [2001] EWHC
Admin 229, [2001] ELR 359 .... 46, **47**, 302

R (on the application of T) v Head Teacher of Wembley High School [2001] EWHC Admin
229, [2001] ELR 359 .... **47**, 299, 303

R v Headteacher and Independent Appeal Committee of Dunraven School, ex p B. See R v
Governors of Dunraven School, ex p B

R v HM Judges sitting as visitors to the Honourable Society of the Middle Temple, ex p
Bullock [1996] ELR 349 .... 575, **578**

R v HM the Queen in Council, ex p Vijayatunga. See R v Committee of the Lords of the
Judicial Committee of the Privy Council acting for the Visitor of the University of
London, ex p Vijayatunga

R (on the application of the University of Cambridge) v HM Treasury: C-380/98 [2000]
All ER (EC) 920, sub nom R v HM Treasury, ex p University of Cambridge [2000] 1
WLR 2514, [2000] 3 CMLR 1359, ECJ 137, 139

R v Hereford and Worcester County Council, ex p Lashford [1987] 1 FLR 508, [1987] Fam
Law 162, 85 LGR 333; affd sub nom R v Secretary of State for Education and Science,
ex p Lashford [1988] 1 FLR 72, [1988] Fam Law 59, 86 LGR 13, CA 352

PAGE

R v Hereford and Worcester County Council, ex p P [1992] 2 FCR 732, [1992] 2 FLR 207,
[1992] Fam Law 431 359
R v Hereford Magistrates' Court, ex p Rowlands [1998] QB 110, [1997] 2 WLR 854, 161 JP
258 292
R v Hillingdon London Borough, ex p Governing Body of Queensmead School [1997] ELR
331 .... 328, **343**, 356
R v Hull Prison Board of Visitors, ex p St Germain (No 2) [1979] 3 All ER 545, [1979] 1 WLR
1401, [1979] Crim LR 726, 123 Sol Jo 768 291
R v Incorporated Froebel Institute, ex p L [1999] ELR 488 571
R v Independent Appeal Panel for Sacred Heart High School, ex p L (2 May 2001,
unreported) 209, 220
R (on the application of L) v Independent Appeal Panel of St Edward's College [2001]
EWHC Admin 108, [2001] ELR 542 245
R v Independent Appeal Panel of Sheffield City Council, ex p N [2000] ELR 700 .... **305**
R v Independent Appeals Tribunal of Hillingdon Borough Council and KM, ex p Governing
Body of Mellow Lane School [2001] ELR 200 .... **309**
R v Inner London Education Authority, ex p Ali (1990) 154 LGR 852, [1990] COD 317, 2
Admin LR 822 .... 156, **158**, 543, **544**, 545, 546
R v Inner West London Coroner, ex p Dallaglio [1994] 4 All ER 139, CA 587
R v Islington London Borough Council, ex p Rixon [1997] ELR 66, 32 BMLR 136, 1 CCL
Rep 119 .... 13, **14**, **545**
R v Kent County Council, ex p C [1998] ELR 108 .... **433**
R (on the application of Rhodes) v Kingston upon Hull City Council [2001] ELR 230 . 20, **513**
R v Kingston upon Thames Council and Hunter [1997] ELR 223 .... **421**
R v Kingston upon Thames Royal London Borough, ex p Emsden [1994] 1 FCR 212,
[1993] 1 FLR 179, [1993] Fam Law 120, 91 LGR 96 .... 221, **222**
R v Lambeth London Borough, ex p N [1996] ELR 299 .... **118**
R v Lambeth London Borough Council, ex p M (1995) 94 LGR 122, 160 LG Rev 61,
sub nom R v Lambeth London Borough Council, ex p MBM [1995] ELR 374 359
R v Lancashire County Council, ex p Foster [1995] 1 FCR 212, [1995] ELR 33 ..... **208**, **440**
R v Lancashire County Council, ex p M [1989] 2 FLR 279; affd (1989) 87 LGR 567,
[1989] 2 FLR 279, [1989] Fam Law 395, 133 Sol Jo 484, [1989] 17 LS Gaz R 37,
CA 357, 359
R v Lancashire County Council, ex p M [1995] ELR 136 .... 244, **569**, 570
R v Lancashire County Council, ex p West (27 July 1994, unreported) **205**
R v Leeds Metropolitan University, ex p Manders [1998] ELR 502 .... 581, **582**, **591**, 596
R v Liverpool John Moores University, ex p Hayes [1998] ELR 261 .... **596**
R v Local Ombudsman, ex p London Borough of Croydon. See R v Comr for Local
Administration, ex p Croydon London Borough Council
R v Lord President of the Privy Council, ex p Page [1993] AC 682, [1992] 3 WLR 1112,
[1993] ICR 114, [1993] 10 LS Gaz R 33, 137 Sol Jo LB 45, sub nom Page v Hull
University Visitor [1993] 1 All ER 97, [1993] NLJR 15, HL **576**
R v Lord Saville of Newdigate, ex p A [1999] 4 All ER 860, [2000] 1 WLR 1855, [1999]
COD 436, [1999] NLJR 1201, CA 348
R v Manchester Metropolitan University, ex p Nolan [1994] ELR 380, DC **134**, 588
R v Muntham House School, ex p R [2000] LGR 255, [2000] ELR 287 571
R v North Yorkshire County Council, ex p Hargreaves (1994) 26 BMLR 121, [1997]
1 CCL Rep 104 14
R v Northamptonshire County Council, ex p K (1993) Times, 27 July **162**
R v Northamptonshire County Council, ex p W [1998] ELR 291, [1998] Ed CR 14 .... **303**
R (on the application of AB and SB) v Nottingham City Council [2001] EWHC Admin 235,
[2001] 3 FCR 350 .... 32, 338
R v Oxfordshire County Council, ex p B. See B (a minor) (special needs education), Re
R v Portsmouth City Council, ex p Faludy [1999] ELR 115, CA **322**
R v Richmond upon Thames London Borough Council, ex p JC [2000] ELR 565, [2000]
Ed CR 587; affd [2001] ELR 21, [2000] All ER (D) 1127, CA 15, **240**, **241**
R v Rochdale Metropolitan Borough Council, ex p S [1993] 1 FCR 306, sub nom
R v Rochdale Metropolitan Borough Council, ex p Schemet 91 LGR 425, [1994]
ELR 89, [1993] COD 113 433

PAGE

R v Roman Catholic Schools, ex p S [1998] ELR 304, [1998] COD 283, [1998] Ed
CR 277 .... **291**

R v Rotherham Metropolitan Borough Council, ex p Clark [1998] 1 FCR 509, 96 LGR 214,
[1998] ELR 152, CA **167**, 212, 231

R v Rotherham Metropolitan Borough Council, ex p LT [2000] ELR 76, CA **204**

R (on the application of O) v St James Roman Catholic Primary School Appeal Panel
[2001] ELR 469 220

R v Schools Adjudicator, ex p Wirral Metropolitan Borough Council [2000] ELR 620,
[2000] Ed CR 355 .... **180**

R v Secretary of State for Education, ex p C [1996] ELR 93 .... **321**

R v Secretary of State for Education, ex p Connon [1996] ELR 454 39

R v Secretary of State for Education, ex p Prior [1994] ICR 877, [1994] ELR 231 546

R v Secretary of State for Education, ex p R and D [1994] ELR 495 .... **448**, **453**, **484**, 537

R v Secretary of State for Education and Employment, ex p Governing Body of West
Horndon County Primary School and the National Association of Head Teachers [1997]
ELR 350 .... **497**

R (on the application of Liverpool Hope University College) v Secretary of State for
Education and Employment [2001] EWCA Civ 362, [2001] ELR 552 137

R v Secretary of State for Education and Employment, ex p Morris [1996] ELR 198, CA .. 518

R v Secretary of State for Education and Employment, ex p RCO [2000] ELR 307 .... **190**

R (on the application of Williamson) v Secretary of State for Education and Employment
(2001) Times, 12 December 282

R v Secretary of State for Education and Employment and the Governors of Southlands
Community Comprehensive School, ex p W [1998] ELR 413, [1998] COD 112,
[1999] Ed CR 135 546

R v Secretary of State for Education and Science, ex p Avon County Council (No 2)
(1990) 88 LGR 737n, [1990] COD 349, CA 155

R v Secretary of State for Education and Science, ex p Chance (26 July 1982, unreported) .. 546

R v Secretary of State for Education and Science, ex p Keating (1985) 84 LGR 469 164

R v Secretary of State for Education and Science, ex p Lashford. See R v Hereford and
Worcester County Council, ex p Lashford

R v Secretary of State for Foreign and Commonwealth Affairs, ex p Council of Civil Service
Unions. See Council of Civil Service Unions v Minister for the Civil Service

R v Secretary of State for Social Services, ex p Association of Metropolitan Authorities
[1986] 1 All ER 164, [1986] 1 WLR 1, 83 LGR 796, 130 Sol Jo 35 .... **112**

R (on the application of Holub) v Secretary of State for the Home Department [2001]
1 WLR 1359, sub nom Holub and Holub v Secretary of State for the Home Department
[2001] ELR 401, [2001] Imm AR 282, CA 44, **45**

R v Senate of the University of Aston, ex p Roffey. See R v Aston University Senate,
ex p Roffey

R v Sheffield City Council, ex p Hague [1999] ELR 242; affd [1999] 32 LS Gaz R 32,
[1999] Ed CR 885, sub nom R v Sheffield City Council, ex p H [1999] ELR 511,
CA 170, 212, **229**, 239

R v Sheffield City Council, ex p M [2000] ELR 85 .... **234**

R v Sheffield Hallam University (Board of Governors), ex p R [1995] ELR 267, [1994]
COD 470 .... **593**, **595**

R v South Bank University, ex p Coggeran [2000] ICR 1342, [2001] ELR 42, [2000]
40 LS Gaz R 41, 144 Sol Jo LB 256, CA 589

R v South Glamorgan Appeals Committee, ex p Evans (10 May 1984, unreported),
DC 231, 232

R v South Gloucestershire Appeals Committee, ex p C [2000] ELR 220 .... **236**, **244**, **570**

R v South Gloucestershire Education Appeals Committee, ex p Bryant [2001] ELR 53,
CA 198, 241

R v South Tyneside Education Department and Governors of Hebburn Comprehensive
School, ex p Cram [1998] ELR 508, 8 Admin LR 477 .... **307**, 309

R v Southend Borough Education Appeals Committee, ex p Southend-on-Sea Borough
Council (17 August 1999, unreported) 231

R v Special Educational Needs Tribunal, ex p South Glamorgan County Council [1996]
ELR 326, CA 368

PAGE

R v Stockton-on-Tees Borough Council, ex p W [2000] ELR 93, CA 193, **194**
R v Surrey County Council Education Committee, ex p H (1984) 83 LGR 219, CA **361**
R (on the application of University of Exeter) v Teacher Training Agency [2001] All ER
    (D) 81 ....**526**
R v Thames Valley University Students Union, ex p Ogilvy [1997] CLY 2149 143
R v Turnbull [1977] QB 224, [1976] 3 All ER 549, [1976] 3 WLR 445, 140 JP 648, 63
    Cr App Rep 132, 120 Sol Jo 486, CA 291
R (on the application of Persaud) v University of Cambridge [2001] EWCA Civ 534,
    [2001] ELR 480 ....**582**
R v University of Central England, ex p Sandhu [1999] ELR 121; on appeal sub nom
    Sandhu v University of Central England [1999] ELR 419, CA 589, **590**, 591
R v University of Humberside, ex p Cousens [1995] CLY 1947, CA 589
R v University of Liverpool, ex p Caesar-Gordon [1991] 1 QB 124, [1990] 3 All ER 821,
    [1990] 3 WLR 667 ....**140**
R v University of London, ex p Vijayatunga. See R v Committee of the Lords of the Judicial
    Committee of the Privy Council acting for the Visitor of the University of London,
    ex p Vijayatunga
R v University of Portsmouth, ex p Lakareber [1999] ELR 135, CA **581**
R (on the application of M) v University of West of England [2001] ELR 458 ....**594**
R (on the application of J) v Vale of Glamorgan County Council [2001] EWCA Civ 593,
    [2001] ELR 758 435
R (on the application of K) v W School (Governors) and West Sussex County Council
    [2001] ELR 311 .... 299, 569
R v Wakefield Metropolitan District Council, ex p G. See G v Wakefield City Metropolitan
    District Council
R v Wiltshire County Council, ex p Razazan [1997] ELR 370, CA **203**
Richardson v Solihull Metropolitan Borough Council [1999] 1 FCR 356, [1998] ELR 319,
    CA **363**
Rogers v Essex County Council. See Essex County Council v Rogers

S

S v Essex County Council and Special Educational Needs Tribunal [2000] ELR 718, [2000]
    Ed CR 471 .... 349, **375**
S (a minor) v Special Educational Needs Tribunal [1996] 1 All ER 171, [1995] 1 WLR
    1627, [1996] 2 FCR 310, [1996] ELR 102; affd [1996] 2 All ER 286, [1996] 1 WLR
    382, [1996] 2 FCR 292, [1996] 1 FLR 663, [1996] Fam Law 405, [1996] ELR 228,
    CA 366, **570**
St Matthias Church of England School (Board of Governors) v Crizzle [1993] ICR 401,
    [1993] IRLR 472, [1993] 15 LS Gaz R 39, EAT 96
Sandhu v University of Central England. See R v University of Central England, ex p Sandhu
Scott v Lothian Regional Council (29 September 1998, unreported) 269
Secretary of State for Education and Science v Tameside Metropolitan Borough Council
    [1977] AC 1014, [1976] 3 All ER 665, [1976] 3 WLR 641, 120 Sol Jo 539, CA;
    on appeal [1977] AC 1014, [1976] 3 All ER 665, [1976] 3 WLR 641, 75 LGR 190,
    120 Sol Jo 735, HL 539, **540**
Secretary of State for Employment v Associated Society of Locomotive Engineers and
    Firemen (No 2) [1972] 2 QB 455, [1972] 2 All ER 949, [1972] 2 WLR 1370,
    [1972] ICR 19, 13 KIR 1, 116 Sol Jo 467, CA 541
Shah v Barnet London Borough Council [1983] 2 AC 309, [1983] 1 All ER 226, [1983]
    2 WLR 16, 81 LGR 305, 127 Sol Jo 36, HL **145**
Simpson v United Kingdom 64 DR 188 (1989), E Com HR 45, **46**, **51**, 348, **402**
Special Educational Needs Tribunal Decision 5/00 [2000] ELR 105 ....**352**
Special Educational Needs Tribunal Decision 39/00 [2000] ELR 632 ....**349**
Special Educational Needs Tribunal Decision 40/00 [2000] ELR 632 ....**352**
Special Educational Needs Tribunal Decision 60/00 [2001] ELR 120 ....**349**

PAGE

Staines UDC's Agreement, Re, Triggs v Staines UDC [1969] 1 Ch 10, [1968] 2 All ER 1,
    132 JP 255, 19 P & CR 450, sub nom Triggs v Staines UDC [1968] 2 WLR 1433, 66
    LGR 618, 206 Estates Gazette 23,112 Sol Jo 171 157
Students' Rights, Re: European Parliament (EC Commission intervening) v EC Council
    (United Kingdom and Netherlands intervening): C-295/90 [1992] ECR I-4193, [1992]
    3 CMLR 281, ECJ 36
Sulak v Turkey 84-A DR 98 (1996), E Com HR **51, 607**
Suriano v Hyde Park 611 NYS 2d 20 (NY SC App Div, 1994) 530
Surrey County Council v P and P [1997] ELR 516 361

T

T and M (minors), Re [1995] ELR 1 .... **454**
Terrington v Lancashire County Council (28 August 1986, unreported) 276
Thomas v University of Bradford [1987] AC 795, [1987] 1 All ER 834, [1987] 2 WLR
    677, [1987] ICR 245, 131 Sol Jo 296, [1987] LS Gaz R 980, [1987] NLJ Rep 220,
    HL 576, 577
Thomson v London University (1864) 33 LJ Ch 625, 10 Jur NS 669, 12 WR 733,
    10 LT 403 602
Thorne v University of London [1966] 2 QB 237, [1966] 2 All ER 338, [1966] 2 WLR
    1080, 110 Sol Jo 231, CA 532, 602
Trietley v Board of Education of Buffalo 409 NYS 2d 912 (App Div, 1978) 463
Triggs v Staines UDC. See Staines UDC's Agreement, Re, Triggs v Staines UDC
Trotman v North Yorkshire County Council [1999] LGR 584, [1998] ELR 625, [1998]
    32 LS Gaz R 29, 142 Sol Jo LB 218, [1999] Ed CR 353, CA **99**, 101, 102
Tyrer v United Kingdom (1978) 2 EHRR 1, E Ct HR 278

V

Valsamis v Greece [1998] ELR 430, E Ct HR **457**, **479**

W

W (Peter) v San Francisco Unified School District 60 Cal App 3d 867 (1976) 530
Wallace v Jaffree 472 US 38 (1985) **459**
Wandsworth London Borough Council v A [2000] 1 WLR 1246, [2000] LGR 81, [2000]
    ELR 257, [2000] 03 LS Gaz R 35, 144 Sol Jo LB 47, CA **80**
Wandsworth London Borough Council v National Association of Schoolmasters/Union of
    Women Teachers [1994] ICR 81, [1993] IRLR 344, 92 LGR 91, [1994] ELR 170,
    [1993] NLJR 655n, CA **418**
Watt v Kesteven County Council [1955] 1 QB 408, [1955] 1 All ER 473, [1955] 2 WLR
    499, 119 JP 220, 53 LGR 254, 99 Sol Jo 149, CA **159**, 543
White v Ealing London Borough Council [1999] 1 FCR 356, [1998] ELR 319, CA **363**
Wilson v Governors of Sacred Heart Roman Catholic School [1998] 1 FLR 663, [1998]
    Fam Law 249, [1998] ELR 637, [1998] PIQR P 145, CA 97

X

X v Bedfordshire County Council [1995] 2 AC 633, [1995] 3 All ER 353, [1995] 3 WLR
    152, [1995] 3 FCR 337, [1995] 2 FLR 276, [1995] Fam Law 537, [1995] ELR 404,
    26 BMLR 15, 160 LG Rev 103, [1995] NLJR 993, HL 346, **388**, 527

Y

Y v United Kingdom (Application 14229/88) (1992) 17 EHRR 238, E Ct HR 280
Yanasik v Turkey 74 DR 14 (1993), E Com HR 47
Young, James and Webster v United Kingdom (1981) 4 EHRR 38, [1981] IRLR 408,
    E Ct HR 480

PAGE

Decisions of the European Court of Justice are listed below numerically.
These decisions are also included in the preceding alphabetical table.

9/74:   Casagrande v Landeshauptstadt München [1974] ECR 773, [1974] 2 CMLR
              423, ECJ 34
39/86:   Lair v University of Hanover [1988] ECR 3161, [1989] 3 CMLR 545, ECJ ... 36
197/86:   Brown v Secretary of State for Scotland [1988] ECR 3205, [1988] 3 CMLR
              403, 1989 SLT 402, ECJ 36
235/87:   Matteucci v Communauté Française de Belgique [1988] ECR 5589, [1989] 1
              CMLR 357, ECJ 36
C-295/90:   Re Students' Rights: European Parliament (EC Commission intervening) v
              EC Council (United Kingdom and Netherlands intervening) [1992] ECR I-4193,
              [1992] 3 CMLR 281, ECJ 36
C-7/94:   Landesamt für Ausbildungsförderung Nordrhein-Westfalen v Gaal
              (Oberbundesanwalt beim Bundesverwaltungsgericht intervening) [1995] All
              ER (EC) 653, [1995] ECR I-1031, [1995] 3 CMLR 17, ECJ 35
C-380/98:   R (on the application of the University of Cambridge) v HM Treasury [2000]
              All ER (EC) 920, sub nom R v HM Treasury, ex p University of Cambridge
              [2000] 1 WLR 2514, [2000] 3 CMLR 1359, ECJ 137, 139

Introduction

Do parents have a legal right to choose the school that their child attends? Who is liable legally when a pupil plays truant from school? Must a pupil take all of the national curriculum subjects? Must all pupils attend sex education classes? If a pupil is bullied at school does the pupil have any legal redress against the bully, the head teacher, the school's governing body or the local education authority? What forms of punishment may a teacher lawfully use? When may a parent appeal to an independent appeal panel where their child is excluded from school? Are religious schools entitled to state funding? Who is legally responsible for the management and conduct of a school? What are the legal rights of disabled pupils and pupils with learning difficulties?

These are just a few of the issues comprising education law. Although education law has its roots in administrative law, it also comprises aspects of the law of tort, human rights, and family law. Education law provides a window on constitutional and social change because it reflects the political, constitutional and economic shifts which affect education policy.

Traditionally, education law was primarily concerned with the duties and powers of local education authorities (LEAs) and central government in the person of the Secretary of State. However, in 1980 the consumer revolution invaded state education when the government decided that parents should have the right to 'choose' a school for their child.

Consumer rights tend to be identified with private sector transactions for goods or services, and the concept fits somewhat uneasily with public sector educational provision in schools, further education and universities. On the other hand parents who send their children to independent schools and pay fees for their children's education are clearly consumers of services in a more orthodox sense.

In the context of education, consumer rights have been subsumed within human rights developments, whereby the right to education is protected by the Human Rights Act 1998 which incorporates the European Convention on Human Rights 1950 (ECHR) into English law. Human rights under the ECHR are primarily concerned with political and social rather than economic rights. The categorisation of the right to education as a human right, as opposed to a consumer right, is more compatible with the public sector provision of education, and in particular the provision by the state of compulsory free education.

Thus the legal regulation of education in the United Kingdom was initially concerned with the legal duties and powers of local and central government. The second stage gave parents, and to some extent students, rights as the consumers of educational services. The third stage recognises that education is a human right, which may lead to pupils as well as parents and students having rights (and obligations) as 'citizens' rather than as 'consumers'.

One consequence of the introduction of 'consumerism' into education has been an increase in litigation by parents and students since 1980. This is likely to continue because the Human Rights Act 1998 has extended the basis and grounds for challenging the legality of decisions taken by schools, universities and other education bodies. However, most education disputes are heard in specialist tribunals rather than in court.

1.   BACKGROUND

Education was regulated primarily by the law of trusts and law of contract until the early part of the nineteenth century. Schools and universities were normally religious or charitable institutions, such as endowed grammar schools, or small businesses, such as dame schools. However, in the nineteenth century as education came to be perceived as necessary for all children and as government became more interventionist, the state started to become involved in educational provision. The independent sector continued to exist and to expand.

The first government grants were made by the Treasury in 1833 to assist school promoters who wished to build schools for poor children. In 1839 the Committee of the Privy Council for Education came into being to administer the distribution of grants for the provision of education for the poor. This was followed in 1840 by the introduction of school inspections, and was part of an expansion of state regulation of activities through inspection, which also saw, for example, inspection of factories and mines.

In 1856 an Education Department was established. The Department was headed by a government minister in 1899 when it became the Board of Education (for an early example of education litigation see *Board of Education v Rice* [1911] AC 179). In 2001 the Department's name was changed from the Department for Education and Employment (DfEE) to the Department for Education and Skills (DfES).

In 1870 local school boards were established, which could set up local schools. Elementary education for children between the ages of five and ten became compulsory in 1880, but fees were only finally abolished for all such pupils in 1918. Secondary and technical or further education expanded from 1902, but pupils or their parents were normally expected to contribute towards the cost. Local education authorities (LEAs) based on local government boundaries replaced the school boards in 1902. LEAs are central to the provision of primary and secondary education, although their powers and responsibilities were reduced during the 1990s. LEAs were also responsible for further education provision until 1992.

At the beginning of the twentieth century there were a handful of universities in England: Oxford, Cambridge, London, Durham and Victoria (Manchester, Liverpool and Leeds). In the first decade of the twentieth century a number of 'red-brick' universities, were established. These included colleges in Birmingham, Manchester, and Bristol, which were given university status, in some cases having been colleges attached to an existing university such as London.

The period 1949 to 1965 saw an expansion in the number of universities. Some existing colleges were given university status, for example, Nottingham, Southampton, and Leicester, as well as other completely new institutions being created, such as Kent at Canterbury.

In 1963 the Robbins Report (Report of the Committee on Higher Education (Cmnd 2154)), led to further expansion of the university sector, and in particular the establishment of nine technological universities, such as Salford and Surrey, which had previously been Colleges of Advanced Technology.

In the late 1960s and early 1970s approximately 30 LEA funded colleges became polytechnics, for example, Middlesex Polytechnic, the Polytechnic of Central London, and Sunderland Polytechnic. Polytechnics were able to award degrees, which were validated by the (CNAA) Council for National Academic Awards. In 1992 polytechnics became the 'new' universities, such as the University of Northumbria, Leeds Metropolitan University, and Sheffield Hallam University. They are now able to award degrees in their own right.

The Education Act 1944 (the Butler Act)

The Education Act 1944 (EA 1944) was of fundamental importance to the education system in England and Wales. The Act regulated the provision of education in schools for almost fifty years. Even now that its provisions have been repealed, many survive in subsequent legislation. It established the framework for public education that exists today.

Education Act 1996, s 1(1) (formerly Education Act 1944, s 7(1))

The statutory system of public education consists of three progressive stages: primary education, secondary education and further education.

The EA 1944 established:
- free compulsory schooling until 15 (now 16)
- transfer from primary to secondary school between the ages of 10 years 6 months and 12 years

- duties (replacing powers) on LEAs to provide secondary, technical and adult education.

The EA 1944 was passed towards the end of the Second World War (1939-1945) and reflected a political consensus. It was not concerned with higher education. The following extract identifies the key reforms introduced by the 1944 Act and some of the factors which influenced its provisions.

Ray Cocks 'Ram, Rab and the civil servants: a lawyer and the making of the "Great Education Act 1944"' 21(1) Legal Studies 15 (March 2001)

The Education Act 1944 has frequently been acclaimed by educational specialists and lawyers but it has rarely been explored by legal historians. By way of an exception to the rule, W R Cornish, as a legal historian, has already commented on the Act's 'sophisticated legal structure'. This allowed it to respond to contrasting policies in different geographical areas. In one place it might allow for grammar schools and secondary modern schools whereas in another area there could be comprehensives. This is what happened in practice. For example:

> In its first phase of operation ... the Attlee government would allow LEAs intent on dividing secondary schools to pursue their establishment, while encouraging some (like London), where their allies were in power, to experiment with comprehensive secondary schools. A decade later this programme would begin to provide evidence undermining the capacities of psychological prediction which for a quarter-century had informed so much educational planning. The Act would prove flexible enough to allow later Labour governments to press towards a comprehensive policy in a much more determined way.

Of course, all of this was understood in highly political terms:

> Conservative governments and local authorities would in general prefer a division at '11-plus' into grammar and secondary modern schools. Much of the Labour movement, sensing in this distinction a social division rather than one truly intellectual, was already drawn to the concept of 'multilateral' or 'comprehensive' education.

One of the major fault-lines of post-war politics was thereby created. The Act had been drafted in such a way that it could be used by mutually antagonistic local politicians to produce radically different educational results across the country as a whole. It had set the stage for local conflict over types of school.

There were numerous other major reforms in the 1944 Act. These included the need for every local education authority (LEA) to survey the educational facilities and needs of its area, and to submit a development plan covering the whole of primary and secondary education. The plan was part of the legislative machinery which allowed for more than one approach to the provision of education. The legislation also created the potential for the full development of a national system of nursery education. Further:

> The role of the religions in education was also secured, not only by the requirement of a daily act of worship in all state schools, together with teaching of religious knowledge, but by financial arrangements which would allow LEAs to take over the full responsibility for the costs of a school in return for a majority on the governing body.

In addition, the Act dealt with the problems of school governance. Primary schools were to have a body of not less than six 'managers', while secondary schools would have 'governors' whose numbers were not limited in this way. The school leaving age was to be raised to 15 without exceptions; and this, in turn, should lead to a later advance to 16. Under a new system of county colleges there would be part-time education in 'work-time' for young persons up to the age of 18 for 300 hours a year. Also, 'the Act ... abolished fees for day pupils in schools maintained by LEAs — secondary as well as primary — and charges for boarding could be remitted'. Meals, milk and other refreshments were to be provided. There was provision for the inspection and registration of private schools. If such a school was regarded as unsatisfactory, it could be refused registration or removed from the register. Direct grant schools were allowed to continue in receipt of state aid for a proportion of local authority places 'while keeping their autonomy over all decision-making and maintaining a largely middle-class intake'. Under certain circumstances there was the possibility of appeals to the Minister. Taken together, reforms such as these created what could, with justice, be called the first full and co-ordinated system of national education for children between nursery age and 18.

The making of the Act

There is no general agreement on how the Act was made. P H J H Gosden's major book on war-time education has opened up the sources in the Public Record Office and revealed the important work of reforming civil servants. But there are disputes about the nature of their work. R G Wallace argues succinctly that the Act was largely the product of a small group of civil servants who, charmingly enough, 'met at the Branksome Dene Hotel, Bournemouth, to which they had been evacuated, between November 1940 and May 1941'. K Jeffereys challenges this with a return to the more traditional view that it was largely the product of senior civil servants in 1942 and 1943 in combination with inspired work by Rab Butler, the last President of the Board of Education and (under the Act) the first Minister of Education. With the assistance of his Labour Parliamentary Secretary, Chuter Ede, Butler, as a Conservative, used his skills to marshal cross-party support for a radical Bill in the war-time coalition government.

In his general study of the measure, Michael Barber points out that:

> The balance of the Bill when it was published was perfectly struck — radical and coherent enough to ensure enthusiastic support from Labour, while being tactful and moderate in settling or avoiding those issues most likely to upset the Conservatives. In this sense it was very much Butler's Bill. The fact that it was being debated at all was also a personal triumph for Butler.

Taking a different approach, Jenny Ozga and Sharon Gerwirtz have revealed in forceful terms the dangers of seeking to explain the Act by reference to the interest groups within the educational 'world' and have argued, instead, that the 1944 Act was not the cornerstone of some form of partnership. It was, rather, 'an attempt by the centre to win back control over a system which was politically problematic because of the raised level of post-war expectation'. If there was any form of partnership it was 'A picture of partnership which puts the emphasis in a closed policy community, operating an already agreed agenda, excluding alternatives and limiting outside access to policy making'. In short, the public appearance of negotiation should not be confused with the internal processes of administrative control.

Changes since 1980

During the period 1944 to 1980 the relationship between central and local government was based on co-operation. Central government had broad discretionary and supervisory powers, whereas local government was primarily responsible for ensuring that suitable education was provided in its area. The LEAs were, for example, normally responsible for planning, making provision for school places, maintenance of school premises, as well as the staffing of many schools.

However, the Education Act 1980 was the dawn of a new era. Under the Education Act 1944 parents and their children had few legal rights and were not perceived to have a formal role in the education of their children. However, that began to change in 1980 with the introduction of the values of consumerism into the education system. This gave parents certain rights, as well as making government more accountable to parents for the education provided to their children. However, this development was linked to increased regulation by central government and a diminution in the role of the LEA.

Neville Harris *Law and Education: Regulation, Consumerism and the Education System* (1993) Sweet & Maxwell

Introduction

p xxix

Since 1980, the Government has legislated in the field of education on an unprecedented scale, to give effect to radical and far-reaching reforms.... Out it is said, goes producer domination, as the vested interests of hitherto all-powerful local education authorities are swept aside and teachers' professional autonomy is undermined. In comes "parent power" and greater institutional autonomy and diversity. Consumer choice becomes the key to the operation of a quasi-market structure in which schools, colleges, and universities are in effect forced to compete with each other to attract pupils and students on whose numbers levels of funding increasingly depend. But central government's wish to control the development and operation of the education system as a whole has resulted in a substantial increase in regulation, which has taken diverse forms...

P xxx

The fostering of educational consumerism in its various forms is claimed to have as its overriding social objective an improvement in the quality of educational provision. This is linked to a wider economic objective concerned with changing the principal basis for the distribution of public financial resources. The theory is that consumer choice will help to determine what is good and worth supporting via public funds, thereby also identifying what is bad and, if necessary improvement does not occur, what should be allowed to wither away. However, this basic theory gives rise to practical difficulties (for example in hindering local planning of provision) and potentially undesirable social consequences, as shall be shown.

Responsibility for what is bad and inefficient has, according to the Government, rested with LEAs. Thus a wider political objective has been to weaken LEA's influence, which may be seen as part of a sustained policy of reducing the role of local government and exerting new forms of control over local authorities. For nearly 40 years the EA 1944 provided more or less the entire legal framework for educational provision at school and FE level in England and Wales. The education service was a national one, locally administered. In the partnership between central and local government, the former was expected to play on a minimal, supervisory role. LEAs, on the other hand, were free to dominate key aspects of local educational provision, planning and management. They controlled the secular curriculum and senior staff appointments and were able to exert substantial influence on school governing bodies. They were responsible for overall planning, which meant that they decided how the local service should be organised (although in some cases needing the approval of the Secretary of State for reorganisation proposals).

However, as shall be shown, LEA domination has been curtailed by the reforms of the 1980s and early 1990s. Part of the rationale for the new, complex and all-pervading regulatory framework for the provision of education in England and Wales, which has enabled central government to exert firmer control over provision, is the need to provide a safeguard against abuse of power by institutions freed from LEA control and enjoying far greater independence and autonomy. Key elements in this framework are the centrally regulated National Curriculum and the new funding regimes, operated by government appointed funding councils, in the further and higher education sectors.

Central regulation has also become a major weapon in the Government's bid to quell the radicalist element among the teaching profession. 'Progressive' teachers were blamed for many of the ills, and in particular falling standards, which the introduction of the National Curriculum, with its prescribed content and administrative arrangements (for example, governing assessment and pupils' records of achievement), aimed to eradicate. As in England and Wales, there is also considerable regulation of teaching in the United States, operating at state and federal levels. Regulation by state authorities, which extends to such matters as textbook selection and the curriculum, is said to provide 'a check on the discretion of local boards of education, administrators and teachers'. But it has been argued that this regulation has created resentment and loss of esteem among teachers by undermining their professional autonomy, and that it is in any event unnecessary in achieving the desired goal of maximising quality and effectiveness in educational provision. The teaching unions' boycott of National Curriculum assessment tests in England and Wales in the summer of 1993 was clearly in part a reaction against the effects of excessive regulation.

It has been suggested that the coincidence of extended freedom of consumer choice with greater central regulation and control, for example in relation to the curriculum ('parents are to be free to choose a school for their children but not free to choose what is taught there, which is the exclusive territory of the Secretary of State'), constitutes one of the major ideological contradictions inherent in recent education reforms in England and Wales. This holds true, but only to a degree. For, as shall be shown, individual freedom of school choice is not guaranteed, and central control of the curriculum, while pervasive, is not absolute.

The changes introduced from 1980 onwards reflect political and social changes since the Education Act 1944 was passed.

P Liell, J Coleman, Wolfe (eds) *Law of Education* (9th edn) Butterworths

Division A[12]

INTRODUCTION

The 1944 Act was one of few pieces of legislation the existence of which was common knowledge. It embodied optimistic hopes for the future, not all of which have been disappointed. It is easy to forget that the abolition of fees for secondary education at maintained schools and the other developments mentioned above marked in their time important progress in popular education. Although the providers were LEAs, 'State education' has long been the common usage—a form of words which has become more apt with the growth of government intervention over the last two decades. The wasting of the 1944 Act has been a symbol of changing perceptions about the purposes of education and the best means of providing it—of the collapse of near consensus which marked at least the earlier half of the post-war period, and was based in part upon shared (or at least widely tolerated) social and constitutional values.

The breakdown in consensus and the emphasis on rights is not always considered to be wholly beneficial.

Rabinowicz, Widdrington and Nicholas Education *Law and Practice* (1996) Pearson

Preface

The involvement of lawyers in the administration of the education system has been likened by some to being as destructive to good management as their introduction into family law and health care. There is perhaps a true parallel in that too often, in the public perception at least, the trust and authority with which schools, heads, teachers and others were regarded seems to have been replaced by cynicism and an absence of respect by the participants in the structure of education for each other. Recent, highly publicised cases involving failing schools and disruptive pupils have done nothing to dispel this perception.

This may be due to enhanced (or perceived) rights parents and pupils have been given by the unprecedented volume of primary and secondary legislation since 1979 on all aspects of school life. This has enabled parents to intervene (or interfere depending on one's perspective) both as governors and when problems (eg admissions, exclusions, special needs) arise.

In May 1997 the Labour Party was elected, ending 18 years of Conservative government. Education was high on the list of priorities for the new government, and a White Paper, *Excellence in Schools* (Cm 3681), was published in July 1997 which was the basis for the School Standards and Framework Act (SSFA) 1998. The government was particularly concerned with raising educational standards for all pupils by improving the quality of teaching and learning.

The government also proposed to abolish grant-maintained status whereby schools were funded directly by central government through the Funding Agency bypassing the local education authority.

White Paper *Excellence in Schools* (Cm 3681, July 1997)

1 Learning can unlock the treasure that lies within us all. In the 21st century, knowledge and skills will be the key to success. Our goal is a society in which everyone is well-educated and able to learn throughout life. Britain's economic prosperity and social cohesion both depend on achieving that goal.

2 Good teachers, using the most effective methods, are the key to higher standards. The government values teachers and intends to build on the knowledge and skills they

have developed over many years. We must make sure that all teachers, whether they are just joining the profession or have many years' experience, understand the best methods of teaching and know how to use them.

3 The first task of the education service is to ensure that every child is taught to read, write and add up. But mastery of the basics is only a foundation. Literacy and numeracy matter so much because they open the door to success across all the other school subjects and beyond.

4 A good education provides access to this country's rich and diverse culture, to its history and to an understanding of its place in the world. It offers opportunities to gain insight into the best that has been thought and said and done.

...

Our policy principles

14 We have consistently made clear that there will be unrelenting pressure on schools and teachers for improvement. But we recognise that successful change will not result from pressure alone. Those whose task it is to work day in, day out to raise standards also need to have access to external expertise and to have their achievements celebrated. Under this government, there will be the right balance of pressure and support which will enable us, together, to rise to the challenges of the new millennium. This is the animating idea behind this White Paper. It informs each of the six principles on which our approach to policy will be based.

The White Paper expressed support for the comprehensive principle, the national curriculum, and parental choice. However, as Harris notes below there was a shift of emphasis in the White Paper from parental choice to quality of provision.

Neville Harris 'The Three "Rs" — Rights, Remedies and Regulation' [1998] XX(I) Liverpool Law Review 7

IV RIGHTS AND REMEDIES : A NEW AND DIFFERENT EMPHASIS ON QUALITY

The plain conclusion which can be drawn from the evidence above is that, in the field of choice of school, parental rights are extremely limited, and the appeal process, while an important means of challenge and accountability, makes an overall difference to choice only at the margins. There is only a very limited scope for individualism, contrary to what one might expect in a competitive market, and despite the previous government's marked emphasis on diversity in the system as an enhancement of choice.

There is, however, a very noticeable shift of emphasis taking place at present from the question of choice to the issue of quality, particularly since the general election. There are already statutory rights of complaint about the quality of provision (either locally or to the Secretary of State). But they are under-utilised, largely ineffective and limited in scope. They do not, for example, cover complaints about the quality of individual teachers and offer only limited redress. However, expectations of higher standards of educational provision and of more accountability on the part of educational institutions have been raised not only by political promises but also by some of the guarantees implied or even expressed in the various parent and student charters and home-school agreements which have been developed ... these charters have brought an increasingly private, contractual and formal basis to relationships between pupils/students and educational institutions and are reflective of the market-orientated approach to educational provision. Although the Labour Government's School Standards and Framework Bill promises more external pressures on schools to improve, the consumer pressures unleashed by the Conservatives' legislation before May 1997 will remain highly potent.

The Labour Party was re-elected in June 2001 and published a second education White Paper, *Schools Achieving Success* (Cm 5230), in September 2001. Standards continued to be important, but whereas 'standards not structures' was one of the six principles in the 1997 White Paper, the 2001 White Paper was particularly concerned with reforming school organisation by providing 'devolution and diversity' in schooling, particularly at secondary school level. Having abolished grant-maintained status in 1998, the impression is that most schools are likely in future to have the freedom and responsibilities enjoyed by those schools with grant-maintained status before its abolition. The Education Bill based on the White Paper is likely to receive the royal assent by the summer of 2002.

White Paper *Schools achieving success* (Cm 5230, September 2001)

Chapter 1

Introduction

1.1 Education remains the government's top priority. The success of our children at school is crucial to the economic health and social cohesion of the country as well as to their own life chances and personal fulfilment. A generation ago Britain tolerated an education system with a long tail of poor achievement because there was a plentiful supply of unskilled and semi-skilled jobs. This is no longer the case. By breaking the cycle of underachievement in education we can extend opportunity across society.

1.2 To prosper in the 21st century competitive global economy, Britain must transform the knowledge and skills of its population. Every child, whatever their circumstances, requires an education that equips them for work and prepares them to succeed in the wider economy and in society. We must harness to the full the commitment of teachers, parents, employers, the voluntary sector, and government — national and local — for our educational mission.

1.3 We have begun this transformation. A child who cannot read is denied access to so much, yet in 1997 nearly half of 11-year-olds were below standard in basic literacy. So our first term priority was to put the basics right in primary schools. The teaching of reading, writing and mathematics was radically improved across the country, thanks to investment in the literacy and numeracy strategies and smaller infant class sizes. We also began the process of raising the rewards and recognition of the teaching profession.

1.4 But the basics are not enough. The talents of each individual child must be developed to the full at secondary level. To achieve this, teachers must be properly supported and rewarded; the curriculum must be modernised; and secondary schools must be given the freedom, capability and incentives to achieve success for as many of their pupils as possible. Our best schools achieve excellent results: our task is to spread this excellence nationwide.

...

1.6 Our second term is dedicated to carrying through this reform of secondary education:
- Giving successful schools the freedom they need to excel and innovate.
- Encouraging all schools to build a distinct ethos and centre of excellence, whether as a specialist school or by some other means.
- Opening secondary education to a new era of engagement with the worlds of enterprise, higher education and civic responsibility.
- Building the curriculum — particularly beyond the age of 14, when the talents of pupils diversify — around the needs of each individual, with far better opportunities for vocational and academic study.
- Intervening where necessary to tackle failure and low standards.

One of the most contentious proposals contained in the White Paper is that relating to diversity in schooling. The establishment of many more specialist schools, such as city academies and Beacon schools, risks introducing selection by the back door, despite the government's apparent commitment to comprehensive education.

In addition, the proposed establishment of more religious or 'faith' schools has the potential to result in educational segregation on the basis of religion and race.

White Paper *Schools achieving success* (Cm 5230, September 2001)

Chapter 5 Excellence, innovation and diversity

WE WILL SUPPORT INCLUSIVE FAITH SCHOOLS

5.30 Faith schools have a significant history as part of the state education system, and play an important role in its diversity. Over the last four years, we have increased the range of faith schools in the maintained sector, including the first Muslim, Sikh and Greek Orthodox schools. There are also many independent faith schools and we know that some faith groups are interested in extending their contribution to state education. We wish to welcome faith schools, with their distinctive ethos and character, into the maintained sector where there is clear local agreement. Guidance to School Organisation Committees will require them to give proposals from faith groups to establish schools the same consideration as those from others, including LEAs. Decisions to establish faith schools should take account of the interests of all sections of the community.

5.31 We note that Lord Dearing's report to the Archbishops' Council recommends that the Church of England increase significantly the number of secondary school places it supports. Where there is local support, we will welcome that. We want these schools to be inclusive, and welcome the recommendation that Church of England schools should serve the whole community, not confining admission to Anglicans. We want faith schools that come into the maintained sector to add to the inclusiveness and diversity of the school system and to be ready to work with non-denominational schools and those of other faiths.

The legal framework

The content of education law has expanded dramatically in the last twenty years because of the need to give legislative effect to the policy changes outlined above. Not only has Parliament passed more than 20 Acts of Parliament since 1979, hundreds of sets of regulations and circulars have also been published. Education litigation has also increased considerably during this period, mainly through use of the judicial review procedure and reference to specialist tribunals (see below). This expansion is an illustration of two more general trends: the creeping legalisation of daily life; and increased intervention by central government in traditionally local concerns.

The principles contained in the Acts of Parliament are supported by detailed provisions set out in statutory instruments (SIs), in the form of regulations and orders. In addition there is departmental and statutory guidance on the practical implementation of the legislation. Hitherto, similar provisions applied in Wales. However, the Welsh Assembly now has responsibility for education and there is likely to be increased divergence in future between the legislation applicable in England and Wales. The education systems in Scotland and Northern Ireland differ from that in England and Wales, and are governed by separate legislation.

Acts of Parliament

More than 20 statutes on education have been passed since 1980, and an Education Bill was introduced in the 2001/2002 parliamentary session. Normally, a Green Paper and a White Paper precede the publication of a Bill, setting out the proposed policy changes that the legislation will implement.

The statutes include:

- Education Act 1980 (enhanced parental choice of school)
- Education Act 1981 (new arrangements for children with special educational needs)
- Education (No 2) Act 1986 (parent governors, new powers and responsibilities for governing bodies)
- Education Reform Act 1988 (national curriculum and grant maintained schools)
- Further and Higher Education Act 1992 (establishment of the 'new' universities and new funding agencies)
- Education (Schools) Act 1992 (league tables)
- Education Act 1993 (grant-maintained, special needs, failing schools)
- Education Act 1994 (training of school teachers, student unions)
- Education Act 1996 (a consolidating statute with 583 sections and 40 Schedules)
- Schools Inspections Act 1996 (consolidating statute)
- Education (Student Loans) Act 1996
- Education Act 1997 (school discipline, inspection of LEAs, careers education)
- School Standards and Framework Act 1998 (raising standards in schools, infant class sizes, new categories of school, independent appeal panels)
- Teaching and Higher Education Act 1998 (higher education funding, teacher training)
- Education (Student Loans) Act 1998
- Learning and Skills Act 2000 (post-16 education)
- Special Educational Needs and Disability Act 2001 (Disability discrimination in education, and SEN).

Statutory instruments

In addition to primary legislation the Department of Education and Skills (DfES), formerly the Department of Education and Employment (DfEE), publishes a considerable number of regulations and orders on educational matters, in the form of statutory instruments.

Examples of regulations and orders are:

- Education (Special Educational Needs) (England) (Consolidation) Regulations 2001, SI 2001/3455
- Education (Student Loans) (Amendment) (England and Wales) Regulations 2001, SI 2001/1627
- Education (Nutritional Standards for School Lunches) (Wales) Regulations 2001, SI 2001/1784
- Education (National Curriculum) (Assessment Arrangements) (England) (Amendment) Order 2001, SI 2001/1286

- *Find out how many regulations and orders on education have been published in the past 12 months. The simplest way to find them is by using the internet. LAWTEL is a useful source for subscribers. Alternatively the Stationery Office website is accessible to the public.*

Guidance

In addition to the primary and secondary legislation the DfES also publishes statutory and non-statutory guidance or advice on how the legislation should be implemented in practice. Guidance is not legally binding. However, the courts will consider that it represents good practice, and should normally be followed.

Statutory guidance means that the guidance has been authorised by an Act of Parliament. It has a higher status than departmental guidance. Guidance used to be issued in the form of 'circulars', but now tends to be described as 'guidance'. On some occasions guidance is given in the form of a code of practice.

Examples of guidance include:

- Code of Practice—School Admissions (DfEE)
- DfEE Circular 10/99 (Social Inclusion: Pupil Support)
- DfEE 0116/2000 (Sex and Relationship Education Guidance)
- DfES 0580/2001 (The Protection of School Playing Fields and Land for City Academies).

- *Find out how many circulars (the name usually given to guidance) have been published by the DfES in the past 12 months. The DfES website is the simplest way of finding out this information.*

In *R v Islington London Borough, ex p Rixon* [1997] ELR 66 the court considered the status of statutory guidance in relation to s 2(1) of the Chronically Sick and Disabled Persons Act 1970 and s 7(1) of the Local Authority Social Services Act 1970. The principles set out are equally applicable to guidance published by the DfES.

R v Islington London Borough, ex p Rixon [1997] ELR 66

Sedley J: This section, therefore, creates a positive duty to arrange for recreational and 'gateway' educational facilities for disabled persons. It is, counsel agree, a duty owed to the individual and not simply a target duty. I will come later to the question of its legal ambit and content. It introduces in turn s 7(1) of the Local Authority Social Services Act 1970:

> Local authorities shall, in the exercise of their social services functions, including the exercise of any discretion conferred by any relevant enactment, act under the general guidance of the Secretary of State.

(By an amendment introduced into the statute, s 7A requires local authorities to exercise their social services functions in accordance with any such *directions* as may be given to them by the Secretary of State.)

What is the meaning and effect of the obligation to 'act under the general guidance of the Secretary of State'? Clearly guidance is less than direction, and the word 'general' emphasises the non-prescriptive nature of what is envisaged. Mr McCarthy, for the local authority, submits that such guidance is no more than one of the many factors to which the local authority is to have regard. Miss Richards submits that, in order to give effect to the words 'shall ... act', a local authority must follow such guidance unless it has and can articulate a good reason for departing from it. In my judgment Parliament in enacting s 7(1) did not intend local authorities to whom ministerial guidance was given to be free, having considered it, to take it or leave it. Such a construction would put this kind of statutory guidance on a par with the many forms of non-statutory guidance issued by departments of state. While guidance and direction are semantically and legally different things, and while 'guidance does not compel any particular decision' (*Laker Airways Ltd v Department of Trade* [1977] QB 643 at 714 per Roskill LJ), especially when prefaced by the word 'general', in my view Parliament by s 7(1) has required local authorities to follow the path charted by the Secretary of State's guidance, with liberty to deviate from it where the local authority judges on admissible grounds that there is good reason to do so, but without freedom to take a substantially different course.

...

A failure to comply with the statutory policy guidance is unlawful and can be corrected by means of judicial review: *R v North Yorkshire County Council, ex p Hargreaves* (1994) 26 BMLR 121, Dyson J. Beyond this, there will always be a variety of factors which the local authority is required on basic public law principles to take into account.

...

A second source of considerations which manifestly must be taken into account in coming to a decision is the practice guidance issued by the Department of Health. This currently takes the form of a practitioners' guide entitled 'Care Management and Assessment', which sets out 'a set of principles' derived from 'current views of practice'.

...

The care plan, as Mr McCarthy readily admits, does not comply either with the policy guidance or the practice guidance issued by central government. There has been a failure to comply with the guidance contained in para 3.24 of the policy document to the effect that following assessment of need, the objectives of social services' intervention as well as the services to be provided or arranged should be agreed in the form of a care plan. For the reasons which I have given, if this statutory guidance is to be departed from it must be with good reason, articulated in the course of some identifiable decision-making process even if not in the care plan itself. In the absence of any such considered decision, the deviation from the statutory guidance is in my judgment a breach of the law;

...

The care plan also fails at a number of points to comply with the practice guidance on, for example, the contents of a care plan, the specification of its objectives, the achievement of agreement on implementation on all those involved, leeway for contingencies and the identification and feeding back of assessed but still unmet need. While such guidance lacks the status accorded by s 7 of the 1970 Act, it is, as I have said, something to which regard must be had in carrying out the statutory functions. While the occasional lacuna would not furnish evidence of such a disregard, the series of lacunae which I have mentioned does, in my view, suggest that the statutory guidance has been overlooked.

In such a situation I am unable to accede to Mr McCarthy's submission that the failures to follow the policy guidance and practice guidance are beyond the purview of the court.

- *What is the legal effect of statutory guidance? How can you find out whether the guidance is statutory or non-statutory? How can a failure to follow such guidance be challenged?*

It is possible to dispute the accuracy of the guidance and refuse to follow it. Where the guidance purports to interpret the law, the court may not agree with the interpretation. For example, in *R v Richmond upon Thames London Borough Council, ex p JC* [2001] ELR 21 Kennedy LJ disagreed with the interpretation of the Education Act 1996, Sch 33, para 11A(1)(a) contained in the Code of Practice on School Admission Appeals.

Modernising education law

The 2001 White Paper, *Schools Achieving Success*, proposes a reform of education law with the emphasis on deregulation and freedom for schools to innovate.

White Paper *Schools Achieving Success* (Cm 5230, September 2001)

Modernising education law

9.4 Education law is a highly complex area, where a great deal of detail is set out in primary legislation, restricting the ability of the education system to innovate and to respond to innovation. Many legal concepts, which served their time extremely well are now outdated. Our view of education itself has evolved over time — Early Years education and Modern Apprenticeships, for example, are just two of the things we are promoting, which could not have been foreseen in earlier Education Acts.

9.5 In addition, much administrative detail is now written into primary education legislation. Compared to other areas of law, this means that there is much greater need to legislate to achieve comparatively minor administrative changes. We believe that much of this detail could more appropriately be placed in secondary legislation — not outside the control of Parliament, but more easily adjusted without extensive legislative change. We will also look to rationalise existing powers, for example to spend money, so that rather than a large range of powers, which apply in narrow circumstances, there will be fewer, broader powers.

These proposals, which are reflected in the Education Bill 2001/02, particularly affect the following areas of education law:
- Organisation and governance of schools, including nursery schools
- School budgets

- School admission arrangements
- School curriculum
- Behaviour in schools
- Weak and failing schools and LEAs
- Teacher employment.

The streamlining of education law has its attractions. In particular the use of legislation to set out the terms of teachers' contracts of employment is archaic. However, the proposals raise a number of questions. Will the new broader powers be legally enforceable, and if so by whom? Will the secondary legislation be subject to adequate parliamentary scrutiny? Will LEAs continue to have obligations which are enforceable by parents and pupils? Will the legal duties and powers currently vested in LEAs be transferred to schools? Do governing bodies have the time, the expertise, and the resources to undertake the responsibilities devolved to them? To whom will schools be accountable for the exercise of their devolved powers? Will an effective formal complaints system be established for parents?

The role of the Secretary of State

The Secretary of State has general and specific legal duties as well as wide-ranging powers including the power to intervene where a governing body is acting unreasonably or unlawfully (see chapter 8), and the power to make regulations in relation to schools as well as further and higher education institutions. A number of ancillary functions of the Secretary of State are set out in the Education Act 1996, Pt IX, Ch I.

The Secretary of State heads the Department for Education and Skills (DfES), which was known as the Department for Education and Employment (DfEE), and had previously been known as the Department of Education and Science (DES).

Education Act 1996, s 10

The Secretary of State shall promote the education of the people of England and Wales.

Education Act 1996, s 11

(1) The Secretary of State shall exercise his powers in respect of those bodies in receipt of public funds which—
(a) carry responsibility for securing that the required provision for primary, secondary or further education is made—
    (i)   in schools, or
    (ii) in institutions within the further education sector,
    in or in any area of England or Wales, or

(b)   conduct schools or institutions within the further education sector in England and Wales,

for the purpose of promoting primary, secondary and further education in England and Wales.

(2) The Secretary of State shall, in the case of his powers to regulate the provision made in schools and institutions within the further education sector in England and Wales, exercise his powers with a view to (among other things) improving standards, encouraging diversity and increasing opportunities for choice.

Note the reference to relevant policy considerations in s 11(2).

A recent example of a new power is that inserted by the School Standards and Framework Act 1998, s 8 which granted the Secretary of State new reserve powers (EA 1996, ss 497A and 497B) to secure proper performance of LEA's functions.

Education Act 1996, s 497A

(1) This section applies to a local education authority's functions (of whatever nature) which relate to the provision of education—
(a)   for persons of compulsory school age (whether at school or otherwise), or
(b)   for persons of any age above or below that age who are registered as pupils at schools maintained by the authority.

(2) If the Secretary of State is satisfied (either on a complaint by any person interested or otherwise) that a local education authority are failing in any respect to perform any function to which this section applies to an adequate standard (or at all), he may exercise his powers under subsection (3) or (4).

(3) The Secretary of State may under this subsection direct an officer of the authority to secure that that function is performed in such a way as to achieve such objectives as are specified in the direction.

(4) The Secretary of State may under this subsection give an officer of the authority such directions as the Secretary of State thinks expedient for the purpose of securing that the function—
(a)   is performed, on behalf of the authority and at their expense, by such person as is specified in the direction, and
(b)   is so performed in such a way as to achieve such objectives as are so specified;

and such directions may require that any contract or other arrangement made by the authority with that person contains such terms and conditions as may be so specified.

(5) Where the Secretary of State considers it expedient that the person specified in directions under subsection (4) should perform other functions to which this section applies in addition to the function to which subsection (2) applies, the directions under subsection (4) may relate to the performance of those other functions as well; and in considering whether it is expedient that that person should perform any such additional functions, the Secretary of State may have regard to financial considerations.

(6) Any direction under this section may either—
(a)   have effect for an indefinite period until revoked by the Secretary of State, or

(b)   have effect until any objectives specified in the direction have been achieved (as determined in accordance with the direction).

(7) Any direction given under subsection (3) or (4) shall be enforceable, on an application made on behalf of the Secretary of State, by an order of mandamus.

- *To which aspects of an LEA's function does this power relate? When may the Secretary of State issue a direction to an LEA? Must the function be performed by the LEA? Where an LEA does not comply with the Secretary of State's direction how may the direction be enforced?*

This provision has a potentially significant impact on LEAs.

Paul Meredith 'The contracting out of LEA functions and the implications for democracy and accountability' (2001) 12(1) Education and the Law 5

The significance of this new provision is enormous: indeed, it is one of the most radical measures of centralised intervention and control seen in recent legislation, though it has more recently been reflected in a much wider local government context in s 15 of the Local Government Act 1999 in respect of the promotion of 'best value' in local authorities generally.

At the time of the passage of the School Standards and Framework Act in 1998, some took the view that this radical power of central intervention would be a measure of last resort and rarely invoked. The then recent experience in Hackney London Borough Council where nominees of the Secretary of State had been sent in on a non-statutory basis was regarded by many as evidence that such measures of central intervention would be fraught with difficulty and would therefore be invoked only on an exceptional basis. This has, however, proved to be far from the case. The indications currently are that the government will not hesitate to intervene at LEA level where OFSTED inspections reveal what the government considers to be significant failings in LEA performance. Clearly the government consider that it is justified in the public interest in intervening in the affairs of failing LEAs, and that this is central to its core policy of enhancing and underpinning educational standards.

...

While it is clear that the goal of improving and underpinning educational standards is entirely laudable, and it would be widely recognised that any failings should be tackled quickly and effectively, the political, social and educational propriety of 'outsourcing' key LEA functions by bringing in private sector educational consultants is less certain. Not only does it potentially undermine the LEA's strategic planning role and its role as a service provider, but it raises essential constitutional questions in terms of local responsibility and accountability. It is entirely possible that a private sector firm operating subject to pre-determined contractual attainment targets and with a focus on the prospect of financial penalties in the event of those targets not being met *may* in some cases offer an efficient means of remedying defective provision of educational services; whether it could be said to be genuinely and sensitively accountable to the people living in the area for the provision of education in the best interests of the community at large is, however, distinctly open to question.

The Education Bill 2001/02 proposes to replace s 497A and to increase further the powers of the Secretary of State. For example, under the Bill the Secretary of State will be able give directions in relation to all the LEA's education functions, not just those relating to compulsory education. In addition the Bill provides that the Secretary of State may direct LEAs to obtain external advisory services where the LEA has made insufficient progress in dealing with weak or failing schools.

The role of the LEA

There are approximately 116 LEAs in England and Wales. Local education authority areas normally correspond to the local government boundary and are the responsibility of the local councils elected by voters in each area.

In England and Wales local education authorities (LEAs) are defined as follows:

Education Act 1996, s 12

(1) The local education authority for a county in England having a county council is the county council.

(2) The local education authority for a district in England which is not in a county having a county council is the district council.

(3) The local education authority for a London borough is the borough council.

(4) The local education authority for the City of London (which for the purposes of this Act shall be treated as including the Inner Temple and the Middle Temple) is the Common Council of the City of London (in their capacity as a local authority).

(5) As respects Wales—
(a)   the local education authority for a county is the county council; and
(b)   the local education authority for a county borough is the county borough council.

(6) Any reference in this Act to the area of a local education authority shall be construed in accordance with the preceding provisions of this section.

...

The education committees of local councils now include representatives of parent governors (s 9 of the SSFA 1998). In the exercise of particular functions the LEA may be under an express or an implied duty to consult interested parties, which normally includes the head teacher, the governing body as well as parents (see for example education development plans below, and school reorganisation in chapter 2).

Local education authorities must appoint a chief education officer to whom the LEA delegate its functions and who is responsible for the operation of the LEA and is accountable to the elected members of the local council. Schools are funded by central government through the LEA which is responsible for determining the education budget. There has been criticism of the amount of the percentage of the schools budget retained by certain LEAs to cover their administrative costs (see chapter 2).

Local education authorities have general duties, in addition to more specific responsibilities which are set out in particular chapters (see for example chapter 3 –

School Admissions). Their legal responsibilities relate mainly to local schools and to pupils and students resident in their area. The majority of their powers in relation to further and higher education have been removed. They are no longer responsible for funding further education colleges, and their former role in the management of polytechnics has ceased.

Education Act 1996, s 13

(1) A local education authority shall (so far as their powers enable them to do so) contribute towards the spiritual, moral, mental and physical development of the community by securing that efficient primary education, secondary education and further education are available to meet the needs of the population of their area.

...

In *R (on the application of Rhodes) v Kingston upon Hull City Council* [2001] ELR 230 parents, concerned about the poor quality of secondary education in Hull, wanted to apply for a declaration that the LEA was in breach of s 13 because it failed to provide an efficent education for children in the LEA. The judge held that an application for judicial review was bound to fail (see extract in chapter 8 for reasons).

The School Standards and Framework Act 1998 placed a new duty on LEAs as part of the government's policy to raise educational standards. It is likely, however, that the courts would consider this duty to be a 'target' duty (see chapter 3) which is enforceable by the Secretary of State rather than by parents.

Education Act 1996, s 13A

(1) A local education authority shall ensure that their functions relating to the provision of education to which this section applies are (so far as they are capable of being so exercised) exercised by the authority with a view to promoting high standards.

(2) This section applies to education for—
(a)   persons of compulsory school age (whether at school or otherwise); and
(b)   persons of any age above or below that age who are registered as pupils at schools maintained by the authority;

and in subsection (1) 'functions' means functions of whatever nature.

Local education authorities are also under a duty to prepare education development plans (ss 6,7 of the SSFA 1998).

School Standards and Framework Act 1998, s 6

(1) Every local education authority shall prepare an education development plan for their area, and shall prepare further such plans at such intervals as may be determined by or in accordance with regulations.

(2) An education development plan shall consist of—

(a)   a statement of proposals, which sets out proposals by the authority for developing their provision of education for children in their area, whether by—

(i)   raising the standards of education provided for such children (whether at schools maintained by the authority or otherwise than at school), or

(ii)   improving the performance of such schools,

or otherwise; and

(b)   annexes to that statement.

...

(6) In preparing an education development plan the authority shall have regard, in particular, to the education of children (within the meaning of subsection (2)) who have special educational needs.

(7) In the course of preparing an education development plan the authority shall consult—

(a)   the governing body and head teacher of every school maintained by the authority;

(b)   the appropriate diocesan authority for any foundation or voluntary school in their area which is a Church of England, Church in Wales or Roman Catholic Church school; and

(c)   such other persons as they consider appropriate.

...

(9) In performing their functions under this section the authority shall have regard to any guidance given from time to time by the Secretary of State.

Note the obligation to consult in s 6(7).

Section 7 of the SSFA 1998 provides for the approval, modification and review of such plans. The statutory provisions are supplemented by regulations (Education Development Plans (England) Regulations 2001, SI 2001/2815, and for Wales SI 1999/1439), and by statutory Codes of Practice on LEA-School Relations for England and Wales respectively under s 127 of the SSFA 1998.

During the 1980s and the first half of the 1990s central government chipped away at the role of LEAS in two ways: by centralisation and by devolution of power. Central government took over control of certain aspects of educational provision, while other aspects were devolved to school governing bodies. This process slowed down when the Labour government was elected in May 1997, published its White Paper *Excellence in Schools* (Cm 3681), and passed the School Standards and Framework Act 1998. However, the 2001 White Paper *Schools Achieving Success* (Cm 5230) emphasises devolution of power to schools as one of its twin objectives.

Paul Meredith 'The Fall and Rise of Local Education Authorities' [1998] XX(1) Liverpool Law Review 41

[A] particular feature of the proposals put forward by the government in its July 1997 White Paper, *Excellence in Schools*, many of which have subsequently been enshrined in the School Standards and Framework Bill presented to Parliament in December 1997, is that a large number of highly significant new powers will be conferred upon LEAs in the drive to improve the standard of educational provision in schools. LEAs will assume a wide range of detailed powers of supervision and intervention to be used in given circumstances in relation to individual schools; and they will assume significant functions in relation to the organisation and planning of the provision of education and the framework of schools in their respective areas. Furthermore, the Secretary of State and OFSTED will assume crucial new powers of supervision and intervention in the affairs of individual LEAs and schools.

...

The balance of power between the central department and LEAs raises the question of the democratic legitimacy of their respective roles and thus takes on a constitutional dimension of the first importance.

...

The overall consequence of these developments was, however, that LEA functions as a whole, and the strategic planning function in particular, had reduced greatly in significance during the tenure of the Conservative government up to May 1997. Arguably, LEAs had thereby lost much of their *raison d'etre*: while they retained a number of important supportive functions in relation to those schools remaining in the LEA-maintained sector, and would have assumed an increasing quality assurance role, they had lost much of their vital role as strategic planners operating with knowledge of and sensitivity to local needs, and accountable democratically to the local electorate.

...

[T]hree of the crucial elements in the government's proposals for improving standards and performance [are]: the setting of targets for individual schools, the formulation of EDPs [Education Development Plans], and specific action to tackle failing schools. What is proposed constitutes an extremely complex network of prescription, monitoring and control from the central department downwards through LEAs to the level of individual schools, backed up by a range of powers of intervention in the event of failure to meet the set goals or standards. What is highly significant is that the network of prescription and control effectively ensures that those goals and standards are formulated at central department level, with the active involvement of the School Standards and Effectiveness Unit and OFSTED. The key mechanism for this is the EDP, incorporating the targets for individual schools and requiring the approval of the Secretary of State: the EDP thus provides a crucial link from the highest level to the lowest. Furthermore, the LEA role of regular monitoring of individual school performance — including in particular the annual review of each school's performance targets — provides another crucial link from the top of the control structure to the bottom: by virtue of the early warning system it may trigger mechanisms for direct involvement in the management of an individual school by the LEA; and the Secretary of State has the capacity to intervene at school level should the school be deemed to require special measures, and to require OFSTED to conduct an inspection of the LEA leading possibly to direct intervention in the running of the authority.

This constitutes a powerful structure of prescription and control, in which LEAs will undoubtedly play a pivotal role. What is, however, quite evident is that it is markedly authoritarian in nature with the main focus of authority very clearly at the centre. Although it is perfectly true that a significant new monitoring role is being forged for LEAs, the overall tenor of what is proposed is highly centralising.

...

It is true that this [the School Standards and Framework] Bill does clearly envisage a crucial role for LEAs in many important respects, particularly in the context of securing the highest possible standards, but it is also beyond doubt that it considerably extends the already well-developed trend towards centralisation in education by the conferment on the Secretary of State of many new powers of regulation, prescription, control and intervention.

On the other hand, while the government declared in *Excellence in Schools* that one of the key principles informing its entire approach to educational reform would be that it would 'work in partnership with all those committed to raising standards', it never declared that that partnership would be evenly balanced. Indeed, in an endeavour as wide-ranging and complex as raising standards in schools across the country, a strong, concerted and centrally driven impetus may well be necessary. In order to achieve the goal of 'zero tolerance of underperformance', it may be necessary to develop a sophisticated network of prescription and control from above: any such centralised prescription and control must, however, be sensitive to the fact that schools in different areas and with different socio-economic backgrounds have different needs and different expectations. In the processes of monitoring schools, setting standards, formulating EDPs, and much else, there needs to be a continuous and constructive dialogue between all the partners in the system to ensure that there is genuine appreciation of and sensitivity towards local needs and variations. In ensuring that this continuous and constructive dialogue takes place, LEAs will play a pivotal role.

In the autumn of 2000 the DfEE published a Policy Paper entitled *The Role of the Local Education Authority in School Education*. The DfEE considered that LEAs should be responsible for ensuring that:
- special educational needs are met
- sufficient school places are available
- transport to school is provided
- schools meet their standards targets
- excluded or ill pupils receive education, and that
- there is a minimum level of bureaucracy.

The Policy Paper proposes new methods of working for LEAs. These include developing systems for identifying good quality providers of 'school improvement services', whether from the private, voluntary or public sector.

Local education authorities are permitted to contract out their functions subject to the exception of key strategic functions. An Order under the Deregulation and Contracting Out Act 1994 is likely to be implemented in 2002 which will permit LEAs to authorise an outside body from the private or voluntary sector to carry out on behalf of the LEA many of the LEA's discretionary functions including:
- the provision of education in pupil referral units
- the assessment and statementing process for children with special educational needs (see chapter 5)
- school admissions
- school attendance
- implementation of the school organisation plan
- implementation of the behaviour support plans.

Local education authorities who 'outsource' these responsibilities will remain legally responsible and democratically accountable for the exercise of these functions. Nevertheless, the risk is that parents will find it more difficult to identify who is in practice responsible for dealing with a specific problem.

(See also Jonathan Greenwold 'Lawyer in the classroom', ch 5, on the increase of LEA liability.)

The role of the 'consumer'

As has already been indicated, parents and their children had few legal rights under the Education Act 1944. Parents were not perceived to have a formal role in the education of their children, although they could be liable if their children did not attend school or were not being educated at home (see chapter 3). Students at universities and college have rights under common law principles and human rights legislation rather than under domestic education legislation.

However, where education legislation identifies factors which should be taken into account in determining, for example, what is a suitable education for a pupil, the economic interests of the LEA tend to predominate over the interests of the parent and pupil.

Parents

The Education Act 1980 gave parents the right to express a preference for a school for their child. This was inaccurately described as the 'right to choose' a school. During the 1980s and early 1990s parents were given additional rights to information including, for example, the right to receive an annual report on their child's progress at school. In addition the appeal processes for admissions, exclusions, and special educational needs were formalised and made independent of the LEA and schools.

Who is a 'parent'?

In *Fairpo v Humberside County Council* [1997] ELR 12 one of the issues before the court was whether a 'local authority foster-parent' within the meaning of the Children Act 1989, s 23(3) was a 'parent' for the purposes of the Education Act 1993. The child was subject to a care order and the local authority had parental responsibility. The question was whether the foster parent had a right to appeal to the Special Educational Needs Tribunal.

Fairpo v Humberside County Council **[1997] ELR 12**

Laws J: That depends on whether she fell within the statutory definition of 'parent', which comes into the Education Act 1993 by a somewhat circuitous route. Schedule 13, para 10 to the Children Act 1989 added a new sub-s (1D) to s 114 of the Education Act 1944. It provides:

> In this Act, unless the context otherwise requires, 'parent', in relation to a child or young person, includes any person—
> (a) who is not a parent of his but who has parental responsibility for him, or
> (b) who has care of him ...

It is plain from the words which follow that (save for irrelevant purposes which are specified) a parent within this definition need not be a natural person, and so may include a local authority. The definition is incorporated into the Education Act 1993 by s 305(3) of that Act, which provides that the 1993 Act is to be construed as one with the Education Act 1944.

...

In truth the whole of the first limb of Mr McCarthy's argument upon analysis is to the effect that there are good policy reasons for excluding a person such as the appellant from the definition of 'parent' in any situation where there is another party possessing and concerned to exercise statutory parental responsibility . ...

But once it is accepted that in their natural sense the words of s 14(1D) are apt to apply to a person in the appellant's position, I cannot think it legitimate to displace their ordinary meaning by appeal to any such proposition. Just as with the first limb of Mr McCarthy's argument, there is no basis for reading the policy concerns which he articulates into the statutory definition.

...

Without wishing to commit the solecism of redefining the statutory definition, I apprehend that the reference in the subsection must be to someone involved in the full-time care of the child on a settled basis. I acknowledge that that is itself a formulation without hard edges, but it seems to me to represent the thrust of what Parliament intended and to conform to the ordinary meaning of the words used. ...

But I do not think that Mr McCarthy has demonstrated that the provisions of the 1989 and 1993 Acts to which he has drawn attention indicate any intention on the part of Parliament that the foster-mother should not be entitled to go to the tribunal.

Children's rights

Pupils under the age of 18 have few rights under education law legislation. It is their parents who have the rights as well as the obligations. This can be compared with the position under the Children Act 1989, where the child has rights which may conflict with those of the parents.

N Lowe 'Children's participation in the family justice system – translating principles into practice' (2001) 13(2) Child and Family Law Quarterly 137

NEW FOCUS ON CHILDREN'S PARTICIPATION IN THE LEGAL PROCESS

Historically, the great shift in English law governing parent and child was the move from the position where children were of no concern at all to one where their welfare was regarded as the court's paramount concern. This fascinating development has been well charted and needs no further elaboration here. Notwithstanding the entrenchment of the welfare principle, traditionally, under English law, children's futures have been decided upon the views of adults, that is, of parents and professionals. In other words, the welfare principle itself is adult-centred and paternalistic. Even so, what we have been witnessing over the last decade or so is an equally significant cultural shift in which children are no longer simply seen as passive victims of family breakdowns, but increasingly as participants and actors in the family justice process. In consequence, in various family proceedings it is incumbent upon the courts to ascertain and to take duly into account children's own wishes and views.

Internationally, impetus for this new focus has been given by Article 12 of the UN Convention on the Rights of the Child 1989, under which:

> States Parties shall assure to the child who is capable of forming his or her own views the right to express those views freely in all matters affecting the child, the views of the child being given due weight in accordance with the age and maturity of the child ... The child shall in particular be provided the opportunity to be heard in any judicial and administrative proceedings affecting the child, either directly, or through a representative or appropriate body, in a manner consistent with procedural rules of national law.

In Europe, the European Convention on the Exercise of Children's Rights 1996 aims to supplement the UN Convention, inter alia, by providing procedural mechanisms by which the voice of the child can be heard in legal proceedings concerning them. In particular, Article 3 provides that a child 'considered by internal law as having sufficient understanding' shall, in the case of judicial proceedings affecting him, be granted and entitled to request the following rights:
(a)   to receive all relevant information;
(b)   to be consulted and express his or her views;
(c)   to be informed of the possible consequences of compliance with these views and the possible consequences of any decision.

While Article 4 further provides for children to have the right:

> to apply, in person or through other persons or bodies, for a special representative in proceedings before a judicial authority affecting the child where internal law precludes the holders of parental responsibilities from representing the child as a result of a conflict of interest with the latter.

...

Children's 'rights' approach

The 'rights of the child' approach is sometimes referred to as being constructed on a liberationist position. This takes the view that children should have similar basic rights to adults, that the distinction between childhood and adulthood is arbitrary and that to apply the traditional best interests approach is to label children as objects of welfare rather than as young citizens who are the subject of rights. This young citizen approach was endorsed by Giddens in his 1999 Reith lectures on the family, in which he advanced the view that modern western family life is increasingly based on a participant democratic approach in which parents consult children when taking important decisions about them.

In addition to these two contrasting approaches, which have largely dominated social-legal discourse on the subject of children, there are signs that two more distinct approaches are emerging from the theoretical worlds of the sociology of childhood and the behavioural sciences. The former views children as social actors in their own terms; the latter adopts the community mental health approach.

The child as social actor

This third approach, which is assuming increasing significance in the developing social research literature of modern childhood, sets out to understand children's experiences 'in their own terms' and to take their words at face value as the primary source of knowledge about their experience. This approach, endorsed incidentally by the Scottish Law Commission, is concerned, as Butler and Williamson point out, with 'hearing the voice of the child, untrammelled by professional discretion or interpretation'. It could, therefore, be argued that, if a court is to understand children's perceptions in their own terms and to appreciate what the experience of divorce and family change means to them, a similar approach should be applied. Yet, as Roche points out, to move from the current position, in which the words of the child are 'filtered through the lens of concern of mediators and other welfare professionals, operating the current family justice system', to one in which the child's concerns are considered in their own terms, will involve a major cultural shift in family law practice. Even so, Roche is an optimist. His plea is that we 'need to be able to hear the unfamiliar and the law could provide one framework in which many voices of childhood can be heard on matters that move and concern them'.

The community mental health approach

This approach starts from the position that the practices and procedures of the family justice system (as other state social care and educational systems) impact on children's lives, whether or not their wishes and feelings are ascertained. This is acknowledged, for example, in section 1(2) of the Children Act 1989, which states that delay is normally to be regarded as detrimental to the child. The underlying thinking behind this principle is that a young person's sense of time is different from that of an adult, and that delay in reaching decisions about a child's future care can add to stress and anxiety, particularly if the child experiences a threat, actual or imagined, of separation from those with whom he is attached. In this sense, therefore, avoidable delay can be described, to use a medical metaphor, as iatrogenic (ie system-induced harm). But the converse is also true: practice and procedures can be designed and operated positively to promote a child's well-being, to buffer the impact of stressful events and even to increase a child's capacity to cope with stressful, critical situations. ... It is notable that this approach is less paternalistic than the conventional child-saving welfare approach and can be used to make a supporting behavioural science case for both the children's rights and the child as social actor approaches, which are outlined above.

VARIABLE COMPETENCE IN CHILDREN: HOW CAN THE FAMILY JUSTICE SYSTEM RESPOND?

The four approaches outlined above in practice represent a spectrum of opinion. As Hendrick observes: 'there are many gradations of perspective amongst scholars and activists'. The issue of assessing a child's competence to participate is central to the whole debate. As Lord Scarman observed in the *Gillick* case:

> The underlying principle of the law ... is that parental rights yield to the child's right to make his own decisions when he reaches a sufficient understanding and intelligence to be capable of making up his own mind on the matter requiring decision.

In practice, the crucial questions that follow from this are: first, how do courts assess when a child has reached sufficient understanding and intelligence; and, secondly, what best is the way to facilitate the child's capacity to participate in proceedings to the extent that they might wish to and to express their wishes and feelings?

In Scotland the law has begun to recognise the concept of children's rights in the area of education.

Paul Meredith 'The child's right to education' (2001) 13(1) Education and the Law 5

[I]n sharp contrast to the position in England and Wales, however, are recent developments in Scottish education law: the Scottish Parliament has recently enacted a wide-ranging and extremely important statute, the Standards in Scotland's Schools, Etc Act 2000. This new Act covers many different aspects of school education in Scotland, and includes provisions for raising standards, school inspection, the ending of self-governing status of schools, School Boards, pre-school children, guidance to education authorities as to the manner of conducting sex education, and changes to the functions and constitution of the General Teaching Council for Scotland. Of particular importance, however, for this discussion of children's rights to education are sections 1 and 2 of the Act which make express provision for children's rights and for the consultation of children over educational matters in ways which are quite unlike education legislation applicable in England and Wales.

Section 1 of the Standards in Scotland's Schools Etc Act provides that:

> It shall be the right of every child of school age to be provided with school education by, or by virtue of arrangements made, or entered into, by, an education authority.

This is unique in education legislation within the UK as a positive assertion of a right to education on the part of children. While it may not in terms of direct practical enforceability be so very different from the oblique right to education enjoyed by children in England and Wales as a correlative to the broad statutory duties placed on LEAs, school governors and headteachers, it nonetheless arguably represents a cultural shift of considerable importance, reflecting in particular the international obligations of the UK under the United Nations Convention on the Rights of the Child and the newly incorporated obligations of public authorities under the European Convention on Human Rights.

Section 2(1) of the Act goes further, imposing a duty on education authorities, where school education is provided to a child or young person by (or through arrangements made by) an education authority, to:

> ...secure that the education is directed to the development of the personality, talents, and mental and physical abilities of the child or young person to their fullest potential.

This in part reflects the wording of Article 29 of the UN Convention on the Rights of the Child and, while culturally significant, may not in itself be of significance in terms of enforceability. Of greater significance arguably is section 2(2) which provides that:

> In carrying out their duty under this section, an education authority shall have due regard, so far as is reasonably practicable, to the views (if there is a wish to express them) of the child or young person in decisions that significantly affect that child or young person, taking account of the child or young person's age and maturity.

Although this section is open to widely divergent interpretations (what, for example, is a decision that 'significantly affects' a child?), and is highly qualified in its terms (it only applies so far as is 'reasonably practicable'), it remains true that the imposition of a duty on education authorities to consult children and young persons over educational decisions of any sort—with its correlative right in the child or young person to be consulted—is unique in education legislation within the UK. Even in the context of crucial decisions affecting the child's future—for example, as to choice of school or the exercise of the parental right to withdraw a child from religious education or worship or from sex education—there has hitherto existed no provision in education law within the UK for consulting the child.

It will be interesting to see whether these issues are also addressed in the context of English and Welsh education law. Recent changes to special educational need legislation (see chapter 5) have begun to recognise the rights of the child. A child is now entitled to attend and give evidence before the Special Educational Needs Tribunal, and the LEA is required to consult the child about the appeal to the tribunal.

The lack of rights for pupils as opposed to their parents may be remedied to some extent by the Human Rights Act 1998 (see below). A claim in tort or for breach of contract may be brought in relation to loss suffered by a pupil under the age of 18. However, a contract claim will only be available where the pupil attends an independent school. For example, a student at an independent school is reported to have threatened to sue her school because she obtained an E grade in her Latin A level.

Students

University students have become increasingly litigious when they fail their programme of study or are not awarded the qualification to which they consider they are entitled. Their challenges to university decisions are normally brought using the judicial review procedure (see chapter 8). However, in *Clark v University of Lincolnshire and Humberside* [2000] ELR 345, the Court of Appeal confirmed that a student may bring a claim against his or her university for breach of contract. Students are likely to be regarded as 'consumers' in the context of consumer protection legislation.

Further education students do not feature in the law reports. This may be because the majority of their qualifications are externally assessed and awarded, which results in fewer complaints against their college.

The role of courts, tribunals, and ombudsmen

Courts

Most education law cases come to court as applications for judicial review of a decision taken by the LEA, or the Secretary of State or the governing body of a school. According to Bridges, Meszaros and Sunkin (*Judicial Review in Perspective* (2nd edn, 1995)) the number of judicial review applications involving education trebled between the late 1970s and the mid 1990s. Many of the applications arose before the Special Educational Needs Tribunal was established. The majority of judicial review applications now involve school admissions, exclusions, or school transport, as well as claims by students against their university.

Negligence claims are also increasing, particularly in the area of special educational needs. Contract claims arise where a child is educated at an independent school, and occasionally where a student sues their university.

Tribunals

Despite the increase in court cases the majority of education appeals are heard in tribunals, which include:

- school admission appeal panels
- school exclusion appeal panels
- Special Educational Needs Tribunal.

The members of admission and exclusion appeal panels are lay volunteers who sit as and when needed. The panels are normally organised by the local education authority. In the case of admission appeals to voluntary aided and foundation schools, the admission appeal panels are organised by the governing body. There are normally three members of a panel, which hears appeals by parents where their child is refused a place at their chosen school, or where their child has been permanently excluded from school.

The Special Educational Needs Tribunal (SENT) was established by the Education Act 1993, partly in response to the increasing number of judicial review applications brought by parents against decisions of the local authority. The tribunal is composed of a legally qualified chairman and two members with relevant experience. The tribunal hears appeals from parents in relation to statutory assessments and statements of their child's special educational needs. From September 2002 the tribunal will also hear claims relating to disability discrimination and will be known as the Special Educational Needs and Disability Tribunal (SENDIST).

In 2001 the Report of the Review of Tribunals, *Tribunals for Users — One System, One Service* (the Leggatt Review) proposed the establishment of a single Education Appeal Tribunal. There would also be a new appellate tribunal. The following proposals were made in relation to admission and exclusion appeal panels which are local government tribunals, and the Special Educational Needs Tribunal.

*Tribunals for Users — One System, One Service,*Report of the Review of Tribunals by Sir Andrew Leggatt, (March 2001)

3.15 Local government tribunals should therefore be included in the Tribunals system. This would have several particular, practical advantages: accommodation alongside other tribunals, a more professional administration, access to IT systems, clear independence, increased accountability, opportunity to share expertise with related tribunals, such as the Special Educational Needs Tribunal (SENT), and access to training for members. We recognise that these tribunals together hear even more cases than the Appeals Service. Their amalgamation into the Tribunals Service, particularly that of the School Admission and Exclusion Appeal Panels, will present large and complex problems. We are, however, convinced that users would benefit significantly if they were included.

3.16 On the face of it, this recommendation might appear to be reducing the independence of local authorities (and in the case of foundation and voluntary aided schools, school governing bodies). In reality it is simply ending a situation in which the local authority is judge in its own cause. It should be noted, however, that the jurisdiction of the SENT has been moved from local to central government without detriment, and reviews of Housing Benefit, which are currently a local responsibility, are shortly to be replaced with a right of appeal to an appeal tribunal, administered by the Appeals Service. The Tribunals Service will have a network of hearing centres across the country. It should aim to provide a responsive local service from that network. Local authorities should be consulted about the issues involved in any transfer.

The Leggatt Review made specific recommendations in relation to school admission and exclusion appeal panels as well as the Special Educational Needs Tribunal. These included:

- improved information for parents
- stronger lay representation on panels
- a legally qualified chairman or clerk where the panel has to consider some aspect of the legislation
- the use of mediation or conciliation before a SENT hearing.

The Special Educational Needs Tribunal as well as other education tribunals, for example, the Registered Inspectors of Schools Tribunal, would also form part of the Education Appeal Tribunal.

Ombudsman

Complaints about maladministration by the LEA or the governing body of a school can be made to the Local Government Ombudsman (see chapter 8). The majority of such complaints relate to special educational needs, school admissions and exclusions.

2. THE LEGAL CONTEXT

Education law forms part of a broader legal picture which includes both domestic and European law. Potentially the most important development in recent years has been the passage of the Human Rights Act 1998. Discrimination legislation was already applicable to schools as well as to further and higher education to a certain extent before 2002, but the impact of the Special Educational Needs and Disability Act 2001 is likely to be considerable.

Employment law

Employment law is outside the scope of this book, but dismissal, discrimination and whistleblowing legislation is applicable to teachers, lecturers, and other employees. The contracting out to private companies of work undertaken by ancillary staff such as dinner ladies and school caretakers is also subject to employment legislation. Teachers' terms and conditions of employment are, however, regulated by specific legislation, including the Protection of Children Act 1999. Educational institutions are subject to the Health and Safety at Work etc Act 1974 which is concerned with the health, safety and welfare of employees, and visitors including pupils and students.

Children Act 1989

Under s 17(1) of the Children Act 1989 a local authority has a general duty to safeguard and promote the welfare of children within its area who are in need (see chapter 5). This may include, for example, day care provision for pre-school children, supervised activities after school and during school holidays. See, for example, *R v Nottingham City Council, ex p AB and SB* [2001] EWHC Admin 235, [2001] 3 FCR 350, in relation to a child protection plan.

Where children are not attending school there are a variety of orders which can be made by a court under either the Education Act 1996 (see chapter 3) or under the Children Act 1989 (CA 1989). A court may issue an education supervision order in certain circumstances (s 36 of and Sch 3 to the CA 1989). The welfare of the child is the paramount consideration under the CA 1989, in contrast to the Education Acts where, as already indicated, it is the parent rather than the pupil who has rights.

Law of the European Union

European Community law is relevant to aspects of education law. In particular, it is relevant to EU nationals who wish to travel to other member states and once there receive publicly funded education either for themselves or their children.

Article 127 of the EC Treaty (formerly Article 128 of the EEC Treaty) recognises the right of workers to receive vocational training. This together with Article 6 EC (prohibition against discrimination on grounds of nationality) and Article 48 EC (free movement of workers) has been recognised by the European Court of Justice as providing the basis for a right to education in certain circumstances. The European Social Charter also recognises a right to vocational education (Article 15).

The distinction between education and vocational training under EU law is important because of the rights attached to the status of 'a worker'.

Ruth Nielsen and Erica Szyszczak *The Social Dimension of the EU* (1997) Handelshøjskolens Forlong, chapter 3

The term 'education' appears for the first time within EC competence as a result of the amendments made by the TEU [Treaty on European Union] 1992 in Article 3(p) EC, Article 126 EC and Article 127 EC. However Article C TEU states that:

> The Union shall be served by a single institutional framework which shall ensure the consistency and the continuity of the activities carried out in order to attain its objectives while respecting and building upon the 'acquis communautaire'.

Since Articles 126 and 127 EC are the successors to Article 128 EEC Article C TEU requires that Articles 126 and 127 EC must be interpreted and applied in such a way that Article 128 EEC is respected and built upon. We must, therefore, examine the *acquis communautaire* in relation to the competence of the EC to develop an education policy.

Competence prior to the TEU

Prior to the TEU, Community competence in the field of education can be discerned in three areas: 1. Education issues were raised under Regulation 1612/68/EEC in relation to rights to facilitate the free movement of workers and for members of their families who wished to study in another Member State. 2. The EC had competence to enact legislation for the mutual recognition of educational and professional qualifications in order to facilitate the free movement of workers under Article 57(1) EC. 3. Legislation was adopted to establish Community schemes in areas such as vocational training, foreign languages, educational exchanges and educational mobility (schemes such as ERASMUS, COMMETT, LINGUA) and to establish a European Training Foundation. This in turn has generated a number of legal base disputes before the ECJ.

Community competence in the field of education after the TEU

There was a gradual shift of balance towards the development of Community vocational training policy through educational institutions as a matter of educational policy, so that from the mid-1980s onwards we find a proliferation of Community vocational training programmes, such as the ERASMUS programme, which created a platform for Community intervention into the further and higher education systems of the member states. This evolution towards a double-track approach to vocational training, with an *educational* track as well as an employment policy track, was decisively confirmed by the TEU 1992. On the employment policy front, Article 123 EEC was amended to make it explicit that vocational training and retraining were the particular means by which the Social Fund was to facilitate adaptation to industrial changes and changes in production systems.

Additionally a new Treaty chapter was created, entitled 'Education, Vocational Training and Youth'. This conferred powers and imposed duties on the Community, which were quite distinct from those relating to the Social Fund, in respect of the development of education (Article 126 EC) and vocational training (Article 127 EC). The importance of Article 127 EC is not, however, in the enlargement of the overall competence of the Community in respect of vocational training, but in the way that it locates some of that competence in the field of education policy rather than employment policy.

The relationship between Articles 127 EC and 128 EC is of major importance, since the content of the Community powers which they delineate is not identical, and neither is the way in which those powers are exercised. The decision-making procedure with regard to education is 'co-decision' (Article 189B EC), whereas that with regard to vocational training is 'cooperation' (Article 189C EC). The demarcation line between education and vocational training has been made more difficult to draw by the fact that the dynamic interpretation which the Court has given to the expression 'vocational training' in connection with Article 128 EEC has caused a number of educational curricular activities to be regarded as vocational training. In the context of the *acquis communautaire* the terms 'education' and 'vocational training' are therefore no longer mutually exclusive, although not all forms of vocational training are provided in an educational context. Now, all forms of education which were not classified as 'vocational training' and falling within Article 128 EC will be covered by the new Article 126 EC. This will include pre-school, primary education, general secondary education and university courses for people wishing to improve their general knowledge rather than prepare themselves for an occupation. Indeed it is arguable that Article 126 EC has become the *lex generalis* with Article 127 the *lex specialis*. The question remains as to whether Articles 126 EC and 127 EC are exhaustive or can Article 235 EC still be used to give the EC competence in matters excluded from the scope of these Articles? Lenaerts predicts that the ECJ will be asked to rule on a number of legal base disputes, possibly initiated by the European Parliament.

The Leonardo Decision is regarded as a key instrument in the new EC policy towards education and vocational training. Article 3 lays down a common framework of objectives for EC action. Freedland calls it 'a new constitution for EC vocational training policy in all but name.' There is now a tendency to see vocational training policy as a matter of educational, rather than employment, policy. This is seen in the Leonardo Decision and also the Education White Paper. Freedland argues that important dimensions of the question, of the scope and purpose of vocational training are lost or down-played if employment policy is not given sufficient emphasis.

The right to receive education in a member state depends upon the status of the pupil or student.

Anthony Robinson 'European Community nationals and their right to receive education in the member state of their choice' (1998) 10(2-3) Education and the Law 113

The right to education under EC law

Until the European Court of Justice (ECJ) decision in *Casagrande v Landeshauptstadt München* [1974] ECR 773, the prevailing view was that entitlement to education, not being an economic activity, was outside the strict scope of Community powers and was solely within the province of the member states. The Court held that the powers which are attributed to the Community to establish a common market could not be limited by the fact that they may affect substantive policy which is formally only within the competence of member states, eg educational policy. The Court declared that:

> Although educational and training policy is not as such included in the spheres which the Treaty has entrusted to the Community institutions, it does not follow that the exercise of powers transferred to the Community is in some way limited if it is of such a nature as to affect the measures taken in the execution of a policy such as that of education and training.

Walter Van Gerven and Peter Van Den Bossche argue that:

> While education remains in the first place a matter for the member states and while the Commission, well aware of the fact that in entering this field the Community is treading on the thin ice of member sates' sensibilities, [it] emphasises time and again its minimalist role under the principle of subsidiarity, [and] the need for a more active and broader involvement of the Community in the field of education is now generally recognised.

The issue that came before the Court for consideration in the *Casagrande* case was the question of the ambit of Article 12 of Council Regulation (EEC) 1612/68 ... on the free movement of workers within the Community, and the right of access to education for children of migrant workers. The Court in the case of *Blaizot v University of Liege* extended this principle of freedom of movement to vocational training under Article 128 of the EEC Treaty. The growing awareness by the Community of the importance of education and its function as a means of realising the goal of the internal market, securing the future wealth and well-being of the Community, and its economic cohesion, led to the EC formally adopting education as an instrument of its policies. In its Communication to the Council of June 1989 on Guidelines for the Medium Term (1989–1992) on Education and Training, the Commission formally recognised the importance of developing its education policy as part of its Internal Market Programme.

In essence the question of whether a student has the right of access to the educational provision of any member state depends upon the strength of the student's claim to be accorded a particular status under Community law.

There are four possible categories of status that the student may claim that may grant them the corollary rights that flow from the 'parcel' of fundamental rights:

1.   The student may be able to invoke the status of a Community citizen.
2.   The student may be able to invoke the status of a Community worker.
3.   The student may [be able to] claim the status of a child of a Community worker.
4.   The student may be able to claim the status of a receiver of services.

...

The Court confirmed in the case of *Gravier v City of Liège* [1985] that member states are responsible for the organisation of their education systems and their teaching policies, and that these matters are not within the Community competence. The Court thereby made clear that the responsibility for determining the educational system and the policies that are pursued remains with the member state, although the member state is responsible for ensuring equality of treatment with other Community nationals who are resident within their area and the Court would interfere to see that such equality is granted.

European Community law expressly protects the rights of children to education where their parents move to work in a different member state.

Council Regulation on Freedom of Movement of Workers within the Community (1612/68/EEC), Art 12

The children of a national of a member state who is or has been employed in the territory of another member state shall be admitted to that state's general educational, apprenticeship and vocational training courses under the same conditions as the nationals of that state, if such children are residing in its territory.

Member states shall encourage all efforts to enable such children to attend these courses under the best possible conditions.

In *Landesamt für Ausbildungsförderung Nordrhein-Westfalen v Gaal*: C-7/94 [1995] All ER (EC) 653 the European Court of Justice held that 'children' were not required to be under 21 or dependent on their parents in order to rely on Article 12 and be eligible for an education allowance. The applicant was a Belgian national who had lived in Germany since the age of two. The principle of equal treatment applies to such 'children'. In this case German nationals remained eligible for an educational allowance when they were over 21 and no longer dependent on their parents.

N Hopkins 'Education and the Children of Migrant Workers: once a child always a child' 18(1) Journal of Social Welfare and Family Law 114

Commentary

Lubor Gaal should be seen in the context of the Court's piecemeal development of a Community education law. The Court's broad interpretation of the material scope of Article 12 (summarised in paras 19 and 24 of its judgment) had already placed the children of migrant workers in a more favourable position under Community law than other students (those with the status of worker and migrant students). The child of a migrant worker can claim equal access to vocational and non-vocational training. This includes equal access to grants for both fees and maintenance. The contribution to the Community education law in *Lubor Gaal* is the broad interpretation of the personal scope of the provision; ie of who can benefit from this favourable position. In defining the personal scope the Court, consistent with its approach in Case 197/86 (*Brown v Secretary of State for Scotland* [1988] ECR 3205) and *Echternach and Moritz*, ... was willing to consider a literal interpretation of the article and the spirit of the regulation. The case can also be seen in the context of the Court's consideration of Regulation 1612/68 generally. In a review of the Court's decisions concerning free movement of workers during 1989–94 Johnson and O'Keeffe noted that the Court had continued a trend of interpreting the material and personal scope of the regulation widely.

The social importance of the decision is that the Court prevented the fact that Mr Gaal had been orphaned from placing him at a disadvantage in relation to education. As Mr Gaal was not of independent means it would seem that he would have been dependent upon his father were his father still alive. If that had been the case then there would probably have been no doubt that he was within Article 12 as a dependant despite his age. While the Court had not previously considered whether the personal scope is subject to an age limit one of the claimants in *Echternach and Moritz* ... was in fact 24 years old at the time of his claim (as Advocate-General Tesauro noted in para 13 of his opinion). In addition, in Case 235/87 (*Matteucci v Communauté française de Belgique* [1988] ECR 5589), Advocate-General Slynn had said that a child should not come outside the scope of the article because of his age (pp. 5601–2). On this analysis the Court's judgment ensured that Mr Gaal was not disadvantaged now that he was dependent upon the state *in loco parentis*.

The Court's interpretation of the personal scope of Article 12 will not only benefit orphans. The decision means that children whose parents are alive are within its personal scope even when the children are 21 years or over and independent. This may even include a child who is a worker.

In the United Kingdom DES Circular 5/81 dated 31 July 1981 (Council Directive of 25 July 1977 on the Education of Children of Migrant Workers) provides guidance to LEAs in relation to language teaching for children of compulsory school age.

Other ECJ decisions of importance in the context of education law include:
- *Lair v Universitat of Hannover*: 39/86 [1988] ECR 3161 (French national who had previously worked in Germany was entitled to a grant on the same basis as German workers under Council Regulation 1612/88);
- *European Parliament v EC Council (Re Students' Residence Directive)*: C-295/90 [1992] 3 CMLR 281 (students have a right of residence in order to pursue their studies in another member state).

One continuing area of debate that is of particular interest in a free market is the mutual recognition of qualifications which will encourage and enable the free movement of workers.

3.   EQUAL OPPORTUNITIES

The Sex Discrimination Act 1975, the Race Relations Act 1976, and the Disability Discrimination Act 1995 apply to the provision of educational services by schools, further education colleges, universities, and LEAs, as well as to the employment of teachers and other staff. In addition the ECHR prohibits discrimination on a wide range of grounds (see Article 14 discussed below).

Sex discrimination

There are three main forms of sex discrimination specified in the Sex Discrimination Act 1975: direct (s 1(1)(a)); indirect (s 1(1)(b)); and victimisation (s 4). (See also ch 3, LEA's duties.)

Sex Discrimination Act 1975, s 1

(1) A person discriminates against a woman in any circumstances relevant for the purposes of any provision of this Act if—
(a)   on the ground of her sex he treats her less favourably than he treats or would treat a man, or
(b)   he applies to her a requirement or condition which he applies or would apply to a man but—
    (i)   which is such that the proportion of women who can comply with it is considerably smaller than the proportion of men who can comply with it, and
    (ii)   which he cannot show to be justifiable irrespective of the sex of the person to whom it is applied, and
    (iii)   which is to her detriment because she cannot comply with it.

The 1975 Act makes it unlawful to discriminate against both male and female pupils and students on the ground of their sex as well as their marital status. Case law has established that sexual harassment falls within the definition of discrimination, and therefore certain types of bullying or name-calling by pupils (or teachers) may amount to sex discrimination.

It is also unlawful to victimise a pupil or student because they have been involved in or made a complaint under the Act; and it is unlawful to discriminate against a pupil or student who is undergoing gender reassignment.

Part III of the Sex Discrimination Act 1975 is concerned with discrimination in education. However, the Act has only been relied on in a limited number of education cases. These have mainly been in the context of the provision of single-sex grammar schools (see chapter 3). Section 22 sets out who is responsible where certain acts of sex discrimination occurs in a particular educational institution.

Sex Discrimination Act 1975, s 22

It is unlawful in relation to an educational establishment falling within column 1 of the following table, for a person indicated in relation to the establishment in column 2 (the 'responsible body') to discriminate against a woman—

(a)   in terms on which it offers to admit her to the establishment as a pupil, or
(b)   by refusing or deliberately omitting to accept an application for her admission to the establishment as a pupil, or
(c)   where she is a pupil of the establishment—
    (i)   in the way it affords her access to any benefits, facilities or services, or by refusing or deliberately omitting to afford her access to them, or
    (ii)   by excluding her from the establishment or subjecting her to any other detriment.

TABLE
ENGLAND AND WALES

Establishment	Responsible body
1. Educational establishment maintained by a local education authority.	Local education authority or … [governing body], according to which of them has the function in question.
2. Independent school not being a special school.	Proprietor.
3. Special school not maintained by a local education authority.	Proprietor … Governing body.]
[3B. Institution within the further education sector (within the meaning of section 91(3) of the Further and Higher Education Act 1992).	Governing body.]
4. University.	Governing body.
4A. Institution, other than a university, within the higher education sector (within the meaning of section 91(5) of the Further and Higher Education Act 1992).	Governing body.]
4. Establishment (not falling within paragraphs 1 [to 4A]) providing full-time or part-time education, being an establishment designated under section 24(1).	Governing body.

Note that s 22 makes it unlawful to discriminate on grounds of sex in four circumstances.

* *Are there any other circumstances where sex discrimination might occur in an educational institution which would therefore not be unlawful?*

In *Debell, Sevket and Teh v London Borough of Bromley* (1984) (reported in Butterworths, *The Law of Education,* F [31]) three female pupils had been kept down a year because of their sex. They claimed that the defendants were in breach of ss 1(1)(a) and s 22(c) of the Sex Discrimination Act 1975 (SDA 1975). Bromley admitted unlawful sex discrimination and paid damages to the claimants.

In *R v Secretary of State for Education, ex p Connon* [1996] COD 454, the only single-sex, non-selective boys school in Gloucestershire proposed to admit girls to Year 10 (the first year of GCSE courses). The Secretary of State rejected the proposal because if adopted it would result in girls but not boys living in the LEA area having the option of receiving single-sex education at that age. A mother of two girls unsuccessfully applied for judicial review of the Secretary of State's decision.

Local education authorities and various funding councils, including the Learning and Skills Council, should not discriminate on grounds of sex when carrying out any of their functions (SDA 1975, ss 23, 23A, 25A). In addition any body providing public sector education is under a duty to provide facilities without sex discrimination (SDA 1975, s 25). There are exemptions for training provision in limited circumstances (SDA 1975, ss 47, 48).

Sections 22 and 25 do not apply to the admission of pupils to single-sex establishments (s 26). Educational charities may apply to the Secretary of State to modify the trust deed where the charity is for the benefit of one sex only.

Where a pupil or a student has been discriminated against in breach of the Sex Discrimination Act 1975, any claim is treated as a claim in tort and can be brought in the county court (s 66 of the SDA 1975). However, damages are not automatically awarded for indirect discrimination (s 1(1)(b)) where the respondent proves that the requirement or condition in question was not applied with the intention of treating the claimant unfavourably on the ground of his sex.

Race discrimination

Racial segregation in education was of central importance to the civil right movement in the United States of America. In *Brown v Board of Education of Topeka* 347 US 483 (1954) the US Supreme Court held that the provision of racially segregated education was in breach of the Fourteenth Amendment of the US Constitution.

A policy of racial segregation in education has never been adopted in the United Kingdom, although in some schools there is arguably de facto segregation on racial or religious grounds. Religious segregation exists in Northern Ireland and may occur more frequently in England and Wales if the government's proposal for an increase in the number of 'faith schools' is implemented.

The relevant provisions of the Race Relations Act 1976 (RRA 1976) are virtually identical to those in the Sex Discrimination Act 1975. Again there are three forms of discrimination: direct (s 1(1)(a)); indirect (s 1(1)(b)); and victimisation (s 2).

Race Relations Act 1976, s 1

(1) A person discriminates against another in any circumstances relevant for the purposes of any provision of this Act if—

(a) on racial grounds he treats that other less favourably than he treats or would treat other persons; or

(b) he applies to that other a requirement or condition which he applies or would apply equally to persons not of the same racial group as that other but—
  (i)   which is such that the proportion of persons of the same racial group as that other who can comply with it is considerably smaller than the proportion of persons not of that racial group who can comply with it; and
  (ii) which he cannot show to be justifiable irrespective of the colour, race, nationality or ethnic or national origins of the person to whom it is applied; and
  (iii) which is to the detriment of that other because he cannot comply with it.

(2) It is hereby declared that, for the purposes of this Act, segregating a person from other persons on racial grounds is treating him less favourably than they are treated.

In *Mandla v Dowell Lee* [1983] 2 AC 548 the House of Lords held that the refusal by the headmaster of an independent school to admit a Sikh boy unless he removed his turban and cut his hair was unlawful. Their Lordships held that Sikhs were a racial group within the meaning of the RRA 1976 and that the headmaster's decision was a breach of s 1(1)(b).

Part III of the Race Relations Act 1976 is concerned with discrimination in education. It is unlawful for LEAs, governors, and governing bodies to discriminate on racial grounds against a person when admitting them to, excluding them from, or affording them access to benefits, facilities or services at the educational establishment in question (RRA 1976, s 17, which is virtually identical to SDA 1975, s 22; see above). In May 2000 the Home Office published a Code of Practice on the recording of racist incidents and crimes by schools as well as other community and voluntary groups.

Local education authorities should not racially discriminate when carrying out any of their functions under the Education Acts (s 18 of the RRA 1976). However, in *R v Cleveland County Council, ex p Commission for Racial Equality* (1992) 91 LGR 139, the Court of Appeal held that the duty not to discriminate did not enable the LEA to refuse to comply with a mother's preference that her daughter attend a predominantly white school, rather than the school with predominately Asian pupils, which she was currently attending (see chapter 3). The duty on the LEA to comply with parental preference was not qualified by the duty not to discriminate.

It is also unlawful for various funding councils, including the Learning and Skills Council, to discriminate on racial grounds (RRA 1976, s 18A). As with sex discrimination there is a general duty on anybody providing public sector education to provide facilities without racial discrimination (RRA 1976, s 19). It is also unlawful for a public authority in carrying out any of its functions to do any act which constitutes discrimination (RRA 1976, s 19B as amended by the Race Relations (Amendment) Act 2000).

In certain circumstances it is permissible and not in breach of the RRA 1976 to provide education specifically for particular racial groups.

Race Relations Act 1976, s 35

Nothing in Parts II to IV shall render unlawful any act done in affording persons of a particular racial group access to facilities or services to meet the special needs of persons of that group in regard to their education, training or welfare, or any ancillary benefits.

There are also more specific exemptions for training (RRA 1976, ss 37, 38).

The Race Relations Act 1976, unlike the Sex Discrimination Act 1975, imposed a general statutory duty on all local authorities. The original section has been replaced by the Race Relations (Amendment) Act 2000 and now reads as follows.

Race Relations Act 1976, s 71

(1) Every body or other person specified in Schedule 1A or of a description falling within that Schedule shall, in carrying out its functions, have due regard to the need—
(a)   to eliminate unlawful racial discrimination; and
(b)   to promote equality of opportunity and good relations between persons of different racial groups.

(2) The Secretary of State may by order impose, on such persons falling within Schedule 1A as he considers appropriate, such duties as he considers appropriate for the purpose of ensuring the better performance by those persons of their duties under subsection (1). ...

The bodies listed in Schedule 1A include local councils, the governing bodies of LEA maintained schools, as well as further and higher education institutions. From May 2002 public bodies, including educational institutions, are under a statutory duty to publish a race equality scheme and to undertake ethnic monitoring of their workforce. A draft Code of Practice on how public authorities should give effect to this section was published in December 2001.

However, the Act has its limitations. It is not unlawful to discriminate on the grounds of religion. This means, for example, that schools 'with a religious character', such as Church of England schools, are permitted to give priority when offering places to children who are christened (see chapter 3).

Similarly, admissions authorities may require children baptised as Catholic attending a Catholic primary school to attend a Catholic secondary school, even though their parents would prefer their child to attend the local community school. Other children attending the primary school would not be required to attend the Catholic secondary school.

Article 14 of the ECHR prohibits discrimination on religious as well as racial grounds (see below), and may provide the basis for claims under the Human Rights Act 1998 where there has been discrimination on religious grounds in the provision of education.

Finally, although the Race Relations Act 1976 made it unlawful to charge overseas students higher tuition fees than home students, a student was not entitled to damages because s 57 provides that damages should not be awarded where there is indirect discrimination but there is no intention to discriminate (*Orphanos v Queen Mary*

College [1985] 2 All ER 233, HL). Overseas students from countries outside the European Union continue to be charged higher fees than UK and EU students.

Disability discrimination

The Disability Discrimination Act (DDA) 1995 originally placed minimal obligations on LEAs and educational institutions. It required schools, colleges and universities to inform parents, pupils and students about the facilities available for disabled people. Schools were required to include information in their annual reports relating to admissions, equal treatment and facilities for disabled pupils (see DfEE Circular 20/99 (What the Disability Discrimination Act (DDA) 1995 Means for Schools and LEAs)).

Further education colleges were required to publish disability statements, and to report to the Government on their progress and future plans for providing FE to students with disabilities. The Higher Education Funding Council was required to take account of the needs of disabled students. Universities and other HE institutions were required to provide disability statements.

None of these provisions gave individual pupils or students an enforceable right with an effective remedy. However, the discrimination provisions of the DDA 1995 have been extended to schools, FE colleges and universities by the Special Educational Needs and Disability Act 2001 (SENDA 2001). The disability provisions start coming into force from September 2002, and the Disability Rights Commission has published two draft codes of practice. The first applies to schools, and the second to post-16 education.

From September 2002 it will be unlawful for LEAs and governing bodies to discriminate against a disabled person when admitting them to or excluding them from school, or in the provision of education or associated services offered to pupils at school (DDA 1995, s 28A). Similar provisions apply to the governing bodies of further and higher education institutions (DDA 1995, s 28R). These provisions are similar but not identical to those in the sex and race discrimination legislation (SDA 1975, s 22, RRA 1976, s 17).

The definition of disability discrimination is contained in the Disability Discrimination Act 1995 as amended by SENDA 2001, ss 12, 13, 27, 28. There are two main forms of discrimination, although there is no concept of indirect discrimination. There are separate definitions for schools (DDA 1995, ss 28B, 28C) and for further and higher education (DDA 1995, ss 28S, 28T).

Disability Discrimination Act 1995, s 28B

(1) For the purposes of section 28A, a responsible body discriminates against a disabled person if—

(a) for a reason which relates to his disability, it treats him less favourably than it treats or would treat others to whom that reason does not or would not apply; and

(b) it cannot show that the treatment in question is justified.

(2) For the purposes of section 28A, a responsible body also discriminates against a disabled person if—

(a)   it fails, to his detriment, to comply with section 28C; and

(b)   it cannot show that its failure to comply is justified.

...

(6) Less favourable treatment of a person is justified if it is the result of a permitted form of selection.

(7) Otherwise, less favourable treatment, or a failure to comply with section 28C, is justified only if the reason for it is both material to the circumstances of the particular case and substantial.

(8) If, in a case falling within subsection (1)—

(a)   the responsible body is under a duty imposed by section 28C in relation to the disabled person, but

(b)   it fails without justification to comply with that duty,

its treatment of that person cannot be justified under subsection (7) unless that treatment would have been justified even if it had complied with that duty.

Disability Discrimination Act 1995, s 28C

Disabled pupils not to be substantially disadvantaged

(1) The responsible body for a school must take such steps as it is reasonable for it to have to take to ensure that—

(a)   in relation to the arrangements it makes for determining the admission of pupils to the school, disabled persons are not placed at a substantial disadvantage in comparison with persons who are not disabled; and

(b)   in relation to education and associated services provided for, or offered to, pupils at the school by it, disabled pupils are not placed at a substantial disadvantage in comparison with pupils who are not disabled.

(2) That does not require the responsible body to—

(a)   remove or alter a physical feature (for example, one arising from the design or construction of the school premises or the location of resources); or

(b)   provide auxiliary aids or services.

Similar provisions apply to further and higher education students (DDA 1995, ss 28S, 28T). Less favourable treatment of a student is justified if it is necessary in order to maintain academic standards or standards of any other prescribed kind (DDA 1995, s 28S(6)). For example, using the same criteria to assess the written work of dyslexic students as other students is unlikely to amount to discrimination.

Many pupils and students with disabilities will also have special educational needs (see chapter 5 for the definition of a disabled person, and the rights and remedies available to disabled pupils and students).

4.   THE HUMAN RIGHTS ACT 1998

The Human Rights Act 1998 came into force in the United Kingdom on 2 October 2000. It incorporates most of the European Convention on Human Rights into English law.

The government should not introduce legislation which is incompatible with the Convention, and courts and tribunals must take into account the provisions of the Convention and its case law when reaching decisions.

The following ECHR Articles are of relevance to education law.

European Convention on Human Rights

Article 3 Prohibition of torture

No one shall be subjected to torture or to inhuman or degrading treatment or punishment.

Article 6 Right to a fair trial

1. In the determination of his civil rights and obligations…everyone is entitled to a fair and public hearing within a reasonable time by an independent and impartial tribunal established by law…

Article 8 Right to respect for family and private life

1.   Everyone has the right to respect for his private and family life, his home and his correspondence.

Article 14 Prohibition of discrimination

The enjoyment of the rights and freedoms set forth in this Convention shall be secured without discrimination on any ground such as sex, race, colour, language, religion, political or other opinion, national or social origin, association with a national minority, property, birth or other status.

The First Protocol

Article 2 Right to education

No person shall be denied the right to education. In the exercise of any functions which it assumes in relation to education and to teaching, the state shall respect the right of parents to ensure such education and teaching in conformity with their own religious and philosophical convictions.

When the United Kingdom signed the First Protocol in 1952 the United Kingdom entered the following reservation:

> …in view of certain provisions of the Education Acts in the United Kingdom, the principle affirmed in the second sentence of Article 2 is accepted by the United Kingdom only so far as it is compatible with the provision of efficient instruction and training, and the avoidance of unreasonable public expenditure.

In *Holub and Holub v Secretary of State for the Home Department* [2001] ELR 401 the Court of Appeal was asked to consider the right to education in the context of an immigration decision which would result in a girl who had been educated in the United Kingdom since 1995 being returned to Poland and continuing her education there.

Holub and Holub v Secretary of State for the Home Department [2001] ELR 401

[25] [We] would adopt as an accurate statement of the law the following passages from Lester and Pannick *Human Rights Law and Practice* (Butterworths, 1999) (paras 4.20.4 and 4.20.6):

> The general right to education comprises four separate rights (none of which is absolute):
> (i)   right of access to such educational establishments as exist;
> (ii)   a right to effective (but not the most effective possible) education;
> (iii) a right to official recognition of academic qualifications ...
> As regards the right to an effective education, for the right to education to be meaningful the quality of the education must reach a minimum standard.

But we do not think that the right is more extensive than this. If Mr Luba's submission that there is a right to an 'appropriate' education means something more than an effective education in the sense described above we do not accept this. There is nothing in the authorities or the literature to which we have been referred which supports such a submission. The Convention does not confer a right to education in any particular country and so does not invite comparison between educational systems.

[26] So Art 2 is limited in scope. Does the evidence show that Luiza's removal from her school in England and return to the Polish education system would breach her Art 2 right? We do not think so. It is certainly not enough to say that Luiza will get a better education in the United Kingdom. Poland clearly has a well developed system of education. It is not surprising that someone who has been out of it for several years will have difficulties getting back into it. But in this case Luiza appears to have the ability to overcome these difficulties. Not only is she extremely bright but she has obviously kept up her Polish to a high standard by attending the Polish Saturday School, no doubt assisted by her mother who is a highly regarded Polish teacher. We do not think that it can be said that Luiza will be denied an effective education if she returns to Poland.

There are four general points relating to the application of the Convention to education law, as well as specific issues, such as corporal punishment, which are considered in the relevant chapters.

1. Is education a civil right within Article 6?

The European Commission of Human Rights considered this point when deciding whether an application under the Convention was admissible. In *Simpson v United Kingdom* (1989) 64 DR 188 the applicant contended that the United Kingdom law and procedures then applicable to him as a pupil with special educational needs were in breach of Article 6.1, Article 2 of the First Protocol, and Article 8 (see also chapter 5).

Simpson v UK (1989) Application 14688/89

Complaints

The applicant complains that the procedures determining his special educational needs and provision were in breach of Article 6 para 1 of the Convention, being a biased, unlawful determination of his civil rights by partial bodies, who created unreasonable delays. He alleges ... that there is no fair, oral or public hearing before the Secretary of State for Education, who himself cannot constitute an independent and impartial tribunal.

...

The law

In analysing complaints of this kind the Convention organs must deal with three questions:
*   whether the case gives rise to a 'contestation' (dispute) concerning a right;
*   if so, whether the right at issue is civil in character;
*   if so, whether there has been compliance with Article 6 para 1 (Art 6–1) of the Convention (cf Eur Court HR, Benthem judgment 23 October 1985, Series A no 97).
As to the first question the Commission considers that the case does give rise to a 'contestation' or dispute over a right. The various Education Acts have created obligations on local education authorities to provide suitable education for all children in their areas. Parents dissatisfied with the education proposed for their children may complain to the Secretary of State and, ultimately, they may seek judicial review of the decisions of the local authority or Minister. Thereby the relevant legislation has created a right which reflects the guarantees of Article 2 of Protocol No 1 (P1–2) to the Convention — a right for children not to be denied an education appropriate to their needs and aptitudes.

However, the Commission does not consider that this right under English domestic law or under Article 2 of Protocol No 1 (P1–2) is of a civil nature for the purposes of Article 6 para 1 (Art 6–1) of the Convention. Although the notion of a civil right under this provision is autonomous of any domestic law definitions, the Commission considers that for the purposes of the domestic law in question and the Convention, the right not to be denied elementary education falls, in the circumstances of the present case, squarely within the domain of public law, having no private law analogy and no repercussions on private rights or obligations (cf Eur Court HR, Deumeland judgment of 29 May 1986, Series A no 100 pp 24–25 paras 71–74). The Commission concludes, therefore, that there is no civil right at issue in the instant case and, accordingly, Article 6 para 1 (Art 6–1) of the Convention is not applicable to the administrative procedures before the domestic education authorities. It follows that this aspect of the applicant's case must be rejected as being incompatible ratione materiae with the provisions of the Convention, pursuant to Article 27 para 2 (Art 27–2) of the Convention.

Note that the facts arose before the establishment of the Special Educational Needs Tribunal. The Commission reached the same decision in *Smith v United Kingdom* (1989) which was decided on the same day as *Simpson*.

*   *Was the applicant the child or the parent?*

The interpretation of 'civil' right has been considered by the English courts in the context of school admission and exclusion appeal panels. In *R (on the appplication of B) v Head Teacher of Alperton Community School;R (on the appplication of T) v*

Head Teacher of Wembley High School; R (on the appplication of C) v The Governing Body of Cardinal Newman High School [2001] EWHC Admin 229, [2001] ELR 359, Newman J rejected the submission that the combined effect of the English education statutes and the Human Rights Act 1998 was to create a civil right to education.

R (on the appplication of B) v Head Teacher of Alperton Community School; R (on the appplication of T) v Head Teacher of Wembley High School; R, ex p C v The Governing Body of Cardinal Newman High School [2001] EWHC Admin 229, [2001] ELR 359

P382

[46] As I read the judgment in *Belgian Linguistics*, the court characterised the right as giving rise to the requirement on the part of the contracting parties to the Protocol to establish a right of access to educational institutions existing at any given time, but excluded from its content a right to education of any particular type or to any particular level. The rationale for the content of the right being so defined is that the scope and content of such education as is available, is for the State to determine. In *Belgian Linguistics* certain children had by a legislative measure been precluded from access to French speaking schools, solely upon the basis of the residence of their parents. As a result, it was held that there had been discrimination, which had led to a failure to secure the right of education which was enshrined in Art 2 of the Protocol. In my judgment the question, whether the right so enshrined was a civil right or not, was not before the court, the court's definition of its content leads to the conclusion that it fell, as the Commission held in *Simpson*, within the domain of public law. As the argument in this case demonstrates the desired goal of the claimant is to establish that the type of education being provided is not suitable. That is the very area, which in accordance with public law principles, has been held to be for the contracting parties to determine and to be outside the scope of the Convention right.

[47] *Yanasik v Turkey* 74 DR 14 (1993), although concerned with advanced education, clearly points in the same direction. The Commission held:

> ... the Commission considers that in principle the right to education cannot be allowed to impinge on the State's right to regulate education ... and that this right does not exclude all disciplinary penalties. It would not be contrary to Article 2 of Protocol No 1 for pupils to be suspended or expelled, provided that the national regulations did not prevent them from enrolling in another establishment in order to further their studies.

The more recent case of *Lalu Hanuman v United Kingdom* [2000] ELR 685, is briefly reported and its exact reasoning cannot be discerned, but it was held that the claimant's rejection by the academic appeal committee of the University of East Anglia did not involve the determination of a civil right or of a criminal charge.

[48] It follows that I reject the submission that there exists in English law a civil right to an education suitable to one's needs.

2. Does a child have a right to education?

The right to education is arguably the right of the child rather than the parent. However, the European Court of Human Rights has tended to regard the parent's and the child's rights as being one and the same. Nevertheless the Human Rights Act 1998 may enable a child to have a right to education which is separate and distinct from that of their parent.

Jane Fortin 'Rights brought home for children' (1999) 62 MLR 350 at 365–7

At least on the face of it, the wording of the Convention appears to provide little scope for challenging the principles of domestic education law which give educational choices to parents rather than to children. In particular Article 2 of the First Protocol seems to reinforce them by directing states to 'respect the right of *parents* to ensure such education and teaching in conformity with their own religious and philosophical convictions'. This provision was clearly designed to protect parents from religious and racial persecution by the state indoctrinating their children through their schooling. ...

Not surprisingly, given its wording, Article 2 of the First Protocol has led to a variety of claims which, despite involving aspects of children's education, are in reality complaints about infringements of parents' own strong philosophical convictions. Indeed, ironically, its terms have been exploited to undermine children's rights to independent thought. For example, the United Kingdom government argued that they justified retaining parents' rights to withdraw their children from the religious instruction and collective school worship provided in state schools and from sex education classes. This argument was unfounded; the European Court had in fact decided that compulsory sex education in schools does not violate parents' rights under that Article as long as it is conveyed in a balanced and objective manner, with no element of indoctrination. But under current legislation British parents are neither required to provide any reason for exercising their right of withdrawal nor to consult their children over such a decision. Domestic law thereby reinforces parents' perceptions that they have a right to dictate their views on all these matters to their children. After incorporation of the European Convention, such provisions might be challenged by an adolescent claiming that whilst these statutory exemptions comply with her parents' rights under Article 2 of the First Protocol of the Convention, her own rights to freedom of expression, of religion and to receive and impart information are all being infringed.

...

To date, the European case law appears to provide little ammunition for those wishing to strengthen children's rights to make their own educational choices rather than allowing their parents to do so for them. There may, however, be grounds for more optimism regarding other aspects of education law. Many have criticised those provisions in the education legislation which exclude children under 18 from being parties to appeals heard by educational tribunals. The children most affected by this aspect of the existing law are those who are permanently excluded from school and those with special educational needs. Giving parents the sole right of appeal to a tribunal over such matters makes a false assumption that children's interests are always identical with those of their parents. A child's inability to become involved in the appeal processes deprives him or her of an important procedural right. This is particularly unjust in cases where, for example, parents are too disinterested or nervous to pursue an appeal on the child's behalf, or where they are incapable of presenting his or her case satisfactorily or objectively. A child might therefore persuade a domestic court that English education law is infringing his or her right to a 'fair and public hearing' under Article 6 and that Strasbourg's early and very narrow interpretation of that Article's scope is now anachronistic. A declaration of incompatibility would force the government to review the present system of appeals. Alternatively, a court confronted with a challenge from an adolescent seeking party status in an appeal hearing might simply comply with its duty to interpret the legislation 'so far as it is possible to do so', in accordance with the terms of Article 6. It might therefore decide that since only a 'relevant person' in the current education legislation can have party status, the term 'relevant person' must be interpreted to include children under the age of 18, despite the obvious contrary intention of the legislative definition.

See also *Campbell and Cosans v United Kingdom* (1982) 4 EHRR 293 on the respective rights of a parent and their child (chapter 4).

3. What is the extent of the right to education?

In the *Belgian Linguistic Case (No 2)* (1968) 1 EHRR 252 the European Court of Human Rights was asked to consider whether Belgium was in breach of Article 2 of the First Protocol 1, Article 8.1, and Article 14 because its domestic law did not enable French-speaking children to be educated at local French-speaking schools.

Belgian Linguistic Case (No 2) (1968) I EHRR 252

Interpretation adopted by the Court

3. By the terms of the first sentence of this Article (P1–2), 'no person shall be denied the right to education'.

In spite of its negative formulation, this provision uses the term 'right' and speaks of a 'right to education'. Likewise the preamble to the Protocol specifies that the object of the Protocol lies in the collective enforcement of 'rights and freedoms'. There is therefore no doubt that Article 2 (P1–2) does enshrine a right.

It remains however to determine the content of this right and the scope of the obligation which is thereby placed upon states.

The negative formulation indicates, as is confirmed by the 'preparatory work' (especially Docs CM/WPVI (51) 7, page 4, and AS/JA (3) 13, page 4), that the Contracting Parties do not recognise such a right to education as would require them to establish at their own expense, or to subsidise, education of any particular type or at any particular level. However, it cannot be concluded from this that the state has no positive obligation to ensure respect for such a right as is protected by Article 2 of the Protocol (P1–2). As a 'right' does exist, it is secured, by virtue of Article 1 (Art 1) of the Convention, to everyone within the jurisdiction of a Contracting State.

To determine the scope of the 'right to education', within the meaning of the first sentence of Article 2 of the Protocol (P1–2), the Court must bear in mind the aim of this provision. It notes in this context that all member States of the Council of Europe possessed, at the time of the opening of the Protocol to their signature, and still do possess, a general and official educational system. There neither was, nor is now, therefore, any question of requiring each State to establish such a system, but merely of guaranteeing to persons subject to the jurisdiction of the Contracting Parties the right, in principle, to avail themselves of the means of instruction existing at a given time.

The Convention lays down no specific obligations concerning the extent of these means and the manner of their organisation or subsidisation. In particular the first sentence of Article 2 (P1–2) does not specify the language in which education must be conducted in order that the right to education should be respected. It does not contain precise provisions similar to those which appear in Articles 5(2) and 6(3)(a) and (e) (art 5–2, art 6–3–a, art 6–

3–e). However the right to education would be meaningless if it did not imply in favour of its beneficiaries, the right to be educated in the national language or in one of the national languages, as the case may be.

4. The first sentence of Article 2 of the Protocol (P1–2) consequently guarantees, in the first place, a right of access to educational institutions existing at a given time, but such access constitutes only a part of the right to education. For the 'right to education' to be effective, it is further necessary that, inter alia, the individual who is the beneficiary should have the possibility of drawing profit from the education received, that is to say, the right to obtain, in conformity with the rules in force in each State, and in one form or another, official recognition of the studies which he has completed.

5. The right to education guaranteed by the first sentence of Article 2 of the Protocol (P1–2) by its very nature calls for regulation by the state, regulation which may vary in time and place according to the needs and resources of the community and of individuals. It goes without saying that such regulation must never injure the substance of the right to education nor conflict with other rights enshrined in the Convention.

The Court considers that the general aim set for themselves by the Contracting Parties through the medium of the European Convention on Human Rights, was to provide effective protection of fundamental human rights, and this, without doubt not only because of the historical context in which the Convention was concluded, but also of the social considerable possibilities for regulating the exercise of these rights. The Convention therefore implies a just balance between the protection of the general interest of the Community and the respect due to fundamental human rights while attaching particular importance to the latter.

6. The second sentence of Article 2 of the Protocol (P1–2) does not guarantee a right to education; this is clearly shown by its wording:

...

In the exercise of any functions which it assumes in relation to education and to teaching, the state shall respect the right of parents to ensure such education and teaching in conformity with their own religious and philosophical convictions.

This provision does not require of states that they should, in the sphere of education or teaching, respect parents' linguistic preferences, but only their religious and philosophical convictions. To interpret the terms 'religious' and 'philosophical' as covering linguistic preferences would amount to a distortion of their ordinary and usual meaning and to read into the Convention something which is not there. Moreover the 'preparatory work' confirms that the object of the second sentence of Article 2 (P1–2) was in no way to secure respect by the state of a right for parents to have education conducted in a language other than that of the country in question; indeed in June 1951 the Committee of Experts which had the task of drafting the Protocol set aside a proposal put forward in this sense. Several members of the Committee believed that it concerned an aspect of the problem of ethnic minorities and that it consequently fell outside the scope of the Convention (see Doc CM (51) 33 final, page 3). The second sentence of Article 2 (P1–2) is therefore irrelevant to the problems raised in the present case.

7. According to the express terms of Article 8(1) (art 8–1) of the Convention, 'everyone has the right to respect for his private and family life, his home and his correspondence'.

This provision by itself in no way guarantees either a right to education or a personal right of parents relating to the education of their children: its object is essentially that of protecting the individual against arbitrary interference by the public authorities in his private family life.

Simpson v UK (1989) Application 14688/89, 4 December 1989

The law

As regards the applicant's personal complaint of a denial of his right to education under Article 2 of Protocol No 1 (P1–2), the Commission observes that Article 2 of Protocol No 1 (P1–2) is not an absolute right which requires Contracting Parties to subsidise private education of a particular type or level. In principle, it guarantees access to public educational facilities which have been created at a given time and the possibility of drawing benefit from the education received. This right 'by its very nature calls for regulation by the state, regulation which may vary in time and place according to the needs and resources of the community and of individuals', as long as the substance of the right to education is preserved (Eur Court HR Belgian Linguistic judgment of 23 July 1968, Series A no 6 pp 30–32 paras 3–5).

Sulak v Turkey (1996) Application 24515/94, 17 January 1996

The Commission recalls that the right to education guaranteed by the first sentence of Article 2 of Protocol No 1 (P1–2) by its very nature calls for regulation by the state provided that such regulation does not injure the substance of the right nor conflict with other rights enshrined in the Convention or its Protocols (cf Campbell and Cosans judgment of 25 February 1982, para 41, Series A, no 98, p 19). The Commission further recalls that the right does not in principle exclude recourse to disciplinary measures, including those of suspension and expulsion from an educational establishment (cf No 14524/89, … pp 14, 27).

4. Does the right to education apply to university education or only to the years of compulsory education?

The Commission addressed this question in *Sulak v Turkey* (1996) which was also an admissibility decision.

Sulak v Turkey (1996) Application No 24515/94, 17 January 1996

Complaints

The applicant complains that his expulsion from the university pursuant to a disciplinary measure deprived him of the right to education. He also alleges that under the national regulations, expelled students are prevented from enrolling in another higher education institution to pursue their studies.

The law

The applicant complains that the disciplinary sanction imposed on him deprived him of the right to education. The Commission examined the applicant's complaint under Article 2 of

Protocol No 1 (P1–2), which, in so far as relevant, provides:

No person shall be denied the right to education...

The Commission recalls that the right to education contemplated in Article 2 of Protocol No 1 (P1–2), mainly concerns elementary education and not necessarily specialist advanced studies (No 14524/89, Dec 6.1.93, DR 74 pp 14, 27).

In the present case the education in question is higher education. However, even assuming that Article 2 of Protocol No 1 (P1–2) is applicable to the present case, the application is in any event manifestly ill-founded...

The impact of the Human Rights Act 1998 on the law of education may be indirect rather than direct. In particular, although the right to education is not regarded as a civil right and so Article 6.1 of the ECHR does not apparently apply to hearings concerned with that right, the general principle of an independent and impartial hearing is likely to be expected politically if not legally. In the longer term the concept of a 'civil' right should be revisited.

- *Why should a 'civil' right be restricted to private law rights? Why should it not mean any public or private right which is accorded to a citizen?*

Anthony Bradley 'Scope for Review: The Convention Right to Education and the Human Rights Act 1998' [1999] EHRLR 395

[Article 2 of the First Protocol] had proved unusually difficult to draft given the sensitivity of many states regarding features of their own educational system, for example the relationship between the state sector and organised religion. Most states, foremost among them the United Kingdom, were reluctant to proclaim that everyone has a right to education, not wishing to impose an open-ended duty on the state to provide it, and instead adopted a negative formulation that, arguably, at its narrowest seeks to exclude improper state interference in the provision of education through arrangements made by parents. It is evident from the *travaux préparatoires* that the strongest single factor that motivated the preparation of an article relating to education was the desire to enable parents to have their children educated in accordance with their own beliefs and to resist 'the overwhelming intrusion of totalitarian propaganda into family life' by 'agencies or quasi-agencies of the state'. The consensus that developed, concentrating on the desire to guard against state ideology in the schools, bridged a wide gap in the Consultative Assembly debates between national delegates who believed that education should be wholly lay and secular and those who would have wished to see greater support for a religious basis for education.

Even the negative formula adopted in Article 2 of the First Protocol would be meaningless if there were no positive right to education, however ill-defined it might be. Indeed, the preamble to the First Protocol confirmed that the states were 'resolved to take steps to ensure the collective enforcement of certain rights and freedoms' additional to those already included in the ECHR. Nonetheless, by contrast with many Convention rights, such as the right to liberty and security (Article 5), the right to a fair trial (Article 6) and the right to freedom of expression (Article 10), the right to education that no person is to be denied is not particularised in any way, apart from the reference to the duty of states in providing education to respect the religious and philosophical convictions of parents.

...

Some Consequences of the Convention Right to Education

...the Strasbourg Court has given little encouragement to parents wishing to secure changes in their national system of education or to secure a position for their child that they have not obtained by using national procedures. Decisions by the Commission have been no more encouraging to such parents. It follows from the *Belgian Linguistic* case that parents have no right to require the state to establish or subsidise school institutions of any particular type or level. However, if Article 2 of the First Protocol does impose positive obligations upon the state, it would seem very difficult for a state to argue that it is not obliged to ensure that school places are available for all children. It has sometimes been argued against the existence of such a positive duty that it is a natural right of parents to educate their own children, but this seems an unrealistic position to adopt if (as the Court has accepted) each of the original signatories to the Convention made educational provision by one means or another available to all children. It is possible to visualise scenarios in which the system of universal provision is interrupted, whether nationally or locally, or where a local authority beset by strikes, maladministration or a shortage of funds is unable to provide schooling for all children in its area. In such situations, central government has the legal power to intervene, but might wish for its own reasons not to do so. A question of the children's right to education could then arise.

...

There is no textual indication in the Convention that education does not refer to all stages of school education. Primary education is the foundation on which later stages are built, but it would be wrong to restrict the Convention right to a level of education that member states would accept as incomplete even for children. And is there any reason for restricting it to the education of children of school age? The religious and philosophical convictions of the parents admittedly drop out of consideration when children become adults. The two sentences in Article 2 of the First Protocol must be read together, but the duty to respect parental convictions cannot cause the first sentence to be read as if it provided that 'No child shall be denied the right to education'. Scenarios involving access to the appropriate level of education might involve (a) a mature student seeking access to higher education; (b) an illiterate adult seeking basic education; (c) immigrants seeking education in the English language; (d) a disabled person seeking continuing education; or (e) a convicted prisoner wishing to take an advanced correspondence course. The position of vocational and technical training is less clear, since this subject is specifically covered in the European Social Charter, but those later provisions ought not to govern interpretation of the Convention.

One difference between a child's access to primary education and an adult's access to higher education must be that the former is a universal right and applies to every child, including those with severe disabilities, whereas it is for the state to regulate access to further or higher education, according to the individual's aptitudes and available resources. Where a student had failed his first year examinations as well as his resit examinations, and for this reason and because of poor attendance had been excluded from the university, it was not difficult for the Commission to hold that he had not been denied the right to education.

Since parents are entitled to respect for their religious and philosophical convictions in their children's schooling, does a similar right arise in respect of an adult student who is undergoing further or higher education? In an era of political correctness, a sensitive student may object to the way in which a subject is taught, but it would need a strong set of facts before a lecturer's attitude or approach to the subject could be said to deny the student a right to education. Such a complaint would be likely to raise issues as to the lecturer's freedom of expression under Article 10 of the ECHR. Academic freedom as such is not secured by the Convention, but if a particular approach in a public college were tantamount to ideological indoctrination, then this could be said to deny the right to *education* by imposing something different on the student. Moreover, both teachers and taught have rights to freedom of thought, conscience and religion under Article 9 of the ECHR that the educational system must respect.

Application of other Convention Rights to Education

...

The complex legal system of education requires innumerable decisions relating to individuals to be made, whether in respect of entry to or exclusion from school or college, the award of educational grants, the examination process, the assessment of special needs or the appointment, disciplining and dismissal of teachers and lecturers. Education is a fertile ground for administrative justice—and injustice. To what extent does the much litigated Article 6(1) require these decisions to accord with the right to a fair trial as being made in the determination of civil rights and obligations or of criminal charges? Article 6(1) applies to disciplinary decisions made in many vocations and professions, but it is not certain whether it applies to the host of decisions that may determine an individual's educational progress and thus his or her access to a vocation or profession. The Strasbourg Court has created no bright line to indicate when a dispute as to an individual's civil rights and obligations arises and thus attracts Article 6(1), and when a dispute is considered merely to arise from the exercise of a public law function so that Article 6(1) does not apply. In *Hornsby v Greece*, the Court held that Greek authorities, who had delayed for many years in permitting English teachers to open a language school, and had even refused to recognise a ruling by the supreme administrative court in Greece, had breached Article 6(1) by failing to decide the matter within a reasonable time. However, in 1989, the Commission ruled that the decision by a local education authority to name a school for a dyslexic child did not affect the child's civil rights and obligations; the decision was outside Article 6(1), since the right not to be denied education was considered to be a public law matter having no analogy in private law. If we extrapolate from this to the proposition that admission questions do not attract due process under Article 6(1), it does not follow that disputes as to exclusion from school or college are outside Article 6(1), particularly where the issues include alleged conduct that might be criminal.

Although the Court has held that the Convention right to education is essentially a right of access to such educational institutions as the state provides, and 'by its very nature calls for regulation by the State' the nature of such regulation is limited by Article 14 (prohibition of discrimination). The very purpose of regulation is to enable choices to be made, and distinctions to be drawn, between different individuals, groups and classes. Such distinctions must not be improperly discriminatory. In one respect the Belgian scheme of education was held to discriminate against certain French-speaking parents. The Court said then that Article 14 'does not prohibit distinctions in treatment which are founded on an objective assessment of essentially different factual circumstances and which ... strike a fair balance' between the interests of the community and respect for Convention rights and freedoms. Yet states appear free to operate schemes that make unequal provision for different classes of institution at the same level of education. In relation to the education system, the potential of Article 14 in raising difficult questions is diminished by the wide discretion in regulation that the *Belgian Linguistic* case perceived states to enjoy. So long as the Court maintains this approach, inequalities in educational provision may well not give rise to breach of the Convention. To illustrate the point, although a serious inequality in selective secondary school provision between boys and girls in Birmingham was held to infringe the Sex Discrimination Act 1975, that inequality might not breach Article 14 of the ECHR read with Article 2 of the First Protocol, given that the Court's emphasis may be limited to establishing that there is no improper discrimination between individuals in their access to existing schools. However, Article 14 introduces into Great Britain new grounds of discrimination, in particular that of religion, in addition to the existing grounds of sex, race and disablement discrimination. The extensive reliance in Britain on church schools, and the fact that such schools may lawfully pursue discriminatory admission policies, may be fertile ground for challenges to educational policy. However, the chances of such challenges succeeding are uncertain, except if a particular policy were to be based on an offensive form of discrimination, such as race, that has never been accepted in the policy of education law in Britain.

Some Effects of the Human Rights Act 1998

The 1998 Act will have an extensive impact on the law of education, even though its practical effects are as yet uncertain. The central departments concerned with education, LEAs, the governors of schools and colleges and the holders of teaching posts in the public sector (notably headteachers) will all constitute 'public authorities' under section 6 of the 1998 Act. Private schools will probably become 'public authorities' only when they are performing functions that derive from the Education Acts and form part of the state's system for providing education. It is in respect of such functions that some decisions of private schools are subject to judicial review in English law. Whereas many universities, but not all, are to a large extent insulated from judicial review by the office of the visitor, and even the visitor's decisions are subject to limited judicial review, the role of universities in the system of higher education is such that they will rank as 'public authorities' for very many of their functions. Schools, colleges and universities may find themselves subject to an increasing number of applications for judicial review based upon alleged breaches of Convention rights or at least those in which Convention rights feature. So too will LEAs and central departments. University visitors will be required when necessary to deal with disputes as to Convention rights.

...Many of these features of the present law are likely to stand up tolerably well to scrutiny on Convention grounds and to this extent the impact of the Human Rights Act on British schools and colleges will be softened. But as society changes, new cultural and community interests develop that are not reflected in our inherited structures, and it is predictable that efforts will be made to further these interests by subjecting aspects of the education system to review on Convention grounds. Whether such efforts succeed will depend on whether British courts are prepared to go beyond the cautious parameters so far set by the Strasbourg Court.

The main cases on the right to education have arisen in the context of corporal punishment (see chapter 4) as well as religious and sex education (see chapter 6). Challenges under the Human Rights Act 1998 have been brought in a number of cases, including school admission and exclusion appeals (see chapters 3 and 4).

International law

In addition to the European Convention on Human Rights there are a number of other international documents recognising a right to education, which have been adopted by the United Kingdom. However, these do not form part of domestic law and are not enforceable in the courts, being subject only to supervision and review by international bodies.

These documents include the Universal Declaration on Human Rights 1948 (Article 26), the Convention on the Elimination of Discrimination in Education 1960 (Article 1(2)), United Nations Convention on the Rights of the Child 1989 (Articles 28, 29), and the International Covenant on Economic, Social and Cultural Rights 1966 (Article 13).

Fons Coomans 'Identifying Violations of the Right to Education' in van Boven, Flintermann and Westendorp (eds) *The Maastricht Guidelines on Violations of Economic, Social and Cultural Rights* (1998) Utrecht

Introduction

It is generally acknowledged that the right to education falls within the category of economic, social and cultural rights. Compared to other rights, such as the right to food or other right to adequate housing, the right to education has always been underexposed. A main feature of the right to education is its mixed character. On the one hand, it affords individuals a claim against the state in respect of receiving education. Realisation of this right requires an effort on the part of the state to make education available and accessible; it implies positive state obligations. This may be called the social dimension of the right to education. On the other hand, the right to education embraces a freedom dimension. There is the freedom of individuals to choose between state-organised and private education, which can be translated, for example, in parents' right to ensure their children's moral and religious education according to their own beliefs. From this also stems the freedom of natural persons or legal entities to establish their own educational institutions. This freedom dimension requires of the state that it conducts a policy of non-interference in private matters; it implies negative state obligations. Both dimensions can be found in Articles 13 and 14 of the International Covenant on Economic, Social and Cultural Rights (hereafter: the Covenant) and in Articles 28 and 29 of the Convention on the Rights of the Child (hereafter: the Convention).

...

1. General Observations

It should be borne in mind that, in comparison to other rights laid down in the Covenant and the Convention, the provisions on the right to education are comprehensive and concrete, setting out the steps to be taken by states in realising the right to education. In performing their duties under these instruments, states do have a margin of discretion in selecting the means to achieve the level of realisation prescribed by the treaties. In particular this is the case for the social dimension of the right to education. Because of the huge costs involved in setting up and maintaining an educational system, state authorities at the central, regional and local level are the major actors in implementing the right to education. But one should not overlook the role played by private organisations in many countries in realising this right: these organisations establish and direct educational institutions based on specific ideas and convictions, operating with, or without, governmental (financial) support. This freedom of education does not imply an obligation for the state to subsidise private educational institutions, but where a state does support private schools, it must do so in a non-discriminatory way. Private educational institutions must conform to minimum (educational) standards laid down by the state.

There is a well-known difference between the norm ('everyone has the right to education'; non-discrimination and equal opportunity with respect to education) and the reality in many countries. The degree of realisation of the right to education is not only dependent on governmental policy and measures, it is also influenced by structural factors dominant in a given society. Structural factors include socioeconomic and cultural development and the economic condition of the family (the need to raise additional income through child labour), discrimination against marginal and vulnerable groups within society, parents' attitudes towards education, as influenced by occupation, class, religion, social and cultural traditions, geographical factors (differences between the (urban) centre and peripheral or remote regions) and demographic factors (composition and growth of the population). These factors have an impact on the level of literacy, access to education, enrolment, drop-out and repetition rates. These structural problems amount to, what may be called, forms of static discrimination. These structural factors should be taken into account when assessing the record of states in implementing the right to education.

...

A number of cases deal with discrimination against girls and women with lower school enrolment and attendance and a lower level of literacy as compared to boys. States have thus failed to take active measures in order to realise equality of treatment between boys and girls with respect to access to education.

In some countries, there is discrimination on religious grounds. In Iran, for example, members of the Bahai minority are denied access to university education. In one case, the CESCR observed that the government of a state party had been unable to prevent or had been unwilling to redress discrimination against the Gypsy minority in education. The government in question had failed to adopt an active non-discrimination policy in order to increase the participation in educational activities of the minority members. With respect to the educational opportunities of children of Albanian nationality within the public school system of the FYROM (Macedonia), the High Commissioner on National Minorities of the OSCE held that further efforts were required to increase the percentage of Albanian pupils continuing their education at secondary school level. The Minister of Foreign Relations of the FYROM replied that his government was making efforts to provide continued education for a great number of persons of Albanian nationality, by allowing quotas in a number of secondary schools. It is submitted that the setting of quotas for pupils of the Albanian minority does not contribute to effective equality, and, in consequence, is discriminatory. The right to education implies after all a right of equal access to the existing public educational institutions.

In a number of other countries, a practice emerged to deny the right to education to asylum-seekers, because they were considered illegal immigrants. In one case, the CESCR considered this situation inconsistent with the obligations under the Covenant. In two other situations, the CRC questioned the compatibility of this practice with Articles 2 and 3 of the Convention.

...

The case of Japan is special, because the government of this state has made a reservation on Article 13(2)(b) and (c), namely the right not to be bound 'in particular by the progressive introduction of free education'. In Japan, many students attend private educational institutions. In general, private education is more expensive than the public education system. According to the Japanese government, it is not able to pay fully for the system of private education. For this reason, the government introduced fees, not only for private secondary and higher education, but also for public education. This reasoning can be criticised, because the Japanese government is shifting the high costs of private education on to students who attend public educational institutions. These students are not able to enjoy private education for financial reasons, but they have to pay fees to maintain the system. In my view, this system of burden-sharing is not justified. States have a primary responsibility to maintain a system of public education which should be accessible to all. It may not put up financial obstacles which hinder the achievement of equal accessibility. In addition, it could be argued that the position of the Japanese economy is sufficiently strong to allow students attending public education to be exempted from paying fees.

...

A clear example of a state deliberately retarding the progressive realisation of the right to education is India. In this country, society is characterised by a strong traditional hierarchic structure and discrimination against specific social groups, in particular the untouchables, scheduled tribes, women, members of minorities and the handicapped. The Indian government and ruling elite give priority to the education of boys over girls. In addition, the government did not pursue an active policy to promote education of all groups and failed to place more emphasis on the elimination of child labour. The national education budget hardly represented three per cent of the Gross National Product. Members of the CESCR observed that, according to many sources, there was a growing disparity between the access to educational opportunities of the rich and the poor in India. Only a very limited number of students from low-income families enrolled in institutes of higher education. There was also a qualitative gap between the public and the private sector: private education was of a much higher standard and usually only accessible to the upper castes. Fees for the private sector were high; people from low-income groups were not able to pay for private education. It has been argued that the lack of progress in making education accessible to all and the irresolute measures against child labour in India are not so much the result of the difficult economic and financial situation of the country. This situation can be better explained by the belief systems of the state bureaucracy and the upper and middle classes in India. Central to these beliefs is [M Weiner *The Child and the State in India — Child Labor and Education Policy in Comparative Perspective* (Princeton, 1991]

> the Indian view of the social order, notions concerning the respective roles of upper and lower social strata, the role of education as a means of maintaining differentiations among social classes ...

Social mobility is limited due to the hierarchic organisation of society which does not allow the mixing of castes. As a result, it is hardly possible for members of the lower castes to attain educational institutions and professions which by tradition are intended for the upper castes. The education system has been an instrument for maintaining the social status quo: those in control of the education system give low priority to mass education as evidenced by the low investment in primary education as compared to other developing countries. They are indifferent to the implementation of compulsory education and to the elimination of child labour.

...

Crucial for the assessment of a state's performance is the nature of the problems in the educational field and the character and effects of the measures a state has taken in order to cope with these problems. In developing countries, the basic infrastructure and resources for an educational system are often inadequate or wanting and the realisation of the right to (primary) education is given a low priority. Many developed states, on the other hand, have an extensive and high-level educational system, which is difficult to maintain because of the huge costs involved. Consequently, these states feel tempted to take retrogressive steps. One of the great challenges for the CESCR and CRC that monitor the implementation of the right to education, is to distinguish between state violations of the right to education and state failures to fulfil the obligations resulting from the right to education. In my view, the latter do not constitute violations. For a fair assessment to be made, a supervisory body must take the economic and financial situation of a country into account and examine whether the government in question has taken concrete measures towards progressive realisation and actual progress has been made and, finally, consider the effects of a state's policy on members of marginal and vulnerable groups.

- *Do you agree with the writer's distinction between 'state violations' and 'state failures to fulfil the obligations resulting from the right to education'?*

CHAPTER 2

Organisation of education (nursery, primary, secondary, further and higher)

1.   INTRODUCTION

There are three main stages of education in England and Wales: primary, secondary, and tertiary. Tertiary education includes further and higher education, that is most colleges and universities. Primary, secondary and further education are regulated by the Education Act 1996, whereas higher education is subject to different statutory provisions. In addition, since 1997 many parents have had the option of their child receiving nursery education.

More than 90 per cent of pupils attend state schools, that is schools funded by the state as opposed to independent schools, which are schools that charge fees normally paid by the pupil's parents. The comprehensive principle was introduced into state schools during the late 1960s. A few local authorities resisted its introduction, and continue to maintain grammar schools or partial selection in their schools.

There was an expansion of higher education in the 1960s and early 1970s.The number of universities was increased in the mid-1960s, and polytechnics were established in the early 1970s. With the increase in the number of institutions and the number of full-time students, the funding of higher education became of greater concern to government. Initially, polytechnics were closely tied to LEAs, although funded mainly by central government. In 1988 the link with LEAs was broken and polytechnics became statutory corporations. In 1992 polytechnics were able to become universities and award their own degrees.

Definitions

'primary education'

Education Act 1996, s 2(1)

(a)   full-time education suitable to the requirements of junior pupils who have not attained the age of ten years and six months; and

(b) full-time education suitable to the requirements of junior pupils who have attained that age and whom it is expedient to educate together with junior pupils within para (a).

Paragraph (b) enables certain middle schools to be categorised as primary schools.

'secondary education'

EA 1996, s 2(2)

(a) full-time education suitable to the requirements of pupils of compulsory school age who are either—
  (i) senior pupils or
  (ii) junior pupils who have attained the age of 10 years and six months and whom it is expedient to educate together with senior pupils of compulsory school age; and
(b) (subject to subsection (5)) full-time education suitable to the requirements of pupils who are over compulsory school age but under the age of 19 which is provided at a school at which education within paragraph (a) is also provided.

Paragraph (a)(ii) enables certain middle schools to be categorised as secondary schools.

EA 1996, s 2(2A)

In England, education is also secondary education for the purposes of the Act (subject to subsection (5)) if it is provided by an institution which—
(a) is maintained by a local education authority, and
(b) is principally concerned with the provision of full-time education suitable to the requirements of pupils who are over compulsory school age but under the age of 19.

EA 1996, s 2(2B)

In addition in England where—
(a) a person is in full-time education,
(b) he receives his education partly at a school and, by virtue of arrangements made by the school, partly at another institution, and
(c) the education which he receives at the school would be secondary education if it was full-time education at the school,

the person's education, both at the school and at the other institution, is secondary education for the purposes of this Act (subject to subsection (5)).

Section 2(2A) and (2B) were inserted by the Learning and Skills Act 2000 (s 110(1)). The provisions form part of the government's policy to make the school curriculum more flexible for 15- and 16-year-olds by, for example, permitting them to attend an FE college or obtain work experience for part of the week.

'further education'

EA 1996, s 2(3)

full-time and part-time education suitable to the requirements of persons who are over compulsory school age (including vocational, social, physical and recreational training), and organised leisure-time occupation provided in connection with the provision of such education, except that it does not include secondary education or higher education.

'higher education'

EA 1996, s 579(1)

education provided by means of a course of any description mentioned in Sch 6 to the Education Reform Act 1988.

The Education Bill 2001/02 provides for revised definitions of nursery, primary and secondary education. Secondary education for 14-16-year-olds will include education at a workplace.

Regulation and control

Until the 1980s LEAs had considerable control over the management of schools and further education colleges, but their role has been diminished by central government, so that each school or college now has considerable autonomy. The role of the governing body has expanded, and parents have a formal role as members of their child's school governing body. However, schools and FE colleges have become subject to increased regulation by central government or its agencies. Similarly universities, which were not subject to statutory regulation, have also become subject to more central government control than hitherto.

These changes are part of a wider changing constitutional picture, which features greater centralisation as well as increased devolution of power. Whether these changes are desirable depends upon a variety of factors including: the competence of the body and individuals managing the school or college; the importance attached to local democratic accountability; and to what extent central government should have a role in delivering local services.

2.   NURSERY EDUCATION AND CHILDCARE

Local education authorities

Local education authorities are now under a duty to provide nursery education for children who have not reached compulsory school age. Nursery education may be provided in a class attached to a primary school, or at a nursery school (see below). Nursery education is defined as:

> full-time or part-time education suitable for children who have not attained compulsory school age (whether provided at schools or elsewhere): SSFAA 1998, s 117(1).

School Standards and Framework Act 1998, s 118

(1) A local education authority shall secure that the provision (whether or not by them) of nursery education for children who—
(a)   have not attained compulsory school age, but
(b)   have attained such age as may be prescribed,

is sufficient for their area.

(2) In determining for the purposes of subsection (1) whether the provision of such education is sufficient for their area a local education authority—
(a)   may have regard to any facilities which they expect to be available outside their area for providing such education; and
(b)   shall have regard to any guidance given from time to time by the Secretary of State.

Regulations have specified the age at which children are entitled to receive nursery education.

Education (Nursery Education and Early Years Development) (England) Regulations 1999, SI 1999/1329, reg 2

(1) For the purposes of section 118(1)(b) of the Act (age of children who have not attained compulsory school age in relation to whom the local education authority's duty to secure sufficient provision of nursery education applies) there is hereby prescribed—
(a)   in the case of a child whose fourth birthday does not fall within one of the periods specified in paragraph (2) below, the age of the child at the start of the first term after his fourth birthday; or
(b)   in the case of a child whose fourth birthday falls within one of the periods specified in paragraph (2) below, the age of the child at the start of the term following the term referred to in that paragraph.

(2) The periods referred to in paragraph (1)(b) above are, in any year—
(a)   the period commencing on 1st April and ending with the start of the Summer term of that year;

(b) the period commencing on 1st September and ending with the start of the Autumn term of that year;

(c)   the period commencing on 1st January and ending with the start of the Spring term of that year.

(3) For the purposes of paragraphs (1) and (2) above, 'term' means the term kept in relation to the education provided, or to be provided, or under consideration, for the child, as the case may be, and, in any year, Spring term, Summer term and Autumn term mean, respectively, the term which starts in January, in April and in September.

- *When should a child whose 4th birthday is (a) on 1 April, or (b) 27 May start to receive nursery education?*

The LEA is required to establish a group known as an 'early years development partnership', whose function is to review the amount of provision available in the LEA area and to work with the LEA in preparing early years development plans. The LEA is required to prepare such plans (s 120 of the SSFA 1998). Nursery education is subject to inspection (s 122 of, Sch 26 to the SSFA 1998).

The Education Bill 2001/02 (Part 9) proposes to amend the definitions of 'nursery school' and 'primary school' so as to make it clear that nursery education is normally part-time (see also p 15, below).

The government's policy is to provide free nursery places for two-thirds of three-year-olds by March 2002 and for all who want one by September 2004 (Green Paper *Schools Building on Success* (Cm 5050, February 2001) p 18).

Local authorities

The provisions in the SSFA 1998 and the CA 1989 overlap to some extent. Local authorities are under a general duty to provide a range of services appropriate to meet the needs of children 'in need' (CA 1989, s 17). In particular local authorities, as opposed to LEAs, are under a duty under the Children Act 1989 to provide day care for pre-school children who are 'in need'. (See also chapter 5 Special Educational Needs.)

'Day-care' is defined as:

any form of care or supervised activity provided for children during the day (whether or not it is provided on a regular basis): s 18(4) of the CA 1989.

Local authorities have the following responsibilities:

Children Act 1989, s 18

(1) Every local authority shall provide such day care for children in need within their area who are—

(a)   aged five or under; and

(b)   not yet attending schools,

as is appropriate.

(2) A local authority may provide day care for children within their area who satisfy the conditions mentioned in subsection (1)(a) and (b) even though they are not in need...

- *What are the differences between the obligations placed on local authorities in s 18(1) and s 18(2)?*

Children Act 1989, s 17(10)

A child is 'in need' if:
(a)   he is unlikely to achieve or maintain, or to have the opportunity of achieving or maintaining, a reasonable standard of health or development without the provision for him of services by a local authority under this Part;
(b)   his health or development is likely to be significantly impaired, or further impaired, without the provision for him of such services; or
(c)   he is disabled.

- *Compare the definition of a child 'in need' under the Children Act 1989, s 17(10) with a child having 'special educational needs' (see chapter 5).*

- *When is a child legally entitled to (a) nursery education; and/or (b) day care?*

Although the prime responsibility for providing day care rests with the local authority, it is required to conduct a triennial review of its day care provision in conjunction with the local education authority (CA 1989, s 19).

The Education Bill 2001/02 (Part 9) proposes to place a new duty on LEAs to review the provision of day care and childminding in their area and to repeal CA 1989, s 19. Early Years Development and Childcare Partnerships will be required to work with LEAs to prepare a plan in respect of both nursery and childcare provision in this area.

3.   SCHOOLS

What is a school?

'School' means an educational institution which is outside the further education sector and the higher education sector and is an institution for providing:
(a)   primary education,
(b)   secondary education or
(c)   both primary and secondary education,
whether or not the institution also provides part-time education suitable to the requirements of junior pupils or further education (Education Act 1996, s 4(1)).

Is a pupil referral unit (PRU) a school?

Education Act 1996, s 19

(1) Each local education authority shall make arrangements for the provision of suitable ... education at school or otherwise than at school for those children of compulsory school age who, by reason of illness, exclusion from school or otherwise, may not for any period receive suitable education unless such arrangements are made for them.

(2) Any school established (whether before or after the commencement of this Act) and maintained by a local education authority which—
(a)   is specially organised to provide education for such children, and
(b)   is not a county school or a special school,

shall be known as a 'pupil referral unit'.

(3) A local education authority may secure the provision of boarding accommodation at any pupil referral unit.

....

Pupil referral units are normally used for pupils who are permanently excluded from school (see chapter 4) or for pupils who are temporarily unable to attend mainstream school because of, for example, school phobia, or their special educational needs.

Schedule 1 contains further detail on pupil referral units, as do the Education (Pupil Referral Units) (Application of Enactments) Regulations 1994, SI 1994/2103.

Compulsory school age

When should a child start school?

The Education Act 1996, s 8(2) states that a child is of compulsory school age (a) when he attains the age of five, if he attains that age on a prescribed day, and (b) otherwise at the beginning of the prescribed day next following his attaining that age.

The 'prescribed days' are 31 August, 31 December, and 31 March (Education (Start of Compulsory School Age) Order 1998, SI 1998/1607).

• *Mary was born four years ago on 8 January. By what date must she start school?*

This is the latest date by which the child should start school (unless the child is going to be educated at home; see chapter 3). However, many local education authorities expect children in their area to start before that date. Parents who are not aware of the local LEA policy may find that they have a limited choice of school if they do not apply in time. In other words it is essential to check the local LEA's admissions policy when a child reaches the age of 3. (see chapter 3).

When does the LEA in which you live expect children to start school?

It may be the September after their fourth birthday, or the beginning of the term in which they become five years old, or the term after their fifth birthday, or some other date.

- *Is a parent legally entitled to refuse to send their child to school before their fifth birthday? Can a parent insist on their child starting school on their fifth birthday?*

When can a young person leave school?

Before 1998 a pupil could leave school on his or her sixteenth birthday. So, for example, if a pupil became 16 on 18 September in Year 11 the pupil could leave immediately without taking any GSCEs or other qualifications. However, pupils are now required to stay until the end of the first half of the summer term. This was introduced in part to encourage pupils to obtain formal qualifications before leaving school.

The date on which compulsory education ends is defined in s 8(3) of the Education Act 1996 which provides that:

A person ceases to be of compulsory school age at the end of the day which is the school leaving date for any calendar year—
(a) if he attains the age of 16 after that day but before the beginning of the school year next following,
(b) if he attains that age on that day, or
(c) (unless paragraph (a) applies) if that day is the school leaving date next following his attaining that age.

The Secretary of State has the power under EA 1996, s 8(4) to set a school leaving date for each year. The Education (School Leaving Date) Order 1997, SI 1997/1970 fixed the date as the last Friday in June from 1998 onwards. See also DfEE Circular 11/97 (School leaving date for 16-year-olds).

- *Sunil has his 16th birthday on 15 October. When can he leave school? What difference would it make, if any, were his birthday to be on the following 15 August?*

Main types of school

There are a number of different legal categories of maintained school, in addition to independent schools. Maintained schools are funded through the LEA, and are regulated primarily by public law principles; whereas independent schools are funded mainly by parents who pay school fees and are regulated by private law principles, in particular the law of contract. Independent schools may be registered with the DfES; the Education Bill 2001/02 (Part 10) provides for a new statutory regime to replace the current provisions in the Education Act 1996. This chapter is concerned with maintained schools.

The type of school affects not just funding arrangements, but also the composition and role of the governing body, as well as admission requirements and the religious curriculum.

The government has stated that it is committed to comprehensive rather than selective education. Nevertheless some grammar schools continue to exist, for example, in Buckinghamshire, Kent, and Lincolnshire. In addition, comprehensive schools may be permitted to select a proportion of their pupils, and specialist schools may have the effect of introducing selection where there are more applicants than places.

The School Standards and Framework Act 1998 introduced the current categories as a consequence of the abolition of grant-maintained status by September 1999. Grant-maintained schools became either foundation or voluntary schools. Community and voluntary schools are very similar to the county and voluntary categories which existed before September 1999.

White Paper *Excellence in Schools* (Cm 3681) chapter 7, pp 66–7, para 3

3 The underlying principles of the new framework are:
- Schools are responsible for their own standards. They should continuously and actively seek to improve their performance so that every child can succeed.
- There is value in encouraging diversity by allowing schools to develop a particular identity, character and expertise.
- The central part which the churches and other foundations have long played in providing schools should be recognised, safeguarding the ethos of voluntary schools.
- Schools should be free to make as many decisions as practical for themselves, in particular on internal management, resource allocation and day-to-day operation.
- But that freedom must be accompanied by accountability to parents, the local community, and the wider public for what they achieve.
- There will be no question of attaching unfair privileges to a particular category of school in funding, admissions arrangements or planning school places. All schools, and all categories of school, must be treated fairly.
- The role of LEAs is not to control schools, but to challenge all schools to improve and support those which need help to raise standards.
- To avoid distraction and disruption for schools, the changes made to establish the new framework should be kept to the essential minimum.

The majority of LEAs divide their schools into primary or secondary schools. Some LEAs also have middle schools. 'Primary school' means a school for providing primary education (see above), and may be divided into infant schools (Reception, Years 1, 2) and junior schools (Years 3, 4, 5 and 6).

Secondary schools provide secondary education (see above). They normally cover the school Years 7 to 11, and may have a sixth form. They may also provide further education.

Middle schools straddle the junior and lower secondary years. They are defined as a 'school providing full-time education suitable to the requirements of pupils who have attained a specified age below 10 years and 6 months and are under a specified age above 12 years': Education Act 1996, s 5(3). The precise age range varies according to the proposals put forward under SSFA 1998, s 28(4) when establishing the school.

Categories of school

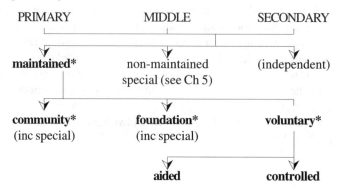

*   These schools are the categories of schools are defined by SSFA 1998, s 20 and Sch 2.

Categories of schools

A 'maintained school' normally means a community, foundation, voluntary (controlled or aided) or special (community or foundation) school. It does not include a maintained nursery school or a pupil referral unit (SSFA 1998, s 20(6)). This is a generic category and refers to the way in which the school is funded.

A 'community school' includes a school which before 1 September 1999 was a county school (SSFA 1998, s 20); and 'community special school' includes a school which was a maintained special school (SSFA 1998, Sch 2). These are the most common types of primary and secondary schools. They are non-denominational and are funded through the LEA.

A 'foundation school' includes a school which before 1 September 1999 was a grant-maintained school; and 'foundation special school' includes a school which was a grant-maintained special school. Although this category was created to replace grant-maintained schools, it is possible for community or voluntary schools to transfer to this category (SSFA 1998, Sch 8). Such a school has a body of persons which holds land or property on trust for the purposes of the school (SSFA 1998, s 21(1)(3)).

A 'voluntary school' is either 'voluntary aided' or 'voluntary controlled'. The majority of such schools are Christian church schools, for example Church of England schools, but they can be of a different religion, or be attached to a non-religious charitable trust (SSFA 1998, s 21(2)). (See also chapter 6 Religion in Schools).

A 'voluntary aided school' includes a school which before 1 September 1999 was (or before becoming a grant-maintained school was) an aided or a special agreement school, or was a grant-maintained school established by promoters. The church or charity to which it is attached is responsible for providing a percentage of the capital costs, and the governing body is responsible for funding the external maintenance of the building (SSFA 1998, s 22, Sch 3, Pts II and III). The teachers are employees of the governing body. The LEA is responsible for maintenance of the interior as well as playgrounds and playing fields.

A 'voluntary controlled school' includes a school which before 1 September 1999 was a controlled school. Such a school is similar to an aided school in its ethos, but neither the founders nor the governing body have any liability for funding the school (SSFA 1998, s 22, Sch 3, Pts I and III). The teachers are employees of the LEA.

A school can change its category in certain circumstances (SSFA 1998, s 35, Sch 8). The detailed requirements are contained in regulations for England and for Wales (see Education (Change of Category of Maintained Schools) (England) 1999, SI 1999/2259; the Welsh regulations are SI 1999/2633).

Other types of schools

There are various other types of schools most of which are not 'maintained schools', but are funded by the government. They include the following schools.

A 'nursery school' is a primary school used mainly to educate children between the ages of 2 and 4 (inclusive) (EA 1996, s 6(1)).

A 'city technology college' (CTC) is a secondary school to which an agreement under s 482 of the Education Act 1996 relates and in which the emphasis of the curriculum is on science and technology (Education Act 1996, s 482(3)(a)). It is an independent but non fee-paying school, which is funded by the Secretary of State for Education and Employment.

A 'city college for the technology of the arts' (CCTA) is the same as a CTC except that the emphasis is on technology in its application to the performing and creative arts.

A 'city academy' is the same as a CTC except that the emphasis is on one of the following subject areas: modern foreign languages; visual, performing or media arts; sport; or any subject specified by order by the Secretary of State (EA 1996, s 482 as amended by LSA 2000, s 130).

A 'grammar school' means a maintained school which had selective admission arrangements at the beginning of the 1997-98 school year and which has been designated a grammar school by the Secretary of State under the SSFA 1998, s 104.

A 'selective school' refers to a maintained school which uses permitted methods of selection as part of its admission arrangements (see chapter 3).

A 'school with a religious character' is a foundation or voluntary school designated as having such a character by the Secretary of State (see chapter 6).

A 'special school' is a school which is organised to make special educational provision for pupils with special educational needs (EA 1996, s 337(1); see chapter 5).

A 'non-maintained special school' means a school which is organised to make special educational provision for pupils with special educational needs and approved by the Secretary of State under the EA 1996, s 342, but which is not a maintained school (see chapter 5).

A 'hospital school' is not defined in education legislation, but as the name implies provides education for children in hospital. The school is a maintained school and may be a voluntary aided school.

- *Which type of primary and secondary school did you attend?*

The government, in its White Paper published in September 2001, proposed to increase the number of specialist schools. Its proposals were included in the Education Bill 2001/02 (Part 5) which provides for the conversion of 'city academies' into 'Academies' which can be established in any part of England, not just in cities. The proposals also favoured a large increase in the number of secondary 'faith' schools, that is schools with a religious character (see chapter 6).

White Paper *Schools Achieving Success* (Cm 5230) paras 5.9–5.13

We will develop and extend the specialist school model

5.9 Specialist schools are a key part of our proposals for a more diverse system because of their proven success in raising standards, as demonstrated by research by Professor David Jesson ... which shows specialist schools adding more value to their pupils' achievements. Following the comments we have received on the Green Paper, we want to clarify and extend our original proposals for specialist schools in a number of areas.

5.10 Firstly, all maintained specialist schools must abide by the same curriculum legislation as other schools and by the law and Code of Practice on Admissions. That will not change.

5.11 There are those who have said that specialist schools will create a two tier system. They won't. We intend to expand the number of specialist schools more rapidly than originally proposed. There will be at least 1,000 specialist schools by 2003 and at least 1,500 by 2005 as a staging post for specialist status for all schools that are ready for it. But we want to do more to make sure that all schools that are ready to do so can achieve a new status. We would like all schools to identify the direction in which they want to move and to work towards it. Each school will be able to choose for itself, and we set out in paragraph 5.34 our proposals for supporting every school to work towards a new role.

5.12 Thirdly, we can confirm our proposals to introduce new specialisms in science; engineering; and business and enterprise. To these we will add a further specialism: mathematics and computing. Schools have said that they want to be able to combine specialisms, where the combinations work sensibly together. We will make sure that can happen. And we will allow schools to work together, so that nearby schools can jointly develop a centre of excellence or combination of complementary specialisms.

5.13 Fourthly, it is imperative that the next phase of school improvement and curriculum development is based on what successful schools do. In *Building on Success*, we said that we wanted to develop advanced specialist colleges as a leading edge of innovative schools. This opportunity will be open to high-performing and successful specialist schools and the first will be designated in September 2002. These schools will work with us to develop the role and to see how they can play a greater role in training teachers.

- *Do these proposals undermine the comprehensive principle?*

The principle of funding schools with a 'religious character' by the state has not attracted a great deal of controversy in the United Kingdom. Although the DfEE did not initially agree to the funding of an Islamic school in the London Borough of Brent, approval was eventually obtained. In addition to Christian schools there are a handful of Jewish, Islamic and Sikh maintained schools.

In the United States and Australia, the funding of such schools reflects two diverging approaches.

D J Stewart, C J Russo 'A comparative analysis of funding non-government schools in Australia and the United States' (2001) 13(1) Education and the Law 29

Introduction

Many similarities may be drawn between the educational systems of Australia and the United States. Yet, a major difference emerges between the systems in these two countries with regard to funding independent, particularly religious, schools. From very early on in Australian history, as in the United States, religious schools have been heavily involved in the nation's education. However, Australia, unlike the United States, currently provides significant public funding to religiously affiliated non-government schools.

...

The DOGS case

As early as 1964, challenges to the funding of non-government schools were facilitated by the establishment, in the Australian State of Victoria, of the Council for the Defence of Government Schools (hence DOGS, the name by which the subsequent challenge in the High Court became known). The efforts of this Council led to the sole challenge to date, on the propriety of using public funds to support non-government schools, to reach the High Court of Australia.

...

In essence, Birch maintained, in language paralleling the American standard as enunciated in *Lemon v Kurtzman*, the laws providing funding to non-government schools and specifically religious schools 'have the purpose and effect of Commonwealth support for religion and to impose on the Commonwealth an excessive entanglement in the affairs of religion.'

In essence, the plaintiffs' reasons for opposing state aid to non-government schools were largely in line with the views of James Madison and Thomas Jefferson who argued for the necessity of separating church and state in America in order, as Birch noted, to 'safeguard the integrity of each as well as to avoid preferential treatment of any one religion.' Other plaintiffs simply did not agree with any form of state aid. Yet others saw state aid as being inimical to the interests of government schools.

Six of the seven members of the High Court, with only Murphy J dissenting, ruled in favour of the Commonwealth. According to the Court, since the sections of the constitution at issue did not deal with establishing a particular religion but were educational in their intent, they did not serve the purpose of establishing any religion or church as part of the Commonwealth. In reaching this judgment, the Court decided that the plaintiffs' submission of similarities between the Constitutions of Australia and the United States, more particularly the Establishment Clause of the First Amendment of the latter, were not sustained.

There is little doubt, then, that while the legality of providing state aid to non-government schools is settled law the level of such aid, together with the decline in government funding will indeed be crucial issues at the 2001 Australian Federal elections.

Government aid and religious schools in the United States

The United States has a more than fifty year history of litigation under the Establishment Clause of the First Amendment contesting the limits of acceptable government aid to students who attend religiously affiliated non-public schools even though religious schools clearly save the taxpayers money. This judicial activity began in 1947 with *Everson v Board of Education*, wherein the Court crafted the Child Benefit Test, under which governmental aid, in the forms of books, transportation, and now, instructional programming and materials, including computers, is available to students who attend religious schools, on the basis that it primarily benefits children and not their schools. Once created, judicial attitudes toward the Child Benefit test have shifted dramatically.

Most recently, *Mitchell v Helms* became the most important case involving state aid to non-public schools since *Lemon*. Writing for the Court in a plurality decision, although not explicitly naming it, Justice Thomas expanded the parameters of the Child Benefit Test, in upholding the constitutionality of Chapter 2 of Title I, now Title VI, of the Elementary and Secondary Education Act, another far-reaching federal law that permits the loan of instructional materials such as library books, computers, television sets, tape recorders, and maps to non-public schools. More specifically, Justice Thomas decided that Chapter 2 did not foster impermissible religious indoctrination since the aid was allocated on the bases of neutral, secular criteria that neither favoured nor disfavoured religion and was available to all schools on a non-discriminatory basis. Further, he applied two principles from *Agostini* in holding that Chapter 2 did not have the effect of advancing religion. First, he noted that Chapter 2 recipients are not defined by reference to religion in noting that the aid is available on a non-discriminatory basis to all schools on the basis of neutral, secular criteria that neither favour nor disfavour religion. Second, he maintained that Chapter 2 did not foster governmental indoctrination of religion since eligibility was not only determined on a neutral basis, using a broad array of criteria, without regard to whether a school was religious but also because parents made private choices in selecting where their children would be educated. As such, Justice Thomas concluded that Chapter 2 did not have the effect of advancing religion even though the aid could be described as direct since it was secular, neutral, and non-ideological and there was no evidence that any of the equipment was diverted to religious purposes.

Conclusion

In examining the situation in Australia and the United States with regard to funding non-public schools, it is interesting to observe how the different histories in both nations have led to such divergent approaches to schooling. In particular, two significant differences emerge.

First, Australia, unlike the United States, has not been restrained by an Establishment Clause or litigation involving other constitutional mechanisms. As such, the Australian approach seems to be more concerned with broadly ensuring that children receive the best quality of education, based on the choices of their parents, and have not generally been as worried about the levels of funding for government and non-government schools. At the same time, it needs to be added that perhaps this situation has developed because Australians are not generally as litigious as their American counterparts. Further, Australians do not appear as passionate about issues such as school funding. To this extent, Australians appear to be more willing to accept the status quo and, apart from the *DOGS* case and the consequent muted dissatisfaction, there has been no overall public desire to bring further legal challenge to the funding of non-government schools. Conversely, in the United States, there has been significant, ongoing legal conflict over the narrower question of the acceptable limits of state aid to religiously affiliated schools.

A second matter worth noting is the apparent disparity that exists, in different ways, in the funding of non-government schools in both countries. That is, while it can be argued that there is too much aid to independent schools in Australia, the converse may be true in the United States where some view the lack of funding to non-public schools as a major inequality in the provision of education.

- *Is the funding of faith schools in England compatible with the provisions of the Human Rights Act 1998?*

Duration of school year and school day

The organisation of the school year is regularly raised as an issue for debate. Suggestions for a four or six term year have been proposed by various organisations, including the Local Government Association. Although the school day is normally divided into a morning and an afternoon session, some LEAs have experimented with a continental approach which involves starting school earlier and ending at lunchtime leaving the afternoon free for other activities.

The decision on how the school day is organised and the responsibility for term dates rests with either the governing body or the LEA depending upon the type of school.

School Standards and Framework Act 1998, s 41

(1) In the case of a community, voluntary controlled or community special school—
(a)   the local education authority shall determine the dates when the school terms and holidays are to begin and end; and
(b)   the governing body shall determine the times of the school sessions.

(2) In the case of a foundation, voluntary aided or foundation special school the governing body shall determine—
(a)   the dates and times when the school terms and holidays are to begin and end, and
(b)   the times of the school sessions.

…

However, in both cases the discretion should be exercised in accordance with the legal requirements which apply to all schools maintained by an LEA and to non-maintained special schools (EA 1996, s 551). The detailed provisions are found in the Education (School Day and School Year) (England) Regulations 1999, SI 1999/3181.

The 'school year' means the period beginning with the first school term to begin after July and ending with the beginning of the first such term to begin after the following July (reg 2). At least 380 sessions shall be held at a school during any school year (reg 3(1)).

The school day 'shall be divided into two sessions which shall be separated by a break in the middle of the day unless exceptional circumstances make this undesirable' (reg 3(1)).

- *What is the minimum number of school days in any school year?*

Nursery classes

Nursery classes are not required to comply with the minimum requirement of 380 sessions a year (reg 3(1)). Nursery schools and nursery classes are required to provide at least three hours of 'suitable activities'. However, it is sufficient to provide each child with one and a half hours of such activities (reg 3(4)). In other words there can be two sessions of one and a half hours.

After school clubs and holiday activities

The Children Act 1989 places legal obligations to provide such activities on local authorities rather than on LEAs. As in the case of day care (see above) the emphasis is on making provision for children 'in need', with the local authority having a discretion to make such provision for other children within their area.

Children Act 1989, s 18(5) and (6)

(5) Every local authority shall provide for children in need within their area who are attending any school such care or supervised activities as is appropriate—
(a)   outside school hours; or
(b)   during school holidays.

(6) A local authority may provide such care or supervised activities for children within their area who are attending any school even though those children are not in need.

4. MANAGEMENT OF MAINTAINED SCHOOLS

The management of a maintained school is the responsibility of the governing body (SSFA 1998, s 38). The head teacher has an important role in practice and also has some legal responsibility. The legal responsibilities vary to some extent according to the type of school. The governing body has been given increased financial responsibility over the past decade. There are five areas of importance to consider. First, the legal status and composition of the governing body; second, the functions and responsibilities of the governing body; third, the financial arrangements for funding the school; fourth the employment of teaching and other staff; and fifth, the issue of vicarious liability in tort claims.

The legislation setting out the functions and responsibilities of the governing body is contained in the SSFA 1998, which is supplemented by regulations, and supported by departmental guidance (e g DfEE Circular 15/98 (New Framework Governing Bodies)).

The Education Bill 2001/02 (Part 3) proposes changes to the government and finance of maintained schools. The Bill implements the Government's consultation paper on school governance: *The Way Forward – A Modernised Framework for School Governance.*

Legal status of the governing body

Every maintained school shall have a governing body, which is a body corporate (SSFA 1998, s 36, Sch 9), which means that the governing body can sue and be sued (see below). The governing body of a foundation, voluntary or foundation special school has charitable status, but the governing body of a community or community special school cannot be a charity (SSFA 1998, s 23). The Education Bill 2001/02 provides that each nursery school should in future have a governing body.

A maintained school is required to have an instrument of government, which sets out the name of the school; the category of school; the name of the governing body; the categories and number of governors; the number of registered pupils (SSFA 1998, s 37, Sch 12). For example s 37(3) provides that:

> The governing body of a maintained school shall not conduct the school under a name other than the one for the time being set out in the school's instrument of government.

The Court of Appeal was asked to consider whether the governing body of a voluntary aided school is an 'emanation of the state', which would mean that an individual could rely directly on the provisions of an EC directive when bringing a case against such a body. The case was concerned with the Acquired Rights Directive (EEC) 77/187, and its transposition into UK law by the Transfer of Undertakings (Protection of Employment) Regulations 1981, SI 1981/1794.

NUT v Governing Body of St Mary's Church of England (Aided) Junior School [1997] ELR 169

Schiemann LJ: This appeal from the Employment Appeal Tribunal arises from the dismissal of three teachers. They were employed at a school which was closed along with its neighbour and were dismissed allegedly for reasons of redundancy. On the day after the closure of their school a new school opened its doors. Most of the teachers who had been employed at the two schools which had been closed down were thereafter employed at the new school. Not so the three appellants. They had no job to go to. On the face of it there was no answer to the assertion that they had been dismissed by the governors of the old school for reasons of redundancy.

Appellants and respondents are agreed that the determinative question before us is whether the governing body of a voluntary-aided school can be regarded as an emanation of the State in the context of the doctrine that an individual can rely on the provisions of a European Community Directive as against the State or an emanation of the State.

...

True it is that in each case the governors volunteered for the task and true it is that the diocese might have chosen not to subject the school to the regime set out in that Order. But the diocese did not so choose but chose instead to enter the State system. True it is that in certain circumstances and subject to certain conditions, the diocese was still free to withdraw the school from the State system, but it did not do so. Whilst the school was in the State system the governors were a public body charged by the State with running the school and with exercising their functions with a view to securing that the school provided the national curriculum.

The legislation already referred to gives extensive powers which may be exercised by the LEA or the Secretary of State to control the actions of the governors. Duties are imposed on the governors both by the general legislation and by the statutory instrument by virtue of which they exercise their powers. The financial position is that the failure to transpose the Directive will, if the present appeal is dismissed, have the effect of allowing the LEA and the State to benefit from the failure to transpose the Directive.

...

(1) Have the governors been made responsible pursuant to a measure adopted by the State for providing a public service?

...

The statutory instrument, made by the LEA under statutory powers, can be regarded as a measure adopted by the State. Education can be regarded as a public service.

(2) Is that service under the control of the State?

...

(3) Do the governors have special powers beyond those which apply between individuals?

Mr Hand submitted that the governors had the power to spend public money and that this was a special power for present purposes. I am not presently persuaded that this was the sort of power which the ECJ had in mind in *Foster v British Gas*.

However, as I have already indicated, I think it inappropriate to apply the tripartite test as though it were a definition section. In my judgment for the purposes of the doctrine of direct vertical effect the governors of the schools must be regarded as emanations of the State and I therefore consider that this appeal must be allowed.

Composition of the governing body

The number and type of governors vary according to the size and category of school. A governor's term of office is four years. The following are normally members of a school's governing body:

- Head teacher
- Parent governors (elected)
- LEA governors
- Foundation/partnership governors (foundation, voluntary schools)
- Teacher governors (elected)
- Staff governors (elected)
- Co-opted governors
- (Additional governors if authorised by regulations).

The School Standards and Framework Act 1998, Sch 9, Pt II sets out the constitution of governing bodies for each category of school. For example, para 9(3) provides that the governing bodies of community schools should be constituted as follows:

School Standards and Framework Act 1998, Sch 9, Pt II, para 9(3)

Category of governor	Secondary school normal basis	Secondary school option if less than 600 pupils	Primary school normal basis	Primary school option if less than 100 pupils
Parent governors	6	5	4 or 5	3
LEA governors	5	4	3 or 4	2
Teacher governors	2	2	1 or 2	1
Staff governors	1	1	1	1 or 0
Co-opted governors	5	4	3 or 4	2

See also the Education (School Government) (England) Regulations 1999, SI 1999/2163; DfEE Circular 15/98 (New Framework Governing Bodies).

The Education Bill 2001/02 proposes changes to the composition of governing bodies.

Functions and responsibilities of the governing body

The SSFA 1998 sets out the functions and responsibilities of the governing body in some detail. They include the following.

CONDUCT OF THE SCHOOL

School Standards and Framework Act 1998, s 38

(1) Subject to any other statutory provision, the conduct of a maintained school shall be under the direction of the school's governing body.

(2) The governing body shall conduct the school with a view to promoting high standards of educational achievement at the school.

...

ESTABLISHMENT OF A COMPLAINTS PROCEDURE

School Standards and Framework Act 1998, s 39

(1) The governing body of a maintained school shall in accordance with regulations—
(a)   establish procedures for dealing with all complaints relating to the school other than

those falling to be dealt with in accordance with any procedures required to be established in relation to the school by virtue of any other statutory provision; and
(b)   publicise the procedures so established;

…

However, no regulations have been approved (see chapter 8). The Education Bill 2001/ 02 has removed the requirement for regulations to be enacted. This means that complaints procedures should be established once the provision is in force. Guidance is likely to be published by the DfES.

PRODUCING A WRITTEN ANNUAL REPORT

School Standards and Framework Act 1998, s 42

(1) Once in every school year the governing body of a maintained school shall prepare a report (a 'governors' report') dealing with such matters, and otherwise complying with such requirements, as may be specified in regulations.

…

HOLDING AN ANNUAL PARENTS' MEETING

School Standards and Framework Act 1998, s 43

(1) Once in every school year the governing body of a maintained school shall hold a meeting (an 'annual parents' meeting') which is open to—
(a)   all parents of registered pupils at the school;
(b)   the head teacher; and
(c)   such other persons as the governing body may invite.

(2) The purpose of the meeting shall be to provide an opportunity for discussion of—
(a)   the governors' report;
(b)   the discharge by the governing body, the head teacher and the local education authority of their functions in relation to the school;
(c)   the aims and values of the school;
(d)   how the spiritual, moral, cultural, mental and physical development of pupils is to be promoted at the school;
(e)   how pupils are to be prepared for the opportunities, responsibilities and experiences of adult life and citizenship;
(f)   the standards of educational achievement of pupils; and
(g)   how the governing body are to promote the good behaviour, discipline and well-being of pupils.

…

PRODUCING A SCHOOL BEHAVIOUR AND DISCIPLINE POLICY

School Standards and Framework Act 1998, s 61

(1) The governing body of a maintained school shall ensure that policies designed to promote good behaviour and discipline on the part of its pupils are pursued at the school.

(2) In particular, the governing body—

(a)   shall make, and from time to time review, a written statement of general principles to which the head teacher is to have regard in determining any measures under subsection (4); and

(b)   where they consider it desirable that any particular measures should be so determined by the head teacher or that he should have regard to any particular matters—

(i)   shall notify him of those measures or matters, and

(ii)   may give him such guidance as they consider appropriate;

and in exercising their functions under this subsection the governing body shall have regard to any guidance given from time to time by the Secretary of State.

(3) Before making or revising the statement required by subsection (2)(a) the governing body shall consult (in such manner as appears to them to be appropriate)—

(a)   the head teacher; and

(b)   parents of registered pupils at the school.

...

(See chapter 4 School Discipline and Exclusions)

ENSURING THAT SCHOOL ATTENDANCE TARGETS ARE SET

School Standards and Framework Act 1998, s 63

(1) Regulations may make provision for and in connection with—

(a)   requiring, or

(b)   enabling the Secretary of State to require,

governing bodies of maintained schools to secure that annual targets are set for reducing the level of unauthorised absences on the part of relevant day pupils at their schools.

See also the Education (School Attendance Targets) (England) Regulations 1999, SI 1999/397; the Education (School Performance and Unauthorised Absence Targets) (Wales) Regulations 1999, SI 1999/1811; the Code of Practice on LEA-School Relations for England 2001; and the Code for Wales 1999.

OTHER RESPONSIBILITIES

These include:

−   producing a school prospectus

−   managing the school's budget (see below)

−   controlling the use of the school premises (SSFA 1998, s 40, Sch 13)

−   fixing school holidays and the times of school sessions (for foundation and voluntary aided schools) (see above)

−   appointing teachers and other staff (see below)

−   agreeing the admission numbers (see chapter 3)

−   considering the case of an excluded pupil (see chapter 4).

In practice the day-to-day operation of the school is the responsibility of the head teacher, although legally the responsibility rests with the governing body. The question whether a head teacher was entitled to ban a parent from the school premises was one of the issues considered by the Court of Appeal in the following case. The ban, on the mother of a six-year-old pupil, was made under the Education Act 1996, s 547, which has been amended by the SSFA 1998.

Wandsworth London Borough Council v A [2000] ELR 257

Buxton LJ:

Summary of the facts

The headmaster of Earlsfield school considered that he had reason to complain of Miss A's conduct on its premises, in particular towards members of his staff. He therefore on 24 November 1997 wrote her a letter (the 24 November 1997 letter) in the following terms:

I am writing to you concerning verbal abuse of staff in our school.

This morning, Miss Denham was in tears after you spoke to her. This was following your comments in [R]'s reading record book, which I found so unacceptable that I have withdrawn the book.

As this is the second instant of verbal abuse of one of our staff, and as you are already on a formal warning from our governors of a ban from our school premises, I must therefore prohibit you from:

(1) Entering school premises (including the playground) beyond the school gate.
(2) Engaging in conversation with our staff without a third party present.

I am taking this action under section 547 of the Education Act 1996.

This ban takes place from Tuesday 25 November and is enforceable in law. I am having the backing of my governing body. You must therefore make the necessary arrangements for [R] to be brought or collected from school if he is to continue to be educated here.

As this is the second school from which you have been banned from the premises, I am informing the relevant officials at Wandsworth Council as there may be issues if [R] is ever educated in another Wandsworth school.

…

The conduct, both in terms of entering the premises and in terms of confrontation with the staff, none the less continued, and Wandsworth accordingly brought proceedings in the Wandsworth County Court seeking an injunction restraining Miss A from trespassing on the premises of Earlsfield school and, what was in the circumstances a formal claim, damages of £1000.

…

The court identified seven issues including:
- Did Miss A have a licence to enter the premises of Earlsfield school? If so, what were its terms?
- If there were public law limits on Wandsworth's freedom to terminate Miss A's licence, was the licence properly terminated in this case?

...

We venture to think that 40 years ago very few people would have thought that parents had any sort of general licence to enter their child's school, or at least had anything more than a most limited licence. But more recently the running of schools has become more informal, and the parents more welcome in them. We entirely agree with Mr Giffin that parents have no licence to roam at will, enter classrooms during lessons, or interfere with the professional work of education. At the same time, however, we think it now puts it too restrictively to see the parents' licence on no higher level than that of the milkman or postman, or of any casual inquirer at a public building who has a licence only to enter to state his business. A parent may, for instance, be permitted, or welcome, to speak to members of staff informally and without prior appointment. He or she may be permitted, or welcome, to enter classrooms before school starts, for instance to see displayed examples of the children's work. He or she may be permitted, or welcome, if arriving to collect the child before the end of school, to wait in the school hall or other convenient place. And so on.

...

In the present case, the headmaster's paramount duty is to secure the proper education of the children for whom he is responsible. The safety and working conditions of his staff are an important factor in pursuit of that aim. He is a professional who must be given a high degree of discretion in taking action against conduct that in his judgment threatens that aim. And he takes that action in the midst of a busy operational life, and not as an adjudicator or as part of some formal decision-making process. The most that can be imposed on him, therefore, in respect of a decision of the type now under scrutiny, is some obligation to inform himself of the parent's position before taking steps against her.

...

Miss A's interest in being on the school premises was more underpinned in public law than are the rights or interests of any citizen to use, say, a recreation ground. But the headmaster's decision not only deprived her of access to the school, but also in so doing treated her differently from, we must assume, other parents. It is therefore a case where an opportunity to make representations should have been given.

In so saying, however, and bearing in mind the features of the headmaster's work to which we have already drawn attention, we wish to guard most strongly against any tendency to impose on a headmaster in this position any obligation to conduct a formal investigation, and much less anything resembling a trial. It would have been sufficient in the present case if the headmaster had, before banning Miss A, written to her asking for her comments, and giving her a short time to reply. If he thought the matter was sufficiently urgent, he could have banned her temporarily, pending fuller consideration. If he received comments, he would have a very wide discretion as to whether his proposed action needed to be reconsidered in the light of them.

...

Applying to our case, therefore, the proper test of whether Wandsworth acted perversely, or otherwise in breach of any public law duty, we immediately come up against the failure to give Miss A any 'hearing', even of the comparatively attenuated nature that we have suggested. Because of that failure, the public law body cannot claim to have properly informed itself as to the facts, and it is that error that grounds Miss A's claim to relief. But if the headmaster had heard Miss A's denials, and not accepted them, then absent any other flaw in the decision-making process his decision could not be challenged. And we should make clear that the opportunity of challenging the decision on grounds of perversity does not grant licence for a retrial of the facts in the hope of establishing an error of that degree when there is nothing on the face of the decision-making process to warrant such an argument.

- *In the light of this decision advise a head teacher what he or she must do where they wish to ban a parent from the school premises.*

Reform of the governing body

Membership of a governing body is a voluntary activity for most of the 370,000 governors in England and Wales. The responsibility and work imposed on governing bodies has expanded dramatically over the past decade. In November 2000 the government published a consultation paper on the duties and responsibilities of school governing bodies. The government's view is that the work of governing bodies needs to be streamlined and they need to be given a less onerous but more strategic role.

The Education Bill 2001/02 purports to give effect to these proposals.

Financial arrangements

Central government is responsible for providing almost all of the money for maintained schools. The money is not paid direct to the schools by the DfEE, but is paid to the local authority, not the LEA, which is responsible for funding individual schools through its LEA.

There have been three main concerns in recent years about the funding arrangements.

The first is that there is a considerable difference in the amount of money spent per pupil depending upon the LEA in which the pupil lives.

The second concern is that some LEAs have creamed off a relatively high percentage of the money allocated to schools by the DfEE in order to cover LEA expenses. The government's policy is to ensure that between 85 per cent and 90 per cent of the money allocated to LEAs actually reaches the schools.

DfEE Press Notice 2000/0291

[In June 2000] the delegation of school budget still ranges from 79.8 per cent at the bottom to 89.8 per cent at the top.

...

49 local education authorities are already delegating at least 85 per cent of their Local Schools Budgets. I believe that the remainder can follow suit. Some authorities are nearly at this level already. For others, the increase will be more challenging. The authorities currently delegating 85 per cent or more are varied in size and include rural and urban authorities.

I am therefore setting a minimum target of 85 per cent delegation for 2001–2002.

I believe there is also room for further savings on central administration, building on the progress that authorities have already made. I therefore propose to lower the present ceilings — £75 per pupil for London and £65 elsewhere — by £5 for 2001–2002.

The third concern has been that even where central government allocates funds for schools the local authority may lawfully decide to spend the money on some service other than education. There have been arguments for increased ring-fencing of money for education to prevent this happening in future.

Summary of financial arrangements

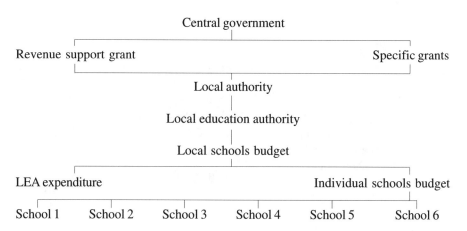

Each school has its delegated budget share.

Role of the LEA

On average approximately 40 per cent of a local authority's budget is spent on education. The funding arrangements for education are set out in primary legislation as follows. A LEA is under a duty to finance all its maintained schools. Section 22 and Sch 3 of the SSFA 1998 contain detailed provisions on the responsibilities of governing bodies, local education authorities and the Secretary of State as to the funding of foundation, voluntary and foundation special schools.

In the case of voluntary aided schools the governing body is responsible for funding certain expenditure, including the provision of premises and some equipment as well as most exterior repairs and maintenance (SSFA 1998, Sch 3, Pt II).

School Standards and Framework Act 1998, s 22

...

(3) In the case of a community school, a community special school or a maintained nursery school, the local education authority's duty to maintain the school includes—
(a)   the duty of defraying all the expenses of maintaining it, and
(b)   the duty of making premises available to be used for the purposes of the school.

(4) In the case of a foundation, voluntary controlled or foundation special school, the local education authority's duty to maintain the school includes—
(a)   the duty of defraying all the expenses of maintaining it, and
(b)   the duty ... of providing new premises for the school ...

(5) In the case of a voluntary aided school, the local education authority's duty to maintain the school includes—

(a)   the duty of defraying all the expenses of maintaining it, except any expenses that by virtue of paragraph 3 of Schedule 3 are payable by the governing body, and

(b)   the duty, under paragraph 4 of Schedule 3 or paragraph 14 of Schedule 6, of providing new premises for the school under and in accordance with that paragraph.

....

The central principle is found in SSFA 1998, s 45:

> For the purposes of the financing of maintained schools by local education authorities, every such school shall have, for each financial year, a budget share which is allocated to it by the authority which maintains it.

The LEA is responsible for preparing a financial scheme which will identify its 'local schools budget', within which there is an 'individual schools budget'. Nearly all maintained schools have a delegated budget, which comprises their 'budget share' of the individual schools budget.

LEAs' financial schemes

Each LEA is required to prepare a financial scheme for the financing of its schools. Such a scheme must comply with requirements laid down in the SSFA 1998 (s 48, Sch 14) or in regulations (see for example the Financing of Maintained Schools (England) Regulations 2000, SI 2000/478). All LEAs are required to prepare two financial statements for each financial year, which runs from April to April. The first, which should be prepared before the beginning of the financial year, comprises an annual estimate of its planned expenditure for the forthcoming year. The second statement sets out the expenditure actually incurred during the previous financial year (SSFA 1998, s 52).

Under the SSFA 1998, s 46(2) and regulations the LEA's financial scheme may deal with, for example:

(a)   the carrying forward from one financial year to another of surpluses and deficits arising in relation to schools' budget shares;

(b)   amounts which may be charged against schools' budget shares;

(c)   amounts received by schools which may be retained by their governing bodies and the purposes for which such amounts may be used;

(d)   the imposition, by or under the scheme, of conditions which must be complied with by schools in relation to the management of their delegated budgets, including conditions prescribing financial controls and procedures;

(e)   terms on which services and facilities are provided by the authority for schools maintained by them.

Local schools budget

The LEA is responsible for determining its 'local schools budget', but is permitted under regulations to deduct certain items of expenditure from this budget to cover its own costs.

School Standards and Framework Act 1998, s 46(1)

(1) ...a local education authority's 'local schools budget' for a financial year is the amount appropriated by the authority for meeting all expenditure by the authority in that year of a class or description prescribed for the purposes of this subsection (which may include expenditure incurred otherwise than in respect of schools).

Prescribed expenditure refers to money spent on the provision of primary and secondary education. It also includes expenditure:
–   supported by specific grants
–   on special educational provision
–   on certain school improvements, and
–   on strategic management.

These four categories of expenditure, together with associated administrative costs and overheads incurred by the LEA, may be deducted by the LEA from the local schools budget before money is allocated to the individual schools (Financing of Maintained Schools (England) Regulations 2000, SI 2000/478, regs 3, 5, and Sch 1).

Individual schools budget

The LEA calculates this budget by deducting the permitted deductions from the local schools budget (see above).

School Standards and Framework Act 1998, s 46(2)

... a local education authority's 'individual schools budget' for a financial year is the amount remaining after deducting from the authority's local schools budget for that year such planned expenditure by the authority in respect of the year as they may determine should be so deducted in accordance with regulations.

School's budget share

Each maintained school is entitled to its 'budget share' of the individual schools budget. Normally every maintained school is to have the budget share delegated (see below) to it, and the governing body is entitled to manage the school's budget share. The SSFA 1998, s 47 sets out how in principle an individual school's budget share should be calculated.

School Standards and Framework Act 1998, s 47

(1) ...a maintained school's budget share for a financial year is such amount as the local education authority may determine, in accordance with regulations, to allocate to the school out of the authority's individual schools budget for that year.

(2) Regulations under this section may, in particular, make provision—

(a)   as to the time when schools' budget shares are to be initially determined by local education authorities;

(b)   specifying—

(i)   factors or criteria which such authorities are to take into account, or

(ii)   requirements as to other matters with which such authorities are to comply,

in determining such shares, whether generally or in such cases as are specified in the regulations;

...

(f)   requiring consultation to be carried out by such authorities in relation to the factors or criteria which are to be taken into account in determining such shares and as to the time and manner of such consultation;...

The factors and criteria which the LEA should take into account when deciding how to allocate budget shares to individual schools are set out in detail in the Financing of Maintained Schools (England) Regulations 2000, SI 2000/478. Note also that an LEA is required to carry out consultation before deciding upon the factors and criteria it will use.

Financing of Maintained Schools (England) Regulations 2000, SI 2000/ 478, reg 10

(1) ...

(2) A local education authority shall have regard to the desirability of such a formula being simple, objective, measurable and predictable in effect, and clearly expressed.

(3) ....

The regulations provide that the LEA must take into account the number of registered pupils at the school (reg 11). The LEA may also take into account the number of places they wish to fund at special schools or boarding schools, or for children with special educational needs (reg 12). Schedule 2 to the regulations lists other factors which an LEA may take into account when drawing up its funding formula. There are 32 factors listed in Sch 2 to the regulations. They include:

–   special educational needs of pupils
–   pupils for whom English is not their first language
–   the presence of a sixth form at a school
–   turnover of pupils
–   admission arrangements at a school
–   the size and condition of a school's buildings and grounds relative to those of other schools maintained by the authority
–   heating and lighting of school premises
–   school milk, meals and other refreshment
–   teachers' salaries at a school
–   social deprivation in the area from which a school derives its pupils.

An LEA should not normally distinguish between types of maintained school when deciding upon the funding to be provided (reg 13). For example, an LEA should not as a matter of general policy decide to give more money to community schools than to voluntary aided schools in its area.

Regulation 22 of the Financing of Maintained Schools (England) Regulations 2000, SI 2000/478 provides that at least 80 per cent of the budget should be allocated to individual schools to cover specific types of costs. This percentage is likely to increase in future years (see above).

Delegated budget

Every maintained school is to have a delegated budget which comprises the school's 'budget share'.

School Standards and Framework Act 1998, s 49

(1) Every maintained school shall have a delegated budget...

(5) Any amount made available by a local education authority to the governing body of a maintained school (whether under section 50 or otherwise)—
(a) shall remain the property of the authority until spent by the governing body or the head teacher; and
(b) when spent by the governing body or the head teacher, shall be taken to be spent by them or him as the authority's agent.

The LEA is required to provide the governing body with the money amounting to the school's budget share. The governing body is entitled to manage the school's budget share, and has a broad discretion as to how the money may be spent; although only certain allowances may be paid to governors. The governing body is permitted to delegate its powers to the head teacher. Governors will not normally be personally liable for the actions of the governing body.

School Standards and Framework Act 1998, s 50

(1) Where a maintained school has a delegated budget in respect of the whole or part of a financial year the local education authority shall secure that in respect of that year there is available to be spent by the governing body—
(a) where the school has a delegated budget in respect of the whole of that year, a sum equal to the school's budget share for the year, or
(b) where the school has a delegated budget in respect of only part of that year, a sum equal to that portion of the school's budget share for the year which has not been spent.

(2) The times at which, and the manner in which, any amounts are made available by the

authority to the governing body in respect of any such sum shall be such as may be provided by or under the scheme.

(3) Subject to any provision made by or under the scheme, the governing body may spend any such amounts as they think fit—
(a)   for any purposes of the school; or
(b)   (subject also to any prescribed conditions) for such purposes as may be prescribed.

(4) In subsection (3) 'purposes of the school' does not include purposes wholly referable to the provision of—
(a)   part-time education suitable to the requirements of persons of any age over compulsory school age, or
(b)   full-time education suitable to the requirements of persons who have attained the age of 19;

but any such purposes may be prescribed by regulations under paragraph (b) of that subsection.

(5) Nothing in subsection (3) shall be read as authorising the payment of allowances to governors otherwise than in accordance with regulations under paragraph 6 of Schedule 11 (or, in the case of temporary governors of a new school, regulations under section 44(5)).

(6) The governing body may delegate to the head teacher, to such extent as may be permitted by or under the scheme, their powers under subsection (3) in relation to any amount such as is mentioned in that subsection.

(7) The governors of a school shall not incur any personal liability in respect of anything done in good faith in the exercise or purported exercise of their powers under subsection (3) or (6).

• *When would individual governors be liable for the actions of the governing body under this section?*

The right of a governing body to a delegated budget can be suspended by the LEA.

School Standards and Framework Act 1998, s 51

Schedule 15 (which provides for the suspension by a local education authority of a governing body's right to a delegated budget in the case of failure to comply with requirements as to delegation or of financial mismanagement, etc) shall have effect.

The LEA may also suspend the delegated budget of a school where the school is subject to a formal warning, has serious weaknesses or requires special measures (SSFA 1998, s 17).

Reform of LEA funding

In September 2000 the government published a Green Paper which proposed separate funding assessments for schools and education authorities. The government also announced that it planned that LEAs should not be able to deduct more than 15 per cent, and preferably only 10 per cent from their local schools budget to cover administrative and other LEA costs.

Department for Transport, Local Government and the Regions Green Paper *Modernising Local Government Finance*

6.6 There are three key issues which the Government believes need to be addressed:
- how best to ensure that funding is properly matched to the separate responsibilities of local authorities and schools;
- how best to ensure that the funds allocated by central Government for education are used for that purpose; and
- how to ensure a fair allocation of funding between authorities and between schools within authorities to reflect pupil needs.

6.7 On the first issue, the Government believes that identifying separately the aggregate funding for schools at both national and local level would enable parents, teachers, heads and governors to see what level of expenditure on schools the Government has planned for each year. The Government believes that the best way forward is to assess and separately identify the resources which it believes should be devoted to schools on the one hand; and the resources required by local authorities on the other. Funding for authorities would support their direct responsibilities in education, including:
- special needs co-ordination;
- making sure that every pupil has a school place;
- support for school transport;
- services for the under fives; and
- the Youth Service.

Such resources would of course be augmented by funding from, for example the Learning and Skills Council for adult education and community learning and separately from Government for the Connexions4 service. This separate identification of budgets would recognise the reality of the current roles and responsibilities in the school system.

6.8 The next issue is how to ensure that resources intended for schools reach them. There are two main options discussed in paragraphs 6.9 to 6.13.

6.9 The first option would be to ring-fence the whole of expenditure for schools through a legal requirement on local authorities to allocate the resources identified by central Government to schools. There are two ways in which such an arrangement might be implemented.
- first, the Government might set a minimum expenditure level, which local authorities were required to allocate to schools, but which they could increase by setting a higher council tax or reprioritising within their total budgets; or
- the whole cost of schools might be met from Government grant, ring-fencing it wholly from other local authority services.

Either of these arrangements would ring-fence school budgets and require legislation. They would guarantee that schools would receive all the funding intended for them and enable schools and parents to have a clearer framework for forward planning.

6.10 But there are arguments against ring-fencing, too:

it could weaken local accountability and democracy and encourage some local authorities to give less attention to their proper responsibilities for strategic planning and quality improvement in schools;

- it could erode local authorities' financial responsibility and freedom;
- it could lead to weaker co-ordination between education and other local services which make a difference to schools and families; and
- it might create pressure for ring-fencing of other services.

6.11 An alternative option, which would not involve a legal duty on authorities to pass on a given level of funding, would instead be based on transparency around schools funding. Under such a system, the funding intended for schools' delegated budgets and for other local education authority responsibilities would be separately identified by central Government as described in paragraph 6.7. Authorities would be required to give their council tax payers and schools a full account of money delivered through spending assessments and through special and specific grants both for schools and for authorities' own service provision; with an indication of the proportions funded through national Government and locally-raised finance; and a comparison with the previous year.

6.12 Such transparency would assist in ensuring local accountability for decisions on funding taken by authorities as it would greatly improve clarity and would put pressure on local authorities to pass on in full the assessments for school budgets. The Government believes that this option would also be more likely to lead local education authorities to continue to add their own resources to the level of funding indicated by central Government.

6.13 In view of the potential difficulties set out in paragraph 6.10 associated with legal ring-fencing, the Government believes that there is a strong case for introducing a system based on transparency as set out in paragraph 6.11. However, the Government would be prepared to legislate to introduce a legal requirement on authorities to pass on funding to their schools if insufficient progress were made through a system based on transparency.

6.14 The third key issue set out in paragraph 6.6 is the need to ensure fairness, on the one hand in the distribution of aggregate resources for schools between local authorities, and on the other, in the distribution of resources between schools within authorities. Some ideas for general revenue grant distribution reform are discussed in paragraph 3. But particularly powerful representations have been made indicating disquiet about the fairness of the distribution of grant for schools between authorities and there is a strong case for reform of the distribution of grant at this level.

6.15 Schools funding could be based on a simpler and more transparent formula. This might comprise a basic entitlement per primary or secondary school pupil, plus enhancements for schools and pupils in authorities where significant deprivation adds to education costs; and a separate enhancement for areas where schools need to pay more to recruit and retain staff. The level of these enhancements would be decided following analysis of evidence about variations in pupil characteristics, cost and achievement, rather than as in the current system by regression analysis against past expenditure. The advantages of such an approach would be greatly increased transparency compared with the existing SSA [standard spending assessment] system; and a system which would be acknowledged as fairer. In introducing such changes, it would be necessary to ensure that no authorities' schools lost in real terms, but that those who are disadvantaged by the current system were subject to levelling up to a fair amount of funding per pupil.

The proposals on education finance are part of a wider package of reform. A new system of funding LEAs and schools is being introduced by amendments to the Local Government Finance Act 1992. The Explanatory Notes to the Education Bill 2001/02 state that 'The new system will involve separate financial assessments for expenditure on school pupils and expenditure on the central functions of LEAs'. The Education

Bill 2001/02 amends education finance legislation accordingly. In particular, there are new definitions of the 'LEA budget' and the 'schools budget', and LEAs will be required to establish a schools forum where schools will be able to be consulted and to advise the LEA on the setting of the schools budget.

Who is the employer?

The LEA forms part of the local authority which may be, for example, a London Borough or a county or city council in England (see chapter 1). The council is a body corporate which means that it has legal personality, and can bring a legal action on its own behalf or be sued.

The governing body of a school is also a corporate body (see above). In the context of education the main question is 'Who may appoint, promote and dismiss teachers and other staff?'. This is also linked to the issue of direct and vicarious liability in tort. To answer the question it is necessary to look at the type of school.

There are detailed regulations relating to the employment of teachers which are beyond the scope of this book. They include health and criminal record checks, as well as ensuring that the prospective teachers are not included on a DfEE list of people (now made under the Protection of Children Act 1999) who should not be employed to work with young children. The Education Bill 2001/02 will replace the current SSFA provisions. The Bill gives the Secretary of State additional powers to make regulations and guidance.

Community, voluntary controlled and community special schools

The LEA is the employer of both teaching and non-teaching staff (SSFA 1998, s 54, Sch 16). The governing body recommends the appointment of a suitable candidate. The LEA may refuse to appoint the candidate in certain circumstances. Different provisions apply where the school's delegated budget is suspended.

The School Standards and Framework Act 1998, Sch 16 sets out in detail the procedures to be followed. They differ according to whether a head teacher, deputy head teacher, other teacher, or non-teaching staff member is to be appointed. The LEA's chief education officer is entitled to attend and advise the governing body on the appointment of all teachers. The head teacher is also entitled to attend and advise, except where a head teacher is being appointed, presumably as a replacement. In the case of most voluntary controlled church schools the governing body may give an officer of the diocesan authority similar rights to the LEA's chief education officer.

The governing body and the LEA should also comply with the requirements of the legislation on sex, race and disability discrimination (see chapter 1 p 37 and chapter 5 p 380). The Code of Practice on LEA-School Relations 2001 provides guidance on LEA representations about headteacher appointments and performance.

APPOINTMENT OF A HEAD TEACHER OR A DEPUTY HEAD TEACHER

Where a head teacher or a deputy head teacher is being appointed, the School Standards and Framework Act 1998, Sch 16, para 7(1) provides:

> Where the governing body approve a recommendation of the selection panel, the local education authority shall appoint the person recommended by the panel unless he does not meet any staff qualification requirements which are applicable in relation to his appointment...

'Staff qualification requirements' are defined in Sch 16, para 1(3) as follows:

> References in this Schedule to staff qualification requirements are to any requirements with respect to—
> (a) qualifications,
> (b) registration,
> (c) health and physical capacity, or
> (d) fitness on educational grounds or in any other respect,
>
> of teachers or other persons employed, or otherwise engaged to provide their services, in work that brings them regularly into contact with persons who have not attained the age of 19 which for the time being apply under regulations under section 218 of the Education Reform Act 1988 (regulations relating to employment of teachers etc) or section 19 of the Teaching and Higher Education Act 1998 (induction training).

- *When may the LEA refuse to appoint as head teacher a person approved by the governing body?*

APPOINTMENT OF OTHER TEACHERS

Where the governing body wishes to appoint a teacher, other than a head or a deputy head, it may advertise, interview and recommend candidates for appointment. In addition the following provisions apply.

School Standards and Framework Act 1998, Sch 16

> 12(1) The local education authority may nominate for consideration for appointment to the post any person who appears to them to be qualified to fill it and who at the time of his nomination either—
> (a) is an employee of theirs or has been appointed to take up employment with them at a future date, or
> (b) is employed by the governing body of a foundation, voluntary aided or foundation special school maintained by them.
>
> (2) No person who is employed at any school maintained by the authority shall be nominated by the authority under sub-paragraph (1) without the consent of the governing body of the school...
>
> 15(1) The local education authority shall appoint the person recommended or accepted

for appointment by the governing body unless he does not meet any staff qualification requirements which are applicable in relation to his appointment...

Regulation 12 enables LEAs to move teachers from one school to another school in the LEA area.

Such staff includes school secretaries, caretakers and laboratory technicians, but school meals staff are not subject to the same provisions. The SSFA 1998, Sch 16 provides that:

20(1) Where the governing body desire the appointment of a person to work in a non-teaching post at the school, they may recommend a person to the local education authority for appointment to the post...

(3) Before selecting a person to recommend under this paragraph and determining in relation to such a recommendation any matters mentioned in sub-paragraph (2), the governing body shall consult—
(a) the head teacher (where he would not otherwise be involved in the decision), and
(b) the chief education officer of the authority...

21(1) The local education authority shall appoint a person recommended to them under paragraph 20 unless he does not meet any staff qualification requirements which are applicable in relation to his appointment.

Schedule 16 also outlines how governing bodies and LEAs should deal with:
– staff conduct, discipline and grievances
– serious concerns about the performance of the head teacher
– suspension and dismissal of staff.

Foundation, voluntary aided and foundation special schools

The main difference in this context between this group of schools and community, voluntary controlled and community special schools is that the governing body is the employer, and the LEA only has an advisory role (SSFA 1998, s 55, Sch 17). For example, para 8 of Sch 17 provides that in relation to the appointment of a head teacher or a deputy head teacher:

Where the governing body approve a recommendation of the selection panel, the governing body shall appoint the person recommended by the panel unless he does not meet any staff qualification requirements which are applicable in relation to his appointment.

Normally non-teaching staff are also employed by the governing body, but it is possible for the governing body and the LEA to agree that a particular appointment is made by the LEA. This could be the case, for example, where the LEA provides a special needs assistant for a pupil.

Schools which have 'a religious character'

In addition there are particular provisions which apply to voluntary aided, foundation and voluntary controlled schools which have 'a religious character' (see above and chapter 6 p 439).

There are special rules relating to the appointment and dismissal of teachers of religious education in such schools. These teachers are described as 'reserved teachers'. The majority of the provisions apply to foundation and voluntary controlled schools with a religious character, rather than voluntary aided schools. In particular:

School Standards and Framework Act 1998, s 58

(1) ....

(2) Where the number of the teaching staff of a school to which this subsection applies is more than two, the teaching staff shall include persons who—
(a)   are selected for their fitness and competence to give religious education as is required in accordance with arrangements under paragraph 3(3) of Schedule 19 (arrangements for religious education in accordance with the school's trust deed or with the tenets of the school's specified religion or religious denomination), and
(b)   are specifically appointed to do so.

(3) The number of reserved teachers in such a school shall not exceed one-fifth of the number of the teaching staff, including the head teacher (and for this purpose, where the number of the teaching staff is not a multiple of five, it shall be treated as if it were the next higher multiple of five).

(4) The head teacher of such a school shall not, while holding the post of head teacher of the school, be a reserved teacher.

(5) Where the appropriate body propose to appoint a person to be a reserved teacher in such a school, that body—
(a)   shall consult the foundation governors, and
(b)   shall not so appoint that person unless the foundation governors are satisfied as to his fitness and competence to give such religious education as is mentioned in subsection (2)(a).

(6) If the foundation governors of such a school consider that a reserved teacher has failed to give such religious education efficiently and suitably, they may require the appropriate body to dismiss him from employment as a reserved teacher in the school.

In addition:

School Standards and Framework Act 1998, s 54(6)

In relation to reserved teachers at a voluntary controlled school, Schedule 16 ... has effect subject to section 58.

• *Compare the appointment procedures for an ordinary teacher and a reserved teacher at a voluntary controlled school.*

In the case of voluntary aided schools there are no specific statutory provisions except where the school does not have a delegated budget. In this case the governing body is not required to obtain the consent of the LEA before dismissing a teacher appointed to give religious education, who has failed to do so efficiently and suitably (SSFA 1998, s 58(7)). Normally, such a school would be required to obtain the LEA's consent before dismissing a teacher.

Religious opinions

Generally no person is to be disqualified from being employed at maintained schools which are non-denominational or do not have a religious character, because of their religious opinions, their attendance or non-attendance at religious worship, or their refusal to give religious education.

School Standards and Framework Act 1998, s 59

(1) This section applies to—
(a)   a community school or a community or foundation special school, or
(b)   a foundation or voluntary school which does not have a religious character.

(2) No person shall be disqualified by reason of his religious opinions, or of his attending or omitting to attend religious worship—
(a)   from being a teacher at the school, or
(b)   from being employed for the purposes of the school otherwise than as a teacher.

(3) No teacher at the school shall be required to give religious education.

(4) No teacher at the school shall receive any less remuneration or be deprived of, or disqualified for, any promotion or other advantage—
(a)   by reason of the fact that he does or does not give religious education, or
(b)   by reason of his religious opinions or of his attending or omitting to attend religious worship.

However, there are three exceptions to these principles where the teacher is appointed as a member of staff at a foundation or voluntary school with a religious character. The exceptions relate to the appointment of head teachers, the appointment of teachers at voluntary aided schools, and the conduct of teachers employed by a voluntary aided school.

School Standards and Framework Act 1998, s 60

...

(4) In connection with the appointment of a person to be head teacher of the school (whether foundation or voluntary controlled) regard may be had to that person's ability and fitness to preserve and develop the religious character of the school.

(5) If the school is a voluntary aided school—
(a)   preference may be given, in connection with the appointment, remuneration or promotion of teachers at the school, to persons—
   (i)   whose religious opinions are in accordance with the tenets of the religion or religious denomination specified in relation to the school under section 69(4), or
   (ii)   who attend religious worship in accordance with those tenets, or
   (iii) who give, or are willing to give, religious education at the school in accordance with those tenets; and
(b)   regard may be had, in connection with the termination of the employment of any teacher at the school, to any conduct on his part which is incompatible with the precepts, or with the upholding of the tenets, of the religion or religious denomination so specified.

...

A member of the non-teaching staff at a voluntary aided school should not be disqualified from employment by reason of his religious opinions, or of his attending or omitting to attend religious worship.

School Standards and Framework Act 1998, s 60(6)

If the school is a voluntary aided school, no person shall be disqualified by reason of his religious opinions, or of his attending or omitting to attend religious worship, from being employed for the purposes of the school otherwise than as a teacher.

In *Board of Governors of St Matthias Church of England School v Crizzle* [1993] ICR 401, the applicant was deputy head teacher at the school. She was a non-practising Roman Catholic of Asian origin. She applied unsuccessfully for the post of head teacher. The EAT held that the board of governors of a Church of England voluntary aided school were justified in making it a condition for the post of head teacher that the applicant was a committed practising Christian, and that such a condition was not a breach of the Race Relations Act 1976.

• *The statutory provisions permit the imposition of such a condition. However, does the legislation conflict with the Human Rights Act 1998 and Art 9 of the ECHR?*

The European Union is introducing an EU directive making it unlawful to discriminate against people at work on the grounds of their religion. However, the EU has also agreed that the provisions contained in the School Standards and Framework Act 1998, which permit a religious school to give preference to teachers who practise the school's faith, will continue to be lawful.

Liability in negligence

The LEA or the governing body may be directly liable in negligence where a pupil is insured because the school does not have a proper system for supervising pupils. As employers they may also be vicariously liable where, for example, a teacher at the school is negligent and as a result a pupil suffers loss or injury. There have been major developments in the tort of negligence in the context of special educational needs (see chapter 5), which also have implications for educational provision generally (see chapter 7).

The standard of care owed by the LEA or the governing body will vary according to the individual child. Cases were traditionally concerned with physical injury suffered by a pupil. In *Nwabudike v Southwark London Borough* [1997] ELR 35 the LEA was held not liable for the injuries suffered by a 6½-year-old boy when he ran out of school during the school lunch hour and was knocked down by a car.

Nwabudike v Southwark London Borough [1997] ELR 35

Judge Zucker QC: It was the duty of those responsible for managing this school to take all reasonable and proper care for the safety of the children. That includes the duty to take all reasonable and adequate steps to prevent the children leaving the school during school hours when they should not have done so. The standard is a high one.

...

I conclude that Mrs Moses took the steps she outlined to me to prevent the children leaving the school. I find that those steps fully and adequately discharged the burden which lay upon her to ensure the safety of the children. I agree that a balance has to be struck between security and preventing a school being turned into a fortress. No school can ensure that accidents never happen. Whatever precautions are taken there is always a risk that they could, particularly if a child is determined to act in a way which breaks the rules designed to protect him or her. What is required of a school is that it takes responsible and proper steps to ensure that its children are safe. That this school did so is evidenced by the fact that there was only one prior similar incident, and that 6 years earlier. I am quite satisfied that it did take reasonable and proper steps to ensure Melvin's safety.

In *Wilson v Governors of Sacred Heart Roman Catholic School* [1998] ELR 637, CA, one pupil, going home after the end of school, whirled his anorak around his head and hit a nine-year-old classmate in the eye. The court held that the governing body of a voluntary primary school was not liable for failing to provide adult supervision between the school building and the school gate at going home time.

The facts of *Nwabudike v Southwark London Borough* [1997] ELR 35 (see above) can be compared with the following case where a similar incident occurred at a mainstream school, but where the pupil had special educational needs. Integrated schooling is common, and demonstrates that mainstream schools should have in place procedures which are appropriate for those children at the school with special educational needs. The case also illustrates the application of the doctrine of res ipsa loquitur in this context.

J v North Lincolnshire County Council [2000] ELR 245

Henry LJ: (2) The accident occurred on 26 November 1996 at approximately 2.35 pm. The claimant J had left the school without permission, and without anyone noticing him. Approximately 1000 metres from the school, on a major road, the A18 Wrawby Road, he was struck by a motor car and sustained serious injuries. The driver of the car was not at fault.

(3) J was one month short of his ninth birthday. He had been at the school for 4 years. He suffered from global development delay, which, as the name implies, meant that his development, mental and emotional, was retarded in comparison with his peers. Evidence as to the extent of this development delay was given by Mr Syme, a consultant psychologist. J's reading age was 7, his IQ 78 to 81 (borderline), he had special educational needs, but was in the top or least serious band of those with such needs. His emotional age was assessed at 4½.

(4) Children with special educational needs are rightly integrated as far as possible into mainstream school life and Brigg Primary School (of which, in all respects other than their perimeter security, we heard nothing but good) did just that. They had two classes for children with such needs. J's form teacher, Mrs Mesher, was specially qualified to teach such children, and each of her two assistants had special experience with such children. The evidence is that they were conscientious and caring.

(5) It was at all times accepted by the school that J could not safely be out of school on his own — 'Absolutely not' — as the headmaster Mr Pearce answered when the question was put to him. He, in common with other like children, had a taxi and escort to and from school.

...

(17) J's absence was noted immediately after the break. At about the same time, this tragic accident occurred. The judge found that the school had been unable to explain how J escaped, or by what gate: '... he might have got out by any of the five gates'.

(18) We take the basic law to be as follows:

> Where the school has accepted the care of children who would be at risk if left alone beside a highway, if a child in their care is injured as a result of being where he should not be (unaccompanied, by a highway) then the onus is on the school to show how it was that he or she came to be where he or she should not be, and to show that that state of affairs had come about through no fault of theirs (see *Carmarthenshire County Council v Lewis* [1955] AC 549 at 561–2, 566, 568 and 570).

(19) This is the application of the maxim res ipsa loquitur, which merely describes the state of the evidence from which it was proper to draw an inference of negligence. It is:

> ...no more than a rule of evidence affecting onus. It is based on common sense, and its purpose is to enable justice to be done when the facts bearing on causation and on the care exercised by the defendant are at the outset unknown to the plaintiff and are or ought to be within the knowledge of the defendant. (*Charlesworth on Negligence* (9th edn), 5–88, citing Lord Normand in *Barkway v South Wales Transport Co* [1950] AC 185.)

...

(32) The school's explanation, such as it was, did not throw any light on how the child got out of school. Had the school been able to do that, then the evidential burden would have

returned to the plaintiff to show why such an escape was negligent. But as that did not happen, the school was driven back to showing that all reasonable precautions were taken to keep the child in: i e to disprove negligence (see Lord Tucker in *Carmarthenshire County Council v Lewis* at 569 …).That answer must be a complete answer, covering all reasonable possibilities (see *Henderson v Henry E. Jenkins & Sons and Evans* [1970] AC 282). Any such disproof of negligence would on the facts before us have to explain why, for instance, the vulnerable Gate 5 exit was not protected (as it now is) by an internal gate on the access road with a catch either high enough or intricate enough to be child-proof. That the school did not succeed in doing. Therefore the school failed to discharge the evidential burden on it to show that the accident was not due to negligence on its part. Accordingly, the plaintiff is entitled to judgment. As the evidential burden does not shift back to him, he need not prove causation. By definition the plaintiff cannot prove how the accident happened, and so cannot put forward any set of facts as causing the accident. And the law does not require him to.

VICARIOUS LIABILITY

The principle of vicarious liability has recently been addressed by the House of Lords in *Lister v Hesley Hall Ltd* [2001] UKHL 22, [2001] 2 WLR 1311. The case concerned the liability of an independent school, which educated pupils with special educational needs, for the sexual abuse of pupils by one of its employees. The House of Lords overruled the decision of the Court of Appeal in *Trotman v North Yorkshire County Council* [1998] ELR 625.

In *Trotman v North Yorkshire County Council* [1998] ELR 625 a 16-year-old pupil, who suffered from epilepsy and mental handicap, alleged that he had been sexually assaulted by the deputy head teacher when they shared a room on a school trip to Spain. They shared a room because the boy suffered from fits and required supervision. The deputy headmaster was subsequently convicted of indecently assaulting other boys, but not the claimant. The court was asked to consider as a preliminary issue whether the LEA could be held vicariously liable for such an assault. The claim was based on trespass, rather than negligence. The judge at first instance held that the LEA was capable of being vicariously liable. The LEA appealed to the Court of Appeal.

Trotman v North Yorkshire County Council [1998] ELR 625

Butler-Sloss LJ: Having looked at some of the relevant decisions on each side of the line, it is useful to stand back and ask: applying general principles, in which category in the *Salmond* test would one expect these facts to fall? A deputy headmaster of a special school, charged with the responsibility of caring for a handicapped teenager on a foreign holiday, sexually assaults him. Is that in principle an improper mode of carrying out an authorised act on behalf of his employer, the council, or an independent act outside the course of his employment? His position of caring for the plaintiff by sharing a bedroom with him gave him the opportunity to carry out the sexual assaults. But availing himself of that opportunity seems to me to be far removed from an unauthorised mode of carrying out a teacher's duties on behalf of his employer. Rather it is a negation of the duty of the council to look after children for whom it was responsible. Acts of physical assault may not be so easy to categorise, since they may range, for instance, from a brutal and unprovoked assault by a teacher to forceful attempts to defend another pupil or the teacher himself. But in the field of serious sexual misconduct, I find it difficult to visualise circumstances in which an act of the teacher can be an unauthorised mode of carrying out an authorised act, although I would not wish to close the door on the possibility.

...

I find it impossible to hold that the commission of acts of indecent assault can be regarded as a mode — albeit, an improper and unauthorised mode — of doing what, on the case advanced, the deputy headmaster was employed by the council to do. In the circumstances alleged, Michael Stevens was employed to supervise the [claimant's] welfare while on the holiday in Spain. The commission by him of acts of indecent assault on a pupil in his charge cannot be regarded as a way of doing that. Rather, it must be regarded as an independent act of self-indulgence or self-gratification ... It is not sufficient to found vicarious liability in the employer that the employment provided the opportunity for the employee to commit the act if the act itself was outside the scope of the employment.

• *Why did the claimant to sue in trespass rather than negligence? Why do you think that the claimant sued the LEA vicariously in trespass rather than directly for negligence?*

Lister v Hesley Hall Ltd [2001] UKHL 22, [2001] 2 WLR 1311

Lord Steyne:

I. The question

1 The central question before the House is whether as a matter of legal principle the employers of the warden of a school boarding house, who sexually abused boys in his care, may depending on the particular circumstances be vicariously liable for the torts of their employee.

II. The sexual abuse

2 In 1979 Axeholme House, a boarding annex of Wilsic Hall School, Wadsworth, Doncaster, was opened. Between 1979 and 1982 the appellants were resident at Axeholme House. At that time the appellants were aged between 12 and 15 years. The school and boarding annex were owned and managed by Hesley Hall Ltd as a commercial enterprise. In the main children with emotional and behavioural difficulties were sent to the school by local authorities. Axeholme House is situated about two miles from the school.

3 The aim was that Axeholme House would provide care to enable the boys to adjust to normal living. It usually accommodated about 18 boys. The company employed Mr and Mrs Grain as warden and housekeeper to take care of the boys. The employers accept that at the material time they were aware of the opportunities of sexual abuse which may present themselves in a boarding school environment.

...

4 The employers accept that, unbeknown to them, the warden systematically sexually abused the appellants in Axeholme House. ... In the early 1990s a police investigation led

to criminal charges in the Crown Court. Grain was sentenced to seven years' imprisonment for multiple offences involving sexual abuse.

6 In 1997 the appellants brought claims for personal injury against the employers.

V. The issues before the House

10 Since the decision in the Court of Appeal the law reports of two landmark decisions in the Canadian Supreme Court, which deal with vicarious liability of employers for sexual abuse of children, have become available: *Bazley v Curry* (1999) 174 DLR (4th) 45; *Jacobi v Griffiths* (1999) 174 DLR (4th) 71. Enunciating a principle of 'close connection' the Supreme Court unanimously held liability established in *Bazley's* case and by a four to three majority came to the opposite conclusion in *Jacobi's* case. The Supreme Court judgments examine in detail the circumstances in which, though an employer is not 'at fault', it may still be 'fair' that it should bear responsibility for the tortious conduct of its employees. These decisions have been described as 'a genuine advance on the unauthorised conduct/unauthorised mode distinction': Peter Cane, 'Vicarious Liability for Sexual Abuse' (2000) 116 LQR 21, 24. Counsel for the appellants invited your Lordships to apply the test developed in *Bazley's* case and in *Jacobi's* case and to conclude that the employers are vicariously liable for the sexual torts of their employee.

11 In another sense the approach to the appeals before the House differs from that adopted in the Court of Appeal. The House is not bound to follow the decision in *Trotman v North Yorkshire County Council* [1999] LGR 584. On the contrary, quite apart from the high persuasive value of the two Canadian decisions, the first task of the House is to consider whether the decision in *Trotman v North Yorkshire County Council*, when examined from a perspective of legal principle, correctly states the position. On the principal point the present appeals therefore in reality challenge the law as stated by the Court of Appeal in *Tortman v North Yorkshire County Council* rather than in the cases under consideration.

15 For nearly a century English judges have adopted Salmond's statement of the applicable test as correct. Salmond said that a wrongful act is deemed to be done by a 'servant' in the course of his employment if 'it is either (a) a wrongful act authorised by the master, or (b) a wrongful and unauthorised *mode* of doing some act authorised by the master': *Salmond, Law of Torts* (1st edn, 1907) 83; and *Salmond & Heuston on the Law of Torts* (21st edn), 443. Situation (a) causes no problems. The difficulty arises in respect of cases under (b). Salmond did, however, offer an explanation which has sometimes been overlooked. He said (*Salmond on Torts* (1st edn, 83–84) that 'a master ... is liable even for acts which he has not authorised, provided they are *so connected* with acts which he has authorised, that they may rightly *be regarded* as modes — although improper modes — of doing them' (my emphasis).

It remains, however, to consider how vicarious liability for intentional wrongdoing fits in with Salmond's formulation. The answer is that it does not cope ideally with such cases. It must, however, be remembered that the great tort writer did not attempt to enunciate precise propositions of law on vicarious liability. At most he propounded a broad test which deems as within the course of employment 'a wrongful and unauthorised mode of doing some *act* authorised by the master'. And he emphasised the connection between the authorised *acts* and the 'improper modes' of doing them. In reality it is simply a practical test serving as a dividing line between cases where it is or is not just to impose vicarious liability. The usefulness of the *Salmond* formulation is, however, crucially dependent on focusing on the right act of the employee.

...

[I]t is not necessary to ask the simplistic question whether in the cases under consideration the acts of sexual abuse were modes of doing authorised acts. It becomes possible to consider the question of vicarious liability on the basis that the employer undertook to care for the boys through the services of the warden and that there is a very close connection between the torts of the warden and his employment. After all, they were committed in the time and on the premises of the employers while the warden was also busy caring for the children.

25 In my view the approach of the Court of Appeal in *Trotman v North Yorkshire County Council* [1999] LGR 584 was wrong. It resulted in the case being treated as one of the employment furnishing a mere opportunity to commit the sexual abuse. The reality was that the county council were responsible for the care of the vulnerable children and employed the deputy headmaster to carry out that duty on its behalf. And the sexual abuse took place while the employee was engaged in duties at the very time and place demanded by his employment. The connection between the employment and the torts was very close. I would overrule *Trotman v North Yorkshire County Council*.

...

VII. The application of the correct test

27 My Lords, I have been greatly assisted by the luminous and illuminating judgments of the Canadian Supreme Court in *Bazley v Curry* (1999) 174 DLR (4th) 45 and *Jacobi v Griffiths* (1999) 174 DLR (4th) 71. Wherever such problems are considered in future in the common law world these judgments will be the starting point. On the other hand, it is unnecessary to express views on the full range of policy considerations examined in those decisions.

28 Employing the traditional methodology of English law, I am satisfied that in the case of the appeals under consideration the evidence showed that the employers entrusted the care of the children in Axeholme House to the warden. The question is whether the warden's torts were so closely connected with his employment that it would be fair and just to hold the employers vicariously liable. On the facts of the case the answer is Yes. After all, the sexual abuse was inextricably interwoven with the carrying out by the warden of his duties in Axeholme House.

...

Lord Clyde:

50 I turn finally to the facts of the present case. It appears that the care and safekeeping of the boys had been entrusted to the respondents and they in turn had entrusted their care and safekeeping, so far as the running of the boarding house was concerned, to the warden. That gave him access to the premises, but the opportunity to be at the premises would not in itself constitute a sufficient connection between his wrongful actings and his employment. In addition to the opportunity which access gave him, his position as warden and the close contact with the boys which that work involved created a sufficient connection between the acts of abuse which he committed and the work which he had been employed to do. It appears that the respondents gave the warden a quite general authority in the supervision and running of the house as well as some particular responsibilities. His general duty was to look after and to care for, among others, the appellants. That function was one which the respondents had delegated to him. That he performed that function in a way which was an abuse of his position and an abnegation of his duty does not sever the connection with his employment. The particular acts which he carried out upon the boys have to be viewed not in isolation but in the context and the circumstances in which they occurred. Given that he had a general authority in the management of the house and in the care and supervision of the boys in it, the employers should be liable for the way in which

he behaved towards them in his capacity as warden of the house. The respondents should then be vicariously liable to the appellants for the injury and damage which they suffered at the hands of the warden.

- *Was this a claim for negligence or for trespass to the person? Is there any difference in the limitation periods applicable to such claims?*

- *If the pupil had been sexually abused (a) by a teacher in the teacher's home, or (b) on school premises by a gardener employed by the school to maintain the grounds, would the school be vicariously liable using the Lister approach?*

In *Lister v Hesley Hall Ltd* [2001] UKHL 22, [2001] 2 WLR 1311, the House of Lords left open the question whether the employee was under a duty to report any psychological damage suffered by the pupil, in the same way as where a pupil suffers physical injury. Lord Hobhouse commented:

> take one of the judge's hypothetical examples, say, there might have been a groundsman at Axeholme House and he might have been the abusing party; Mr Grain might have discovered what had happened and the distress it had caused to the boy but did nothing about it and did not report the incident to the defendants. The defendants might not be liable for what the groundsman did; he was employed to look after the grounds, not to have anything to do with the boys. But the defendants would be liable for the breach of Mr Grain who was employed to care for the boys and their welfare. The liability of the defendants might not be so grave or extensive as if Mr Grain had been the abuser himself but it would in principle be capable of existing.

PSYCHOLOGICAL INJURY

Recently the courts have been asked to consider claims based on psychiatric or psychological damage, and financial loss. The House of Lords has considered the issue of vicarious liability in negligence claims arising out of special educational needs provision (see also chapter 5). The case concerned the liability of the LEA for the actions of an educational psychologist employed by the LEA, and the House of Lords considered the policy implications of holding LEAs liable for the actions of educational psychologists and teachers.

Phelps v Hillingdon London Borough Council [2000] ELR 499

Lord Slynn of Hadley: If the educational psychologist does have a duty of care on the facts is it to be held that it is not just and reasonable that the local education authority should be vicariously liable if there is a breach of that duty? Are there reasons of public policy why the courts should not recognise such a liability? I am very conscious of the need to be cautious in recognising such a duty of care where so much is discretionary in these as in other areas of social policy. As has been said, it is obviously important that those engaged in the provision of educational services under the statutes should not be hampered by the imposition of such a vicarious liability. I do not, however, see that to recognise the existence of the duties necessarily leads or is likely to lead to that result. The recognition of the duty of care does not of itself impose unreasonably high standards. The courts have long recognised that there is no negligence if a doctor 'exercises the ordinary skill of an ordinary competent man exercising that particular art':

...

It would make no sense to say that educational psychologists owe a duty of care to under-performing pupils they are asked to assess, but teachers owe no duty of care to under-performing pupils in their charge or about whom they give educational advice under the statutory scheme. In the same way as an educational psychologist owes a duty of care in respect of matters falling within the scope of his professional expertise, by parity of reasoning so must a teacher owe a duty of care to a child with learning difficulties in respect of matters which fall within his field of competence. A teacher must exercise due skill and care to respond appropriately to the manifest problems of such a child, including informing the headteacher or others about the child's problems and carrying out any instructions he is given. If he does not do so, he will be in breach of duty he owes the child, as well as being in breach of the duties he owes his employer, and his employer will be vicariously liable accordingly.

My third illustration raises a particularly controversial issue. It cannot be that a teacher owes a duty of care only to children with special educational needs. The law would be in an extraordinary state if, in carrying out their teaching responsibilities, teachers owed duties to some of their pupils but not others. So the question which arises, and cannot be shirked, is whether teachers owe duties of care to all their pupils in respect of the way they discharge their teaching responsibilities. This question has far-reaching implications. Different legal systems have given different answers to this question.

I can see no escape from the conclusion that teachers do, indeed, owe such duties. The principle objection raised to this conclusion is the spectre of a rash of 'gold digging' actions brought on behalf of under-achieving children by discontented parents, perhaps years after the events complained of. If teachers are liable, education authorities will be vicariously liable, since the negligent acts or omissions were committed in the course of the teachers' employment. So, it is said, the limited resources of education authorities and the time of teaching staff will be diverted away from teaching and into defending unmeritorious legal claims. Further, schools will have to prepare and keep full records, lest they be unable to rebut negligence allegations, brought out of the blue years later. For one or more of these reasons, the overall standard of education given to children is likely to suffer if a legal duty of care were held to exist.

I am not persuaded by these fears.

...

In the present case I am not persuaded that there are sufficient grounds to exclude these claims even on grounds of public policy alone. It does not seem to me that there is any wider interest of the law which would require that no remedy in damages be available. I am not persuaded that the recognition of a liability upon employees of the education authority for damages for negligence in education would lead to a flood of claims, or even vexatious claims, which would overwhelm the school authorities, nor that it would add burdens and distractions to the already intensive life of teachers. Nor should it inspire some peculiarly defensive attitude in the performance of their professional responsibilities. On the contrary it may have the healthy effect of securing that high standards are sought and secured. If it is thought that there would only be a few claims and for that reason the duty should not be recognised, the answer must be that if there are only a few claims there is the less reason to refuse to allow them to be entertained. As regards the need for this remedy, even if there are alternative procedures by which some form of redress might be obtained, such as resort to judicial review, or to an ombudsman, or the adoption of such statutory procedures as are open to parents, which might achieve some correction of the situation for the future, it may only be through a claim for damages at common law that compensation for the damage done to the child may be secured for the past as well as the future.

5. SCHOOL ORGANISATION IN A LOCAL EDUCATION AUTHORITY

When grant-maintained status was introduced by the Education Reform Act 1988, LEAs had no control over schools which acquired that status, because they were funded directly from central government. With the abolition of grant-maintained status in 1999 and the creation of foundation status LEAs have regained overall responsibility for the provision of schools in their area. However, all types of schools now have more autonomy from their LEA than they did in the 1980s. The School Standards and Framework Act 1998 has established new structures in an attempt to rationalise school provision within individual LEAs.

The LEA has legal responsibility for ensuring the provision of sufficient school places in its area (see also chapters 1 and 3).

Education Act 1996, s 14

(1) A local education authority shall secure that sufficient schools for providing—
(a) primary education, and
(b) education that is secondary education by virtue of section 2(2)(a),

are available for their area.

...

(3) In subsection (2) 'appropriate education' means education which offers such variety of instruction and training as may be desirable in view of—
(a) the pupils' different ages, abilities and aptitudes, and
(b) the different periods for which they may be expected to remain at school,

including practical instruction and training appropriate to their different needs.

...

(6) In exercising their functions under this section, a local education authority shall in particular have regard to—
(a) the need for securing that primary and secondary education are provided in separate schools;
(b) the need for securing that special educational provision is made for pupils who have special educational needs; and
(c) the expediency of securing the provision of boarding accommodation (in boarding schools or otherwise) for pupils for whom education as boarders is considered by their parents and the authority to be desirable.

....

School organisation committees

Under the SSFA 1998 every English LEA is required to set up a school organisation committee for its area (s 24 of, Sch 4 to the SSFA 1998). The membership of the committees is to be set out in regulations, but SSFA 1998, s 24(3) states that:

(3) Those regulations must be so framed as to secure that every school organisation committee includes at least one person within each of the following categories—

(a) a member of the local education authority;

(b) a person nominated by the Diocesan Board of Education for any diocese of the Church of England any part of which is comprised in the authority's area; and

(c) a person nominated by the bishop of any Roman Catholic Church diocese any part of which is comprised in the authority's area.

Regulation 5 of the Education (School Organisation Committees) (England) Regulations 1999, SI 1999/700 provides more detail on the composition of the committee, which must comprise five categories of members, and may, if the LEA chooses, include a sixth category.

Regulation 5

(1) Each school organisation committee shall consist of the following members appointed by the authority—

(a) at least one and not more than 7 members who are members of the authority;

(b) at least one and not more than 7 members nominated in accordance with paragraph (2);

(c) at least one and not more than 7 members nominated in accordance with paragraph (4);

(d) at least one and not more than 7 members nominated by the Further Education Funding Council for England;

(e) the number of members referred to in paragraph (6), each of whom is a member of the governing body of a relevant school, other than a governor who is appointed to the school's governing body by the authority and is also a member of the authority (members appointed under this sub-paragraph constituting the 'schools group'); and

(f) if the authority so determine, up to 7 other members who are not members of the authority, from persons appearing to them to represent the interests of any section of the local community determined by the authority.

(2) Members falling within paragraph (1)(b) shall be nominated by the Diocesan Board of Education for the diocese of the Church of England which comprises the area of the authority and where the area of the authority is comprised in more than one such diocese—

(a) the members shall be nominated by the Diocesan Board for one diocese with the agreement of the Diocesan Boards for the other dioceses; or

(b) if the Diocesan Boards are unable to agree, at least one and not more than the relevant number of members shall be nominated by the Diocesan Board for each such diocese.

(3) In paragraph (2) above 'the relevant number' is 7 divided by the number of dioceses of the Church of England in which the area of the local education authority is comprised, rounded down to the nearest whole number.

(4) Members falling within paragraph (1)(c) shall be nominated by the bishop of the Roman Catholic Church diocese which comprises the area of the local education authority and where the area of the authority is comprised in more than one such diocese, paragraphs (2)(a) and (b) and (3) above shall apply with the substitution of references to the bishop of the Roman Catholic Church diocese for references to the Diocesan Board of Education for the diocese of the Church of England.

...

School organisation plans

All LEAs are required to prepare a five-year school organisation plan for their area. Again details as to the procedures to be followed in drawing up a plan may be found in regulations (Education (School Organisation Plans) (England) Regulations 1999, SI 1999/701), but the key principles are contained in primary legislation.

School Standards and Framework Act 1998, s 26

...

(2) A school organisation plan is a statement which sets out—
(a) how the authority propose to exercise their functions during the prescribed period with a view to securing the provision of primary and secondary education that will meet the needs of the population of their area during that period; and
(b) any facilities which the authority expect to be available outside their area for providing such education.

(3) A school organisation plan must deal with such matters, and take such form, as may be prescribed.

(4) The matters prescribed for the purposes of subsection (3) shall include the provision which the authority propose to make during the period in question for children with special educational needs.

(5) A school organisation plan prepared by a local education authority in England requires the approval of the school organisation committee or the adjudicator...and regulations may make provision with regard to the procedure to be followed in connection with the preparation and approval of such plans.

Section 26 of the SSFA 1998 and the regulations also provide that LEAs in England should publish draft school organisation plans and allow for objections to the proposal to be made. Both the draft plan and any objections should be submitted to the school organisation committee. The committee may approve the draft plan or prepare its own plan. Certain matters may be referred to an adjudicator. The procedure in Welsh LEAs is different because they do not have school organisation committees (SSFA 1998, s 27).

Adjudicators

Adjudicators are to be appointed to resolve disputes within the school organisation committee (s 26 of the SSFA 1998). They are appointed by the Secretary of State (SSFA 1998, s 25, Sch 5). School organisation committees are required to reach unanimous decisions on school organisation plans (Education (School Organisation Plans) (England) Regulations 1999, SI 1999/701, reg 8). Where they are unable to do so they are required to refer the matter to an adjudicator. The LEA may also refer the plan to the adjudicator where the committee has not voted on the plan within two months of the LEA submitting it to the committee (reg 12).

The adjudicator's powers are to be found both in the SSFA 1998 and in regulations, for example the Education (School Organisation Proposals) (England) Regulations 1999, SI 1999/2213, which are supplemented by guidance (DfEE circular 9/99 (organisation of school places)). They include the following power:

School Standards and Framework Act 1998, s 26(6)(e)

(i)   to approve a draft plan either with modifications proposed by the committee or without modifications, or

(ii) to make proposals to the committee for modifications to be made to the draft plan...

Education (School Organisation Plans) (England) Regulations 1999, SI 1999/701, reg 9

(1) The adjudicator may—

(a) approve the draft plan as submitted to him; or

(b) approve the draft plan with the modifications contained in any proposals referred to him under regulation 8(5)(b); or

(c) make his own proposals for modifications to the draft plan (which may relate to any aspect of the plan).

(2) Where the adjudicator makes his own proposals for modifications to the draft plan he shall send a copy of his proposals to the committee.

The committee may either approve the draft plan with the modifications proposed by the adjudicator, or refer the draft plan back to the adjudicator (reg 10). The regulations provide for further references between the committee and the adjudicator.

Ultimately the committee or the adjudicator should approve a draft school organisation plan, which is then published in its final form by the LEA.

The adjudicators may also hear objections relating to admission arrangements (see chapter 3).

Establishment, closure and reorganisation of schools

The introduction of school organisation plans and committees was part of an attempt to rationalise the number of school places available in individual LEAs. Such rationalisation may result in the need to establish new schools, close existing schools or reorganise the existing provision. The legal powers and duties are primarily vested in the LEA, although the Secretary of State has residual powers.

Parents often object where a LEA proposes to close or reorganise local schools. Litigation may now be less likely where there is an effective school organisation committee. However, parent representatives do not automatically have the right to sit on such a committee (see above).

The legislation gives LEAs the power to:

– establish or alter community, foundation or voluntary schools
– discontinue community, foundation, voluntary or maintained nursery schools
– establish, alter or discontinue community, or foundation special schools.

The SSFA 1998 now sets out the legislation dealing with the establishment, reorganisation and closure of schools. It replaces similar provisions found in the Education Act 1996 and earlier legislation. However, the requirement that these procedures should apply wherever there is a 'significant change of character' has been replaced by a list of circumstances, described as 'prescribed alterations' which will trigger these procedures. The procedures vary slightly according to whether or not the school is a special school.

In addition to the legislative provisions contained in the SSFA 1998 and the Education (School Organisation Proposals) (England) Regulations 1999, SI 1999/2213, guidance is given in DfEE circular 9/99 (organisation of school places) as amended (see below).

In addition there are regulations where a school wishes to change its category, for example from a foundation to a voluntary aided school (Education (Change of Category of Maintained Schools) (England) Regulations 2000, SI 2000/2195).

The Education Bill 2001/02 (Part 5) provides that LEAs may invite other people or organisations, such as the Church of England, to make proposals for the establishment of a new school. The Learning and Skills Council may propose the establishment, alteration, or closure of school sixth forms. Governing bodies of community schools will be given the power to propose alterations to their school. At the moment only LEAs may make such a proposal. Voluntary and foundation school governing bodies already have such a power. The Bill also provides that the Secretary of State will have the power to direct that an LEA increase the number of school places where they are insufficient. The Bill also amends the existing procedures.

Mainstream schools maintained by LEAs

ESTABLISHMENT AND ALTERATION OF SCHOOLS

An LEA may establish a new community school or alter an existing one. Voluntary and foundation schools may be established by 'promoters', or altered by their governing body. Where there is an intention to establish or alter a mainstream school the body concerned is required to publish proposals.

- *What is meant by the word 'establish'? Does it mean 'open' a school, or merely to start the process necessary to open a school?*

R v Buckinghamshire County Council, ex p Milton Keynes Borough Council (1996) 9 Admin LR 159

Facts:

Milton Keynes Borough Council [sought] a declaration that the decision of Buckinghamshire County Council, as local education authority for an area including Milton Keynes, on 18 May 1995 to publish notices ... of its intention to establish a new grammar school in Milton Keynes was ultra vires.

...

The county council was aware that from 1 April 1997 the borough council was to replace it as the local education authority for the area and it was also aware that if its proposals for the establishment of a grammar school got beyond a particular stage, by the time the borough council became the education authority there would be little it could do to alter or modify the proposals. It would therefore be saddled with the establishment of a grammar school to which it was strongly opposed.

Ognall J said that the county argued, inter alia, that 'establish' meant no more than to put in train procedures for the establishment of a school; that the concept of a local education authority was that it was an institution which was always there irrespective of the identity of the particular authority.

...

While his Lordship had every sympathy with the strong feelings of the borough, which were sincerely held, his Lordship was persuaded by the reasoning and arguments of the county which were to be preferred over those of the borough.

'Alter' in this context includes the transfer of the school to a new site but excludes any change in the religious character of the school (s 28(11)). 'Alter' also includes the introduction of certain admission arrangements, as well as the revision of admission arrangements for a grammar school.

A school can change category from, for example, foundation, to voluntary aided but certain procedures must be followed (SSFA 1998, s 35, Sch 8, and Education (Change of Category of Maintained Schools) (England) Regulations 2000, SI 2000/2195).

Consultation

Before LEAs or promoters publish any proposals they are required to consult 'appropriate persons' in accordance with any guidance issued by the Secretary of State.

School Standards and Framework Act 1998, s 28

(1) Where a local education authority propose—
(a)   to establish a new community or foundation school, or
(b)   to make any prescribed alteration to a community school, or

(c) to make any prescribed alteration to a foundation school consisting of an enlargement of the premises of the school,

the authority shall publish their proposals under this section.

(2) Where—
(a) any persons (referred to in this Part as 'promoters') propose to establish a new foundation or voluntary school, or
(b) the governing body of a foundation or voluntary school propose to make any prescribed alteration to the school,

those persons or (as the case may be) the governing body shall publish their proposals under this section.

...

(6) Before publishing any proposals under this section, the relevant body or promoters shall consult such persons as appear to them to be appropriate; and in discharging their duty under this subsection the relevant body or promoters shall have regard to any guidance given from time to time by the Secretary of State.

What is meant by any 'prescribed alteration'?
This is set out in SSFA 1998, ss 28(11); 101(1) and (3), 109(2), and the Education (School Organisation Proposals) (England) Regulations 1999, SI 1999/2213, reg 3 and Sch 1, paras 1-9. A useful summary is provided in the guidance.

DfEE circular 9/99 (organisation of school places)

7. The changes that require the publication of proposals (other than in special schools) are:
* the opening of a new community, foundation or voluntary school;
* the closure of an existing maintained school;
* the enlargement of the premises of a school where this would increase the capacity of the school by more than 30 pupils; and, taken together with any previous enlargement from the appropriate date, represents an increase in the capacity of the school by 25%, or at least 200 pupils whichever is the lesser; unless the school is expected to revert to its existing physical capacity within three years. ...
* a change in the age range of a school by a year or more, including the addition or removal of a sixth form, but excluding the introduction or discontinuing of part-time or full-time FE or providing or removing provision for pupils over compulsory school age who are repeating a course of education completed before they reached compulsory school age;
* the addition or removal of provision which is recognised by the Local Education Authority as reserved for pupils with special educational needs;
* the introduction of banding arrangements for the admission of pupils (section 101 of the 1998 Act);
* proposals by the governing body of a designated grammar school to end selection (section 109 of the 1998 Act);
* changing a school from single-sex to mixed or vice versa. (For the purposes of deciding whether statutory proposals are necessary, a school is treated as admitting pupils of one sex only if the admission of pupils of the other sex is limited to pupils over compulsory school age, and does not exceed 25% of the age group in question);

- the introduction or ending of boarding, or an increase or decrease in boarding provision by 50 pupils or 50% of capacity, whichever is the greater;
- the transfer of a school to a new site, except where the transfer is to the school's playing fields; or where the premises cannot (a) be brought up to the prescribed standards (currently the Education (School Premises) Regulations 1999), or (b) it is not reasonably practicable to enlarge the teaching accommodation to the required size, and the new site is within 3.2 kilometres (2 miles) of the existing site;
- a reduction or increase in a school's standard number;
- a change of category of a school (ie from community, foundation, voluntary aided, or voluntary controlled) to another of these categories, under Schedule 8 of the Act;
- an increase (other than a temporary increase) in the number of pupils in any relevant age group by 27 or more pupils…
- the closure of one site of a multi-sited school if it is 1.6 kilometres (one mile) or more from the main entrance of any remaining site.

What is meant by 'consult'?

This issue was considered in the following case which was concerned with the statutory obligation of the Secretary of State to consult representative organisations before making housing benefit regulations. The case contains useful statements of principle.

R v Secretary of State for Social Services, ex p Association of Metropolitan Authorities [1986] I All ER 164 at 167

Webster J: The issue, however, is whether the Secretary of State thereby consulted the applicants within the meaning of that word in s 36(1). The applicants contend that the Secretary of State failed to comply with his obligation to consult within the meaning of that subsection, because the time allowed to them within which to comment on the proposals was insufficient and because the information provided was inadequate or misleading, with the effect that they were unable sufficiently or properly to comment on the proposals. The respondent, the Secretary of State, contends that, in the light of the need to amend the regulations urgently, the time allowed and the information provided were each sufficient to enable the applicants to make sufficiently considered comments.

There is no general principle to be extracted from the case law as to what kind or amount of consultation is required before delegated legislation, of which consultation is a precondition, can validly be made. But in any context the essence of consultation is the communication of a genuine invitation to give advice and a genuine consideration of that advice. In my view it must go without saying that to achieve consultation sufficient information must be supplied by the consulting to the consulted party to enable it to tender helpful advice. Sufficient time must be given by the consulting to the consulted party to enable it to do that, and sufficient time must be available for such advice to be considered by the consulting party. Sufficient, in that context, does not mean ample, but at least enough to enable the relevant purpose to be fulfilled. By helpful advice, in this context, I mean sufficiently informed and considered information or advice about aspects of the form or substance of the proposals, or their implications for the consulted party, being aspects material to the implementation of the proposal as to which the Secretary of State might not be fully informed or advised and as to which the party consulted might have relevant information or advice to offer.

- *Who are 'persons as appear to them to be appropriate'? (see below).What remedy is available to such persons who have not been consulted?*

Publication of statutory proposals

Local education authorities and promoters are required to publish their proposals in accordance with any regulations which may require the proposals to contain certain information, and be published in a particular manner (SSFA 1998, s 28(3)).

See also the Education (School Organisation Proposals) (Wales) Regulations 1999, SI 1999/1671; and the Education (School Organisation Proposals) (England) Regulations 1999, SI 1999/2213. For example reg 5(2) of SI 1999/2213 provides:

> Any proposals for the establishment of a school shall be published—
> (a) by being posted in a conspicuous place in the area to be served by the school; and
> (b) in at least one newspaper circulating in that area.
>
> ...

In England LEAs and promoters are required to send to the local school organisation committee:
(a) a copy of the published proposals, and
(b) such information in connection with those proposals as may be prescribed by regulations (SSFA 1998, s 28 (6)).

Objections to statutory proposals

Schedule 6 to the SSFA 1998 contains further provisions which apply to both England and Wales in relation to the procedures to be followed once the proposals have been published. Schedule 6 applies to the establishment, alteration or discontinuance of both mainstream and special schools. The Schedule is concerned with making objections to, approving and implementing statutory proposals. For example in relation to England, para 2 of Pt I of Sch 6 provides that objections to the proposals may be made by 'any person'.

> (1) Any person may make objections to any proposals published under section 28, 29 or 31.
>
> (2) Where the proposals were published by a local education authority—
> (a) any objections under this paragraph shall be sent to the authority within such period as may be prescribed ('the objection period'); and
> (b) within such period as may be prescribed the authority shall send to the relevant committee copies of all objections made (and not withdrawn in writing) within the objection period, together with the authority's observations on them.
>
> (3) Where the proposals were published by a governing body or promoters, any objections under this paragraph shall be sent to the relevant committee within such period as may be prescribed.

The 'relevant committee' is the school organisation committee in England. See *R v Brent London Borough Council, ex p Gunning* (1985) 84 LGR 168 (below) where the period of time allowed to make objections and the decision of the local authority to close two schools were challenged by parents.

Approval

Proposals require the approval of the school organisation committee where, for example, objections are made to the statutory proposals. If the committee does not approve the proposals the matter is referred to the adjudicator (SSFA 1998, Sch 6, para 3(5), (6)). In addition:

School Standards and Framework Act 1998, Sch 6, Pt I, para 3

…

(4) When deciding whether or not to give any approval under this paragraph the committee shall have regard to—

(a)   any guidance given from time to time by the Secretary of State, and

(b)   the school organisation plan for the committee's area;

and the committee shall not give any such approval unless they are satisfied that adequate financial resources will be available to enable the proposals to be implemented.

…

(7) Where any proposals are referred to the adjudicator under sub-paragraph (5) or (6)—

(a)   he shall consider the proposals afresh; and

(b)   sub-paragraphs (2) to (4) shall apply to him in connection with his decision on the proposals as they apply to the committee.

DISCONTINUANCE OF SCHOOLS

A community school can be closed by its LEA, and a foundation or voluntary school by its governing body. The discontinuance provisions, unlike the establishment and alteration provisions, also apply to maintained nursery schools (SSFA 1998, ss 29(1)(b), 33(1)(c)).

As in the situation where there is a proposal to establish a school, there is an obligation on the LEA or the governing body to:

– consult appropriate persons
– publish their proposals
– send a copy of the proposals and other relevant information to the local school organisation committee (England) or the Secretary of State (Wales) (SSFA 1998 s 29).

• *Compare the publication requirements for establishing a school (see above) to the following requirements where it is proposed to alter or close a school.*

Education (School Organisation Proposals) (England) Regulations 1999, SI 1999/2213

5. Manner of publication of proposals

(3) Any proposals—

(a) for the making of a prescribed alteration to a school which would not alter the area to be served by the school;
(b) for the discontinuance of the school;
(c) to apply to the school organisation committee to vary any standard number which applies to the school;

shall be published—
(d) by being posted in a conspicuous place in the area served by the school;
(e) in at least one newspaper circulating in that area; and
(f) by being posted at or near the main entrance to the school or, if there is more than one main entrance, all of them.

(4) Any proposals for the making of a prescribed alteration to a school which would alter the area proposed to be served by the school, shall be published—
(a) by being posted in a conspicuous place in the area served by the school and the area proposed to be served by the school;
(b) in at least one newspaper circulating in the areas referred to in sub-paragraph (a) above; and
(c) by being posted at or near the main entrance to the school, or, if there is more than one entrance, all of them.

Are parents 'appropriate persons' to be consulted?

The following case was concerned with provisions contained in the Education Acts 1944 and 1980, but the principle expressed by the judge is of relevance to the current legislation.

R v Brent London Borough Council, ex p Gunning (1985) 84 LGR 168

Hodgson J: In this case the applicants seek judicial review of the two decisions of the respondent local authority made on 12 July 1984 and the publication on 20 July 1984 of notices in respect of those decisions. The decisions arrived at by the local authority were to make proposals under section 12 of the Education Act 1980 which, if approved by the Secretary of State, would effectively result in the closure of two schools, Sladebrook High School and South Kilburn High School, and their amalgamation with and accommodation upon the premises of two other schools.

...

The grounds upon which relief is sought are set out in detail and at length. In brief, they amount to allegations of breaches of the requirements of the Education Acts 1944 and 1980, failure to have proper consultation before reaching the decisions and unreasonable behaviour on the grounds set out in *Associated Provincial Picture Houses Ltd v Wednesbury Corporation* [1948] 1 KB 223; 45 LGR 635. There has, it is alleged, been both 'procedural impropriety' and 'irrationality' of the three category headings set out in the speech of Lord Diplock in *Council of Civil Service Unions v Minister for Civil Service* [1985] AC 374.

...

The parents had no statutory right to be consulted, but that they had a legitimate expectation that they would be consulted seems to me to be beyond question. The interest of parents in the educational arrangements in the area in which they live is self-evident. It is explicitly recognised in the legislation (see, for example, section 6 of the Education Act 1980). The legislation places clear duties upon parents, backed by draconian criminal sanctions. Local education authorities habitually do consult on these matters. In 1980 and 1983 this local authority itself had had comprehensive consultations which had led to the decision in 1983 to retain all school sites. Local education authorities are exhorted by the Secretary of State to consult, and the results of the consultations are something which he takes into account. On any test of legitimate expectation, it seems to me that these parents qualify (see *Council of Civil Service Unions v Minister for the Civil Service*).

If I am right that the parents had this legitimate expectation, then they have the same legal right to consultation as they would have had if it had been given to them specifically by statute.

...

Circular 4/1984, para 10 ... does point to the desirability that consultation should be upon proposals of some specificity into which those consulted can get their teeth, whether the proposals be framed in general policy terms or in terms of specific options.

Mr Sedley submits that these basic requirements are essential if the consultation process is to have a sensible content. First, that consultation must be at a time when proposals are still at a formative stage. Second, that the proposer must give sufficient reasons for any proposal to permit of intelligent consideration and response. Third, to which I shall return, that adequate time must be given for consideration and response and, finally, fourth, that the product of consultation must be conscientiously taken into account in finalising any statutory proposals.

Following the decision to consult taken at the meeting on 10 May, the director prepared a consultative document which, because of the colour of its paper, became known as the gold document.

...

In my judgment that document, on the most favourable criteria to the local authority, was wholly inadequate, and it is clear from the evidence that, at the public meetings, no real attempt was made to flesh it out.

...

For consultation upon the fundamental change of a policy thought, with reason, to have been finally decided upon for the foreseeable future in the previous year, the period for consultation seems to me to have been wholly inadequate.

In *Lee v Department of Education and Science* (1967) 66 LGR 211, where the length of time to be given to governors by the Minister under s 17(5) of the Education Act 1944 was in issue, Donaldson J held that anything less than one month in term time would be unreasonably short. The matter which had to be considered in that case was very much simpler and came within a far narrower compass than was here the case, where fundamental changes in the whole structure of education in Brent were in issue.

I am left in no doubt that the consultation process was woefully deficient, both as to content and timing and, on that ground also, in my judgment, any decision based upon the consultation should be struck down.

Governing bodies wishing to close a foundation or voluntary school are subject to additional requirements. For example:

School Standards and Framework Act 1998, s 30

(1) Subject to the following provisions of this section, the governing body of a foundation or voluntary school may discontinue the school by serving on the Secretary of State and the local education authority at least two years' notice of their intention to do so.

(2) If expenditure has been incurred on the school premises (otherwise than in connection with repairs)—
(a)   by the Secretary of State,
(b)   by the Funding Agency for Schools,

(c)   by any local education authority, or

(d)   by an authority which was a local education authority within the meaning of any enactment repealed by the Education Act 1944 or an earlier Act,

no such notice may be served without the consent of the Secretary of State.

(3) If discontinuing the school would affect the facilities for full-time education suitable to the requirements of persons over compulsory school age who have not attained the age of 19, the governing body shall, before serving a notice under this section, consult the appropriate further education funding council.

...

(7) A notice served under subsection (1) may not be withdrawn without the consent of the local education authority.

(8) If a foundation or voluntary school is discontinued under this section, the duty of the local education authority to maintain the school as a foundation or voluntary school shall cease.

In addition SSFA 1998, s 30(4) and (5) provide for the LEA to take over the management of the school where the governing body is not prepared to do so during the notice period. Section 30(10) to (13) also contain detailed provisions relating to the rights of trustees over land occupied by a foundation or voluntary school.

• *What is the minimum period of notice which a governing body must give in order to close a school? To whom must the notice be given? Does the governing body have to consult parents before giving such notice?*

Special schools maintained by LEAs

The statutory requirements are the same irrespective of whether the special school is being established, altered or discontinued. Where it is a foundation special school the governing body has the power to publish proposals as well as the LEA. As in the case of mainstream schools there is an obligation to consult 'appropriate' persons, publish proposals in a prescribed form, and send a copy of the proposals to either the school organisation committee (England) or the Secretary of State (Wales) (SSFA 1998, s 31).

The Secretary of State has a reserve power to direct an LEA to close a community or foundation special school where he considers that closure would be in the interests of the health, safety or welfare of the pupils (SSFA 1998, s 32(1)).

The provisions in the SSFA 1998 have been modified in certain respects by the Education (Maintained Special Schools) (England) Regulations 1999, SI 1999/2212. Guidance is contained in DfEE circular 15/99 (maintained special schools).

There is a statutory obligation to consult 'appropriate persons' where a special school is likely to merge or be closed (SSFA 1998, s 31(4)).

- *Is the parent of a pupil at a special school an 'appropriate person'? What amounts to 'consultation'?*

In *R v Lambeth London Borough* , *ex p N* [1996] ELR 299 the LEA proposed to close a boarding school for special educational needs pupils which it maintained in Berkshire. A statutory notice was published in accordance with the Education Act 1993 and the Education (Special Schools) Regulations 1994. The statutory provisions required the LEA to consult parents on its proposals. Guidance was provided in circular 3/94. The applicant sought to quash the statutory notice on three grounds, one of which being that the consultation which took place was general and took place with the head teacher and governors, not with the parents. The LEA's position was that it had relied on the head teacher to solicit parents' views. Latham J applied the four requirements set out in *R v Brent London Borough Council, ex p Gunning* (1985) (see above) and held that the notice of closure of the school was ultra vires and unlawful for the following reasons.

R v Lambeth London Borough, ex p N **[1996] ELR 299**

Latham J: In my view, no consultation took place as required by s 184(1) of the 1993 Act. The obligation is to consult on the proposal relating to the school in question; and the guidance in the Ministerial circular makes it clear that parents are particularly important consultees. The respondents were therefore required to take reasonable steps to ensure that the parents were not only informed of the proposal to close the school, but also invited to make representations to the respondents either orally at a meeting or in writing, not on generalities of policy, but with specific regard to the closure of the school which would include the proposed timetable and the effect that that would have on them and their child or children. The consultations which took place before January 1995 went nowhere near meeting these criteria. The respondents have been unable to point to any invitation to the parents to make such representations. The best that can be gleaned from the documents is the general exhortation to headteachers in October 1993. That was, in my view, insufficient as an instruction to meet the requirements of the 1993 Act, and was not designed to meet them. The mistake was made in December 1994 when the proposal to cease to maintain the school was confirmed. All the necessary consultees should then have been notified of the proposal in relation to each school and a fair opportunity given to them, particularly the parents, to respond.

Rationalisation of school places

The Secretary of State has powers initially granted by the EA 1996 (ss 500-506) and now contained in SSFA 1998, to direct LEAs to expand or reduce the number of school places. Previously the LEA and the governing bodies had usually determined the number of school places available in an area.

School Standards and Framework Act 1998, s 34

Schedule 7 (which provides for the Secretary of State to give directions to local education authorities and governing bodies to bring forward proposals for the rationalisation of school places, and for such proposals to be made by him) shall have effect.

The School Standards and Framework Act 1998, Sch 7 gives to the Secretary of State the power to direct an LEA to make proposals to alter the number of schools in its area, where the Secretary of State is of the opinion that the number of schools in the LEA area is 'excessive' or 'insufficient'. The Secretary of State may similarly direct the governing body of a foundation or voluntary school in relation to its school.

Education action zones

The School Standards and Framework Act 1998 introduced the concept of Education Action Zones (EAZs). The Secretary of State has the power to establish EAZs in certain areas in order to improve educational standards at the schools within the area.

School Standards and Framework Act 1998, s 10

(1) If the Secretary of State considers that it is expedient to do so with a view to improving standards in the provision of education at any particular maintained schools, he may by order provide for those schools to constitute collectively an education action zone for the purposes of this Chapter.

(2) An education action zone shall be established in the first instance for three years; but the Secretary of State may, by an order made before the end of that period, provide for the zone to continue in existence for a further two years.

(3) ....

(4) No order shall be made by the Secretary of State under subsection (1), (2) or (3) except on an application made for the purpose with the consent of the governing body of every school which it is proposed should be a participating school.

...

Twenty five EAZs were established in the summer of 1998, and more have followed in 1999, 2000 and 2001. Some of the original EAZs have been extended for a further two years. In practice an EAZ contains a group of approximately 20 primary, secondary and, if appropriate, special schools in the same geographical area. In April 2000 the DfEE announced the creation of 14 new 'small' EAZs. Each zone concentrates on a secondary school and its feeder primaries. Fourteen more 'small' zones were announced in September 2000, and a further 42 were planned for 2001.

Schools in an EAZ may opt out of the statutory national conditions on teachers' pay and terms of employment. This enables schools to pay higher salaries to teachers.

Each EAZ has an Education Action Forum (SSFA 1998, s 11), whose main functions are set out in s 12.

School Standards and Framework Act 1998, s 12

(1) An Education Action Forum shall have as its main object the improvement of standards in the provision of education at each of the participating schools.

(2) A Forum may, under arrangements made by the governing body of a participating school in respect of any prescribed function of that body relating to the conduct of the school, either—
- (a) discharge that function on behalf of the governing body until such time as they may specify in a request to the Forum to cease discharging the function on their behalf; or
- (b) assume full responsibility for the discharge of that function during the whole of the period for which the Forum remains in existence.

...

The Order (statutory instrument) establishing an EAZ normally lists the schools which are included within the zone, and sets out the membership of the Education Action Forum. An example of an EAZ Order is the Great Yarmouth Achievement Education Action Zone Order 2000, SI 2000/86, which came into force on 17 April 2000.

- *Look at an example of a recent order, or an order that applies to an area with which you are familiar. Note who are the 'partners' in the zone, how many primary and secondary schools are included within the zone, and who is represented in the Education Action Forum.*

The Education Bill 2001/02 (Part 11) provides for minor amendments to the EAZ provisions in the SSFA 1998.

6.   FURTHER EDUCATION AND SIXTH FORM COLLEGES

In 1991 the government published a White Paper *Education and Training for the 21st Century: The Challenge to Colleges* (Cm 1536) which proposed giving 'colleges more freedom to expand their provision and respond more flexibly to the demands of customers'. The emphasis was on institutional autonomy, so that such institutions would no longer be subject to LEA funding or control. However, the price of freedom to manage their own affairs and to generate income was more supervision by central government through its funding agencies, the Further Education Funding Councils (FEFCs) (replaced by the Learning and Skills Councils).

The White Paper led to the passing of the Further and Higher Education Act (FHEA) 1992. Nevertheless FE was still seen as the 'Cinderella' of educational provision, despite catering for more than two and a half million students in more than 500 colleges. Further changes were introduced by the Learning and Skills Act 2000, which is aimed at improving and expanding the educational provision available for 16- to 19-year-olds. In particular, the government wants to raise standards, increase student numbers, and modernise the infrastructure of FE. In addition to changing the funding regime, the LSA 2000 gives the Secretary of State powers to establish new support services, and establishes new powers of inspection (see chapter 7).

Jane Johnson 'The Learning and Skills Act 2000: Impact and change for further education' (2000) 12(4) Education and the Law 259 at 260

In spite of the rapid development of the sector, reports indicate that UK skill levels are low, and there is a national consensus that many students in the UK are under-educated and under-trained in comparison with our competitors. Over 160,000 16 to 18-year-olds (about 1 in 11 of the age group) are neither learning nor in work. This figure has remained constant since 1994. Currently, an average of 1 in 5 courses taken by young people in further education colleges are not completed and as many as a half of those in government-funded training, leave their programmes early. Additionally, 7 million adults have severe problems with basic skills and 1 in 5 have a lower level of literacy than is expected of an 11-year-old. Adults wishing to study find that there are too many barriers to returning to college and generally there is a lack of advice available for both adults and young students. There are also skills gaps in the labour market; 80% of IT companies recruiting in 1997 experienced difficulty in recruiting suitable staff, and productivity levels in the UK are lower than in other major economies. Our gross domestic product per worker lags behind the US by 40% and France and Germany by 20%. The government intends to address these issues by restructuring the organisation of the sector to attract more students including adult learners, and develop their skills and educational achievements to reshape the learning culture in the UK.

National targets underpin this commitment to widen and increase participation in learning.

The Learning and Skills Act 2000 provides the mechanism for these changes which demand a 'substantial expansion and restructuring of post-16 education and training'.

Institutions within the further education sector include: general further education colleges, and specialist further education colleges, for example, art colleges; sixth form colleges; and tertiary colleges.

There has been very little litigation in the FE sector, compared with the HE sector, where the main area of litigation has arisen out of assessment decisions by the universities (see chapter 8). In FE students mainly take externally assessed courses, which students may in practice find more difficult to challenge.

Further education is defined as follows:

Education Act 1996, s 2

...

(3) Subject to subsection (5), in this Act 'further education' means—

(a) full-time and part-time education suitable to the requirements of persons who are over compulsory school age (including vocational, social, physical and recreational training), and

(b)   organised leisure-time occupation provided in connection with the provision of such education,

except that it does not include secondary education or (in accordance with subsection (7)) higher education.

(4) Accordingly, unless it is education within subsection (2)(b), full-time education suitable to the requirements of persons over compulsory school age who have not attained the age of 19 is further education for the purposes of this Act and not secondary education.

(5) For the purposes of this Act education provided for persons who have attained the age of 19 is further education not secondary education; but where a person—
(a)   has begun a particular course of secondary education before attaining the age of 18, and
(b)   continues to attend that course,

the education does not cease to be secondary education by reason of his having attained the age of 19.

(6) In subsection (3)(b) 'organised leisure-time occupation' means leisure-time occupation, in such organised cultural training and recreative activities as are suited to their requirements, for any persons over compulsory school age who are able and willing to profit by facilities provided for that purpose.

(7) References in this section to education do not include references to higher education.

It is possible in limited circumstances for secondary education to be provided in further education institutions (Education (Secondary Education in FE Institutions) Regulations 1999, SI 1999/954), and for further education to be provided in secondary schools (Education (Further Education in Schools) Regulations 1999, SI 1999/1867).

• Are further education institutions lawfully entitled to provide sports activities for their students?

Further education institutions

Further education institutions are classified legally as :
(a)   FE colleges
(b)   sixth-form colleges (FHEA 1992, s 15).
As a consequence of FHEA 1992 sixth-form colleges became further education institutions rather than schools, and as a consequence were funded by FEFC rather than by their LEA. However, the LSA 2000 provides that LEAs may again establish and maintain secondary schools that provide full-time education for 16- to 19-year-olds without providing education for children of compulsory school age.

The FHEA 1992, s 16 allowed the Secretary of State or the National Assembly (Wales) to incorporate into the FE sector LEA-maintained institutions for 16- to 19-year-olds. The LSA 2000, s 111 simplifies the powers contained in s 16 of the FHEA 1992.

Further education corporations were established under the FHEA 1992, s 15(4). They have charitable status (s 22 of the FHEA 1992). Their powers relate to the provision of further (and higher) education, as well as the supply of related goods and services (ss18, 19 of the FHEA 1992). Legislation removed these institutions from LEA control. Property, rights and liabilities including contracts of employment were transferred from LEAs (and grant-maintained schools) to the new corporations. LEAs may still provide further education in the form of, for example, evening classes and adult education classes.

Further and Higher Education Act 1992, s 18

(1) A further education corporation may—
(a)   provide further and higher education,
(aa) in pursuance of arrangements made—
    (i)   by a local education authority, or
    (ii) by the governing body of a school on behalf of such an authority,

provide secondary education to pupils in the fourth key stage, and
(b)   supply goods or services in connection with their provision of education...

* *Compare and contrast the principal powers of a further education corporation with those of a higher education corporation (see below).*

More detailed supplementary powers are spelt out in s 19.

Further and Higher Education Act 1992, s 19

(1) A further education corporation may do anything (including in particular the things referred to in subsections (2) to (4) below) which appears to the corporation to be necessary or expedient for the purpose of or in connection with the exercise of any of their principal powers.

(2) A further education corporation may conduct an educational institution for the purpose of carrying on activities undertaken in the exercise of their powers to provide further or higher education and, in particular, may assume as from the operative date the conduct of the institution in respect of which the corporation is established.

(3) A further education corporation may provide facilities of any description appearing to the corporation to be necessary or desirable for the purposes of or in connection with carrying on any activities undertaken in the exercise of their principal powers (including boarding accommodation and recreational facilities for students and staff and facilities to meet the needs of students having learning difficulties within the meaning of section 4(6) of this Act).

(4) A further education corporation may—
(a)   acquire and dispose of land and other property,
(b)   enter into contracts, including in particular—
    (i)   contracts for the employment of teachers and other staff for the purposes of or in connection with carrying on any activities undertaken in the exercise of their principal powers, and
    (ii) contracts with respect to the carrying on by the corporation of any such activities,

(c)   borrow such sums as the corporation think fit for the purposes of carrying on any activities they have power to carry on or meeting any liability transferred to them under sections 23 to 27 of this Act and, in connection with such borrowing, may grant any mortgage, charge or other security in respect of any land or other property of the corporation,

(d)   invest any sums not immediately required for the purposes of carrying on any activities they have power to carry on,

(e)   accept gifts of money, land or other property and apply it, or hold and administer it on trust for, any of those purposes, and

(f)   do anything incidental to the conduct of an educational institution providing further or higher education, including founding scholarships or exhibitions, making grants and giving prizes.

Each FE and sixth-form college, as a statutory corporation, is required to have a constitution together with an instrument and articles of government which regulate the conduct of the college (Further and Higher Education Act 1992, ss 20, 21, 22).

All FE institutions are required in the same way as HE institutions to secure freedom of speech at the college (see p 139) and ensure that any student union operates in a fair and democratic manner (see p 142).

There have been a number of investigations into mismanagement at FE colleges (see also chapter 7).

A Hussain and J Boardman 'Governance in Further Education: A Road to Failure Paved with Good Intentions' [2000] Education LJ 60

The unpaid watchdog

The effectiveness of the board of governors depends upon the calibre of person it attracts and the quality of input that person is able to make. So what sort of a person will want to take up the job of an unpaid watchdog? Jonathan Rée, a former staff governor at Middlesex University, gave a highly revealing interview to Phil Baty of *The Times Higher Education Supplement* at the end of 1998. Professor Rée is stated to believe that 'most university governors are simply not of the right calibre for overseeing the proper management of billions of pounds of public money'. Indeed, in his open letter of resignation he explains that as all the governors are volunteers:

> most of them have onerous business outside the board: even with the best will in the world they cannot be expected to form genuinely independent judgments on every matter that comes before them.

Peter Scott and Catherine Bargh conducted research into the social composition of the board of governors. They found that governors were atypical of the student community and the population at large. They were aged between 46–56, 98% were white, 83% were men, 40% had a professional background and almost 50% voted Conservative in the 1992 General Election.

Whilst this in itself does not smack of poor governance (and indeed may no longer be too much of a problem for colleges), a fuller appreciation of the other 'stakeholder interests' can really only be had where the composition is reflective. Indeed, where the composition of governing bodies is not reflective of the stakeholder groups this undermines the decision-making and can lead to claims of cronyism.

Furthermore, we think Professor Rée's conclusion is telling and shows that a system based upon what Sir Geoffrey Holland calls 'the British tradition of public service and giving to the community' is fundamentally flawed. Professor Rée is quoted as saying:

It is [all] very well congratulating yourselves on being Nolan-pure and conforming to a code of practice but if you have got no gumption you will not be a good governor. Governors are either retired civil servants or people too busy to do the job properly.

This aspect of governance is also based upon the generosity and spirit of individuals; another good intention.

...

Governmental laissez-faire in the face of a kulturkampf

The *kulturkampf* ('culture struggle') facing the education sector is substantial. This is noticeable if we compare the situation immediately before and after the deregulation of the sector. From a pre-incorporation situation, when the funding and control for most of the sector was under the control of the LEA, to a position where the individual institutions are given direct control over their budgets, there has been a great leap by any measure.

The way in which the sector is expected to function has also changed significantly. The previous Conservative government was keen on the idea that colleges should adopt an 'entrepreneurial' outlook. The government encouraged innovation and, as a part of this, franchising. This change in the expectation of colleges — whose previous goal had been limited exclusively to providing and promoting education — has led to a culture struggle which has not been addressed by successive governments. We suggest that the colleges have not been given the powers they need to adopt this entrepreneurial outlook. Colleges as exempt charities having a limited power as statutory corporations are not appropriately constituted to conduct a business.

Rather than simplifying things, the new Labour government seems to have burdened colleges even further. There is now evidence of a further change in culture being brought about by the government. The new culture involves the notion of 'partnership'. The colleges are now being encouraged to work in partnership with other institutions and with the wider community, again, with similar problems of powers. This is leading to a further *kulturkampf.*

Learning and Skills Council

The FHEA 1992 provided that further education was to be funded by the Further Education Funding Councils for England and Wales. The Councils were appointed by and financed by grants from the Secretary of State (FHEA 1992, ss 1, 7). In 2001 they were dissolved by the LSA 2000 and replaced by the Learning and Skills Council.

The Learning and Skills Council (LSC) is the sole national body responsible for planning and funding post-16 learning in England. There is also a new Council for Education and Training in Wales, and there are 47 local Learning Skills Councils. Forty per cent of the places on the national and local councils are reserved for people with recent business experience.

Sections 2, 3, and 4 of the LSA 2000 impose statutory duties on the national LSC.

Learning and Skills Act 2000, ss 2 and 3

2(1) The Council must secure the provision of proper facilities for—
(a)   education (other than higher education) suitable to the requirements of persons who are above compulsory school age but have not attained the age of 19,
(b)   training suitable to the requirements of such persons,
(c)   organised leisure-time occupation connected with such education, and
(d)   organised leisure-time occupation connected with such training.

(2) Facilities are proper if they are—
(a)   of a quantity sufficient to meet the reasonable needs of individuals, and
(b)   of a quality adequate to meet those needs.

(3) In performing the duty imposed on it by subsection (1) the Council must—
(a)   take account of the places where facilities are provided, the character of facilities and the way they are equipped;
(b)   take account of the different abilities and aptitudes of different persons;
(c)   take account of the education and training required in different sectors of employment for employees and potential employees;
(d)   take account of facilities whose provision the Council thinks might reasonably be secured by other persons;
(e)   make the best use of the Council's resources and in particular avoid provision which might give rise to disproportionate expenditure.

(4) Provision is not to be considered as giving rise to disproportionate expenditure only because that provision is more expensive than comparable provision.

(5) For the purposes of this section—
(a)   education includes both full-time and part-time education;
(b)   training includes both full-time and part-time training;
(c)   training includes vocational, social, physical and recreational training;
(d)   higher education is education provided by means of a course of any description mentioned in Schedule 6 to the Education Reform Act 1988.

3(1) The Council must secure the provision of reasonable facilities for—
(a)   education (other than higher education) suitable to the requirements of persons who have attained the age of 19,
(b)   training suitable to the requirements of such persons,
(c)   organised leisure-time occupation connected with such education, and
(d)   organised leisure-time occupation connected with such training.

(2) Facilities are reasonable if (taking account of the Council's resources) the facilities are of such a quantity and quality that the Council can reasonably be expected to secure their provision...

• *Compare (a) the age groups; and (b) the different level of duty imposed on the LSC in sections 2 and 3. Should the LSC give preference to either age group?*

Learning and Skills Act 2000, s 4

The Council must—
(a)   encourage individuals to undergo post-16 education and training;

(b)   encourage employers to participate in the provision of post-16 education and training;
(c)   encourage employers to contribute to the costs of post-16 education and training.

Financing of further education

The LSC is financed by grants from the Secretary of State. It has wide powers enabling it to make payments to a range of bodies including FE colleges, schools and private training providers. The LSC may also make direct grants to students. Payments may include money intended to be paid as awards to students, and which is normally distributed by the institutions, for example, through Access Funds.

Learning and Skills Act 2000, s 5

(1) The Council may secure the provision of financial resources to—
(a)   persons providing or proposing to provide post-16 education or training;
(b)   persons providing or proposing to provide goods or services in connection with the provision by others of post-16 education or training;
(c)   persons receiving or proposing to receive post-16 education or training;
(d)   persons providing or proposing to provide courses falling within paragraph 1(g) or (h) of Schedule 6 to the Education Reform Act 1988 (courses in preparation for professional examinations at a higher level or providing education at a higher level);
(e)   institutions within the further or higher education sector (within the meaning of section 91 of the Further and Higher Education Act 1992) which provide or propose to provide secondary education (other than post-16 education);
(f)   persons undertaking or proposing to undertake research relating to education or training;
(g)   persons providing or proposing to provide facilities described in section 8(1) or (2);
(h)   persons carrying out means tests under arrangements made under section 9;
(i)   persons providing or proposing to provide information, advice or guidance about education or training or connected matters (including employment).

....

Sixth forms in schools will receive their funds from the LSC, but it will be paid via the school's LEA (LSA 2000, s 7). This change is unlikely to be introduced before 2002-03. All LEAs have the power to provide additional funding.

FE and HE institutions are enabled to collaborate with LEAs on provision for 14-to16-year-olds (FHEA 1992, s 18 as amended by s 146 of the LSA 2000). Such institutions are able to provide secondary education to certain pupils at Key Stage 4 and for whom a variation on the national curriculum has been agreed to enable them to undertake work-related learning (see chapter 6). In practice it is more likely that FE institutions will make such provision.

Whether the Learning and Skills Act 2000 will achieve the impact desired by the government remains to be seen. In the following extract Jane Johnson looks at the result of a survey she undertook to find out the views of college principals on the proposed new structure of FE.

Jane Johnson 'The Learning and Skills Act 2000: Impact and change for further education' (2000) 12(4) Education and the Law 259 at 265, 266

Comment

Although it was premature to distribute a questionnaire on the impact of the new Act, reactions of college principals are interesting. Clearly, some were reluctant to comment, but many seemed genuinely concerned over the new funding arrangements, and were sceptical over the idea that by removing the TECs and the Further Education Funding Council bureaucracy would be reduced.

The composition of the local Skills and Learning Council seemed a cause of concern for some principals, their point being that if members were selected from the old TECs, then there may be little change. Clearly, it is vital that these bodies are made up of new enthusiastic representatives of commerce and industry in order to meet the challenge ahead. Further, college principals doubted that employer domination of the Council would lead to a better match of supply and demand for skills. It remains to be seen whether there will be any impact on this issue.

Table 1.

Advantages	Disadvantages
Fast response to changes	Competition from private sector
Intelligent planning	Bureaucracy — less funds for colleges
Demise of TEC/FEFC divide	Unclear role for Local Skills Council
Single funding regime	Could create more inspection at the expense of learning
Promise of greater funding	Two sets of inspectors — unrealistic split
Reduced bureaucracy — removal of TECs	Potential for increased bureaucracy
More emphasis on teaching and learning	FE becomes a provider rather than a collegiate sector with community responsibilities
More focus on funding and planning	Uncertainty over new funding arrangements
Creation of learning partnerships	Centralised system seems to favour employers
Separation of inspection from quality improvements	Removal of understanding with FEFC which has taken many years

The list of advantages recorded [in Table 1] demonstrates that some principals are more positive about the potentially good things in the new system, for example, more emphasis on planning and local control. Surprisingly, some principals had little knowledge of the potential impact of the legislation which suggests a lack of communication and does not provide a sound foundation for the changes ahead.

Financial support for FE students

Most students were entitled to an 'Individual Learning Account' (ILA) which enabled them to receive education up to the value of £150 at a specified institution (LSA 2000, ss 104, 105). Employers could contribute towards the cost of studying, and tax relief was available for employees. There were two types of ILA from which the student could choose. The first allowed for the option of developing a dedicated bank account model (s 104). The second allowed students to register with a central provider in order to qualify for financial assistance (s 105). Grants were also available to eligible students.

Detailed provisions are contained in the Individual Learning Accounts (England) Regulations 2000, SI 2000/2146. However, the DfES suspended the operation of the ILA scheme from December 2001 because of allegations of poor quality provision and high costs.

Funding for 16- to 19-year-olds

Some FE (or school) students may be eligible for one of the new forms of financial support authorised by the Education Act 1996, s 518 (as substituted by the School Standards and Framework Act 1998, s 129).

Education Act 1996, s 518

(1) A local education authority, for the purpose of enabling persons to take advantage of any educational facilities available to them, may in such circumstances as may be specified in or determined in accordance with regulations—
(a) pay such expenses of children attending community, foundation, voluntary or special schools as may be necessary to enable them to take part in any school activities,
(b) grant scholarships, exhibitions, bursaries and other allowances in respect of persons over compulsory school age.

(2) Regulations may make provision—
(a) for requiring a local education authority to make, in relation to each financial year, a determination relating to the extent to which they propose to exercise their power under subsection (1)(b) in that year; and
(b) for authorising an authority to determine not to exercise that power in a financial year—
    (i) generally,
    (ii) in such cases as may be prescribed, or
    (iii) in such cases as may be determined by the authority.

In certain circumstances LEAs may pay school expenses (Local Education Authority (Payment of School Expenses) Regulations 1999, SI 1999/1727).

The nature of the LEA power under the previous version of EA 1996, s 518 and the Scholarship and Other Benefits Regulations 1977, SI 1977/1443, which have been replaced by new provisions, was considered in the following case, which illustrates the discretionary nature of such awards. The parents of a 13-year-old boy applied on his behalf to the LEA for a discretionary grant to enable him to attend full-time a residential vocational dance school.

R v Birmingham City Council, ex p Youngson (a child) [2001] LGR 218

Scott Baker J: ... the parents had contended that nothing comparable to the courses available at Elmhurst was obtainable elsewhere in the West Midlands. They wished Jacob to stay at the school until he was 16, amounting to approximately £55,000 in funding over five years.

Section 9 of the 1996 Act provided that in exercising all their respective powers and duties under the Education Acts, local education authorities should have regard to the general principle that pupils were to be educated in accordance with the wishes of their parents in so far as that was compatible with the provision of efficient instruction and training and the avoidance of unreasonable public expenditure.

The education authority had power to make an award by virtue of section 518 of the 1996 Act, which provided that regulations empowered local education authorities, in certain circumstances, to grant awards to pupils.

Regulation 4(d) of the Scholarship and Other Benefits Regulations, SI 1977 No 1443 provided that subject to regulation 6, every authority 'may' for the purpose of enabling pupils to take advantage without hardship to themselves or their parents of any educational facilities available to them, pay the whole or any part of the tuition fees, boarding or lodging fees and expenses payable in respect of children attending schools at which fees were payable.

Regulation 6 provided that no payment would be made under the regulations unless (a) it was required to be made in order to prevent or relieve financial hardship; (b) except in the case of a payment under regulation 4(e)(ii), the amount of the payment was related to the means of the parents; and (e) the authority was satisfied that the course of education to which payment relates was suitable to the pupil.

His Lordship said that the natural meaning of that legislation was that local authorities had a discretion whether to make payments in individual cases.

The word 'may' in regulation 4 had its ordinary natural meaning, and it did not mean 'shall'. A discretionary, not mandatory power in regulation 4 was consistent with section 518 of the 1996 Act, which had granted a power to the local authority rather than imposed a duty on it.

By contrast, regulation 6 imposed a duty not to make payments unless certain criteria were fulfilled and the discretion could not be exercised in favour of making a payment unless the regulation 6 conditions were satisfied.

In the exercise of its discretion, the education authority's policy of only granting an award where the applicant could show (i) evidence of severe financial hardship, (ii) that funding was unobtainable from other sources, (iii) compelling reasons why alternative forms of study achieving the same qualifications were unavailable of inappropriate, or (iv) other exceptional circumstances, was lawful.

Post-compulsory education awards

A LEA has the power under s 518 of the EA 1996 and the regulations (see below) to decide which students will be eligible for the post-compulsory education awards. The LEAs are likely to restrict their availability to students from less well-off families. The students should be ordinarily resident in the UK or be, for example, refugees or EU nationals (Education (Fees and Awards) Regulations1997, SI 1997/1972). The awards include a school access fund award. All LEAs are required to decide each year whether or not they will make any awards under these regulations.

Local Education Authority (Post-Compulsory Education) Awards Regulations 1999, SI 1999/229 (as amended), regs 3 and 4

3(1) Subject to paragraph (2) a local education authority shall have power to grant a post-compulsory education award, that is to say—
(a) a scholarship
(b) an exhibition
(c) a bursary, or
(d) any other allowance

granted in respect of an eligible person for the purpose of enabling that person to take advantage of any educational facilities available to him.

...

4(1) A local education authority shall determine, in respect of each financial year, whether they should exercise the power in regulation 3(1) in respect of post-compulsory education awards other than school access fund awards and if they are to do so in that year whether to do so—
(a) generally, or
(b) only in the cases of eligible persons who satisfy such criteria as may be determined by the authority.

Education maintenance allowance

In addition to these awards an education maintenance allowance was introduced in some parts of England in 1999 also under s 518 of the EA 1996. The current regulations for these allowances are the Education Maintenance Allowance (Pilot Areas) Regulations 2000, SI 2000/2012 as amended by SI 2001/797.

Local education authorities involved in the original scheme included Cornwall, Lewisham and Stoke-on-Trent (reg 2 and Part 1 of the Schedule). The areas were expanded considerably in 2000, and include Birmingham, most inner London LEAs, and Sunderland (reg 2 and Part 2 of the Schedule).

The nature of the allowance varies according to the LEA. The allowance is generally available to certain groups of students, for example 'vulnerable' students, students who have been in care ('looked after') and student estranged from their families ('independent'). The students are required to satisfy a residence condition, and their parents' income should not exceed a specified amount (which varies according to where they live) The allowance takes different forms, which vary according to the LEA. The four types of allowances are: weekly allowance, termly bonus, special allowance, and achievement bonus.

An education maintenance allowance learning agreement must be signed by a parent, the student and by a person on behalf of the institution where the student will study.

The education maintenance allowance has provided the template for clauses in the Education Bill 2001/02 (Part 11). These provisions will enable the Secretary of State to make regulations which will be applicable nationally, and which will entitle certain pupils and students in secondary or further education, or training to receive such an allowance.

7. HIGHER EDUCATION

The White Paper *Higher Education: a New Framework* (Cm 1541, 1991) proposed a 'cost effective expansion [of HE via] greater competition for funds and students'.

'Higher education' is not defined other than by reference to specified courses, which are predominantly undergraduate and postgraduate degree courses and higher professional courses. A higher education course is defined in the Education Reform Act 1988, Sch 6, para 1.

Education Reform Act 1988, Sch 6

1 ...
(a) a course for the further training of teachers or youth and community workers;
(b) a postgraduate course (including a higher degree course);
(c) a first degree course;
(d) a course for the Diploma of Higher Education;
(e) a course for the Higher National Diploma or Higher National Certificate of the Business & Technician Education Council, or the Diploma in Management Studies;
(f) a course for the Certificate in Education;
(g) a course in preparation for a professional examination at higher level;
(h) a course providing education at a higher level (whether or not in preparation for an examination).

2 For the purposes of paragraph 1(g) above a professional examination is at higher level if its standard is higher than the standard of examinations at advanced level for the General Certificate of Education or the examination for the National Certificate or the National Diploma of the Business & Technician Education Council.

3 For the purposes of paragraph 1(h) above a course is to be regarded as providing education at a higher level if its standard is higher than the standard of courses providing education in preparation for any of the examinations mentioned in paragraph 2 above.

The higher education sector comprises:

(a) universities;

(b) colleges of Higher Education.

Legal status of higher education institutions

'Old' or 'pre-existing' universities are normally corporations created by Royal Charter, and in practice have few limitations on their legal capacity. Their powers are found in their individual charters and rules.

From 1 April 1989 specified polytechnics and advanced FE colleges maintained by LEAs became higher education corporations (statutory corporations), which have charitable status (ERA 1988, s 125A). Property, rights and liabilities, and staff were transferred to the new corporations. A few 'new' universities are companies limited by guarantee, for example Guildhall University and the University of Greenwich, rather than statutory corporations.

In 1992 polytechnics were able to call themselves 'universities' subject to the approval of the Privy Council (s 77 of the FHEA 1992), and to award degrees (s 76 of the FHEA 1992). The Council for National Academic Awards (CNAA) which had been the degree awarding body for polytechnics was dissolved.

The 'new' universities' statutory powers are found in the Education Reform Act 1988, s 124.

Education Reform Act 1988, s 124

(1) A higher education corporation shall have power—

(a)   to provide higher education;

(b)   to provide further education; and

(c)   to carry out research and to publish the results of the research or any other material arising out of or connected with it in such manner as the corporation think fit.

(2) A higher education corporation shall also have power to do anything which appears to the corporation to be necessary or expedient for the purpose of or in connection with the exercise of any of the powers conferred on the corporation by subsection (1) above...

Their constitution and powers are set out in ERA 1988, as amended, and the institution's instrument of government (ERA 1988, s 124A, Sch 7 and 7A) and articles of government.

Education Reform Act 1988, s 125

(1) Any institution conducted by a higher education corporation shall be conducted in accordance with articles of government, to be made by the corporation with the approval of the Privy Council.

(2) The articles of government—

(a) shall determine the functions to be exercised in relation to the institution by the board of governors of the institution, the principal of the institution and the academic board of the institution; and

(b) may regulate the constitution and functions of committees of the corporation and of the academic board of the institution and provide for the delegation of functions of the board of governors and the academic board to such committees, to the chairman of the corporation or to the principal.

(3) The articles of government shall also make provision with respect to the procedure for meetings of the board of governors, of the academic board and of committees of the corporation and the procedure in relation to the appointment of members of the corporation (including in either case quorum and proxies), and may make provision with respect to—

(a) procedures for the appointment, promotion, suspension and dismissal of staff;

(b) procedures for the admission, suspension and expulsion of students; and

(c) the appointment and functions of a clerk to the board of governors.

(4) The articles of government may also make provision authorising the board of governors to make rules or byelaws for the government and conduct of the institution, including in particular rules or byelaws with respect to—

(a) the conduct of students and staff or either of them; and

(b) any such procedures as are mentioned in subsection (3)(a) or (b) above.

....

The powers relating to the procedures for the admission, suspension and expulsion of students (ERA 1988, s 125(3)(b)) and to the conduct of students (ERA 1988, s 125(4)(a)) have given rise to litigation (see chapter 8). As statutory corporations the new universities must not exceed or abuse their powers. For example, they are required to take into account relevant considerations when reaching decisions made under those powers. In *R v Manchester Metropolitan Univeristy, ex p Nolan* [1994] ELR 380 failure by the CPE board of examiners to take into account mitigating factors invalidated the decision taken by the board in September 1992.

R v Manchester Metropolitan University, ex p Nolan [1994] ELR 380

Sedley J: The applicant sat the Common Professional Examination at the respondent university on 1 June 1992. On that day and again on 4 June 1992 he was found by the respective chief invigilators, Mr Rayburn and Mr Grout, to have brought in with him several pages of notes which were on his desk. He was not prevented from completing the examinations, but was told on each occasion that there would be a disciplinary hearing.

The hearing which was accordingly held on 25 June 1992 before the Faculty Examinations Disciplinary Committee was the only oral hearing accorded at any stage to the applicant under the rules. No complaint is or could be made of its procedure or outcome save in one (now immaterial) respect. The committee had before it an allegation that the applicant had 'cheated and/or sought to gain an unfair academic advantage by using unauthorised notes in his possession'. The applicant was present and had representation, and evidence was called on his behalf both as to fact and as to character. In addition to evidence of the detail of the alleged offence, the committee read testimonials from the applicant's tutors from the University of Wales, his MP and a family friend, and a short report from a psychiatrist. His personal tutor, Miss Deehan, gave oral evidence strongly in his favour which is summarised in the minutes of the meeting. The formal memorandum to the chairman of the CPE board of examiners reported.

> The Examinations Disciplinary Panel found the student guilty of attempting to gain an unfair academic advantage by bringing unauthorised material into the examination room, where it was maintained on the desk and available for use by the student if he so wished.
>
> The panel found, however, that there were mitigating circumstances in terms of the student's mental state prior to and during the examination period.
>
> The panel makes no formal recommendations but would ask the board of examiners to determine appropriate academic action or penalty in the light of the panel's findings.'
>
> ...

I find that there were not before the board [of examiners] the testimonials from the applicant's tutors at Cardiff and his MP, nor the letter from the consultant psychotherapist, all of which had been before the disciplinary committee on 25 June 1992 and had palpably influenced that committee in the applicant's favour. Nor, apparently, were the minutes of the disciplinary committee before the academic board.

...

(c) Did the board take into consideration all the factors it should have done?

In approaching its task, however, the board had limited material. The academic registrar in para 15 of his second affidavit says:

> I have no doubt having attended the meeting in person that the board was aware of the mitigating circumstances. They were referred to in discussion the board was aware of the applicant's previous achievements and certainly approached its decision on the basis that he was of excellent character. It was fully aware and certainly accepted that he was under stress at the time of the examination. As against this however the board had to deal with infraction of an important regulation governing a professional examination.

If there had been a full oral hearing before the board it would have been up to the applicant to present what material he wished to them, but he had no right to attend and was entirely dependent on what was placed before the board in his absence. It emerges from the evidence — as I have found — that this did not include some important statements in mitigation. In the absence of the recommendation as to penalty which the disciplinary committee should have made and of the disciplinary committee's own minutes and (inevitably) of the applicant himself, this lacuna was certainly significant and may well have been crucial. I am unable to accept Mr Richardson's submission that everything material was substantially known to the board.

I am reinforced in this by three further factors. First, this was the same body as had taken the ultra vires decision on 9 July 1992. While, on good advice, it had rescinded that decision and started again, it behove the board to be doubly cautious in what it then did. Secondly, anticipating for a moment the next head of argument, it was on any view a surprising decision that was reached, suggesting that something material in the applicant's favour may well have been overlooked. Thirdly, I am not convinced that the mere presence of the applicant's personal tutor Miss Deehan affords an assurance that the powerful mitigation which she is minuted as having advanced for him on 25 June 1992 was repeated at the board meeting on 22 September 1992. In the applicant's absence and in the absence of any evidence of what role she played at the latter meeting it would not be right to infer that her voice was heard, or as clearly heard, in the applicant's favour as it had been before the disciplinary committee.

I would therefore hold that there was a material failure on the part of the board of examiners on 22 September 1992 to take into account matters which it was incumbent on them to take into account, namely the full evidence in mitigation which had been placed before and accepted by the disciplinary committee. Such a failure will ordinarily vitiate the material proceedings and nullify the decision.

Use of the title 'university'

The use of the title 'university' by an institution is regulated by statute. Only approved HE institutions are entitled to use the word 'university' in their name. Approval must be given by the Privy Council. The name should not be confusing. This requirement was included to address the problem of new universities existing alongside old universities in the same town or city. For example, in Manchester there is Manchester University and Manchester Metropolitan University (formerly Manchester Polytechnic).

The use of the phrase 'university college' in the title of an institution is also regulated. Normally, such an institution is not a university.

Further and Higher Education Act 1992, s 77

(1) Where—
(a)   power is conferred by any enactment or instrument to change the name of any educational institution or any body corporate carrying on such an institution, and
(b)   the educational institution is within the higher education sector,

then, if the power is exercisable with the consent of the Privy Council, it may (whether or not the institution would apart from this section be a university) be exercised with the consent of the Privy Council so as to include the word 'university' in the name of the institution and, if it is carried on by a body corporate, in the name of the body.

...

(3) In exercising any power exercisable by virtue of this section to consent to a change in any name the Privy Council shall have regard to the need to avoid names which are or may be confusing.

(4) Any educational institution whose name includes the word 'university' by virtue of the exercise of any power as extended by subsection (1) above is to be treated as a university for all purposes, unless in that name that word is immediately followed by the word 'college' or 'collegiate'.

This section is supplemented by s 39 of the Teaching and Higher Education Act (THEA) 1998 which prohibits the marketing of an institution as a university unless the use of the word 'university' in its name has been approved. The section does not apply to 'old' universities, but encompasses foreign universities offering educational services within the United Kingdom.

Teaching and Higher Education Act 1998, s 39

(1) A relevant institution in England or Wales shall not, when making available (or offering to make available) educational services, do so under a name which includes the word 'university' unless the inclusion of that word in that name is—
(a)   authorised by or by virtue of any Act or Royal Charter, or
(b)   approved by the Privy Council for the purposes of this section.

(2) A person carrying on such an institution shall not, when making available (or offering to make available) educational services through the institution, use with reference either to himself or the institution a name which includes the word 'university' unless the inclusion of that word in that name is authorised or approved as mentioned in subsection (1).

(3) Subsection (1) or (2) applies where the educational services are made available, or (as the case may be) the offer to make such services available is made, in any part of the United Kingdom.

....

(5) In approving the inclusion of the word 'university' in any name for the purposes of this section the Privy Council shall have regard to the need to avoid names which are or may be confusing.

(6) The Privy Council's power of approval under subsection (1) or (2) shall not be exercisable in a case where the inclusion of the word 'university' in the name in question may be authorised by virtue of any other Act or any Royal Charter.

...

In *R v Secretary of State for Education and Employment, ex p Liverpool Hope University College* [2001] EWCA Civ 362, [2001] ELR 552, the Court of Appeal upheld the decision of the Secretary of State to bring into force s 39 of the THEA 1992. The college argued unsuccessfully that the Secretary of State had indicated that such institutions were to be given sufficient time to apply for university status before the section was implemented. The Secretary of State established that all that had been proposed was that such institutions should be given a reasonable time to comply with the change, for example sufficient time to print new prospectuses and other publicity material.

This case is symptomatic of the changes that have taken place in higher and further education. Institutions no longer operate outside the market place (see also Case C-380/98: *R v HM Treasury, ex p Cambridge University* [2000] 1 WLR 2514 below). Although they receive public funding they are selling a service to consumers. If the service is not in demand, the institution may fall into financial difficulties and may not survive.

S van Bijsterveld and K Mouwen 'The Hybrid University as a Concept for the Future' [2001] Education Law Journal 26

Introduction

All over Western European countries, radical shifts are taking place in the relations between the state, society and the market. The role of the state is subject to profound reconsideration: traditional bulwarks of state activity are being privatised or are transformed into (semi) autonomous structures. Society is changing and the market is stepping in.

Universities, too, are subject to these general trends. Whatever the precise relationship between governments and universities and the precise position of universities under the law in various countries, similar developments have taken place in the field of research and higher education. Over the last decades, governments in Western European countries have realised profound budget cuts in the field of higher education. In general terms, they have also changed their policies as regards universities from direct intervention to indirect steering methods (steering at a distance). The combination of these two developments has encouraged and facilitated universities to operate on the market.

...

If no prolific cooperation with third parties can be established within the framework of the traditional academic concepts and presuppositions, then a new concept needs to be created. The focal point in this new concept is the hybridity of the academic organisation: the new university must be capable of accommodating the elements of its traditional task as well as market-based elements.

In our view, the solution to this problem of hybridity is in essence the quest for a new *overarching, binding principle* that is capable of bringing together and keeping together the interests and cultures of both the traditional task-oriented university and the market.

...

We are well aware that the mere acceptance of hybridity as a characteristic of the university does not offer the final word. We do not ignore that the promotion of the hybrid university, as the university for the future, still leaves many real questions unanswered and that in itself it offers no solution for problems that are encountered. With this, the university does not fall out of line with other hybrid organisations that face similar problems and questions. Defining the conceptual starting point, however, is the essential condition for clarifying the institutional structures of the university and the legal conditions under which it operates and for enabling the university to fulfil the newly perceived tasks.

...

The legal status of the hybrid university

The acceptance and introduction of the hybrid university obviously poses questions with regard to the legal status of the university. Without going into the details of the laws relating to universities in the various particular legal systems, there are a few general observations which can be made in this respect.

There are, basically, two dimensions to the issue of the legal aspects of the hybrid university. First of all, the introduction of the hybrid university poses the question of the consequences for the internal structure of the university. University structures will have to be adapted to the new mission, which focuses both on the traditional academic core tasks and on the market. This adaptation involves legal issues. Secondly, external legal dimensions relating to the introduction of the hybrid university need to be considered. These basically concern the relation of the hybrid university to the 'market' in general and to government.

...

As to the *external* legal dimension, a few elements need special consideration. First, it is clear that much of the resistance surrounding the hybridity of the university is caused by the fear of competition distortions and unfair cross-subsidisation. It is feared that universities, with their solid infrastructure and their subsidised first flow of funds, will (be tempted to) operate under market price and, therefore, engage in unfair competition. This fear is often used as an argument against the acceptance of hybrid organisations in general.

Financing of higher education institutions

Higher Education Funding Councils for England and Wales have been appointed by the Secretary of State, who makes grants to the Councils (ss 62, 68 of the FHEA 1992). The Secretary of State may attach general requirements (s 68) and directions (s 81) to such grants.

The Councils have the power to make grants, loans, or other payments to higher education institutions (s 65) and to 'connected institutions' (s 65(3A)) They are required to consult institutional representatives and governing bodies, and should have 'regard to the desirability of not discouraging any institution' from obtaining funding from other sources (s 66). However, the Secretary of State has indicated that universities should not charge top-up fees for tuition.

The Councils assess the quality of education in universities and other higher education institutions through Quality Assessment Committees (s 70). The governing bodies of higher education institutions are required to provide information to the Councils.

In the United Kingdom universities are normally regarded as public bodies. For example, even those universities, such as Oxford and Cambridge, which have considerable wealth receive public funds, and decisions made in relation to the academic progress of university students are subject to judicial review.

One consequence of the changing role of universities (see above) is that they are entering into an increased number of external contracts. In Case C-380/98: *R v HM Treasury, ex p Cambridge University* [2000] 1 WLR 2514, the European Court of Justice gave a preliminary ruling to the effect that an English university is a 'contracting authority' and so subject to the public procurement directives where, for example, at least half its income comes from payments by public authorities. This is the position where the majority of its income is derived from tuition fees paid by LEAs or awards or grants for the support of research for which the university gave no consideration.

Freedom of speech

Universities, colleges of higher education, university colleges, and further education colleges are required to secure freedom of speech on their premises.

Education (No 2) Act 1986, s 43

(1) Every individual and body of persons concerned in the government of any establishment to which this section applies shall take such steps as are reasonably practicable to ensure that freedom of speech within the law is secured for members, students and employees of the establishment and for visiting speakers.

(2) The duty imposed by subsection (1) above includes (in particular) the duty to ensure, so far as is reasonably practicable, that the use of any premises of the establishment is not denied to any individual or body of persons on any ground connected with—

(a)   the beliefs or views of that individual or of any member of that body; or
(b)   the policy or objectives of that body.

(3) The governing body of every such establishment shall, with a view to facilitating the discharge of the duty imposed by subsection (1) above in relation to that establishment, issue and keep up to date a code of practice setting out—
(a)   the procedures to be followed by members, students and employees of the establishment in connection with the organisation—
    (i)   of meetings which are to be held on premises of the establishment and which fall within any class of meeting specified in the code; and
    (ii)   of other activities which are to take place on those premises and which fall within any class of activity so specified; and
(b)   the conduct required of such persons in connection with any such meeting or activity;

and dealing with such other matters as the governing body consider appropriate.

(4) Every individual and body of persons concerned in the government of any such establishment shall take such steps as are reasonably practicable (including where appropriate the initiation of disciplinary measures) to secure that the requirements of the code of practice for that establishment, issued under subsection (3) above, are complied with.

Each institution is required to have a code of practice setting out certain matters.

- *If you are a student at a university or a college, consider whether your institution's code of practice complies with the requirements of this section.*

In *R v University of Liverpool, ex p Caesar-Gordon* [1990] 3 All ER 821 the court was asked to consider whether the university was in breach of this section when it banned a meeting, organised by the student Conservative Association, which was to be addressed by speakers from the South African embassy in London.

The university was fearful that anti-apartheid protesters would disrupt the meeting. The ban was imposed in part because the university considered that it would have no control over some of the protesters, because they would be members of the public rather than members of the university, and that the disorder might also occur off the university premises in a public place.

R v University of Liverpool, ex p Caesar-Gordon [1990] 3 All ER 821

Watkins LJ: Succinctly stated s 43(1) imposes on the university a positive duty to take steps to ensure that freedom of speech within the law is secured for members, students and employees and visiting speakers. This duty is of course qualified. The university need only take: 'Such steps as are reasonably practicable to ensure that freedom of speech within the law is secured ...'

In our opinion the words 'reasonably practicable' qualify the steps which must be taken to ensure freedom of speech. The extent of that duty is made clear by sub-ss (3) and (4), which define the manner in which the duty imposed by sub-s (1) is to be discharged. The governing body of the university is required to issue a code of practice to be followed by *members of the university* in connection with the organisation of meetings and other activities *held on the premise of the university.*And the governing body of the university must take such steps as are reasonably practicable to secure that the requirements of the code of practice (*which apply to its members and its premises*) are complied with. Thus, we conclude, that on a true construction of s 43 the duty imposed on the university by sub-s (1) is local to the members of the university and its premises. Its duty is to ensure, so far as is reasonably practicable, that those whom it may control, that is to say its members, students and employees, do not prevent the exercise of freedom of speech within the law by other members, students and employees and by visiting speakers in places under its control. To require the university in the discharge of its duty under sub-s (1) to take into consideration persons and places outside its control would be, in our view, to impose on it an intolerable burden which Parliament cannot possibly have intended the university to bear.

It is stated in para 2(h) of the code as to the registrar:

> If not satisfied that adequate arrangements can be made to maintain good order, may refuse or withdrawn permission for the meeting or activity.

'Good order' can only, in our opinion, relate to good order within the precincts of the university. The code is concerned with procedures to be followed at meetings on university premises and does not envisage the university taking steps to ensure good order elsewhere. Such steps would be beyond the de facto powers of the university in any event.

Had they confined their reasons when refusing permission for the meetings to take place to the risk of disorder on university premises and among university members, it may be that no objection could have been taken to either of their decisions. Where, however, the threat was of public disorder without the university, then, unless the threat was posed by members of the university, the matter was, in our opinion, entirely for the police.

Student unions

Students at a higher education (or a further education) institution are not required to be members of its student union. However, most student unions must be operated in accordance with the Education Act 1994, ss 20-22. The Education Act 1994, s 21 sets out those institutions to which its provisions apply.

Education Act 1994, s 20

(1) In this Part a 'students' union' means—

(a) an association of the generality of students at an establishment to which this Part applies whose principal purposes include promoting the general interests of its members as students; or

(b) a representative body (whether an association or not) whose principal purposes include representing the generality of students at an establishment to which this Part applies in academic, disciplinary or other matters relating to the government of the establishment.

(2) References in this Part to a students' union include an association or body which would fall within subsection (1) if for the references to the generality of students at the establishment there were substituted a reference to—

(a) the generality of undergraduate students, or graduate students, at the establishment; or

(b) the generality of students at a particular hall of residence of the establishment.

(3) References in this Part to a students' union include an association or body which consists wholly or mainly of—

(a)   constituent or affiliated associations or bodies which are themselves students' unions within subsection (1) or (2), or

(b)   representatives of such constituent or affiliated associations,

and which fulfils the functions of a students' union within subsection (1) or (2) in relation to students at an establishment to which this Part applies.

(4) An association or body may be a students' union within the meaning of this Part in relation to more than one establishment but not in relation to establishments generally in the United Kingdom or a part of the United Kingdom.

...

- *Would a club devoted to philosophy or football, or the Junior Common Room at an Oxford College come within this definition of a 'student union'?*

Each governing body is legally responsible for many aspects of the operation of the student union at its institution.

Education Act 1994, s 22

(1) The governing body of every establishment to which this Part applies shall take such steps as are reasonably practicable to secure that any students' union for students at the establishment operates in a fair and democratic manner and is accountable for its finances.

(2) The governing body shall in particular take such steps as are reasonably practicable to secure that the following requirements are observed by or in relation to any students' union for students at the establishment—

(a)   the union should have a written constitution;

(b)   the provisions of the constitution should be subject to the approval of the governing body and to review by that body at intervals of not more than five years;

(c)   a student should have the right—

(i)   not to be a member of the union, or

(ii)   in the case of a representative body which is not an association, to signify that he does not wish to be represented by it,

and students who exercise that right should not be unfairly disadvantaged, with regard to the provision of services or otherwise, by reason of their having done so...

The Education Act 1994, s 22(2) further provides that the governing body's responsibility extends to:

-   elections of officers
-   the financial affairs of the student union, including the allocation of funds to clubs and societies
-   affiliation to external organisations
-   the availability of an effective complaints procedure
-   informing students annually of, for example, their right not to join a union
-   issuing a code of practice setting out the above arrangements.

The provisions in relation to elections do not apply to open learning or distance learning students:

Education Act 1994, s 22(9)

Subsection (2)(d) and (l)(ii) (elections and affiliations: requirements to hold secret ballot of all members) do not apply in the case of an open or distance learning establishment, that is, an establishment where the students, or the great majority of them, are provided with materials for private study and are not required to attend the establishment to any significant extent or at all.

In *R v Thames Valley University Students Union, ex p Ogilvy* [1997] CLY 2149, the court held that the action of a student union in excluding a student from its premises could not be challenged by way of judicial review. The legislation did not give a public law dimension to the actions of student unions.

In *Anyanwu v South Bank Student Union* [2001] UKHL 14, [2001] 2 All ER 353 two students who were elected as officers of the student union unsuccessfully applied for judicial review of the decision by the student union to exclude them from the student union premises. They subsequently brought a racial discrimination claim before an industrial tribunal. The claim was against the student union and the university. The preliminary issue, whether the claim against the university should be struck out, was heard by the House of Lords.

Anyanwu v South Bank Student Union [2001] UKHL 14, [2001] 2 All ER 353

Lord Bingham of Cornhill: My Lords, this appeal turns on the correct interpretation and application of s 33(1) of the Race Relations Act 1976. Section 33 of the Act (as amended) provides:

(1) A person who knowingly aids another person to do an act made unlawful by this Act shall be treated for the purposes of this Act as himself doing an unlawful act of the like description.

...

[5] The expression 'aids' in s 33(1) is a familiar word in everyday use and it bears no technical or special meaning in this context. A person aids another if he helps or assists him. He does so whether his help is substantial and productive or whether it is not, provided the help is not so insignificant as to be negligible. While any gloss on the clear statutory language is better avoided, the subsection points towards a relationship of co-operation or collaboration; it does not matter who instigates or initiates the relationship. It is plain that, depending on the facts, a party who aids another to do an unlawful act may also procure or induce that other to do it.

[6] Mr Anyanwu and Mr Ebuzoeme, the appellants, were students at and members of the South Bank University. As a result of elections held in May 1995 they were engaged to serve as full-time salaried officers of the South Bank Student Union for a fixed term of one year beginning on 1 August 1995. In that capacity they were trustees of the funds of the

student union, which was treated as an educational charity. Questions were raised by the university about their conduct as trustees, and disciplinary proceedings were instituted. The university suspended both appellants as members of the university by letters dated 22 February 1996, which also forbade them from entering any university building including the student union until given permission to do so. Following the appellants' non-appearance at the disciplinary proceedings the university expelled them from the university with immediate effect by letters dated 29 March 1996 which again forbade them from entering any university building including the student union. It was of course impossible for the appellants to perform their duties as employees of the student union if they were unable to enter its premises and by letters dated 2 April 1996 to each appellant the student union treated the appellants' employment contracts as at an end.

...

[16] The first question which must be asked is: what is the act of the student union made unlawful by Pt II of the Act which it is said that the university knowingly aided the student union to do? The answer, in each case, is that the student union dismissed the appellant on discriminatory racial grounds. ...

[17] The second question is: what is it alleged that the university did which knowingly aided the doing of that unlawful act by the student union? ...

[18] The third question is: do those allegations (if fully established) bring the appellants' complaints against the university within s 33(1) of the Act? The House is not concerned with allegations that the appellants might have made against the university in the county court under s 17 of the Act, but only with knowing aid given by the university to the student union in dismissing the appellants. I would for my part have doubted whether the appellants' allegations were sufficient to support their claim against the university on this limited basis under s 33(1), and I would have questioned whether the appellants' general claims against the university of racial prejudice, intimidation and interference (even if established) could have been said to satisfy the subsection. A majority of your Lordships do not however share my doubts, and having read the compelling opinions of my noble and learned friends Lord Steyn and Lord Hope of Craighead my reservations are assuaged if not entirely dispelled. I am content to acquiesce in the view which commends itself to the majority.

[19] I would accordingly allow the appeal, set aside the order of the Court of Appeal and remit the matter to an employment tribunal for a hearing, long overdue, against both the student union and the university. In resolving the claim against the university, the tribunal should apply the plain terms of s 33(1) as explained by your Lordships. The subsection will apply if the university is shown to have knowingly aided (or helped or assisted) the student union to dismiss the appellants. It is not helpful to introduce 'free agents' and 'prime movers', which can only distract attention from the essentially simple test which (however complicated and controversial the facts) is the test to be applied.

Lord Steyn: [33] Lord Bingham of Cornhill set out the scheme of the 1976 Act and has explained with great care and precision how s 33(1) ought to be construed. I am in full agreement with his interpretation of this provision. It is therefore unnecessary for me to cover all the same ground. I do, however, state the major points germane to the present appeal. The correct approach is to construe the words of s 33(1) in its contextual setting. It creates a form of derivative liability predicated on the commission of an unlawful act by another person. For present purposes the unlawful act against which s 33(1) must be considered is the alleged dismissal of the appellants by their employers (the student union) on discriminatory racial grounds. The issue of knowledge does not need to be considered on the present appeal. Focusing on the concept of knowingly *aiding*, the word is used in its ordinary sense. While there is no exact synonym the words help, assist, co-operate, or collaborate convey more or less the right nuance. The word 'aid' is therefore not used in either an extensive or a restrictive sense. The critical question is: Does the word aid in its contextual sense cover the conduct of the secondary party? It follows that it is wrong to be diverted by any inquiries not mandated by the statute as to whether the alleged aider was or was not a prime mover or a free agent.

This case illustrates that in limited circumstances a university may be legally liable for 'aiding' the actions of the student union.

Student finance

Major changes to student funding resulted from the passing of the Teaching and Higher Education Act 1998 as amended, although the changes had been heralded by a reduction in the value of student grants and the introduction in 1990 of student loans.

Mandatory and discretionary awards

Before September 1998 LEAs were required to make awards (mandatory grants) to persons ordinarily resident in their area who attended first degree, initial teacher training and other designated courses at a university etc maintained or assisted by public funds (s 1 of the EA 1962, repealed by the Teaching and Higher Education Act 1998).

Local education authorities also had the power to make discretionary awards to persons over compulsory school age attending courses such as the Legal Practice Course, or the Bar Vocational Course (s 2 of the EA 1962 repealed by the Teaching and Higher Education Act 1998). LEAs now have the power to make post-compulsory education awards for 16- to 19-year-olds (see above).

The Secretary of State had a discretionary power (s 3 of the EA 1962) to make awards to postgraduate students and others, but that power has also been repealed.

Mandatory and discretionary grants to cover living expenses have been abolished for most courses, other than teacher training. However, the concept of 'ordinarily resident' remains important where students apply for an award for tuition fees, a maintenance grant, or in order to be eligible for a student loan.

'ORDINARILY RESIDENT'

Shah v Barnet London Borough Council [1983] AC 309

Lord Scarman: Each student has applied for judicial review on the ground that the local education authority had erred in law in reaching the conclusion that the student had failed to prove that he had been ordinarily resident in the United Kingdom throughout the three years preceding the first year of the course in question.

The Act of 1962 and the Regulations are to be construed by giving to the words 'ordinarily resident in the United Kingdom' their natural and ordinary meaning.

Ordinary residence is not a term of art in English law. But it embodies an idea of which Parliament has made increasing use in the statute law of the United Kingdom since the beginning of the 19th century.

...

Unless, therefore, it can be shown that the statutory framework or the legal context in which the words are used requires a different meaning, I unhesitatingly subscribe to the view that 'ordinarily resident' refers to a man's abode in a particular place or country which he has adopted voluntarily and for settled purposes as part of the regular order of his life for the time being, whether of short or long duration.

There is, of course, one important exception. If a man's presence in a particular place or country is unlawful, e g in breach of the immigration laws, he cannot rely on his unlawful residence as constituting ordinary residence.

...

The legal advantage of adopting the natural and ordinary meaning, as accepted by the House of Lords in 1928 and recognised by Lord Denning MR in this case, is that it results in the proof of ordinary residence, which is ultimately a question of fact, depending more upon the evidence of matters susceptible of objective proof than upon evidence as to state of mind. Templeman LJ emphasised in the Court of Appeal the need for a simple test for local education authorities to apply: and I agree with him. The ordinary and natural meaning of the words supplies one. For if there be proved a regular, habitual mode of life in a particular place, the continuity of which has persisted despite temporary absences, ordinary residence is established provided only it is adopted voluntarily and for a settled purpose.

Fees, grants and loans

Grants, which include fees and awards to cover the cost of living, and loans are authorised by the Teaching and Higher Education Act 1998. Section 22 applies to further as well as higher education, which reflects a change in policy whereby further education students are potentially treated in the same way as university students.

Teaching and Higher Education Act 1998, s 22(1)

(1) Regulations shall make provision authorising or requiring the Secretary of State to make grants or loans, for any prescribed purposes, to eligible students in connection with their undertaking—
(a)   higher education courses, or
(b)   further education courses,

which are designated for the purposes of this section by or under the regulations.

The main regulations are the Education (Student Support) Regulations 2001, SI 2001/951. The regulations are amended or replaced each year. They provide for grants for certain fees, supplementary grants for living costs for certain students, and loans for living costs.

The regulations set out the categories of 'eligible' and 'ineligible' students. One of the requirements is that the student should be 'ordinarily resident' (see above). The student should also be attending a 'designated course'. Some part-time courses are included. Postgraduate courses, other than teacher training, do not come within this provision.

Tuition fees

The THEA 1998 and regulations made under the Act introduced means-tested payment of tuition fees (see e g Education (Mandatory Awards) Regulations 2001, SI 2001/1734).

Universities and other higher education institutions normally charge higher tuition fees to overseas non-EU students.

Orphanos v Queen Mary College [1985] 2 All ER 233

Lord Fraser of Tullybelton: My Lords, the appellant is a citizen of Cyprus, of Greek nationality, who has been a student at the respondent college since October 1982, when he entered on a three-year course in mechanical engineering. He came to the United Kingdom in December 1978 and since then he has been resident in the United Kingdom for the purpose of education. The first issue in the appeal is whether he was liable to pay fees to the college for the academic year 1982–83 as an overseas student, for whom the appropriate rate was £3,600, or as a home student, for whom the appropriate rate in that year was only £480. The solution of that issue depends on the true construction of the contract between the appellant and the college. Both the judge in the county court (his Honour Judge McDonnell) and the Court of Appeal (Griffiths and May LJJ) decided this issue in favour of the college and held that the appellant was liable as an overseas student. The second issue is whether, if the appellant is liable to pay fees at the overseas students' rate, the college, by charging him at that rate, has unlawfully discriminated against him on racial grounds, contrary to the Race Relations Act 1976. The solution of that issue depends on the construction of the 1976 Act, particularly of s 1(1)(b).

On the assumption that the residence qualification is therefore caught by s 1(1)(b)(i), it is necessary to consider under s 1(1)(b)(ii) whether the requirement is 'justifiable irrespective of the colour, race, nationality or ethnic or national origins of the [student] to whom it is applied'. Nationality is the only one of these grounds which is in question in this appeal. 'Justifiable' means, in my opinion, 'capable of being justified'. 'Irrespective of' in that subsection means 'without regard to', as I said in *Mandla v Dowell Lee* [1983] 1 All ER 1062 at 1070, [1983] 2 AC 548 at 566, and I see no reason to alter that opinion. No doubt the main reason for introducing the residence requirement was, as counsel for the college said, to curtail public expenditure on education in the interest of economy. That reason itself did not involve discrimination on racial grounds. But the particular method of curtailment may have done so. Various methods of curtailing the expenditure were possible: grants to all students could have been cut by an equal percentage, and their fees could have been correspondingly increased, or grants could have been restricted by reference to the academic qualifications of applicants. No doubt many other methods were possible. The method chosen was to concentrate grants on home students, and to cease subsidising foreign students. The justification relied on by the college is set out in more detail in further and better particulars of their defence, which includes statements to the following effect:

3. The fees of home students are subsidised. There is no good reason why the fees of

overseas students should be subsidised from public funds ... 4. The government cannot afford to subsidise overseas students ... 6. The use of fees is a legitimate means of regulating the admission of overseas students and has the advantage of reducing public expense ... 7. The previous system had resulted in a large increase in numbers and a large increase in the cost to the British taxpayers with little relationship between the pattern of those large student numbers and Britain's own long-term priorities ...

These statements show that the main motive for introducing the residence requirement was economy. But the economy was to be effected at the expense of foreign students. That may have been a perfectly reasonable and justifiable policy for the British government to adopt but in my opinion the college, on whom the onus lies under s 1(1)(b)(ii), has not been able to justify the requirement without having regard to the nationality of the applicants at whose expense the policy was carried into effect.

...

A claim for damages would be made on the basis that the appellant has suffered damage to the extent to which he has been overcharged for the first year's fees, namely £1,320, perhaps with the addition of a further sum for loss of interest on that sum or for the cost of borrowing it. I shall assume, without deciding, that a claim for damages could be properly mounted on that basis. The question then arises whether it would be excluded by s 57(3) of the 1976 Act.

...

Section 57(3) provides:

As respects an unlawful act of discrimination falling within section 1(1)(b), no award of damages shall be made if the respondent proves that the requirement or condition in question was not applied with the intention of treating the claimant unfavourably on racial grounds.

May LJ in the Court of Appeal had no difficulty in holding that, although the college had, in his view, discriminated against the appellant on racial grounds, it had done so unintentionally. I have reached the same conclusion, though with rather more difficulty. I approach the consideration of s 57(3) with two points in mind. First, the subsection applies only to an unlawful act of discrimination under s 1(1)(b), that is to acts of indirect discrimination, and it does not apply to acts of direct discrimination under s 1(1)(a). No doubt the reason is that an act of direct discrimination falling with s 1(1)(a) would necessarily be done with the intention of treating the claimant unfairly on racial grounds. Second, the subsection evidently assumes that not all acts of indirect discrimination falling within s 1(1)(b) need be done with that intent; without that assumption the subsection would be useless. So it is not right to say that any discrimination on racial grounds which (like the college's residence requirement) cannot be justified under s 1(1)(b)(ii) irrespective of the nationality of the claimant must necessarily have been applied with the intention of treating him unfairly on racial grounds. Section 57(3) is looking at the subjective intention of the discriminator. Section 1(1)(b)(ii), on the other hand, is looking at the objective possibility of justifying the discrimination without reference to any of the racial grounds. When the college applied the residence test to the appellant its intention was to discriminate against persons who did not reside in the EEC area but there is, in my opinion, no ground for suggesting that it was intending to discriminate against them on the ground of their nationality or on any other racial grounds. Unfortunately, the discrimination on the grounds of residence cannot be justified irrespective of nationality, and it is therefore unlawful under the 1976 Act, but its unlawfulness is unintentional and accidental. I would therefore hold that, the requirement in question not having been applied with the intention of treating the appellant unfavourably on racial grounds, he is precluded by the provisions of s 57(3) from obtaining an award of damages.

Thus the charging of higher fees to overseas students amounts to unlawful discrimination but there is no effective remedy for the students under the Race Relations Act 1976. In *Nabadda v Westminster City Council* [2000] ELR 489 a student attempted to claim damages under EC law for injury to feelings caused by indirect racial discrimination.

Nabadda v Westminster City Council [2000] ELR 489

Buxton LJ: (1) In these proceedings four Swedish nationals, currently students in the UK, sue two local authorities, Westminster and Haringuey. The four students have identical interests, as do the two authorities.

(2) The students are pursuing a variety of courses which do not need to be described further. Each of the students has for the purposes of their course both a grant and a loan from a Swedish organisation, shortly called SNB. Each of the students applied to the relevant English local authority for what is conveniently called a 'fees only' award: that is, an award not in relation to their maintenance, but in order to defray the costs of their education. That award is a 'mandatory' award: meaning that, if the student fulfils the qualifications laid down in the subordinate legislation creating the award, the local authority is obliged by that legislation to make the award.

(3) The relevant legislation in this case is the Education (Mandatory Awards) Regulations 1997. The crucial regulation for this case is reg 23, which provides that a qualifying student shall not receive an award if he receives from other sources any scholarship or similar award equalling the amount of his fees. There is not to be taken into account in that process of calculation any award or loan made under various English statutes. The authorities both took the view that that required them to take into account the SNB loans: with the result that the students received less than a full award. In so determining, the authorities acted on the regulations as they stood in 1997. The regulations were significantly amended in 1998 to add to the 'exempted' loans or awards any award made under legislation of any other Member State of the Community. An explanatory note to the amending regulations said that the change had been made in order to avoid discrimination against students supported by other Member States.

(4) As a direct result of that change, all of the students were informed in February 1998 that they would receive a full award for that and any subsequent years of their studies. Two of them had commenced judicial review proceedings in relation to the authorities' earlier decision, but those proceedings were necessarily and properly abandoned. With the students having received full grants, and it being provided by the regulations that anyone in their position was entitled to such a grant, that might have been thought to be the end of it so far as the law was concerned. In these proceedings, however, the students seek damages in respect of the initial refusal of a grant, though only in terms of damages for injury to their feelings.

...

For the purpose of the present applications it is assumed, though very emphatically not conceded, that the students' courses consisted of vocational training. On that basis, the authorities concede that the withholding of the grant because of the SNB loan constituted discrimination contrary to the terms of Art 6 [EC Treaty, now Art 12 EU Treaty]. Such discrimination was what, in English terms, would be characterised as indirect: that is to say, that the students were not refused the grant because they were Swedish, but because they were subject to a condition that, although not confined to Swedish persons (because it would appear that a person of another nationality living in Sweden would be eligible for an

SNB loan), was plainly much more likely to affect Swedish nationals than nationals of other EU countries.

(7) So far so good. The next and crucial step in the students' case is, however, that they are by reason of such discrimination entitled to damages within the English system under the Race Relations Act 1976 (the 1976 Act). To the extent that (as is the case) certain provisions of the 1976 Act stand in the way of granting the remedy sought in this case in respect of the breach of Art 6, those provisions must be disapplied or ignored, in deference to the primacy of Community law.

...

Although the argument was not put in quite this way, it amounted to saying that the court should characterise the Community claim in terms that approached as close as possible to a type of liability to be found in domestic law, and then apply to that claim the provisions for relief provided for that domestic claim. Thus, the students' claim was in respect of discrimination on grounds of nationality by a local education authority: such as is prohibited in domestic law by a combination of ss 3(1) and 18 of the 1976 Act.

...

(16) In my judgment, therefore, the claim made under the 1976 Act fails in limine. No such third principle as contended for by Mr Allen exists, and there is therefore no basis for bringing the claim under the 1976 Act, and much less for requiring the 1976 Act to be applied in an amended form in order to accommodate the claim.

Student loans

Student loans are available to students on specified higher education courses. The loans are to cover maintenance costs and originally were obtained from the Student Loans Company (s 1 of the Education (Student Loans) Act 1990). The Education (Student Loans) Act 1996 gave the Secretary of State power to pay subsidies to private sector financial institutions to enable them to make loans to students on the same 'favourable' terms as the Student Loans Company. As from 1998 existing loans have been transferred to the private sector (Education (Student Loans) Act 1998; Student Loans Regulations 1998, SI 1998/211).

Means-tested 'low interest' loans are now made under the THEA 1998, s 22 and ensuing regulations. The loans can be repaid in one of three ways. Where students are employed, deductions from their salaries are made by their employers in the same way as income tax is deducted, once their income reaches a prescribed level.

The legislation sets out in detail the provisions which the regulations may contain.

Teaching and Higher Education Act 1998, s 22

(1) Regulations shall make provision authorising or requiring the Secretary of State to make grants or loans, for any prescribed purposes, to eligible students in connection with their undertaking—
(a)   higher education courses, or
(b)   further education courses,

which are designated for the purposes of this section by or under the regulations.

(2) Regulations under this section may, in particular, make provision—

(a) for determining whether a person is an eligible student in relation to any grant or loan available under this section;

(b) prescribing, in relation to any such grant or loan and an academic year, the maximum amount available to any person for any prescribed purpose for that year;

(c) where the amount of any such grant or loan may vary to any extent according to a person's circumstances, for determining, or enabling the determination of, the amount required or authorised to be paid to him;

(d) prescribing categories of attendance on higher education courses or further education courses which are to qualify for any purposes of the regulations;

...

Section 22 goes on to set out the numerous matters which may be included within regulations. These include:

– payment and repayment of loans
– grounds of and procedures for appeals
– rates of interest
– obligations of employers to keep records.

The rate of interest is spelt out in s 22(9).

Teaching and Higher Education Act 1998, s 22(9)

In subsection (4)(a) 'the specified rate for low interest loans' means the rate for the time being specified for the purposes of any exemption conferred by virtue of section 16(5)(b) of the Consumer Credit Act 1974 (exemption of certain consumer credit agreements by reference to the rate of the total charge for credit).

The current regulations are the Education (Student Support) Regulations 2001, SI 2001/951, and the Education (Student Loans) (Repayment) Regulations 2000, SI 2000/944.

For example, the regulations provide that liability to repay the loan and interest is cancelled in limited circumstances.

Education (Student Loans) (Repayment) Regulations 2000, SI 2000/944

12. Cancellation

(1) Subject to paragraph (4) where a borrower is not in breach of any obligation to repay his loan in accordance with Part V or in breach of any obligation to repay any other loan mentioned in paragraph (2) and the Secretary of State is satisfied that he—

(a) has died;

(b) has attained the age of 65; or

(c) receives a disability related benefit and because of his disability he is permanently unfit for work

the Secretary of State shall cancel his liability to repay his student loan.

The government has indicated that it plans to pay off loans for newly-qualified teachers in shortage subjects in mainatined schools or the FE sector. The Education Bill 2001/02 (Part 11) gives effect to this policy.

Grants for living costs

Grants for living costs are still available for students on undergraduate courses who:
–   have dependants
–   are disabled
–   incur certain travel costs
–   have recently left care.
The detailed provisions are found in the Education (Student Support) Regulations 2001, SI 2001/951. There is also additional funding for medical, dental and nursing courses.

Postgraduate students

There is limited public funding for postgraduate students. Funding is available for:
–   teacher training
–   disabled students
–   research council studentships.
Grants are also available for students studying in Europe (Education (Student Support) (European Institutions) Regulations 2000, SI 2000/2197).

CHAPTER 3

School admissions

1. INTRODUCTION

The right to choose a school for their child is perceived by many parents as being of fundamental importance, and is linked to the duty placed on parents to ensure that their children receive suitable full-time education. However, school admission arrangements are concerned as much with the responsibilities of LEAs and governing bodies as with the rights and duties of parents. Nevertheless, parental choice has dominated the political agenda.

In 1980 the Conservative government introduced legislation which was interpreted as giving parents the right to choose a school for their child. For many parents this interpretation proved to be of limited value, because the right was not to choose a school, but the more limited right to express a preference for a school.

In 1996 the Audit Commission published a report which was based on empirical research and which looked at aspects of the supply and allocation of school places in England and Wales. The following extract sets out the considerations the Commission considered should be taken into account by central government and local education authorities when making decisions about the number of school places.

The Audit Commission 'Trading Places — The Supply and Allocation of School Places' National Report, 1996

1. 'Which school should my child attend?' is one of the most important questions facing any parent. For the vast majority of parents, the answer involves state education: 93 per cent of pupils attend state-funded schools. This situation generates a need for high-quality public provision that meets parents' desires and expectations to get the best education for their child. One of the key functions of LEAs is to respond to these needs, desires and expectations, by ensuring a supply of places at schools to meet the 'demand' for education created by pupils in their area.

...

3. In their attempts to secure value for money, the principal challenge for LEAs is to provide the right number of school places in the right locations. This involves the pursuit of both **economy** and **effectiveness** ... The aim should be to achieve a good match between pupils and places within an infrastructure of high-quality school buildings and facilities, where all schools are of a sufficient size and calibre to deliver the curriculum cost-effectively. But there is a third consideration — **parents' right to express a preference** for their child's school. The scope for parents in any area to secure a place for their child at the preferred school will depend crucially on how an LEA has organised school places and admissions policies, and on whether it has been able to achieve a consistently high quality of education across all local schools.

In July 1997 the White Paper *Excellence in Schools* (Cm 3681) set out the government's policy on school admissions.

School admissions

28 We want as many parents as possible to be able to send their children to their preferred school. But where demand exceeds supply and one school is more popular than another, some parents will be disappointed. A recent survey by the Audit Commission ... estimated that nearly one parent in five did not get a place for their child at their genuine first preference school. Yet the Commission also drew attention to the level of unfilled school places; currently over 800,000 in England.

In 2001 the government published a White Paper *Schools Achieving Success* (Cm 5230) proposing the establishment of more specialist schools, which is likely to add even more complexity to the admissions process and further dilute the comprehensive principle. Parents may already have to express a preference between, for example, a community school, a voluntary aided school, a foundation school, or a City Technical College (CTC). Each school is likely to have different admission criteria. Some children may not in practice be able to obtain a place at any of the popular schools because they live too far away, do not attend church, or do not achieve a high enough grade in an entrance test.

Therefore, the right of a parent to express a preference for a particular school has to be considered in the context of the other legal duties imposed on parents and LEAs in relation to school attendance and the provision of school places, and the practical difficulties facing parents where there are a number of schools with different admission criteria which their child may or may not meet.

2.   LOCAL EDUCATION AUTHORITIES' DUTIES

All LEAs are required to ensure that there are sufficient school places available for children living in their area, and to comply with parental wishes as to their child's schooling. However, the duties relating to parental wishes are subject to major qualifications.

Sufficient schools

Despite the shift of power from LEAs in recent years (see chapter 1), LEAs remain responsible for ensuring that there are 'sufficient' primary and secondary schools in their area. The legal duty is set out in the Education Act 1996, s 14.

Education Act 1996, s 14

(1) A local education authority shall secure that sufficient schools for providing—
(a)   primary education, and
(b)   education that is secondary education by virtue of section 2(2)(a),

are available for their area.

(2) The schools available for an area shall not be regarded as sufficient for the purposes of subsection (1) unless they are sufficient in number, character and equipment to provide for all pupils the opportunity of appropriate education.

(3) In subsection (2) 'appropriate education' means education which offers such variety of instruction and training as may be desirable in view of—
(a)   the pupils' different ages, abilities and aptitudes, and
(b)   the different periods for which they may be expected to remain at school,

including practical instruction and training appropriate to their different needs.

...

(6) In exercising their functions under this section, a local education authority shall in particular have regard to—
(a)   the need for securing that primary and secondary education are provided in separate schools;
(b)   the need for securing that special educational provision is made for pupils who have special educational needs; and
(c)   the expediency of securing the provision of boarding accommodation (in boarding schools or otherwise) for pupils for whom education as boarders is considered by their parents and the authority to be desirable.

(7) The duty imposed by subsection (6)(a) does not apply in relation to middle schools or special schools.

When considering whether or not there are 'sufficient' schools the LEA may take into account places available at CTCs and city academies as well as at all maintained schools, and may take into account the fact that some children will attend independent schools (*R v Secretary of State for Education and Science, ex p Avon County Council (No 2)* (1990) 88 LGR 737n).

'Sufficient schools' and 'appropriate education' are considered to apply to the quantitative rather than qualitative aspects of provision. In other words parents are unlikely to be able to rely on this section when arguing that the quality of the educational provision in schools maintained by the LEA falls below an acceptable standard.

The nature of the duty imposed on LEAs by s 14 has been considered by the courts, which have interpreted it restrictively, treating it is a target rather than an absolute duty. The section has not provided parents with an effective remedy where, for example, the local education authority has closed the schools because of industrial action by caretakers (see *Meade v London Borough of Haringey* [1979] 2 All ER 1016, CA), or where there is a shortage of school places (see *R v ILEA, ex p Ali and Murshid* (1990) 2 Admin LR 822).

In addition the courts consider that parents should normally complain to the Secretary of State under s 497 of the Education Act 1996 (formerly s 99 of the Education Act 1944) (see chapter 8) before seeking redress in the courts.

Meade v London Borough of Haringey [1979] 2 All ER 1016

Lord Denning MR: On Monday 22 January 1979 the caretakers at the schools in Haringey came out on strike. There were very few of them. Only one or two for a school of 500 or 600 children. Their duties were simple enough. To look after the buildings and the heating system. To unblock drains. To lock up at night and open up in the morning. And so forth. Yet by coming out on strike they succeeded in paralysing the educational system of the great London Borough of Haringey. The borough council closed over 100 schools for weeks on end. 37,000 children were deprived of the teaching they should have had. They were put back in their examinations and their careers. Some ran loose in the streets while their mothers were out working.

The parents of the children were much upset by all this. They went to their lawyers to see if there was any way to get the schools reopened. The lawyers looked up the statute and found that it was the duty of the borough council under s 8 of the Education Act 1944 'to secure that there shall be available for their area sufficient schools ... for providing ... full-time education suitable to the requirements of [the] pupils'.

...

Now here is the point of the case. The borough council say that they had just cause or excuse for closing the schools: because they feared that to open them would cause industrial strife or make it worse. Counsel for the borough council acknowledged before us that they could have opened them. They could have got the keys from the caretakers. They could have got other people to do the work of the caretakers; or got volunteers to do it. But they felt that if they did so the trade unions would cause so much trouble that it would make things worse. So they kept the schools closed, until they could get agreement with the unions to call off the strike. In contrast some other London boroughs did keep their schools open.

To see whether this is a good answer, I propose to go through the history of events as disclosed in the affidavits. It will show that the branch secretaries of the two unions exercised a dominating influence over the borough council; and that the closure of the schools was the result of a combination of the unions and the council acting together.

...

The point of law which arises is this: if the local education authority have failed to perform their duty (to keep open the schools), have the parents any remedy in the courts of law? There is a remedy given by the statute itself. It is to complain to the Secretary of State under s 99 of the 1944 Act. But that remedy has proved to be of no use to the parents. Can they now come to the courts? This depends on the true construction of the statute.

...

Now although that section does give a remedy, by complaint to a Minister, it does not exclude any other remedy. To my mind it leaves open all the established remedies which the law provides in cases where a public authority fails to perform its statutory duty either by the act of commission or omission.

...

This case

Applying these principles, I am clearly of opinion that if the borough council, of their own free will, deliberately closed one school in their borough for one week, without just cause or excuse, it would be ultra vires: and each of the parents whose child suffered thereby would have an action for damages. All the more so if they closed it for five weeks or more. Or for all schools. No one can suppose that Parliament authorised the borough council to renounce their duties to such an extent as deliberately to close the schools without just cause or excuse. To use Lord Reid's words *Padfield v Minister of Agriculture, Fisheries and Food* [1968] 1 All ER 694 at 701, it was their duty 'not to act so as to frustrate the policy and objects of the Act'.

Just cause or excuse

Now comes the great question in this case: had the borough council any just cause or excuse for closing the schools as they did? On the evidence as it stands, the borough council were acting under the influence of the trade unions and indeed in combination with them. And the trade unions and their secretaries were, as I see it, acting quite unlawfully. They were calling on the local education authority to break their statutory duty, to close the schools instead of keeping them open as they should have done. Now s 13 of the Trade Union and Labour Relations Act 1974 as amended gives them immunity if they induce a person to break a contract. But it gives them no immunity if they induce a local authority to break its statutory duty. The law is well-established that a public authority cannot enter into any contract or take any action incompatible with the due exercise of its statutory powers or the discharge of its statutory duties: see *Birkdale District Electric Supply Co Ltd v Southport Corpn* [1926] AC 355 at 364 by Lord Birkenhead. It cannot effectively contract not to exercise its statutory powers or to abdicate its statutory duties: see *Staines Urban District Council's Agreement, Triggs v Staines Urban District Council* [1968] 2 All ER 1 at 5 ... by Cross J. It seems to me that if the local education authority closed the schools, at the behest of the trade unions, or in agreement with them, they were acting unlawfully. The trade unions had no right whatever to ask the borough council to close the schools. The borough council had no business whatever to agree to it. Instead they should have kept the schools open, and risked the consequences of the dispute escalating. Or they should have moved the court for an injunction to restrain the leaders of the trade unions from interfering with the due opening of the schools. I am confident that the people at large would have supported such a move and expect the trade union leaders to obey it, and they would have obeyed it.

...

Conclusion

On the evidence as it stands before us, it appears that the trade unions were the dominating influence in requiring the schools to be closed and not reopened: and the borough council closed them at the behest of the trade unions or in agreement with them. In so doing the borough council were breaking their statutory duty: and the trade unions' leaders were inducing them to break it. Such conduct was in my view unlawful: and the trade unions' leaders have no immunity in respect of it. It was open to the parents to come to the courts of law and to complain of it, and to ask the courts to restrain any further breach of the statutory duty. There remains the question whether the court should grant an injunction. That depends on the balance of convenience. If the strike had been still continuing, I should have been in favour of granting an injunction. But that is now unnecessary. The very imminence of an injunction seems to have brought everyone to their senses. During the hearing before us the strike was called off. The schools opened. The teachers went back. The pupils returned to their desks. All's well that ends well. But it must not happen again.

In *R v Inner London Education Authority, ex p Ali* (1990) 2 Admin LR 822 between 400 and 500 children living in the Stepney area did not have a school place because of an increase in the number of children of school age. Some of the children had been out of school for a year or more. This increase had not apparently been foreseen by the LEA. The applicants were, respectively, the father of a schoolboy and the director of a local advice centre. Woolf LJ considered the nature of the duty which was then contained in the Education Act 1944, s 8. (See also chapter 8.)

R v Inner London Education Authority, ex p Ali (1990) 2 Admin LR 822

Woolf LJ: This type of duty can be described as a 'target duty'. In the language of Mr Goudie there is built into s 8 a 'degree of elasticity'. While there are a number of standards which are required to be achieved by the local education authority, the setting of those standards is, in the first instance, for the local education authority alone to determine as long as those standards are not outside the tolerance provided by the section.

There are going to be situations, some of which can and others which cannot be reasonably be anticipated, where the education provided falls below the statutory standard and the standards which the local education authority would set for itself. It is undoubtedly the position that within the area for which ILEA is responsible at the present time, the statutory standards and the standards that it would set for itself are not being met but this does not mean that ILEA [is] necessarily in breach of [its] duty under s 8. The question is whether ILEA has taken the steps which the statute requires to remedy the situation which exists.

...

The duty under s 8 is, therefore, not absolute. A local education authority which is faced with a situation where, without any fault on its part, it has not complied with the standard which the section sets for a limited period is not automatically in breach of the section. Here I refer to changing situations which could not be anticipated, not questions of resources or priorities.

Furthermore, even where there is a breach of s 8 the court in their discretion may not intervene if by the time the matter comes before the court the local education authority is doing all that it reasonably can to remedy the situation. The situation is best left in the hands of the bodies to whom Parliament has entrusted performance of the statutory duty, if they are seeking to fulfil that duty.

Children to be educated in accordance with parental wishes

The EA 1944, s 76 imposed a general duty on LEAs to educate children in accordance with their parents' wishes. This provision is now contained in s 9 of the EA 1996, and should be distinguished from the right of parents to express a preference for a school (see below) which is normally of more practical importance to parents.

Education Act 1996, s 9

In exercising or performing all their respective powers and duties under the Education Acts, the Secretary of [State and local education authorities] shall have regard to the general principle that pupils are to be educated in accordance with the wishes of their parents, so far as that is compatible with the provision of efficient instruction and training and the avoidance of unreasonable public expenditure.

The obligation is qualified by the section itself, in that the LEA may also take into account efficiency and cost factors. In addition the courts have held that the section does not require LEAs to comply with parental wishes as to the *type* of school their child should attend.

In *Watt v Kesteven County Council* [1955] 1 QB 408 twin brothers had passed the necessary examinations which entitled them to receive a grammar school education. However, there was no such school in the LEA. The LEA agreed to pay the fees for the two boys so that they could attend an independent school in the area. The boys' father, the claimant, wanted the LEA to pay the fees so that they could attend a Roman Catholic boarding school elsewhere. The case went to the Court of Appeal.

Watt v Kesteven County Council [1955] 1 QB 408

Denning LJ: I desire to say at the outset that the question in this case does not depend in the least on the religious views of the parent. The question would be the same if a member of the Church of England living in Stamford wished, for some reason or other, to send his boys away to a boarding school in some other part of the country. He might wish to send them there because it was his old school, or because the classics were well taught there, or because it was a co-educational school. The question in such a case would be just the same as this: Is the parent entitled to have the tuition fees paid by the county council?
...
The short answer to the father's argument is, I think, this: Whilst education is free in this country, it is only free at the schools which the county council make available. I can find nothing in the Act which compels the county council to pay the fees at any school which the father chooses. The duty of the county council is plain. They must make schools available for all the pupils in their area. But they can fulfil this duty, not only by maintaining schools themselves, but also by making arrangements with certain other schools. They may, for instance, make a grant to aid a school and in return get a right to a number of free places. Or they may make arrangements with some particular independent school to take the boys. At all the schools which the county council maintain themselves, no fees are payable. At the other schools with which they make arrangements, they must provide free places or pay the fees in full. Once they have fulfilled their duty in one or other of these ways — either by maintaining schools themselves, or by making arrangements with certain other schools — there is no more which they are bound to do.
...
Section 76 [of the EA 1944] does not say that pupils must in all cases be educated in accordance with the wishes of their parents. It only lays down a general principle in which the county council must have regard. This leaves it open to the county council to have regard to other things as well, and also to make exceptions to the general principle if it thinks fit to do so. It cannot therefore be said that a county council is at fault simply because it does not see fit to comply with the parent's wishes.

Similarly in *Cumings v Birkenhead Corpn* [1972] Ch 12, parents unsuccessfully challenged the LEA's admissions policy which restricted the choice of secondary school for children attending Roman Catholic primary schools. Such children could normally only apply to Roman Catholic secondary schools because the non-denominational secondary schools were only likely to have sufficient places for children from non-denominational and Church of England primary schools.

Cumings v Birkenhead Corpn [1972] Ch 12

Lord Denning MR: So here, if this education authority were to allocate boys to particular schools according to the colour of their hair or, for that matter, the colour of their skin, it would be so unreasonable, so capricious, so irrelevant to any proper system of education that it would be ultra vires altogether, and this court would strike it down at once. But, if there were valid educational reasons for a policy, as, for instance, in an area where immigrant children were backward in the English tongue and needed special teaching, then it would be perfectly right to allocate those in need to special schools where they would be given extra facilities for learning English. In short, if the policy is one which could reasonably be upheld for good educational reasons it is valid. But if it is so unreasonable that no reasonable authority could entertain it, it is invalid: see the judgment of Lord Greene MR in *Associated Provincial Picture Houses Ltd v Wednesbury Corporation* [1948] 1 KB 223, 228–9. Applying those considerations in the present case, it is quite impossible to suggest that the education authority have gone outside their powers. They have laid down a policy and given good reasons for it.

...

It seems to me that in the conditions foreseen in January 1968 it would have been really pointless to allow the parents of children at the Roman Catholic primary schools to opt for non-Roman Catholic secondary schools when there seemed no possibility at all of being able to give effect to such a choice if it were made; and for my part I can see no reason at all for thinking the education authority unreasonable in acting as they did, and the submission that their action was so unreasonable as to be ultra vires seems to me, with respect, to be plainly wrong.

Therefore, parents cannot rely upon s 9 of the EA 1996 to insist that their child attends a school of a particular religious denomination, or a school where the pupils are predominantly from a particular racial ethnic group, or a single-sex school. However, if a parent expresses a preference for such a school and the school has places then the admissions authority is under a duty to comply with the parent's preference (see below).

The issue of whether a parent can demand that their daughter attends a single-sex school has come before the courts on at least one occasion. In *R v Governors of the Buss Foundation Camden School for Girls, ex p Lukasiewicz* [1991] COD 98 the parents of an academically able 11-year-old girl wished her to attend the voluntary-aided Camden School for Girls which was less than a mile from where she lived. Pupils were grouped into ability bands (see below) and places allocated within each band on the basis of having sisters already attending the school, any special or social need, or living nearest to the school. Their daughter was not offered a place although girls who were less able academically and who lived further away were offered places. The parents unsuccessfully appealed to the appeal committee (see below) and subsequently applied for judicial review of the original refusal and the committee's decision. One of the grounds of their challenge was that their wish that their daughter attended a single-sex school was a 'social need' and this was not taken into account. They were unsuccessful.

R v Governors of the Buss Foundation Camden School for Girls, ex p Lukasiewicz [1991] COD 98

Otton J: It was clear that the Governors, when they considered the applicant's application, did take into account the fact that the parental preference was for single sex education and that their preferential school was Camden School.

...

(5) The way in which the parents had filled in the application form did not raise and could not be construed as raising a social need or social reason over and above all the other applicants who had specified their preference for a single sex school. In any event, the parents always knew that a mere preference might not and would not, in certain circumstances suffice. The admission booklet clearly stated that it was not possible to guarantee that parents' wishes in respect of a single sex school could be met. In the absence of any material supporting the parents' desire for a single sex school on the basis of a social need, social requirement or social reason, there was no possibility of their wish overriding the wishes of any other parent. The obligation was to consider the wishes not only of the individual parent but the other parents who were affected as well.

• *Is failure to provide a single-sex secondary education to, for example, the daughter of a devout Muslim a breach of the Human Rights Act 1998?*

• *Is it lawful for a parent to express a preference for a school with a majority of white English children? (See R v Cleveland County Council, ex p CRE [1994] ELR 44.)*

Duty not to discriminate against applicants

It is unlawful for LEAs, governing bodies of schools, and other educational institutions to discriminate against an applicant or a pupil on the grounds of her or his sex (ss 22 (see p 38), 23, 25 of the Sex Discrimination Act 1975). Virtually identical provisions dealing with racial discrimination are to be found in ss 17, 18 and 19 of the Race Relations Act 1976 (as amended by the Race Relations (Amendment) Act 2000) (see p 40). Similar provisions are contained in DDA 1995, s 28A which comes into force in September 2002 (see p 42).

Single-sex educational schools are permitted by the Sex Discrimination Act 1975, s 26.

These provisions are enforced in the county court by bringing a claim for damages or making an application for a declaration or an injunction (Sex Discrimination Act 1975, s 66).

Sections 23 and 25 of the Sex Discrimination Act 1975 have been the subject of several cases where there has been a discrepancy in the number of places available for girls and for boys at single-sex schools in the LEA.

Sex Discrimination Act 1975, ss 22 and 23

22 It is unlawful in relation to an educational establishment ... to discriminate against a woman—
(a) in terms on which it offers to admit her to the establishment as a pupil, or
(b) by refusing or deliberately omitting to accept an application for her admission to the establishment as a pupil, or ...

23(1) It is unlawful for a local education authority in carrying out such of its functions under [the Education Acts] as do not fall under section 22, to do any act which constitutes sex discrimination...

In *R v Northamptonshire County Council, ex p K* (1993) Times, 27 July, s 23 of the Sex Discrimination Act 1975 and s 8 of the Education Act 1944 (now EA 1996, s 14) were considered when the Secretary of State approved the LEA's proposal to close its only single-sex boys' school because of the falling roll.

R v Northamptonshire County Council, ex p K (1993) Times, 27 July

Hutchinson J: ... the council proposed to close the school as the only viable option given that the falling numbers on school rolls nationally was reflected in that of the school.
...
[T]he only other single-sex school in the area admitted only girls and accordingly the council was aware that closure of the school would have risked a breach of the 1975 Act.
...
In his Lordship's judgment, accepting the council's argument that it could not have performed its statutory duties under section 8 of the 1944 Act nor under section 23 of the 1975 Act because of the future lack of educational opportunities at the school, there was nothing which was repugnant or unlawful in the council's approach.

The Secretary of State had accepted that the duty of the local education authority under the 1975 Act had been an important factor for him to take into account in deciding whether to give his approval. Accordingly his decision was also reasonable and valid and there was no ground for impugning it.

The Sex Discrimination Act 1975 also imposes a general duty on LEAs and governing bodies, but it may only be enforced by the Secretary of State.

Sex Discrimination Act, 1975, s 25

(1) Without prejudice to its obligation to comply with any other provision of this Act, a body to which this subsection applies shall be under a general duty to secure that facilities for education provided by it, and any ancillary benefits or services, are provided without sex discrimination.

(2) The following provisions of [the Education Act 1996], namely—
(a) [section 496](power of Secretary of State to require duties under that Act to be exercised reasonably), and
(b) [section 497](powers of Secretary of State where local education authorities etc are in default), shall apply to the performance by a body to which subsection (1) applies of the duties imposed by sections 22 [23, 23A, 23C and 23D] and shall also apply to the performance of the general duty imposed by subsection (1), as they apply to the performance by a local education authority of a duty imposed by that Act...

(4) The sanctions in subsections (2) and (3) shall be the only sanctions for breach of the general duty in subsection (1), but without prejudice to the enforcement of sections 22 [23, 23A, 23C and 23D] under section 66 or otherwise (where the breach is also a contravention of [any] of those sections)....

(6) Subsection (1) applies to—
(a) local education authorities in England and Wales;...
(c) any other body which is a responsible body in relation to—
  (i) an establishment falling within paragraph 1, 3, [3A], [3B] or 7 of the table in section 22;

...

(See chapter 1 p 38 for meaning of 'responsible body'.)

In *Birmingham City Council v Equal Opportunities Commission* [1989] AC 1155 there were selective single-sex grammar schools in the LEA which provided education for about 5 per cent of the 11-year-old children in the area. Selection was made on the basis of pupils' examination results. However, while there were 390 grammar school places for boys, there were only 210 places available for girls. One consequence of this disparity was that a girl had to achieve a higher mark than a boy in the entrance examination in order to obtain a place. The Equal Opportunities Commission challenged the legality of the LEA's provision. The House of Lords upheld the Commission's claim.

Birmingham City Council v EOC [1989] AC 1155

Lord Goff of Chieveley: The first argument advanced by the council before your Lordships' House was that there had not been, in the present case, less favourable treatment of the girls on grounds of sex.

Here two points were taken. It was submitted (1) that it could not be established that there was less favourable treatment of the girls by reason of their having been denied the same opportunities as the boys for selective education unless it was shown that selective education was better than non-selective education, and that no evidence to that effect was called before McCullough J; and (2) that, if that burden had been discharged, it still had to be shown that there was less favourable treatment on grounds of sex, and that involved establishing an intention or motive on the part of the council to discriminate against the girls. In my opinion, neither of these submissions is well-founded.

As to the first it is not, in my opinion, necessary for the commission to show that selective education is 'better' than non-selective education. It is enough that, by denying the girls the same opportunity as the boys, the council is depriving them of a choice which (as the facts show) is valued by them, or at least by their parents, and which (even though others may take a different view) is a choice obviously valued, on reasonable grounds, by many others. This conclusion has been reached by all the judges involved in the present case; and it is consistent with previous authority: see, in particular, *Gill v El Vino Co Ltd* [1983] QB 425 and *R v Secretary of State for Education and Science, ex p Keating* (1985) 84 LGR 469. I have no doubt that it is right. As to the second point, it is, in my opinion, contrary to the terms of the statute. There is discrimination under the statute if there is less favourable treatment on the ground of sex, in other words if the relevant girl or girls would have received the same treatment as the boys had for their sex. The intention or motive of the defendant to discriminate, though it may be relevant so far as remedies are concerned (see section 66(3) of the Act of 1975), is not a necessary condition to liability; it is perfectly possible to envisage cases where the defendant had no such motive, and yet did in fact discriminate on the ground of sex. Indeed, as Mr Lester pointed out in the course of his argument, if the council's submission were correct it would be a good defence for an employer to show that he discriminated against women not because he intended to do so but (for example) because of customer preference, or to save money, or even to avoid controversy. In the present case, whatever may have been the intention or motive of the council, nevertheless it is because of their sex that the girls in question receive less favourable treatment than the boys, and so are the subject of discrimination under the Act of 1975. This is well established in a long line of authority: see, in particular, *Jenkins v Kingsgate (Clothing Productions) Ltd* [1981] 1 WLR 1485, 1494, per Browne-Wilkinson J, and *Ex p Keating*, per Taylor J, at p 475; see also *Ministry of Defence v Jeremiah* [1980] QB 87, 98, per Lord Denning MR. I can see no reason to depart from this established view.

I turn then to the most substantial issue in the case. This turns upon the true construction of section 23 of the Act of 1975, and its relationship with section 25.

...

Section 25, however, is, as I read it, concerned with something different. It is concerned with a positive duty placed upon bodies in the public sector, including local education authorities, to secure that 'facilities for education provided by it, and any ancillary benefits or services, are provided without sex discrimination.' This section is therefore intended, not to outlaw acts of discrimination as such, but to place upon such bodies a positive role in relation to the elimination of sex discrimination. The idea appears to have been to see that such bodies are, so to speak, put on their toes to ensure that sex discrimination does not occur in areas within their responsibility. It must not be forgotten that, in the field of education, there must be some reluctance on the part of parents to become entangled in disputes with their children's schools, or with the authorities responsible for them, on this subject. Quite apart from fear of prejudicing their children's prospects, the simple fact is that children pass rapidly on to other things, and a complaint of this kind may soon become irrelevant in relation to them.

...

All that is necessary for the commission to show is that the council, in carrying out its functions under the section, did an act (or deliberately omitted to do an act) where such act or omission constituted sex discrimination. Were that not so, there would be a serious gap in the legislation. This conclusion is consistent with the decision of Taylor J in *Ex p Keating*, 84 LGR 469, which appears to me to be correctly decided. Nor, with all respect, is it right, in my opinion, to restrict section 23 as Woolf LJ would do, with reference to the word 'constitutes' in the phrase 'to do any act which constitutes sex discrimination.' I myself do not attach such significance to that word. As I read them, the effect of sections 22 and 23 is to render unlawful all cases of particular acts or (deliberate) omissions by local education authorities which are discriminatory in the sense laid down in section 1 (and section 2) of the Act of 1975. Where there is at the same time a failure by an authority to fulfil its general duty under section 25, a person discriminated against by an act or deliberate omission made unlawful by sections 22 or 23 can still bring proceedings against the local education authority.

...

The time has come for the Birmingham City Council to accept that it is in breach of section 23 of the Act of 1975, and that something has got to be done about it. Its proper course must surely be to respond to the proposal of the commission that it should begin the necessary proceed of consultation, with a view to finding the most practical solution available which accords with the obligations imposed upon by Parliament.

I would dismiss the appeal.

Following the House of Lords' decision, Birmingham City Council considered how the ruling should be implemented. The LEA proposed changing one of the boys' grammar schools into a mixed-sex school. However, in October 1989 the school's governors refused to accept this proposal. In October 1990 the Secretary of State approved grant-maintained status for the school.

The LEA argued that once the school became grant-maintained the LEA was no longer in breach of s 23 of the Sex Discrimination Act 1975 because the disparity in numbers of places provided by the LEA available for boys and girls at local grammar schools would be reduced. The EOC disagreed with the LEA's interpretation of the law, and the Secretary of State was not prepared to give an assurance that the interpretation was correct. In June 1991 the EOC sought judicial review of the LEA's decision that it did not have to take into account the number of places available at a grant-maintained boys' grammar school when performing its duties under the Sex Discrimination Act 1975. The case was heard by the Court of Appeal in 1992, which considered the obligation of the LEA to provide sufficient schools under of s 8 of the Education Act 1944 (now s 14 of the Education Act 1996; see above).

R v Birmingham City Council, ex p EOC (No 2) [1994] ELR 282

Neill LJ: Mr Beloff for the council felt obliged to concede that in considering their obligations under the 1975 Act the council were entitled to take advantage of any places provided in grant-maintained schools. Thus if before Handsworth Grammar School had changed its status there had been a satisfactory equilibrium in Birmingham between the places provided for boys and the places provided for girls, the council would not have been required to provide extra places for boys to make up for the loss of the Handsworth Grammar School places. We consider that this concession was rightly made. It serves to emphasise, however, the force of Mr Lester's submission that in considering the extent of the duty under s 8 of the 1944 Act one looks at all the schools in the area and not merely at the schools which are maintained by the local education authority.

It is not necessary in the present case to reach a final conclusion with regard to independent schools. It seems to us, however, in considering whether sufficient schools are available, the local education authority has to take account, and only take account, of places which are available free. The relevant 'pool', as we would term it, is the pool of free places in single-sex schools providing a grammar school education. This pool may include assisted places at independent schools, but in our judgment it certainly includes grant-maintained schools.

The duty of securing that sufficient schools are available for providing secondary education of a suitable kind is a different duty from the duty to provide such schools.

In these circumstances the appeal by the Birmingham City Council will be dismissed.
...
Before parting with the case, however, we think it right to draw attention to some of the problems which in our view remain.

It is noteworthy that in the important paper entitled 'Choice and Diversity, a New Framework for Schools', which was presented to Parliament by the Secretaries of State for Education and Wales in July 1992, no reference was made to the requirements of the Sex Discrimination Act. This Act, and comparable legislation in the field of race relations, requires close examination when the duties and obligations of bodies responsible for the provision of public sector education are being formulated.

It seems to us that if and when further legislation in the field of education is being considered it is important that account shall be taken of:
(a)   the fact that both the Secretary of State and local education authorities retain under the present legislation some overall responsibilities for public sector education as a whole;
(b)   the fact that the discrimination with which a court would be likely to be primarily concerned would be discrimination against an individual boy or girl or groups of boys or girls.
In these circumstances we consider that amendments should be introduced to enable the elimination of discrimination to take place in accordance with a suitable and sensible time-scale. Schools and school places cannot be provided at the drop of a hat. Furthermore, account must be taken of the fact that the risks of discrimination may vary from year to year or even from term to term. Even if precisely equal numbers of places are provided at particular types of school both for boys and for girls, girls may require to achieve a higher mark to obtain admission. Under the present legislation this might constitute a form of unlawful discrimination. But the disparities would be likely to vary from year to year and be due to factors over which local education authorities or governing bodies could not possibly exercise control. It may therefore be right to provide that unlawful discrimination could only be proved if over a period a pattern of discrimination could be established.

These are only some of the questions which need to be addressed. It seems to us that the impact of civil rights legislation in the field of education requires to be looked at comprehensively as a matter of urgency. The present case has served to expose only one or two of the difficulties which exist in this field.

- *To what extent has subsequent legislation or guidance addressed the issues identified by Neill LJ as requiring consideration? (See section 3 Admission Arrangements below.)*

Although grant-maintained status has been abolished, similar difficulties may arise with foundation schools or with CTCs or city academies.

Duty to comply with parental preference

The Education Act 1980 introduced this duty which is now contained in s 86 of the SSFA 1998. However, as will be seen below the duty is subject to important qualifications.

School Standards and Framework Act 1998, s 86

(1) A local education authority shall make arrangements for enabling the parent of a child in the area of the authority—

(a)   to express a preference as to the school at which he wishes education to be provided for his child in the exercise of the authority's functions, and

(b)   to give reasons for his preference.

(2) Subject to subsections (3) and (6) and section 87 (children excluded from two or more schools), a local education authority and the governing body of a maintained school shall comply with any preference expressed in accordance with arrangements made under subsection (1).

In *R v Rotherham Metropolitan Borough Council, ex p Clark* [1998] ELR 152 the Court of Appeal was asked to consider whether the LEA's admission arrangements enabled parents to 'express a preference' and 'to give reasons' as required by the legislation (s 411 of the EA 1996 which is now s 86 of the SSFA 1998).

R v Rotherham Metropolitan Borough Council, ex p Clark [1998] ELR 152

Buxton LJ: This appeal concerns the implementation by the Rotherham MBC Local Education Authority (LEA) of statutory provisions concerning the recognition of parental preferences as to the secondary school at which their children should be educated. The two secondary schools involved in this case are called respectively Old Hall and Kimberworth. The allocation policies for each of those schools, as for all 'county' (as opposed to aided) schools in Rotherham, is based on (an expression that for the moment I use neutrally) a catchment area drawn for each school, priority for the allocation of places being given to children living within the school's catchment area. Old Hall is generally perceived by parents as being a better, or at least a more sought-after, school than Kimberworth. The applicants in this case are 10 out of some 55 children living in the Kimberworth catchment area whose parents none the less expressed a preference to attend Old Hall, but were unsuccessful in those applications.

...

With regard to s 411(1)(a), I am unable to agree with the applicants' argument and the judge's view and, I respectfully regret, with the view taken by my Lords, that the LEA's arrangements as described above did not 'enable' the parents of children in the Old Hall catchment area to express a preference as to their wish for education to be provided for their children at Old Hall.

The arrangements clearly enabled parents, such as the present applicants, in other catchment areas to express such a preference, because in such case the parent was required to indicate that he wished education to be provided at Old Hall and not at the catchment area school. Those within the Old Hall catchment area were by contrast told that if they wanted their children to attend that school they need take no action, since a place would be reserved for the child. I of course agree with what I think must have been the judge's assumption that inertia, devoid of other considerations, could not amount to the expression of a preference. The question is, however, not simply what the parent in fact does, but what the LEA's arrangements enable him to do. To judge that, those arrangements must be looked at as a whole.

The arrangements set out in, in particular, section 5 of the information booklet do in my view enable the parent to express a wish that his child should be educated at his catchment area school. As a recipient of a letter written in the terms of the policy, he is enabled to express a preference to the LEA by not taking steps to contest or dissent from the allocation of his child to the catchment area school. As the recipients of the letters were told, if you want your child to attend the school in which you live, you need take no action. If the parent complies with that indication, that is not mere inaction, but a relevant response in the context of the LEA's arrangements, and of what those arrangements have told the parent about how he can ensure that his child goes to the catchment area school. Those arrangements can thus in my view fairly be said to enable the parent who wishes his child to attend the catchment area school to express a preference as to the school at which he wishes education to be provided for that child.

The judge may have been deflected from that conclusion at least partly because he accepted the argument of the applicants that parents who take no action may not in fact have a preference for the catchment area school, but 'simply sit back and accept that the child goes to that school without really considering positively whether there is a preference for that as opposed to some other school' ... There are I think two points to be made about what at first sight seems to be a robustly commonsense conclusion.

First, when considering the application of s 411(1)(a) the point is irrelevant. The question is not whether the parents *in fact* expressed a preference, but whether the arrangements *enabled* them to express a preference; which in my view the arrangements clearly did. Secondly, however, I recognise that at the next stage of the process, when the LEA has to choose between oversubscribing 'preferences', it may be said with more force, and indeed is said, that the arrangements are insufficient to distinguish between failures to respond that connote preferences and failures to respond that merely reflect inertia. I would however wish to be cautious before attributing mere inertia to parents who are not before the court, and in particular before attributing such attitudes to many, or indeed any, of the parents who fell within the Old Hall catchment area. The evidence was that Old Hall was a very sought-after school: 54 children from outside its catchment area, equivalent to more than 25 per cent of its intake from within its catchment area, originally wanted to go there. I am afraid that I see no justification for assuming a point on which we have no evidence, that parents within the Old Hall catchment area who took no action on receipt of the LEA's circular did not in fact wish their children to attend Old Hall: just as other parents from outside the catchment area had the same wish.

I would therefore hold, differing from the judge, that the LEA's arrangements looked at as a whole did enable parents within a given catchment area to express a preference not only for a school outside the catchment area but also for the catchment area school itself.

The lawfulness of the LEA's policy: the parents' giving of reasons

I have much more difficulty in respect of s 411(1)(b) of the 1996 Act, an issue that, because of his conclusion as to s 411(1)(a), did not need to be explored in detail by the judge.

Why the parent is required to give reasons, and how and to what extent those reasons are acted on in the subsequent process, are matters of some difficulty to which I shall have to return. The immediate issue is whether, on the assumption that I adopt that the LEA's arrangements enabled a parent of a child within the Old Hall catchment area to express a preference for Old Hall, those arrangements also enabled the parent to give reasons for that preference. It seems to me quite plain that they did not. The LEA's letter indicated in terms that, if a parent in the catchment area wished his child to be educated at Old Hall, he need do nothing. His lack of reply would be sufficient to indicate agreement with the assumption that he wished his child to be educated at the catchment area school: but, not least because no possible reasons for that decision were adumbrated in the LEA's letter, lack of reply cannot possibly be construed as the giving of reasons for that preference. A parent might have many reasons for wanting his child to go to Old Hall other than the fact, or the mere fact, that he lived in the Old Hall catchment area; as, again, many parents from outside the area had reasons, on the small sample of evidence in this case often differing reasons, for their children to go to Old Hall. The LEA's arrangements do not enable any conclusions at all to be drawn as to what the catchment area parents' reasons were.

...

[T]he LEA is free to ignore whatever reasons the parents expressing preferences may have given, and choose between them by the application of a general policy in what may be, except as an application of that policy, an arbitrary fashion. It is therefore not easy to see what the role or effect can be of the reasons given by parents, or why the LEA should be obliged to enable the parents to give reasons: which, if given, it can then ignore. That difficulty is reinforced by the fact that all that the LEA is required to do is to enable the parent to give reasons. As I understand the view of s 411(1)(b) that is taken by my Lords, as well as by myself, all that would have been necessary in the present case to comply with that s 411(1)(b) would have been for the LEA to include in its circular a statement such as 'You may if you wish state on the enclosed form any reasons that you have for your preference': whether that preference was expressed by silence (as I consider to be sufficient) or by the positive expression of choice that my Lords consider to be necessary. But, in actually allocating places, the LEA can act without reference to whether a parent has taken advantage of that invitation, and without reference to any reasons that he does express.

...

Bingham LCJ: It was the evident purpose of the legislation, first introduced in 1980, to give primacy and effect to parental choice save insofar as so to do would 'prejudice the provision of efficient education or the efficient use of resources'. The omission of a parent of a child living within the catchment area to respond to the letter sent to him is not necessarily indicative of any preference for the school within the catchment area. But to treat it as if it is to give to the fact of residence within the catchment area a primacy, as an expressed preference, it does not necessarily have. Further if the allocation of a place to a child living within the catchment area whose parent did not respond necessitates refusing such a place to a child who lives outside it whose parent expressed a preference for that school then the reason why the preference of the latter is not complied with has nothing to do with prejudice to efficient education or the efficient use of resources. In other words the provisions of s 411(2) and (3) presuppose that the expression of a preference is a positive act. Further the language used in s 411 is, in my view, inconsistent with the submissions of the local education authority. In ordinary English a failure to respond is not an expression of anything. Likewise silence is not indicative of a preference for it is equally consistent with indifference. It follows that in my view the arrangements made by the local education authority did not enable the parents to express a preference as required by s 411(1).

The arrangements required to be made by a local education authority are ones designed to enable the parent not only to express a preference but also to give reasons for his preference. The reasons may be of importance at a later stage of the process if it is not possible to give effect to all expressed preferences. But whilst the parent cannot be required to do either the arrangements must enable him to do both. The arrangements made by this local education authority do not enable a parent whose child lives within the catchment area and who fails to respond to the letter to give any reasons. In my view this is another pointer to the correctness of the judge's conclusion that inaction in the face of the letter of 7 October 1996 cannot be an expression of a preference. It is also another reason why the policy adopted by the local education authority fails to comply with s 411(1).

...

The duty on the LEA, it is pointed out, is to:

... make arrangements for enabling the parent of a child in the area of the authority—
(a) to express a preference ...

In other words, the authority must establish a system which gives parents the opportunity to express a preference. That, it is said, the LEA did, both to parents who preferred another school to that provisionally allocated and to parents who (by silence or acquiescence) were taken to express a preference for the school provisionally allocated. They were only entitled to an opportunity, and that they had.

On a wholly literal approach to the statutory language that argument is sustainable. But it does not in my view give effect to the spirit or purpose of the section. For the section should lead to the allocation of places on the basis of parental choice, restricted so far as necessary by limitations of space and the other s 411(3) constraints. What the scheme operated by the LEA here achieved was in my view something rather different, allocation of places on the basis of catchment areas, supplemented by parental choice. That must necessarily have been so unless it be assumed (to my mind unrealistically) that all parents in the Old Hall catchment area preferred that school as distinct from being indifferent or having a marginal but unexpressed preference for another school. In truth, we do not know what the Old Hall catchment area parents preferred because they were never invited to say. I do not think the scheme operated by the LEA gave parental choice the priority which the Act intended.

Because parents who were happy with the provisionally allocated school (in whose catchment area they lived) were not invited to express a preference, it followed that they were not invited to give reasons. On no reasonable reading of the language used could it be said that the LEA made arrangements which enabled parents happy to accept their provisional allocation to give reasons. The system which the LEA established was not in any meaningful sense such as to give them that opportunity. That was, in truth, because they were not invited to express a preference either. While, therefore, I agree with what Buxton LJ has said about reasons, I (like the judge and Morritt LJ) consider that the LEA's scheme as operated failed to give effect to s 411(1)(a) as well as s 411(1)(b).

In the event, almost all the places available at Old Hall went to Old Hall catchment area parents who had never expressed a preference or given reasons or been invited to do so. The same result might have followed if they had expressed a preference. We cannot know. If parental choice is to be given the weight which, I think, Parliament intended, the first and important step must be to invite parents to express a preference and give reasons if they choose to do so. That step was not taken; and the preferences expressed by the applicants' parents were not complied with (in the first instance) when, had the step been taken, it may well be that they could and should have been. I would accordingly grant a declaration that the arrangements made by the LEA did not comply with the requirements of s 411(1) of the 1996 Act.

- *Compare the view expressed by Buxton LJ with that of the majority in the Court of Appeal.*

- *Note the criticisms of s 411(1)(b) of the EA 1980, now s 86(1)(b) of the SSFA 1998, expressed by Buxton LJ and Bingham LCJ.*

Admission arrangements in Sheffield, which did not enable parents to set out the reasons why their catchment school was their first preference, were held to be unlawful in *R v Sheffield City Council, ex p Hague* [1999] ELR 242.

In 1999 the DfEE published statutory guidance on school admissions which contains the following advice on parental preference.

Code of Practice on School Admissions (1999)

Parental Preference

3.13 LEAs and governing bodies have an overriding duty, except in some specified circumstances, to comply with parents' declared preference(s) as to the school where they would like their child to be educated. The 1997 Rotherham judgment made clear that when allocating places at schools, the LEA must consider those parents who have expressed a preference ahead of those who have expressed no preference. Consequently, LEAs should make every effort to ensure that parents do express a preference and are fully aware of the likely consequences if they do not. This may entail producing literature in community languages, for instance. It will mean monitoring as far as possible the plans of parents of children who are transferring into primary or secondary education and following up cases where no preference has been received. As an example of good practice, LEAs may involve primary schools in the process, by routing applications through them so that parents who have not expressed a preference can be identified.

3. ADMISSIONS ARRANGEMENTS

Admissions authorities

In any particular LEA there are likely to be at least two, if not more, admissions authorities. Under the School Standards and Framework Act 1998, s 88 the admissions authority in the case of community and voluntary controlled schools will normally be the LEA (or the governing body where the power has been delegated to it); and in the case of foundation and voluntary aided schools it will be the governing body. The admissions authority for CTCs and city academies is the governing body.

The SSFA 1998 introduced several changes in an attempt to enable the LEA to co-ordinate admission arrangements in its area. In some LEAs where there are a large number of voluntary or foundation schools there could be as many as 30 admission authorities.

The legislative provisions have been supplemented by two statutory (SSFA 1998, s 84) Codes of Practice which came into effect in 1999:
- School Admissions
- School Admission Appeals.

The government's policy in relation to school admissions was set out in the White Paper *Excellence in Schools* (Cm 3681) which was published in July 1997, and the Technical Consultation Paper *Framework for the Organisation of Schools* published in August 1997.

White Paper *Excellence in Schools* (Cm 3681, July 1997)

School admissions

29 Parents must have the information they need to see what different schools can offer and to assess their choices realistically. Where a school is over-subscribed, there must be clear and fair criteria for deciding applications. Church schools may reasonably carry out interviews to assess religious or denominational commitment. Places should not otherwise be offered on the basis of an interview with the pupil or parent.

30 At present LEAs are 'admission authorities' for county and controlled schools but governing bodies play that role in GM, voluntary aided and special agreement schools. This can lead to difficulties, and uncertainty for parents. We will therefore expect to see the development of local forums of headteachers and governors from community, aided and foundation schools, to share information about their schools' admissions arrangements, with administrative support from LEAs. We will expect the forums to develop helpful and timely information for parents and common timetables for applications for their local area. Guidance on the establishment and operation of such forums will be provided by the DfEE.

The Code of Practice on School Admissions (1999) provides that:

2.3 School admission arrangements should work for the benefit of all parents and children in an area. The arrangements should be as simple as possible for parents to use, and help them to take the best decisions on the school for their children.

2.4 In drawing up admission arrangements, admission authorities should aim to ensure that:
- the arrangements enable parents' preferences for the schools of their choice to be met to the maximum extent possible
- admission criteria are clear, fair and objective, for the benefit of all children including those with special educational needs or with disabilities
- local admission arrangements contribute to improving standards for all pupils
- local admission authorities consult each other and co-ordinate their arrangements, including over the rapid reintegration wherever sensible of children who have been excluded from other schools
- parents have easy access to helpful admissions information
- local admission arrangements achieve full compliance with all relevant legislation and guidance – including on infant class sizes and on equal opportunities – and take full account of the guidance in this Code.

Admission arrangements are concerned with, for example, deciding the basis on which children should be offered a place at a particular school. These 'admission criteria' may be based on the distance between home and school, religious affiliation, academic ability, or aptitude in a particular subject.

A foundation or voluntary aided school which has a religious character may include criteria or enter into arrangements which preserve the religious character of the school (SSFA 1998, s 91). Where such arrangements are agreed to by the LEA the normal procedure is followed (s 91(2) of the SSFA 1998). Where the LEA does not agree to the governing body's proposals (s 91(3) of the SSFA 1998), the proposed admissions arrangements have to be referred to the adjudicator and be agreed by the adjudicator, or in certain circumstances the Secretary of State.

Consultation

The School Standards and Framework Act 1998 introduced a new procedure for determining admission arrangements. This requires admission authorities for maintained schools in the LEA to consult each other annually before deciding upon their admission arrangements, and provides for certain matters to be referred to an independent adjudicator. Where the LEA is the admission authority for a school it should consult the governing body of each school as part of any consultation process (s 89(9) of the SSFA 1998).

School Standards and Framework Act 1998, s 89

(1) The admission authority for a maintained school shall, before the beginning of each school year, determine in accordance with this section the admission arrangements which are to apply for that year.

(2) Before determining the admission arrangements which are to apply for a particular school year, the admission authority shall consult the following about the proposed arrangements, namely—
(a)   the local education authority (where the governing body are the admission authority),
(b)   the admission authorities for all other maintained schools in the relevant area or for such class of such schools as may be prescribed, and
(c)   the admission authorities for maintained schools of any prescribed description.

(3) In subsection (2) 'the relevant area' means—
(a)   the area of the local education authority; or

....

LEAs may be required by the Education Bill 2001/02 to co-ordinate school admission arrangements in their area. The Bill also contains amendments to the admission arrangements procedures set out in SSFA 1998, ss 89, 90 and 91.

The Code of Practice on School Admissions recommends the establishment of local Admission Forums. The Education Bill 2001/02 replaces this voluntary arrangement. LEAs will be required to establish admission forums. The new legislative provisions will be implemented by regulations, which will replace the current guidance in the Code of Practice set out below.

The Code of Practice on School Admissions (1999)

Admissions Forums

4.5 LEAs, together with other school admission authorities, should set up local Admissions Forums to be the vehicle for consultation and discussion of issues arising from proposed admission arrangements. These new Forums should help to develop a real consensus at a local level. Local Admissions Forums will be an important way for headteachers, governors, local education authorities, special educational needs and diocesan representatives to work together to arrive at satisfactory admission arrangements. Forums should enable all admission authorities in an area to consider how local arrangements can best meet the needs of parents and how admission arrangements mesh in with other issues such as planning, children with special needs and children with difficult behaviour.

4.6 As regards planning, it is recommended that Admissions Forums are used to consider proposals for change in planned admission numbers, whether proposals are made by schools which are their own admission authority or schools for which the local education authority is the admission authority.

Having consulted other admission authorities each admission authority decides what its admission arrangements will be for the school year in question, and informs other admission authorities in the area. For example, an LEA should decide by March 2002 what admission arrangements will be in place for community schools for the school year starting in September 2003.

School Standards and Framework Act 1998, s 89(4)

Once the admission authority have carried out any such consultation, the authority shall—
(a)   determine that their proposed arrangements (either in their original form or with such modifications as the authority think fit) shall be the admission arrangements for the school year in question; and
(b)   (except in such cases as may be prescribed) notify the bodies whom they consulted under subsection (2) of those admission arrangements.

Variation

Where the LEA or governing body subsequently decides to vary these admission arrangements it should refer the proposed variations to the adjudicator and notify the other admission authorities.

School Standards and Framework Act 1998, s 89(5) to (7)

(5) Where an admission authority—
(a)   have in accordance with subsection (4) determined the admission arrangements which are to apply for a particular school year, but
(b)   at any time before the end of that year consider that the arrangements should be varied in view of a major change in circumstances occurring since they were so determined,

the authority shall (except in a case where their proposed variations fall within any description of variations prescribed for the purposes of this subsection) refer the proposed variations to the adjudicator, and shall (in every case) notify the bodies whom they consulted under subsection (2) of the proposed variations.

(6) The adjudicator shall consider whether the arrangements should have effect with those variations until the end of that year; and if he determines that the arrangements should so have effect or that they should so have effect subject to such modification of those variations as he may determine—
(a)   the arrangements shall have effect accordingly as from the date of his determination; and
(b)   the admission authority shall (except in such cases as may be prescribed) notify the bodies whom they consulted under subsection (2) of the variations subject to which the arrangements are to have effect.

(7) In relation to a maintained school in Wales any reference to the adjudicator in subsection (5) or (6) shall be read as a reference to the Secretary of State...

The provisions in s 89 are supplemented by regulations: Education (Relevant Areas for Consultation on Admission Arrangements) Regulations 1999, SI 1999/124; Education (Determination of Admission Arrangements) Regulations 1999, SI 1999/ 126.

The Code of Practice on School Admissions provides detailed guidance on the consultation which should be undertaken by the admission authorities, and when agreed admission arrangements may be varied. Such variation may only occur in limited circumstances. The Code of Practice sets out the DfEE's view on the law relating to variation.

The Code of Practice on School Admissions (1999)

A.14 Once admission arrangements have been determined, they can be varied only as permitted by section 89 of the 1998 Act and the Regulations. So:

(i) where an admission authority considers that the arrangements should be varied because of a major change in circumstances, that authority must refer the proposed variations to the Adjudicator, notifying all the bodies who had to be consulted before the arrangements were determined. The Regulations define a major change of circumstances as a serious and unexpected event affecting the provision of education at the school. An example of a serious and unexpected event might be a fire which destroyed classroom space.

(ii) where there is no major change in circumstances, variations may be made only where a genuine error, omission or misprint occurred when an admission authority determined its admission arrangements, or where an admission authority sees a need to revise its admission arrangements in the light of an Adjudicator or Secretary of State determination on another school with the same or substantially the same admission arrangements. In these cases, the admission authority responsible must notify all the admission authorities who had to be consulted earlier, as above; and such an admission authority may refer the variation to the Adjudicator for a determination.

The adjudicator

The LEA and governing bodies may object to the admission arrangements adopted by an LEA or governing body. Parents have the right to object about pre-existing selection arrangements. In England the objections are made to an adjudicator, whereas in Wales they are made to the Secretary of State.

The Education (Objections to Admission Arrangements) Regulations 1999, SI 1999/125 make further provision in relation to objections, For example, objections should normally be made within six weeks from the date when details of the admission arrangements became available (reg 3).

School Standards and Framework Act 1998, s 90

(1) Where—
(a)   admission arrangements have been determined by an admission authority under section 89(4), but
(b)   a body consulted by the admission authority under section 89(2) wish to make an objection about those arrangements, and
(c)   the objection does not fall within any description of objections prescribed for the purposes of this paragraph,

that body may refer the objection to the adjudicator.

(2) Where—
(a)   admission arrangements have been determined by an admission authority under section 89(4), but
(b)   any parent of a prescribed description wishes to make an objection about those arrangements, and
(c)   the objection falls within any description of objections prescribed for the purposes of this paragraph,

that person may refer the objection to the adjudicator.

(3) On a reference under subsection (1) or (2) the adjudicator shall either—
(a)   decide whether, and (if so) to what extent, the objection should be upheld, or
(b)   in such cases as may be prescribed, refer the objection to the Secretary of State for that question to be decided by him.

(4) Where the objection is referred to the Secretary of State under subsection (3)(b), the adjudicator shall, if the Secretary of State so requests, give his advice on the question referred to in that provision.

(5) ....

(6) Where the adjudicator or the Secretary of State decides that an objection referred to him under this section should be upheld to any extent, his decision on the objection may specify the modifications that are to be made to the admission arrangements in question.

(7) In the case of any objection referred to him under this section, the adjudicator or the Secretary of State (as the case may be) shall publish his decision on the objection and the reasons for it.

(8) The decision of the adjudicator or the Secretary of State on the objection shall, in relation to the admission arrangements in question, be binding on the admission authority and on all persons by whom an objection about those arrangements may be made under subsection (1) or (2); and if that decision is to uphold the objection to any extent, those arrangements shall forthwith be revised by the admission authority in such a way as to give effect to the decision.

....

Only certain 'objections' may be referred to the adjudicator by the admission authorities. For example objections to selection may not be referred where the school is a grammar school or a school where partial selection has been permitted (SI 1999/125, reg 2).

However, ten or more parents can object about pre-existing selection arrangements (SI 1999/125, regs 5, 6). Parents have no right to make objections about any other aspect of the admission arrangements. Generally, only parents of a child at primary school who are resident in the LEA area are eligible to refer such an objection to the adjudicator (SI 1999/125, reg 4).

The adjudicator is under a duty to decide whether or not to uphold the objection or to refer the matter to the Secretary of State. The adjudicator's decision must be published.

The Code of Practice on School Admissions sets out the factors considered relevant in determining objections to partial selection.

The Code of Practice on School Admissions (1999)

5.12 Local parents or a local admission authority may make an objection to partially selective admission arrangements. Where such an objection is to the principle that the school is partially selective, the Adjudicator will need to consider whether the arrangements act in the best interests of local children, including those with special educational needs, and parents, or work against those interests; whether they disrupt the sensible and efficient provision of education locally; and whether they have a detrimental effect on parental choice.

Relevant pointers include whether:
* local pupils, who could otherwise expect to be admitted to a school, are in effect being denied admission
* other schools in the area are suffering adverse changes in their pupil profile as a result of the partially selective school 'creaming off' high ability pupils
* partially selective arrangements are causing significant difficulties for pupil placement across the whole area
* relatively high numbers of children are having to travel an unreasonable distance to school because of the pressure on school places in their local area caused by partial selection
* the LEA can show that partially selective admission arrangements are causing it difficulties in discharging its duty to ensure that there are school places available for all children in its area
* an already limited choice of school in isolated rural areas is being further limited
* children are being adversely affected, for example, because they have to sit a number of different tests to gain a place in a local school.

One of the first cases involving a challenge to an adjudicator's decision was *R v Downes, ex p Wandsworth London Borough Council* [2000] ELR 425 which was concerned with whether the objections to partial selection came within the adjudicator's jurisdiction. The judgment contains useful comments on the role of the adjudicator and the court.

R v Downes, ex p Wandsworth LBC [2000] ELR 425

Sullivan J: This is an application for judicial review by Wandsworth London Borough Council (the council), which is the local education authority for its area, of three decisions made on 4 August 1999 by the respondent who is an adjudicator appointed under the School Standards and Framework Act 1998 (the Act), in respect of the admission arrangements to be made for three secondary schools within the council's area: the

Ernest Bevin, Burntwood and Graveney schools, for the school year commencing September 2000.

...

In the case of all three schools the admission authority decided to maintain the pre-existing arrangements for admission, whereby part of the intake each year was based on selection by a test of general ability: 50% of the intake at Graveney and Ernest Bevin and 32% of the intake in Burntwood would be selected in that way. The remainder of the schools' intakes would be selected by applying other criteria: siblings in the schools, medical/social grounds and proximity to the school....

Partial selection was introduced at Burntwood and Graveney in September 1995 and at Ernest Bevin in September 1996. It is not in dispute that the admission arrangements determined for the three schools for the year 2000 by the admission authorities were permitted within the terms of s 100. One of the bodies consulted under s 89(2) was Honeywell Infant and Junior Schools (Honeywell).

Honeywell objected to the admission arrangements.

...

In the case of Graveney, but not Ernest Bevin and Burntwood, there were also parental objections. These objections largely echoed those advanced by Honeywell.

...

[The adjudicator] stated that he was satisfied that he had jurisdiction to determine the objections and proceeded to analyse the evidence by reference to the various considerations which are referred to in para 5(12) of the Code. Principally on two grounds, access for local children and the adverse effect on other schools, but also noting the need for increased travelling by pupils, he concluded that the admission arrangements in each of the three schools was 'not in the best interests of local children'.

...

The adjudicator then determined that at Ernest Bevin and Graveney the percentage of pupils admitted by selection should be reduced from 50% to 25% and at Burntwood from 32% to 25%. It is these determinations which are the subject of these proceedings.

...

In a nutshell, Mr Griffin on behalf of the council argues that in substance Honeywell's objections sought the substitution of pupil banding for partial selection or at the very least the abolition of the latter as the basis for admission and on either basis there was no power to refer those objections to the adjudicator, and that the adjudicator's decision to reduce the number of pupils chosen by reference to general ability at Graveney from 50% to 25% would constitute a significant change of character of that school and was therefore outwith the adjudicator's powers by virtue of s 103 of the Act as modified.

It is common ground that it is for the court to decide what is the substance of an objection under s 90(1). If the court concludes that in substance Honeywell's objections sought an alteration to the admission arrangements by the introduction of pupil banding, the applications in respect of Ernest Bevin and Burntwood must succeed. If the court concludes that Honeywell's objection was not seeking the introduction of pupil banding then the question arises as to whether the alterations sought to the admission arrangements would constitute a significant change in the character of those schools.

...

Whilst the court is competent to decide what is the substance of an objection, such an exercise will involve no more than construing the objection document, it is singularly ill-equipped to decide whether a proposed alteration to admission arrangements would constitute a significant change in the character of a school. Such a decision necessarily involves a very substantial degree of expert educational judgment.

...

[O]n the particular facts of these cases the court is bound to form its own view. I expressly leave open the question whether that would be an appropriate course to adopt in any future case arising under these provisions.

Turning to the Honeywell objections, reg 2(2) requires me to look at the substance rather than the form. Most objections will not be made by those who are legally trained, thus it would be particularly inappropriate to subject them to minute legal analysis. The objection should be read as a whole in a commonsense manner bearing in mind as part of the background factual matrix that admission arrangements must be made each year for each school.

...

[M]y view [is] that the substance of Honeywell's objection was to seek the abolition of partial selection as a basis for admission and its replacement by pupil banding. It follows that there was no power to refer Honeywell's objections to the adjudicator.

...

Graveney is a different case because there was no question that the adjudicator had jurisdiction to entertain the parents' objections. Did his determination that the number of a pupils selected by reference to general ability was to be reduced from 50% to 25% alter the admission arrangements to such an extent as to constitute a significant change of character at the school and thus fall foul of the provisions of s 103 as modified?

The adjudicator is obliged to give reasons for his decision. It is trite law that those reasons must deal with the substantial issues. Whether raised by the parties or not, the constraint imposed by s 103 was of fundamental importance. Given the advice in the circulars to which I have referred, if the adjudicator had intended to say, 'I propose a reduction in the number of pupils admitted by selection on the basis of ability from 50% to 25% and I am satisfied that for the following reasons ... this would not amount to a significant change in the character of the school', one would have expected him to say so in express terms.

It follows that the Graveney determination is liable to be quashed even if the court is limited to reviewing this aspect of the adjudicator's decision on *Wednesbury* grounds. Quite simply, the adjudicator has not addressed his mind to this issue. On a *Wednesbury* approach, it would not be right, as a matter of discretion, to quash the determination if it was obvious that on redetermination the adjudicator would be able to reach the conclusion that such a reduction in partial selection would not fall foul of s 103(2).

For the reasons set out above in relation to the abolition of partial selection, I am very far from convinced that this would be the case. A halving of the number of pupils admitted by selection on the basis of ability in any year is clearly a less radical alteration than the abolition of partial selection, but in the light of my interpretation of s 573(4) and (5), of the way in which the introduction of partial selection at these schools was dealt with in the relatively recent past and of the advice in the circulars to which I have referred, one would require very clear justification indeed for the proposition that such a reduction would not result in a significant change in the character of this particular school. Whether the change would be desirable or undesirable is not the question.

One of the important issues discussed in this case was whether the reduction or abolition of partial selection amounted to a significant change in the character of the school. If it did, certain statutory procedures (see chapter 2) had to be invoked, and the adjudicator did not have jurisdiction. The concept of 'significant change of character' has been removed from the legislation, and in future the adjudicator may have jurisdiction in this situation.

T Lewis Brooke 'The Future of Partial Selection: Issues Raised by *R v Downes, ex p Wandsworth LBC*' [2000] Education Law Journal 159

Under the new system, alterations which do constitute a significant change of character may not require the publication of proposals. Sullivan J found that the abolition of partial selection, or its reduction from 50% to 25%, does constitute a significant change to the character of the school. Such a change can come about in future by the less formal procedure of a referral of an objection to the adjudicator. However, the abolition or reduction of partial selection is not on the list of prescribed alterations notwithstanding that it would clearly have been caught under the old provisions. This change represents an important procedural alteration, clearly based on a significant shift of policy. The policy is well documented and repeated by the Secretary of State in his introductory message to the DfEE *Code of Practice on School Admissions*:

> I am not in favour of any further selection based on academic ability … nor do I believe that partial selection based on academic ability is the best way to achieve higher standards.

However, the adjudicator has tended to reduce rather than abolish partial selection where objections have been referred to him. Furthermore, in the *Wandsworth* case the adjudicator found the retention of some level of partial selection was necessary to maintain a balanced intake at the schools in question. Presumably, this principle will apply more widely than the London Borough of Wandsworth. It must therefore be doubtful whether the Government will be able to fulfil the pledge in the White Paper *Excellence in Schools*, that by 2002 'there will be … no more partial selection by general academic ability'.

The first case where an adjudicator's decision was judicially reviewed was heard in December 1999. The case was concerned with the fairness of new admission arrangements being introduced as a consequence of the abolition of grant-maintained status by the SSFA 1998. The Code of Practice on School Admissions (1999) requires admission arrangements and admission criteria to be fair.

R v Schools Adjudicator, ex p Metropolitan Borough of Wirral [2000] ELR 620

Latham J: Admission arrangements to secondary schools in the applicants' area have to change next year because of the provisions of the Act. The applicants therefore undertook detailed consultation on its proposals for new arrangements for admissions for the year 2000/01 with school governing bodies, with parent teacher associations, guidance authorities and teachers' associations. …

(8) Results of the consultation were first considered by the Education Committee in April 1999, and a decision was taken to hold a further round of consultation, the results of which were considered by the Education Committee in June 1999. The Committee was there faced with two options in relation to the way in which admissions procedures should operate.

(9) The first has been described in the papers as the 'rank order option'. Put simply, that entitled a parent to indicate in order of preference which school he or she wished the child to attend.

(10) The second option was known as the 'elevated preference option'. This option was to take account of the fact that the applicants, although at the moment a Labour-controlled authority, have a number of grammar schools (indeed, well-known grammar schools) within the area. In order to provide, it was thought, some protection for those parents whose children were able enough to consider admission to a grammar school, this option enabled such parents to give a first preference for a grammar school but then also to give — in the event that the child was unable to attend the grammar school — a first preference in relation to what was to be known as an 'all-ability' school.

(11) On 23 June 1999 the Committee decided to adopt the elevated preference option. It is to be noted that the elevated preference option is not one which operates before the parent knows whether or not a child has met the academic or ability requirements of the grammar school. By the time such a parent seeks to make his or her choice, he or she will have been told whether or not the child meets the academic or ability criteria. However, the parent will not have been told how many parents have named the particular grammar school as their first preference; the number of children with particular justifications for choosing that school, the geographical pattern of preferences, or the reasons put forward by other parents for admission to that particular school.
...
The schools adjudicator identified that the issue which he had to determine was whether or not the admissions procedure met the criterion of fairness which was set out in the Code of Practice. He said as follows:

The issue of fairness or unfairness arises where the all-ability school is oversubscribed either before the process of 'elevation' or as a result of it. In both events a second preference elevated to a first preference can displace a parentally expressed first preference, and it is a direct consequence of the arrangements that this should be enabled to happen. At the point at which a preference is expressed under the LEA's proposed arrangements, one parent has already expressed a preference for a grammar school and another is, for the first time, enabled to express a preference for an all-ability school. If, as result of that process which includes 'elevation', the first choice of the second parent is not met, whilst the second choice of the second parent is, the process operates in a way which to the second parent will in my view appear not to be 'fair' to use the word of paragraph 5.2 of the Code. This will apply equally to parents living inside or outside the LEA.

I do not regard the elevation of the preferences expressed by one group of parents over those of some others, in the particular circumstances of the arrangements proposed by the LEA, as fair, in that some parents are by reason of these arrangements given less opportunity than others to have their preference met, and therefore uphold the objection to this element in the LEA's arrangements ...

(17) In effect, the schools adjudicator, therefore preferred, and therefore imposed, the first option, ie the rank order option.

(18) The applicants challenge that decision on three grounds. The first ground is that it is said that the adjudicator misdirected himself in law by substituting his judgment for that of the authority, in deciding that the admission arrangements were unfair under the Code of Practice.

(19) It seems to me that, put in that way, the applicants' argument is misconceived. The provisions of the Act that I have already cited make it plain that the schools adjudicator has what is, in effect, an original jurisdiction to determine the objection. Naturally, he will take into account all the matters which are submitted to him by all interested parties. The background will include the local education authority's decision. The local education authority is comprised of elected representatives who can be expected to know the area which they represent.

(20) Clearly, when considering the submissions made by or on behalf of the local education authority, the schools adjudicator will be bound to take that into account when assessing their validity. But, at the end of the day, as the passage from the Code of Practice which I have also cited makes clear, it is for the schools adjudicator to come to his own decision on the merits of the objection.

…

(22) The second ground upon which the applicants challenge the decision is that the schools adjudicator was in breach of his duty to act fairly in failing to give the applicants an opportunity to meet the complaint that the admission procedure was unfair.

…

(28) I remind myself that the challenge under this head is essentially a challenge on the basis that the applicants have been treated unfairly. In my judgment, they were not. They were told clearly the basis upon which it was considered by the objector that the admissions procedures were unfair. That remained the nature of the objection, and the schools adjudicator came to a conclusion on that precise issue. He gave to the applicants every opportunity in the letter that I have referred to, to put before him everything which they considered to be appropriate and important for the purposes of his determination.

(29) In those circumstances, I do not consider that there is any justification for the argument that they were not given a proper opportunity to present the case fully and adequately.

…

(32) The third ground of challenge is essentially that the schools adjudicator came to an irrational or perverse decision. It is said that he failed to take into consideration, for example, the matters which I have already referred to as to the background against which the decision by the applicants came to be made and that he gave no consideration to the applications' own views which, as I have already indicated when dealing with the first ground, I believe certainly that he was obliged to do.

…

(40) I can see nothing irrational in his approach. What was identified by the objector can properly be described as unfairness. That unfairness exists and cannot be gainsaid. So, in those circumstances, the only question could be whether there was anything in the material before the schools adjudicator which could enable him to come to the conclusion that there was a countervailing argument as to fairness which justified coming to the opposite conclusion. Namely that although apparently unfair, none the less it, in fact, was designed in order to secure what could properly be described as overall fairness.

(41) There seems to me to be nothing in the material before me that suggests that the schools adjudicator came to a conclusion which was perverse.

Wirral attempted to introduce the same arrangements the following year. Objections were raised on the basis that the process effectively enabled some parents to have an alternative first preference. The Chief Schools Adjudicator decided that Wirral's proposals were unfair to parents not applying to the grammar schools, and that parents should be required to express their preference for a secondary school before the selection process for grammar schools was completed.

This meant that parents who expressed a preference for a grammar school would be gambling on their child obtaining a place. Where the child did not obtain a place, the parents would be unlikely to be offered a place at their second preference school if it was a popular school which more parents had selected as their first preference than there were places available.

Wirral challenged the adjudicator's decision. The judge upheld the adjudicator's decision and considered that the adjudicator's revised system gave truer effect to real first preferences (*R (on the Application of Wirral Metropolitan Borough Council) v Chief Schools Adjudicator* [2001] ELR 574).

Objections relating to religious admission criteria must be referred to the Secretary of State (SSFA 1998, s 90(3)(b)). These objections are defined in the regulations.

Education (Objections to Admission Arrangements) Regulations 1999, SI 1999/125, reg 7

(1) The adjudicator shall refer an objection to the Secretary of State under section 90(3)(b) in a case where the objection is about any criterion for admission to a school relating to a person's religion, religious denomination or religious practice.

(2) This regulation does not apply to Wales.

Guidance is contained in the Code of Practice on School Admissions on the role of adjudicators. For example:

The Code of Practice on School Admissions (1999)

Adjudicators

4.9 Section 25 of the 1998 Act empowers the Secretary of State to appoint Adjudicators to consider school organisation and admissions issues where it has not been possible to reach local agreement. Adjudicators are independent of the Secretary of State. They will look afresh at the issues raised by objections referred to them, considering each objection on its individual merits and taking account of the reasons for disagreement at local level, in the light of the legislation and the guidance in this Code (see Annex A, paragraphs A.16 to A.22).

...

A.17 Admissions Forums should enable differences to be settled between admission authorities before admission arrangements are determined. Under the 1998 Act, particularly section 90, Adjudicators have the responsibility for determining disputes between local admission authorities over admission arrangements, including admissions policies and oversubscription criteria...

A.18 ... The Adjudicator must also have regard to the effect of any decision taken on the obligations on admission authorities under the Sex Discrimination Act 1975 and the Race Relations Act 1976.

• *Does the decision of the adjudicator (or the Secretary of State) have to be published? (See SSFA 1998, s 90(7) above.)*

Selective schools

Selection is a political 'hot potato'. In *Excellence in Schools* (Cm 3681, July 1997), the government agreed that the 163 existing grammar schools could continue in existence. Admission to such schools should be wholly based on high ability and aptitude. However, in November 1998 the government proposed allowing parents to vote against grammar schools continuing to exist in their area.

General restriction on selection 'by ability' and 'by aptitude'

Since September 1997 partial selection on the basis of academic ability has been ruled out, although existing arrangements continue to operate. Selection by banding is acceptable. The continued existence of CTCs, the introduction of city academies and the expansion of specialist schools may well amount to more selection via the back door. Separate provisions (see below) apply to grammar schools.

School Standards and Framework Act 1998, s 99(1), (3)

(1) No admission arrangements for a maintained school may make provision for selection by ability unless—
(a)   they make provision for a permitted form of such selection; or
(b)   the school is a grammar school (as defined by section 104(7)).

(3) No admission arrangements for a maintained school may make provision for selection by aptitude unless they make provision for a permitted form of such selection.

Selection by ability

However, selection by ability is permitted in three situations: where partial selection was used in 1997-98; where selection is on the basis of pupil banding; and for entry to a sixth form. Unlike selection 'by aptitude' it may not be introduced as part of new or revised admission arrangements.

School Standards and Framework Act 1998, s 99(2)

(2) The following are permitted forms of selection by ability—
(a)   any selection by ability authorised by section 100 (pre-existing arrangements);
(b)   any selection by ability authorised by section 101 (pupil banding); and
(c)   any selection by ability conducted in connection with the admission of pupils to the school for secondary education suitable to the requirements of pupils who are over compulsory school age.

School Standards and Framework Act 1998, s 100

(1) Where at the beginning of the 1997–98 school year the admission arrangements for a maintained school made provision for selection by ability or by aptitude (and they have at all times since that date continued to do so), the admission arrangements for the school may continue to make such provision so long as there is, as compared with the arrangements in force at the beginning of that year—
(a)   no increase in the proportion of selective admissions in any relevant age group, and
(b)   no significant change in the basis of selection.

Such arrangements are concerned with partial selection, for example where 10 per cent of the intake is selected on the basis of ability (see Education (Proportion of Selective Admissions) Regulations 1998, SI 1998/2229).

BANDING

School Standards and Framework Act 1998, s 101

(1) Subject to subsections (2) to (4), the admission arrangements for a maintained school may make provision for selection by ability to the extent that the arrangements are designed to secure—
(a)   that in any year the pupils admitted to the school in any relevant age group are representative of all levels of ability among applicants for admission to the school in that age group, and
(b)   that no level of ability is substantially over-represented or substantially under-represented.

(2) Subsection (1) does not apply if the arrangements have the effect that, where an applicant for admission has been allocated to a particular range of ability by means of some process of selection by reference to ability, some further such process is required or authorised to be carried out in relation to him for the purpose of determining whether or not he is to be admitted to the school.

...

(5) Where the admission arrangements for a school make both such provision for selection by ability as is mentioned in subsection (1) above and such provision for selection by aptitude as is mentioned in section 102(1), nothing in this section shall be taken to prevent those arrangements—
(a)   from authorising or requiring a process of selection to be carried out at any stage for the purpose of establishing that an applicant for admission has a relevant aptitude; or
(b)   from having the effect of giving priority to such an applicant with a relevant aptitude irrespective of his level of ability.

Schools are able to adopt admission arrangements which combine banding with selection by aptitude (see SSFA 1998, s 102(3) below). The Code of Practice sets out the government's policy on banding.

The Code of Practice on School Admissions (1999)

Banding

5.13 The government believes that banding arrangements can be compatible with the comprehensive principle, provided the arrangements are fair, objective and are not used as a means of admitting a disproportionate number of high ability children. Annex A, paragraphs A.64 to A.68 set out the legal requirements for banding. The Secretary of State does not intend to suggest how many ability bands an admission authority should have, or what percentage of children should be admitted in each band. That is for individual admission authorities to decide. But any banding arrangements should ensure that the intake represents the range of applicants' abilities.

5.14 It is up to the relevant admission authority to decide which tests should be used to determine the band in which to place an individual child. There are various ways of testing children for this purpose. A reading test was adopted by the former ILEA. Some admission authorities use a verbal or non-verbal reasoning test, some both. Some have developed their own tests. Whatever form of test is used to band, it must be objective. The admission authority must ensure that the tests and the arrangements for them do not discriminate against children on grounds of sex or race.

Banding is not uncommon. It can be used to ensure a mixed ability intake. For example, it formed part of the admission arrangements in *R v Governors of the Buss Foundation Camden School for Girls, ex p Lukasiewicz* [1991] COD 98 (see above) where the school sorted the applications for admission into three ability bands. The applicant lived beyond the distance from the school at which applicants in her band of ability were admitted, but within the distance at which applicants in band 3 lived.

Banding was used within the Inner London Education Authority (ILEA) until ILEA was abolished in April 1990, but by 1995 only 8 of the 12 London boroughs, which had taken over responsibility for education from ILEA, retained banding.

Research into the use of banding provides a valuable insight into its aims and effects.

H Pennell and A West 'Changing Schools: Secondary Schools' Admissions Policies in Inner London in 1995' LSE, Centre for Educational Research, Clare Market Papers No 9

2.4 The effectiveness of banding

Banding can only be considered to be effective if it succeeds in providing a balanced intake to secondary schools, with limited variation in the intake between schools. Variation in the intake between schools is felt to be particularly likely when there is a large voluntary sector when former grammar schools are perceived as such, when there are many single-sex schools and when there are surplus places in the system. The presence of grant-maintained schools and City Technology Colleges (CTCs) could be an additional factor.

The existence of surplus places in the ILEA was considered to be the prime reason why the percentage of children with VR Band 1 in each secondary school varied from 3.0 to 37.5 and the percentage in VR Band 3 from 46.3 to 6.3 (1986 secondary intakes). Banding across inner London was thus not as effective as it might have been.

2.5 The effects of an unbalanced intake

There is extensive work comparing selective systems (grammar plus secondary modern) with comprehensive systems, but most of the results are equivocal. A Scottish study is regarded as being one of the best and reveals more clear-cut results (McPherson & Willms, 1987). Its main findings were that:
- pupil attainment suffered in 'creamed' comprehensive schools;
- attainment improved as the severity of creaming declined;
- attainment improved the longer the school had been comprehensive all through;
- the gap between the attainment of middle-class and working-class pupils decreased after comprehensive reorganisation.

Research carried out in the ILEA's Research and Statistics Branch (ILEA, 1990) found that the proportion of VR Band 1 pupils appears to have a significant effect on the average 16-plus performance score — a higher proportion enhances the performance score over and above the enhancement expected as a result of the presence of the number of VR Band 1 students. The reverse of this is, of course, that the higher the proportion of VR Band 2 and 3 pupils, the lower the level of achievement. These findings suggest that a balanced intake leads to the most equitable results.

...

4 Discussion

Since the abolition of the ILEA, the system of 'banding' which aimed to ensure that secondary schools had an intake balanced in terms of ability, has successively been abandoned by the new inner London LEAs. The three Conservative-run councils dropped banding as soon as they took control of education in April 1990 and the policy was clearly stated in their Development Plans. By 1992, only half the inner London LEAs had retained banding and by 1995 it was only retained by four LEAs, all Labour controlled.

From the point of view of educational policy, it is perhaps not surprising that the Conservative-controlled LEAs (Kensington and Chelsea, Wandsworth and Westminster), have given up banding, seeing it in some cases as incompatible with the concept of parental choice. What is more interesting is that a majority of Labour-controlled LEAs (Camden, Islington, Hammersmith and Fulham, Lambeth and Southwark) have, for other reasons also decided not to use banding.

In geographical terms, the boroughs that are continuing to band are in adjoining areas of the north and east of London and in the south-east. Policy changes in relation to secondary schools admissions thus seem to be affected by the procedures adopted by neighbouring boroughs; where there is significant movement of pupils across borough boundaries at the secondary level, administrative factors may well play a part in determining policy changes in relation to the system of banding. The existence of a large number of schools that are voluntary-aided or grant-maintained, which are responsible for their own admissions, also appears to be an important factor in these decisions.

It appears that the decision to end banding has led some voluntary-aided and grant-maintained schools to introduce their own school-based banding systems. A minority of grant-maintained schools have also begun to select part of their intake specifically on the basis of pupils' ability.

Whilst some of the voluntary-aided schools that have introduced their own form of banding still aim to recruit in the same proportions as the ILEA banding procedure (i e 25% most able, 50% average, 25% below average), others aim to recruit more pupils from the able and average groups (e g 40%, 40%, 20%). As well as these differences, the methods used to place pupils into different bands also differ from school to school and in particular in the different types of tests used.

There are undoubtedly questions that these new admissions criteria raise for issues related to equity. Those pupils who are less able will inevitably have a reduced choice and this is a cause for concern. Moreover, the continued use of interviews as part of the transfer process means that there is scope in some voluntary-aided schools, some grant-maintained schools and all CTCs for pupils to be selected covertly even where there is a commitment to obtaining a balanced intake. In these cases there remains the likelihood of more motivated pupils from advantaged family backgrounds being offered places at the expense of those who are from a more deprived background and/or where learning is not valued so highly. (For a more detailed discussion of these issues, see West and Pennell, 1995.)

Selection 'by aptitude for particular subjects'

Although selection by 'ability' is not normally permissible, selection on the basis of 'aptitude' is permitted either under pre-existing arrangements or in the form permitted by s 102 of the SSFA 1998.

School Standards and Framework Act 1998, s 99(4), (5)

(4) The following are permitted forms of selection by aptitude—
(a) any selection by aptitude authorised by section 100 (pre-existing arrangements); and
(b) any selection by aptitude authorised by section 102 (aptitude for particular subjects).

(5) For the purposes of this Chapter—
(a) a school's admission arrangements make provision for selection by ability or by aptitude if they make provision for all or any of the pupils who are to be admitted to the school in any relevant age group to be so admitted by reference to ability or to aptitude (as the case may be);
(b) 'ability' means either general ability or ability in any particular subject or subjects;
(c) 'admission arrangements' has the meaning given by section 88(2); and
(d) 'maintained school' means a community, foundation or voluntary school.

School Standards and Framework Act 1998, s 102

(1) Subject to subsection (2), the admission arrangements for a maintained school may make provision for the selection of pupils for admission to the school by reference to their aptitude for one or more prescribed subjects where—
(a) the admission authority for the school are satisfied that the school has a specialism in the subject or subjects in question; and
(b) the proportion of selective admissions in any relevant age group does not exceed 10 per cent.

(2) Subsection (1) does not apply if the admission arrangements make provision for any test to be carried out in relation to an applicant for admission which is either a test of ability or one designed to elicit any aptitude of his other than for the subject or subjects in question.

(3) Where, however, the admission arrangements for a school make both such provision for selection by aptitude as is mentioned in subsection (1) and such provision for selection

by ability as is mentioned in section 101(1), the reference in subsection (2) above to a test of ability does not include any such test for which provision may be made under that section.

(4) In this section 'the proportion of selective admissions', in relation to a relevant age group, means the proportion of the total number of pupils admitted to the school in that age group (determined in the prescribed manner) which is represented by the number of pupils so admitted by reference to aptitude for the subject or subjects in question.

(5) In this section 'test' includes assessment and examination.

- *Can any maintained school introduce selection criteria based on aptitude?*

- *What percentage of pupils may be selected on the basis of aptitude?*

- *Could a school select that percentage for different subjects or is that the maximum total percentage permitted?*

- *What is the difference between 'ability' and 'aptitude'?*

The introduction, variation or abandonment of partial selection on the basis of aptitude (SSFA 1998, s 103) may result in objections being referred to the adjudicator (see above).

Code of Practice on School Admissions (1999)

4.12 The Adjudicator will be able to determine that an admission authority seeking to continue to make provision for partial selection should cease to do so, even where that selection was introduced following the approval of statutory proposals under the previous legislation. The 1998 Act prevents new selection by ability being introduced; the Adjudicator can make a determination on an objection by an admission authority where another admission authority is seeking to give priority to some pupils on the basis of aptitude, for example as to whether the school does have a specialism in that particular subject or whether the proposed test assesses ability rather than aptitude.

Grammar schools

Grammar schools continue to exist in a number of LEAs, for example Kent, and Buckinghamshire.

School Standards and Framework Act 1998, s 104

(1) Where the Secretary of State is satisfied that a maintained school had selective admission arrangements at the beginning of the 1997–98 school year, he may by order designate the school as a grammar school for the purposes of this Chapter.

(2) A school has selective admission arrangements for the purposes of this Chapter if its admission arrangements make provision for all (or substantially all) of its pupils to be selected by reference to general ability, with a view to admitting only pupils with high ability.

...

BALLOTS

There is provision in the legislation for parents who object to grammar schools to request that a ballot of parents is held to decide whether the selective admission arrangements should be retained. The legislation sets out in detail which parents are entitled to vote in a ballot (s 106 of the SSFA 1998). The provisions have proved so complex that a ballot has only been held in one area (Ripon), and the parents voted in favour of keeping selection.

School Standards and Framework Act 1998, s 105

The Secretary of State may by regulations make provision for ballots of parents to be held, at their request, for determining whether the grammar schools to which such ballots relate should retain selective admission arrangements.

A ballot will only be held if at least 20 per cent of eligible parents request such a ballot (s 106(3) of the SSFA 1998). Eligible parents include parents of pupils attending schools within the relevant area, as well as parents of pupils resident in and attending independent schools in that area (s 106(1) of the SSFA 1998, Education (Grammar School Ballots) Regulations 1998, SI 1998/2876). Whether parents of pupils already attending one of the grammar schools should be entitled to vote was the issue in the following case.

R v Secretary of State for Education and Employment, ex p RCO [2000] ELR 307

Scott Baker J: The applicant is a year 7 pupil at St Michael's Catholic Grammar School in the London Borough of Barnet. This is a voluntary aided selective school controlled by a foundation board and ultimately by the Roman Catholic Diocese with the responsibility for Barnet. The school has existed for many years as a grammar school. There are two other grammar schools within the London Borough of Barnet, namely the Henrietta Barnet School and Queen Elizabeth Boys' School.

By s 104 of the School Standards and Framework Act 1998 the Secretary of State for Education and Employment may, by order, designate a maintained school such as St Michael's, which had selective admission arrangements at the beginning of the 1997/98 school year, as a grammar school. Regulations have been made under the 1998 Act to that effect, namely the Education (Grammar School Designation) Order 1998. Where a grammar school has been so designated, the Secretary of State may make regulations providing for a ballot of parents to be held at their request to decide whether the school or schools to which the ballot relates should retain selective admission arrangements. Such regulations have been made.

For balloting purposes schools fall into one of three categories: (1) all grammar schools within a relevant area; (2) a group of grammar schools; and (3) a stand-alone grammar school.

St Michael's comes into the second category, a group of grammar schools, along with the Queen Elizabeth School and the Henrietta Barnet School. If enough parents petition a specified body or organisation (the Electoral Reform Society) for a ballot, a ballot must then be held. The complaint in this case is that the regulations are so drawn that only parents of feeder schools to these three grammar schools can participate in the ballot. A parent of a child who is already a pupil at the school does not qualify. This, argues Mr Engelman, is unjust. It may result in the abolition of selective admission arrangements when such a course is quite contrary to the wishes of all, or most, of the parents of the current pupils in the school.

The illogicality and injustice, says Mr Engelman, is emphasised when one sees that were St Michael's in category (1) — that is all grammar schools within a relevant area — then the parents of current pupils would be able to take part in the ballot.

...

Mr Singh says that it is a logical distinction to categorise in Sch 1 all those schools falling within areas of the country that as a matter of generality do offer selective arrangements. Since that is the overall policy of the area concerned, he says that it is perfectly logical and that it makes sense to bring all the parents within the ambit and under the umbrella of the provisions of the balloting arrangements so that they are entitled to have a vote — not only the parents of those children who are in feeder schools who will in the foreseeable future be going to the school in question, but also the parents of those children who are already there. This is because any change would effectively be a change of policy right across the board as opposed to a change of policy with regard to an individual school or a small group of schools.

Looking at the position from the angle of Schs 2 and 3, one can see the logic behind saying that there can be a distinction between the parents of children who will be affected by going into the school and parents of children who are already there, because the age group of the children who are already there has been subject to the selection process and they will not be so directly affected as the children who may come in from the feeder schools in the future.

...

Mr Engleman says that it does not wholly depend upon the primary legislation because the detail of the subsidiary legislation goes further and when one examines it one can categorise as irrational the decision to exclude from the right to vote the parents of children who are already in the school. I cannot accept that submission. It seems to me that the decision to create legislation to achieve that is entirely within the bounds of what is permissible. One might take one view about it, one might take another. But that is a matter for the legislator's decision and not a matter on which, in my judgment, the courts should interfere.

Local education authorities and governing bodies of LEA maintained schools are not permitted to publish material which is designed to influence the outcome of the ballot. They are, however, permitted to provide factual information together with a fair and reasonable assessment of the consequences were the ballot to result in the school no longer being wholly selective (s 107 of the SSFA 1998).

A simple majority of votes cast in the ballot results in the grammar school ceasing to have selective admission arrangements (s 108 of the SSFA 1998).

Admissions information

The School Standards and Framework Act 1998 sets out the general obligations imposed on LEAs, the governing bodies of foundation or voluntary aided schools, and the governing bodies of LEA maintained schools to publish information on school admissions. The information should include the admission number normally admitted, and the policy followed in deciding admissions (see admissions criteria below).

School Standards and Framework Act 1998, s 92

(1) A local education authority shall, for each school year, publish the prescribed information about—
(a) the admission arrangements for each of the following, namely—
(i) the maintained schools in their area, and
(ii) if regulations so provide, such maintained schools outside their area as may be determined by or in accordance with the regulations;
(b) the authority's arrangements for the provision of education at schools maintained by another local education authority or not maintained by a local education authority;
(c) the arrangements made by the authority under sections 86(1) (parental preferences) and 94(1) (admission appeals); and
(d) such other matters of interest to parents of pupils seeking admission to schools within paragraph (a) or (b) above as may be prescribed.

(2) The governing body of a foundation or voluntary aided school shall, for each school year, publish the prescribed information about—
(a) the admission arrangements for the school;
(b) the arrangements made by the governing body under section 94(2) (admission appeals); and
(c) such other matters of interest to parents of pupils seeking admission to the school as may be prescribed.

(3) The governing body of a school maintained by a local education authority—
(a) shall publish such information as respects that school as may be required by regulations; and
(b) may publish such other information with respect to the school as they think fit.

(4) For the purposes of subsection (3) information about the continuing education of pupils leaving a school, or the employment or training taken up by such pupils on leaving, is to be treated as information about the school.

(5) A local education authority may, with the agreement of the governing body of any school maintained by the authority, publish on behalf of the governing body the information referred to in subsection (2) or (3).

....

Note that under subsection (5) the LEA may publish information on behalf of one or more of the schools in its area. For example, the admissions information for all community and voluntary controlled secondary schools may be contained in a single secondary schools prospectus.

Detailed provisions are contained in regulations, and guidance on the content of the information is set out in the Code of Practice.

Code of Practice on School Admissions (1999)

3.6 Experience suggests that published admissions information is most helpful where it:
- offers clear guidance in plain English and in commonly-used community languages to steer parents through the procedure
- sets out clearly the timescale for each stage of the admissions process, particularly the deadline for receipt of applications
- explains briefly each school's admission policy and oversubscription criteria and how they are applied
- gives the number of applicants who were successful in previous years and the criteria under which they were accepted
- explains what is expected from parents, and what the parent can expect from the school and the LEA, at each stage
- makes clear when parents will know whether or not their applications have been successful, and how to take up their statutory right of appeal
- gives a name and details of a contact point for further information.

3.7 Published admission arrangements must include the oversubscription criteria which will be used to allocate places if there turn out to be more applicants than places available at a particular school. Paragraphs 5.1 onwards give guidance on oversubscription criteria. The criteria chosen may in turn give rise to a need to publish more information to help parental choice. For instance, where catchment areas are used, admission authorities should consider whether a map of the areas should be made available to parents on request or, if practical, included in the admissions information. Where priority is given by admission authorities to children transferring from named feeder primary schools, details should be given. And, in general, LEAs should consider publishing information on whether and to what extent schools in their area have been oversubscribed in the past (for example in the previous year), commenting on whether that is likely to be a good guide for the future.

3.8 The annual school performance tables help inform parents over admissions decisions. The published reports of recent school inspections will also be relevant. In the case of a school which is found by inspection to be in need of special measures or seriously weak, the LEA will want to provide parents with additional information about the urgent steps which are being taken to ensure pupils are not disadvantaged. Parents choosing a school need to be assured that all causes for concern will be tackled and removed very quickly, as required by new national policies.

- *Contact a local school or LEA and obtain a copy of their current admissions information. Does the information contain the details required by this section and recommended in the guidance?*

In *R v Stockton on Tees Borough Council, ex p W* [2000] ELR 93 parents alleged that the LEA failed to publish the admission criteria in sufficient detail; in particular that parents should have been provided with a map of the admission zone for the school. The parents applied for permission to apply for judicial review of decisions of the LEA and the appeal committee, both of which declined to offer places at the school chosen by the six applicants.

R v Stockton on Tees Borough Council, ex p W [2000] ELR 93

Stuart-Smith LJ: The complaint in this case is that, although it was clear that there were admission zones, there was not sent out with the criteria a map, so the parents could not see, if they wanted to, whether they were in a particular zone. What happened is that in the October of the previous year the parents are sent a letter which tells them in which admission zone they are and in the case of these parents they were told that they were not in the admission zone of the school but of BC School.·

So the first and the principal ground of complaint is that the council did not comply with the statutory obligation because they did not send a map of the area.

…

There is no doubt here that the local education authority in the admissions information indicated that further information could be obtained on request from the council, so they resolved the matter in that way. They did not send a map out with each of these documents. They left it to the people concerned, if they were in any doubt as to what admission zone they were in, to make that inquiry.

For my part I can see nothing wrong with that and I would decline to hold that that was a breach of the statutory duty.

…

The second ground relates to the question of a child moving into the area. The complaint is that the local education authority did not publish what is alleged to be their policy: that, if after the admission date referred to somebody moves into the area, the local authority will admit to the school in question a child who lives in the relevant admission zone.

…

The admissions policy does refer to the question of people moving but is silent, it is true, about what the position would be if somebody moves into the area after the relevant date. But it seems to me that it is a matter which the local authority have to deal with on an ad hoc basis. I do not read Miss Donnelly's statement as being a guarantee that, if somebody moves into the are at a date after the admission date has passed, that person will necessarily be granted a place in that school; but rather that the local authority will do their best in a sensible way to accommodate a child who has moved into the area after the relevant date in the nearest and most appropriate school.

I can see nothing wrong with having approached the matter in that way and, in my judgment, again that is not a breach of the statutory obligation.

Buxton LJ: It seems to me wholly impossible to suggest that Parliament has intended that each such parent should receive a copy of the map: which must be the implication of the argument pressed upon us that the map was a necessary part of the published information.

What map should be published in that connection would be another serious problem. My Lord has referred to the, understandably, formidable nature of the map that we were shown. It would not be possible for the local authority simply to distribute the catchment area map for one particular school, because it would not be possible to say with certainty what schools which parents were interested in. In my judgment, the local authority in this case more than fully fulfilled its requirements by the information that it did publish.

Number of places

The *standard number* is the minimum number of pupils which can be admitted by a community or voluntary school for a particular year group. This can be increased by the admissions authority after consultation between the LEA and the governing body. The new number is known as the *admission number*. This number is important for parents, because where, for example, a community school does not have that number of pupils in the year group, and a parent expresses a preference for a place in that year group for their child, the LEA must offer the child a place at the school (see above). However, where that number is met or exceeded the LEA is unlikely to offer the child a place on the ground that the year group is full.

There are no legislative minimum or maximum numbers for a class or a year group, except for infant classes (reception, Year 1, and Year 2) where the number of pupils in the class should not exceed 30 (see below).

The fixing of admission numbers is regulated by the School Standards and Framework Act 1998, s 93 and Sch 23.

School Standards and Framework Act 1998, s 93

(1) The admission authority for a maintained school shall not fix as the admission number for any relevant age group and any school year a number which is less than the relevant standard number.

(2) Subject to section 1(6) (duty of local education authority and governing body to comply with limit on infant class sizes), the admission authority may fix as the admission number for any relevant age group and any school year a number which exceeds the relevant standard number.

(3) Schedule 23 (determination, variation and review of standard numbers) shall have effect.

...

Variations in the standard number may be proposed by the governing body or the LEA. In certain circumstances the proposal should be considered by the School Organisation Committee, and the adjudicator. The Education Bill 2001/02 removes the requirement for a school to have a standard number.

Infant class size

In relation to infant classes, the LEA and the governing body are under a duty to comply with the statutory requirement that there should not be more than 30 children in these classes (reception, Year 1, and Year 2). Although s 1(6) of the SSFA 1998 only applied to admission after September 2001, regulations provided that the limit applied to admissions to:
- reception classes in September 1999 onwards
- Year 1 classes in September 2000 onwards, and
- Year 2 classes in September 2001 onwards.

The Code of Practice on School Admissions (1999), para 3.17 states that the reason for the introduction of maximum class sizes in infant classes is that:

'The government has pledged to reduce infant class sizes, in support of its agenda of raising standards.'

School Standards and Framework Act 1998, s 1

(1) The Secretary of State shall by regulations—
(a)   impose a limit on class sizes for infant classes at maintained schools; and
(b)   specify the school years in relation to which any such limit is to have effect.

(2) Any limit imposed under this section shall specify the maximum number of pupils that a class to which the limit applies may contain while an ordinary teaching session is conducted by a single qualified teacher.

(3) Subject to subsections (4) and (5), regulations under this section shall be so framed that—
(a)   the maximum number specified in pursuance of subsection (2) is 30, and
(b)   that limit has effect in relation to the 2001–02 school year and any subsequent year.

...

(5) The Secretary of State may by order amend subsection (3)—
(a)   by substituting for '30' such other number as is specified in the order; or
(b)   by substituting for the reference to the 2001–02 school year a reference to such other school year as is so specified.

(6) Where any limit imposed under this section applies to an infant class at a maintained school, the local education authority and the governing body shall exercise their functions with a view to securing that that limit is complied with in relation to that class.

The limit is given effect by the following regulations, which also permit the admission authority to exceed the infant class size limit in certain circumstances.

Education (Infant Class Sizes) (England) Regulations 1998, SI 1998/1973

3   Limit on infant class sizes

(1) This regulation has effect for limiting class sizes for infant classes at schools in England for the purposes of section 1 of the 1998 Act.

(2) No infant class at such a school shall contain more than 30 pupils while an ordinary teaching session is conducted by a single qualified teacher.

(3) Where an ordinary teaching session in the case of any such class is conducted by more than one qualified teacher, paragraph (2) shall be taken to prohibit the class from containing more than 30 pupils for every one of those teachers.

(4) Where an infant class at such a school contains any excepted pupil (as defined by regulation 4), paragraph (2) or (3) shall apply as if he were not included in the class.

(5) Any limit imposed by this regulation shall apply in relation to the 2001–2002 school year and any subsequent year.

(6) References in the 1998 Act to any limit imposed under section 1 of that Act shall, in relation to schools in England, be construed in accordance with this regulation.

4 Excepted pupils

(1) For the purposes of regulation 3, a child to whom any of paragraphs 2 to 7 of the Schedule applies is an excepted pupil in relation to an infant class at a school unless suitable education could be provided for him in another infant class at that school without relevant measures having to be taken.

(2) In paragraph (1) 'relevant measures' means measures which would—
(a) be required to be taken to ensure compliance with the duty imposed by section 1(6) of the 1998 Act, and
(b) prejudice the provision of efficient education or the efficient use of resources.

SCHEDULE
EXCEPTED PUPILS

Regulation 4

1 In this Schedule—

'child' means a child who is a pupil in any infant class;

'the school' means the school of which that class forms part; and

'governing body' means the governing body of that school.

2 This paragraph applies at any time during the admission school year to any child with a statement admitted to the school by virtue of section 324(5)(b) of the 1996 Act outside a normal admission round.

3 This paragraph applies at any time during the admission school year to a child admitted to the school outside a normal admission round who
(a) was initially refused admission to the school owing to a failure properly to implement the school's admission arrangements; but
(b) was subsequently offered a place there by virtue of a determination made by the relevant person that there had been such a failure in relation to the child.

4 This paragraph applies at any time during the admission school year to a child admitted to the school outside a normal admission round by virtue of a determination of an appeal panel in accordance with paragraph 12 of Schedule 24 to the 1998 Act.

5(1) This paragraph applies at any time during the admission school year to a child admitted to the school outside a normal admission round—
(a) in relation to whom that school is the only school (apart from any school to which he has been refused admission or from which he has been permanently excluded) which—
    (i) is within a reasonable distance from his home, and
    (ii) provides suitable education; and
(b) who did not, at the relevant time, ordinarily reside at a place which was within a reasonable distance from that school.

(2) In sub-paragraph (1)(b) 'the relevant time'—
(a) in relation to a child to whom regulation 2(3) applies, means the time when the majority of pupils in the age group in which he falls were admitted to the school; and
(b) in relation to a child to whom regulation 2(4) applies, means the time referred to in subparagraph (c) of that paragraph.

6 This paragraph applies to a child—

(a)   who is a registered pupil at a special school, and

(b)   who, by arrangement with another school which is not a special school, receives part of his education at the other school,

at any time when he is in an infant class at the other school.

7(1) In this paragraph, 'designated pupil' means a pupil with special educational needs who—

(a)   is a registered pupil at a school which is not a special school; and

(b)   is normally educated in a unit which—

    (i)   forms part of that school, and

    (ii) is specially organised to provide education for pupils with special educational needs.

(2) This paragraph applies to a child who is a designated pupil at any time when he is in an infant class which does not form part of the unit referred to in sub-paragraph (1)(b).

(3) Where this paragraph applies to a child, regulation 4(1) shall have effect in relation to that child as if after 'in another infant class at that school' there were inserted '(other than a class which comprises or forms part of a unit referred to in paragraph 7(1)(b) of the Schedule)'.

8 Paragraphs 3 to 5 do not apply to a child with a statement.

• *Identify the six circumstances where the admission authority is permitted by regulation 4 and the Schedule to exceed the infant class size limit by admitting an 'excepted pupil'.*

Note that these provisions only apply where the infant classes in other schools have 30 or more pupils (reg 4), and that three of the six circumstances apply only to children with special educational needs.

• *Mr and Mrs Smith move from Essex to the London Borough of Fleet in December. They apply for a place in the reception class of the nearby community primary school for their daughter to start in January. The class has 30 pupils who started school at the beginning of the autumn term. Is their daughter an 'excepted pupil' who can be offered a place?*

Admissions criteria

Admissions criteria are the principles by which the admissions authority, that is the LEA or the governing body, allocates the places available at each school to children who have applied for a place at that school. There are two main entry points to school. First, with the start of compulsory schooling at primary school, and second, on the transfer to secondary school. Where a school is popular with parents and there are more applications than places the criteria are used to determine which children will be offered a place. Some admissions criteria lack clarity (see for example *R v South Gloucestershire Education Appeals Committee, ex p Bryant* [2001] ELR 53, CA, where the criterion of 'nearest to/furthest from' appears to have caused confusion to both the parent and the appeals committee).

Different schools may have different admissions criteria and this often leads to confusion among parents. For example, community schools will normally give preference to siblings and to children living close to the school, whereas schools with a religious character will give preference to children who regularly worship at a specified local church, and selective schools will give preference to children who pass an entrance test.

The variety of admissions criteria can result in some children not satisfying the admissions criteria for any of their local schools. The legality of particular admissions criteria has been challenged in a number of cases, but rarely successfully. The Code of Practice gives guidance on what the DfEE considered to be acceptable admission criteria.

Code of Practice on School Admissions (1999)

Oversubscription and Oversubscription Criteria

5.1 Where more parents have expressed a preference for a particular school in a particular year than it has places in that year, the admission authority must apply the oversubscription criteria in its published admission policy in deciding which parents' preferences it should meet.

5.2 Admission authorities have a fairly wide discretion to determine their own oversubscription criteria provided these criteria are objective, clear, fair, compatible with admissions and equal opportunities legislation, and have been subject to the consultation the 1998 Act requires (see Chapter 4). Admission authorities should consider how best to monitor school admission applications, refusals of places and admission appeals to ensure that the admission process is fair and offers equal opportunities to all pupils.

5.3 Commonly used and acceptable criteria include sibling links, distance from the school, ease of access by public transport, medical or social grounds, catchment areas and transfer from named feeder primary schools, as well as parents' ranking of preference (see paragraph 3.14). Admission authorities should make clear the order of priority in which the criteria will be applied, and how any tie-break decisions will be made. Admission authorities should not give priority to parents based on the date order in which applications were received before the deadline...

5.7 Bearing in mind the provisions of the Sex Discrimination Act 1975 and the Race Relations Act 1976, admission authorities should carefully consider the possible impact, direct or indirect, on equal opportunities of their proposed oversubscription criteria. For example, criteria which gave preference to children whose parents had attended the school or followed particular occupations could disproportionately disadvantage ethnic minority, Traveller or refugee families who have more recently moved into the area. In such cases, the criteria could be unlawful unless objectively justified. And it would not generally be good practice for admission authorities to set or seek to apply oversubscription criteria which had the effect of disadvantaging certain social groups in the local community. Such criteria might legitimately be challenged in Admissions Forums, or referred to the Adjudicator for a determination of whether they served the interests of all local children. Examples would be explicit or implicit discrimination on the basis of parental occupation, employment, income range, standard of living or home facilities.

5.8 Where a school is named in a statement of special educational needs, the admission authority has a duty to admit the child to the school. An admission authority should determine oversubscription criteria, and apply them, as fairly to children with special educational needs but no statement or a disability as to other applicants.

Distance between home and school

Admission authorities can give priority to children living closer to the school. However, it is important to note that an LEA cannot discriminate against children living in a different LEA by giving priority to children who live in its area. The right of a parent to express a preference (s 86(1) of the SSFA 1998; see below), and the obligation placed on the admission authority to comply with that preference (s 86(2) of the SSFA 1998) apply whether or not the parent lives within the LEA area.

School Standards and Framework Act 1998, s 86(8)

The duty imposed by subsection (2) in relation to a preference expressed in accordance with arrangements made under subsection (1) shall apply also in relation to—
(a)   any application for the admission to a maintained school of a child who is not in the area of the authority maintaining the school, and
(b)   ...

and references in subsection (3) to a preference and a preferred school shall be construed accordingly.

This statutory provision can make it difficult for LEAs to plan for future demand for school places because they have to respond to demand from outside their own area. In addition parents living in the LEA feel aggrieved when their child does not obtain a place in their local LEA school because the school is popular and close to the LEA boundary and children living in the adjacent LEA who live closer to the school have priority over their child. Parents often feel, perhaps understandably, that because they pay their council tax to the local authority their child should have priority over children living in neighbouring authorities.

Section 86(8)(a) of the SSFA 1998 in effect re-enacts s 6(5) of the Education Act 1980 which was the subject of the *Greenwich* decision, which is famous, if not notorious, in education law.

R v Greenwich London Borough Council, ex p Governors of John Ball Primary School (1989) 88 LGR 589

Lloyd LJ: For many years there has been what Parker LJ called 'a two-way traffic' between the boroughs. Children living near the border would attend a primary school in one borough and a secondary school in the other, depending on which was nearest. This worked well under ILEA. If a particualr school was overscribed, preference would be given to children with a brother or sister at the school in question. Thereafter preference would be given to children within the shortest walking distance, irrespective of the borough in which they happened to live. In this way cross-border links developed between primary schools in one borough and secondary schools in the other. I take one example. For many years, a high proportion of children from John Ball primary school in Lewisham have been accustomed to go on to Thomas Tallis secondary school, which is just over the border in Greenwich. That suited both schools and it suited the parents. The nearest secondary school in Lewisham is much further away, a walking distance of between two and three miles.

The effect of the Education Reform Act 1988 is that the Inner London councils will each become the local education authority for their areas. They have each established Shadow Education Committees to prepare for the transfer of functions. They were each required to prepare and publish a development plan, setting out the manner in which they proposed to discharge their functions.

At first it seemed that there would be little if any change, at any rate in the short run. Paragraph 4.15 of the development plan prepared and published by Greenwich stated:

Admissions to County Secondary Schools

Greenwich will continue with the existing transfer arrangements for admissions to secondary schools in September 1990. A statement to this effect will be included in the published arrangements (October 1989) for admissions to secondary schools.

That was in February 1989. Thereafter Greenwich council carried out a consultation exercise. As a result the policy for admissions to Greenwich secondary schools changed radically. Instead of the old arrangements it was decided to give Greenwich residents priority over residents of all other areas, including Lewisham, unless there happened to be a current sibling connection. That decision was taken by the Shadow Education Committee of Greenwich on 27 July 1989. It is that decision which is now the subject of this application for judicial review.

...

I agree that the purpose of section 6 is to impose a duty, subject to the exceptions set out in section 6(3), and not to lay down a policy. Policy lies within the discretion of the local education authorities. But the discretion must be exercised consistently with and so as not to thwart the provisions of section 6(5). I cannot agree that section 6(5) is confined to cases where there is no oversubscription. I do not accept that its sole purpose is to ensure that places are filled which would otherwise go a-begging, or to prevent what in argument came to be called 'a dog-in-the-manger attitude' on the part of local education authorities. Its purpose is much wider. It is to ensure that all children from within or without the area rank pari passu, that they all come to the starting gate at the same time, if I may adopt the sporting metaphor coined by Farquharson LJ in the course of argument. I can give no other meaning to the language of section 6(2) and section 6(5), when read together. Nor would any other construction make much sense in the context of London education, where schools may lie on or very close to the border between two boroughs.

...

It is said that to allow an influx of children from Lewisham to Greenwich would or might make it impossible for Greenwich to comply with their duty under section 7 of the Act of 1944, namely, to secure that efficient education is available to meet the needs of the population of their area. Greenwich might, it is said, have fulfilled their duty under section 8 of the Act to secure that sufficient schools are available in their area. But if, for example, Thomas Tallis were then filled entirely by children from Lewisham, Greenwich children who would otherwise have gone to Thomas Tallis would necessarily be displaced. There might be nowhere else for them to go within the Greenwich area. Greenwich would have fulfilled their duty under section 8, but would be in breach of their duty under section 7. That could not, it is said, be right. I see here the seeds of a theoretical difficulty which may not have been fully resolved in the legislation as it stands. But I see little (if any) practical difficulty. In the first place the application of the proximity rule will prevent any large scale influx of children from one borough to another. Secondly, the traffic is unlikely to be all one way. What Greenwich lose on the swings they will gain on the roundabouts. Thirdly, we have not heard of any practical difficulties arising out of Greenwich children being displaced under the old arrangements, that is to say, prior to the announcement of the new policy. So far as we know, the old policy worked reasonably satisfactorily under the aegis of the ILEA. I see no reason why the same or similar policy should not continue to work well in the future. So the practical difficulties of complying with section 6(5) may have been exaggerated. As for the theoretical difficulties. I accept of course that section 6(5) must be read as one with sections 7 and 8 of the Act of 1944. But I see no reason to cut down or qualify in any way the perfectly clear statutory provision to be found in section 6(5).

...

It may well have been understandable for Greenwich to give their own residents priority over all others in Greenwich schools. But it conflicts with the clear provision of sections 6(2) and 6(5) read together. It is on that short ground that I would dismiss this appeal.

Despite criticism the government did not amend the principle now enshrined in s 86(8) of the SSFA 1998 and the *Greenwich* decision. Its approach was set out in the Technical Consultation Paper *Framework for the Organisation of Schools*, and the Code of Practice on School Admissions (1999).

Framework for the Organisation of Schools — Technical Consultation Paper (1997)

School Admissions

5. We do not propose to reverse the 'Greenwich judgment', which prohibited LEAs and schools from giving preference to children living in the LEA area over children from elsewhere. But we recognise the importance of admission authorities working more closely together with those in neighbouring LEA areas so that sensible planning can take place. We will encourage the proposed new forums described below to address such issues.

Code of Practice on School Admissions (1999)

5.4 Often parents live in one LEA but find they are close to schools in a neighbouring authority. Parents in inner cities, particularly London, have long chosen schools across borough boundaries, not least under the former Inner London Education Authority (ILEA). The 1989 Greenwich judgment established that LEA maintained schools may not give priority to children simply because of the fact that they live in the authority's administrative area. Applications for the authority's schools by parents living outside the LEA area must be considered equally. The Greenwich judgment was a sensible recognition of these patterns, prohibiting LEAs from giving priority to children solely on account of the fact that they live in the authority's administrative area.

- *To what extent do admissions forums (see above) address the issue raised in the Greenwich case?*

Catchment areas

Where a school has a catchment area it should not normally correspond with borough boundaries. The case of *R v Wiltshire County Council, ex p Razazan* [1997] ELR 370, CA, illustrates how an LEA may lawfully operate a catchment area which in effect excludes some children living in another LEA. The case is concerned with s 6(1), (2), (3) and (5) of the Education Act 1980. The equivalent provisions are now found in s 86(2), (3), (8) of the SSFA 1998.

R v Wiltshire County Council, ex p Razazan [1997] ELR 370

Thorpe LJ: Tom Razazan lives with his parents at Farleigh Hungerford, which is just beyond the Wiltshire county boundary into Somerset. His parents wanted him to start his secondary education in Wiltshire at St Lawrence School, Bradford on Avon, in September 1995. However in February 1995 the local education authority (LEA) rejected their application for a place at St Lawrence on the ground that the school was oversubscribed and that all available places had been allocated elsewhere in accordance with the LEA's admissions policy, a copy of which had been sent to them in August 1994. The parents then pursued their right of appeal under s 8 of the Education Act 1980, but to no avail.

Accordingly they challenged the lawfulness of the LEA's admission policy by an application for judicial review.

...

I will set out the material parts [of Wiltshire's policy] in full ...

Where any particular county or controlled school is oversubscribed the admission policies of all other maintained schools in the surrounding area are considered to determine whether or not there are any children who have no priority of admission to any of the other schools. Children who have no priority of a place at another school are then given first consideration for the oversubscribed school. The effect of this is that, if a school is oversubscribed, children who live in its designated area will be given priority over children from outside the area who have access to another school. Remaining places are allocated to applicants who match the following criteria in the order stated.

The 'following criteria' are medical condition, older sibling attending, stated family or social reasons, and stated educational reasons.

The parents' fundamental submission below was that their preference had been overridden by a policy that gives priority to children living within the school's designated area over children living outside that area.

...

Wiltshire had a designated area policy which treated alike those resident and those non-resident within the county. Within the county those living within the vicinity of a grant-maintained as opposed to a maintained school were within a catchment area that was not designated and therefore had no guaranteed place. Therefore in applying for a place at a maintained school of their choice within the county they had first priority. An application from a child beyond the county boundary without a guaranteed place would have the same priority. Equally, children were treated as category B applications if they had a guaranteed place at another school, whether that school was within or without the county. Those resident in Westwood, for instance, although resident within the county and much closer to St Lawrence, were no better off than Farleigh Hungerford residents.

...
So in the present case it is abundantly clear to me that Wiltshire have adopted reasonable criteria by which to determine those applications to an oversubscribed school that will be accepted and those which will be rejected. Mr Engelman's submission that the criteria are not only unreasonable but unlawful for breach of the duty contained in s 6(5)(a) plainly fails. An analysis of the facts shows that there is no discrimination against those resident outside the county. The statement at the head of the policy criteria, namely 'applications for places at county and controlled schools for pupils living outside the county are treated as if children are resident in Wiltshire' is not specious but is justified on an appreciation of the policy as a whole.

The DfEE provided the following guidance on the use of catchment areas.

Code of Practice on School Admissions (1999)

5.5 The Rotherham judgment [1998] ... confirmed that there is nothing unlawful in the principle of admission authorities operating catchment areas as part of oversubscription criteria and thereby giving priority to some local children. In view of an admission authority's duty in allocating places to give priority to parents who have expressed a preference, it should not make any firm guarantees of places to parents in a local catchment area, particularly if those parents do not express a preference for the school.

In 1999 Rotherham parents again challenged the admission arrangements in the LEA, but this time the challenge was to the legality of the catchment area for a particular school.

R v Rotherham Metropolitan Borough Council, ex p LT [2000] ELR 76

Stuart-Smith LJ: To use the jargon of local education authorities, the children were outside the catchment area of the school in question and outside the respondent local education authority's area. The catchment area of the school in question is shown in a plan which is within the bundle. The relevant catchment area is that of the Dinnington Comprehensive School. There are 15 schools within the respondent's area. Each has its own catchment area. The catchment areas are drawn on a geographical basis. So far as the relevant one is concerned, the Dinnington Comprehensive School's catchment area, on its eastern boundary, follows the boundary of the local education authority. The school itself is situated more or less centrally within the catchment area and there is no criticism in this case of the catchment area itself. The criticism is that the policy of the local education authority is said to conflict with the relevant provisions of the statute.
...
The appellant submits that the concept of catchment as giving first priority in this case necessarily discriminates against the out-borough children because some of those who are in-borough, namely those in the catchment area, have priority over all those who are outside the borough. Miss Appleby accepts that it can be lawful for a local education authority to have a catchment area but not, it seems, if it coincides to any extent with the local education authority's boundary. I cannot accept this argument. It is obvious that proximity to a school is a proper and valid consideration. One cannot simply place the point to a pair of compasses on the school and draw a circle of so many miles radius around it. If you did that with each school you would have a series of circles, some of which

overlap, so some people might live in two or more catchment areas and some people might miss out altogether. Catchment areas have to be carefully considered so that they interlock with each other and have regard to areas of population and bus routes, safe walking distance and matters of that sort.

The essence of Owen J's judgment is, first, that if the geographical location is lawful, as it is, then a catchment qualification is also lawful. Secondly, the reason why the appellant did not have priority was not because they were outside the local education authority but because they were outside the catchment area of the school. In that respect they were like every other person inside the borough but not within the catchment area. Unless there is any challenge to the geographical nature of the catchment area, which there is not, it is not rendered unlawful simply because one of the boundaries of the catchment area lies along the borough. It seems to me that the logic of Miss Appleby's submission would result, if she is right, in preference being given to out-borough residents over those in the borough but outside the catchment area. That plainly cannot be what Parliament intended. One can envisage a situation where the school in question is located very close to the boundary, where the catchment area is drawn in such a way that it is entirely, save for some small and insignificant extent, within the LEA boundary. If that were the position, it might give rise to a challenge to the catchment area itself or the policy.

Selection by lottery

Allocating school places by lottery now appears rather quaint, and perhaps reflected the attitude that which school a child attended was not that important. This criterion only fell out of favour in the mid-1990s.

R v Lancashire County Council, ex p West (27 July 1994, QBD, unreported) (taken from Liell, Coleman, Poole (eds), The Law of Education F[111.2])

Background

This application for judicial review concerned four applications in respect of Habergham High School and one in relation to Ormskirk Grammar School, both of which schools are maintained by Lancashire County Council as the LEA.

...

In the case of Habergham the 173 places available are divided among four geographical areas of the Borough of Burnley. Children with 'relevant brothers and sisters' and children with special reasons are first offered places. The remaining places are then allocated as follows. Children who live in the Borough of Burnley are considered first. They are divided into four groups according to which primary school they attend and:

> A random selection procedure using random selection tables will then be used. Each remaining application will be numbered and the tables used to select those to be allocated places.

In the case of Ormskirk, brothers and sisters of children already attending the school at the time of the transfer were at the top of the list. Special reasons were part of the consideration and, in the cases of all schools except Ormskirk Grammar and one other, proximity was considered. In the case of those two schools places were allocated first to children with brother and sister connections and then to children with special reasons.

The remaining places were allocated first to children living within specified districts and where there were more children than places available, after which a random selection procedure was used to allocate places.

The system, including random selection, had been in operation for more than ten years.

...

Macpherson of Cluny J: Where the selection is random the chances are equal, or at least they are the same depending on the number of places and the number of people competing for them. Therefore, parents confronted with option one (random selection) as opposed to option two (drawing lines on maps) might well choose the former rather than the latter.

...

[I have] come to the conclusion that there was nothing unlawful in the system adopted, and followed for 12 years by the Local Education Authority. The Secretary of State does not like it very much. Of course I understand fully why the parents who are disappointed do not like it now. But I am wholly unable to see that it is unlawful. Indeed, I do not regard it as unfair in the circumstances. It could be much more unfair in some cases to draw lines on maps than to take the cases and apply them to the table as has been done in this case.

It should be noted that selection by lot is no longer included in the Secretary of State's guidance as a recommended admission criterion.

Religious affiliation

Voluntary and foundation schools with a religious character are permitted to include admission criteria which will preserve the religious character of the school (s 91 of the SSFA 1998; see section 3 Admissions Arrangements, above). This was also permitted under earlier legislation (s 413 of the EA 1996, s 6(6) of the EA 1980), although the procedures were different.

Code of Practice on School Admissions (1999)

5.6 Schools supported by religious foundations often give preference to members of a particular faith or denomination. Where they do, their admission arrangements should make clear whether a statement of religious affiliation or commitment would be sufficient; whether it is to be 'tested' for admission purposes and if so, how; and what, if any, references would be required from the family's priest, minister or other religious leader and how they will be used. Church schools may frame their oversubscription criteria in accordance with any Trust Deed, providing this does not conflict with general legislation.

Normally voluntary schools or foundation schools with a religious character require adherence to a particular faith and sometimes regular attendance at a particular place of worship. In *R v Governors of the Bishop Challoner Roman Catholic Comprehensive Girls' School, ex p Choudhury* [1992] 2 AC 182, the House of Lords was asked to decide whether a voluntary aided school could refuse to give a place to a pupil who did not satisfy any of the admission criteria, but whose parent had expressed a preference for a place. The admission criteria required pupils at the very least to be

'Christian'. There was no provision for the admission of non-Christian pupils. Most such schools now include adherence to another faith as one of their admission criteria. Their Lordships were considering s 6 of the EA 1980; the relevant provisions are now in s 86, in particular s 86(3)(b) of the SSFA 1998.

R v Governors of the Bishop Challoner Roman Catholic Comprehensive Girls' School, ex p Choudhury [1992] 2 AC 182

Lord Browne-Wilkinson: My Lords, this case raises the important question whether the governors of a voluntary aided school which is oversubscribed (ie has more candidates for admission than it can accommodate) is entitled to operate an admissions policy which gives preference to children of a particular religious persuasion notwithstanding the statutory provisions which give parents a right to send their children to the school of their choice.

...

Shortly stated, the main issue is whether a school which is oversubscribed so that it cannot accept all the applications for admission can adopt religious criteria (ie criteria intended to preserve the character of the school) in selecting the successful applicants for admission and thereby exempt itself under section 69(3)(a) from the duty under section 6(2) to give effect to the preferences expressed by parents whose children do not meet such criteria.

In the present case, the voluntary aided school in question, The Bishop Challoner Roman Catholic Comprehensive Girls' School in the London Borough of Tower Hamlets, adopted the following admission policy:

Admission Policy

Bishop Challoner is a Roman Catholic school. We expect all parents to support our aims fully and to uphold our Catholic ethos. The school admits pupils in accordance with the following criteria in order of priority: 1. Baptised Catholics. 2. Children of baptised Catholic parent/s. 3. Practising Christians. Priority will be given to those with sisters at the school. 4. Other Christians. Priority will be given to those with sisters at the school.

It is common ground that in the year starting September 1991 the school had more applicants for admission than it could accommodate without prejudicing the provision of efficient education. The appellants ('the applicants') are the parents of two girls, one a Hindu the other a Muslim. In November 1990 each of the applicants expressed a preference that his daughter should be educated at the school. Their applications were refused on the grounds that they did not meet the admission criteria. Both appealed to the appeal committee established under the Act of 1980. On 6 June 1991 both appeals were dismissed.

Each of the applicants applied for judicial review of (a) the refusal of the governors to admit his daughter to the school and (b) the decision of the appeal committee.

...

[W]here a school is undersubscribed and yet seeks to refuse certain applicants who have expressed a preference for that school, Parliament has indicated that if spaces are to remain unfilled because of admission criteria such criteria have to be agreed with the local education authority. It does not follow that Parliament had the same intention when, whatever criteria are adopted, all spaces in the school will be filled in any event.

...

Church voluntary aided schools are, as I have said, a sort of partnership between the church which established them and the local education authority. From the outset many, if not most of them, have reflected their religious foundation in the admissions policy they pursue by favouring those of their own faith. Nobody suggests that, apart from section 6, it was anything but proper for the governors to adopt religious criteria for selection. Views may differ as to whether the religious leaning of the school or parental preference should prevail. In the circumstances, I find it inconceivable that, if Parliament wished to restrict the governors' established right to adopt religious criteria for admission, it would have legislated to produce such a basic departure from the existing law by implication rather than by clear enactment.

...

It is one thing to provide (as in section 6(3)(b)) that in the absence of special arrangements parental preferences is to prevail over a desire to keep places vacant on, for example, religious grounds: it is quite another to say that when some parental preferences are to be denied in any event as must be the case under section 6(3)(a)) the choice of those parental preferences which are to prevail and those which are to be defeated should not be based on religious criteria. The crucial fact is that if the school is over-subscribed, the parental wishes of some parents *must* be defeated whatever criteria are adopted.

...

For these reasons, I can see no grounds for giving anything other than the literal meaning to section 6(3). Since the school was oversubscribed, the case falls within section 6(3)(a). Therefore, there was no duty on the school to give effect to the applicants' preferences that their daughters should be educated at the school.

- *If the school had not been oversubscribed would the governing body still have been acting lawfully in refusing the girls a place at the school?*

Arguably the admission criteria used were in breach of the Race Relations Act 1976 if it could be demonstrated that a considerably smaller proportion of Asians could satisfy the requirement to be Christian than the ethnic majority.

In *R v Lancashire County Council, ex p F* [1995] ELR 33 parents challenged the legality of the LEA's policy of allocating secondary school places in community and voluntary controlled schools to children attending Roman Catholic primary schools only after other applicants had been offered places. The LEA's reason for the policy was that because the places at Roman Catholic secondary schools would not be offered to non-Roman Catholic pupils, but places at community schools could be offered to Roman Catholic pupils, as a consequence Roman Catholic pupils had a wider choice than non-Catholic pupils. In addition were the Catholic pupils to take up places at the non-Catholic schools this might result in the non-Catholic pupils not having any school place.

R v Lancashire County Council, ex p F [1995] ELR 33

Kennedy LJ: This is an application for judicial review of a decision of Lancashire County Council's education officer in a letter, dated 1 March 1994, refusing F, aged 10, a place in September 1994 in Highfield School, and offering him a place in St Mary's High School, Blackpool. Although the challenge is in the form of a challenge to an individual decision in relation to a particular child, it is in reality a challenge to an important part of the policy of the Lancashire County Council, which becomes effective whenever more parents wish to send children to a particular non-denominational school than it can accommodate. In other words, it is oversubscribed.

...

There are 22 Roman Catholic schools and six Church of England schools out of a total of 99 schools, and 20% of the children attend the Roman Catholic secondary schools.

...

That provision [EA 1980, s 6(6)] enables the governing bodies of Roman Catholic schools to agree with the local education authority a limit of the non-Roman Catholic children who may be admitted, and many such agreements have been made between governing bodies and Lancashire County Council. Some of the agreements provide that no children who are not Roman Catholic shall be admitted; others provide for the admission of a small percentage of the non-Catholic children. In the case of St Mary's High School the percentage is 10%.

...

Compliance with the preferences of all parents would, therefore, prejudice the provision of efficient education and the efficient use of resources. The policy which has been promulgated for application when a school is oversubscribed must, therefore, be applied and this application can only succeed if that policy is shown to be one which in Lord Diplock's words 'no sensible authority acting with due appreciation of its responsibilities would have decided to adopt'. Standing in isolation and without explanation a policy which allocates places to Roman Catholic children attending a Roman Catholic primary school only after other applications have been met sounds discriminatory and unsustainable, but when set out in the context, as it exists in this local education authority's area, it seems to me to be impossible for this court to say that it is so unreasonable that the court should interfere. Put very simply, the situation is that a large number of children have to be accommodated in a finite number of secondary schools which fall into two groups: the county high schools and the Roman Catholic schools. Because of arrangements made between the Roman Catholic diocesan authorities and the local education authority pursuant to the 1980 Act, very few non-Catholic children can be accommodated in Roman Catholic schools even if they wanted to go there.

If too many Roman Catholic children from the Roman Catholic primary schools express a preference to go to county schools and those preferences are considered in the same way as all other preferences, then the local education authority will be left with a number of children who cannot be given places, as they should be, in the areas in which they live, so the local education authority has formulated its policy and, after carefully considering the advice of the Department for Education, has decided to adhere to it. It may be that for those who have to formulate the policy the arguments are, as the Roman Catholic and diocesan authorities observed, finely balanced, but we are not entrusted with that task.

Accordingly, in my judgment, this application fails and should be dismissed.

- *Compare the case of Cumings v Birkenhead Corpn 1971 (see p 160 above).*

Normally the governing body determines whether a particular applicant satisfies the religious requirements set out in the admissions criteria. In *R v Independent Appeal Panel for Sacred Heart High School, ex p L* (LAWTEL 2 May 2001) the claimant was not offered a place at a Roman Catholic secondary school for girls by the governing body because her Catholicism did not meet their requirements. The admission criterion stated that she should be from a practising Roman Catholic family, committed to the local community and in possession of a certificate of proof from the parish priest. The claimant's father and grandparents, but not her mother, were Catholics; the claimant attended mass fortnightly, and her mother attended occasionally; and the priest stated that he supported the application. Scott Baker J held that regular attendance at mass was clearly understood by all the parties to be weekly attendance and there was no error of law by either the governing body or the appeal panel (see also *R v Governors of La Sainte Union Convent School, ex p T* [1996] ELR 98).

- *Should there be uniform admissions criteria according to the category of school?*

- *Should all schools have catchment areas, so that if a child lives at a particular address they would have the right to attend a particular school?*

Withdrawal of the offer of a place

Once the admission authority has made an offer of a place to a parent, the Code of Practice indicates that it should only be with drawn in exceptional circumstances.

Code of Practice on School Admissions (1999)

5.28 Once an admission authority has made an offer of a school place, it may only lawfully withdraw that offer in very limited circumstances. These may include when the admission authority offered the place on the basis of a fraudulent or intentionally misleading application from a parent (for example, a false claim to residence in a catchment area) which effectively denied a place to a child with a stronger claim; or where a parent has not responded to the offer within a reasonable time. It would not generally be lawful for an admission authority to withdraw a school place once the child was attending that school, except where that place was fraudulently obtained. In deciding whether to withdraw in such a case, the length of time that the child had been at the school should also be taken into account. Where a place is withdrawn, the application must then be considered afresh, and a right of appeal offered if a place is refused.

However, in *R v Beatrix Potter School, ex p K* [1997] ELR 468 the court held the withdrawal of an offer was not unreasonable.

R v Beatrix Potter School, ex p K [1997] ELR 468

Popplewell J: This is an application by K to challenge the decision of the headteacher of Beatrix Potter Primary School dated 22 July 1996 to withdraw an offer of a place which had been made on 19 July 1996. The facts of this case can be fairly shortly stated…

There was an application in November 1995 for admission by this child to the school and in May 1996 that application was refused, the evidence being that there were something like 250 applicants and only a few places. In May 1996 there was an appeal against the refusal and that appeal was unsuccessful.

...

Two of the children who had got places moved away and therefore on one view there were two spare places. As appears from the headteacher's affidavit, he decided to offer one of those places to this applicant.

...

What then happened was that the applicant was informed that there was a place available and that was confirmed by a letter stating that '... your child will enter school on the morning of September 9' and setting out the arrangements for lunch and how the class was to be divided, and 'Information on the school uniform for 8 September was included in your information pack and we expect all the parents to comply with it'. It ends, 'May I formally welcome you to the school and wish you a long and happy association with us'.

...

What then happened was the applicant and the mother went off and bought a school uniform. Later that day, within hours, the headteacher having told the respondents that there was now a place because of the council policy, rang up and told Mrs Neilson that the offer was withdrawn. That is what gives rise to this claim.

...

There are two substantive arguments which I have to consider. First, it is said that there has been a breach of the Education Act in that the parents' preference had not been adhered to. Secondly, that the offer made on 19 July 1996 gave rise to a legitimate expectation and that legitimate expectation was based on an express promise and it was relied on and gave rise to some detriment on the part of the applicant and the mother, and that entitles that the applicant at set aside the withdrawal and in effect allow the child to go to this school.

...

All the facts necessary to give rise to legitimate expectation are there. There has been a clear express promise. It has been relied on and there has been some detriment. It is not only to the detriment in the cost of buying clothes, but the upset that was caused to the mother and child. That is more particularly so when one has regard to the fact that there is in the school a brother of this applicant, and the family unit would be upset in the broadest sense from the withdrawal of this offer.

Legitimate expectation is in my view a factor to be taken into account in deciding whether the respondents have acted *Wednesbury* unreasonably. In some cases it may be the only factor and would therefore be wholly decisive in an applicant's claim. In other cases it may be no more than one of the matters to be taken into account. It is really an aspect of the general public law obligation and the obligation on the respondents not to act unreasonably.

...

I therefore turn to consider the *Wednesbury* principle and consider if the withdrawal by the respondents of this offer was unreasonable. I look at the policy behind the respondents' decision. I look at the effect that it had on the applicant and the length of it and I come to the clearest possible conclusion that it is impossible to categorise the decision to withdraw as *Wednesbury* unreasonable. If there were a test of fairness I would also take the same view, that given the short period of time in which these parents were mistakenly of the view that the child had a place is of itself extremely relevant. Nothing that I can say of course should encourage the idea that an offer is other than a very serious matter. Parents who receive an offer are likely to treat it very seriously and I entirely accept that the upset which was caused to the child and to the parents was a very real one. But given all the circumstances of this case this application must fail.

- *What difference would it make legally were Beatrix Potter School an independent school?*

4.   RIGHTS OF PARENTS

Right to express a preference

Parents have the right to express a preference as to which school their child should attend, and the admissions authority (the LEA or the governing body) must comply with that preference (see p 166), subject to certain exceptions. (See p 217 below.)

School Standards and Framework Act 1998, s 86(1)

A local education authority shall make arrangements for enabling the parent of a child in the area of the authority—

(a) to express a preference as to the school at which he wishes education to be provided for his child in the exercise of the authority's functions, and

(b) to give reasons for his preference.

See *R v Rotherham Metropolitan Borough Council, ex p Clark* [1998] ELR 152 and *R v Sheffield City Council, ex p H* [1999] ELR 511 (above) on the meaning of this subsection. The Education Bill 2001/02 amends and clarifies SSFA 1998, s 86. In particular parents will be able to express a preference for more than one school, and the right to express a preference will also apply to sixth forms.

The duty to comply with the parent's preference arises even where the reason for the preference is based on racial grounds. In *R v Cleveland County Council, ex p The Commission for Racial Equality* [1994] ELR 44 the mother of a five-year-old girl asked the LEA to transfer her daughter 'to a school with a majority of white children because she did not want her daughter to learn songs in Pakistani, did not want her to be taught Pakistani at the expense of English and did not think it fair on her daughter to attend a school in which Pakistani children, with whom her daughter did not associate, were in the majority'. The Commission for Racial Equality challenged the decision of the council to transfer the girl to the school requested by her mother, and the decision of the Secretary of State not to intervene. The CRE regarded the issue as an important point of principle.

R v Cleveland County Council, ex p Commission for Racial Equality **[1994] ELR 44**

Parker LJ: In the present case it is accepted that non-compliance with the request for admission to primary school B could not have been justified under any of the exceptions set out in s 6(3). On the face of it therefore the council were obliged to comply with Mrs C's request. They could not do otherwise without being in breach in s 6.

The CRE contend however that the mandatory and apparently unqualified duty under s 6 is qualified or overridden by s 18 of the Race Relations Act 1976, as amended by s 33(1) of the 1980 Act.

As so amended s 18(1) provides:

It is unlawful for a local education authority, in carrying out such of its functions under the Education Acts 1944 to [1980] as do not fall under section 17, to do any act which constitutes racial discrimination.

...

Accordingly, I hold that the council's duty under s 6 is unqualified by s 18. Assuming, however, that this is wrong the question arises whether the child's transfer amounted in law to segregation by the council on racial grounds.

...

Mr Sedley submits that by complying with the preference the council were, on racial grounds, segregating the child from the pupils at primary school A within the meaning of s 1(2) of the 1976 Act. The act of discrimination, if there was one, can in my judgment only be a failure to refuse admission to primary school B. The questions to be answered are therefore:

(a) Can such a failure amount to an 'act' within s 18(1) of the Act?
(b) If so, was it on racial grounds?
(c) If so, did it amount to segregation?

(a) Did the failure amount to an 'act'?

It appears to me that the ordinary meaning of an act is the taking of a positive step rather than the omission to take such a step. Thus one has negligent acts or omissions and I can see no reason why the same should not apply in the present case. Suppose the council had refused admission to primary school B it would as it seems to me be an attempt to enforce the stay of K at primary school A which is no part of the LEA's duty or function. Furthermore, on Mr Sedley's submissions it would, I think, follow in the circumstances that such refusal amounted to segregation from the pupils at primary school B. I do not consider that the council's failure to refuse admission was an act within s 18(1) of the 1976 Act. This makes it unnecessary to deal with questions (b) and (c) above mentioned, but I regard it as desirable that I should do so.

(b) Was the council's 'act' on racial grounds?

It appears to me that to this there can only be one answer and that is 'No'. The council 'acted' or failed to refuse admission on the simple ground that they had been advised that in law they had no option but to do so.

(c) Did the council's 'act' amount to segregation?

If there was any segregation here at all it consisted in my view in the removal of K from primary school A, which was the lawful act of her mother. But it is said that in compliance with her mother's preference the council itself segregated the child from the pupils at primary school A. On any ordinary use of language it does not appear to me that the council did any such thing. Mr Sedley relied on certain international conventions, but they could only assist him if there were ambiguity or uncertainty in the language of the Act itself. I do not consider that there is any. To submit, as Mr Sedley does, that one segregated a person who is admitted to school A from the pupils at all other schools is in my view to put a construction on the word much too strained to be acceptable.

...

The CRE, I have no doubt, instituted the present proceedings to establish what they considered to be an important principle. In the course of argument, however, the nature of that principle varied considerably until in the end it became one which, if accepted, would be of no avail to them. It would compel a council to reject a preference plainly based on a desire to further racial equality and would announce to all racists that they could further their prejudices by the simple means of making bare applications or, if they had been misguided enough to make an application which revealed racial grounds and had had it rejected, they will only have to resubmit it as a bare application and it would then be accepted.

I would dismiss this appeal.

Research has indicated that parents choose a particular school for a variety of reasons, and that some parents are more able to make an informed decision. Research undertaken in the London Borough of Haringey in 1999 looked at admissions and admission appeals for places in three secondary and six primary schools in September 1999. One aspect of the research was to find out why and how parents chose a particular school as their first preference.

'Parental Perceptions of the School Admissions Appeal Process in the London Borough of Haringey Summer 1999', Anne Ruff with Andrew Dorn, Middlesex University, 2000

Reason for first preference

3.1.4 The reason given by most parents for choosing a particular school as their first preference, was that the school had a good reputation (96). This was important for 65% of secondary school parents (55) and for 51% of primary school parents (31).

3.1.5 The second most frequent reason given (72) was that it was the nearest school to home. This was important for 66% of primary school parents (40) and for 38% of secondary school parents (32). The choice of nearest school to home is also likely to be influenced by the admissions criteria applicable to most new pupils, which is based on distance between school and home for all schools other than Hornsey School for Girls.

3.1.6 For 40 out of the 48 parents who had children already attending the school the attendance of the sibling was a factor in making the school their first preference.

3.1.7 Some parents wanted their son or daughter to attend the school because other relatives did so (17). Nine parents commented that in practice they had no choice but to choose the school as their first preference. This reinforces the views expressed by some parents in relation to the provision of information (see 3.1.4).

3.1.8 In the case of Hornsey School for Girls eight parents selected the school as their first preference because it was a single-sex school. For three primary school parents childcare arrangements affected their preference.

4.1 'Parents as choosers'

4.1.1 ....

4.1.2 ... a small number of studies have included consideration of parental perceptions and responses to school admissions procedures and particularly at how parents understand, exercise and cope with 'choice'.

4.1.3 Most notably Gewirtz, Ball and Bowe (1995) [*Markets, Choice and Equity in Education,* OUP] in a study of eleven LEAs produced a typology of 'parents as choosers' which claimed that parents could be categorised according to their understanding of admissions procedures, the extent to which they felt comfortable with the notion of choice and their ability to play the system to their perceived advantage. According to Gewirtz and her colleagues there are three types of parent choosers: the privileged/skilled chooser, the semi-skilled chooser and the disconnected chooser.

4.1.4 The privileged chooser values choice and has the economic, social and cultural capital to enter the education market and utilise the opportunities of choice. These parents are able to 'decode' school systems and organisation and understand sometimes complex admissions arrangements and criteria. Often these parents have some kind of inside knowledge of how education systems work and economically, are more likely to be able to move house, pay for travel or turn to the private sector. These parents, according to Gewirtz et al, are attracted to high status, academic schools (often selective) and will go to great lengths to get their child admitted. Apparently this type of parent is most likely to appeal if they do not get their first preference.

4.1.5 The second type of chooser, the semi-skilled, though aware of the importance of parental choice is less 'at ease' when it comes to operationalising it: 'the biographies and family histories of these families have not provided them with the experiences or inside knowledge of the school system and the social contacts and cultural skills to pursue their choice effectively'.

4.1.6 In the Gewirtz study the semi-skilled choosers come across as slightly sad in that though they are highly conscientious of their role as parents and want to do the best for their child they don't quite know how to play the system. They are like outsiders looking in on a system they don't understand yet are desperate to exercise the 'rights' and the promise of choice proclaimed by government policy. According to the study theses parents were much less likely to appeal if they did not get the school of their choice.

4.1.7 The third type of parent chooser, according to the Gewirtz study, are the disconnected who regard choice as a necessity rather than as an opportunity. Though these parents were as concerned about their children's education as others, choice was not a concept they understood and there was an element of fatalism about the difference a school could make to their child's ability to achieve. These parents did not undertake comparative research on the schools available, choice appeared to them to be predetermined and these parents were less concerned with exam results than with facilities, safety and nearness. There was also a strong element of 'localism' in their school preference as compared to the 'cosmopolitanism' of the skilled/privileged chooser.

4.1.8 For information about schools the disconnected chooser relied more on the gossip of local networks than on public information. In the language of the Gerwirtz study these parents were least likely to possess the 'cultural capital' to make comparisons between schools, comprehend complex admissions criteria or play the system. They were also least likely to appeal against non-admission.

4.1.9 Gerwirtz and her colleagues were convinced that 'choice is very directly and powerfully related to social class' and that their typology of parents is strongly class based with the disconnected choosers being overwhelmingly working class, the privileged/skilled choosers predominantly middle class and the semi-skilled choosers being a mixed class group. In other words parents' perceptions of school choice and admissions, their ability to understand the system and indeed their perceptions of the fairness or otherwise of admission appeals will be strongly influenced by their socio-economic position.

4.1.10 Whether or not one can make the same conclusions regarding Haringey parents remains an open question since the survey of parents did not control for this factor. In addition, as Gerwirtz points out, class is an increasingly 'slippery' concept to apply and that any typology of parents is probably best seen as a continuum than as any fixed set of categories. Nonetheless, the notion that parents' perceptions of admissions, choice and appeals are likely to by related to class, and particularly its cultural aspects, seems highly plausible.

4.2 Reasons for parental choice

4.2.1 A second important (and more recent) piece of research on parents and school admissions is that by Woods, Bagley and Glatter (1998) [*School Choice and Competition*, Routledge] in three LEAs and involving 6000 completed questionnaires from parents over a three-year period. As with other studies in the field the focus is not simply on parents but on school adaptations to so-called market forces and competition.

4.2.2 The Woods, Bagley and Glatter study included discussion of the different criteria parents used to make their choice, the types of information they relied on in making that choice and the sources of parental dissatisfaction with admission arrangements. Again, the issue of parental perceptions of admissions *appeal* arrangements was not directly addressed.

4.2.3 According to Woods and his colleagues, parents' reasons for choosing schools can be broadly categorised into *academic-centred and child-centred* factors.

4.2.4 Academic included factors such as exam results and having a sixth form whereas child-centred covered whether the child would be happy with the school, nearness and maintenance of friendship networks.

4.2.5 The Haringey research confirms the importance of these two factors to the parents who completed the questionnaires.

4.2.6 In contrast to the Gerwirtz study, Woods et al are much less certain about any correlation between social class and parents' reasons for choosing a school. In only one of the LEAs they studied did there appear to be a strong connection between class and parental choice criteria with 35% of middle class parents prioritising academic factors over child-centred compared to 19% of working class parents. In the other LEAs no similar relationship could be established and Woods and his colleagues concluded that the efficacy of class as a determinant of parental reasons for choosing a school 'will be bound up with the particular context and culture of the area'. In addition they identified three 'core factors' that were mentioned by virtually all parents to varying degrees (whatever their social class): academic standards, nearness to home/convenience for travel, the child's happiness at the school.

4.2.7 The most useful sources of information identified by the parents in the Woods study were: school visits, sibling connections, parents' friends, school brochures, league tables. Visits to schools was overwhelmingly the most important factor and the study found little social class variation apart from some tendency for middle class parents to make greater use of league tables and working class parents to rely more on family networks and connections.

4.2.8 As one would expect the Woods study confirmed that the extent to which parents perceived that they had real 'choice' varied between the LEAs concerned with 25% of parents in one LEA believing that they could realistically choose between three or more schools to 67% in another. The limiting factors perceived by parents were: insufficient places in popular schools, poor quality of education in some schools, 'problems' in certain schools (e g drugs, bullying), restricted choice in terms of types of schools (e g church schools, single sex schools) and transport problems. Interestingly, very few parents said that they would like to see more selective grammar schools. The first two limiting factors were identified by a number of the Haringey parents who completed the questionnaires.

4.2.9 In terms of admissions arrangements and criteria parents were critical of the use of rigid catchment areas and nearness rules (if they lived outside those areas) and the fact that no account was taken of the length of time that the child had lived in the area.

Exceptions

Section 86(2) of the SSFA 1998 provides that the admissions authority must comply with parental preference unless one or more of the three exceptions contained in s 86(3) of the SSFA 1998 apply. These exceptions mean in practice that many parents do not have the right to choose a school.

School Standards and Framework Act 1998, s 86(3)

The duty imposed by subsection (2) does not apply—
(a) if compliance with the preference would prejudice the provision of efficient education or the efficient use of resources;
(b) if the preferred school is a foundation or voluntary aided school and compliance with the preference would be incompatible with any special arrangements under section 91 (admission arrangements to preserve the religious character of a foundation or voluntary aided school); or
(c) if the arrangements for admission to the preferred school—
(i) are wholly based on selection by reference to ability or aptitude, and
(ii) are so based with a view to admitting only pupils with high ability or with aptitude,

and compliance with the preference would be incompatible with selection under those arrangements.

In addition to these three general exceptions to the duty to comply with parental preference, there is an additional exception where the pupil has been permanently excluded from two or more schools. The duty to comply with parental preference is waived for a two-year period from the date of the last exclusion (s 87 of the SSFA 1998; see below).

Parents can challenge the refusal of a place in three ways. First, they can challenge the legality of the admissions criteria used by the admissions authority (see above). Secondly, they can appeal to an independent admissions appeal panel (see below). Thirdly, parents can argue that none of the SSFA 1998, s 86(3) exceptions apply.

(A) SECTION 86(3)(A) EXCEPTION

[I]f compliance with the preference would prejudice the provision of efficient education or the efficient use of resources ...

This exception is the one most commonly applied at the two main entry years (reception class for primary school and Year 7 for secondary schools), because it is relevant to all types of schools where there is oversubscription; that is where there are more applications than places available. The admissions authority will argue that the approved admission number has been reached because offers have been made to children according to the published admissions criteria. In other words the admissions authority states that the school is full, and that it would be prejudicial to teachers and pupils to admit any additional children.

In *R v Governors of the Hasmonean High School, ex p N and E* [1994] ELR 343 parents argued without success that the refusal to offer a place to their children on the ground that the school was oversubscribed was, in reality, a refusal on academic grounds which was not an admission criterion for the school and therefore did not come within s 86(3)(c).

R v Governors of the Hasmonean High School, ex p N and E [1994] ELR 343

Glidewell LJ: The appellant in the first case, N, is just 12 years of age. She was born on 28 September 1981. She has learning difficulties in some subjects, and as a result the local education authority for the area in which she lives, Barnet London Borough Council, has issued a statement of special needs relating to her under s 7 of the Education Act 1981.

N and her parents are of the orthodox Jewish faith. She has, until July 1993, been at the Independent Jewish Day School. Her parents wish her now to attend the Hasmonean High School (which I shall call 'the school'). The school is a voluntary aided school providing secondary education in the orthodox Jewish tradition. It admits only children of the Jewish faith. There are separate schools for boys and girls on separate sites some distance from each other, both in the London Borough of Barnet. N's elder brother is a pupil at the boys' school.

N's parents applied to the school for a place for her to enter in September 1993. On 24 February 1993 the parents were notified that the school would not offer N a place.

...

As to the second case, E is 12 years of age. She also has learning difficulties in some subjects. In her case, Barnet have indicated that they are in the process of assessing her for a statement of special needs, but they have not issued such a statement, even in draft. She and her parents are also orthodox Jews. Her older sister is already at the school and her parents naturally wish her to go there. Indeed, they assumed that as a sibling she would be able to enter the school. But this was not to be.

...

Nevertheless, it is agreed that in considering her parents' application for her to be admitted to the school, the governors were required to decide in accordance with their own published criteria for admission. If they failed to do so, it might properly be said that they had taken into account an irrelevant factor or failed to take a relevant factor into account.

The criteria for admission to Hasmonean add to the criteria laid down by Barnet.

...

Then para (c) which is the critical one for the purposes of this appeal:

Applications are controlled by the governors and head teacher. The school will seek to establish that the child satisfies the overriding criteria for admission referred to in the paragraph above and that the child can be offered within the school a suitable education to meet his/her needs and without prejudicing the welfare and educational needs of other children in the school. These criteria will be satisfied by questionnaire and/or interview to be conducted by the head teacher or other senior member of his staff ...

...

The main ground of N's appeal and of the renewal of E's application is, putting it bluntly, that the decisions to refuse both girls admission — and in E's case to dismiss her appeal — have not been made for the stated reasons. The allegation is that the decision had been made, taking into account academic ability or lack of it, as the major, if not the sole criterion. That, it is submitted, does not fall within criterion (c) and thus is an irrelevant consideration.

Those reasons [given by the governors] mean inevitably that for both girls lack of academic ability was a factor in the decision not to admit them. Mr Clayton, appearing for both N and E, accepted in this appeal (I am not sure how far he was minded to accept earlier), that a school may not be able to offer education to meet the needs of a child of low academic ability and/or that to admit such a child may prejudice other children in her class. So to that extent he accepts that academic ability or standard can be relevant to the governors' consideration of the matters set out in criterion (c).

...

The real issues on this appeal are as to the extent to which the governors took academic quality into account in their decisions in relation to N and E, and whether, taking it into account to that extent, was proper within criterion (c) of the school's admission criteria.

...

I am not satisfied that the evidence in either case justifies the court in concluding that either the governors or, in E's case, the appeal committee, when reading the decisions challenged, acted unlawfully by taking into account an irrelevant consideration. I realise, of course, that this will be a grave disappointment for all four parents, and one can only sympathise with them deeply, but in my view the judge was right to take the view that neither of these was a proper case for the court exercising its power to quash the decisions of the governors or the appeal committee, or to make the declaration sought.

The facts of this case arose under earlier SEN legislation and before the Special Educational Needs Tribunal was established (see chapter 5). Both the applicants had siblings at the school or a connected school and would normally have expected to have been offered a place because of the family connection. The argument that admitting children with special educational needs prejudices the welfare and educational needs of other children at the school is unlikely to be successful with the increased emphasis on inclusion. The reason that the application was unsuccessful is a consequence of the general nature of the admission criteria in paragraph (c) which gave the governing body considerable discretion.

The current guidance indicates that children with special educational needs but without a statement should be treated in the same way as other applicants.

Code of Practice on School Admissions (1999)

5.19 Children with special educational needs but without statements must be treated as fairly as other applicants. Admission authorities may not refuse to admit a pupil because they consider themselves unable to cater for his or her special educational needs. Admission authorities must consider applications from children who have special educational needs but no statement, on the basis of the school's published admission criteria. They cannot refuse to admit a pupil on the grounds that he or she does not have a statement of special educational needs, or is currently being assessed for one. Where admission authorities give some priority to children with special educational needs but without a statement, their published admission arrangements should state in what way their arrangements differ for such children.

(See the Code of Practice on School Admission para 5.8 and chapter 5 (below) for the position in relation to the admission of children with statements of special educational needs.)

Where a parent applies for a place outside the normal admission rounds the Code of Practice indicates that an admission authority may be able to refuse to admit a child with challenging behaviour in certain circumstances.

Code of Practice on School Admissions (1999)

5.24 Unless it is to the normal year of entry, admission authorities can decide that they should refuse to admit a child where there are places available, where to do so would prejudice the provision of efficient education or the efficient use of resources. This is only likely to be appropriate in circumstances where a school has a particularly high concentration of pupils with challenging behaviour, and where it is trying to improve its standards from a low base as part of its achievement of targets and its development plan, that is schools which are under special measures or have recently come out of them (within the last two years), or have been identified by OFSTED or the LEA as having serious weaknesses.

(B) SECTION 86(3)(B) EXCEPTION

[I]f the preferred school is a foundation or voluntary aided school and compliance with the preference would be incompatible with any special arrangements under section 91 (admission arrangements to preserve the religious character of a foundation or voluntary aided school) ...

A church school can lawfully refuse to offer a place to a child who does not satisfy its admissions criteria which are based on religious affiliation. Such a refusal is lawful where the school is oversubscribed as well as where it has spare places (see above: *R v Governors of the Bishop Challoner Roman Catholic Comprehensive Girls' School, ex p Choudhury* [1992] 2 AC 182; *R v Independent Appeal Panel for Sacred Heart High School, ex p L* (LAWTEL 2 May 2001).

In *R (on the application of O (by her litigation friend Mr O)) v St James Roman Catholic Primary School Appeal Panel* [2001] ELR 469 Newman J accepted that

Article 8 of the ECHR (the right to respect for family life) and Article 2 of Protocol 1 (the right to respect for parents' religious convictions) can be engaged by an admissions decision to a religious school which one sibling is already attending. He considered that Article 8 would be satisfied where there is a sibling criterion in the admissions policy, which raises the possibility that where there is no such a criterion there may be a breach of Article 8.

(C) SECTION 86(3)(C) EXCEPTION

[I]f the arrangements for admission to the preferred school—
(i)   are wholly based on selection by reference to ability or aptitude, and
(ii) are so based with a view to admitting only pupils with high ability or with aptitude,

and compliance with the preference would be incompatible with selection under those arrangements.

Selection of pupils is permissible where the school is a grammar school, or a comprehensive school with a small percentage of the pupils being selected on the basis of aptitude or ability. This is nearly always a secondary school. The Code of Practice School Admissions (1999) states that academic selection should not be used to decide entry into primary education (para 5.9).

In selective schools the admissions authority may refuse to comply with parental preference either because there are no places or because the child has not, for example, obtained a high enough mark in an entrance test.

Selection *by ability* is permitted (s 99(1), (2) of the SSFA 1998; see above) in the following situations:
–   pre-existing arrangements
–   pupil banding
–   admission to a sixth form
–   the school is a grammar school.
Selection *by aptitude* is permitted (s 99(4) of the SSFA 1998; see above) in the following situations:
–   pre-existing arrangements
–   aptitude for particular subject(s).
Popular selective schools may combine selection criteria with geographical or religious criteria.

In *R v Kingston upon Thames Royal London Borough Council, ex p Emsden* [1993] 1 FLR 179 the admissions authority for two grammar schools attempted to combine selection on the basis of ability with a geographical criterion. This was because the previous policy of selection on the basis of ability alone was unpopular with parents living in the LEA as it resulted in fewer children living in the LEA obtaining places than before.

R v Kingston upon Thames Royal London Borough Council, ex p Emsden **[1993] 1 FLR 179**

Schiemann J:

Introduction

In the Royal Borough of Kingston upon Thames there have been for years a boys' grammar school known as Tiffin School and a girls' grammar school known as Tiffin Girls' School. Each has an excellent reputation and many applications for entry are made by parents of children — both those who live within the borough (whom I shall call 'insiders') and those who live outside it (whom I shall call 'outsiders'). Tiffin School is a voluntary controlled secondary school and is wholly maintained by the local education authority, which is the respondent council. Tiffin Girls' School is a county secondary school and is both owned and maintained by the council. They are both, and have been for years, regularly oversubscribed.

...

By a resolution dated 23 July 1991 the council changed its policy to one which consists of two stages. The first stage is one in which the children who want to get in take tests and a pool of the most academically successful is established as a result of that process. The pool contains significantly more pupils than can be accepted by the schools that year. It is therefore necessary to shrink the pool so that it corresponds to the number of places available. This is done by the application of a second stage. This second stage has nothing to do with ability, but is geographical: places are awarded on the basis of who is nearest the school in question. I shall refer to this as the 'geographical policy'. The result of the adoption of this policy is likely to be that: (1) fewer outsiders will secure entry to the schools than was the case under the ability only policy; and (2) no one in the extreme south of the Borough of Kingston will secure entry — this is because the schools are broadly in the north of the borough. The brightest child in the borough might live in the south. It would get into the pool, but would then promptly be thrown out again because it lived too far away from the school.

...

The applicants live in the extreme south. They want their children to go to one of the Tiffin schools. They were happy with the limit outsiders policy, but accept that it is unlawful and therefore not open to the council. They were happy with the ability only policy which, in any event, gave their children a chance to be selected for a Tiffin school. They naturally object to the geographical policy because that is likely to have the effect of excluding their children, however good they may be academically, from the benefits which they apparently consider can be secured if one attends one or other of the Tiffin schools and which they apparently consider are not available elsewhere in the borough.

...

In my judgment there is nothing intrinsically or inevitably unlawful in a local education authority maintaining a selective school to which some of the pupils residing in that local education authority's area are effectively denied a right of access. That was the essence of Mr Thompson's first submission and it fails. However, there can be circumstances in which the adoption of a policy which has this result is attended by a motivation which renders the adoption of that policy illegal. That brings me on to Mr Thompson's second submission.

The second submission

The applicants' case is that the geographical policy was adopted without there being any educational grounds for it, but mainly or solely in order to advantage insiders and disadvantage outsiders. Although the applicants are insiders, they are disadvantaged under the geographical policy and they say that their disadvantage has come about as a result of the local education authority trying to produce a situation which was not on its face discriminatory so as to fall foul of the *Greenwich* ruling.

It is established law that an administrative body must not be motivated by impermissible reasons. Thus a council may award a contract to the son of the chairman, but they must not do it *because* he is the son of the chairman.

In the present case it is agreed that, *absent any educational grounds for adopting the geographical policy*, a desire to improve opportunities for insiders to secure admission and correlatively decrease opportunities for outsiders would be an impermissible motive. That follows from the *Greenwich* case. The issue between the parties is whether the applicants have proved that there were no educational grounds for the change and that the council was so motivated.

...

Fortunately in the context of this case I do not need to make a finding. This is because I have no doubt that I should refuse the relief sought by the applicants. This is because of the delay in launching these proceedings. The decision complained of was made on 23 July 1991. The application for leave was not made until 7 January 1992.

- *If parents do not obtain a place at the school of their choice and the LEA offers them a place at a failing school, what options are open to the parents? Should their child have the right to a place at a school which is not failing?*

Where a pupil has been permanently excluded from two or more schools

Where the pupil has been permanently excluded from two or more schools the duty to comply with parental preference is waived for a two-year period from the date of the last exclusion. This provision was introduced by s 11 of the EA 1997, and is now contained in s 87 of the SSFA 1998.

School Standards and Framework Act 1998, s 87

(1) The duty imposed by section 86(2) does not apply in the case of a child to whom subsection (2) below applies.

(2) Where a child has been permanently excluded from two or more schools, this subsection applies to him during the period of two years beginning with the date on which the latest of those exclusions took effect.

(3) Subsection (2) applies to a child whatever the length of the period or periods elapsing between those exclusions and regardless of whether it has applied to him on a previous occasion.

(4) However, a child shall not be regarded as permanently excluded from a school for the purposes of this section if—
(a) although so excluded he was reinstated as a pupil at the school following the giving of a direction to that effect to the head teacher of the school; or
(b) he was so excluded at a time when he had not attained compulsory school age.

...

(6) For the purposes of this section the permanent exclusion of a child from a school shall be regarded as having taken effect on the school day as from which the head teacher decided that he should be permanently excluded.

The Education Bill 2001/02 provides that a child should not be regarded as permanently excluded where the governing body of the independent appeal panel would have directed reinstatement (see chapter 4), but reinstatement was not practicable.

One effect of this provision is that the parent has no right of appeal against the refusal of the admission authority to offer the child a place at the school, even where the school has space. The LEA, as the admission authority for a community or voluntary controlled school, may decide to admit such a child because, for example, the LEA is under a duty to provide a school place for children in its area. Where the LEA does so decide, the school's governing body has a right of appeal to an independent appeal panel (s 95 of the SSFA 1998).

LEA power to direct admission

The LEA has the power to direct that a child should be admitted to a specified school which is a reasonable distance from his home. This power arises where the child has been refused admission because, for example, the year group is full, or he has been permanently excluded from school. The power may be used where there is a shortage of school places in the LEA, and may result in schools being required to accept pupils in excess of the approved number for the year group.

School Standards and Framework Act 1998, s 96

(1) The local education authority may give a direction under this section if, in the case of any child in their area, either (or both) of the following conditions is satisfied in relation to each school which is a reasonable distance from his home and provides suitable education, that is—
(a)   he has been refused admission to the school, or
(b)   he is permanently excluded from the school.

(2) A direction under this section shall specify a school—
(a)   which is a reasonable distance from the child's home, and
(b)   from which the child is not permanently excluded.

The LEA is required to consult the pupil's parent and the governing body before deciding to give a direction, and the governing body has the right to refer the matter to the Secretary of State (SSFA 1998, s 97(3)). However, a direction cannot require a school to admit a child if the effect would be that an infant class would exceed 30 pupils. The Education Bill 2001/02 amends SSFA 1998, ss 96 and 97 so that the LEA may only direct admission to a school for which it is not the admission authority. Where the LEA is the admission authority the Secretary of State (or the National Assembly for Wales) may direct admission to such a school.

Admission appeals

The admissions authority must give parents the opportunity to appeal to an independent appeal panel where their child is refused a place at the school of their choice. The independent appeal panel's decision is binding on the admissions authority. The panels replaced the appeal committees which were perceived as lacking independence because a member of the admission authority (that is a local councillor or a school governor) was eligible to sit on the committee.

An appeal must be in writing and parents should be given at least 14 days from receiving the decision in which to appeal. Parents must be given the opportunity to attend the appeal in person and to make oral representations. If they wish they may be represented by a friend or by a lawyer. The child may attend the hearing at the discretion of the panel. The panel's decision and its reasons should be communicated to the parents in writing.

The panels have been given additional powers under the Special Educational Needs and Disability Act 2001 (see chapter 5) to hear admission appeals relating to disability discrimination. These powers are likely to come into force in September 2002.

School Standards and Framework Act 1998, s 94

(1) A local education authority shall make arrangements for enabling the parent of a child to appeal against—

(a) any decision made by or on behalf of the authority as to the school at which education is to be provided for the child in the exercise of the authority's functions, other than a decision leading to or embodied in a direction under section 96 (directions for admission), and

(b) in the case of a community or voluntary controlled school maintained by the authority, any decision made by or on behalf of the governing body refusing the child admission to the school.

(2) The governing body of a foundation or voluntary aided school shall make arrangements for enabling the parent of a child to appeal against any decision made by or on behalf of the governing body refusing the child admission to the school.

...

(5) Schedule 24 has effect in relation to the making and hearing of appeals pursuant to arrangements made under this section.

(6) The decision of an appeal panel on an appeal under Schedule 24 shall be binding on—

(a) the local education authority or the governing body by whom or on whose behalf the decision under appeal was made, and

(b) in the case of a decision made by or on behalf of a local education authority, the governing body of a community or voluntary controlled school at which the appeal panel determines that a place should be offered to the child in question.

The statutory provisions are supplemented by guidance, which is now contained in the Code of Practice on School Admission Appeals (1999). The DfEE's view of the aims and objectives of the appeal process is set out in the Code of Practice.

Code of Practice on School Admission Appeals (1999)

Aims and Objectives of the Appeals Process

1.9 School admission appeals should work for the benefit of parents, children, school admission authorities and schools themselves. The appeal arrangements should be as simple and clear as possible for everybody who is involved in the process. It is particularly important that parents find appeal arrangements easy to understand. ...

1.11 The fundamental objectives of admission appeals should be to:
* provide an independent, impartial and informal forum for parents and the admission authority concerned to present their respective cases, and to be confident that they will be given a fair hearing
* ensure that appeal panels weigh up all the evidence presented to them carefully and objectively before reaching a final decision on the appeal
* operate within education legislation, and also have regard to the implications of other legislation such as the Sex Discrimination Act 1975; the Race Relations Act 1976; the Disability Discrimination Act 1995; and the Human Rights Act 1998 (which will come into force in full in 2000). Appeal panels are carrying out a judicial function and must apply the principles of natural justice (see Annex A, paragraph A.3)
* have regard to all relevant guidelines in conducting appeal arrangements, including this Code; the Admissions Code of Practice; and the Code of Practice on the Identification and Assessment of Special Educational Needs
* to provide a system which is clear and consistent and as easy to understand as possible by everyone involved
* make workable the class size reduction legislation

Who may sit on an appeal panel?

The SSFA 1998, Sch 24 replaced the provisions contained in the EA 1996, ss 423, 429, Sch 33. The main change was that councillors and governors of the school are disqualified from sitting on an appeal panel, as are teachers at the school in question, employees of the LEA or governing body, and anyone who has a close connection with the school.

School Standards and Framework Act 1998, Sch 24

PART I

CONSTITUTION OF APPEAL PANELS

Appeal arrangements made by local education authorities

1(1) An appeal pursuant to arrangements made by a local education authority under section 94(1) shall be to an appeal panel constituted in accordance with this paragraph.

(2) An appeal panel shall consist of three or five members appointed by the authority from—

(a)   persons who are eligible to be lay members; and

(b)   persons who have experience in education, are acquainted with educational conditions in the area of the authority or are parents of registered pupils at a school.

(3) Of the members of an appeal panel—

(a)   at least one must be a person who is eligible to be a lay member and is appointed as such; and

(b)   at least one must be a person falling within sub-paragraph (2)(b).

(4) For the purposes of this paragraph a person is eligible to be a lay member if he is a person without personal experience in the management of any school or the provision of education in any school (disregarding any such experience as a governor or in any other voluntary capacity).

(5) Sufficient persons may be appointed by the authority under this paragraph to enable two or more appeal panels to sit at the same time.

(6) No person shall be a member of an appeal panel if he is disqualified by virtue of sub-paragraph (7).

(7) The following persons are disqualified for membership of an appeal panel—

(a)   any member of the authority or of the governing body of the school in question;

(b)   any person employed by the authority or the governing body, other than a person employed as a teacher;

(c)   any person who has, or at any time has had, any connection with the authority or the school, or with any person within paragraph (b), of a kind which might reasonably be taken to raise doubts about his ability to act impartially in relation to the authority or the school.

(8) A person employed as a teacher by the authority shall not be taken, by reason only of that employment, to have such a connection with the authority as is mentioned in sub-paragraph (7)(c).

(9) A person shall not be a member of an appeal panel for the consideration of an appeal against a decision if he was among those who made the decision or took part in discussions as to whether the decision should be made.

(10) A person who is a teacher at a school shall not be a member of an appeal panel for the consideration of an appeal involving a question whether a child is to be admitted to that school.

(11) Where, at any time after an appeal panel consisting of five members have begun to consider an appeal, any of the members—

(a)   dies, or

(b)   becomes unable through illness to continue as a member,

the panel may continue with their consideration and determination of the appeal so long as the number of the remaining members is not less than three and the requirements of sub-paragraph (3) are satisfied.

Almost identical provisions (Sch 25, para 2) apply to appeal arrangements made by governing bodies where they are the admissions authority. Panel members are not paid, although they may claim certain allowances. Panels, which normally comprise three members, may sit in the evenings or during the day. The great majority of appeals relate to admission to reception class at the start of primary school or on transfer to secondary school (Year 7). One appeal panel should hear all the appeals for a particular school. Where there are tens if not hundreds of parents appealing for a school the panels may have to sit for many hours. The panels are supported and advised by a clerk. Both panel members and clerks should receive training on the law and the procedures to be followed by the panel.

The Education Bill 2001/02 proposes the repeal of SSFA 1998, Schs 24 and 25. The contents of the Schedules will in future be contained in regulations rather than in primary legislation. Regulations are easier to amend and are subject to less parliamentary scrutiny than Acts of Parliament. This repeal is part of the government's aim to modernise education law (see chapter 1). One change of substance is that any pupil already in a secondary school will have a right of appeal where he or she is refused entry to the school's sixth form.

• *Should panel members be paid? Should there be a legally qualified chairman? Note the recommendations of the Leggatt Review (see Ch 1).*

The role of the appeal panel

School Standards and Framework Act 1998, Sch 24, para 11

The matters to be taken into account by an appeal panel in considering an appeal shall include—
(a) any preference expressed by the appellant in respect of the child as mentioned in section 86, and
(b) the arrangements for the admission of pupils published by the local education authority or the governing body under section 92.

The panels can hear three types of appeal, and their powers vary accordingly. The three types of appeal are:
–   appeals by parents against the refusal of a place in Years 3-13 (prejudice appeals)
–   appeals by parents against the refusal of a place in reception, Years 1 or 3 (infant class size appeals)
–   appeals by the governing body of a community or voluntary controlled school, against the decision of the LEA to admit a child who has been permanently excluded from other schools on two or more occasions (see above).
Appeal panels have been given the power to hear claims that admission decisions breach the Disability Discrimination Act 1995 (s 28K as inserted by s 20 of the SENDA 2001). This provision is likely to come into force in September 2002. The Disability Rights Commission has drafted two codes of practice on disability discrimination in education.

The DfEE's views on the powers of appeal panels are set out in the Code of Practice School Admission Appeals.

Code of Practice on School Admission Appeals (1999)

The powers of appeal panels

2.13 Appeal panels cannot hear complaints or objections on wider aspects of local admission policies and practice. This is the role of the Adjudicator or, in limited cases, the Secretary of State. Nor do appeal panels have a role in consultations through local Admissions Forums. Appeal panels can consider concerns about an individual admission authority's admission arrangements raised by a parent in the context of their appeal in so far as they may have a bearing on their child's admission. Panels should not get drawn into or allow general discussion about admission policies and practices at appeal hearings. They must focus on the case put forward by the admission authority for refusing to admit the child and the parents' case for admission.

However, in *R v Sheffield City Council, ex p H* [1999] ELR 511 the majority of the Court of Appeal (Laws LJ dissenting) considered that the appeal committee (as it was then called under the EA 1996) could consider the legality of LEA admission arrangements. Owen J had held that the LEA's admission procedure was unlawful (see above). Lord Justice Laws gives a powerful dissenting judgment setting out why in his opinion the committees (now known as panels) do not and should not have the jurisdiction to consider the legality of the LEA policy.

R v Sheffield City Council, ex p H [1999] ELR 511

Laws LJ: The conception that the committee might review the legality of LEA policy is to my mind inconsistent with the single role allotted to it: that is, as I have said, the determination of the merits of individual appeals. An adjudication to the effect that an admissions policy is unlawful would as a matter of logic be material not merely to the outcome of the individual appeal, but to the case of every child affected by the policy. That is only consonant with a general supervisory jurisdiction, as is possessed by the High Court, but which the committee certainly lacks. Moreover, the committee is not given the power to grant any remedy affecting a class of cases as opposed to the individual case: contrast the High Court's jurisdiction to give declaratory relief or, as appropriate, to issue one or more of the prerogative orders.

While Sch 33, para 11 is not as I have said drafted in exclusory terms, nevertheless its provisions constitute a powerful indication of the kind of exercise upon which the committee is enjoined to embark. It must 'take into account' the matters there set out, with a view to deciding whether the parents' choice of school in the individual case should prevail over the allocation made by the LEA pursuant to its policy. A requirement to 'take into account' any particular matter is in my judgment apt only to impose a duty to consider factual material. It is entirely inapt to impose a duty to adjudicate upon issues of law.

It was suggested in the course of argument that if the committee was not *obliged* 'to take into account' a legal error made by the LEA, nevertheless it was at least *entitled* to do so. I do not think this can be right. Quite aside from the sense to be given to the expression 'take into account', I cannot see how it can be asserted that the committee may *choose* whether or not to adjudicate upon a question of law, unless the suggestion is that the exercise of its jurisdiction, or some aspect of it, is discretionary, by analogy with the supervisory jurisdiction of the High Court. But such a proposition cannot possibly be got out of the statute.

Moreover, the suggestion that the committee possess a jurisdiction akin to judicial review is to my mind hopelessly impractical. The committee is made up of lay persons (they have, I understand, a legally qualified clerk) who are required to hear, year by year, a large number of individual appeals, and to do it speedily and relatively informally. We were told that in 1998 there were 49 such appeals from the Sheffield LEA. The prospect that the committee in disposing of its difficult and important workload might be obliged to hear intricate legal argument upon which it would then have to adjudicate with possibly far-reaching consequences seems to me to be nothing short of a recipe for chaos. I do not of course mean that the committee members would not do their duty thoroughly and conscientiously as they do at present, nor that they would necessarily be likely to arrive at the wrong result. But hearings would be lengthened. Lawyers would be briefed much more frequently than at present. Decision after decision of the committee would be challenged in judicial review proceedings. There would be much uncertainty while such proceedings were pending. The efficient administration of school admissions would be gravely undermined.

   ...

Pill LJ: The appeal committee's duty is, of course, to determine the merits of individual appeals. The idea that it can do so without some reference to the lawfulness of the arrangements made by the LEA under s 411 is, however, unrealistic. An appeal committee is not obliged to treat those arrangements as if set in stone and beyond challenge. They may lack clarity or, as in this case, be unlawful. Mr McManus accepted, in the course of argument, that the appeal committee should not be obliged to enforce arrangements which were contrary to basic human rights or were racially or sexually discriminatory. Whether they do so offend, involves a legal judgment by the appeal committee. Mr Bean was doing no more than submitting that, if it knew of the illegality present in this case, the appeal committee might have come to a different conclusion. I disagree with that submission on the facts, as already stated, but I cannot agree that, as a matter of jurisdiction, the appeal committee is disentitled from considering legal issues.

Laws LJ, whose judgment I have had the opportunity of reading in draft, refers to the existence of the power claimed for an appeal committee as 'hopelessly impractical'. Laws LJ goes on to accept, however, that were a committee faced with school admission arrangements which had already been condemned in the High Court as unlawful in some respect no doubt it might have regard to that fact if there was any practical sense in which it could properly affect the outcome of individual appeals. Far from being a 'far cry from what is suggested here', it is in my view exactly what Mr Bean was suggesting. The Court of Appeal had held, prior to the appeal committee decision, that arrangements not materially different from those in the present case were unlawful. Mr Bean submitted that, had the committee known of such illegality, its decision in the particular case might have been different. On the facts, I disagree with Mr Bean but he is in my view not defeated by a lack of jurisdiction.

   ...

The difficulty of defining the jurisdiction of an appeal committee which is intended to reassure parents by virtue of its independence is plain. There is no simple answer to the conflict which may follow from a wish to create, on the one hand, a quasi-judicial procedure which aggrieved parents may use and, on the other hand, a procedure which does not interfere unduly with the needs of good administration. The powers of an appeal committee in the present context have been stated briefly in the statute but generally. The statutory scheme does not provide specific answers to the difficulties of definition which arise. Good sense can be expected of committees in their approach to LEA arrangements. A committee is not obliged to ignore illegality if the merits of a particular case require adherence to legality.

   ...

Peter Gibson LJ: The appeal committee was plainly intended by Parliament to be an independent tribunal to which parents aggrieved by local education authority decisions relating to the schools in which their children are to be placed could turn to have those decisions impartially reviewed, and no restriction was placed on the grounds of the appeal or the nature of the representations which could be made to the committee.

...

If it is permissible for the appeal committee to consider some questions of law, I cannot think that there can be any objection in principle to the committee considering other questions of law relevant to the appeal. Having said that, I fully recognise the practical difficulties to which Laws LJ rightly draws attention in his judgment. The primary function of the appeal committee is to determine the merits of the particular appeal. The appeal committee plainly has no power to quash the council's policy decision, but if the point had been taken (which it was not) on the appeals in respect of the appellants that the admissions procedure was unlawful by reason of the *R v Rotherham Metropolitan Borough Council, ex p Clark* decision, I take the view that the appeal committee could not shut its eyes to that fact; nor could a fresh appeal committee do so. In each case it would have had to consider the effect of that illegality on the appeal before it.

In this case the appeals committee was not aware of the decision of the Court of Appeal in *R v Rotherham Metropolitan Borough Council, ex p Clark* [1998] ELR 152 which held that similar admission arrangements to those in Sheffield were unlawful. Where, for example, a parent raises the issue of the legality of the arrangements for the first time before the panel, the panel may choose to make a decision on the point or may prefer to decide that objections should have been lodged with the adjudicator (see above).

The Code of Practice School Admission Appeals recommends that parents should receive the documents from the admission authorities at least one week before the hearing. There is no statutory time limit for parents to submit information about their appeal.

However, in *R v Southend Borough Education Appeals Committee, ex p Southend-on-Sea Borough Council* (1999) LAWTEL 17/8/99, Hooper J considered that there were important policy reasons why those responsible for the child ought to put all relevant evidence regarding the child's admission before the LEA when it made its original admission decision. In this case the local authority challenged unsuccessfully the decision of the appeal committee, which had allowed the appeals brought by two parents and thereby admitted two children to an infant class.

'Prejudice' appeals

Where the admissions authority has not offered a place to a child because the school is full then 'prejudice' has to be established (see SSFA 1998, s 86(3)(a) above) by the admissions authority. This is the first part of the 'two-stage process' which was set out in *R v South Glamorgan Appeal Committee, ex p Evans* (10 May 1984, unreported), by Forbes J, and applied by Woolf LJ in *R v Comr for Local Administration, ex p Croydon London Borough Council* [1989] 1 All ER 1033. The hearing by the appeal panel is a rehearing rather than a review of the decision not to offer a place.

R v Comr for Local Administration, ex p Croydon LBC [1989] I All ER 1033

Woolf LJ: This is an application for judicial review by Croydon London Borough Council (Croydon) in respect of a report which was made by Dr Yardley (the commissioner), who is chairman of the Commission for Local Administration in England. In the report the commissioner concluded that there had been maladministration by an education appeal committee (the committee) set up by Croydon in the course of considering an appeal by parents who lived in the adjoining borough of Sutton against the refusal of Croydon to allow their daughter to attend a secondary school in Croydon in accordance with the preference which they had expressed. The application raises a general issue as to the extent of the jurisdiction of a local commissioner and education appeal committees. In addition it raises specific issues as to the manner in which the committee came to its decision to dismiss the appeal and the basis for the commissioner's conclusion that there had been maladministration by the committee.

The facts

For the purposes of the application the facts can be briefly summarised. In October 1984 the parents indicated that they would prefer their daughter to commence her secondary education the following year at one of three schools which they named. One of those schools, the school with which this application is concerned, was Woodcote High School, which was the school which the daughter's elder sister attended. The daughter was in fact allocated to none of the schools for which the parents had expressed a preference and instead she was allocated to a fourth school. On 6 June 1985 the parents appealed against the decision of Croydon in relation to the Woodcote High School. The appeal was heard by the committee and the appeal was dismissed. On 20 June 1985 a complaint was referred by a councillor to the commissioner in relation to dismissal of that appeal and the other appeals which were heard as a result of the refusal to admit the daughter to any of the preferred schools.

Although the decision of Forbes J in *R v South Glamorgan Appeals Committee, ex p Evans* (10 May 1984) is unreported, it is regarded as being of considerable significance by those concerned with pupil admissions.

...

The procedure adopted by these committees is one agreed with the Council on Tribunals as applicable to all county educational authorities ... It might be helpful, therefore, if the procedure were looked at again, particularly to indicate to these committees that it is indeed a two-stage exercise on which they embark: the first being to decide what is really a question of fact, is there or would there be prejudice to the efficient education etc if this child were admitted and the second, the question of discretion, balancing between the degree of prejudice and the extent of applicability of the parental factors. The onus seems to me to be clearly on the education authority in stage 1. As the Act can be read as indicating that its primary object is to support parental choice, it may be that it should be considered that the onus remains on the education authority to demonstrate that the prejudice is of sufficiently serious degree to outweigh the parental factor.

I have no doubt that Forbes J was perfectly right to take the view that there should be a two-stage exercise. Unless an appeal committee comes to the conclusion that compliance with the parents' preference would prejudice the provision of efficient education or the efficient use of resources, the local education authority remains under a duty to comply with the expressed preference and if they fail to do so they are in breach of duty. Accordingly, an appeal will automatically be allowed if an appeal committee do not consider that to give effect to the preference would result in such prejudice. If, however, an appeal committee comes to the conclusion that efficiency would be prejudiced by complying with the preference, then the appeal committee will have to proceed to the second stage and decide how to exercise its discretion, by weighing up the advantages which would be achieved by complying with the preference as against the prejudice this would cause. In general therefore I indorse Forbes J's approach.

- • *What did Woolf LJ state that the committee should consider at the first stage?*

The approach which should be adopted by the committee at the first stage was further explained in *R v Appeal Committee of Brighouse School, ex p G* [1997] ELR 39 where the court considered whether the role of the appeal committee was correctly explained by the document provided by the school to parents.

R v Appeal Committee of Brighouse School, ex p G [1997] ELR 39

Sedley J: Paragraph 10 of these notes reads as follows in its first three sub-paragraphs:

The Appeal Committee must adopt a two-stage process in reaching its decision. First, it must decide whether allowing more pupils into the school would prejudice the provision of efficient education and the efficient use of resources. If not, then some pupils must be admitted.

If it decides that the school has a reasonable case, it must move on to the second stage and consider the argument for each child. If, on balance, it decides that the parents' argument is stronger than that of the school, then it will decide that the child should be admitted.

You will receive a letter informing you of the Appeal Committee's decision after all appeals have been heard.

It can be seen that while the first of these subparagraphs poses the issue correctly, the second poses an incorrect test. It is not enough for the school to show the appeal committee that it has a reasonable case. It would be a surprising school that had a numbers limit without having a reasonable case for it. It is for the school to satisfy the appeal committee that the numbers limit is a justified numbers limit and upon that the appeal committee must ultimately form its own view.

...

The decision letter in para 2 begins by stating a conclusion which was indeed framed in terms appropriate to the legal obligation of the committee. It begins, 'The committee decided'. It then indicates its reasons for limiting itself to the domestic arrangements arrived at by the school itself. It gives no indication of having made any independent appraisal of the school's reasoning which had been testified to in detail by the headteacher before the committee. When one turns to the affidavit to see whether the affidavit can supply the want and show that the appeal committee had in fact independently appraised the school's own views and evidence in coming to its own conclusion, one finds on the contrary that it appears to have fallen into the error which the notes for guidance also fall into of simply asking whether the school had a case, as undoubtedly it did have, for its numbers limit.

In *R v Blackpool Borough Council Education Committee, ex p Taylor* [1999] ELR 237 parents argued that the committee had taken into account irrelevant information in reaching the decision that the school was full and could not admit any more pupils.

R v Blackpool Borough Council Education Committee, ex p Taylor [1999] ELR 237

Kay J: What is said, and what is the heart of this proposed challenge, is that there was evidence placed before the committee in the form of a report which not only referred to the problems that would be created at the school if extra children were admitted to it, but also that an efficient use of educational resources required consideration of problems at other schools where numbers would, as a result, be short. It is submitted that that is a factor which it was appropriate for the committee to take into account.

...

Thus, argues the proposed respondent, by analogy with a similar situation where similar wording is used in relation to special education needs, there is the authority of the Court of Appeal that it is open to an education committee to take into account not only the particular resources at that particular school, but other educational resources as well. The authority in question is *B v London Borough of Harrow and Special Educational Needs Tribunal* [1998] ELR 351.

If that were the only issue that was raised in this case, it would be my conclusion that there was at least an arguable point, and it may be that in an appropriate case it would be proper for such a matter to be argued and resolved by the court. I certainly would not be prepared to shut out such an application at this stage.

In *R v Sheffield City Council, ex p M* [2000] ELR 85 the court refused to grant leave to apply for judicial review of the LEA and appeal committee's decision that the school was full.

R v Sheffield City Council, ex p M [2000] ELR 85

Burton J: At the end of the day, looked at in the round, this is a question of whether a local authority, in the light of s 411(2)(a), just because there is a physical possibility of having 30 children in a class, can properly reach an informed decision to have a lesser limit and, notwithstanding the preference of a parent to have a child in, not to accede to that preference if it takes the number over that limit.

It seems to me clear that this committee took a decision that to increase the number of pupils and to allow G and the others in would prejudice the provision of efficient education or the efficient use of resources and their decision is not capable of challenge.

• *What did Woolf LJ state that the appeal committee should consider at the second stage?*

An illustration of the approach which should be adopted by the committee at the second stage is provided by *R v Essex County Council, ex p Jacobs* [1997] ELR 190.

R v Essex County Council, ex p Jacobs [1997] ELR 190

Collins J: The applicant, Kevin Jacobs, is the father of twins, Bradley and Zoe, who were born on 8 May 1985. He wants the twins to attend as their secondary school, Roding Valley High School in Loughton. That school is conveniently close and, perhaps, more importantly, their two elder sisters attended it. The oldest has just left, but the younger, now aged 13, is still there.

...

The applicant lives in Chigwell about a mile outside the boundary of the catchment area. He is divorced, and his ex-wife lives in the London Borough of Redbridge, again, about a mile outside the catchment area. Thus Roding Valley High School is particularly convenient for both parents since the children spend time at each of their addresses.

The original applications to enter the school were made by Mrs Jacobs using her address on 9 April 1995. They were, of course, applications for the school year beginning in September 1996.

On 9 February 1996 the applications were refused by the local education authority.

...

Suffice it to say, that on the evidence that was put before the committee, which I have referred to, it seems to me that it was perfectly proper for the committee to decide that in relation to that school alone — quite apart from any knock on effect in the education authority's area overall — there was established a prejudice to efficient education, and that brings into play s 6(3)(a) of the 1980 Act.

Furthermore, the evidence was sufficient to satisfy the committee, and clearly did satisfy the committee, that that was the position before any of the 32 appeals before it was considered. So, each appellant had the burden of satisfying the committee that notwithstanding that there would be a prejudice to efficient education, the child in question should be admitted because there were special circumstances arising in relation to that child.

...

There are, as it seems to me, two major flaws in what is set out on the face of those notes of the matters which weighed with the committee.

First of all, they seemed to believe that the sibling issue could be resolved by moving the child who was already at Roding Valley, presumably, hoping to place her at Woodbridge, although there was no evidence, as far as I am aware, before the committee that the child would be able to go to Woodbridge. Be that as it may, Mr Lane, who has appeared on behalf of the local education authority, accepts that that is something which the committee should not have had in mind. It clearly was an irrelevant consideration and was not a proper way of approaching the issue in relation to whether having a sibling at the school was a matter which should weigh in the favour of the parents. Quite apart from anything else, it is obviously thoroughly undesirable to move a child from a school where the child is happy and settled and remove her to another school in the middle of her secondary education. It was a proposition which really ought not to have been made at all.

...

It will be apparent from a combination of the notes and the recollections of Mr Wilkins, such as they are, and of Mr Convoy, that the committee clearly focused on the mother's address and the fact that there was available Woodbridge School from that address. What the committee seem to have failed to have appreciated is the relevance of father's address.

Now, it is not so much that the children would live at father's address and that that therefore is the appropriate address for the purpose of considering whether Roding Valley was the correct school, but that the children would spend a considerable part of the time at father's address. It was quite impossible to exclude consideration of that address as being a relevant factor to be taken into account in deciding whether Mr and Mrs Jacobs had raised sufficient exceptional circumstances to enable their children to qualify for Roding Valley School, notwithstanding that the numbers had already been filled.

It seems to me, that the committee ought to have considered both addresses in the light of the desirability of a school which was able to cater easily for both addresses, and that was the added relevance of the father's address. When one adds that to the sibling already at the school, and one bears in mind that that sibling too would have to go to both addresses that on the face of it might have provided a more powerful reason for the sibling connection to prevail in the circumstances of this case. Certainly, it is something which, as it seems to me, the committee ought to have taken into account.

Unfortunately, on the face of the material before me it did not. That together with the reference to the possibility of taking the elder child away from Roding Valley seems to me to indicate that the committee did indeed fail to have regard to all the relevant circumstances. More importantly, as a result, they may well not have attached sufficient weight to the matters which were being put forward on behalf of the Jacobs, as amounting to special circumstances to outweigh the prejudice to efficient education.

Where there is a dispute of fact between the admissions authority and the parent, the panel must make a finding of fact on the evidence.

R v Birmingham City Council Education Appeals Committee, ex p B [1999] ELR 305

Scott Baker J: Where an appeal committee of this nature is minded to disbelieve a case that is being advanced by an appellant, they should give that appellant an opportunity of dealing specifically with the points that are troubling them and are leading them towards making such a finding and give the appellant an opportunity of dealing with them. That did not happen in this case.

The balancing exercise which is undertaken by the panel at this stage is a matter of judgment, and it is difficult for parents to argue that the decision reached is unlawful.

R v South Gloucestershire Appeals Committee, ex p C [2000] ELR 220

Dyson J: I turn, therefore, to the balancing exercise itself. The question of the weight to be accorded to the parental factors and the prejudice to the provision of efficient education or the efficient use of resources is a matter of judgment. It is often difficult if not impossible to say why a decision which involves an exercise of judgment is made one way rather than another. In the present case, the committee felt that the prejudice that would be caused by the admission of the applicant slightly outweighed the parental factors. It might well be unrealistic to ask the committee in such a case: why? I suggest that the members of the panel would be likely to respond 'because that is the judgment we reached on the basis of our experience in education'.

In practice most parents appeal on the basis that their child would be prejudiced were he or she not to be offered a place. Tim Kaye argues that parents might have more chance of winning their appeal if they challenged the admission authority's statement that admitting another child would prejudice efficient education or the efficient use of resources (that is the first-stage issue).

Tim Kaye 'Admissions to school: efficiency versus parental choice?' (1998) 10 Education and the Law 19

It is worth reiterating that if those on the appeal committee are not satisfied that the LEA or governors have made out the case that there would be prejudice to efficient education or the efficient use of resources, then the committee is bound forthwith to allow the appeal — so that the child be admitted into the preferred school — because of the nature of the duty in s 411 of the EA 1996. There is then no need to consider the second stage at all. It is therefore of vital importance that the concept of efficiency in this context is better understood than appears to be the case at present. It is also important to emphasise, however, that an appellant parent must set out in writing beforehand the reasons for an appeal. This means that an appeal committee can only adjudicate upon the question of whether or not there would be any prejudice to efficient education or the efficient use of resources by the admission of the child in question to the preferred school if the claim of the LEA or governors to that effect is specifically challenged by the appellant parent.

...

In a typical appeal, it is clear that the only extra expenditure that would be required of a school if it were to admit the pupil concerned would be the sum of the cost of extra textbooks, incidental stationery, a chair and a desk. Yet, except for new textbooks, most schools carry a surplus of each of these items, so that the admission of one more child would not necessitate further expenditure and could not therefore be prejudicial to efficiency. Moreover, even where a school could show that it would have to spend more money than it had planned because of the admission of this particular pupil, the fact that the question of prejudice to efficiency has to be judged over at least the whole LEA area means that prejudice will remain hard to establish. For although the preferred school may be compelled to spend an additional sum of money, the admission of the pupil to another school in the area would usually necessitate the latter school's purchasing much the same books and equipment at much the same cost. Thus, although the immediate burden would fall on different schools depending on which of them actually admitted the pupil in question, the same costs would be incurred on behalf of council tax payers no matter which school admitted the pupil. It could not therefore be argued that the admission of the pupil into the preferred school would prejudice the efficient use of resources, since those resources would be used in an equally efficient way whichever school were to admit this pupil. The LEA or governors would therefore be unable to establish such prejudice and the parent's appeal would therefore have to be allowed at the first, factual stage of the hearing without any need for a consideration of the second stage.

The statistics available (see below) do not indicate the grounds on which parents win their appeal. Although casual appeals where only one or two parents are appealing may be won at stage one, it is unlikely that where there are multiple appeals that parents will succeed at stage one.

MULTIPLE APPEALS

Where there are multiple appeals for one school, which is likely in relation to popular schools, the same appeal panel should hear all the appeals. The previous Code of Practice recommended that each parent's appeal should be heard individually rather than as a grouped appeal. However, the current Code does not favour one method over the other. In any event, no decision should be taken by the panel until it has heard all the appeals.

Code of Practice on School Admission Appeals (1999)

Procedures for dealing with multiple appeals

4.65 Appeal panels may wish to deal with multiple appeals in one of two ways:

Grouped appeals: where the admission authority's case in respect of a school is heard once for the first stage of the appeal ... In this case, the admission authority presents its general case (the factual stage) in the presence of all parents (and any representatives) who may question the case. If the panel concludes that 'prejudice' exists, it will be necessary to move to the second stage. At this stage the appeals of the individual parents should be heard without the presence of the others and no decisions should be taken until all the appeals have been heard.

Individual appeals: where the admission authority presents its case, followed by the individual parents' cases, as in the order of the hearing set out in paragraph 4.46. In these circumstances, it will be necessary for the panel to hear the admission authority's case repeatedly. In the first stage, where the admission authority is arguing that prejudice would arise, the case will always be the same. The admission authority must not produce new evidence, or expand upon its case as the appeals proceed, because parents earlier in the process will not have had an opportunity to consider that evidence and respond accordingly. The clerk should explain at the start of the hearing that the admission authority may not do this. If, however, material new evidence comes out in the questioning of the admission authority's evidence, the clerk should ensure that the appeal panel considers what bearing the evidence may have on all the appeals and should decide how best to advise so that the panel deals with the matter fairly. This may entail adjourning the appeals to give parents the opportunity to consider and challenge the new evidence.

In *R (on the application of C) v Governing Body of Cardinal Newman High School* [2001] ELR 359 Newman J held that the admissions appeal panel did not follow the Code of Practice in a multiple appeal. In particular, the panel should have admitted seven children because the governing body had not established that the school had reached its admission number. Only then should the second stage of the two-stage test be considered by the panel in relation to other appeals. (See also chapter 1 on the human rights aspects of this case.)

In multiple appeals should the committee compare one child's case with another?

This issue was addressed in *R v Education Appeal Committee of Leicestershire County Council, ex p Tarmohamed* [1997] ELR 48.

R v Education Appeal Committee of Leicestershire County Council, ex p Tarmohamed [1997] ELR 48

Sedley J: In my judgment it is where fairness is unattainable without some process of comparison that the law steps in and demands it. For the reasons that I have given, comparison is not called for when in the committee's judgment only one of a number of appeals for admission to the same school merits success on the ground that the parental preference has greater weight than the resultant prejudice to educational provision. It is true that this is implicitly a comparative exercise because one child will have succeeded where others have failed, but this is because it provides a basis upon which others may make comparison, not because it itself was being carried out by the making of a comparison.

Where, however, the first stage of establishing prejudice in the event of further admissions has been reached, if on matching the individual grounds for parental preference against the established level of prejudice a number of children, say six out of the present 15, come through as each meriting admission, then there may well arise a further problem. The problem is whether, even though the school might have withstood the stress of one or perhaps two further admissions, the admission of all six (in the postulated case) may create such further stress upon the school's provision and resources that they cannot, in the committee's judgment, all be admitted.

In this event there is in my view — and Mr McCarthy for the local education authority accepts this — no alternative but to rank the children in order of priority. This, however, is not because it is something which the Act spells out. It is what fairness demands in order to enable the committee to make properly informed individual decisions pursuant to the Act in a case where the number of appeals which have succeeded in the face of the initial test of prejudice creates a further level of prejudice to the provision and resources of the school.

'Infant class size' appeals

The power of the appeal panel is restricted where the child is applying for a place in an infant class. The panel does not go through the second or balancing stage of the process which applies to 'prejudice' appeals. There are only two grounds on which the appeal panel can allow an appeal where the child is refused a place in an infant class (reception, Year 1, and Year 2).

School Standards and Framework Act 1998, Sch 24, para 12

Where the decision under appeal was made on the ground that prejudice of the kind referred to in section 86(3)(a) would arise as mentioned in subsection (4) of that section, an appeal panel shall determine that a place is to be offered to the child only if they are satisfied—

(a)   that the decision was not one which a reasonable admission authority would make in the circumstances of the case; or

(b)   that the child would have been offered a place if the admission arrangements (as published under section 92) had been properly implemented.

Two issues have come before the courts. The first is the nature of the appeal hearing; and the second is whether or not fresh evidence may be presented to the appeal panel.

SCHOOL STANDARDS AND FRAMEWORK ACT 1998, SCH 24, PARA 12(a)

In *R v Sheffield City Council, ex p H* [1999] ELR 511 at 520 Laws LJ stated that para 12(a) 'may indeed be said to confer a jurisdiction akin to judicial review, although very plainly circumscribed so as to apply only to the particular appellant's individual circumstances'.

In *R v Richmond upon Thames London Borough Council and Education Appeal Committee, ex p JC (Secretary of State for Education and Employment intervening)* [2000] ELR 565 Kay J held that appeals under the predecessor to para 12(a) were reviews rather than rehearings. In his view this meant that no fresh evidence could be submitted by the parents to the appeal hearing, but this was not the view taken by the Court of Appeal. Kennedy LJ also disagreed with Kay J's interpretation of para (a) in the Code of Practice School Admission Appeals (1999), considering that it was too restrictive.

R v Richmond upon Thames London Borough Council and Education Appeal Committee, ex p JC [2001] ELR 21

Kennedy LJ: Still confining myself to the words of the paragraph, I turn to para 11A(1)(a) [now SSFA 1998, Sch 24, para 12(a)]. Here the test is not, as in (b), what the original admissions authority would have done. Its decision is accepted, and exposed to a rationality test. Was it a decision 'which a reasonable admission authority *would make* in the circumstances of the case?' The words underlined — 'would make' — suggest that the appeal committee has to envisage the admission authority making its decision now. It does not have to envisage what decision a reasonable admission authority *would have made*, and that I regard as significant, particularly when contrasted with the tenses of the verbs in para 11A(1)(b). If the appeal committee has to envisage the admissions authority making its decision now I see no reason why the appeal committee should not have regard to any information now available, but it will need to be persuasive. Taken together with the rest of the information, and any other relevant circumstances, it must render the original decision irrational, or the original decision stands.

    ...

    If my interpretation of para 11A(1)(a) is correct then the appeals committee can have regard to fresh evidence, but it cannot conduct a rehearing. It can only ask itself whether the decision not to admit the child was not one which a reasonable admissions authority would (now) make in the circumstances of the case. Those circumstances may include, as they do in this case, the fact that the fresh evidence sought to be relied upon could have been placed before the admissions authority which made the original decision, and the fact that all of the available places have already been allocated. That approach is to some extent less restrictive than the approach adopted by Kay J, and for which Mr Swift, for the respondents, contended before us. But I doubt whether in the vast majority of cases that distinction will make any difference to the outcome. However, the approach which commends itself to me does have this advantage — it allows the appeal committee to have regard to powerful evidence of a highly significant change of circumstances which for one reason or another could not have been placed before the original admissions authority, and thus to do justice, without undermining the purpose of the legislation as a whole.

SCHOOL STANDARDS AND FRAMEWORK ACT 1998, SCH 24, PARA 12(b)

Although a para 12(b) hearing is still regarded as a review of the original decision fresh evidence may also be admissible in certain circumstances.

R v Richmond upon Thames London Borough Council and Education Appeal Committee, ex p JC (Secretary of State for Education and Employment intervening) [2000] ELR 565 (QBD)

Kay J: I would only add that in considering subpara (b), deciding whether the admission arrangements have properly been applied may well raise questions of whether the decision is *Wednesbury* unreasonable. Where some factual criterion is involved such as proximity, it will not be difficult to resolve the issue and if the admissions authority has made a mistake which is crucial to the decision, the appeal will be allowed. Where, however, there is a question of judgment involved such as in consideration of the weight to be attached to special circumstances, the admissions authority will not have 'properly implemented' the admissions arrangements if they reached a conclusion on the weight that was *Wednesbury* unreasonable.

The information upon which the decision is to be judged will be that which was before the admissions authority, together, I would add, with evidence of which they should have been aware if they had acted reasonably. Thus the only time that it will be possible to put fresh information before the appeal committee is when it can be demonstrated that it is information of which the admissions authority should have been aware if they had acted reasonably. If, for example, the parents could show that there was information which they had not provided because they had never been given any indication that it should be provided, or that they had been misled into thinking that the admissions authority would seek such information itself then fresh evidence may be admissible, but it will only be in limited circumstances of that kind.

Kennedy LJ in the Court of Appeal stated that he agreed with Kay J's interpretation of (b), although he added ([2001] ELR at 31):

As a matter of statutory construction it seems to me that para 11A(1)(b) is really a slip clause empowering the appeal committee to put right any error made by the admissions authority (in this case the sub-committee) on the information available to it. For example, if it failed to notice that the applicant had a sibling in the school despite that information being given on the application form, or if it miscalculated the distance between the applicant's home and the school. The tense of the verbs in para 11A(1)(b) seems to me to make it clear that in general in considering this sub-paragraph the appeal committee cannot look at anything not available to the original admission authority.

A fresh statement or a fresh letter might be a convenient way in which to highlight the original error, but it would have to be discernible without recourse to additional material, and if the appellant is to succeed there has to be no doubt as to what the sub-committee would have decided if the admission arrangements had been properly implemented.

In *R v South Gloucestershire Education Appeals Committee, ex p Bryant* [2001] ELR 53 the parents were unable to persuade the Court of Appeal that the appeal committee was wrong to accept that the LEA had properly implemented the admission arrangements.

- *Compare and contrast the situations where parents are able when appealing under either para 12(a) or para 12(b) to produce 'fresh evidence' to the independent appeal panel.*

- *To what extent does the limit on the size of infant classes restrict parental preference and the right to appeal?*

A further complication arises where the admission for the infant class is less than 30, for example, 27. Should the appeal panel apply the prejudice test or the infant class size test?

Anne Ruff 'Admission appeals in 1999: the impact of the 1998 Regulations and R v Birmingham CC, ex parte M (1998)' (1999) 11 Education and the Law 77

In this case the 'standard' two-stage prejudice test would presumably apply until 30 children have been offered places. Once 30 children have places the 'new' [infant class size] prejudice test would apply to other appeals. If, for example, the approved number is 27, and there are 15 parents appealing for a place, the appeal committee, having heard all the appeals, should rank them using the standard test. The committee could then allow no, one, two or three appeals. If it wished to allow further appeals, the committee would be required to use the new [infant class size] prejudice test for the remaining cases.

Permanently excluded pupil admission appeals

The parent of a pupil who has been permanently excluded on two or more occasions may not appeal against the refusal of a place within two years of the most recent exclusion (see above, s 95(1) of the SSFA 1998). However, where the LEA decides to admit such a child to a school, the governing body of the school can appeal to an appeal panel against this decision (s 95(2) of the SSFA 1998).

The appeal panel is similar to a school admissions appeal panel. However, no member can sit on the panel if they have previously been involved in considering whether the child should have been reinstated after a permanent exclusion or in any other admission appeal during the two-year period (SSFA 1998, Sch 25, para 3(2)). Schedule 25 sets out the procedures for hearing these appeals. The decision of the appeal panel is binding on the LEA and the governing body.

School Standards and Framework Act 1998, Sch 25

7 On an appeal the panel shall allow—
(a)   the local education authority and the governing body to make written representations;
(b)   an officer of the authority nominated by the authority, and a governor nominated by the governing body, to appear and make oral representations; and
(c)   the governing body to be represented.

8 In considering an appeal the appeal panel shall have regard to—
(a)   the reasons for the local education authority's decision that the child in question should be admitted; and
(b)   any reasons put forward by the governing body as to why the child's admission would be inappropriate.

The panel's decision

The parents, the LEA, and the governing body should be informed in writing of the panel's decision 'and the grounds on which it is made' (Sch 24, para 15 to the SSFA 1998). In the case of a permanently excluded pupil admission appeal the decision of the panel and the grounds on which it is made should be communicated in writing to the LEA and the governing body within two days (Sch 25, para 12 to the SSFA 1998).

Code of Practice on School Admission Appeals (1999)

Notification of the decision to parents

4.83 Schedule 24 to the 1998 Act requires that the decision and the grounds on which it is made be communicated in writing to parents and the admission authority. The decision letter should make reference to the two-stage process (see paragraphs 4.55 to 4.61) – unless that was not followed, e g because the appeal involved a class size issue (see paragraphs 4.52 to 4.54 and Annex B) – and indicate the establishment of prejudice by the admission authority. The letter should also explain in full why the panel decided that the individual circumstances of the parents' case were considered sufficient or insufficient to outweigh the prejudice arguments of the admission authority.

4.84 The written decision should be sent by the clerk and it should be expressed clearly, using straightforward language that can be understood by a lay person. The letter should be sent as soon as possible after the appeal panel has made its decision and ideally within seven days, although this may not always be possible where there are multiple appeals for one school.

The contents of such decision letters have been sometimes criticised for merely reciting, for example, the two-stage process undertaken by the appeal panel and not specifically addressing the grounds of appeal raised by the parents. This was central to the case of *R v Birmingham City Council Education Appeals Committee, ex p B* [1999] ELR 305.

R v Birmingham City Council Education Appeals Committee, ex p B [1999] ELR 305

Scott Baker J: This is an application for judicial review of a decision of the Birmingham City Council Education Appeals Committee.

The applicant is aged 11 and was due to commence secondary school education in September 1998. His parents want him to go to John Wilmott school which was their expressed preference. However, the education authority allocated him to Washwood Heath school.

...

The applicant's parents live in Erdington. That is where the local education authority regarded him as living. That is the address that was given to Brookvale Primary School where the applicant attended until July 1998. But the position is, says the applicant's father, that the applicant was showing signs of being a difficult child. Apparently this was put down to him being an only child. In order to address the problem he went to live with his father's twin brother in Sutton Coldfield. The twin brother has two girls also living at the same address. One already has been going to the John Wilmott school for some time and the other started September 1998. The evidence before the education authority was to an extent equivocal about when the applicant started living in Sutton Coldfield and the extent to which he lived there.

...

In this case the decision emerged from the panel dated the very same day that the panel had concluded hearing these appeals. It had concluded, so the evidence tells us, on the afternoon of 1 May 1998. A letter dated that day was sent to the applicant's parents.

...

It seems plain to me and indeed it is conceded that that was a standard form letter. It tells the reader absolutely nothing in my judgment about the particular facts or circumstances of this applicant's appeal.

...

Miss Mountfield relies on the decision of Macpherson J in *R v Lancashire County Council, ex p M* [1995] ELR 136 where he said that it was sufficient under the provision that preceded para 14 to give the grounds of the decision and that the grounds were distinguishable from detailed reasons. Putting it shortly, the appeal committee did not have to go into detail in saying why it had come to the conclusion that it had.

...

In my judgment, there was a failure here to give, as the statute required, the grounds on which this particular decision was made. Whilst I accept entirely the observations of Macpherson J that it is quite unnecessary for an appeal committee of this kind to go into detailed reasons, it does seem to me that the statute requires that an appellant is entitled to know the basis for the decision beyond simply a ritual incantation of the two-stage test. Then it is said that the committee erred in failing to follow the city council's published policy and to allocate M a place, in the light of the apparent finding of the committee that the boy was not living in Sutton Coldfield. If that is indeed the finding that was being made, they never reached the further stage of assessing the boy's situation in the context of where his case lay in the priority scale. It was, in my judgment, absolutely fundamental for a finding to be made as to where the boy was living. This could give rise to difficulty if it be the case that M was living for 4 days a week at his uncle's address and at the weekends with his parents, particularly if he had been doing so over a significant period of time. But it was up to the committee to decide what the facts were and then make a finding.

R v South Gloucestershire Appeals Committee, ex p C [2000] ELR 220

Dyson J: I do not believe that the decision in *R v Birmingham City Council Education Appeals Committee, ex p B* lays down any general principle save perhaps to say that a minimum requirement of the grounds of a decision is that they explain broadly the basis of the decision. I respectfully agree with what Macpherson J said in *R v Lancashire County Council, ex p M* [1995] ELR 136: the statute requires broad grounds rather than detailed reasons. What is required will depend on the issues that have been raised on the appeal. In a complex case the grounds may well have to be more elaborate than in a simple one. Where however there is no dispute as to the primary facts, I do not consider that the grounds are required to make findings about those facts.

...

It seems to me that in a case such as the present, to insist on the committee giving reasons for its exercise of judgment would be to treat the grounds of its decision as equivalent to the detailed reasons for it. Parliament has not required detailed reasons. All that the appellant needs to know is how on the undisputed facts or on the facts as found (whichever is the case), the committee has exercised its judgment in the weighing of the scales.

However, in *R (on the application of L) v Independent Appeal Panel of St Edward's College* [2001] EWHC Admin 108, [2001] ELR 542 Morison J considered that the decision letter fell below the standard required. He approved *R v Birmingham City Council Education Appeals Committee, ex p B* [1999] ELR 305 stating that where there were issues of fact to be resolved, or new material, or a new point raised, the 'standard letter would need to be tailored to deal with such an appeal'.

Anne Ruff 'Admission appeals in 1999: the impact of the 1998 Regulations and *R v Birmingham City Council, ex parte M* (1998)' (1999) 11 Education and the Law 77

Second, in view of recent judicial decisions, in particular the *Birmingham* case, as well as the comments of the Local Government Ombudsman, the letter notifying the parents of the appeal committee's decision should set out the specific grounds for their decision. The decision should specifically address the main ground(s) of appeal. This is likely to be the position for all types of admissions appeals, not just 'prejudice' appeals.

This does not mean that standard form letters can never be used; nor does it mean that detailed reasons have to be given. However, local authorities and governing bodies should review the letters they currently use and if necessary adapt them so that the specific grounds for the committee's decision may be included. In the long run it may be simpler to adopt this approach for all admission appeals. It may be undesirable, if not difficult, to distinguish 'run-of-the-mill-cases' from unusual cases. Therefore, it would be advisable for the notes taken by the clerk at the appeal hearing and when recording the committee's decision to be sufficiently detailed to provide these specific grounds. The clerk may find it necessary to ensure that the committee has identified and addressed the central issues raised by each appeal.

The difficulty faced by local authorities and governing bodies is that if the specific grounds for the appeal committee's decision are set out in the decision letter, parents are likely to find it easier to challenge the decision than hitherto. On the other hand, if local authorities decide, for whatever reason, to continue using the standard form 'ritual incantation', the decision may equally be open to challenge by parents.

Alternatively, a compromise would be for local authorities and governing bodies to inform parents in the decision letter of their right under the Tribunals and Inquiries Act 1992 to request further reasons for the decision. However, this may prove more time-consuming than automatically providing specific grounds in all decision letters.

Statistics

The statistics available indicate that parents do not often succeed with their appeal.

Audit Commission 'Trading Places — The Supply and Allocation of School Places' (1996)

Admissions appeals in England 1991/92 to 1994/95

Appeals have increased by 58 per cent in the primary sector and 35 per cent in the secondary sector.

Number of appeals (000s)

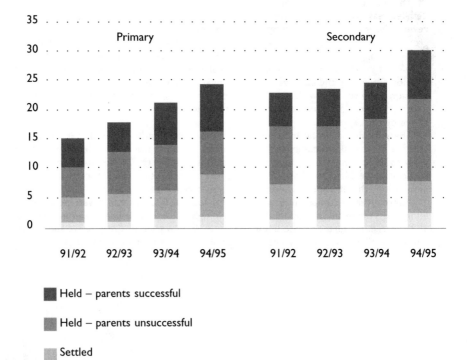

Held – parents successful

Held – parents unsuccessful

Settled

Withdrawn

Research on admission appeals in the London Borough of Haringey in 1999 indicated that the success rate for community schools could be particularly low.

Anne Ruff with Andrew Dorn 'Parental Perceptions of the School Admissions Appeal Process in the London Borough of Haringey Summer 1999' Middlesex University (2000)

APPEALS HEARD	PRIMARY National 1997/98	Haringey 1997/8	Haringey 1999	Haringey 1999
Number heard (%)	16,621 (100)	155 (100)	32 (100)	14 (100)
Number upheld (%)	8,125 (49)	43 (28)	10 (31)	2 (14)
Number not upheld (%)	8,496 (51)	112 (72)	22 (69)	12 (86)

APPEALS HEARD	SECONDARY National 1997/98	Haringey 1997/8	Haringey 1999	Haringey 1999
Number heard (%)	20,519 (100)	110 (100)	166 (100)	65 (100)
Number upheld (%)	7,838 (38)	9 (8)	7 (4)	1 (2)
Number not upheld (%)	12,681 (62)	101 (92)	159 (96)	64 (98)

The most significant feature of these figures is the low number of appeals that are upheld by Haringey appeal committees compared with the national figures. This was the position in 1998 as well as in 1999. One reason for this may be that the admissions criteria for Haringey schools are relatively clear-cut. The admissions authority has no discretion in most cases. There is no element of selection based on aptitude or ability. Therefore, so long as the admissions criteria have been applied properly it is more difficult for parents to persuade the committee that their child has been unduly prejudiced. A second reason may be that the LEA is normally able to present a strong case when arguing that a particular school is unable to accommodate additional pupils in a specific year group.

Admission statistics published by the DfES in June 2001 confirm that only a minority of appeals are successful.

DfEs 'Admission Appeals for Maintained Primary and Secondary Schools in England 1999/00'

Table I Appeals lodged by parents against non-admission of their children to maintained primary and secondary schools: England 1995/96 to 1999/00

		1995/96	1996/97	1997/98	1998/99	1999/00
Primary						
Admissions (1)	Number:	580,778	572,989	563,205	569,478	547,761
Appeals lodged by parents	Number:	27,996	32,643	30,868	32,194	28,728
Number of appeals lodged per 1,000 new admissions	Number:	48.2	57.0	54.8	56.5	52.4
Heard by appeals committee	Number:	18,794	21,817	20,178	21,219	18,712
	Percentage (2)	67	67	65	66	65
Appeals decided in parents' favour	Number:	9,056	10,580	9,564	9,341	7,290
	Percentage (3)	48	48	47	44	39
Secondary						
Admissions	Number:	582,184	602,151	604,063	617,681	628,613
Appeals lodged by parents	Number:	34,860	40,021	46,103	53,739	60,454
Number of appeals lodged per 1,000 new admissions	Number:	59.9	66.5	76.3	87.0	96.2
Heard by appeals committee	Number:	25,206	29,472	33,192	38,961	43,943
	Percentage (2)	72	74	72	73	73
Appeals decided in parents' favour	Number:	7,921	9,234	10,752	12,642	14,182
	Percentage (3)	31	31	32	32	32
All Schools						
Admissions	Number:	1,162,962	1,175,140	1,167,268	1,187,159	1,176,374
Appeals lodged by parents	Number:	62,856	72,664	76,971	85,933	89,182
Number of appeals lodged per 1,000 new admissions	Number:	54.0	61.8	65.9	72.4	75.8
Heard by appeals committee	Number:	44,000	51,289	53,370	60,180	62,655
	Percentage (2)	70	71	69	70	70
Appeals decided in parents' favour	Number:	16,977	19,814	20,316	21,983	21,472
	Percentage (3)	39	39	38	37	34

(1) Admissions in primary schools collected for the first two terms only
(2) Number of appeals heard by a committee expressed as a percentage of the number of appeals lodged by parents
(3) Number of appeals decided in favour of the parents expressed as a percentage of the number of appeals heard by a committee

Table 2 Appeals lodged by parents against non-admission of their children to maintained primary and secondary schools by type of school England 1999/000

England	Number of schools admissions	Percentage of school admissions for which there was no appeal	Number of appeals lodged by parents	Appeals withdrawn before reaching an appeal committee		Number of appeals heard by appeals committee		Appeals decided in parents' favour	
				Number	% (1)	Number	% (1)	Number	% (2)
PRIMARY									
Community (3) and voluntary controlled	436,700	94	25,202	7,354	29	15,769	63	6,306	40
Voluntary aided and aided (4)	93,690	97	2,856	462	16	2,394	84	829	35
Foundation (5)	17,371	96	670	121	18	549	82	155	28
Total Primary	**547,761**	**95**	**28,728**	**7,937**	**27**	**18,712**	**65**	**7,290**	**40**
SECONDARY									
Community (3) and voluntary controlled	444,767	90	41,353	9,842	24	28,209	68	10,604	38
Voluntary aided and aided (4)	61,142	91	5,660	820	14	4,840	86	1,133	23
Foundation (5)	122,704	89	13,441	2,547	19	10,894	81	2,445	22
Total Secondary	**628,613**	**90**	**60,454**	**13,209**	**22**	**43,943**	**73**	**14,182**	**32**
ALL SCHOOLS									
Community (3) and voluntary controlled	881,467	92	66,555	17,196	26	43,978	66	16,910	38
Voluntary aided and aided (4)	154,832	94	8,516	1,282	15	7,234	86	1,962	27
Foundation (5)	140,075	90	14,111	2,668	19	11,443	81	2,600	23
TOTAL	**1,176,374**	**92**	**89,182**	**21,146**	**24**	**62,655**	**70**	**21,472**	**34**

(1) Number of appeals expressed as a percentage of the number of appeals lodged by parents
(2) Number of appeals decided in favour of the parents expressed as a percentage of the number of appeals heard by a committee
(3) Community schools, previously county schools
(4) Aided schools, previously special agreement schools
(5) Foundation schools, previously grant maintained schools

Unfortunately, the DfES figures for primary schools do not distinguish between infant and junior appeals. This was the second year (1999/2000) that the infant class test applied. This test makes it more difficult for parents to appeal successfully. It is likely to be the main reason for the 11 per cent reduction in the number of appeals lodged and a 5 per cent reduction in the number of successful primary school admission appeals, because reception class appeals make up the great majority of primary school appeals.

There are considerable variations between LEAs and regions in the percentage of appeals lodged and the success rate for appeals. In 1999/2000 the national average for successful primary school appeals was 39 per cent. In the East Riding of Yorkshire, however, 71 per cent (157) of primary school appeals heard were successful, whereas in the London Borough of Southwark only 6 per cent (15) of appeals heard were successful.

The variation for secondary school appeals is similar. The national average for successful appeals in 1999/2000 was 32 per cent. In North Lincolnshire, however, 76 per cent (42) of appeals were successful, whereas in the London Borough of Hammersmith and Fulham only 5 per cent (10) of appeals were successful.

There are likely to be a number of factors causing the variation in success rates. These may include admission criteria which contain ambiguities or give discretion to the admission authority, for example in relation to religious affiliation or academic ability; and a shortage of local school places.

89,200 appeals were lodged by parents in 1999/2000 out of approximately 1,162,962 admissions. The DfES considers that the great majority of parents obtain the school of their choice. To support this claim the Department relies on a report it commissioned from Sheffield Hallam University and the Office of National Statistics, which was published in June 2001. Nearly 3,000 parents of secondary school pupils were interviewed. The findings show that:

– 91 per cent of the parents said they were satisfied with the outcome of the application process
– 96 per cent received an offer for a place at a school for which they had expressed a preference
– 92 per cent were offered a place at either the school they ranked first on their LEA application form or one they applied to direct; and
– 85 per cent were offered a place at their favourite school — the one they most wanted their child to go to.

Can parents challenge the appeal panel's decision?

The committee's decision is binding on the LEA, the governing body and the parents. However, in certain circumstances parents can ask the Secretary of State to review a committee's decision (see e g *R v Beatrix Potter School, ex p K* [1997] ELR 468 above); make an application for judicial review (see also e g *R v Appeal Committee of Brighouse School, ex p G* [1997] ELR 39); or make a complaint to the Local Government Ombudsman.

The Local Government Ombudsman can investigate complaints where the committee has failed to comply with procedural requirements. *R v Comr for Local Administration, ex p Croydon London Borough Council* (1989) (see also above) provides a valuable illustration of the respective roles of the Ombudsman and the court in this context.

R v Comr for Local Administration, ex p Croydon London Borough Council [1989] I All ER 1033

Woolf LJ: In that report the commissioner set out the results of his inquiries, and his reasons for coming to the conclusion that there was maladministration in the way the committee dealt with the appeal and the injustice which he concluded had occurred as a result. He also expressed the opinion that the only fair way to remedy the maladministration was for the appeal to be reheard by a fresh committee with all the available evidence before them. He also made certain general recommendations as to how appeal committees should perform their functions in the future. There was then a meeting between officers of the council and the commissioner and subsequently the commissioner wrote a letter on 20 November 1986 clarifying his conclusions and recommendations.

...

The jurisdiction issue

...

In short, the specific criticisms are, first, that the committee acted on inadequate evidence and did not seek, as it should have done, further evidence and, second, that the committee in reaching its decision applied its policy to the exclusion of the merits of the particular case which was before it. These are matters of complaint which I regard the commissioner as having jurisdiction to consider within the terms of s 26(1).

...

The problem in this case is that the commissioner apparently never appreciated that there was a conflict between his jurisdiction and that of the court. In my view he should have done so at least before he concluded his investigation and then he should have exercised his discretion whether to discontinue his investigation. However, as he indicates that if he had considered the question of discretion he would undoubtedly have decided to proceed, I would not be prepared to grant relief solely on this basis.

However, counsel for Croydon also complains about the two grounds on which the commissioner found maladministration. She says that his own report makes it clear that there was no justification for either finding. I accept that this submission is well founded.

The commissioner apparently has taken the view in para 43 that the committee was not entitled, on the basis that the daughter's admission would result in an increase above the 210 figure which was the planned admission limit for the school, to conclude that to allow the appeal of the parents would cause prejudice. However, as the report makes clear, this limit was part of Croydon's transitional arrangements to establish a new sixth form entry under a reorganisation scheme approved in December 1982 by the Secretary of State. The committee had the statement of Croydon which explained the circumstances in which that limit had been determined. The committee was aware that it was Croydon's policy that apart from 30 pupils from a specific area in Sutton, all the places at the school had to be offered to children who, unlike the daughter, were resident in Croydon. 272 children living in Croydon had in fact given the school as a first preference and in consequence

97 parents from Croydon still had their names on the school's waiting list. In these circumstances there was ample material available which entitled the committee to come to the conclusion that admission of the daughter would be prejudicial.

The substance of the second criticism made by the commissioner was that the committee not only took into account the policy but in the case of three out of five of the members regarded that policy as constituting good cause for not considering the appeal at all. However, the commissioner in his report carefully sets out the reasoning of the five members and the contents of his own report make it clear that this criticism is just not justified. The members of the committee, as they were entitled to, took different views of the importance of the policy, but in no case did any member decide the case on policy considerations alone. It follows that as criticisms are unjustified there is no foundation for the commissioner's finding of maladministration.

Complaints about admissions procedures, in particular the procedures followed by appeal committees, comprise approximately 25 per cent of the complaints concerning education that are referred to the Ombudsman. (See also chapter 8 on complaints procedure and the section in that chapter on local government ombudsmen.)

5.   DUTIES OF PARENTS

Children aged 5-16 years

Parents are under a legal duty to ensure that any of their children who are aged 5–16 years are in full-time education.

Education Act 1996, s 7

The parent of every child of compulsory school age shall cause him to receive efficient full-time education suitable—
(a)   to his age, ability and aptitude, and
(b)   to any special educational needs he may have,

either by regular attendance at school or otherwise.

The following definitions should be noted.
(1)   'Suitable' means that 'the education (a) prepares the child for life in modern civilised society; (b) enables the child to achieve his full potential' (*Harrison v Stevenson* (1981) unreported; see Liell, Coleman and Poole (eds) *The Law of Education* B[3008]).
(2)   'Regular attendance' means 'for the periods prescribed by the person upon whom the duty to provide education is laid' (per Lord Parker CJ, *Hinchley v Rankin* [1961] 1 WLR 421 at 425). In other words a child who arrives late after the register is closed may be deemed not to have attended school that day.
(3)   'Otherwise' than at school includes home education, and education at a Pupil Referral Unit (PRU), which may only amount to four or five hours tuition a week.
An LEA can serve a school attendance order on a parent who is in breach of this duty, and failure to comply with the order will make a parent liable to prosecution. This may

occur where the parent is educating their child at home, but the LEA considers that the education being given is not 'suitable'.

School attendance orders

Education Act 1996, ss 437 and 443

437(1) If it appears to a local education authority that a child of compulsory school age in their area is not receiving suitable education, either by regular attendance at school or otherwise, they shall serve a notice in writing on the parent requiring him to satisfy them within the period specified in the notice that the child is receiving such education.

...

443(1) If a parent on whom a school attendance order is served fails to comply with the requirements of the order, he is guilty of an offence, unless he proves that he is causing the child to receive suitable education otherwise than at school.

Registered pupil

Where the child is a registered pupil at a school, but does not attend, the parent is liable to be prosecuted under s 444 of the EA 1996. This section is likely to be used where a pupil truants regularly.

Education Act 1996, s 444(1)

(1) If a child of compulsory school age who is a registered pupil at a school fails to attend regularly at the school, his parent is guilty of an offence.

The following case illustrates how this section is applied.

Bath and North East Somerset District Council v Warman [1999] ELR 81

Rose LJ: This is a prosecutor's appeal by way of case stated against a decision of the Bath and Wansdyke magistrates. On 11 June 1998 they acquitted the respondent, Mrs Warman, in relation to an information which alleged that she was the parent of a child of compulsory school age who had failed to attend school regularly over a period of 6 months, prior to the date of the information, contrary to s 444 of the Education Act 1996.

The girl was born on 8 October 1981. Her sixteenth birthday in consequence fell at or about the midpoint of the autumn term in 1997. She was undoubtedly, as the justices found, of compulsory school age at the period to which the information related. She was one of 10 children born to her mother, the respondent. Eight children live at home, six at this time were of compulsory school age and all, save the eldest, the girl featuring in this information, attended school regularly. In June/July 1997 the girl in question, as I have said then being a few months off her sixteenth birthday, left home to live with her long-term boyfriend. The justices found that she went to live some considerable distance away in Devon. They further found that her mother did not know where she was living until Christmas 1997, by which time of course the girl was over 16. The attendance certificate before the justices (dated 3 February 1998) showed, as I have indicated, that the girl failed to attend school at all during the 1997 autumn term. The justices found that the mother objected to her daughter leaving home but could not stop her.

...

However hard it may appear to be, in my judgment, the construction placed upon this statutory provision in the authorities to which I have referred, makes the conclusion inescapable that the circumstances of this case did not give rise to unavoidable cause for the child's absence from school. It might be thought a little surprising that the mother in this case, having regard to the history of the family, insofar as it appears from the facts found by the justices, was prosecuted in relation to this matter, bearing in mind that, as I have said, the girl was, albeit of compulsory school age, on the verge of her sixteenth birthday. She was also, as the justices found a girl of some maturity. One can well understand that it is of the highest importance that the parents of children should be persuaded to comply with the statutory obligation which bears upon them in the terms of the section of the Act to ensure that their children do go to school. But, for my part, I have some doubt as to whether, in the particular circumstances of this case, the prosecution of the mother for a criminal offence was a wholly desirable exercise. That said, for the reasons already given, there can be no doubt that the justices were wrong in finding as they did.

Accordingly I, for my part, would remit the matter with a direction that they convict. I would echo the words of the Lord Chief Justice in *Crump v Gillmore*. Although the question of penalty is a matter for them, the justices might very well think that the appropriate penalty, in the present case, is one of absolute discharge.

- *If the facts arose now, when would a pupil aged 16 on 8 October be able to leave school?*

Parents are strictly liable under s 444, in other words there is no defence that they have done all that could be reasonably expected to ensure that their child attends school. However, s 444(3)–(6) provide 'statutory excuses' or defences.

Education Act 1996, s 444

(3) The child shall not be taken to have failed to attend regularly at the school by reason of his absence from the school—
(a) with leave,
(b) at any time when he was prevented from attending by reason of sickness or any unavoidable cause, or
(c) on any day exclusively set apart for religious observance by the religious body to which his parent belongs.

(4) The child shall not be taken to have failed to attend regularly at the school if the parent proves—
(a) that the school at which the child is a registered pupil is not within walking distance of the child's home, and
(b) that no suitable arrangements have been made by the local education authority ... for any of the following—
    (i)   his transport to and from the school,
    (ii) boarding accommodation for him at or near the school, or
    (iii) enabling him to become a registered pupil at a school nearer to his home.

(5) In subsection (4) 'walking distance'—
(a)   in relation to a child who is under the age of eight, means 3.218688 kilometres (two miles), and
(b)   in relation to a child who has attained the age of eight, means 4.828032 kilometres (three miles),

in each case measured by the nearest available route.

(6) If it is proved that the child has no fixed abode, subsection (4) shall not apply, but the parent shall be acquitted if he proves—
(a)   that he is engaged in a trade or business of such a nature as to require him to travel from place to place,
(b)   that the child has attended at a school as a registered pupil as regularly as the nature of that trade or business permits, and
(c)   if the child has attained the age of six, that he has made at least 200 attendances during the period of 12 months ending with the date on which the proceedings were instituted.

...

(8) A person guilty of an offence under this section is liable on summary conviction to a fine not exceeding level 3 on the standard scale.

The Criminal Justice and Court Services Act 2000, s 72 has raised the fine which can be imposed on parents of truanting pupils to £2,500, or three months imprisonment. Parents who can show that they have reasonable justification for their child not attending will have a defence to this aggravated offence. The police now have the power to arrest parents who do not attend court.

The Education Act 1996, s 444(4) and (5) are often relied upon where there is a dispute between parents and the LEA over the provision of free transport to school (see chapter 6). In May 1994 the DFE issued Guidance on 'School attendance: Policy and practice on categorisation of absence'.

Home-school agreements

The Education Act 1997, s 13, which was passed by the Conservative government, gave county and voluntary schools the option of introducing home-school partnership documents, acceptance of which would be a condition of admission to the school. In July 1997 the Labour government in its White Paper (chapter 6, paras 7 and 8) indicated that all schools would be expected to have home-school contracts, but they would not be legally binding. The provisions in the Education Act 1997 were repealed and replaced by s 110 of the School Standards and Framework Act 1998. Schools must carry out a consultation exercise before adopting or revising the agreement or declaration.

School Standards and Framework Act 1998, s 110

(1) The governing body of a school which is—
(a)   a maintained school, or

(b)   a city technology college, a city college for the technology of the arts or a city academy,

shall adopt a home-school agreement for the school, together with a parental declaration to be used in connection with the agreement.

(2) For the purposes of this section and section 111 a 'home-school agreement' is a statement specifying—
(a)   the school's aims and values;
(b)   the school's responsibilities, namely the responsibilities which the school intends to discharge in connection with the education of pupils at the school who are of compulsory school age;
(c)   the parental responsibilities, namely the responsibilities which the parents of such pupils are expected to discharge in connection with the education of their children while they are registered pupils at the school; and
(d)   the school's expectations of its pupils, namely the expectations of the school as regards the conduct of such pupils while they are registered pupils there;

and 'parental declaration' means a document to be used by qualifying parents for recording that they take note of the school's aims and values and its responsibilities and that they acknowledge and accept the parental responsibilities and the school's expectations of its pupils.

(3) The governing body shall take reasonable steps to secure that the parental declaration is signed by every qualifying parent.

(4) Subsection (3) does not, however, require the governing body to seek the signature of a qualifying parent if, having regard to any special circumstances relating to the parent or the pupil in question, they consider that it would be inappropriate to do so.

(5) Where the governing body consider that a registered pupil at the school has a sufficient understanding of the home-school agreement as it relates to him, they may invite the pupil to sign the parental declaration as an indication that he acknowledges and accepts the school's expectations of its pupils.

(6) The governing body shall discharge their duty under subsection (3), and (where they decide to exercise it) shall exercise their power under subsection (5), as follows—
(a)   in the case of a pupil attending the school on the relevant date, as soon after that date as is reasonably practicable; and
(b)   in the case of a pupil admitted to the school after the relevant date, as soon after the date of his admission as is reasonably practicable.

...

The 1998 Act expressly states that the requirement to sign the parental declaration must not be made a condition of admission; but is ambiguous as to the legal effect of the home-school agreement.

School Standards and Framework Act 1998, s 111

...

(4) Neither the governing body of a school to which section 110(1) applies nor the local education authority where it is the admission authority for such a school shall—

(a)   invite any person to sign the parental declaration at a time when the child in question has not been admitted to the school;

(b)   make it a condition of a child being admitted to the school that the parental declaration is signed in respect of the child; or

(c)   make any decision as to whether or not to admit a child to the school by reference to whether any such declaration is or is not likely to be signed in respect of the child;

and in this subsection 'admission authority' has the meaning given by section 88(1).

(5) No person shall be excluded from such a school or suffer any other adverse consequences on account of any failure to comply with any invitation to sign the parental declaration.

(6) A home-school agreement shall not be capable of creating any obligation in respect of whose breach any liability arises in contract or in tort.

It is questionable whether these agreements have any significant impact on the attitude or behaviour of parents or pupils.

Ann Blair 'Home-School Agreements: A Legislative Framework for Soft Control of Parents' [2001] Education LJ 79

Home-school agreements are one legislative response to problems of exclusion and participation. As will be demonstrated, recent legislation has placed legal obligations on schools, it creates quasi-legal obligations on the part of parents, but the legislation does this to 'enforce' (or perhaps just to reinforce) what are clearly seen to be predominantly moral rather than legal obligations. The obligations of parenthood in respect of schooling no longer fall solely within the norms of law that relate to attendance etc, but now are deemed to include an obligation to be a 'good parent'.

This article aims to show that home-school agreements are both instruments of participation and instruments of coercion. The question is whether the aim of using them to address the direct failings of the 'antisocial' parent and the problem of the 'antisocial' child is compatible with their use as an instrument of participation and community. However, one can see that their appeal for those converted to the New Labour mission is that these seemingly slight documents, and the obligations that surround them, hold the ability to touch multiple aspects of the government's ideology and inclinations all at the same time.

...

Conclusion

There is little that can be identified as wrong with the desire to clarify respective roles and expectations and to encourage parents to sign up to a school's values system. However, because the DfEE has been unable to let go of the legislation's coercive origins and refuse the opportunity to 'impose' the Secretary of State's most pressing concerns on schools and parents through its introduction, the model the legislation has settled on compromises partnership by forcing this particular form of it upon potentially unwilling participants.

A further strand of 'third way' thought is a belief that pragmatism should guide policy not ideology. Government should introduce only that which works. Interestingly, this particular initiative was mooted at a time when there was next to no evidence of its effectiveness or otherwise. Only time will tell whether these agreements will, in the end, foster partnerships where they would not have arisen otherwise. However, it is already becoming clear that those who would prefer such agreements to have 'teeth' feel that 'soft control' in this case amounts, effectively, to no control. Equally, those felt to be in most need of being drawn into partnership, the most socially excluded, seem to date to be the least likely to be involved in negotiating the terms of these agreements, and most likely to refuse to sign up or to be able to comply with the obligations such 'agreements' set out. Equally, the child/pupil, who is after all one of the principal objects of concern, features only as a footnote to the process. Overall they seem more a triumph of New Labour ideology than an embodiment of pragmatic policy-making. If antisocial behaviour is to be addressed in part by engaging parents with their social responsibilities, it would perhaps be more fruitful to jettison compulsory home-school agreements with their coercive undertones and to concentrate on building genuine partnerships in a variety of ways that can be tailored to the needs of the individual school and community. If coercion is then still required in relation to the minority of parents who are letting down their child and their community by failing in the duties of a 'good parent', then it is argued that a great deal more agreement is needed as to what exactly these duties are, and a great deal more transparency in the development of appropriate interventions.

6.   ALTERNATIVES TO PARENTAL PREFERENCE

Parental preference, which is central to the law and policy on school admissions, is meaningless unless a school has spare places. Generally, only unpopular schools have spare capacity. In practice most parents do not have a choice. They have to express a preference for the school to which their child has the greatest chance of obtaining a place, or else gamble with their child's education. The operation of parental preference often gives rise to uncertainty and unfairness, and frequently does not achieve its objective of providing choice.

The Audit Commission set out its views on what needs to be done in its 1996 report which looked at the issue from the perspective of encouraging LEAs and schools to operate more efficiently and effectively. The Commission recommended that the government should review the national framework for planning school places.

Audit Commission 'Trading Places — The Supply and Allocation of School Places' (1996)

Action at a national level

68. The old system was largely planned, but such planning was by no means simple. The LEA had to take into account important players such as the Diocesan School Boards. And the success of the LEAs in operating the planned system was patchy, leading to critical Audit Commission reports. The reform programme has diminished the capacity of LEAs to plan and control the system directly, by affording a degree of local self-management to schools and by introducing a market for school places. The emerging system contains a balance between market forces and planning. The key issue is where to strike that balance.

69. Where the balance is struck is a matter for political choice. However, the evidence of this study is that the price of the market system is rising. Moreover, it is not evident that a greater emphasis on the planning role of LEAs and other agencies … would interfere with any beneficial effects of the school market. Rather, local agencies need to harness the strength of the market to identify pressure points. There is a need to cope with success by enabling successful schools to expand and manage failure by identifying, intervening in and sometimes closing schools in difficulty. This requires bodies to manage the local school market. Redoubled efforts to make existing mechanisms work more effectively will help. But it is likely that those efforts will prove insufficient. There are options for readjustment to the framework, which retain the strength of the market to spur performance, while supplementing it with further features likely to improve value for money. The analysis in the previous chapter suggests that reform should be guided by three key principles:

- **achieving clarity and consistency** — the government could avoid the risk of system gridlock by choosing a clear order of priority between competing policies, or by finding a different way of striking balance between them;
- **allowing local action** — the national framework should ensure that the powers and responsibilities of local agencies are consistent with effective intervention at the local level; and
- **creating incentives** — the government could explore options for strengthening incentives within the system, particularly for tackling surplus places and unpopular or failing schools.

None of these suggestions eliminates the possibility of conflicts between policies; rather, they redress the balance in favour of value for money.

…

81. Recent changes to the education system, where they result in rising standards, are to be welcomed. But such successes should not distract attention from continuing problems. The designed outcomes of economy, efficiency and effectiveness, as well as the satisfaction of parental choice, will not be achieved automatically through the operation of the market alone. These outcomes, and the balances that will inevitably be struck between them given limited resources, can be achieved only by active intervention to manage the market. The analysis and arguments in this report suggest that such intervention and management is best undertaken at a local level. But local efforts are currently hampered … sometimes by poor LEA performance, but also by the defects of the national framework. There is no simple solution. But it is possible to achieve greater value for money than at present.

A simple solution has been proposed by Joan Sallis, a respected school governor and writer.

Joan Sallis 'Making nonsense of parental choice' ACE Bulletin 83, June 1998, p 10

School admissions criteria may soon be the subject of broadly based local discussion. We can only hope that this will be brisk and business-like and will bring to an end the farce which parental choice has become. But while the government may genuinely wish to bring better planning and equity to the process, they are doing so within a framework originally designed to allow market forces to operate freely. This includes the publication of performance data, open enrolment up to standard numbers (I have no quarrel with these) and finally (and this is the provision that needs review) the principle that admission criteria have to be applied without reference to LEA boundaries. The interpretation of this principle (originally s 31 of the 1980 [Education] Act) is generally referred to as the Greenwich decision, following a challenge in the courts.

…

What it means, simply, is that no preference may be given to an LEA's own children in the allocation of school places. It is creating chaos and the government won't change it. The absurdity is that it has denied to many parents the simplest right of all which is to choose the school nearest their homes. It has also left many a well-planned local system seriously short of places to sort its own needs.

In the end the interests of all children require that parents and fellow taxpayers fight in their own area for better local resourcing, and better planning.

Although the government has made provision for local fora and adjudicators in order to rationalise admission arrangements, it still pays lip-service to the concept of parental choice. It remains to be seen whether the new arrangements will address the current difficulties faced by parents and LEAs.

CHAPTER 4

School discipline and exclusions

1. INTRODUCTION

The phrase 'school discipline' may bring to mind images from Dickens and from *Tom Brown's Schooldays* with their descriptions of harsh punishments for schoolboys who broke the school rules. Corporal punishment (not to be confused with capital punishment) is no longer considered lawful in United Kingdom schools, but the extent to which teachers may discipline pupils is still controversial as can be seen by the occasional criminal prosecution of teachers for assault.

The use of 'exclusion', which is the term now used for suspension and expulsion, has been particularly problematic during the past few years. Government policy has been aimed at reducing the number of pupils permanently excluded from school. The balance between the need to maintain a reasonable standard of behaviour in school and the importance of ensuring that pupils are not unreasonably excluded has led to a number of court cases.

Government policy emphasises the importance of encouraging good behaviour among pupils and of 'social inclusion', which means keeping pupils within the mainstream education system. One of the consequences of this focus on behaviour is that the issue of bullying has come to the fore. This is reflected both in the legislative provisions, and also in recent case law.

In addition to the legislative provisions and the case law there are a number of circulars which are of particular importance in this area. These are:

- DfEE Circular 10/98 (Section 550A of the Education Act 1996: The Use of Force to Control or Restrain Pupils)
- DfEE Circular 10/99 (Social Inclusion: Pupil Support)
- DfEE Circular 11/99 (Social Inclusion: the LEA Role in Pupil Support)

Circular 10/99 is particularly important, and has been criticised for its complexity and bias towards keeping pupils in school. The sections dealing with exclusion have been amended three times since the circular was introduced in September 1999. In January

2002 the DfES published draft guidance on permanent exclusion, which will replace the existing sections of Circular 10/99 on permanent exclusion. The main changes proposed include the advice that bullying can warrant permanent exclusion, and clarification on when permanent exclusion is appropriate for a first or one-off offence.

The White Paper *Excellence in Schools* (Cm 3681, July 1997) set out the government's policy on discipline, which was aimed at improving school discipline and school attendance while also reducing exclusions and introducing LEA behaviour support plans.

Ofsted published a report in February 2001 setting out strategies to promote educational inclusion (*Improving Attendance and Behaviour in Secondary Schools*).

2.   SCHOOL DISCIPLINE

In the White Paper *Excellence in Schools* (Cm 3681, July 1997), the government focused on improving pupil behaviour.

White Paper *Excellence in Schools* (Cm 3681, July 1997) Paras 13–16

Discipline and attendance

IMPROVING DISCIPLINE

13   Good discipline also depends on partnership. It starts in the home and must continue into school. Most schools are well-ordered communities but it is vital, in the interests of all pupils, that standards of behaviour are improved where they are not satisfactory.

14   Improving home/school links and the quality of teaching will make a major contribution to reducing indiscipline, but schools can also act directly to improve pupil behaviour. We will be consulting on detailed new guidance for schools, reflecting the provisions of the Education Act 1997 on school discipline policies and after-school detention, and offering advice on good practice. This will emphasise the need for every school to have a clear behaviour policy which sets out the boundaries of what is acceptable, the hierarchy of sanctions, arrangements for their consistent application, and a linked system of rewards for good behaviour. We will support local initiatives to tackle behaviour problems, take more active steps to spread information on good practice emerging from these, and expect LEAs to offer schools proactive support in tackling unacceptable behaviour.

15   In particular, we shall ensure wider knowledge of the benefits which schools have gained from the careful introduction of 'assertive discipline'. This involves the whole school in a concerted effort to improve and maintain discipline through a clearly understood behaviour framework, emphasising positive encouragement as well as clear sanctions.

16   As part of their behaviour policies, all schools need effective strategies to deal with bullying. These work particularly well when the whole school community, including pupils, is involved in their development and application. The emotional and mental distress caused by bullying can have a severe adverse effect on pupils' achievement — both directly and where it leads to truancy.

Legally and practically the head teacher is responsible for the day-to-day implementation of the school rules, usually now described as the school behaviour policy. The governing body has overall responsibility for the conduct of the school, and the LEA has a strategic role. Individual teachers are also responsible for their own behaviour, and their employer (the LEA or the governing body depending upon the type of school) will normally be vicariously liable for the teacher's actions.

The governing body

The governing body of an LEA maintained school is responsible for:
* ensuring that the school has behaviour and discipline policies
* producing written principles on behaviour and discipline, having consulted the head teacher and parents
* giving guidance to the head teacher where appropriate
* setting school attendance targets aimed at reducing truancy.

Parents and others who are concerned about the validity of a particular punishment or exclusion should always obtain a copy of these policies in order to establish whether the school has complied with its own policies. The head teacher is responsible for publicising the policies (see below).

School Standards and Framework Act 1998, s 61

(1) The governing body of a maintained school shall ensure that policies designed to promote good behaviour and discipline on the part of its pupils are pursued at the school.

(2) In particular, the governing body—
(a)   shall make, and from time to time review, a written statement of general principles to which the head teacher is to have regard in determining any measures under subsection (4); and
(b)   where they consider it desirable that any particular measures should be so determined by the head teacher or that he should have regard to any particular matters—
    (i)   shall notify him of those measures or matters, and
    (ii)   may give him such guidance as they consider appropriate;

and in exercising their functions under this subsection the governing body shall have regard to any guidance given from time to time by the Secretary of State.

Regulations (made under SSFA 1998, s 63) have been passed which give the Secretary of State power to require governing bodies to set annual targets for reducing the level of unauthorised absences by pupils at their schools.

School Standards and Framework Act 1998, s 63(4)

'unauthorised absence', in relation to such a pupil, [ie a 'relevant day pupil'] means any occasion on which the pupil is recorded as absent without authority pursuant to regulations under section 434 of the Education Act 1996 (registration of pupils).

See the Education (School Attendance Targets) (England) Regulations 1999, SI 1999/ 397; the Education (School Performance and Unauthorised Absence Targets) (Wales) Regulations 1999, SI 1999/1811; the Code of Practice on LEA-School Relations.

The head teacher

Where the governing body has not decided what is an acceptable standard of behaviour at the school, the head teacher has the responsibility for doing so (s 61(6) of the SSFA 1998). In addition the head teacher has a duty to take 'measures' to ensure that pupils behave in accordance with the school's behaviour and discipline policy and any guidance given by the governing body (s 61(5) of the SSFA 1998).

School Standards and Framework Act 1998, s 61(4) and (7)

(4) The head teacher shall determine measures (which may include the making of rules and provision for enforcing them) to be taken with a view to—
(a)   promoting, among pupils, self-discipline and proper regard for authority;
(b)   encouraging good behaviour and respect for others on the part of pupils and, in particular, preventing all forms of bullying among pupils;
(c)   securing that the standard of behaviour of pupils is acceptable; and
(d)   otherwise regulating the conduct of pupils. ...

(7) The measures determined by the head teacher under subsection (4) shall be publicised by him in the form of a written document as follows—
(a)   he shall make the measures generally known within the school and to parents of registered pupils at the school; and
(b)   he shall in particular, at least once in every school year, take steps to bring them to the attention of all such pupils and parents and all persons employed, or otherwise engaged to provide their services, at the school.

The measures should include any school rules, which may range from banning weapons to banning the wearing of jewellery or the dyeing of hair. Sanctions should also be included, and the measures should explain what sanctions are likely to be regarded as appropriate for the breach of which rules.

* *How often, in what form and to whom must the 'measures' be publicised?*

* *Why would a school ban the wearing of jewellery?*

Bullying

Bullying occurs at most, if not all, schools. Newspaper stories often report children running away from home or even committing suicide because they have been bullied at school. Section 61(4)(b) of the SSFA 1998 places a statutory duty on head teachers to 'determine measures' which should prevent 'all forms of bullying among pupils'.

In December 2000 the DfEE published non-statutory guidance on bullying, which recommends that schools should adopt a whole school policy and suggests strategies which schools can put in place to deal with bullying. The link between the anti-bullying policy and the school's behaviour policy is spelt out.

Bullying: Don't Suffer in Silence—an anti-bullying pack for schools: DfEE Non-statutory Guidance 64/2000

10. The anti-bullying policy should dovetail with the school's behaviour policy. It should be clear what the sanctions are for bullying and in what circumstances they will apply. Strong sanctions such as exclusion may be necessary in cases of severe and persistent bullying.

What amounts to 'bullying'?

The DfEE has identified three main types of bullying.

DfEE Circular 10/95: Protecting Children from Abuse: The Role of the Education Service

Bullying

35. Bullying is defined as deliberately hurtful behaviour, repeated over a period of time, where it is difficult for those being bullied to defend themselves. It can take many forms, but the three main types are physical (e g hitting, kicking, theft), verbal (e g name calling, racist remarks) or indirect (e g spreading rumours, excluding someone from social groups). It is important for schools to have a whole school policy against bullying and vital that they should act promptly and firmly to combat it whenever and wherever it occurs (see Circular 8/94). Pupils should be aware of how they can draw their concerns about bullying to the attention of staff in the confidence that these will be carefully investigated and, if substantiated, taken seriously and acted upon.

This definition has been expanded in the non-statutory guidance 64/2000 published by the DfEE in December 2000.

The nature of bullying

1. There are many definitions of bullying, but most consider it to be:
   - deliberately hurtful (including aggression)
   - repeated often over a period of time
   - difficult for victims to defend themselves against
2. Bullying can take many forms, but three main types are:
   - physical – hitting, kicking, taking belongings
   - verbal – name calling, insulting, making offensive remarks
   - indirect – spreading nasty stories about someone, exclusion from social groups, being made the subject of malicious rumours

3. Name calling is the most common direct form. This may be because of individual characteristics, but pupils can be called nasty names because of their ethnic origin, nationality or colour; sexual orientation; or some form of disability.

Who is likely to be bullied?

Bullying: Don't Suffer in Silence—an anti-bullying pack for schools: DfEE Non-statutory Guidance 64/2000

Who is involved in bullying – and where?

4. A survey of 5 primary schools and 14 secondary schools across England in 1997, taking evidence from 2,308 pupils aged 10 to 14 years, showed that bullying is widespread (Fig 1). There was bullying in all schools, although a comparison with earlier work indicates a reduction during the 1990s.

FIGURE 1: INCIDENCE OF BULLYING IN SCHOOLS

	Not at all	Only once or twice	Sometimes (2–3 times per month)	Once per week	Several times per week
BEEN BULLIED %					
Overall	55.5	32.3	4.3	3.8	4.1
Boys	56.8	30.5	4.9	4.0	3.8
Girls	53.9	34.3	3.7	3.6	4.5
BULLY OTHERS %					
Overall	73.4	23.7	1.3	1.0	0.6
Boys	71.9	24.1	1.7	1.5	0.8
Girls	75.1	23.1	0.9	0.5	0.4

...

8. Any child can be bullied, and although *none* of these characteristics can excuse it, certain factors can make bullying more likely:
*   lacking close friends in school
*   being shy
*   an over-protective family environment
*   being from a different racial or ethnic group to the majority
*   being different in some obvious respect – such as stammering
*   having Special Educational Needs or a disability
*   behaving inappropriately, intruding or being a 'nuisance'
*   possessing expensive accessories such as mobile [phones]
    ...

10. Verbal bullying is common amongst boys and girls. Boys experience more physical violence and threats than girls, although physical attacks on girls by other girls are becoming more frequent. Girls tend to use indirect methods which can be more difficult to detect.

11. Being bullied tends to decrease with age (Fig 2), probably because older pupils are developing coping skills. In addition, older pupils meet fewer people who are physically stronger than them. However, attitudes to victims tend to become less sympathetic over

the age range 8 to 15 years, especially in older boys. Physical bullying declines with age, but indirect bullying increases.

FIGURE 2: AGES OF CHILDREN INVOLVED IN BULLYING '2 OR 3 TIMES A MONTH OR MORE OFTEN'

	Year 6 (10 yrs)	Year 7 (11 yrs)	Year 8 (12 yrs)	Year 9 (13 yrs)	Year 10 (14 yrs)
Been bullied	18.7	13.1	12.1	10.5	7.5
Bully others	5.3	1.4	2.8	3.6	3.3

The guidance addresses bullying by race, gender, sexual orientation or disability in more detail.

What is the effect of bullying on a pupil?

DfEE Circular 10/99 Social Inclusion: Pupil Support

Dealing with bullying

4.29 The emotional distress caused by bullying in whatever form – be it racial, or as a result of a child's appearance, behaviour or special educational needs, or related to sexual orientation – can prejudice school achievement, lead to lateness or truancy and, in extreme cases, end with suicide. A third of girls and a quarter of boys are at some time afraid of going to school because of bullying. Bullying is usually part of a pattern of behaviour rather than an isolated incident. Pupils should be encouraged to report any bullying to staff or to older pupils they can trust. Low report rates should not of themselves be taken as proof that bullying is not occurring.

4.30 Head teachers have a legal duty to take measures to prevent all forms of bullying among pupils. All teaching and non-teaching staff, including lunchtime supervisors, should be alert to signs of bullying and act promptly and firmly. Pupils may see failure to respond to incidents or allegations as tolerating bullying. As bullying tends to occur during break time, schools will wish to ensure they have strategies covering play and break time, and all relevant staff receive appropriate training.

What should schools do?

Bullying: Don't Suffer in Silence—an anti-bullying pack for schools: DfEE Non-statutory Guidance 64/2000

1   Bullying should be discussed as part of the curriculum, but teachers also need general strategies to deal with the problem. Whilst they should try strategies such as those described below, schools may find that stronger measures are needed in the more serious and persistent cases.

2   *Where other strategies do not resolve the problem, permanent exclusion may be justified in the most serious and persistent cases, particularly where violence is involved.* The Department's updated guidance for local education authority exclusion appeal panels makes clear that pupils responsible for violence or threatened violence should not normally be reinstated.

3   Five key points:
  * never ignore suspected bullying
  * don't make premature assumptions
  * listen carefully to all accounts – several pupils saying the same does not necessarily mean they are telling the truth
  * adopt a problem-solving approach which moves pupils on from justifying themselves
  * follow-up repeatedly, checking bullying has not resumed.

The DfEE guidance recommends the use of a variety of strategies. These include activities which enable pupils to discuss bullying and to respect one another. For example theses issues can be addressed in:
* co-operative group work from age 5
* circle time from age 5
* circles of friends from age 5
* befriending from age 9
* schoolwatch from age 9
* the support group approach from age 9
* mediation by adults from age 9
* mediation by peers from age 9

LIABILITY IN THE TORT OF NEGLIGENCE

Where schools do not take reasonable steps to deal with the bullies the LEA or, in the case of voluntary aided and foundation schools, the governing body will be vicariously liable for the negligence of the school staff.

There are several cases where pupils have been awarded compensation in out of court settlements as a consequence of being bullied and suffering either physical or psychological trauma.

In *Cotton v Trafford Borough Council* (6 October 2000, unreported) a judge at Manchester County Court awarded damages of £1,500 to a boy who was bullied over a twelve-month period while a pupil at Sale Grammar School. The damages were awarded for psychiatric injury suffered by the boy when he was 12 years old as a consequence of predominantly verbal homophobic bullying by other pupils. He was unable to attend school for two years as a consequence and received psychiatric treatment.

The judge held that the school was in breach of its duty of care because it did not do enough in the light of the information available to staff. The school should have been more proactive by, for example, adopting a new strategy to deal with the bullying. In particular there was a failure to investigate, a failure to keep colleagues informed, a failure to collect evidence, and a failure to monitor effectively the agreed strategy.

This appears to be the first case where damages have been awarded for verbal as opposed to physical bullying.

Bullying is most likely to take place at break times. It can also take place off school premises. In the following case the claimant who was born on 19 May 1981 claimed damages for bullying which occurred at her middle school. Her mother applied for a place at an out of catchment secondary school for her daughter, but the application was unsuccessful. The claimant was educated at home for a year before attending the local FE college although she was only 13-years-old. In June 1995 she obtained three GCSEs with very low grades. In 1996 she sought medical help and was diagnosed as suffering from episodes of depression caused by severe bullying.

Bradford-Smart v West Sussex County Council [2001] ELR 138

Garland J: Leah Bradford-Smart, the claimant, seeks damages against the defendant council for psychiatric injury caused by bullying when she was a pupil at Ifield Middle School between September 1990 and July 1993, a maintained primary school for which the defendant was responsible. Apart from a claim for general damages, there is an unqualified claim for loss of future earnings and quantified claims for special damage totalling £16,950.

...

There was, so far as counsel were aware, no direct authority on liability for bullying. In Scotland there is the opinion of Lord MacLean in *Scott v Lothian Regional Council* (unreported), 29 September 1998 given in the Court of Session, and the very recent decision of His Honour Judge Holman in Manchester County Court, *Cotton v Trafford Borough Council* (unreported), 6 October 2000. The former involved name-calling and taunting followed by two serious and humiliating indecent assaults at the school; the latter also involved homophobic name-calling and taunting for the most part at the school, but the judge excluded from the scope of the duty of care a serious indecent assault on the basis that it was unforeseeable. I therefore approach this case as raising issues of principle, although I am assisted by the Scottish and county court decisions.

...

In both *Scott* and *Cotton*, the fact that the claimants had been bullied was not in issue and the bullying had taken place almost entirely on the school premises. In *Cotton's* case the serious assault which was held to be unforeseeable had taken place on a school trip to France. In both cases the judges approached the question of breach with the assistance of expert evidence. Lord MacLean held that the teachers concerned had not fallen below the standard to be expected of a guidance teacher of ordinary skill acting with ordinary care, whereas His Honour Judge Holman found that the conduct of the teachers had fallen short of the school's own procedures and strategies... A major difficulty was that the conduct complained of by Leah and Mrs Bradford-Smart in 1992–93 took place outside the school either on the estate where Leah lived with her mother or on the public service bus going to and from school.

...

I have no hesitation in finding that from July 1992 Leah was seriously bullied at home and on the bus going to and from school. I also find that threats were made as to what would happen in school. However, as I have already indicated, I accept Mrs Ashworth as a reliable and truthful witness although Mr Ullstein QC suggested that I should find her rather too ready to see the good in people and not firm enough in rejecting the bad. Mrs Ashworth was continuously in contact with Mrs Bradford-Smart, she was fully aware of what was happening and as a class teacher did all that she could to safeguard Leah while she was at school. I do not consider that her conduct fell short of that to be expected of an ordinarily competent class teacher or that she did or failed to do anything which no class teacher of ordinary skill would have done or refrained from doing if acting with ordinary care. The school had in 'Working Together' a policy and procedures which both experts agreed were thoroughly up to date and satisfactory; Mrs Ashworth allowed Leah to stay with her if she felt threatened; if one of the gang came looking for her, Mrs Ashworth told her to go away; in order not to be over-protective, Mrs Ashworth encouraged Leah to go out and play if she thought it was safe and then kept an eye on her; Leah never made any complaint to her about any occurrence at school, and Mrs Ashworth kept Mr Harvey fully informed, contrary to what he asserted in his witness statement. Mrs Ashworth's role was essentially a defensive one. The question that lies at the heart of this case is whether the school was under a duty to be pro-active, that is, to go out beyond the school gate to the children and their parents in order to prevent or mitigate the bullying to which Leah was being subjected. This is of fundamental importance because I have taken the view that although Leah suffered disappointment and unhappiness during her first two years at school she was not in fact bullied. In the third year Mrs Ashworth's defensive actions prevented bullying in school although Leah was fearful as a result of what happened outside school. It follows that if Leah suffered psychiatric illness caused by bullying (matters to which I shall turn), then the causative bullying was at home and on the bus going to and from school, not in the school itself. Three questions arise:

1   Did the school owe any and, if so, what duty to Leah in respect of bullying outside the school gates?
2   If there was such a duty what steps could the school reasonably be expected to have taken in order to comply with it?
3   Was there a failure to take appropriate action with the result that the bullying was neither mitigated nor prevented?
    …

I make no secret of the fact that I find this a most anxious case. Advancing the boundaries of negligence requires the most careful consideration of whether it is fair, just and reasonable to impose a duty granted that there is foreseeability of damage and proximity. There was proximity and I have no difficulty with foreseeability: that sustained persecution by third parties can go beyond misery to psychiatric illness. The boundaries of negligence have been moved forward in *Gower v London Borough of Bromley* [1999] ELR 356 and *Phelps v Hillingdon London Borough Council; Anderton v Clwyd County Council; G (A Minor) v Bromley London Borough Council; Jarvis v Hampshire County Council* [2000] 3 WLR 776. In both cases the extent of the duty and the nature of the particular breach could in my view be ascertained with greater precision than is possible in the present case. Is a school to be concerned with bullying only at the bus stop immediately outside the school gate, on the bus itself or arising from anti-social behaviour between families on a housing estate? A school's powers are limited to what might best be described as inquiry and counselling which may in certain circumstances exacerbate rather than ameliorate the situation. I have come to the conclusion that granted a school knows that a pupil is being bullied at home or on the way to and from school, it would not be practical let alone fair, just and reasonable, to impose upon it a greater duty than to take reasonable steps to prevent that bullying spilling over into the school. That appears to me to be the consensus between Mr Watling and Mr Lomas although they could not agree what those steps should be. I would regard the duty as going no further than to prevent the bullying actually happening inside the school; in other words, to take effective, defensive measures. If the school chooses, as a matter of judgement, to be pro-active then that is a matter of discretion not obligation. Talking to the children or to their parents may or may not produce any benefit. Taken to extremes, excluding the bullies from the school, would probably greatly exacerbate the situation. In my judgement, a school cannot reasonably be expected to do more than to take reasonable steps to prevent a child being bullied while it is actually at the school. I have decided that whatever Mr Harvey may or may not have done, Mrs Ashworth did take reasonable steps to safeguard Leah while she was actually at school. Accordingly, the claim must fail at this point.

The Court of Appeal dismissed the pupil's appeal. However, unlike Garland J, the court considered that there could be circumstances where the failure by a head teacher to use his disciplinary powers against a pupil, who attacked another pupil outside school, would be a breach of the duty of care owed by the school to the victim (*Bradford-Smart v West Sussex County Council* [2002] NLJR 142).

Would the LEA be liable if the bullying had occurred on a school bus provided by the LEA?

The DfEE's guidance addresses the problem of bullying occurring outside school, but is not legally binding, and relies on the High Court rather than the Court of Appeal decision in *Bradford-Smart*.

Bullying: Don't Suffer in Silence—an anti-bullying pack for schools: DfEE Non-statutory Guidance 64/2000

Bullying outside a school's premises

19. Schools are not directly responsible for bullying off their premises. This was recently confirmed in a Court judgment which ruled that the head's duty of care to prevent bullying only applied within the precincts of a school (*Leah Bradford-Smart v West Sussex County Council...*). But a good deal of bullying takes place outside the school gates, and on journeys to and from school. The bullying may be by pupils of the school or pupils of other schools or people not at school at all.

20. A school's anti-bullying policy should encourage pupils not to suffer in silence. Where a pupil tells of bullying off the school premises, a range of steps could be taken:
- talk to the local police about problems on local streets (if necessary seek a police presence at trouble spots);
- talk to the transport company about bullying on buses or trains;
- talk to the head of another school whose pupils are bullying off the premises;
- map safe routes to school, and tell pupils about them (software available from Map IT Ltd 01487 813745);
- talk to pupils about how to avoid or handle bullying outside the school premises.

- *Will a head teacher be liable in the tort of negligence if the 'measures' adopted by the head teacher under s 61(4) of the SSFA 1998 do not include an anti-bullying strategy?*

BULLYING AND CRIMINAL LIABILITY

Bullying can amount to one or more criminal offences, including assault, battery and harassment. However, the police are rarely asked to intervene in incidents of bullying.

Clare Furniss 'Bullying in schools: it's not a crime—is it?' (2000) 12 (1) Education and the Law 9

Introduction

Each term, bullying in school causes widespread fear, misery and distress. Bullying leaves in its wake physical injury and mental trauma. Victims of bullying experience feelings of anxiety, anger, vengefulness and helplessness (Slee, 1994; Borg, 1998). For some children, bullying can affect them so much that they try to commit suicide, run away, refuse to go to school or develop chronic illnesses (Elliott, 1992). In turn, these reactions detrimentally affect their progress and attainment at school. Resultant low self-esteem can have a long-term impact upon the victim, sometimes lasting well into adulthood. Borg (1998) has described school bullying as 'a serious psychological problem ... responsible for widespread suffering and pain among children and equally widespread apprehension, concern and anxiety among parents'. The Department of Education and Employment (DfEE et al, 1999) estimates that about one-third of girls and a quarter of boys at some time are afraid to go to school because of bullying.

In view of the often serious impact of school bullying upon its victims, this article aims to explore who should be responsible for managing and reducing the problem in schools.

Teachers rarely see school bullying as a matter for the police. Apart from occasional one-off cases, police are rarely involved and prosecutions are extremely few. This is partly because of social attitudes to bullying which prevent its construction as a crime. It is also because of the existence of the school's internal disciplinary structure, which provides an alternative means of intervention. I will argue that, for older children (children under ten are in any event deemed incapable of forming criminal intent), despite the existence of the school's disciplinary mechanism there is a role for criminal justice agencies in two situations. The first is where school mechanisms are ineffective: in this situation, police action could be seen as a last resort. The second is where the bullying is too serious for the school to deal with (and I discuss different measures of seriousness below). From a victim's perspective, I argue for greater recognition that some bullying activities are criminal offences. This ensures that criminal justice agencies are not simply overlooked when planning effective intervention that meets the needs of the victims for support and protection, as well as providing for future prevention and deterrence.

...

There is some evidence that pupils and parents encounter situations where teachers are unable or unwilling to take action against bullying, although the scale of this problem is not known. Because teachers may feel overwhelmed with other responsibilities, action against bullying may not be seen as a priority. Bullying does not tend to make classroom management difficult, unlike other disruptive behaviour such as insolence or unruly behaviour towards the teacher. Teachers may see bullying as an inevitable part of growing up, may feel powerless to prevent it, or feel that intervention may make the situation worse. Morgan and Zedner (1992, p 93) found that, where children and their families did involve the school, they 'were generally less than satisfied with the response they received. The majority did not feel that the school took them seriously.' The Children's Legal Centre (1996) issued legal guidance on the law to parents and children in response to a number of calls to their helpline asking about practical advice where schools do not accept that bullying is taking place, or do not take action to stop bullying. It seems that legislation placing duties upon schools cannot alone tackle this problem. Numerous letters from children to the Child Ombudsman in Sweden indicated that despite the existence of legal responsibilities, 'adults at school do not see, or do not want to see, the bullying that goes on among the students' (Olweus, 1999). The best answer would obviously be to encourage all schools to take all bullying more seriously. In the meantime. If victims are faced with school inaction, then the criminal justice system may provide a last-resort choice. If police action (cautioning, prosecuting) is seen as a possibility, a threat to call the police may be sufficient to prevent further bullying (Waddington, 1993), or to motivate the school into taking action (Children's Legal Centre, 1996).

The school teacher

The teacher was traditionally regarded as being in loco parentis, that is having the same rights and duties as a parent while a child was their responsibility. This common law principle has been supplemented by statutory provisions (see now ss 2(9) and 3(1) and (5) of the Children Act 1989).

Children Act 1989, s 3

(5) A person who—
(a) does not have parental responsibility for a particular child; but
(b) has care of the child,

may (subject to the provisions of this Act) do what is reasonable in all the circumstances of the case for the purpose of safeguarding or promoting the child's welfare.

An LEA is vicariously liable where improper punishment is used by a teacher. The concept of vicarious liability in the teacher/employer context has recently been examined by the House of Lords (*Lister v Hesley Hall Ltd* [2001] UKHL 22, [2001] 2 WLR 1311; see chapter 2).

Role of the LEA

In addition to being potentially vicariously liable for their employees, LEAs have reserve powers to prevent a breakdown of discipline at a particular maintained school, as well as having a duty to provide support for pupils with behavioural difficulties.
Guidance is provided in the:
• Codes of Practice on LEA-School Relations 2001
• Circular 1/98 (LEA Behaviour Support Plans)
• Circular 11/99 (Social Inclusion: the LEA Role in Pupil Support).

School Standards and Framework Act 1998, s 62

(1) The local education authority may, in the circumstances mentioned in subsection (2) or where subsection (3) applies, take such steps in relation to a maintained school as they consider are required to prevent the breakdown, or continuing breakdown, of discipline at the school.

(2) The circumstances are that—
(a) in the opinion of the authority—
　　(i)　the behaviour of registered pupils at the school, or
　　(ii)　any action taken by such pupils or their parents,
　　is such that the education of any registered pupils at the school is (or is likely in the immediate future to become) severely prejudiced; and
(b) the governing body have been informed in writing of the authority's opinion.

(3) This subsection applies where—
(a) a warning notice has been given in accordance with section 15(2) referring to the safety of pupils or staff at the school being threatened by a breakdown of discipline at the school,
(b) the governing body have failed to comply, or secure compliance, with the notice to the authority's satisfaction within the compliance period, and
(c) the authority have given reasonable notice in writing to the governing body that they propose to exercise their powers under subsection (1) of this section (whether or not in conjunction with exercising their powers under either or both of sections 16 and 17);

and a notice under paragraph (c) of this subsection may be combined with a notice under section 15(1)(c).

(4) Steps taken by a local education authority under subsection (1) may include the giving of any direction to the governing body or head teacher.

• *What is the LEA required to do under SSFA 1998, s 62(3) before intervening?*

Behaviour support plans

Behaviour support plans were introduced by the Education Act 1997. The White Paper *Excellence in Schools* (Cm 3681, July 1997) proposed using these plans as a springboard for a multi-agency approach.

White Paper 'Excellence in Schools' (Cm 3681, July 1997) para 22

LEA behaviour support plans

22 An effective multi-agency approach to support good discipline and behaviour at local level is vital. We expect that preparation of the behaviour support plans required under the 1997 Act will prompt many LEAs to review the range of their provision in this area and to improve co-ordination with social services and other agencies locally. We will be consulting widely on guidance for these plans, which we envisage covering:
•   LEA support for schools in improving the management of pupil behaviour, with a view amongst other things to preventing unauthorised absence and exclusions;
•   the type and nature of provision available outside mainstream schools for pupils with behaviour problems;
•   arrangements for supporting the education of excluded pupils; and
•   arrangements for effective co-ordination between relevant local agencies, and for involving the youth service and the voluntary sector.

The statutory provisions are contained in the EA 1996, s 527A (which was inserted by the Education Act 1997, s 9), and in Local Education Authorities (Behaviour Support Plans) Regulations 1998, SI 1998/644. An LEA is required to publish and review these plans which must set out the arrangements made by the LEA to support and assist schools to promote good behaviour and discipline.

Education Act 1996, s 527A

Duty of LEA to prepare plan relating to children with behavioural difficulties

(1) Every local education authority shall prepare, and from time to time review, a statement setting out the arrangements made or proposed to be made by the authority in connection with the education of children with behavioural difficulties.

(2) The arrangements to be covered by the statement include in particular—
(a)   the arrangements made or to be made by the authority for the provision of advice and resources to relevant schools, and other arrangements made or to be made by them, with a view to—
  (i)   meeting requests by such schools for support and assistance in connection with the promotion of good behaviour and discipline on the part of their pupils, and
  (ii)   assisting such schools to deal with general behavioural problems and the behavioural difficulties of individual pupils;
(b)   the arrangements made or to be made by the authority in pursuance of section 19(1) (exceptional provision of education for children not receiving education by reason of being excluded or otherwise); and
(c)   other arrangements made or to be made by them for assisting children with behavioural difficulties to find places at suitable schools.

(3) The statement shall also deal with the interaction between the arrangements referred to in subsection (2) and those made by the authority in relation to pupils with behavioural difficulties who have special educational needs.

(4) In the course of preparing the statement required by this section or any revision of it the authority shall carry out such consultation as may be prescribed.

(5) The authority shall—
(a)   publish the statement in such manner and by such date, and
(b)   publish revised statements in such manner and at such intervals,

as may be prescribed, and shall provide such persons as may be prescribed with copies of the statement or any revised statement.

(6) In discharging their functions under this section a local education authority shall have regard to any guidance given from time to time by the Secretary of State.

(7) In this section 'relevant school', in relation to a local education authority, means a school maintained by the authority (whether situated in their area or not).

Note that a LEA's responsibilities are not limited to children who have special educational needs as a consequence of their behavioural difficulties (see EA 1996, s 527A(3)).

• *Does s 527A give a parent a remedy where the parent considers, for example, that the LEA has failed to provide sufficient resources to help the school address their child's behavioural difficulties?*

3.   DETENTION

The use of detention as a punishment by teachers has a long history. Unlawfully detaining a pupil will normally amount to false imprisonment. The following case was primarily concerned with the lawfulness of corporal punishment, but Phillimore J in the Court of Appeal also considered the legality of detention.

Mansell v Griffin [1908] 1 KB 160

It is, I suppose, false imprisonment to keep a child locked up in a classroom, or even to order it to stop, under penalties, in a room for a longer period than the ordinary school time without lawful authority. Could it be said that a teacher who kept a child back during play hours to learn over and say his lesson again, or who directed a child to stand up and kept him standing perhaps for an hour, subjecting him thus to fatigue and to the derision of all his class-mates, or who put upon him a dunce's cap, as was frequently done in earlier days in the case of stupid or backward children — could it be said that such a teacher would be liable in an action for trespass to the person? The cases I have instanced are not cases of the infliction of blows, but they are cases of interference with the liberty of the subject, and it seems to me that the principle must be the same for all these cases.

In 1986 a father sued the LEA for damages for false imprisonment where his son was a member of a class which was kept in after the end of school for ten minutes as a punishment. The father claimed that (1) he had withdrawn permission to the school, to detain his son for minor indiscipline, and (2) blanket detention of a class was unreasonable. The judge rejected the father's claim, holding that the detention was a reasonable punishment, but also stated:

Punishment must not be indiscriminate. A blanket detention such as the punishment of a whole class must only be used as a last resort, otherwise people who are quite innocent may be detained incorrectly and unlawfully. (*Terrington v Lancashire County Council* (unreported), *The Law of Education* (9th edn) Butterworths, Division F56.)

The question as to when detention outside school hours is lawful is now regulated by statute. Detention after school may raise health and safety issues where pupils have a long journey by public transport. Such a detention may cause a pupil to miss a bus or train and result in the pupil having to wait an hour or more on their own for the next one.

The detention on disciplinary grounds of a pupil outside school hours is permitted despite the absence of express parental consent so long as certain conditions are satisfied.

Education Act 1996, s 550B

(1) Where a pupil to whom this section applies is required on disciplinary grounds to spend a period of time in detention at his school after the end of any school session, his detention shall not be rendered unlawful by virtue of the absence of his parent's consent to it if the conditions set out in subsection (3) are satisfied.

(2) This section applies to any pupil who has not attained the age of 18 and is attending—
(a)   a school maintained by a local education authority;...

or
(c)   a city technology college [, city college for the technology of the arts or city academy].

(3) The conditions referred to in subsection (1) are as follows—
(a)   the head teacher of the school must have previously determined, and have—
       (i)   made generally known within the school, and
       (ii)   taken steps to bring to the attention of the parent of every person who is for
              the time being a registered pupil there,
       that the detention of pupils after the end of a school session is one of the measures
       that may be taken with a view to regulating the conduct of pupils;
(b)   the detention must be imposed by the head teacher or by another teacher at the
       school specifically or generally authorised by him for the purpose;
(c)   the detention must be reasonable in all the circumstances; and
(d)   the pupil's parent must have been given at least 24 hours' notice in writing that the
       detention was due to take place.

(4) In determining for the purposes of subsection (3)(c) whether a pupil's detention is
reasonable, the following matters in particular shall be taken into account—
(a)   whether the detention constitutes a proportionate punishment in the circumstances
       of the case; and
(b)   any special circumstances relevant to its imposition on the pupil which are known to
       the person imposing it (or of which he ought reasonably to be aware) including in
       particular—
       (i)   the pupil's age,
       (ii)   any special educational needs he may have,
       (iii) any religious requirements affecting him, and
       (iv)   where arrangements have to be made for him to travel from the school to his
              home, whether suitable alternative arrangements can reasonably be made by his
              parent.
       ...

- *Does this section apply to independent schools?*

- *What should a head teacher do in order to ensure that after school detention is one of
  the sanctions which can be used by the school?*

- *What matters should be taken into account before a detention is imposed?*

- *Were the facts of Terrington v Lancashire County Council (see above) to arise again
  would the detention be lawful under s 550B?*

4.   CORPORAL PUNISHMENT AND PHYSICAL FORCE

The use of physical force and corporal punishment in schools declined during the
second half of the twentieth century. However, it continued to be used in independent
schools and in some state schools. A series of cases brought under the European

Convention on Human Rights 1950 led to the abolition of corporal punishment first in state schools and subsequently in independent schools.

The current position is that the use of physical force or corporal punishment by teachers normally gives rise to civil and criminal liability. However, physical restraint, which may involve a 'battery', is lawful in limited circumstances.

Abolition of corporal punishment

Corporal punishment had been used by the courts for many years as a method of punishing juvenile offenders. In 1968 it was abolished in England and Wales, but continued to be used in the Isle of Man. In *Tyrer v United Kingdom* (1978) 2 EHRR 1 the applicant had been sentenced in the Isle of Man to three strokes of the birch for assault occasioning actual bodily harm. The applicant complained to the European Commission that the punishment was in breach of Article 3 of the ECHR. The European Court of Human Rights held that the punishment was not inhuman and did not amount to torture, but that it was degrading and therefore in breach of Article 3.

This decision clearly implied that where corporal punishment was still administered in schools, it was also likely to be in breach of Article 3. The issue was tested by the parents of two boys attending Scottish state schools.

Campbell and Cosans v UK (1982) 4 EHRR 293

24. Mrs Campbell and Mrs Cosans claimed that, on account of the use of corporal punishment as a disciplinary measure in school, their sons Gordon and Jeffrey were victims of a violation of Article 3, which reads: 'No one shall be subjected to torture or to inhuman or degrading treatment or punishment'.

The Commission found no such violation. The government agreed with this conclusion.

25. Neither Gordon Campbell nor Jeffrey Cosans was, in fact, strapped with the tawse. Accordingly, the Court does not in the present case have to consider under Article 3 an actual application of corporal punishment.

26. However, the Court is of the opinion that, provided it is sufficiently real and immediate, a mere threat of conduct prohibited by Article 3 may itself be in conflict with that provision. Thus, to threaten an individual with torture might in some circumstances constitute at least 'inhuman treatment'.

27. Although the system of corporal punishment can cause a certain degree of apprehension in those who may be subject to it, the Court nevertheless shares the Commission's view that the situation in which the applicants' sons found themselves did not amount to 'torture' or 'inhuman treatment', within the meaning of Article 3: there is no evidence that they underwent suffering of the level inherent in these notions as they were interpreted and applied in *Ireland v United Kingdom* [(1978) 2 EHRR 25].

28. The Court's judgment in the *Tyrer* case [(1978) 2 EHRR 1] does indicate certain criteria concerning the notion of 'degrading punishment'. In the present case, no 'punishment' has actually been inflicted. Nevertheless, it follows from that judgment that 'treatment' itself will not be 'degrading' unless the person concerned has undergone—either in the eyes of

others or in his own eyes—humiliation or debasement attaining a minimum level of severity. That level has to be assessed with regard to the circumstances of the case.

...

Jeffrey Cosans may well have experienced feelings of apprehension or disquiet when he came close to an infliction of the tawse ... but such feelings are not sufficient to amount to degrading treatment, within the meaning of Article 3.

The same applies, a fortiori, to Gordon Campbell since he was never directly threatened with corporal punishment ... . It is true that counsel for his mother alleged at the hearings that group tension and a sense of alienation in the pupil are induced by the very existence of this practice but, even if this be so, these effects fall into a different category from humilation or debasement.

...

32. Article 2 of Protocol No 1 reads as follows:

No person shall be denied the right to education. In the exercise of any functions which it assumes in relation to education and to teaching, the State shall respect the right of parents to ensure such education and teaching in conformity with their own religious and philosophical convictions.

Mrs Campbell and Mrs Cosans alleged that their rights under the second sentence of this Article were violated on account of the existence of corporal punishment as a disciplinary measure in the schools attended by their children.

...

Having regard to the Convention as a whole, including Article 17, the expression 'philosophical convictions' in the present context denotes, in the Court's opinion, such convictions as are worthy of respect in a 'democratic society' and are not incompatible with human dignity; in addition, they must not conflict with the fundamental right of the child to education, the whole of Article 2 being dominated by its first sentence.

The applicants' views relate to a weighty and substantial aspect of human life and behaviour, namely the integrity of the person, the propriety or otherwise of the infliction of corporal punishment and the exclusion of the distress which the risk of such punishment entails. They are views which satisfy each of the various criteria listed above; it is this that distinguishes them from opinions that might be held on other methods of discipline or on discipline in general.

...

38. Mrs Campbell and Mrs Cosans have accordingly been victims of a violation of the second sentence of Article 2 of Protocol No 1.

III. The alleged violation of the first sentence of Article 2 of Protocol No 1

39. Mrs Cosans alleged that, by reason of his suspension from school ... her son Jeffrey had been denied the right to education, contrary to the first sentence of Article 2.

...

Again, Article 2 constitutes a whole that is dominated by its first sentence, the right set out in the second sentence being an adjunct of the fundamental right to education.

Finally, there is also a substantial difference between the legal basis of the two claims, for one concerns a right of a parent and the other a right of a child.

The issue arising under the first sentence is therefore not absorbed by the finding of a violation of the second.

41. The right to education guaranteed by the first sentence of Article 2 by its very nature calls for regulation by the State, but such regulation must never injure the substance of the right nor conflict with other rights enshrined in the Convention or its Protocols.

The suspension of Jeffrey Cosans—which remained in force for nearly a whole school year—was motivated by his and his parents' refusal to accept that he receive or be liable to corporal chastisement ... . His return to school could have been secured only if his parents had acted contrary to their convictions, convictions which the United Kingdom is obliged to respect under the second sentence of Article 2 ... . A condition of access to an educational establishment that conflicts in this way with another right enshrined in Protocol No 1 cannot be described as reasonable and in any event falls outside the State's power of regulation under Article 2.

There has accordingly also been, as regards Jeffrey Cosans, breach of the first sentence of that Article.

- *Which provision of the Convention did the Court hold had been breached by the school having a policy of using corporal punishment?*

Corporal punishment of publicly funded pupils in state schools and in independent schools in Scotland and England was abolished by the Education (Scotland) Act 1980, s 48A and the Education (No 2) Act 1986, s 47. Meanwhile the United Kingdom paid £2,000 in compensation and costs to a pupil who was caned (*X v UK* 24 YB ECHR 403 (1981)).

The legislation did not apply to most pupils at independent schools. Therefore, it was not unlawful for such pupils to be subjected to corporal punishment. In *Y v UK* (1992) 17 EHRR 238 Y was a pupil at a private school. He was caned across the buttocks by the headmaster. Although he was clothed the caning left four weals. There was no prosecution of the headmaster and a civil claim was dismissed. The European Commission of Human Rights found that there was a breach of Articles 3 and 13. The United Kingdom agreed to pay Y £8,000 before the case went to the court.

In 1993 the United Kingdom was once more brought before the European Court of Human Rights which was again asked to consider the legality of the form of punishment used in an independent school.

Costello-Roberts v UK (1993) 19 EHRR 112

7. In September 1985 Mrs Costello-Roberts sent the applicant, who was then aged seven, to an independent boarding preparatory school in Barnstaple, Devon. The school had approximately 180 pupils, none of whose fees were paid out of public funds, and received no direct financial support from the government.

8. In the school's prospectus it was stated that a high standard of discipline was maintained, but no mention was made of the use of corporal punishment. Mrs Costello-Roberts had

made no inquiry about the school's disciplinary regime and did not at the outset make known her opposition to corporal punishment. The school in question operated a system whereby such punishment was administered upon acquisition of five demerit marks. On 3 October 1985 the applicant received his fifth demerit mark for talking in the corridor. The other demerit marks were for similar conduct and for being a little late for bed on one occasion. Having discussed the matter with his colleagues, the headmaster decided that the only answer to the applicant's lack of discipline, about which he had received three warnings from the headmaster, was to give him three 'whacks' on the bottom through his shorts with a rubber-soled gym shoe. He so informed the applicant on 8 October.

9. The punishment was administered by the headmaster three days later, eight days after Jeremy had received his fifth demerit mark. No other persons were present.

...

10. The applicant's mother complained to the police some time between 4 and 16 November 1985, but was told that there was no action they could take without any visible bruising on the child's buttocks. A complaint by her to the National Society for the Prevention of Cruelty to Children received a similar response.

...

Judgment

Mr Costello-Roberts was a young boy punished in accordance with the disciplinary rules in force within the school in which he was a boarder. This amounted to being slippered three times on his buttocks through his shorts with a rubber-soled gym shoe by the headmaster in private. Mr Tyrer, on the other hand, was a young man sentenced in the local juvenile court to three strokes of the birch on the bare posterior. His punishment was administered some three weeks later in a police station where he was held by two policemen whilst a third administered the punishment, pieces of the birch breaking at the first stroke.

32. Beyond the consequences to be expected from measures taken on a purely disciplinary plane, the applicant has adduced no evidence of any severe or long-lasting effects as a result of the treatment complained of. A punishment which does not occasion such effects may fall within the ambit of Article 3, provided that in the particular circumstances of the case, it may be said to have reached the minimum threshold of severity required. While the Court has certain misgivings about the automatic nature of the punishment and the three-day wait before its imposition, it considers that minimum level of severity not to have been attained in this case.

Accordingly, no violation of Article 3 has been established.

III. Alleged violation of Article 8

33. The applicant alleged that his corporal punishment had also given rise to a breach of Article 8 of the Convention, which reads:

1. Everyone has the right to respect for his private and family life, his home and his correspondence.

2. There shall be no interference by a public authority with the exercise of this right except such as is in accordance with the law and is necessary in a democratic society in

the interests of national security, public safety or the economic well-being of the country, for the prevention of disorder or crime, for the protection of health or morals, or for the protection of the rights and freedoms of others.

...

The Court does not exclude the possibility that there might be circumstances in which Article 8 could be regarded as affording in relating to disciplinary measures a protection which goes beyond that given by Article 3. Having regard, however, to the purpose and aim of the Convention taken as a whole, and bearing in mind that the sending of a child to school necessarily involves some degree of interference with his or her private life, the Court considers that the treatment complained of by the applicant did not entail adverse effects for his physical or moral integrity sufficient to bring it within the scope of the prohibition contained in Article 8. While not wishing to be taken to approve in any way the retention of corporal punishment as part of the disciplinary regime of a school, the Court therefore concludes that in the circumstances of this case there has also been no violation of that Article.

...

40. For the following reasons the Court agrees in substance with the government's submission that an effective remedy was available to the applicant in respect of his Article 3 and 8 complaints.

First, it was not disputed that it would have been open to the applicant to institute civil proceedings for assault and that, had they succeeded, the English courts would have been in a position to grant him appropriate relief in respect of the punishment which he had received.

Secondly, the effectiveness of a remedy for the purposes of Article 13 does not depend on the certainty of a favourable outcome: in any event it is not for the Court to speculate as to what decision the English courts would have reached, given particularly the latitude which those courts would have to apply relevant contemporary standards.

In so far as the applicant's arguments relate to the more general question of the scope of the relevant domestic law, the Court recalls that Article 13 does not go so far as to guarantee a remedy allowing a Contracting State's laws as such to be challenged before a national authority on the ground of being contrary to the Convention or to equivalent domestic legal norms.

There has accordingly been no breach of Article 13.

For these reasons, the court
1.   *holds* by five votes to four that there has been no violation of Article 3;
2.   *holds* unanimously that there has been no violation of Article 8 or Article 13.

It was only in September 1999 that corporal punishment in independent schools was abolished (s 548 of the EA 1996 substituted by SSFA 1998 (s 131(1)). It has been reported that certain religious schools, including the Christian Fellowship School in Liverpool, argue that banning corporal punishment is an interference with the right of parents to have their children educated as they wish in accordance with Article 1 of Protocol 2 of the ECHR. However, their argument was rejected in *R (Williamson) v Secretary of State for Education and Employment* (2001) Times, 12 December. Elias J held that 'the belief that corporal punishment should be imposed could not properly be described as a philosophical or religious conviction'.

The section now applies to all types of schools as well as organisations providing nursery education.

Education Act 1996, s 548

(1) Corporal punishment given by, or on the authority of, a member of staff to a child—
(a)   for whom education is provided at any school, or
(b)   for whom education is provided, otherwise than at school, under any arrangements made by a local education authority, or
(c)   for whom specified nursery education is provided otherwise than at school,

cannot be justified in any proceedings on the ground that it was given in pursuance of a right exercisable by the member of staff by virtue of his position as such.

(2) Subsection (1) applies to corporal punishment so given to a child at any time, whether at the school or other place at which education is provided for the child, or elsewhere.

(3) The following provisions have effect for the purposes of this section.

(4) Any reference to giving corporal punishment to a child is to doing anything for the purpose of punishing that child (whether or not there are other reasons for doing it) which, apart from any justification, would constitute battery.

...

Note that the effect of s 548(1) is to remove a defence; the defence being that the teacher (or other authorised person) was acting as a reasonable parent and was therefore entitled to administer reasonable chastisement.

* *What amounts to 'battery'? How, if at all, would this provision assist the parents in Campbell and Cosans v UK (1982) 4 EHRR 293?*

The section goes on to provide a defence in certain circumstances, which can apply to teachers, other employees, and voluntary helpers such as parents.

Education Act 1996, s 548(5)

However, corporal punishment shall not be taken to be given to a child by virtue of anything done for reasons that include averting—
(a)   an immediate danger of personal injury to, or
(b)   an immediate danger to the property of,

any person (including the child himself).

* *Identify a situation where this defence would arise. Do these provisions provide a defence for both a criminal charge and a civil claim?*

Power to restrain pupils

In addition to being permitted to commit a 'battery' in limited circumstances under s 548(5) of the EA 1996, a member of the school staff has statutory authority to use reasonable force to restrain a pupil in certain situations (s 550A(1) of the EA 1996 as inserted by s 4 of the EA 1997). This defence also applies to anyone who, with the authority of the head teacher, has lawful control or charge of pupils at the school.

Education Act 1996, s 550A

(1) A member of the staff of a school may use, in relation to any pupil at the school, such force as is reasonable in the circumstances for the purpose of preventing the pupil from doing (or continuing to do) any of the following, namely—
(a) committing any offence,
(b) causing personal injury to, or damage to the property of, any person (including the pupil himself), or
(c) engaging in any behaviour prejudicial to the maintenance of good order and discipline at the school or among any of its pupils, whether that behaviour occurs during a teaching session or otherwise.

(2) Subsection (1) applies where a member of the staff of a school is—
(b) on the premises of the school, or
(b) elsewhere at a time when, as a member of its staff, he has lawful control or charge of the pupil concerned;

but it does not authorise anything to be done in relation to a pupil which constitutes the giving of corporal punishment within the meaning of section 548.

(3) Subsection (1) shall not be taken to prevent any person from relying on any defence available to him otherwise than by virtue of this section.

Detailed guidance is contained in DfEE Circular 10/98 (Section 550A of the Education Act 1996: the Use of Force to Control or Restrain Pupils.)

DfEE Circular 10/98: Section 550A of the Education Act 1996: the Use of Force to Control or Restrain Pupils

Summary of Contents

A new provision comes into force on 1 September 1998 (Section 550A of the Education Act 1996). This clarifies the powers of teachers, and other staff who have lawful control or charge of pupils, to use reasonable force to prevent pupils committing a crime; causing injury or damage; or causing disruption. Such powers already existed under common law but they have often been misunderstood.

Neither the Act, nor this circular, authorise the use of corporal punishment in any circumstances. Nor are they intended to encourage the use of inappropriate force.

The circular:
- gives examples of circumstances in which physical intervention might be appropriate, and factors that teachers should bear in mind when deciding whether to intervene;
- discusses the meaning of 'reasonable force';
- advises that schools should have a policy about the use of reasonable force, and should tell parents about it; and,
- advises that schools should record incidents in which force is used to control or restrain a pupil, and tell parents of any such incidents involving their child.

The meaning of 'reasonable force' is explained as follows.

DfEE Circular 10/98: Section 550A of the Education Act 1996: the Use of Force to Control or Restrain Pupils

16. There is no legal definition of 'reasonable force'. So it is not possible to set out comprehensively when it is reasonable to use force, or the degree of force that may reasonably be used. It will always depend on all the circumstances of the case.

17. There are two relevant considerations:
- the use of force can be regarded as reasonable only if the circumstances of the particular incident warrant it. The use of *any* degree of force is unlawful if the particular circumstances do not warrant the use of physical force. Therefore physical force could not be justified to prevent a pupil from committing a trivial misdemeanour, or in a situation that clearly could be resolved without force;
- the degree of force employed must be in proportion to the circumstances of the incident and the seriousness of the behaviour or the consequences it is intended to prevent. Any force used should always be the minimum needed to achieve the desired result.

18. Whether it is reasonable to use force, and the degree of force that could reasonably be employed, might also depend on the age, understanding, and sex of the pupil.

The case of the Welsh head teacher who slapped a ten-year-old boy after he pushed her backwards onto a bench highlights the difficulties which may arise in interpreting s 550A. She was eventually acquitted on appeal of assaulting the boy (*R v Evans* (LAWTEL 18 May 2001), but was immediately suspended again by the governing body (*Evans v Monmouthshire County Council and the Governing Body of St Mary's Junior School, Caldicot* LAWTEL 14 June 2001).

- *Do you think that s 550A and the guidance have made it clear when reasonable force may be used by a teacher?*

5.   EXCLUSIONS AND REINSTATEMENT

Where a pupil persistently misbehaves or commits a single serious breach of the school behaviour policy, the head teacher may consider it appropriate to suspend or expel the pupil. The terminology used in the legislation and guidance for suspension is 'fixed term exclusion' and for expulsion is 'permanent exclusion'. 'Indefinite' exclusions are no longer permissible. 'Voluntary' exclusions, where a school asks parents to withdraw their child from school under the express or implied threat that if the child is not withdrawn the child will be excluded, have no legal status.

White Paper: *Excellence in Schools* (Cm 3681, July 1997)

Exclusions

19 Schools need the ultimate sanction of excluding pupils; but the present number of exclusions is too high. We are concerned in particular about the unjustified variation in exclusion rates between schools and the disproportionate exclusion of pupils from certain ethnic minorities and children looked after by local authorities. We will be consulting shortly on detailed new guidance for schools and LEAs about the appropriate circumstances for exclusion, about appeals and arrangements for pupils' subsequent education, and about the merits of financial incentives for schools to admit pupils excluded by others.

20 Where pupils are out of school, LEAs have a duty to arrange suitable education. Such arrangements have not always been adequate. For example, home tuition should be sufficient to meet pupils' educational needs, not just what it is convenient for the LEA to provide. The quality and cost-effectiveness of many pupil referral units need to be substantially improved—taking advantage of the opportunities presented by the new inspection arrangements. For older pupils alternative approaches—such as that offered by Cities in Schools, which successfully engages disaffected pupils in a carefully organised programme that includes work experience—should be considered. There should be a specific learning programme for each excluded pupil, with clear targets, a full timetable, and the objective of a return to mainstream schooling wherever sensible.

21 As well as being a cause of low achievement, especially amongst boys, truancy and exclusion are also associated with crime. A survey for the recent Audit Commission study *Misspent Youth* indicated that 65 per cent of school-age offenders sentenced in court had also been excluded from school or were persistent truants. Action to improve attendance and reduce the need for exclusion should therefore contribute significantly to the government's wider strategy to prevent anti-social and criminal behaviour by young people and to reduce the associated public costs.

In 1999 the government introduced new statutory guidance (DfEE circular 10/99 (Social Inclusion Pupil Support), DfEE circular 11/99 (Social Inclusion: the LEA Role in Pupil Support)). Circular 10/99 has proved controversial in relation to exclusions and those provisions have been amended three times since September 1999 and are likely to be revised and replaced in 2002. Head teachers, governing bodies, LEAs, and independent appeals panels are required to take into account the statutory guidance (SSFA 1998, s 68).

One of the aims of the guidance was to reduce the number of exclusions. Figures published by the DfES indicate that the number of permanent exclusions peaked in 1996/97 and has declined in subsequent years. The decline is unlikely to be attributable to the guidance because that only came into effect on 1 September 1999.

Statistical First Release (SFR 20/2001)

Table 1 Number of permanent exclusions by type of school, England 1995/96 to 1999/00

	1995/96	1996/97	1997/98	1998/99	1999/00 (5)
PRIMARY SCHOOLS(3)					
Number of permanent exclusions	1,608	1,573	1,539	1,366	1,200
Percentage of permanent exclusions(1)	13	12	13	13	14
Percentage of school population(2)	0.04	0.04	0.03	0.03	0.03
SECONDARY SCHOOLS(3)					
Number of permanent exclusions	10,344	10,463	10,187	8,636	7,000
Percentage of permanent exclusions(1)	83	83	83	83	82
Percentage of school population(2)	0.34	0.34	0.33	0.28	0.22
SPECIAL SCHOOLS(4)					
Number of permanent exclusions	524	632	572	436	400
Percentage of permanent exclusions(1)	4	5	5	4	5
Percentage of school population(2)	0.54	0.64	0.58	0.45	0.41
ALL SCHOOLS					
Number of permanent exclusions	12,476	12,668	12,298	10,438	8,600
Percentage of permanent exclusions(1)	100	100	100	100	100
Percentage of school population(2)	0.17	0.17	0.16	0.14	0.11

(1)   The number of permanent exclusions expressed as a percentage of the total number.

(2)   The number of permanent exclusions expressed as a percentage of the number (headcount) of full and part-time pupils of all ages (excluding dually registered pupils in special schools) in January each year.

(3)   Includes middle schools as deemed.

(4)   Includes both maintained and non-maintained special schools.

(5)   Provisional estimate. Permanent exclusions for 1999/00 are estimated as a number of LEAs did not confirm the data for their schools.

Table 2: Number of permanent exclusions by gender, age, special educational needs and ethnic group, England 1999/2000

	Number of permanent exclusions	Percentage of permanent exclusions [1]	Percentage of population [2]
Gender:			
Boys	7,032	84.5	0.18
Girls	1,291	15.5	0.03
Age [3]:			
4	9	0.1	0.00
5	59	0.7	0.01
6	86	1.0	0.01
7	132	1.6	0.02
8	202	2.4	0.03
9	312	3.7	0.05
10	460	5.5	0.08
11	519	6.2	0.09
12	1,180	14.2	0.20
13	1,766	21.2	0.31
14	2,200	26.4	0.39
15	1,288	15.5	0.24
16	92	1.1	0.05
17	16	0.2	0.01
18	2	0.0	0.01
19	0	0.0	0.00
Special Educational Needs;			
Pupils with statements of SEN	1,494	18.0	0.61
Pupils without statements of SEN	6,829	82.0	0.09

	Number of permanent exclusions	Percentage of permanent exclusions [1]	Percentage of population [2]
Ethnic group :			
Number	8,314	100.0	0.12
White	6,890	82.9	0.12
Black Caribbean	455	5.5	0.46
Black African	145	1.7	0.17
Black other	218	2.6	0.37
Indian	54	0.6	0.03
Pakistani	129	1.6	0.07
Bangladeshi	53	0.6	0.08
Chinese	2	0.0	0.01
Any other ethnic group	289	3.5	0.20
Ethnicity not known	79	1.0	–

1. The number of permanent exclusions expressed as a percentage of the total number.
2. The number of permanent exclusions expressed as a percentage of the number (headcount) of full time and part time, boys and girls of all ages, pupils of each age,

pupils of all ages with and without statements of SEN, in primary, secondary and special schools (excluding dually registered pupils in special schools) in January 2000.
3.   Age at 31 August 1999.
4.   The number of permanent exclusions of compulsory school age and above expressed as a percentage of the total number of permanent exclusions of compulsory school age and above.
5.   The number of permanent exclusions of compulsory school age and above expressed as a percentage of the number (headcount) of pupils of compulsory school age and above in each ethnic group in primary, secondary and special schools (excluding dually registered pupils in special schools) in January 2000.

However, there has been a backlash by teachers and their unions against the decisions of the independent appeal panels which have ordered reinstatement of pupils who have been permanently excluded (see below).

The current legislative provisions are found in the School Standards and Framework Act 1998, ss 64 to 68, and Sch 18, together with the following regulations:

- Education (Exclusion from School) (Prescribed Periods) Regulations 1999, SI 1999/1868 as amended by SI 2000/294
- School Standards and Framework Act 1998 (Amendment of Schedule 18) (England) Order 2001, SI 2001/2086.

The School Standards and Framework Act 1998 gives the head teacher the power to exclude pupils on disciplinary grounds; and the pupil's parents the right to make representations to the governing body and, in the case of a permanent exclusion, to appeal further to an independent appeal panel. Both the governing body and the independent appeal panel have the power to direct that the pupil be reinstated.

The Education Bill 2001/02 proposes to transfer most of the existing primary legislation on exclusion to regulations as part of the government's endeavour to modernise education law. The content is likely to remain much the same, except that a right of appeal will be given to parents whose children have been excluded from PRUs (Pupil Referral Units), and maintained nursery schools will come within the legislative provisions for the first time.

Role of the head teacher

In addition to having the power to exclude a pupil the head teacher has a duty to inform the pupil's parents and other bodies that a pupil has been excluded. Before excluding a pupil the head teacher must take into account the statutory guidance contained in Circular 10/99.

Power to exclude

School Standards and Framework Act 1998, s 64

(1) The head teacher of a maintained school may exclude a pupil from the school for a fixed period or permanently.

(2) The head teacher may not exercise the power to exclude a pupil from the school for one or more fixed periods such that the pupil is so excluded for more than 45 school days in any one school year.

(3) A pupil may not be excluded from a maintained school (whether by suspension, expulsion or otherwise) except by the head teacher in accordance with this section.

(4) In this Act 'exclude', in relation to the exclusion of a child from a school, means exclude on disciplinary grounds (and 'exclusion' shall be construed accordingly).

If the head teacher is absent from school may an acting or a deputy head teacher exclude a pupil?

Education Act 1996, s 579

(1) In this Act, unless the context otherwise requires—

...

'head teacher' includes acting head teacher;

...

* *What is the maximum period for which a pupil may be subject to one or more fixed term exclusions in any one school year?*

* *How many weeks is 45 school days?*

WHEN IS EXCLUSION APPROPRIATE?

Before excluding a pupil the head teacher should consider the guidance contained in Circular 10/99. Where a head teacher fails to take into account or ignores the guidance, the governing body or the independent appeals panel should normally direct reinstatement of the pupil.

The head teacher should follow a two-stage process. First, the head teacher should ascertain what actually happened. Where the evidence indicates that there has been a serious breach of the school discipline policy, the head teacher should secondly decide whether exclusion is a reasonable response to the incident.

The guidance gives advice on the approach to be followed by the head teacher in gathering evidence on which to base a decision. The fact-finding aspect of the head's role has also been considered by the courts. This can be particularly problematic where the incident being investigated may also give rise to a criminal charge. For example, the question arises whether a head teacher is in the same position as a police officer investigating an allegation.

DfEE Circular 10/99: Social Inclusion: Pupil Support

Chapter 6, The Use of Exclusion

6.3 Before reaching a decision, the head teacher should:
- consider all the relevant facts and firm evidence to support the allegations made, and take into account the school's policy on equal opportunities. If there is doubt that the pupil actually did what is alleged, the head teacher should not exclude the pupil;
- allow the pupil to give their version of events;
- check whether an incident appeared to be provoked by racial or sexual harassment;
- if necessary consult others, being careful not to involve anyone who may later take part in the statutory review of their decision, eg a member of the Discipline Committee.

Where there is a dispute as to the identification of the alleged culprit, the head teacher is not required to comply with rules of criminal procedure when investigating the incident. However, great care should be taken to ensure that the identification is not tainted by suggestion. In the following case the court recognised the difficulties faced by the head teacher in gathering the evidence, and reserved its criticisms for the hearings before the governing body and appeal committee.

R v Roman Catholic Schools, ex p S [1998] ELR 304

Moses J: In this case the essential issue was the correctness of identification of Mrs Taylor. Since identification was the only issue, it was of importance that those conducting the inquiry should remind themselves of the dangers of identification evidence and the need for safeguards to avoid such dangers. It was, therefore incumbent upon them to examine carefully the circumstances in which the identification was made and consider the extent to which those safeguards necessary to avoid the dangers of visual identification were in place. Such safeguards normally require an account of the initial description given by the witness of the culprit before the identification took place, an account of the process of identification and the steps taken to avoid any identification being tainted by suggestion. For example, the first description given by a witness is important. It provides a measure for testing the accuracy of any subsequent identification and avoids the danger that a description given after identification may have been added or coloured by the appearance at the time of identification. I am not suggesting that those conducting an inquiry where the identification of a pupil at a school in issue must have available the decision of *R v Turnbull* [1977] QB 224. But fairness requires that, in such a case, they should have had well in mind the dangers of identification evidence and the need for safeguards to avoid them. A careful, even if not searching inquiry, will at least raise questions as to the circumstances in which the original identification was made, whether any description was available before such an identification and whether any description might have been tainted by the process of identification. In order to resolve issues arising as to the accuracy of an identification and the circumstances in which it was made, it will usually be necessary to have oral evidence from the identifying witness not least so as to be able to probe the circumstances in which the identification was made. In *R v Board of Visitors of Hull Prison, ex p St Germain (No 2)* [1979] 1 WLR 1401, a prison visitors' case, Geoffrey Lane LJ used the example of identification evidence to support the proposition that there may be cases where in order to be given a fair opportunity to controvert the charge a prisoner should have the opportunity of cross-examination of the witness who had purported to identify him.

The Court of Appeal considered the relationship between the roles of the head teacher, the discipline committee and the independent appeal panel in *R v Headteacher and Independent Appeal Committee of Dunraven School, ex p B* [2000] ELR 156. The court was primarily concerned with whether the pupil had received a fair hearing, and secondly whether the identity of an informant should be revealed.

R v Dunraven School, ex p B [2000] ELR 156

Sedley LJ: The application was made on behalf of a pupil at Dunraven School, a grant-maintained comprehensive school in the London Borough of Lambeth, by his mother. The applicant, 15 years old at the time of the hearing before us, was born in November 1984. At the opening of the appeal the court continued the order protecting him from disclosure of his identity.

The case before the deputy judge, and before us, concerns the way in which the applicant came to be permanently excluded from Dunraven School. On 9 December 1998 a handbag belonging to a teacher was stolen from the staffroom. Suspicion came to rest on the applicant and two other pupils, identified in these proceedings as D and M. Some weeks later, on 11 January 1999, the three were interviewed separately by the headteacher, Richard Townsend. I will return to the detail of what was elicited and how it was elicited, but the outcome of the interviews was that all three boys were temporarily excluded the following day and permanently excluded a fortnight later by the headteacher.

The exclusions came, as they were required to do, before a committee of the governing body which heard D's case first, then the applicant's, then M's. The applicant was not told what D had said about him and his part in the episode. His representative did, however, challenge the headteacher's account of how the applicant had initially come to admit being present at the time of the theft, something which he had subsequently resiled from. The governing body upheld the decision of the headteacher to exclude the applicant and M permanently from the school. In respect of D they reversed the head's decision.

The applicant appealed to the statutory appeal committee, which came to the same conclusions, and on the same materials, as the governors.

...

Did the applicant have a fair hearing?

It is a proposition too obvious to require authority that what fairness demands in a particular situation will depend on the circumstances. In relation to permanent exclusion from a grant-maintained school Parliament has made it clear—as the common law would otherwise have done, given what is at stake in such cases—that the pupil, through his or her parent, has a right to be heard. Such a right is worthless unless the parent knows in some adequate form what is being said against the child. Where what is being said has taken at least two different and arguably inconsistent forms, fairness will ordinarily require enough disclosure to reveal the inconsistency.

A second, related principle is that it is unfair for the decision-maker to have access to damaging material to which the person at risk—here the pupil through his parent—has no access.

In my judgment both of these principles were breached in the course of the hearing before the governors. They were also breached in the hearing before the appeal committee, with the consequence that no question can arise (as it might otherwise have done: see

Calvin v Carr [1980] AC 574; cf *R v Hereford Magistrates Court, ex p Rowlands* [1998] QB 110) of a fair appeal having cured a deficient hearing.

...

Section 76(2) of PACE, put shortly, requires the prosecution to prove beyond reasonable doubt, where the issue is raised, that a confession on which it proposes to rely has not been obtained by oppression or by any inducement likely to render it unreliable. Code C translates this into police practice. While PACE and its Codes may serve as a touchstone of fair procedure outside the criminal justice process, they can logically do no more than this. Thus para 11.14 of Code C indicates that a juvenile should ordinarily not be interviewed in the absence of an appropriate adult. Paragraph 11.3 forbids the use of oppression or threats or promises to elicit answers or obtain a statement. A headteacher, while not in the same position as a parent, is not in the same position as a police officer. This does not license him to use oppression, but it does help in deciding what amounts to improper pressure on a pupil. Without doubt an admission made to a headteacher who has told a child that he will be kept in until he confesses, or who has untruthfully told a child that he has been seen committing the offence, would be worthless; but I do not consider that what happened here, accepting that it may well have had the distressing effect which the applicant described, was such as to make his admission of presence unreliable or the manner of obtaining it oppressive. In particular it is clear that the applicant has in his recollection condensed the headteacher's justifiable remark—that exclusion was more likely if he had taken part in the theft and was now denying it—into a threat of exclusion whether he admitted the theft or whether he did not. Such a threat would so obviously have been self-defeating that I see no realistic prospect of a finding that it was made.

...

Brooke LJ: Mr Townsend [the headteacher] saw B and his mother on 14 January 1999, and on 27 January 1999 he decided to convert the temporary exclusions into permanent exclusions for all three boys. He had concluded that they had all been present at the incident. He justified his decision in D's case because he had admitted he had asked the other boys for money, and he did not tell any member of staff about the theft when it occurred. Indeed, he had only admitted his involvement when Mr Townsend interviewed him.

This, then, was the state of affairs when the school's governors became involved. They faced what turned out to be a formidably difficult task. It is quite clear, in my judgment, that they did their level best to set about it fairly. Understandably, they did not incur the heavy expense of seeking legal advice, although in retrospect it might have been better if they had.

The reason why their task was so difficult was that B was still denying that he had been present in the staffroom at all. His defence was that Mr Townsend had used oppressive behaviour to force a 'confession' out of him. That defence was rejected twice on the facts, and I see no reason why that issue should be reopened on this judicial review application, particularly since, like Sedley LJ, I do not consider that the 'confession' takes things very much further forward. Its existence, however, led to the admission of a good deal of evidence which would not normally have been before the committee on the question whether he had indeed been culpably involved in this theft. A further problem arose from the fact that Mr Townsend told the exclusion committee that he considered that D had given him his written statement in confidence, and he was not willing to disclose it, even when B's mother pressed him for the statement by her son's accuser.

Circular 10/99 gives guidance to head teachers on when exclusion is and is not an appropriate response.

DfEE Circular 10/99: Social Inclusion: Pupil Support

Chapter 6, The Use of Exclusion

6.2 A decision to exclude a child should be taken only:
- in response to serious breaches of a school's discipline policy; and
- if allowing the pupil to remain in school would seriously harm the education or welfare of the pupil or of others in the school.

Before excluding a child, *in most cases* a range of alternative strategies such as those included in Section 4 [Handling Signs of Disaffection] should be tried. This is not meant to prevent immediate action to protect pupils and staff, including period exclusion. A permanent exclusion can be given for a first offence, for example involving violence, but only when the head teacher has had further opportunity (not in the 'heat of the moment') to consider the incident in question.

If, when they review an exclusion, the Discipline Committee or the independent appeal panel consider that the guidance in this Section and Annex D was not followed, they should normally direct re-instatement.

...

6.4 Exclusion should not be used for:
- minor incidents such as failure to do homework or to bring dinner money;
- poor academic performance;
- lateness or truancy (more information about improving attendance is in Section 4);
- pregnancy (see Section 3);
- breaching school uniform policy including hairstyle or wearing jewellery;
- punishing pupils for the behaviour of the parents, for example, by extending a fixed period exclusion until the parents agree to attend a meeting.

Permanent exclusion should be used as a last resort, when all else has failed. Normally it should not be used for a first offence. ...

6.6 A decision to exclude a child permanently is a serious one. It is a final step in the process for dealing with disciplinary offences when a wide range of other strategies have been tried and have failed, including the use of a Pastoral Support Programme. It is also an acknowledgement by the school that it can no longer cope with the child. The Secretary of State does not expect a head teacher normally to exclude permanently a pupil for a 'one-off' or first offence.

Specific guidance is also given where the exclusion is drugs-related, and where the excluded child has special educational needs. ...

DRUGS-RELATED EXCLUSION

6.9 In many cases exclusion will be the appropriate course. But it is for schools to decide whether or not to exclude permanently for all incidents connected with drug misuse. Fixed period exclusions may in some cases be more appropriate. Schools need to ensure that the course of action takes into account the needs of the individuals involved (as well as their peers) both in terms of their educational and personal development, and in terms of recognising that permanent exclusion may make a young person more vulnerable to exposure to drugs.

PUPILS WITH SPECIAL EDUCATIONAL NEEDS (SEN)[1]

6.10 The level of exclusions for pupils with a statement of SEN is extremely high; the most recent data show that the permanent exclusion rate for such pupils was seven times higher than for pupils without a statement. Other than in the most exceptional circumstances, schools should avoid permanently excluding pupils with statements. In most cases, the head teacher will be aware that the school, whether mainstream or special, is having difficulty managing a statemented pupil's behaviour well before the situation has escalated. Schools should try every practicable means to maintain placements, including seeking LEA and other professional advice as appropriate. Where this process has been exhausted, the school should liaise with the LEA about initiating an 'interim' annual review of the statement.

6.11 Where a child is excluded from a special school during the period between the head teacher's initial decision and the meeting of the governing body, the head teacher should work with the LEA to see whether more support can be made available, or whether the statement can be changed to name a new school. If either of these options is possible, the head teacher should normally withdraw the exclusion.

6.12 There is some evidence that a significant number of pupils are being excluded from mainstream schools part way through the assessment process. Head teachers should make every effort to avoid this. Although a large and increasing number of exclusions are from schools catering for pupils with EBD [emotional and behavioural difficulties], there is evidence that the most effective special schools are very reluctant to exclude their pupils.

1   More information: The Education of Children with Emotional and Behavioural Difficulties. DFE Circular 9/94; Meeting special educational needs: a programme of action DfEE 1998. Includes measures to improve arrangements for EBD children; Truancy and School Exclusion: Report by the Social Exclusion Unit. The Stationery Office 1998; Effective schooling for pupils with emotional and behavioural difficulties. Cole E, Visser J, Uptown G David Futon Publishing 1998; Advisory Centre for Education Exclusions helpline 020 7704 9822.

Exclusions procedure

School Standards and Framework Act 1998, s 65

(1) Where the head teacher of a maintained school excludes any pupil, the head teacher shall (without delay) take reasonable steps to inform the relevant person of the following matters—
(a) the period of the exclusion (or, if the pupil is being permanently excluded, that he is being so excluded);
(b) the reasons for the exclusion;
(c) that he may make representations about the exclusion to the governing body, and
(d) the means by which such representations may be made.

(2) Where the head teacher decides that any exclusion of a pupil for a fixed period should be made permanent, he shall (without delay) take reasonable steps to inform the relevant person of—
(a) his decision, and
(b) the matters specified in paragraphs (b) to (d) of subsection (1).

(3) Subsection (4) applies where the head teacher—
(a)   excludes any pupil in circumstances where the pupil would, as a result of the exclusion—
    (i)   be excluded from the school for a total of more than five school days in any one term, or
    (ii)   lose an opportunity to take any public examination,
(b)   excludes a pupil permanently, or
(c)   decides that any exclusion of a pupil should be made permanent.

(4) Where this subsection applies, the head teacher shall (without delay) inform the local education authority and the governing body of the following matters—
(a)   the period of the exclusion (or, if the pupil is being permanently excluded, that he is being so excluded), or
(b)   his decision that any exclusion of a pupil for a fixed period should be made permanent, and (in either case) of the reasons for it.

(5) In this section and in sections 66 and 67 'the relevant person' means—
(a)   in relation to a pupil under the age of 18, a parent of his;
(b)   in relation to a pupil who has attained that age, the pupil himself.

(6) Where regulations under paragraph 4 of Schedule 11 require the governing body of a maintained school to establish a discipline committee, references in this section and sections 66 to 68 to the governing body of such a school shall be construed as references to their discipline committee.

Where, for example, a bully is being excluded, does the parent of a pupil who has been bullied have the right to know that the bully has been excluded?

Annex D of circular 10/99 gives detailed guidance on how and when parents should be informed, as well as what should be contained in the letter sent to the parents. For example:

A head teacher who excludes a pupil should make sure the parent is notified immediately, ideally by telephone, and that the telephone call is followed by a letter within one school day. An exclusion should normally begin on the next school day.

Role of the governing body

The pupil's parent has the right to make representations to the governing body. Normally the powers of the governing body in relation to exclusions are exercised by a pupil discipline sub-committee (Education (School Government) (England) Regulations 1999, SI 1999/2163, para 48). The LEA also has the right to make representations as to the appropriateness of the exclusion, but no longer has the right to direct that the pupil should be reinstated.

School Standards and Framework Act 1998, s 66

(1) Subsections (2) to (6) apply where the governing body of a maintained school are informed under section 65(4) of any exclusion or decision to which that provision applies.

(2) The governing body shall in any such case—
(a)   consider the circumstances in which the pupil was excluded;
(b)   consider any representations about the exclusion made to the governing body—
    (i)   by the relevant person in pursuance of section 65(1)(c) or (2)(b), or
    (ii)   by the local education authority;
(c)   allow each of the following, namely—
    (i)   the relevant person, and
    (ii)   an officer of the local education authority nominated by the authority,

to attend a meeting of the governing body and to make oral representations about the exclusion; and

(d)   consider any oral representations so made.

...

(5) The head teacher shall comply with any direction of the governing body for the reinstatement of a pupil who has been excluded from the school.

...

(7) Where—
(a)   the head teacher of a maintained school excludes a pupil otherwise than as mentioned in section 65(3), and
(b)   the governing body receive any representations made in pursuance of section 65(1)(c) or (2)(b) by the relevant person about the exclusion,

they shall consider those representations.

....

- *When does a parent have the right to make oral representations to the discipline committee of the governing body? Look at s 66(1) and (2), and s 65(3) and (4).*

- *Does a parent have the right to make oral representations where their child is excluded for four days?*

- *Where a pupil has been excluded for four days may the discipline committee direct reinstatement?*

The discipline committee has the power to direct that the head teacher should reinstate the pupil immediately or on a particular date, or not at all, but only where the right to make oral representations exists. Normally, the discipline committee need only consider oral representations within 50 school days of the decision to exclude (Education (Exclusion from School)(Prescribed Periods) Regulations 1999, SI 1999/1868, as amended for England by SI 2000/294). Most fixed term exclusions will in practice be over by the time the committee meets. Nevertheless, parents may wish to make representations and if the committee considers that reinstatement was appropriate, this should be noted on the pupil's school record.

The role of the discipline committee of the governing body has been considered by the Court of Appeal. Brooke LJ considered the standard of proof required.

R v Headteacher and Independent Appeal Committee of Dunraven School, ex p B [2000] ELR 156

Sedley LJ: It follows that any action taken by the governing body will be predicated upon inquiries already made by the head teacher. This does not mean that the governing body is limited to considering the consequences of whatever the head teacher has established. On the contrary, its role must be precisely to ensure that exclusion (including the facts on which it is founded) is properly reconsidered in a manner which ensures that the pupil is being fairly treated—something which a head teacher's initial inquiry and conclusion may not always be able to achieve in the difficult conditions of a large urban comprehensive with a hundred different demands on the head's time and attention. This, it seems to me, is why, where an appeal from the governors is provided by statute, there is no such statutory distancing of the governors from the head teacher. Because the latter is for practical reasons in the successive positions of investigator, accuser, jury and judge, the governors are there to provide an essential independent check on his judgment.

I would therefore reject Mr Oldham's submission that the governors' only duty was to decide whether the head teacher had acted reasonably. In my view it was their duty to establish to their own satisfaction what the primary facts were—as in fact they did. In doing so they were entitled to start from the head teacher's findings. For his part, the head teacher was entitled to reach what was in practice, and arguably too in law, a provisional decision in the way he did precisely because it had to be fully and fairly reviewed by the governors. It was the governing body which then had to afford a fair hearing.

...

[T]he governors needed to proceed in this way: first, they wished to take D's account into consideration, which necessarily meant letting the pupil and his parent know what it was, they had to consider whether his identity could be concealed; if it could not, then they had to consider whether to go ahead without reliance on anything D had said (by, for example, simply considering the applicant's admission, albeit withdrawn by him, that he had been there) or to drop the case and reinstate the applicant. The one thing which in my judgment the governors could not fairly do was decide to take into account a written statement made by D which the applicant had not seen and D's oral testimony to them which the applicant had not heard. Nor would it have been fair to disclose these without also disclosing (to the governors as well as to the applicant) what D had originally said to the head teacher.

...

Brooke LJ: What difference did it make that D's statement (or the gist of it) was not disclosed to B? I have considered this question anxiously, and have finally come to the firm conclusion that it transferred a fair procedure into an unfair procedure, and that the result cannot stand.

...

Justice demanded that if B denied he had been guilty of theft, he should know the nature of the case against him. In the event, lacking legal advice, the exclusion committee thought they could shortcircuit matters by not disclosing D's statement or requiring D to give oral evidence against B, but confining their inquiry to an examination of the terms of B's 'confession'.

...

I mention the requisite standard of proof, although it was not mentioned on the appeal, because I have had to bear it in mind when deciding how to respond to the issues raised on the appeal. Since B was being charged with an offence of dishonesty, the law requires that proof should not be on the ordinary balance of probabilities, but that it should be distinctly more probable that he was dishonestly involved in stealing from the teacher's handbag than that he was not.

...

I can understand the reasons why schools wish to proceed with exclusion proceedings in serious cases of theft without waiting for the outcome of police inquiries. But if they do, it is incumbent on them to follow the rules of fair process prescribed by the courts before they taint a pupil with the stigma of a finding of theft and the potentially devastating consequences of a permanent exclusion for theft. While I would hate to see these hearings dominated by lawyers, there are certain minimum standards of fairness that have to be applied, and for the reasons given by Sedley LJ, with which I agree, I would allow the appeal.

Brooke LJ's approach to the standard of proof was applied in *R (on the application of K) v Governors of the W School and West Sussex County Council* [2001] ELR 311, where a pupil was excluded following allegations of sexual abuse, and in *R (on the application of T) v Head Teacher of Wembley High School* [2001] EWHC Admin 229, [2001] ELR 359 where the pupil was alleged to have assaulted a pupil and a teacher (see chapter 1 on the human rights aspects of this and two other cases heard together by Newman J).

Circular 10/99 also gives guidance on what should happen once the discipline committee has reached its decision.

DfEE Circular 10/99: Social Inclusion: Pupil Support

Annex D, procedures for excluding a pupil

13 If the Discipline Committee decides to direct reinstatement it should discuss with the LEA whether extra short term support would help to ensure successful reintegration. If the Discipline Committee confirms a head teacher's decision to exclude, it should be satisfied that there are satisfactory arrangements for the pupil to continue their education while away from school.

14 The Discipline Committee should notify the parent and the LEA of its decision, within one school day of the hearing, giving the reasons. The Committee may not attach conditions to the reinstatement of the pupil.

15 If the Discipline Committee upholds the head teacher's decision to exclude a pupil permanently, it should write within one school day to the parent:
- giving the reasons for the decision;
- explaining the parent's right to appeal to an independent appeal panel to which the parents can make oral and written statements;
- giving the name and address of the person the parents should contact if they wish to appeal, explaining that any notice of appeal should explain the grounds of appeal and stating the last date for giving notice (15 school days from the Discipline Committee's decision). The parent has the right to appeal to the panel even if they did not make a case to the Discipline Committee.

AFTER THE MEETING

16 A note of the Discipline Committee's views on the exclusion should normally be placed on the pupil's record with a copy of the head teacher's exclusion letter.

- *Can a Discipline Committee change a fixed term exclusion into a permanent exclusion or vice versa? Can the committee reduce the length of a fixed term exclusion?*

The decision of the governing body can be challenged by way of judicial review on the grounds for example that it has failed to consider relevant matters.

R v Camden London Borough and Governors of Hampstead School, ex p H [1996] ELR 360

Kennedy LJ: [W]here, as here, there was a child victim the overall case did require some serious investigation of the effect that the proposed setting aside of the head's decision would have on the injured boy. Although, for no reason obvious to me, his name was concealed on all of the documents seen by the governors and Mr Wilkinson, the committee knew that H 'had had some less than happy experience in other schools and that he was the subject of a statement of special educational needs'.

...

In other words in so far as the future of H was a relevant consideration the governors were content to proceed upon the assumption that if the permanent exclusion of A and B were lifted H would not only remain in the school but would also be able to come to terms with what had occurred.

...

But was it a valid assumption? That was something about which, as it seems to me, Mr Rabinder Singh is right in suggesting that the governors and the LEA could quite easily, and therefore should, have obtained more information. Mr H and H himself might have helped, and so could others such as not only the head, H's head of year and the education social worker, but also the education psychologist (who it was known would be involved because it was known that there was a statement of special educational need) and perhaps also the GP, Dr Parkes, whose report of 9 May 1996 we have seen.

In my judgment this was an important line of inquiry because when the matter was considered in the round the evidence might have indicated that in reality a choice had to be made between maintaining H in the school and reversing the head's decision in relation to A and B.

Similarly, in *R v Governors of Bacon's City Technology College, ex p W* [1998] ELR 488, the procedure followed by the governors at the hearing together with their failure to give reasons for their decision was held to be unlawful.

The independent appeal panel

Local education authorities must enable an appeal to be brought against the decision of the governing body not to reinstate a pupil who has been permanently excluded from school. This right of appeal is limited to permanent exclusions. The LEA is responsible for arranging appeals for all maintained schools, including voluntary and foundation schools. The appeal is made to an independent appeal panel whose membership is similar to that of an admission appeal panel. The members are volunteers who normally receive some training from the LEA. Before September 1999 the panels were called committees and could include members of the governing body or local councillors.

Procedural flaws at the governors' hearing can be remedied by a fair hearing before the panel (*R v Governors of St Gregory's RC Aided High School, ex p Roberts* (1995) Times, 27 January; *R v Headteacher and Independent Appeal Committee of Dunraven School, ex p B* [2000] ELR 156 at 190).

Composition of appeal panels

School Standards and Framework Act 1998, Sch 18

2 (1) An appeal pursuant to arrangements made by a local education authority under section 67(1) shall be to an appeal panel constituted in accordance with this paragraph.

(2) An appeal panel shall consist of three or five members appointed by the authority from—
(a)   persons who are eligible to be lay members; and
(b)   persons who have experience in education, are acquainted with educational conditions in the area of the authority or are parents of registered pupils at a school.

(3) Of the members of an appeal panel—
(a)   at least one must be a person who is eligible to be a lay member and is appointed as such; and
(b)   at least one must be a person falling within sub-paragraph (2)(b).

(4) For the purposes of this paragraph a person is eligible to be a lay member if he is a person without personal experience in the management of any school or the provision of education in any school (disregarding any such experience as a governor or in any other voluntary capacity).

(5) Sufficient persons may be appointed by the authority under this paragraph to enable two or more appeal panels to sit at the same time.

(6) No person shall be a member of an appeal panel if he is disqualified by virtue of sub-paragraph (7).

(7) The following persons are disqualified for membership of an appeal panel—
(a)   any member of the authority or of the governing body of the school in question;
(b)   any person employed by the authority or the governing body, other than a person employed as a teacher;
(c)   any person who has, or at any time has had, any connection with—
     (i)   the authority or the school, or with any person within paragraph (b), or
     (ii) the pupil in question or the incident leading to his exclusion, of a kind which might reasonably be taken to raise doubts about his ability to act impartially in relation to the authority, the school or the pupil in question.

(8) A person employed by the authority as a teacher shall not be taken, by reason only of that employment, to have such a connection with the authority as is mentioned in sub-paragraph (7)(c).

...

• *Can a parent of a pupil or a teacher, or a governor of the school from which the pupil has been excluded be a member of the panel hearing the appeal? Can a local authority councillor sit on an appeal panel?*

In *R (on the application of B) v Head Teacher of Alperton Community School* [2001] EWHC 229, [2001] ELR 359 the decision of the independent panel to uphold the decision to exclude a 15-year-old pupil was quashed because the chair of the governing body of the school was a member of the independent panel. The pupil also claimed that as a consequence the hearing was not 'independent and impartial' and was in breach of Article 6.1 of the ECHR because he had been excluded for a criminal offence (assault on another pupil) and his reputation was affected. The court rejected this argument and held that Article 6.1 does not apply to school exclusion proceedings (see chapter 1).

Role of the appeal panel

The main role of the appeal panel is to determine whether the pupil should be reinstated. Panels should meet within 15 days of the date on which the parent lodged the appeal.

School Standards and Framework Act 1998, s 67

(1) A local education authority shall make arrangements for enabling the relevant person to appeal against any decision of the governing body under section 66 not to reinstate a pupil who has been permanently excluded from a school maintained by the authority.

(2) Schedule 18 has effect in relation to the making and hearing of appeals pursuant to arrangements made under subsection (1); and in subsections (3) and (4) 'appeal panel' means an appeal panel constituted in accordance with paragraph 2 of that Schedule.

(3) The decision of an appeal panel on an appeal pursuant to arrangements made under subsection (1) shall be binding on the relevant person, the governing body, the head teacher and the local education authority.

(4) Where on such an appeal the appeal panel determines that the pupil in question should be reinstated, the panel shall either—
(a)   direct that he is to be reinstated immediately, or
(b)   direct that he is to be reinstated by a date specified in the direction.

The statutory provisions are supplemented by detailed guidance. Where the guidance has not been complied with by either the head teacher or the governing body the panel should normally reinstate the pupil.

DfEE Circular 10/99: Social Inclusion: Pupil Support

Annex D, procedures for excluding a pupil

32. In considering an appeal, the panel should decide what the pupil has actually done. If more than one incident of misconduct is alleged, they should decide in relation to each one. Once they are satisfied as to the pupil's responsibility on the balance of probabilities the panel should then consider whether in their opinion permanent exclusion is a

reasonable response to that behaviour. Relevant factors that must be taken into account include:

- whether permanent exclusion was used in accordance with the Secretary of State's guidance (where there is doubt the appeal panel should normally direct reinstatement);
- the broader interests of other pupils and staff in the school, as well as those of the excluded pupil;
- the school's published discipline policy; where other pupils were involved and have been punished for the same incident, whether permanent exclusion in the case before the panel is an excessive sanction.

1. Where, having regard to their findings, the panel decide that the pupil in question should not be permanently excluded, they must then consider whether to direct that the pupil is to be reinstated immediately or at some future date. However, where (for example) the parent does not wish the pupil to be reinstated, or the pupil is now too old to remain at the school, it would not be appropriate for the panel to direct reinstatement. Nevertheless, the panel should indicate in their decision letter that but for those circumstances they would have directed reinstatement. The letter should be added to the pupil's school record for future reference.

- *What are the two stages that the panel should go through before reaching its decision?*

- *Can the appeal panel hear an appeal where a parent does not wish their child to be reinstated, but merely wishes to clear their child's name?*

Paragraph 32 was revised in January 2001 and now specifically refers to the standard of proof. However, Brooke LJ stated (see *R v Headteacher and Independent Appeal Committee of Dunraven School, ex p B* [2000] ELR 156 above) that where the incident amounts to an offence of dishonesty, a discipline committee or an appeal panel should be more sure that the evidence supports the decision than where a less serious incident is alleged.

- *What did Brooke LJ consider to be the requisite standard of proof where an offence of dishonesty was alleged? Does that standard apply whenever a criminal offence arises from the facts giving rise to the exclusion? How often is that likely to be?*

There is no legal requirement on the panel to call witnesses so that they may be cross-examined (*R (on the application of T) v Head Teacher of Wembley High School* [2001] EWHC Admin 229, [2001] ELR 359). Therefore, the panel can rely on written statements, but the panel is required to explain the reason(s) for its decision.

R v Northamptonshire County Council, ex p W [1998] ELR 291

Laws J: If the decision letter written in this case were adequate, it might readily be thought that the assertion that permanent exclusion was a reasonable course for the school and that the child was responsible for the actions in question would be a sufficient statement of grounds in every instance where the committee decides to uphold permanent exclusion in this kind of case. That could not be right. While I do not think that I am by any means entitled to find on the evidence that this committee writes such a standard form letter in every case, there is I think a danger that such a committee, having regard in perfect good faith, as no doubt it will, to a code of the kind adopted here by the respondents, may simply follow the words of what in this case is para 11(e)(i). That is not sufficient. Something which explains the decision in the particular case is required.

See also chapter 3 p 343 (the panel's decision).

Responsibility of LEA where exclusion upheld

Where the pupil has not been reinstated the LEA is responsible for providing the child with education while he or she is out of school (EA 1996, s 19). DfEE Circulars 10/99 and 11/99 place considerable emphasis on the reintegration of excluded pupils into school within weeks if not days. In practice pupils who are permanently excluded often only receive part-time education for weeks if not months either by way of work sent home by their school or by attendance at a PRU.

Where a pupil has been permanently excluded on two or more occasions, the LEA is no longer under an obligation to comply with parental preference as to the choice of alternative school for a two-year period, beginning with the date of the most recent exclusion (SSFA 1998, s 87, see chapter 3).

Challenging the decision of the appeal panel

The decision of the panel can be challenged by way of judicial review or by way of complaint to the local government ombudsman (see chapter 8). Normally it is the parents who have challenged the decision of the panel not to reinstate their child. However, in *R v Exclusion Appeal Panel of Bristol City Council, ex p Governing Body of Fairfield High School* (2000) LTL 3/11/2000 the governing body unsuccessfully applied for judicial review of the appeal panel's decision to direct reinstatement of an excluded pupil.

The majority of judicial review challenges relate to the fairness of the hearing. Three issues of particular interest have come before the courts recently. The first is where the incident giving rise to the exclusion is also the subject of a criminal investigation; the second is what is meant by reinstatement; and the third relates to the position of the school and the teachers who refuse to teach a reinstated pupil.

Criminal prosecution pending

Panels are required to meet within 15 days of the parent of the excluded pupil lodging an appeal. Where the incident giving rise to the exclusion is also the subject of a criminal prosecution the possibility of parallel proceedings gives rise to certain problems which were highlighted in the following case.

R v Independent Appeal Panel of Sheffield City Council, ex p N [2000] ELR 700

Moses J: (1) This is an application for permission to quash a decision of an independent appeal panel of Sheffield City Council. It arises out of an allegation made by a girl pupil at the school in question of a sexual assault by another pupil. The matter was reported, the police took an interest and the evidence was such that it satisfied both the evidential test and the public interest test (or so I am entitled to assume) because a prosecution is being brought.

(2) The question arose as to what should happen where, in a school of some 1200 pupils, the boy against whom the allegation had been made and the victim attended the same school.

...

First, it seems to me the point is of great significance. I do not know how often it happens, but it is bound to happen again that there is a criminal charge pending involving two pupils at the same school where the consideration of whether one should be excluded will arise. I am told that on the present researches of counsel it is accepted that as a matter of law the panel is bound to consider whether the proposed defendant in the criminal proceedings is in fact guilty of the offence. I find that a startling proposition, and I would, were I deciding it, require a lot of persuasion that that was the true position in law.

(6) It seems to me that by far the best approach would be for the panel to accept that it cannot investigate the truth or otherwise of the charge and consider a free-standing separate issue, namely whether it is in the best interests of the school, all the pupils, the other pupil particularly concerned and of course the pupil who is charged, for that pupil to be excluded, bearing in mind that the truth or otherwise of the accusation cannot be determined until the criminal proceedings. It seems to me that the panel is making all sorts of difficulties for itself in attempting to decide the issue of guilt or innocence with its hands tied behind its back. There will be many pupils who feel unable, on legal advice, to assist the panel because they will want to keep their defence fresh for the criminal charge. Indeed, the complainant herself might regard it as wholly undesirable that she should have to give an account to the panel while the criminal charge is pending.

...

(8) Secondly, whilst of course I have been assisted and accept what the father has told me today, there is another aspect to that, namely that if there has been an error by the panel which has led to the girl in question staying away from the school, she has rights which ought to be vindicated (if she be right) by a conclusion given by the court.

The application for leave to apply for judicial review was granted, but the case was settled before the full hearing. Since June 2001 the panel has the power to adjourn the hearing where, for example, a pupil faces criminal charges arising out of the incident which led to the permanent exclusion (School Standards and Framework Act 1998 (Amendment of Schedule 18) (England) Order 2001, SI 2001/2086). Therefore, were the facts of *ex p N* to arise in the future, the appeal panel is likely to adjourn the hearing. This may be to the excluded pupil's detriment as he or she may be out of school for many months pending the outcome of the criminal case.

What is meant by 'reinstatement'?

In *R (on the application of C) v Governors of B School* [2001] ELR 285 an independent appeal panel directed that the pupil should be reinstated from 2 May 2000. A large majority of the staff wrote to the Secretary of State expressing their disquiet at the decision, and threatened industrial action if they were directed to teach the pupil, although they were prepared to set and mark work for her. During the summer term the pupil spent the morning working at a desk outside the principal's office. From half way through the term she went to a pupil support centre in the afternoons. This continued with minor variations in the autumn term. The pupil's parents complained to the Secretary of State in May 2000 whose view was that it is for the school to determine how best to reintegrate a pupil following an appeal panel's decision that the pupil should be reinstated. C's parents considered that their daughter had not been reinstated and applied for judicial review. The key question was the meaning of the term 'reinstatement'.

R (on the application of C) v Governors of B School [2001] ELR 285

Richards J: (26) It is common ground in this case that the effect of the panel's decision was to direct reinstatement on 2 May. There has been no legal challenge to the decision which is therefore binding on the governing body under s 67(3). There is an absolute duty on the governing body to comply with it. The first issue is whether the governing body is in breach of that duty. That requires consideration of what reinstatement means.

...

In my judgment reinstatement is not to be given any elaborate meaning; what is intended to be achieved is the removal of the exclusion. It does not follow that everything has to be put back exactly as it was before the exclusion. What matters is that the regime applied to the pupil after the date for reinstatement is a regime that does not involve the continuing exclusion of the pupil from the school. It does not have to be an identical regime to that which prevailed before the pupil was excluded.

(35) I do not think that reinstatement necessarily entails full reintegration into the classroom even where that was the previous state of affairs. Full reintegration may be wholly inappropriate after a long absence—I have already referred to the fact that the principal thought that some phased reintroduction would be required after C's 45-day absence, leaving aside the problems created by the stance taken by the staff.

...

(38) So far as the first issue is concerned, I am satisfied that C is no longer being excluded from the school and that there has therefore been compliance with the duty to reinstate.

(39) My conclusion in relation to that issue means that the governing body has a discretion as to how it goes about the process of reinstatement so that there is no longer an exclusion of the pupil. The question then arises—and this is the second issue—whether there has been a lawful exercise of discretion in this case.

(46) In any event, absent clear and binding authority, I would be very reluctant to hold that the governing body is precluded, as a matter of law, from taking into account a threat of industrial action by teachers in deciding on the appropriate course of action to adopt. That is all the more important when one bears in mind that the governing body has to consider the interests of all the pupils at the school. If, for example, the circumstances were such that a particular course of action would inevitably lead to the effective closure of the school, with none of the pupils being taught, and their examination prospects being prejudiced in consequence, it would be very surprising if that consideration could not lawfully affect the governing body's decision whether or not to take that course of action.

In my judgment the action of the staff and unions in proceeding on a basis which is inconsistent with the appeal panel's findings cannot be imputed to the governing body. The stance that staff and unions have adopted is a matter that the governing body can lawfully take into account in reaching its own decisions, even if that stance is not soundly based. Of course, if the governing body had itself acted with a view to defeating the appeal panel's decision, or on the basis that the panel's factual findings were mistaken and could be somehow disapplied, then it could be said to have acted for an improper purpose and to have taken an irrelevant consideration into account. But on the evidence that cannot be said to be the position.

- *What difference would it have made if the governing body had refused to reinstate the pupil?*

- *Could the 'reintegration' process go on indefinitely?*

Refusal of school to comply with reinstatement direction

In *R (on the application of C) v Governors of B School* [2001] ELR 285, and in *R v Governors of W School and T Education Authority (Borough Council), ex p H* [2001] ELR 192 neither the governing body nor the head teacher had refused in principle to reinstate the pupil, although the teaching and support staff had threatened industrial action.

This was not the position in the next case, where it was agreed that the governing body was in breach of its statutory obligation to educate the pupil as a consequence of the teachers threatening industrial action were the pupil to return to the school. The judge accepted the argument of the LEA and the governing body that he should exercise his discretion and refuse to issue an order of mandamus ordering the governing body to reinstate the excluded pupil.

R v South Tyneside Education Department, and Governors of Hebburn Comprehensive School, ex p Cram [1998] ELR 508

Ognall J: This is an unusual, unhappy and troublesome matter. The applicant, the father and guardian ad litem of his 14-year-old son, Graham, (G), seeks an order of mandamus requiring the respondents to reinstate his son into mainstream teaching at Hebburn Comprehensive School in South Tyneside.

...

It is accepted that the first and second respondents have a statutory duty to provide G with education suitable to his requirements. It is also accepted that the second respondents have not, in fact, reintegrated G into the normal curriculum of full-time mainstream teaching at Hebburn School. Accordingly, there is a clear prima facie breach of the statutory duty imposed upon the respondents to educate G according to the requirements of the law.

Additionally, there is a clear non-compliance with the direction of the School Exclusion Panel of 17 November 1995 directing G's reinstatement with a view to his reintegration into mainstream schooling.

...

Mr Cohen, in attractive and cogent arguments, submitted that if I were to decline relief here then it would be on the basis of the refusal of the teachers through their trade union to comply with their contractual duty owed to the second respondents. That, he submitted, would be unlawful conduct by the teachers. In those circumstances, for the court to decline relief when confronted with the threat of industrial action would be, he suggested, a complete abdication of the court's responsibility to uphold the rule of the law. It would be, he suggested, a charter for irresponsible persons to set the law at defiance—industrial might would become in the context legal right.

My instinct, therefore, would be to question whether giving significant account to the response or potential response of the NASUWT is properly characterised as an abdication of the rule of law. That is more especially so when the conduct in question has a potential, it should be noted, for affecting the lawful rights of many hundreds of children and their parents.

Ognall J also noted that the Secretary of State had decided not to use her power under what is now s 497 of the EA 1996 to direct the governing body to reinstate the pupil, and considered that to be a matter which he could take into account when deciding whether or not to exercise his discretion.

In *R v Governors of W School and T Education Authority (Borough Council), ex p H* [2001] ELR 192 the pupil sought judicial review because of the governing body's failure not to reinstate him. The court refused the application for the following reasons. However, the judge expressed concern about the role of the teachers and their unions as well as the decision in *ex p Cram*.

R v Governors of W School and T Education Authority (Borough Council), ex p H [2001] ELR 192

Blofeld J: (30) I am satisfied that the headteacher, the governors and the second respondent did genuinely attempt to reinstate H to the best of their ability after the panel's decision, which rightly or wrongly disappointed them all. I have come to the conclusion that I accept that both unions and their members are genuine in their determination not to teach H. I therefore accept that the head teacher and the governors and the LEA have done all they reasonably could to persuade the teachers in those unions to continue to teach H and not to take industrial action. I bear in mind that I have heard no representations from either of those unions.

(31) In those circumstances I go no further than to say, on the face of it, their actions appear to be unlawful. I express my anxiety that where there is an independent appeal panel which sits and hears a case that that decision is not accepted, however reluctantly, by the unions and their members. If something has gone wrong with the panel's decision (and I am far from saying it did) then I consider it unfortunate that it was not appealed. If it is not appealed then it must be accepted.

(32) This country has always prided itself on acting according to the law and long may that continue. I dislike the idea that Parliament sets up detailed procedures for dealing with unruly children and yet in specific circumstances teachers, through their unions, are able to circumvent the law.

(33) I do not consider that Ognall J in the *R v South Tyneside Education Department and the Governors of Hebburn Comprehensive School, ex p Cram* [1998] ELR 508 case was setting down a precedent that necessarily applied in analogous cases.

...

(36) I come to the same conclusion as he did but I add that I do not do so with the same confidence that he displayed. It seems to me to be the better of the two options, but I do not find either really satisfactory.

Trade dispute?

In *ex p Cram* (see above) the governing body suggested that the parents should have considered bringing a claim against the teaching unions involved. This suggestion was merely noted by the judge in that case.

However, it formed the basis of the action in *P v National Association of Schoolmasters and Union of Women Teachers* [2001] EWCA Civ 652, [2001] ELR 607. Teachers refused to teach a pupil who had been reinstated by the governing body. The excluded pupil brought a claim for damages against the teachers' trade union. One of the issues was whether there was a trade dispute within the meaning of s 244 of the Trade Union and Labour Relations (Consolidation) Act 1992.

Waller LJ held that the dispute related to the teachers' terms and conditions of employment because the dispute between the teachers and the head teacher, or possibly the governing body, was whether it was reasonable to teach the excluded pupil in class. Therefore, there was a trade dispute, and the union's inducement to the teachers, after a ballot, not to teach P was not unlawful.

New evidence after the appeal panel has reached its decision

In *R v Independent Appeals Tribunal of Hillingdon Borough Council and KM, ex p Governing Body of Mellow Lane School* [2001] ELR 200 the governing body successfully applied for leave to apply for judicial review of the independent appeal panel's decision to reinstate the pupil. The governing body wanted the court to quash the decision, and the panel was supportive because after the panel's decision to reinstate evidence became available which confirmed that the pupil had been in possession of cannabis.

R v Independent Appeals Tribunal of Hillingdon Borough Council and KM, ex p Governing Body of Mellow Lane School [2001] ELR 200

Newman J: The pupil is the beneficiary of a decision from the panel body for so long as the panel body properly considers the decision which it reached, one to which in law it was right to come. Had there been no application for judicial review by the applicant governing body of the school but merely a representation to the panel that it reconsider its decision. I know not the details, but I assume it had powers to reconsider the position, it would have been entitled to do so, as with any public body, in light of the material put before it. In such a case the pupil would obviously be entitled to make representations in respect of the new material giving rise to the need for the reconsideration of its original decision.

The court appears to have decided that a decision which may have been rational at the time the decision was made may become irrational because of evidence which subsequently comes to light. The court is entitled to quash such a decision.

- *Is this a correct statement of the law?*

- *Does the panel have the legal authority to hear representations from the governing body after it has reached a decision to reinstate, and change its decision in the light of those representations?*

- *Where a point of fact can be resolved within a reasonable time should the panel reach a decision or use its recently acquired power to adjourn?*

Statistics

Annual statistics are published on the success rates of appeals to the independent panels. The 1999/2000 statistics cover the period when Circular 10/99 was first introduced. The statistics for the earlier years cover appeals heard when the previous Circular (10/94) was in force. The statistics show that overall the number of appeals lodged declined between 1996 and 1999, but that the number of appeals decided in the parents' favour increased. However, only approximately one in four appeals was successful. Many parents do not appeal, and the DfEE estimated that in 1999/2000 only one in 30 exclusions resulted in successful appeals.

Statistical First Release (SFR20/2001)

Table 2: Summary of school exclusion and reinstatement appeals in academic years 1997/98, 1998/99 and 1999/00 (provisional)

		Exclusion and Reinstatement Appeals by Parents					Exclusion and Reinstatement Appeals by Governors				
		Lodged	Heard		Decided in parents' favour		Lodged	Heard		Decided in governors' favour	
		Number	Number	%(1)	Number	%(2)	Number	Number	%(1)	Number	%(2)
Primary, Secondary and Special Schools	1997/98	1287	1011	78.6	204	20.2	122	118	96.7	50	42.4
	1998/99	1216	964	79.3	220	22.8	97	93	95.9	48	51.6
	1999/00	948	863	91.0	317	36.7	8	6	75.0	4	66.7

(1) Shown as a percentage of appeals lodged.
(2) Shown as a percentage of appeals heard.

How competent are the appeal panels?

In *Challenges to School Exclusion* (2000, Routledge Falmer) the authors provide an account and an evaluation of the work of exclusion appeal panels in seven LEA areas. The research was conducted between 1997 and 1999.

Neville Harris and Karen Eden with Ann Blair *Challenges to School Exclusion*

Chapter 7, The Exclusion Appeal Panels

The reforms under the 1998 Act have set in place a framework for independent decision-making. However, whether that will result in greater impartiality in practice depends upon the way the membership of the appeal panels go about their task and how they perceive their role, which the Act has not changed. As already noted, the absence of a judicial approach has in the past been criticised by the Council on Tribunals. Our research finds further, disturbing evidence to reinforce the Council's observations. In our view, this evidence, which is presented in Chapter 9, strengthens the case not only for better training of panel members but also for a further change to the constitution of exclusion appeal panels—the introduction of lawyer chairs.

Having said this, the present system is generally successful in recruiting people with wide-ranging and mostly relevant experience. Often they are people who have additional adjudicative experience: 60 per cent of appeal panel members in our survey had experience of serving on other appeal bodies (in many cases school admissions appeal panels) or as magistrates. A majority of LEAs in our survey (64 per cent) considered that the panels contain an appropriate balance of expertise (as opposed to 24 per cent who did not and 12 per cent who were unsure). Nevertheless, there is clearly a need for more guidance on the recruitment of members, particularly with a view to ensuring greater representation of ethnic minorities. Indeed, a number of LEAs admitted that one of the major flaws with the current appeal panels is the under-representation of ethnic minorities among the membership. Consideration should also be given to an upper age limit, in order to ensure consistency with other tribunals exercising judicial functions and thereby reinforce the judicial role of the panel which members often fail to appreciate fully.

If exclusion appeals were brought within the jurisdiction of the SENT, as the Council on Tribunals has repeatedly recommended, one of the advantages would be that they would be part of a national system. The SENT has a national President and a secretariat based in two offices serving the whole country. Transfer of this work to the SENT would help to ensure consistency in relation to training matters in addition to quality control. As the Council on Tribunals has commented, exclusion appeals 'are part of the workload of what is essentially a very busy tribunal system, with no central organisation to guide and monitor the standard of the tribunals' work or decision-making' (Council on Tribunals 1995: para 2.32). When recommending a judicial head for individual tribunal systems the Council has, however, excluded 'the locally-based tribunal systems such as the Education Appeal Committees' (Council on Tribunals 1997c: para 2.26). A judicial head would be desirable, however, as he or she could also monitor appointments to panels, which does not happen centrally at present. On this basis, there may well be a case for putting the exclusion appeal system on a national footing, although this would involve an (albeit relatively small) additional financial cost (see further Chapter 10).

A report published by The Children's Society looked at the experience of children and young people and their families after an exclusion from school. The research was particularly concerned with developing preventative and reintegrative strategies.

Carol Hayden, Simon Dunne 'Outside, looking in, children's and families experiences of exclusion from school' (2001, The Children's Society)

Discussion—welfare or justice?

A central issue in relation to the prevention and management of exclusion is the potential tension between child welfare and justice. It is clear from some of the parents' reports that the process of exclusion did not feel just. Also, children often expressed the view that their exclusion was unfair and they were angry about this. Certainly, the emphasis within the formal process is not conducive to a focus on child welfare. In the changing educational context outlined at the start of this chapter, it is obvious that the focus needs to be on both justice and welfare, but that a focus on procedural fairness alone does not necessarily address welfare issues fully. We agree with Harris and Eden (2000) when they conclude that this is a consequence of the appeal system having a disciplinary rather than a welfare focus.

Procedural fairness and adherence to principles of natural justice are very important issues and ones that may require more training in schools to ensure that they occur. However, although they may lead to more procedurally correct exclusions, it may not prevent exclusion. These comments are not made in an attempt to discount the importance of fairness and justice in the business of exclusions, but rather to highlight the potential for following a route that may have adverse consequences, both for the way resources in the education service are used and the way schools go about their work. The biggest losers in all of this are likely to be children in need of sympathy and support.

Reinstatement in the same school did work in a few cases but not others. Representations and appeals generally decide in the school's favour and were usually negative experiences for parents. It must be queried whether resources are best spent in this way, especially when SEN and social needs are such glaring issues, and inadequate resources, particularly the time of skilled staff, are part of the problem. There is a clear need for a problem-solving approach to avoid children being out of school for very long periods: both the SEN/statementing route and the exclusion route generally do not work in the immediate interests of the child. Furthermore, statementing appears to be no guarantee of expert help or protection from exclusion.

The primary focus should be on child welfare and a minimisation of the damage already incurred by exclusion. A support focus is needed even more at the point of exclusion; however, this is precisely when parents feel that support is at its weakest. There is an urgent need to make sure that support is in place both during and immediately following an exclusion, in order to minimise the loss of education and 'getting behind', which is likely to make reintegration more difficult.

...

The research has illustrated the complexity of the issues that surround exclusion from school. It has shown the devastating effects exclusion can have on the well-being of families. Many of the children in our study were very angry about how they had been treated. Comments from children remind us of what our focus must be, in that less than half thought that their exclusion was fair. Often this sense of unfairness was because children had retaliated in a fight, other children had been involved, or the children said that they had not done what they had been accused of. This sense of injustice, coupled with reduced educational opportunities, is a dangerous mix. Children were still spending considerable periods of time outside full-time education. The Home Office Youth Lifestyles Survey indicates that attachment to school protects children—especially 12–16-year-old boys—from involvement in criminal activity. Success in school is an even stronger protective factor. Achievement in school is an even stronger protective factor. (Flood—Page et al, 2000).

- *What difference would it make were the appeal system to have a welfare rather than a disciplinary focus? Should the welfare of other pupils and staff as well as that of the excluded pupil be taken into account?*

Chapter 5

Special educational needs

1. INTRODUCTION

The law regulates the educational provision for both children and young people with special educational needs. The Education Act 1996 (EA 1996) contains the primary legislation, but should be considered in the context of other statutory provisions such as the Children Act 1989, the Disability Discrimination Act 1995, and the Special Educational Needs and Disability Act 2001 (SENDA 2001), as well as the tort of negligence.

A child has 'special educational needs' for the purposes of the EA 1996 if he has a learning difficulty which calls for special educational provision to be made for him (EA 1996, s 312(1)). In 1978 the Warnock Committee Report was published (*Special Educational Needs*, the Report of the Committee of Enquiry into the Education of Handicapped Children and Young People). The Committee estimated that 20 per cent of all pupils in schools have learning difficulties of one kind or another. These may vary from mild dyslexia to severe physical and mental impairment. The recommendations contained in the Warnock Report were implemented by the Education Act 1981.

The Education Act 1981 emphasised the integration of children with special educational needs into mainstream schools wherever possible, as opposed to sending them to special schools, and established procedures for assessing such children and providing education for them. The selection of a suitable school is often a matter of dispute between the parent and the LEA partly because of a particular school's suitability but also because of the question of cost (see below).

The Education Act 1993 reaffirmed the principle of integration and also:
- established the Special Educational Needs Tribunal (SENT)
- extended parental choice
- introduced a Code of Practice.

The current legislation is contained in the EA 1996, as amended by SENDA 2001, as well as in regulations. Statutory guidance is given in the form of a Code of Practice, which is of great practical importance.

In October 1997 the government published a Green Paper, *Excellence for All Children – Meeting Special Educational Needs* (Cm 3785). The Green Paper stated that the government's approach to improving the achievement of children with special educational needs had six themes. These are:

- high expectations for children with special educational needs (SEN)
- inclusion of children with SEN within mainstream schooling wherever possible
- effective support for parents of children with SEN
- shifting resources from expensive remediation and the emphasis on procedures to cost-effective prevention and practical support
- boosting opportunities for staff development
- local provision based on partnership.

These proposals were criticised by parents' groups.

'Law is vital' says SEN action group

A new grouping of SEN organisations, which includes ACE, has written to David Blunkett, Secretary of State for Education expressing concern over the implications of proposals in the Green Paper, Excellence for All Children. The group, Action for Entitlement seeks an assurance that the current legal framework protecting children with special educational needs is not weakened or reduced as a result of the Green Paper.

'Many of the people we represent, and with whom we work everyday, find that getting the provision their children need is only possible with the law in place,' says the letter, which adds that the plan to switch resources from statemented to non-statemented children with special needs is a switch from provision protected by statute to provision which is discretionary and variable. The letter expresses alarm at the suggestion of setting national criteria for who is statemented and who isn't, pointing out that where this practice is in operation, very needy children are refused assessment because their needs as individuals have not been taken into account. 'It is the force of law alone that protects these vulnerable children's interests: a reduction in statements will result in fewer children having a guarantee that their needs will be met.'

What the LEAs say

ACE noted an interesting convergence of views between a number of LEAs and the views expressed in the Green Paper. Some LEAs, however, clearly recognise the real problem is a lack of resources. The following selection gives a flavour:

- **Wandsworth:** 'The Green Paper makes it clear the government is committed to working to reduce this percentage (2.8% of children with statements) nationally to 2%.'
- **Hertfordshire** identifies the problem of switching the focus to early intervention — when LEAs still have the legal duty to make provision for older pupils 'A short-term problem for local authorities (sometimes referred to as the "Statement time-bomb") is that until the number of older pupils with SEN reduces, the earlier identification process will result in an increased pressure on already committed budgets.'

[*Advisory Centre for Education Bulletin*, 81 February 1998]

In September 1998 the Audit Commission published an update on its 1992 report (*Getting In On the Act*) which found that: 'the money spent on SEN services now accounts for about 15 per cent of the money spent in schools, an increase of 25 per cent since 1992. The update considered that there had been some improvements since the 1992 Report, but that were still problems.

The government consulted on its proposals and there remained considerable concern among parents' groups that the rights of children with SEN would be diminished were those proposals to be implemented. Eventually the SEN and Disability Bill 2000 was introduced. At its second reading in the House of Commons on 20 March 2001 the Secretary of State for Education and Employment, David Blunkett stated:

House of Commons Hansard Debates for 20 Mar 2001, col 218

Mr Blunkett: ...
I want to make it absolutely clear that the controversy that arose last year about the consultation on the code of practice needs to be put to rest. We were seeking to ensure that a flexible and responsive way forward existed. Clear views were expressed across the range of opinions, suggesting that it would be better if we could secure specificity and clarity through the code of practice.

We shall make it clear that education authorities are required to specify provision in statements, as they always have been. We shall retain the requirement in the regulations for provision to be specified, matching the terms of the duty on education authorities set out in the Education Act 1996. The code will state clearly that statements should

describe clearly all of the child's special educational needs in full; set out the main objectives that the special educational provision aims to meet; specify clearly and in detail the provision required to meet each of the child's needs; describe the arrangements for setting shorter term objectives for the child; describe any special arrangements for the annual review of the statement; stress the importance of the school monitoring and evaluating the child's progress during the year; emphasise the importance of the local education authority monitoring the child's progress toward identified outcomes — with the school.

The guidance will make it clear that provision may often need to be expressed in terms of hours, equipment or personnel. It will make it absolutely clear that education authorities must not, in any circumstance, have a blanket policy not to quantify the provision in statements.

The Special Educational Needs and Disability Act 2001:
–   reinforces the presumption that children with SEN will be educated in mainstream schools
–   requires schools to inform parents that they are making SEN provision for their child
–   gives schools the right to request the LEA to carry out a statutory assessment of a pupil
–   requires LEAs to provide information to parents and schools about SEN services available

- requires LEAs to provide a parent partnership service
- requires LEAs to establish mediation arrangements for resolving disputes with parents
- requires LEAs to comply with orders of the SEN.

New regulations were introduced in 2001. The relevant regulations for England include:
- Education (Special Educational Needs)(England)(Consolidation) Regulations 2001, SI 2001/3455;
- Special Education Needs (Provision of Information by Local Education Authorities)(England) Regulations 2001, SI 2001/2218;
- Education (Special Educational Needs)(Information)(England) Regulations 1999, SI 1999/2506.

New statutory guidance, which came into effect in January 2002, is contained in:
- Special Educational Needs Code of Practice DfES/581/2001;
- Inclusive Schooling – Children with Special Educational Needs DfES 0774/2001.

Additional non-statutory guidance can be found in the SEN Toolkit published by the DfES.

In addition to amending the legislation relating to special educational needs, the Special Educational Needs and Stability Act 2001 has extended the anti-discrimination provisions contained in the Disability Discrimination Act 1995 (DDA 1995) to schools, FE colleges and universities. In relation to schools, most claims under the DDA 1995 will be heard by the renamed Special Educational Needs and Disability Tribunal (SENDIST). Claims brought by students at FE colleges or universities will be heard in the county court. The disability discrimination provisions are likely to come into effect from September 2002.

2. DEFINITIONS

The EA 1996 sets out the key terms, which are 'special educational needs', 'learning difficulty', 'child', and 'special educational provision'.

Education Act, s 312

(1) A child has 'special educational needs' for the purposes of this Act if he has a learning difficulty which calls for special educational provision to be made for him.

(2) Subject to subsection (3) (and except for the purposes of section 15(5)) a child has a 'learning difficulty' for the purposes of this Act if—
(a) he has a significantly greater difficulty in learning than the majority of children of his age,
(b) he has a disability which either prevents or hinders him from making use of educational facilities of a kind generally provided for children of his age in schools within the area of the local education authority, or
(c) he is under compulsory school age and is, or would be if special educational provision were not made for him, likely to fall within paragraph (a) or (b) when of ... that age.

...

(4) In this Act 'special educational provision' means—

(a) in relation to a child who has attained the age of two, educational provision which is additional to, or otherwise different from, the educational provision made generally for children of his age in schools maintained by the local education authority (other than special schools) ..., and

(b) in relation to a child under that age, educational provision of any kind.

A 'child' with special needs includes any person under the age of 19 so long as they are a registered pupil at a school (s 312(5) of the EA 1996). However, where a 16- to18-year-old with SEN attends, for example, a further education college they do not fall within the definition of a 'child' and their educational rights are more limited. A child is not regarded as having a 'learning difficulty' solely because English is not or has not been the language spoken in their home (s 312(3) of the EA 1996).

A child with serious learning difficulties will normally have a 'statement of special educational needs', which entitles the child to minimum levels of support. However, in practice parents often have difficulty in obtaining a statement for their child, and even when they do the contents of the statement may not be sufficiently precise or be enforceable against the LEA (see 'Contents of the statement', p 356, below).

Statistics relating to appeals to the SENT illustrate the range of special educational needs that exists.

Nature of SEN

The types of disability with which the [SENT] dealt last year, and the proportion of each, are set out below. They remained very similar to the previous year, although the number of cases concerning literacy difficulties (including specific learning difficulties), which has always been the Tribunal's major concern, recorded a rise.

Nature of SEN	99/00 Total	%	98/99 Total	%
Autism	319	13.0%	313	13.0%
Emotional & Behavioural Difficulties	315	12.8%	272	11.3%
Epilepsy	31	1.3%	23	1.0%
Hearing Impairment	75	3.0%	73	3.0%
Literacy (Including SpLD)	932	37.8%	818	33.9%
Moderate Learning Difficulties	142	5.8%	153	6.3%
Multi Sensory Impairment	4	0.2%	4	0.2%
Physical Handicap	124	5.0%	142	5.9%
Severe Learning Difficulties	75	3.0%	91	3.8%
Speech & Language Difficulties	274	11.1%	287	11.9%
Visual Impairment	31	1.3%	31	1.3%
Other/Unknown	141	5.7%	205	8.5%
Total appeals registered	2463		2412	

(SENT Annual Report 1999/2000)

Local authorities also have responsibilities towards 'children in need', including disabled children (Children Act 1989, s 17). Pupils and students with disabilities have the right not to be discriminated against because of their disability (Disability Discrimination Act 1995), and LEAs have a responsibility to provide suitable education to sick children who are unable to attend school (see below, p 325).

What amounts to a learning difficulty?

R v Hampshire Education Authority, ex p J (1985) 84 LGR 547

The applicant was highly intelligent but suffered from dyslexia which caused a continued weakness in spelling, reading and continuous essay writing. The combined effect of high intelligence and dyslexia caused the applicant depression and frustration.

Taylor J found that dyslexia was clearly a disability and the only reasonable conclusion in this case was that the applicant did have a learning difficulty within s 1 of the Education Act 1981. The crux of the case was the meaning of 'special educational provision' in s 1(3).

The definition in subsection (3) could not be read alone. It had to be read in conjunction with subsection (1).

That made it clear that a special educational provision had to be one which was called for by a learning difficulty. Thus assistance for dyslexia would come within the definition, tuition in Greek or music would not.

What is meant by 'special educational provision'?

In *B v Isle of Wight Council* [1997] ELR 279 the child's parents appealed to the High Court on a point of law against the decision of the SENT.

McCullough J: A is aged 7. (I will refer to her as A and to her parents as 'Mr and Mrs B'.) A cannot make skilled movements with accuracy. The medical name for her condition is dyspraxia. Because of it she has special educational needs within the meaning of the Education Act 1993. (Unless otherwise stated references to statutory provisions are to provisions in this Act.)

A lives in the Isle of Wight. The Council of the Isle of Wight, as the local education authority, has made a statement of her special educational needs. Such a statement must be in the form required by the Act and the Education (Special Educational Needs) Regulations 1983 (which I will call 'the regulations') and must specify the authority's assessment of the child's special educational needs (in part II), the special educational provision which the authority considers appropriate to meet those needs (in part III), the type of school which the authority considers appropriate (in part IV) and any available additional non-educational provision of which, in the opinion of the authority, advantage should be taken if the child is to benefit from the special educational provision specified (in part V).

The 'needs' in part II are for the 'provision' in part III. A child does not have 'special *educational* needs' unless his difficulty calls for 'special *educational* provision'. It is not every 'learning difficulty' that calls for 'special *educational* provision'. A child within s 156(2)(a) will obviously have a learning difficulty that calls for some *educational* provision (very likely a 'special' one), but this will not necessarily be so for those within s 168(2)(b): a child with bad sight or hearing may have 'a disability which prevents or hinders him from making use of educational facilities of a kind generally provided', but if all he needs is a pair of spectacles or a hearing aid he has no need for any special *educational* provision and therefore has no 'special *educational* needs'. The same would be so of a diabetic or epileptic child who needed only drug therapy and of a child unable to walk who needed only a wheelchair.

In truth the phrase could hardly be more explicitly defined. There is nothing difficult about 'provision'. 'Special' is defined. As for 'educational', it is not surprising that the Act contains no section telling one what it means. All that anyone can do when judging whether a 'provision' is 'educational' or 'non-educational' is to recognise that there is an obvious spectrum from the clearly educational (in the ordinary 'schools' sense of that word) at one end to the clearly medical at the other, take all the relevant facts into account, apply common sense and do one's best.

See also the extract from the case below (p 357). Compare the approach taken by the Court of Appeal in the following case.

Bromley London Borough v SENT [1999] ELR 260

Sedley LJ: ... What is special about special educational provision is that it is additional to or different from ordinary educational provision (see s 312(4)). So far the meaning is open-ended. It is when it comes to the statement under s 324 that the LEA is required to distinguish between special educational provision and non-educational provision; and the prescribed form is divided up accordingly. Two possibilities arise here: either the two categories share a common frontier, so that where the one stops the other begins; or there is between the unequivocally educational and the unequivocally non-educational a share territory of provision which can be intelligibly allocated to either. It seems to me that to adopt the first approach would be to read into the legislation a sharp dichotomy for which Parliament could easily have made express provision had it wished to do so, but which finds no expression or reflection where one would expect to find it, namely in s 312. Moreover, to interpose a hard edge or a common frontier does not get rid of definitional problems: it simply makes them more acute. And this is one of the reasons why, in my judgment, the second approach is the one to be attributed to Parliament. The potentially large intermediate area of provision which is capable of ranking as educational or non-educational is not made the subject of any statutory prescription precisely because it is for the local education authority, and if necessary the SENT, to exercise a case-by-case judgment which no prescriptive legislation could ever hope to anticipate.

See also the extract from the case below (p 358). Being exceptionally able is not regarded as a 'learning difficulty'. However, having learning difficulty should not be equated with low ability.

R v Secretary of State for Education, ex p C [1996] ELR 93

Schiemann J: ... The proposition of law is that:

The fact that [C] is able to compensate, as a result of her exceptionally high intelligence, to a level *above* that achieved by the majority of children of her chronological age does not mean that she does not have SEN within the definition now contained in s 156.

It is based on part of a Taylor J's judgment in *R v Hampshire Education Authority, ex p J* (1985) 84 LGR 547 where he said:

The fact that [a child] has a very high intelligence and may therefore be able to some extent to compensate for [dyslexia] is neither here nor there.

This proposition however is accepted on behalf of the Secretary of State and there is in fact no dispute between the parties as to the law.

In *R v Portsmouth City Council, ex p Faludy* [1999] ELR 115 the High Court was asked to consider whether an LEA should fund the attendance at Cambridge University of an intellectually gifted pupil who also had special educational needs.

R v Portsmouth City Council, ex p Faludy [1999] ELR 115

Simon Brown LJ: The applicant, Alexander Faludy, is a very clever 15-year-old who has just gone up to Peterhouse College, Cambridge to read theology and history of art. He is, as the very extensive publicity surrounding this case has already pointed out, the youngest undergraduate since William Pitt the Younger. However, he is also severely dyslexic and has dyspraxic difficulties which even his intellectual giftedness cannot wholly overcome.

He applies today for leave to appeal from the judgment of Tucker J given on 25 August 1998, refusing his application for judicial review to challenge his local education authority's decision not to carry out a statutory assessment of his special educational needs, or to provide for them.

The essential factual background to the application is that the applicant has been attending Milton Abbey School, a private school in Dorset, for some years past, funded by his parents with some assistance from an American charity. The plan now is that while completing his 3-year course at Cambridge he should during part of his vacations continue to attend that same school. Cambridge has three 8-week terms. The proposal is that in addition to spending those 24 weeks pa at Cambridge, the applicant will spend a further 8 or 9 weeks at Milton Abbey.

The applicant's parents first sought the respondent's assistance in funding the applicant's education in January 1998. His father's letter of 26 January 1998 asks the respondents to fund the remaining years of his education up to the age of 19. In particular, however, the funding being sought was for the applicant's placement at Cambridge, rather than his school fees at Milton Abbey. ...

What then is the position with regard to the basic expense of the applicant's attendance at Cambridge ... in particular can [the LEA] be required to fund it under the statements procedure for children with special educational needs?

... [Section] 1(4) of the Education Act 1996 ... provides that, apart from an immaterial exception, 'nothing in this Act confers any functions with respect to higher education'.

... [Section] 319 of the Act ... enables the local education authority in certain circumstances to make special educational provision 'otherwise than in a school'. Obviously the word 'otherwise' is apt on its face to include a university, just as it is apt to include a sixth form college, home tuition and no doubt other possibilities... That still does not overcome his central difficulty, which is that s 1(4), clearly the governing provision with regard to the Act in its entirety, provides that the local education authority has no powers or duties with regards to higher education. Even, therefore, construing s 319 as Mr Engelman would have us do, in my judgment that cannot overcome the impossibility of requiring a local education authority to fund higher education.

... Mr Engelman has sought, ... to seek also the funding by the respondent authority of Alexander's 8 or 9 weeks a year at Milton Abbey during his Cambridge career. That he seeks to do so by reference to s 324 of the Act, arguing that there was a need here to make a statement under s 324(4)(a) and that that statement could well — he would no doubt contend should — have specified Milton Abbey as a school appropriate to provide for Alexander's continuing special educational needs.

...

It is quite clear that what was being put forward as the applicant's case was the totality of Alexander's needs, of which the education at Peterhouse College was the major part. ... I do not believe that Parliament contemplated that a student would attend both Peterhouse, Cambridge and a school.

Children with disabilities

The Special Educational Needs and Disability Act 2001 (SENDA 2001) has extended the anti-discrimination provisions into the field of education. Schools as well as FE colleges and universities now fall within these provisions. Many children with SEN will also be a 'disabled pupil'.

* Look at the definition of a 'disabled pupil' and consider whether all 'disabled pupils' will be children with special educational needs

The Disability Discrimination Act 1995, s 28Q(2) as inserted by SENDA 2001, s 25 states that: ' "Disabled pupil" means a pupil who is a disabled person'. This definition refers to the definition contained in the Disability Discrimination Act 1995.

Disability Discrimination Act 1995, ss 1, 2 and Sch 1

1. Meaning of 'disability' and 'disabled person'

(1) Subject to the provisions of Schedule 1, a person has a disability for the purposes of this Act if he has a physical or mental impairment which has a substantial and long-term adverse effect on his ability to carry out normal day-to-day activities.

(2) In this Act 'disabled person' means a person who has a disability.

2. Past disabilities

(1) The provisions of this Part and Parts II and III apply in relation to a person who has had a disability as they apply in relation to a person who has that disability

...

Schedule 1
Impairment

1. (1) 'Mental impairment' includes an impairment resulting from or consisting of a mental illness only if the illness is a clinically well-recognised illness.

...

Long-term effects

2. (1) The effect of an impairment is a long-term effect if—
(a)   it has lasted at least 12 months;
(b)   the period for which it lasts is likely to be at least 12 months; or

(c)   it is likely to last for the rest of the life of the person affected.

(2) Where an impairment ceases to have a substantial adverse effect on a person's ability to carry out normal day-to-day activities, it is to be treated as continuing to have that effect if that effect is likely to recur.

(3) ….

Severe disfigurement

3. (1) An impairment which consists of a severe disfigurement is to be treated as having a substantial adverse effect on the ability of the person concerned to carry out normal day-to-day activities.

(2) ….

Normal day-to-day activities

4. (1) An impairment is to be taken to affect the ability of the person concerned to carry out normal day-to-day activities only if it affects one of the following—
(a)   mobility;
(b)   manual dexterity;
(c)   physical co-ordination;
(d)   continence;
(e)   ability to lift, carry or otherwise move everyday objects;
(f)   speech, hearing or eyesight;
(g)   memory or ability to concentrate, learn or understand; or
(h)   perception of the risk of physical danger.

(2) ….

Substantial adverse effects

5. Regulations may make provision for the purposes of this Act—
(a)   for an effect of a prescribed kind on the ability of a person to carry out normal day-to-day activities to be treated as a substantial adverse effect;
(b)   for an effect of a prescribed kind on the ability of a person to carry out normal day-to-day activities to be treated as not being a substantial adverse effect.

Effect of medical treatment

6. (1) An impairment which would be likely to have a substantial adverse effect on the ability of the person concerned to carry out normal day-to-day activities, but for the fact that measures are being taken to treat or correct it, is to be treated as having that effect.

(2) In sub-paragraph (1) 'measures' includes, in particular, medical treatment and the use of a prosthesis or other aid.

(3) Sub-paragraph (1) does not apply—
(a)   in relation to the impairment of a person's sight, to the extent that the impairment is, in his case, correctable by spectacles or contact lenses or in such other ways as may be prescribed; or
(b)   in relation to such other impairments as may be prescribed, in such circumstances as may be prescribed.

Progressive conditions

8. (1) Where—
(a)   a person has a progressive condition (such as cancer, multiple sclerosis or muscular dystrophy or infection by the human immunodeficiency virus),

(b)   as a result of that condition, he has an impairment which has (or had) an effect on his ability to carry out normal day-to-day activities, but

(c)   that effect is not (or was not) a substantial adverse effect, he shall be taken to have an impairment which has such a substantial adverse effect if the condition is likely to result in his having such an impairment.

(2) ....

The meaning of disability is expanded in the Disability Discrimination (Meaning of Disability) Regulations 1996, SI 1996/1455; and advice is contained in *DDA 1995: Guidance on Matters to be Taken into Account in Determining Questions Relating to the Definition of Disability* (HMSO 1996).

• *Compare the definitions under the Education Act 1996 and the Disability Discrimination Act 1995 with the Children Act 1989 definitions of a child 'in need' and a 'child who is disabled'.*

Children unable to attend school through illness

A child who is suffering from a long-term illness does not necessarily have a 'learning difficulty'. However an LEA has a legal obligation to provide education for a sick child who is unable to attend school. The education may be provided at a pupil referral unit or at home, in a hospital or elsewhere; it is likely to be part-time rather than full-time.

Education Act 1996, s 19

(1) Each local education authority shall make arrangements for the provision of suitable ... education at school or otherwise than at school for those children of compulsory school age who, by reason of illness, exclusion from school or otherwise, may not for any period receive suitable education unless such arrangements are made for them.

...

(6) In this section 'suitable education', in relation to a child or young person, means efficient education suitable to his age, ability and aptitude and to any special educational needs he may have.

The House of Lords considered the nature of this duty to provide a 'suitable education' in the following case; and in particular whether the LEA's resources are relevant in determining what is 'suitable'.

R v East Sussex County Council, ex p Tandy [1998] ELR 251

Lord Browne-Wilkinson: The appellant, T, was born on 8 February 1982 and was a child of compulsory school age until 8 February 1998. She has suffered from myalgic encephalomyelitis (ME) since she was 7 in consequence of which she has found it very difficult and at times impossible to attend school. From May 1992 onwards, the LEA provided 5 hours per week home tuition for her. Originally this home tuition was provided pursuant to a statement of special needs: T was mildly dyslexic. However that statement of special needs was withdrawn in July 1995 and from then onwards home tuition has been continued under s 298. T's progress has been kept under constant review and every effort made to reintegrate her into her school environment. But her medical condition meant that she only attended school on a handful of occasions. Her prime source of education was home tuition.

In July 1996 Dr Bacon, the manager of pupil services for the LEA, wrote to T's parents telling them of a general review of the LEA's home tuition services and warning them that 'the level of tuition may reduce from the previous standard of 5 hours per week as part of a package of measures which aims to facilitate a pupil's early return to full-time education'. There was a report in the Press that the LEA's home tuition budget had been cut from £100,000 a year to £25,000 a year but in July 1996 T's parents were told — as will appear rather surprisingly — that the LEA had not yet concluded its policy on home tuition. At that time T's ability to attend school had not improved. At a meeting held on 10 September 1996 the LEA's case work officer told T's parents that the maximum number of hours of home tuition would be cut from 5 hours per week to 3 hours per week, a decision which, the case worker said, was dictated purely by financial considerations and not by T's illness or educational needs.

...

It was in those circumstances that these proceedings for judicial review were launched on 30 November 1996 attacking the LEA's decision to reduce the number of hours of home tuition provided for T from 5 to 3 hours per week. The decision has been attacked on three separate grounds: (1) that the local authority in reaching its decision to cut the number of hours took into account an irrelevant consideration, namely, its financial resources; (2) that the decision was reached in pursuance of an improper purpose, viz, to save money; (3) that the decision was irrational. For reasons which will appear, it is only necessary for me to consider the first of those grounds. But for that purpose it is necessary to consider the reasons for the decision of the LEA to reduce the number of hours of home tuition provided for T.

Like all other local authorities, the respondent county council is in an unenviable position. It is now prevented from obtaining either from central government or from local taxation the financial resources necessary to discharge its functions as it would like to do. In a period when the aim of central government, of whatever political colour, has been to achieve a reduction in public spending, local authorities have not been relieved of statutory duties imposed upon them by Parliament in times past when different attitudes prevailed. Thus, in preparing its budget the respondent county council had to find ways of saving expenditure.

... There is nothing in the 1993 Act to suggest that resource considerations are relevant to the question of what is 'suitable education'. On their face those words connote a standard to be determined purely by educational considerations. This view is much strengthened by the definition of 'suitable education' in s 298(7) which spells out expressly the facts which are relevant to the determination of suitability, viz the education must be 'efficient' and 'suitable to his age, ability and aptitude' and also suitable 'to any special educational needs he may have'. All these express factors relate to educational considerations and nothing else. There is nothing to indicate that the resources available are relevant. ... [The] LEA owes the statutory duty to each sick child individually and not to sick children as a class ... The duty is to make arrangements for what constitutes suitable education for each child. That duty will not be fulfilled unless the arrangements do in fact provide suitable education for each child.

For these reasons as a matter of pure construction I can see no reason to treat the resources of the LEA as a relevant factor in determining what constitutes 'suitable education'. But I should make it clear, as did Keene J and Staughton LJ in their judgments, that if there is more than one way of providing 'suitable education', the LEA would be entitled to have regard to its resources in choosing between different ways of providing suitable education.

Does the decision in *R v Gloucestershire County Council ex p Barry* lead to a different conclusion? That case concerns s 2(1) of the Chronically Sick and Disabled Persons Act 1970 ...

The applicant was disabled and had been in receipt under s 2(1) of home care for shopping, pension, laundry, cleaning and meals on wheels. He was then informed that the provision of cleaning and laundry would be withdrawn because the local authority had insufficient resources. It was held by the majority of your Lordships' House, Lord Nicholls of Birkenhead, Lord Hoffmann and Lord Clyde (Lord Lloyd of Berwick and Lord Steyn dissenting) that it was lawful for the local authority in deciding what was necessary to meet the needs of the applicant to take into account the scarcity of the resources available to it.

The position in the present case is quite different. Under s 298 the LEA is not required to make any prior determination of T's need for education nor of the necessity for making provision for such education. The statute imposes an immediate obligation to make arrangements to provide suitable education. Moreover it then expressly defines what is meant by 'suitable education' by reference to wholly objective educational criteria. For these reasons, in my judgment the *R v Gloucestershire County Council ex p Barry* decision does not affect the present case.

There remains the suggestion that, given the control which central government now exercises over local authority spending, the court cannot, or at least should not, require performance of a statutory duty by a local authority which it is unable to afford. In the present case, the LEA does not contend that lack of resources is any defence to a failure to perform the statutory duty if it has arisen. But lack of resources is relied upon to preclude any statutory duty arising. My Lords I believe your Lordships should resist this approach to statutory duties.

First, the county council has as a matter of strict legality the resources necessary to perform its statutory duty under s 298. Very understandably it does not wish to bleed its other functions of resources so as to enable it to perform the statutory duty under s 298. But it can, if it wishes, divert money from other educational, or other, applications which are merely discretionary so as to apply such diverted moneys to discharge the statutory duty laid down by s 298. The argument is not one of insufficient resources to discharge the duty but of a preference for using the money for other purposes. To permit a local authority to avoid performing a statutory duty on the grounds that it prefers to spend the money in other ways is to downgrade a statutory duty to a discretionary power. A similar argument was put forward in the *R v Gloucestershire County Council ex p Barry* case but dismissed by Lord Nicholls (at p 470F–G) apparently on the ground that the complainant could control the failure of a local authority to carry out its statutory duty by showing that it was acting in a way which was *Wednesbury* unreasonable in failing to allocate the necessary resources.

... Parliament has chosen to impose a statutory duty, as opposed to a power, requiring the local authority to do certain things. In my judgment the courts should be slow to downgrade such duties into what are, in effect, mere discretions over which the court would have very little real control. If Parliament wishes to reduce public expenditure on meeting the needs of sick children then it is up to Parliament so to provide. It is not for the courts to adjust the order of priorities as between statutory duties and statutory discretions.

- *To what extent may a LEA take into account its financial resources when deciding what amounts to a 'suitable education' for a particular child?*

- *On what grounds did Lord Browne-Wilkinson distinguish ex p Barry?*

- *Would Ms Tandy now have any protection under the Disability Discrimination Act 1995?*

See the comment on Lord Browne-Wilkinson's judgment in J Hogg 'Preferred Option Shortfall – Children in Need' [2000] Fam Law (February) 114 (below, p 338).

3.   ROLE OF THE LEA

Local education authorities have overall legal responsibility for special educational provision in their area, and are required to consult with governing bodies where necessary. Additional duties, relating to the provision of advice and information, as well as mediation, have been imposed on LEAs by SENDA 2001 (see below). LEAs are responsible for identifying and assessing children with SEN, as well as deciding whether or not the child requires a statement.

Education Act 1996, s 315

(1) A local education authority shall keep under review the arrangements made by them for special educational provision.

(2) In doing so the authority shall, to the extent that it appears necessary or desirable for the purpose of co-ordinating provision for children with special educational needs, consult the governing bodies of community, foundation and voluntary and community and foundation special schools in their area.

See below *R v Hillingdon London Borough, ex p Governing Body of Queensmead School* [1997] ELR 331 on the relationship between the LEA and a governing body.

Duty to educate in mainstream education

Under the original provision contained in EA 1996, s 316 the presumption was that children with SEN should be educated in mainstream rather than special or independent schools. This fundamental principle, which is derived from the Warnock Committee Report, was enshrined in the EA 1980 and underpins current government policy. However, a new stronger version of s 316 of the EA 1996 has been substituted by SENDA 2001, s 1 which came into effect in September 2001, together with a new s 316A.

Note that the original presumption in the EA 1996 (before substitution) was subject to four conditions being met, the first being that mainstream education should be compatible with the parent's wishes. However, parents cannot veto a mainstream school selected by the LEA, so long as that school is appropriate (see below). The second, third and fourth conditions were set out in the original s 316(2) of the EA 1996, with (c) being of particular importance in practice.

Education Act 1996, s 316

(1) Any person exercising any functions under this Part in respect of a child with special educational needs who should be educated in a school shall secure that, if the conditions mentioned in subsection (2) are satisfied, the child is educated in a school which is not a special school unless that is incompatible with the wishes of his parent.

(2) The conditions are that educating the child in a school which is not a special school is compatible with—
(a)   his receiving the special educational provision which his learning difficulty calls for,
(b)   the provision of efficient education for the children with whom he will be educated, and
(c)   the efficient use of resources.

The substituted version of s 316, which replaces the presumption with a duty, is as follows:

Education Act 1996, s 316

Duty to educate children with special educational needs in mainstream schools

(1) This section applies to a child with special educational needs who should be educated in a school.

(2) If no statement is maintained under s 324 for the child, he must be educated in a mainstream school.

(3) If a statement is maintained under s 324 for the child, he must be educated in a mainstream school unless that is incompatible with –
(a)   the wishes of his parent, or
(b)   the provision of efficient education for other children.

(4) In this section and section 316A 'mainstream school' means any school other than—
(a)   a special school, or
(b)   an independent school which is not—
        (i)   a city technology college,
        (ii)   a city college for the technology of the arts, or
        (iii)   a city academy.

- *Compare the compatibility requirements under the 'old' and 'new' s 316. Consider what differences the changes may make in practice.*

- *Note the definition of mainstream school under the 'new' s 316.*

Education Act 1996, s 316A

Education otherwise than in mainstream schools

(1) Section 316 does not prevent a child from being educated in—
(a)   an independent school which is not a mainstream school, or
(b)   a school approved under section 342,

if the cost is met otherwise than by a local education authority.

The section goes on to provide that in certain exceptional temporary circumstances the LEA may fund a child without a statement who is attending an independent or non-maintained special school; and that the LEA may fund such a place where the school is named in the child's statement of special educational needs.

The LEA is not obliged under either version of s 316 of the EA 1996 to make provision for the child in a mainstream school if the parents object, but may still do so if that is the most appropriate provision.

The relationship between s 9 of the EA 1996, which requires an LEA to have regard to parental wishes, s 411 of the EA 1996, which requires an LEA to comply with parental preference subject to certain exceptions, and s 316 of the EA 1996 was considered by the Court of Appeal in *L v Worcestershire County Council and Hughes* [2000] ELR 674.

L v Worcestershire County Council and Hughes [2000] ELR 674

Hale LJ: ...[The tribunal] accepted a proposed amended statement drawn up in November 1998 as a working document for the hearing. This proposed that K should attend a 'day school able to provide physical and curricular access and appropriate support for children with physical difficulties'. The LEA put forward two mainstream schools, St Peter's and St John's, and a maintained special school for children with physical handicap, Rosehill. The cost of placement at St Peter's or St John's was £15,430, at Rosehill it was £18,418, while at A Manor School it was £44,044.

... They concluded that K did not need either the conductive education or the extended school day provided at A Manor School. She did need physiotherapy but that could be provided for in an amended statement as could other requirements to meet her physical disabilities.

... Four points were taken before the judge but only one is pursued in this court. Essentially this is how the LEA and tribunal are to treat parental wishes in cases such as this where the child has special educational needs and the parent wishes that child to attend a private, non-maintained special school, which is very much more expensive than the state-provided alternatives.

[Hale LJ considered the relevant statutory provisions and how the law on parental choice had developed since the Education Act 1944.]

The words [in s 316(1)] 'unless that is incompatible with the wishes of his parent' were inserted by the 1993 Act. Previously, the duty to secure mainstream schooling had inevitably arisen once the qualifying conditions were met. It was argued before Carnwath J that these words introduced a parental veto over mainstream education. He rejected that argument. In doing so he followed a decision of Owen J in *Forbes v London Borough of Ealing* (unreported) 30 September 1999, which he considered 'absolutely right': the authority's duty to provide education in a mainstream school did not apply if the parent objected, but the primary duty to provide education appropriate to the child's needs still did so, and if those needs were met by a mainstream school then that primary duty was met, even if the parents did not agree. There is no appeal against that aspect of the decision.

It is argued, however, that a similar balancing exercise arises in relation to the duty in s 316 as arises in relation to the duties in s 411 (for children without statements) and Sch 27 (for children with statements whose parents choose maintained schools). In other words, the LEA or tribunal should first have asked themselves whether the conditions for mainstream schooling in s 316(2) applied so as to bring the duty to provide mainstream schooling into play. If they did, then the tribunal should have asked whether this duty was incompatible with parental wishes. If it was, they should have proceeded to the second stage, and carried out a balancing exercise, weighing the strength and depth and reasons for those parental objections against the financial and other advantages of mainstream education. This would, it was argued, require the tribunal to give far more weight to parental objections to mainstream schooling than is required by s 9.

This is a subtle argument. It depends, not upon the existence of the duty to provide mainstream schooling in s 316, but upon the fact that parental objection has negatived that duty. But, argues Mr Gordon QC for the mother, the same applies to s 411 and para 3 of Sch 27. The prejudicial factor, be it resources or another, has negatived the duty to comply with parental choice. Nevertheless, the case-law suggests that there is still a balancing act to be performed between parental preference and the resource objections. Why should it not also be so here?

... It is quite clear that the choice of school provisions in s 411 and para 3 of Sch 27 do not arise in this case. The cases which suggest that a second stage balancing exercise arises once those duties have been negatived by resource considerations clearly relied upon the existence of other provisions requiring LEAs, appeal committees and the tribunal to take account of parental views. No one suggests that parental views are irrelevant in this case. The duty to 'have regard to the general principle' in s 9 clearly does apply, as does the duty to take account of parental representations. Indeed we wonder whether the references to a second stage balancing exercise in the *Glamorgan, Croydon* and *Harrow* cases reflect anything more than this.

Equally it is clear that the duty to secure mainstream schooling in s 316(1) has been negatived by the mother's objections.

...

Carnwath J [stated below]

... once the parents have made clear their opposition to mainstream education, then one is taken outside [section 316] altogether, and indeed one is simply left with the ordinary obligations under section 324.

Those ordinary obligations are, as we have seen, to determine in detail the special educational provision which is called for by the child's special educational needs, including the type of school or other institution which would be appropriate, and naming a particular school if they think that should be done. That determination, as we have already seen, is to be informed by the views expressed by the parents and account must be taken of the general principle in s 9. It called for an informed exercise of judgment and that, in our view, was what was required in this case, it was also in our view exactly what the tribunal made.

Mainstream school or special school?

Whereas in *L v Worcestershire County Council and Hughes* [2000] ELR 674 the mother wanted her daughter to attend an independent school rather than a mainstream or special school, some parents may want their child to attend a mainstream school in preference to a special school.

Haringey London Borough Council v SENT 1996 CO/2469/96, 10 September 1996 ([1996] CLY 2486)

H appealed against a decision of the Special Education Needs Tribunal as to the provision of mainstream secondary education for a girl with athetoid cerebral palsy, who was the subject of a special educational needs statement made under the Education Act 1993, s 168 and Sch 10. The school of parental choice was closer to the girl's home and permitted her to retain contact with her established peer group, although it did not offer ease of access and other adapted facilities present at the school selected by H.

Held, dismissing the appeal, that although suitability was an issue that could override parental choice under Sch 10, para 3(3)(b) of the 1993 Act and that resources were a factor to be taken into account under this head, the decision was one that the tribunal was fully entitled to reach on the facts of the case. Placing the girl in H's preferred school meant that she would be with other disabled children in an environment which would not stretch her intellectually. The reasons given by the tribunal were sufficient to show how the decision had been reached and did not need to detail the adaptations needed at the chosen school, and showed, by implication, that any sums to be spent in doing so were not incompatible with the efficient use of resources.

Other parents may want their child to attend a special school rather than a mainstream school.

R v London Borough of Brent and Vassie, ex p AF [2000] ELR 550

Owen J: Mr F, the appellant, is the father of AF. A is 10 years old. A is the applicant in the judicial review proceedings. He has a mild degree of autism. In addition he has a severe specific language disorder and this is his major disability. For these reasons he has special educational needs.

The main problem here is that the first respondent, the LEA, wish A to continue to attend OM School, formerly a grant-maintained mainstream primary school, which it now maintains and where A attends a special language unit. Mr F wants A to attend SH School, a special school for autistic children maintained by the borough of Ealing. His reasons are:
(1) that A needs specialist teaching from a teacher with experience of educating autistic children, and
(2) A is too vulnerable for a mainstream school.
...

[Mr F] is to be admired for the love and concern which he shows for his son, but such qualities do not necessarily lead to a correct diagnosis. Mr F maintains that A is autistic and needs to be educated in a specialist school for autistic children, his choice being SH School. The respondent's case was that this was not so since '[A]'s degree of autism was mild and ... his main difficulties were his severe specific language disorder'. ... [T]he tribunal concluded 'on the evidence that placement at Oakington Manor language unit did meet

[A]'s special educational needs'. I see no reason to think that this was a perverse finding. A's special educational needs were those of one suffering from mild autism and a complex communication disorder. The fact that the teacher did not have the experience which was desirable and specified did not mean, of itself, that OM School could not and would not meet A's special educational needs.

Does a child with SEN have to attend a school?

The short answer is 'No'. Parents may choose to educate their child at home (see chapter 3) or at a specialist centre. Local education authorities have the power to arrange for the child to be educated 'otherwise than in a school' (EA 1996, s 319). This may be applicable where the child is unwell (see EA 1996, s 19; *R v East Sussex County Council, ex p Tandy* [1998] ELR 251, above).

Some parents may want their child to be educated at a specialist centre abroad. Local education authorities have the power to make such provision in the case of a child with a statement of special educational needs (EA 1996, s 320).

Although LEAs have the power to make these arrangements, an LEA may not be prepared to fund the cost where it considers that appropriate education may be provided at, for example, a local school. Note that s 320(3) of the EA 1996 does not require the LEA to pay all of the costs of education outside the UK.

Education Act 1996, s 319

(1) Where a local education authority are satisfied that it would be inappropriate for—
(a)   the special educational provision which a learning difficulty of a child in their area calls for, or
(b)   any part of any such provision,

to be made in a school, they may arrange for the provision (or, as the case may be, for that part of it) to be made otherwise than in a school.

(2) Before making an arrangement under this section, a local education authority shall consult the child's parent.

Education Act 1996, s 320

(1) A local education authority may make such arrangements as they think fit to enable a child for whom they maintain a statement under section 324 to attend an institution outside England and Wales which specialises in providing for children with special needs.

…

(3) Where a local education authority make arrangements under this section in respect of a child, those arrangements may in particular include contributing to or paying—
(a)   fees charged by the institution,

(b) expenses reasonably incurred in maintaining him while he is at the institution or travelling to or from it,
(c) his travelling expenses, and
(d) expenses reasonably incurred by any person accompanying him while he is travelling or staying at the institution.

(4) This section is without prejudice to any other powers of a local education authority.

Disputes arise where the parent wants a particular school named in Part 4 of their child's statement of special educational needs, and the LEA disagrees (see below). An example of such a case involving the Higashi School in Boston, USA is *R v Cheshire County Council, exp C* [1998] ELR 66. The case in the High Court was concerned with whether the SENT should have granted a request by the parent for an adjournment because her expert witness was unwell. However, the court was also asked to consider the question of part-funding under s 164(3) of the EA 1993, which has been replaced by s 320(3) of the EA 1996.

R v Cheshire County Council, ex p C [1998] ELR 66

Sedley J: Mrs C, the appellant, has two autistic children of whom H, the elder, is now almost 7 years old. Her needs, which are profound, have been met with some apparent success by the Higashi School in Boston, Massachusetts. The fees there are, however, extremely high, amounting to almost £53,000 pa. The appellant herself placed H there in September 1993 without local authority funding, but in May 1995 the authority agreed retrospectively to fund her placement from November 1994 to August 1995. At the end of May 1995, however, the authority produced H's final statement of special educational needs, naming an independent special autistic school, Lambs House School, Cheshire, in the statement. The total fees at Lambs House are something over £44,000 pa for a residential placement and a little over £35,000 pa for a day placement.

… A benefactor who learned of H's difficulties offered to pay the difference between the Lambs House fees and the Higashi fees so as to enable her to continue in the Boston school, part-funded by the local education authority under s 164(3). The local education authority, however, has stood by its own judgment to the extent of paying Lambs House School to keep an unoccupied place available for H. H, however, was kept at the Higashi school until funds ran out earlier this year, since when she has been at home, placing her mother potentially in breach of the law and perpetuating the waste of resources. It was in the course of this process that in June 1995 notice of appeal to the tribunal was given. The grounds were these:
1. Lack of specificity in part 3 of the statement.
2. The need for a boarding 7 days a week placement.
3. A highly specialised provision is required only available with the Higashi method at the Higashi School in Boston, USA.

… To begin with, part-funding is possible only for schools outside England and Wales; there is no means of introducing a parental or other contribution to the cost of domestic special education. Secondly, if there is more than one appropriate institution outside Britain, parental means will ordinarily be available to offset both in the same amount, so that the less expensive choice will still be lawful for the local authority. It is only where the choice is between fully funding a placement in Britain and part-funding a placement abroad in exactly the same net amount that there will be, as there is in this case, a true parity of financial considerations. In these circumstances, although — so far as I can see — in no others, the choice can and should be made on purely educational grounds.

....

On the tribunal's present findings, of course, the Higashi School is rated below Lambs House in terms of appropriateness to H's needs, so that the foregoing paradigm would not apply. But if on a full hearing the tribunal concludes that the Higashi School is either as good as or better than Lambs House in relation to H's needs, and if the offer of part-funding is still there and still sufficient to equalise the net cost to the education budget, the tribunal will in my judgment have jurisdiction to substitute the Higashi School for Lambs House in part 4 of the statement.

District health authorities and local authorities

Local education authorities may ask district health authorities and local authorities to assist LEAs with SEN provision. The authorities should normally comply with the request. However, they are permitted to refuse on several grounds, including lack of resources.

Education Act 1996, s 322

(1) Where it appears to a local education authority that any Health Authority, Primary Care Trust or local authority could, by taking any specified action, help in the exercise of any of their functions under this Part, they may request the help of the authority or trust, specifying the action in question.

(2) An authority or a trust whose help is so requested shall comply with the request unless—
(a) they consider that the help requested is not necessary for the purpose of the exercise by the local education authority of those functions, or
(b) subsection (3) applies.

(3) This subsection applies—
(a) in the case of a Health Authority or Primary Care Trust, if that authority or trust consider that, having regard to the resources available to them for the purpose of the exercise of their functions under the National Health Service Act 1977, it is not reasonable for them to comply with the request, or
(b) in the case of a local authority, if that authority consider that the request is not compatible with their own statutory or other duties and obligations or unduly prejudices the discharge of any of their functions.

....

The question of where the primary legal responsibility lies for providing and paying for special educational provision was considered in a pair of cases involving the London Borough of Harrow (*R v Harrow London Borough Council, ex p M* [1997] ELR 62; *R v Brent and Harrow Health Authority, ex p Harrow London Borough Council* [1997] ELR 187). The Education Act 1993, s 166, which was superseded by s 322 of the EA 1996, was the provision in force at the relevant time.

R v Harrow London Borough Council, ex p M [1997] ELR 62

Turner J: This is an application for judicial review of the respondent local education authority's alleged failure to comply with the statement of special educational needs made in respect of the infant applicant. There is a parallel application by the present respondent against the local health authority, Brent and Harrow Health Authority, in respect of their alleged failure to help in the exercise of the respondent borough's functions under Part 2 of the Education Act 1993.

The applicant is now aged 6 years. At the time of her birth she suffered cerebral palsy in consequence of which she has, and has had a statement made in respect of her special educational needs. That is not the problem. What lies at the heart of the present dispute is which of two public bodies should take the steps necessary to comply with that statement. Behind this dispute lies the problem of chronic underfunding of public bodies who have a statutory duty to fulfil but only a limited budget out of which to meet their statutory obligations. The date when the statement was issued was 3 February 1996. Part 3 provides that the applicant requires the following provision:

(a) occupational therapy, one hour a week;
(b) speech and language therapy, one hour a week; and
(c) physiotherapy, not less than 45 minutes a week.

In the period 26 February to 7 June 1996, the applicant did receive therapy, but only at about half the rates specified in the statement. Since 7 June 1996 she has received none at all. As early as 13 March 1996 the applicant's parents were writing to the LEA complaining of its failure fully to implement the statement. As the letter sets out ... the parents had earlier complained on a number of occasions by telephone, but without achieving any constructive response from the LEA. The reply which this letter provoked ... in essence consists of an assertion that the LEA are relieved of the necessity of complying with the statement because of a failure by the health authority to provide the requisite resources.

... For many months, as will be seen from the judgment to be given in the LEA's application against the health authority, the LEA had been fully alive to, as well as having discussed the financial problems confronting the health authority, just how that authority was planning to cope with those problems. The LEA knew that the health authority was only able to, and would provide, half the service that any statement of special educational needs required. This was because its finances effectively prevented it from doing anything else. Equally clearly, the LEA also knew that its duty was not one which fell to be met as an 'ultimate' one, but was its own primary responsibility.

The argument put forward by the LEA was that 'having requested a public body which, in the circumstances, is duty bound to provide the therapy they have arranged that the special educational provision has been made for the applicant'. This argument has to fail.

If, as was the case here, the LEA knew that for reasons of financial stringency, the health authority was only going to provide approximately one half the required therapy, the LEA knew that they had not made arrangements that the special educational provision was made as were required of them by s 168(5) of the 1993 Act. They also knew that the health authority were not in breach of any statutory duty in not meeting the help that had been requested of them because of the (lack of) 'resources available to them'. The argument that the LEA were entitled to rely on s 166 when they knew of the position of the health authority in regard to that section and the reasons for it, is in my judgment untenable.

The LEA argued that under s 166 (now s 322) 'there is no room for partial compliance' by the Health Authority.

R v Brent and Harrow Health Authority, ex p Harrow London Borough Council [1997] ELR 187

Turner J: This is an application for judicial review of the decision of the respondent health authority dated 14 May 1996 to refuse to meet the request of the applicants to provide speech, occupational and physiotherapy to the infant applicant in the application brought against the new applicants. For the sake of simplicity, in this judgment the infant applicant just referred to will be so described. The obligation of a district health authority to help an education authority (LEA) in the provision of special educational needs is set out in s 166 of the Education Act 1993.

...

The respondents drew attention to their general duty under the 1977 Act which requires them to continue the promotion of a comprehensive health service in their district which involves the delivery of appropriate health services for all its resident population. The point implicit in these introductory submissions was that a health authority is a many-faceted organisation with a number of separate functions to perform under the general umbrella of providing a comprehensive service to the population in its area. The allocation of resources is a function which will ordinarily be performed on an annual but continuing basis according to a number of competing priorities, just one of which will be the provision of help to a LEA under s 166 of the 1993 Act. Such an authority could not reasonably be expected to recalculate and reallocate resources according to a particular demand which arises at any particular moment. Under s 166, the health authority is required to have regard to the total resources available to it which it is likely to do when setting its annual budget. The resources available to a health authority cannot sensibly be understood to mean that they are to be considered on a daily basis. There is no practical scope for a LEA to require a health authority to reorder its priorities in a way which the LEA might approve. That is peculiarly the function of a health authority to perform.

... The respondents do, in fact, prioritise the needs of individual 'clients' according to their assessed needs and have decided how to allocate resources between 'clients' having particular levels of need. The respondents have deposed that their 'guiding principle' is equity between patients of similar need, regardless of whether or not the patient has been statemented.

...

Such an approach is, in my judgment, impeccable. The provisions of s 166 do not render it without the power of a district health authority to seek to ration its scarce resources in the manner in which the respondents did in the present case. Accordingly, at the conclusion of the oral argument in this case I indicated that the application for judicial review would be refused.

Children 'in need'

In addition to their obligation to co-operate with LEAs under the Education Act 1996, local authorities have responsibilities under the Children Act 1989 to 'children in need' and to their families.

Children Act 1989, s 17

(1) It shall be the general duty of every local authority (in addition to the other duties imposed on them by this Part)—

(a) to safeguard and promote the welfare of children within their area who are in need; and

(b) so far as is consistent with that duty, to promote the upbringing of such children by their families, by providing a range and level of services appropriate to those children's needs.

...

(2) Any service provided by an authority in the exercise of functions conferred on them by this section may be provided for the family of a particular child in need or for any member of his family, if it is provided with a view to safeguarding or promoting the child's welfare.

...

(8) Before giving any assistance or imposing any conditions, a local authority shall have regard to the means of the child concerned and of each of his parents.

...

(10) For the purposes of this Part a child shall be taken to be in need if—

(a) he is unlikely to achieve or maintain, or to have the opportunity of achieving or maintaining, a reasonable standard of health or development without the provision for him of services by a local authority under this Part;

(b) his health or development is likely to be significantly impaired, or further impaired, without the provision for him of such services; or

(c) he is disabled

and 'family', in relation to such a child, includes any person who has parental responsibility for the child and any other person with whom he has been living.

(11) For the purposes of this Part, a child is disabled if he is blind, deaf or dumb or suffers from mental disorder of any kind or is substantially and permanently handicapped by illness, injury or congenital deformity or such other disability as may be prescribed; and in this Part—

'development' means physical, intellectual, emotional, social or behavioural development; and 'health' means physical or mental health.

- *Compare the definition of 'in need' with 'special educational needs' and the definition of 'a child who is disabled' with the definition of a 'disabled pupil' (see above).*

A case which illustrates the responsibilities of a local authority in relation to a child 'in need', who also had profound learning difficulties is *R (on the application of AB and SB) v Nottingham City Council* [2001] EWHC Admin 235, [2001] 3 FCR 350.

'Preferred Option Shortfall — Children In Need' J Hogg [2000] Fam Law (February) 114

Recent developments in community care law have significant implications for children services. This, taken together with the gradual evolution of a corpus of law relating to children 'in need', rather than just children who are subject to care proceedings, may lead to a somewhat overdue change in approach to the provision of children services as a whole, making them more on a par with adult services.

...

The general duty (s 17) is qualified by its use as are the duties in Sch 2, para 8 (advice and guidance, activities, home help service, travel assistance, and holidays), and day care (s 18). In fact the only duty not qualified in this way is the duty under s 20 to provide accommodation. It only arises where it appears to the local authority that the child requires accommodation. The difficulty with this approach is that it leaves the possibility of unmet need unaddressed.

Resource considerations

A more subtle approach may be to import financial considerations into the determination of what is a 'need' in the first place, as Lord Nicholls did in *R v Gloucestershire County Council* by taking the view that each local authority determines need by reference to, among other things, its own resources. There is decided authority in cases in the sphere of community care law, not least *R v Gloucestershire County Council*, that the courts would wish to adopt this approach and thereby avoid unmet need.

... If whether a person has a need is determined to some extent by the local authority's resources it is unlikely that there can be general agreement about what 'a need' is because it can only be what the authority determines it to be. This point was recognised by the House of Lords in *R v East Sussex County Council ex p Tandy* [1998] AC 714. In this case Lord Browne-Wilkinson gave the judgment of a unanimous House of Lords. In considering the case under the Education Act 1993 he took the view that lack of resources was not relevant to the issue of service provision for a child's education. Although once again this was a different statutory framework (now s 19 of the Education Act 1996) no mention was made in the relevant section about financial considerations, although it was mentioned elsewhere in the Act, unlike the 1989 Act.

...

The only argument here, in his Lordship's view, was 'were the needs of the child being met by the LEA?'. There was no issue as to whether the needs of the child were correctly identified as such. I would suggest the approach adopted by the House of Lords in this case is not likely to be applicable to cases under the 1989 Act because of the duty to assess need first.

...

My own view is that his Lordship's approach appears to be something of a masterful sleight of hand. In determining what is suitable education for a child the local education authority (LEA) must necessarily assess the educational needs of the child, if only on the basis that what is suitable education for one child may well not be suitable for another. Given that an assessment is in fact involved, Lord Nicholls' approach in *R v Gloucestershire County Council* would appear to apply and be preferable — in determining whether a need exists, resources are a relevant consideration.

Provision of advice, information and mediation

The Special Educational Needs and Disability Act 2001 has imposed additional duties on an LEA partly as an attempt to ensure that parents are better informed at an earlier stage in the process. This may reduce the number of disputes arising between parents, schools and the LEA.

Education Act 1996, s 332A

Advice and information for parents

(1) A local education authority must arrange for the parent of any child in their area with special educational needs to be provided with advice and information about matters relating to those needs.

...

(3) The authority must take such steps as they consider appropriate for making the services provided under subsection (1) known to—
(a)   the parents of children in their area,
(b)   the head teachers and proprietors of schools in their area, and
(c)   such other persons as they consider appropriate.

More detail on these requirements is set out in Special Educational Needs (Provision of Information by Local Education Authorities) (England) Regulations 2001, SI 2001/2218. For example, the regulations require LEAs to explain what element of SEN provision should be funded by schools and the LEA respectively for pupils who are not statemented.

Many LEAs already provide such advice and information through parent partnership services. This provision requires all LEAs to make such provision. In addition SENDA 2001 requires LEAs to appoint independent mediators to resolve disputes informally between parents and schools (governing bodies) and the LEA.

Education Act 1996, s 332B

Resolution of disputes

(1) A local education authority must make arrangements with a view to avoiding or resolving disagreements between authorities (on the one hand) and parents of children in their area (on the other) about the exercise by authorities of functions under this Part.

(2) A local education authority must also make arrangements with a view to avoiding or resolving, in each relevant school, disagreements between the parents of a relevant child and the proprietor of the school about the special educational provision made for that child.

(3) The arrangements must provide for the appointment of independent persons with the function of facilitating the avoidance or resolution of such disagreements.

...

(5) The authority must take such steps as they consider appropriate for making the arrangements made under subsections (1) and (2) known to—
(a)   the parents of children in their area,
(b)   the head teachers and proprietors of schools in their area, and
(c)   such other persons as they consider appropriate.

(6) The arrangements cannot affect the entitlement of a parent to appeal to the Tribunal.

Compliance with SENT orders

Until SENDA 2001 there was no legal obligation on LEAs to comply with Tribunal orders, although complaints could be made to the Local Government Ombudsman (see chapter 8). However, the following provision has now been introduced.

Education Act 1996, s 336A (as inserted by SENDA 2001, s 3)

Compliance with orders

(1) If the Tribunal makes an order, the local education authority concerned must comply with the order before the end of the prescribed period beginning with the date on which it is made.

(2) Regulations under this section, so far as they relate to Wales, require the agreement of the National Assembly for Wales.

4.   ROLE OF THE GOVERNING BODY

The governing body of a community, voluntary or foundation school has a general duty in relation to children with SEN who are attending the school. In the case of a nursery school the duty rests with the LEA.

The Special Educational Needs and Disability Act 2001 requires schools to give certain information to parents of children with SEN, and also gives schools the right to request a statutory assessment (see below).

Secure appropriate provision

The importance of integration of pupils with SEN is reflected in the requirement that the governing body should try to ensure that, where practicable, a child with SEN is able to participate in all school activities which are available to children without SEN. Local education authorities can supply and charge governing bodies of schools for goods or services provided to assist schools perform their statutory obligations in relation to pupils with SEN (EA 1996, s 318).

Education Act 1996, s 317

(1) The governing body, in the case of a community, foundation or voluntary school and the local education authority, in the case of a maintained nursery school, shall—
(a)   use their best endeavours, in exercising their functions in relation to the school, to secure that, if any registered pupil has special educational needs, the special educational provision which his learning difficulty calls for is made,

(b)   secure that, where the responsible person has been informed by the local education authority that a registered pupil has special educational needs, those needs are made known to all who are likely to teach him, and

(c)   secure that the teachers in the school are aware of the importance of identifying, and providing for, those registered pupils who have special educational needs.

(2) In subsection (1)(b) 'the responsible person' means—

(a)   in the case of a community, foundation or voluntary school the head teacher or the appropriate governor (that is, the chairman of the governing body or, where the governing body have designated another governor for the purposes of this paragraph, that other governor), and

(b)   in the case of a nursery school, the head teacher.

…

(4) Where a child who has special educational needs is being educated in a community, foundation or voluntary school or a maintained nursery school, those concerned with making special educational provision for the child shall secure, so far as is reasonably practicable and is compatible with—

(a)   the child receiving the special educational provision which his learning difficulty calls for,

(b)   the provision of efficient education for the children with whom he will be educated, and

(c)   the efficient use of resources,

that the child engages in the activities of the school together with children who do not have special educational needs.

• *Compare with the obligation not to discriminate under Disability Discrimination Act 1995, s 28A(2).*

Provide information to parents

The governing body owes a specific duty to individual parents as well as a general duty to the parent body as a whole. The Special Educational Needs and Disability Act 2001 requires the governing body to provide information to parents of children with SEN as soon as special educational provision is being made for their child. Perhaps surprisingly parents have sometimes been unaware for several years that such provision was being made for their child.

Education Act 1996, s 317A

Duty to inform parent where special educational provision made

(1) This section applies if—

(a)   a child for whom no statement is maintained under section 324 is a registered pupil at—

(i)   a community, foundation or voluntary school, or

(ii)   a pupil referral unit,

(b) special educational provision is made for him at the school because it is considered that he has special educational needs, and

(c) his parent has not previously been informed under this section of special educational provision made for him at the school.

(2) If the school is a pupil referral unit, the local education authority must secure that the head teacher informs the child's parent that special educational provision is being made for him at the school because it is considered that he has special educational needs.

(3) In any other case, the governing body must inform the child's parent that special educational provision is being made for him there because it is considered that he has special educational needs.

In addition the governing body is also required to include in their annual report to parents details of the implementation of their policy for pupils with SEN, together with information as to:

(a) the arrangements for the admission of disabled pupils;
(b) the steps taken to prevent disabled pupils from being treated less favourably than other pupils; and
(c) the facilities provided to assist access to the school by disabled pupils;

and for this purpose 'disabled pupils' means pupils who are disabled persons for the purposes of the Disability Discrimination Act 1995 (s 317(6) of the EA 1996). (See above for the definition of 'disabled pupil'.)

Relationship with LEA

In *R v Hillingdon London Borough, ex p Governing Body of Queensmead School* [1997] ELR 331 the governing body challenged the legality of the decision by the LEA to reduce the amount of money provided by the LEA to the governing body for the education of children with SEN attending the school. The school was a grant-maintained school but was nevertheless subject to the duty now contained in s 316 of the EA 1996 (previously s 161 of the EA 1993).

The judge considered not only the relevant statutory provisions, but also the Code of Practice on the Identification and Assessment of Special Educational Needs (1994), DFE Circular 2/94 on the Local Management of Schools, and Circular 11/90 on Staffing for Pupils with Special Educational Needs.

R v Hillingdon London Borough, ex p Governing Body of Queensmead School [1997] ELR 331

Collins J: On 7 March 1996 the authority was faced with the need to implement savings of at least £2m for 1996/97. Since 12 of the 15 secondary schools in its area were grant-maintained, the authority was unable to make any cuts in their overall budgets since these were determined by the CFF allocation formula. The LMS scheme had determined that LEA schools should not be funded any differently so that they were not disadvantaged.

Thus, any cuts could only be achieved by reducing the sums allocated for statemented pupils.

The savings required of the education committee had to amount to some £1.5m. On 11 March 1996 Mr Duggan, Queensmead's Headmaster, was informed in his capacity as chairman of the Hillingdon Association of Headteachers of proposed cuts in secondary schools' budgets for statemented pupils of £500,000. He was, understandably appalled, since he recognised that his school was facing a cut of about 60%. As he has pointed out in his affidavit in these proceedings, almost all the money received was spent by Queensmead on the extra teachers and SSAs required to provide for the statemented needs of the pupils concerned. Any sums left over were spent on equipment. In November 1994 an OFSTED inspection team had reported most favourably on the school's provision for statemented pupils. It followed that any cuts would mean that the extra tuition needed for the children could not be provided and their statemented needs could not be met from the sums provided by the LEA for those purposes.

...

The education committee approved the cuts on 18 March 1996.

...

Budgetary constraints and lack of funds can play no part in the assessment of a child's special educational needs. This seems to me to follow from the decision of the Court of Appeal in R v Gloucestershire County Council ex p Barry [1996] 4 All ER 421, at p 442A. Financial constraints can be considered in deciding how those needs are to be met, provided always that they are met. It cannot be said that a need exists but it would be too expensive to provide for it. The requirement is to meet the needs, but the provision made may be the minimum necessary to meet them. The LEA has a duty, which is non-delegable, to arrange that the special educational provision specified in a statement is made for the child: 1993 Act, s 168(5)(a)(i). The way in which the provision is made may be the most economical so long as it is made. The governors of the school in their turn have a duty to use their best endeavours to secure that the special educational provision is made: 1993 Act, s 161(1)(a).

The problem in this case arises largely because there has been no discussion with the school but the LEA (as it is entitled to do) has decided to adopt a formulaic approach. The general principles of course apply: if the formula produces a sufficient sum, the school cannot complain. But if the formula does not in fact produce a sum sufficient to meet the special educational provisions set out in the statements, the LEA must give more. It cannot require the school to make up the balance. It is for the LEA to decide what is sufficient but it must take all relevant matters into consideration and, as it seems to me, unless it discusses the matter with the school, it is likely to fail to have regard to the actual needs of all the relevant pupils and, where a change is being made, to whether the formula is indeed sufficient to enable the school to provide for the needs. In addition, it is essential that the formula is properly applied so that sufficient sums are provided.

...

One of the major objectives of the 1993 Act is to ensure that statemented pupils should, if possible, be educated in mainstream schools in order to obtain the benefit of the national curriculum and contact with ordinary pupils and the school's facilities.

...

Even if the LEA was correct to apply the formula as it did, it is clear on the evidence that the sums do not provide sufficient to meet the needs. Each side relies on the delegation of funding to the governors and the lack of any requirement for them to use sums in any particular manner to support their cases. The LEA says it has provided enough following the formula correctly. The school must then use it as it sees fit and if the school chooses to spend more it must make up the difference. The applicants say that there is no power in the LEA to require them to use their funds in any particular way or for any particular purpose and so the requirement to fund the difference is unlawful. In my judgment, one returns to the duty upon the LEA to arrange for the needs to be met in accordance with the statement. As I have already said, if the formula does not produce enough money for that to be done, the LEA must make up the balance and cannot require the school to use its funds for that purpose.

In those circumstances, the reduction of the funds was unlawful and the decision of the education committee cannot stand.

The judge also considered that the LEA was in breach of its obligation to consult the governing body where a reduction in funding is likely to have a significant impact on its overall budget.

5. IDENTIFICATION AND ASSESSMENT OF SPECIAL EDUCATIONAL NEEDS

Identification

Local education authorities are responsible for identifying most, but not all, children in their area who have special educational needs.

Education Act 1996, s 321

(1) A local education authority shall exercise their powers with a view to securing that, of the children for whom they are responsible, they identify those to whom subsection (2) below applies.

(2) This subsection applies to a child if—
(a)   he has special educational needs, and
(b)   it is necessary for the authority to determine the special educational provision which any learning difficulty he may have calls for.

(3) For the purposes of this Part a local education authority are responsible for a child if he is in their area and—
(a)   he is a registered pupil at a maintained school,
(b)   education is provided for him at a school which is not a maintained school but is so provided at the expense of the authority,
(c)   he does not come within paragraph (a) or (b) above but is a registered pupil at a school and has been brought to the authority's attention as having (or probably having) special educational needs, or
(d)   he is not a registered pupil at a school but is not under the age of two or over compulsory school age and has been brought to their attention as having (or probably having) special educational needs.

For which children are an LEA not responsible under this section?

In *Holtom v Barnet London Borough* [1999] ELR 255 the claimant's claim for breach of this statutory duty (under the EA 1944) was struck out by the Court of Appeal, which relied on the reasoning of the House of Lords in *X v Bedfordshire County Council* [1995] 2 AC 633 (see below).

Holtom v Barnet London Borough [1999] ELR 255

Hale LJ

...

However, in *X (Minors) v Bedfordshire County Council; M (A Minor) and Another v Newham London Borough Council and Others; E (A Minor) v Dorset County Council; Christmas v Hampshire County Council; Keating v Bromley London Borough Council* [1995] 2 AC 633, [1995] ELR 404 the House of Lords held that there was no private right of action for breach of a local education authority's duties in the Education Act 1944, including the sections relevant here, on its own.

The 1994 Code of Practice advocated a 5-stage model. The responsibility for pupils at stages 1-3 rested with the school; whereas for pupils at stages 4 or 5 the LEA and the school shared the responsibility. However, the Code of Practice published in November 2001 (DfES 581/2001) no longer refers to a 5-stage model. The Code prefers instead a 'graduated approach through *School Action* and *School Action Plus*' (*Early Years Action* and *Early Years Action Plus* in early education settings). The '*Action Plus*' approach will involve external specialists and is equivalent to stage 3 of the old model.

Assessment

A formal statutory assessment of a child's needs is undertaken by the LEA where the child's needs have not been met by the school-based strategies (known as *School Action* and *Action Plus*). The assessment enables the LEA to determine the special education provision required. This assessment was Stage 4 of the process under the 5-stage approach. In practice informal non-statutory assessment may take place at any time. Where a child is identified as having severe learning difficulties it is possible for the LEA to move straight to a statutory assessment.

Education Act 1996, s 323

(1) Where a local education authority are of the opinion that a child for whom they are responsible falls, or probably falls, within subsection (2), they shall serve a notice on the child's parent informing him—
(a) that they are considering whether to make an assessment of the child's educational needs,
(b) of the procedure to be followed in making the assessment,
(c) of the name of the officer of the authority from whom further information may be obtained, and

(d)   of the parent's right to make representations, and submit written evidence, to the authority within such period (which must not be less than 29 days beginning with the date on which the notice is served) as may be specified in the notice.

(2) A child falls within this subsection if—
(a)   he has special educational needs, and
(b)   it is necessary for the authority to determine the special educational provision which any learning difficulty he may have calls for.

...

(6)   Where, at any time after serving a notice under subsection (1), a local education authority decide not to assess the educational needs of the child concerned they shall give notice in writing to the child's parent of their decision.

- *What is the test which the LEA must rely on in deciding whether or not to make a statutory assessment of a particular child?*

The LEA should make a decision within six weeks of issuing the notice (or receiving a request for an assessment from, for example, the child's parent – see below).

Where the LEA decides to proceed with an assessment under this section the LEA must give written notice to the child's parent. If the LEA decides not to proceed the parent can appeal to SENT and then to the High Court.

An example of such a case is *H v Kent County Council and the Special Educational Needs Tribunal* [2000] ELR 660. The appellant was the father of a 10-year-old girl who suffered from epilepsy. She had medical and educational difficulties which were fully documented in a number of reports from various specialists including educational psychologists. She had been on the LEA's SEN Register since she was 5 years old, from which time her condition had been monitored. In May 1998 when she was 8 years old the LEA agreed to carry out a second statutory assessment, but did not do so, and in January 1999 in effect refused to make a statutory assessment. The appellant appealed to the SENT, which concluded that it was not necessary for the LEA to undertake a further statutory assessment of his daughter's needs. The appellant appealed to the High Court.

H v Kent County Council and SENT [2000] ELR 660

Grigson J: (42) I ... the aggrieved party should be able to identify the basis of the decision with sufficient clarity to be able to determine whether or not the Tribunal had gone wrong in law. Further, that statements of reasons should deal in short form with the substantial issues raised in order that the parties can understand why the decision has been reached; in other words, what evidence is rejected and what evidence is accepted.

(43) Here the question that the Tribunal had to decide was whether it was necessary for the local education authority to make a statutory assessment and, consequently, a statement. The question can be put in another form. The local education authority have a complex grading system in respect of special educational needs. There is a scale running from 1 to 6.

The policy is that no statutory assessment will take place and so no statement be made, unless the child is within level 4. Abigail was at level 3.

...

It is not possible to ascertain from this decision how the Tribunal viewed the evidence of Dr Muter and Dr McCormick and the recommendations they made, based upon their findings. I add that the assertion in the Tribunal's judgment that there had been no substantial change in circumstances since the previous statutory assessment is unsustainable, unless the evidence of Dr Muter and Dr McCormick was simply rejected. There was no such finding.

...

(53) I was referred to the standard textbook, de Smith, Woolf and Jowell *Judicial Review of Administrative Action* (Sweet & Maxwell). At p 466 of that book, the following passage appears:

The reasons must generally state the Tribunal's material finding of fact and meet the substance of the principle arguments that the Tribunal was required to consider.

(54) This decision does not meet those requirements and such an omission is, in my judgment, a fundamental error of law.

(55) The matter does not end there, because the appellant goes on to argue, that no reasonable Tribunal, properly directing itself as to the evidence, could have reached the conclusion that Abigail did not require a statutory assessment of her special educational needs.

(56) It is argued on the basis of the judgment of the Court of Appeal in the case of *R v Lord Saville of Newdigate and Others ex p A and Others* [1999] 4 All ER 860, that to refuse Abigail statutory assessment is a breach of her fundamental right to effective education under Art 2 of Protocol I of the Convention. It is argued that in these circumstances where the court has to consider the rationality of the decision of a Tribunal, the threshold to be achieved so as to trigger the court's intervention should be lower because of a potential or actual breach of a fundamental right being involved.

...

(58) That the right to effective education is a fundamental right is plain. Here, as a matter of fact, we are not dealing with deprivation of Abigail's right to education. What is at issue is the machinery by which her educational needs are to be assessed and subsequently met.

(59) In considering this part of the application, I accept and adopt the reasoning of the European Commission of Human Rights in the application of *Simpson v UK* (Application No 14688/89) (1989) 64 DR 188. I am not going to go through that.

(60) The appellant relies on the decision of the European Court of Human Rights in *Belgian Linguistics Case (No 2)* (1968) I EHRR 252. I think it is sufficient to refer to two matters in the headnote:
(a)   In spite of its negative formulation, the first sentence of Article 2 of the Protocol did enshrine a 'right'.
(b)   The negative formulation indicated, however, that the Contracting Parties did not recognise such a right to education as would have required them to establish at their own expense, or to subsidise, education of any particular type or at any particular level.

(61) It follows that whatever test is applied, I do not accept that the local education authority's refusal to make a statutory assessment or the Tribunal's rejections of the appeal amount to a breach of the right to education enshrined in Protocol I.

Parent's right to request an assessment

The child's parent can ask the LEA to arrange for an assessment to be made where no statement is maintained.

Education Act 1996, s 329

(1) Where—
(a) the parent of a child for whom a local education authority are responsible but for whom no statement is maintained under section 324 asks the authority to arrange for an assessment to be made in respect of the child under section 323,
(b) no such assessment has been made within the period of six months ending with the date on which the request is made, and
(c) it is necessary for the authority to make an assessment under that section, the authority shall comply with the request.

(2) If in any case where subsection (1)(a) and (b) applies the authority determine not to comply with the request—
(a) they shall give notice in writing of that fact to the child's parent, and
(b) the parent may appeal to the Tribunal against the determination.

....

The LEA must comply with the request where it is 'necessary' for the authority to make an assessment under s 323 of the EA 1996.

The following are examples of cases where a parent's request has been refused and the parent has appealed to SENT.

[2000] ELR 632, 39/00

X, a girl of 11, had specific learning difficulties. The tribunal concluded that although she had made progress in reading, she had made little or none in spelling. The information about her abilities and performance in maths was confusing. The evidence of X's overall needs was incomplete and confused, the picture given by the LEA was unclear and the tribunal did not consider that X's present school, let alone her secondary school, could plan appropriately without sufficient information. Accordingly, the tribunal considered that an assessment was urgently needed and ordered the LEA to arrange one.

[2001] ELR 120, 60/00

X was a boy of 16 with medical problems, low esteem and a record of poor school attendance. His mother appealed against the LEA's decision not to arrange an assessment. X was enrolled at a sixth form college. The LEA contended that the tribunal had no jurisdiction, because X was no longer within the definition of a 'child' in s 312(5). It argued that the decision in *S v Essex County Council and the Special Educational Needs Tribunal* [2000] ELR 718, where the tribunal was held to have jurisdiction, should be distinguished because the child in that case had a statement. The tribunal held that it had jurisdiction, and dismissed the application to strike out, on the basis that X came within the definition of 'child' at the date of the LEA's decision.

School's right to request an assessment

This right was introduced by SENDA 2001, s 8. Previously where a school had requested a statutory assessment and the LEA refused to agree to undertake one, neither the school nor the child's parents had a right of appeal to SENT. This was problematic where the parents were initially unable or unwilling to request a statutory assessment for their child.

Education Act 1996, s 329A

(1) This section applies if—

(a)   a child is a registered pupil at a relevant school (whether or not he is a child in respect of whom a statement is maintained under section 324),

(b)   the responsible body asks the local education authority to arrange for an assessment to be made in respect of him under section 323, and

(c)   no such assessment has been made within the period of six months ending with the date on which the request is made.

(2) If it is necessary for the authority to make an assessment or further assessment under section 323, they must comply with the request.

...

(7) If, as a result of this section, a local education authority decide to make an assessment under section 323, they must give written notice to the child's parent and to the responsible body which made the request, of the decision and of their reasons for making it.

(8) If, after serving a notice under subsection (3), the authority decide not to assess the educational needs of the child—

(a)   they must give written notice of the decision and of their reasons for making it to his parent and to the responsible body which made the request, and

(b)   the parent may appeal to the Tribunal against the decision.

...

(11) 'Relevant school' means—

(a)   a maintained school,

(b)   a maintained nursery school,

(c)   a pupil referral unit,

(d)   a city technology college,

(e)   a city college for the technology of the arts,

(f)   a city academy.

(12) 'The responsible body' means—

(a)   in relation to a maintained nursery school or a pupil referral unit, the head teacher, and

(b)   in relation to any other relevant school, the proprietor. ...

- *Where the school's request is refused who has a right of appeal to the SENT?*

Statutory assessment procedure

The assessment itself is governed by Sch 26 of the EA 1996 and the Education (Special Educational Needs) (England) (Consolidation) Regulations 2001, SI 2001/3455. The 1994 Regulations (SI 1994/1047) continue to apply to Wales.

Where the child is also 'in need' under the Children Act 1989 a single assessment may be undertaken (Children Act 1989, Sch 2, para 3, as amended).

Normally the LEA must seek advice from the child's parent, educational advice, medical advice, psychological advice, advice from social services and other relevant advice as to the child's needs etc. Schedule 26, for example, makes it an offence in certain circumstances where a parent does not ensure that their child attends a medical examination.

Education Act 1996, Sch 26

4(1) Where a local education authority propose to make an assessment, they may serve a notice on the parent of the child concerned requiring the child's attendance for examination in accordance with the provisions of the notice.

(2) The parent of a child examined under this paragraph may be present at the examination if he so desires.

(3) A notice under this paragraph shall—
(a) state the purpose of the examination,
(b) state the time and place at which the examination will be held,
(c) name an officer of the authority from whom further information may be obtained,
(d) inform the parent that he may submit such information to the authority as he may wish, and
(e) inform the parent of his right to be present at the examination.

5(1) Any parent who fails without reasonable excuse to comply with any requirements of a notice served on him under paragraph 4 commits an offence if the notice relates to a child who is not over compulsory school age at the time stated in it as the time for holding the examination.

(2) A person guilty of an offence under this paragraph is liable on summary conviction to a fine not exceeding level 2 on the standard scale.

6.   STATEMENT OF SEN

After the statutory assessment has been completed the LEA decides whether or not to issue or continue with a statement of special educational needs.

Education Act 1996, s 324(1)

If, in the light of an assessment under section 323 of any child's educational needs and of any representations made by the child's parent in pursuance of Schedule 27, it is necessary for the local education authority to determine the special educational provision which any learning difficulty he may have calls for, the authority shall make and maintain a statement of his special educational needs.

- *What is the statutory test which should be used by the LEA in deciding whether to make or maintain a statement of special educational needs?*

Where the LEA considers that a statement is not necessary the parent has a right of appeal to SENT.

Education Act 1996, s 325

(1) If, after making an assessment under section 323 of the educational needs of any child for whom no statement is maintained under section 324, the local education authority do not propose to make such a statement, they shall give notice in writing of their decision, and of the effect of subsection (2) below, to the child's parent.

(2) In such a case, the child's parent may appeal to the Tribunal against the decision.

...

The following are examples of cases where the parent has appealed to SENT.

[2000] ELR 632, 40/00

X was a boy of 10, for whom a statement in lieu had been issued. He had complex difficulties, was making slow progress both educationally and socially, and had poor language comprehension. The tribunal concluded that X's learning difficulties were severe and complex, ordered the LEA to make a statement and expressed the view that it should anticipate the circumstances he would encounter at secondary school.

[2000] ELR 105, 5/00

X, a girl of 11, had a rare bone abnormality which resulted in her being of very small stature. Although bright, she had some gaps in her knowledge as a result of the teaching at her previous school. X's parents considered that she was well placed at her present school, but feared that without a statement she could not be guaranteed the support she needed. They appealed against the LEA's refusal to make a statement. The tribunal concluded that X needed to receive the in-class support she was currently receiving, and would need physical adaptations to allow her to participate in practical lessons. All that could be made available from the school's existing resources. The appeal was dismissed.

See also *R v Hereford and Worcester County Council, ex p Lashford* [1987] 1 FLR 508.

Form and content of the statement

Education Act 1996, s 324

...

(2) The statement shall be in such form and contain such information as may be prescribed.

(3) In particular, the statement shall—
(a) give details of the authority's assessment of the child's special educational needs, and
(b) specify the special educational provision to be made for the purpose of meeting those needs, including the particulars required by subsection (4).

(4) The statement shall—
(a) specify the type of school or other institution which the local education authority consider would be appropriate for the child,
(b) if they are not required under Schedule 27 to specify the name of any school in the statement, specify the name of any school or institution (whether in the United Kingdom or elsewhere) which they consider would be appropriate for the child and should be specified in the statement, and
(c) specify any provision for the child for which they make arrangements under section 319 and which they consider should be specified in the statement.

(4A) Subsection (4)(b) does not require the name of a school or institution to be specified if the child's parent has made suitable arrangements for the special educational provision specified in the statement to be made for the child.

(5) Where a local education authority maintain a statement under this section, then—
(a) unless the child's parent has made suitable arrangements, the authority—
   (i)   shall arrange that the special educational provision specified in the statement is made for the child, and
   (ii) may arrange that any non-educational provision specified in the statement is made for him in such manner as they consider appropriate, and
(b) if the name of a [maintained school] is specified in the statement, the governing body of the school shall admit the child to the school.

...

(6) Subsection (5)(b) does not affect any power to exclude from a school a pupil who is already a registered pupil there.

....

Subsection (4A) was inserted by SENDA 2001, s 9. This provision is likely to apply where the child's parent has arranged for the child to attend an independent school, or to educate the child at home.

Schedule 27 to the EA 1996 and regulations (Education (Special Educational Needs) (England) (Consolidation) Regulations 2001, SI 2001/3455) contain more detail on the procedures for making and maintaining statements.

• *Bearing in mind s 324(6) of the EA 1996, consider the guidance contained in Circular 10/99 (Social Inclusion: Pupil Support) on exclusions in such circumstances.*

The Education (Special Educational Needs) (England) (Consolidation) Regulations 2001, SI 2001/3455 contains details of the procedure and time limits applicable to all stages of the process. For example, a draft statement should be issued within two weeks of the decision to statement, and a final statement within a further eight weeks. The total time from the beginning of the assessment process to the issuing of a final statement is supposed to be twenty-six weeks.

A useful summary of the time limits applicable to the assessment and statementing process is contained in the SEN Code of Practice 2001.

CODE OF PRACTICE SUMMARY

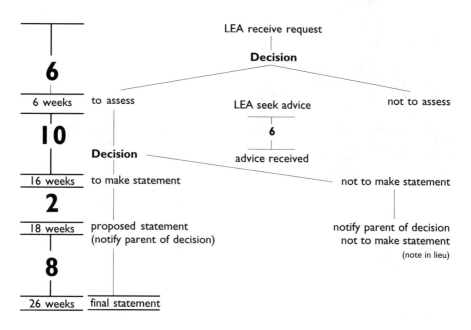

Form of the statement

The statement must be in the form prescribed in Schedule 2 to the regulations (SI 2001/3455). The statement must follow the format and contain the information required by the regulations (reg 16). The Code of Practice provides the following guidance on the contents of a statement.

Writing the Statement

Where an LEA, having made an assessment of a child, decide to make a statement, they shall serve a copy of a proposed statement and a written notice on the child's parent

within two weeks of the date on which the assessment was completed.
See Education Act 1996, Sch 27 and the Education (Special Educational Needs) (England) (Consolidation) Regulations 2001

8.29   The notice must be in the form prescribed in Part B of the Schedule to the Regulations. The statement of special educational needs must follow the format and contain the information prescribed by the Regulations (see Schedule 2 to the Regualtions):

Part 1 *Introduction:* The child's name and address and date of birth. The child's home language and religion. The names and address(es) of the child's parents.

Part 2 *Special Educational Needs* (learning difficulties): Details of each and every one of the child's special educational needs as identified by the LEA during statutory assessment and of the advice received and attached as appendices to the statement.

Part 3 *Special Educational Provision:* The special educational provision that the LEA consider necessary to meet the child's special educational needs.
(a)   The *objectives that* the special educational provision should aim to meet.
(b)   The *special educational provision* which the LEA consider appropriate to meet the needs set out in Part 2 and to meet the objectives.
(c)   The arrangements to be made for monitoring progress in meeting those objectives, particularly for setting short-term targets for the child's progress and for reviewing his or her progress on a regular basis.

Part 4 *Placement:* The type and name of school where the special educational provision set out in Part 3 is to be made or the LEA's arrangements for the education to be made otherwise than in school.

Part 5 *Non-Educational Needs:* All relevant non-educational needs of the child as agreed between the health services, social services or other agencies and the LEA.

Part 6 *Non-Educational Provision:* Details of relevant non-educational provision required to meet the non-educational needs of the child as agreed between the health services and/or social services and the LEA, including the agreed arrangements for its provision.

Signature and date

8.30   All the advice obtained and taken into consideration during the assessment process must be attached as appendices to the statement:

The advice appended to the statement must include:
1.   Parental evidence
2.   Educational advice
3.   Medical advice
4.   Psychological advice
5.   Social services advice
6.   Any other advice, such as the views of the child, which the LEA or any other body from whom advice is sought consider desirable. In particular, where the child's parent is a serving member of the armed forces, advice from the Service Children's Education (SCE).

Parts 2 and 3 of the statement are particularly important because they specify the educational needs of the child and the educational provision required to meet those needs which should be provided by the LEA. The LEA is not legally required to provide for the non-educational needs of a child. Therefore, it is important whether a particular need is categorised as 'educational' or 'non-educational'.

The primary duty to arrange for therapy specified in a statement rests on the LEA (see above *R v Harrow Borough Council, ex p M* [1997] ELR 62; *R v Brent and Harrow Health Authority, ex p Harrow London Borough Council* [1997] ELR 187; *R v Hillingdon London Borough Council, ex p Governing Body of Queensmead School* [1997] ELR 331).

Contents of the statement

The contents of the statement from the parent's perspective should be as specific as possible in order that the parent can monitor effectively what provision is being made for their child. However, LEAs often prefer to keep some flexibility in the provision.

L v Clarke and Somerset County Council [1998] ELR 129

Laws J: ...

In my judgment a requirement that the help to be given should be specified in a statement in terms of hours per week is not an absolute and universal precondition of the legality of any statement. One can appreciate the force of the comment in the guidance. There will be some cases where flexibility should be retained. However it is plain that the statute requires a very high degree of specificity. The main legislation itself (and I refer to s 324(3)(a) and (b)) requires the statement to give details of the child's special educational needs and to specify the provision to be made.

The terms of form B in the regulation, part of which I have read, are plainly mandatory and it seems to me that in very many cases it will not be possible to fulfil the requirement to specify the special educational provision considered appropriate to meet the child's needs, including specification of staffing arrangements and curriculum, unless hours per week are set out.

The real question, as it seems to me, in relation to any particular statement is whether it is so specific and so clear as to leave no room for doubt as to what has been decided is necessary in the individual case. Very often a specification of hours per week will no doubt be necessary and there will be a need for that to be done.

In *P v Swansea City and County* (2000) Times, 1 December, Elias J held that the tribunal's decision was too vague. In particular the tribunal had failed to direct which parts of the national curriculum should be excluded or how assessments of progress would be modified.

SPECIAL EDUCATIONAL NEEDS

* *What is meant by special educational needs in Part 2 of the statement? (see definitions above)*

Dyslexia was not legally recognised as constituting a learning difficulty and therefore a special educational need until the case of *R v Hampshire Education Authority, ex p J* (1985) 84 LGR 547) (*Butterworths Law of Education* (9th edn, 1997) vol 5, para F 87).

SPECIAL EDUCATIONAL PROVISION

- *What is meant by special educational provision in Part 3 of the statement? (see definitions above)*

- *Does it include speech therapy, occupational therapy, or physiotherapy? Does it include stress free transport to school? Does it include the installation of a lift in a primary school?*

B v Isle of Wight Council [1997] ELR 279

McCullough J: Both parties agreed that occupational therapy and physiotherapy would help A to benefit properly from her education. The tribunal did not disagree and, by implication at least, they accepted that they would assist her with PE and music and movement and games, which the tribunal must have known were part of the National Curriculum. That, however, was not the question. Spectacles and hearing aids assist those who need them in every classroom lesson. What has to be considered is the nature of the provision itself.

Speech therapy called for consideration in *R v Lancashire County Council ex p CM (A Minor)* [1989] 2 FLR 279. M was a boy with a severe language problem; he needed intensive speech therapy. The Court of Appeal, affirming the decision of the Divisional Court, said at p 301:

> ... to teach a child who has never been able to communicate by language ... seems to us just as much educational provision as to teach a child to communicate by writing.

The therapy was teaching M to speak. The reports in this case do not suggest that the therapies will teach A PE or music and movement or any other school subject, whether part of the National Curriculum or not. As Dr Watson said, they are directed to improving muscle tone, balance and co-ordination, tracking and motor and perceptual skills. All the reports are to the same general effect. Improve these things and benefits result: improved writing, visual ability, more confidence and co-operation, etc. There is nothing to suggest that the tribunal disagreed with any of that. But that, as I have said, was not the question. The writers of the reports on which Mr Brown relies appear to have thought that because the proposed therapy would have undoubted educational benefits, and was intended to do so, this made the therapy itself educational rather than non-educational.

For these reasons I do not accept Mr Brown's submission that the tribunal came to a conclusion 'contrary to the evidence'. I see no contradiction between the *evidence* and their conclusion. The departure came in not accepting the *opinions* expressed in the reports on which Mr Brown relies. The tribunal was entitled, indeed bound, to make its own judgment.

The tribunal held (conclusions para 2e) that the physiotherapy was designed to enable A properly to benefit from the regime to be provided for her as described in part III of her statement. Not only was that a conclusion fairly open to them on the material before them, I would go so far as to say that it was the only reasonable conclusion to reach. No doubt the council were right to accept that some occupational therapy and some physiotherapy might be 'educational' in some cases, but I cannot think that this would be other than exceptional.

See also extract from case above.

Bromley London Borough v SENT [1999] ELR 260

Sedley LJ: ... S is now 12 years old. At his birth on 4 July 1986 he suffered severe trauma which has resulted in life-long mental and physical incapacitation. S's disability, and the central question of law arising from it, are set out in the following passage of Owen J's judgment:

> To understand the problem which S presented and presents to his parents and to the LEA it is necessary to have some realisation of S's disability. S, who is now 12 years of age, has spastic, quadriplegic cerebral palsy, epilepsy and impaired vision. He cannot walk, sit up or stand and is totally reliant on adults for all his mobility needs with the exception of head movements. He is totally reliant on adults for dressing, washing, toileting and feeding: he cannot feed himself. At most he understands some words and phrases but only in contexts which are very familiar to him. DC says that S has no speech. Others say that he communicates "... through simple vocalising, facial expressions and some body movement. He is considerably *developmentally* delayed and much of his functioning is said to be *below* the 12-month level" (emphasis added).

...

The central issue is the meaning and ambit of 'special educational provision' in Part IV of the Education Act 1996. It arises out of the tribunal's conclusion that S's acknowledged need for physiotherapy, occupational therapy and speech and language therapy formed part of his special educational needs, with the consequence that the provision of these therapies was part of the special educational provision which the LEA must make for him. This, as will be seen, had major consequences for S's placement and, in turn, for the cost to the LEA of providing for his special educational needs.

...

The concrete challenge offered by S's parents to the statement was to the proposal to keep him at R School. Their reason, however — and this is what raises the present question of law — was that S's needs for therapy out of school hours and out of term-time were, at least in part, educational needs, and that these could not be addressed at a day school such as R School. Their contention was that the special educational provision which the LEA was obliged to make for S was residential provision throughout the year.

...

The material conclusions of the SENT were, first, that physiotherapy, occupational therapy and speech therapy were all part of S's educational needs, and that part 2 and 3 of the statement should be correspondingly amended; and secondly, that S should be placed at C School, with an appropriate amendment to part 4.

Before us, as before Owen J, the principal critique advanced by the London Borough of Bromley of the tribunal's decision is that it classifies or treats as educational provision forms of treatment which in law cannot be so classified or treated.

...

In *G v Wakefield Metropolitan District Council and Another* (1998) 96 LGR 69, Laws J (as he then was) said:

It will be obvious that, notwithstanding Parliament's lexicon in section 312, the concepts of 'learning difficulty' and 'special educational provision' are not tightly defined. The Court of Appeal has held in *R v Lancashire County Council ex p Moore* (1989) 86 LGR 567 that speech therapy may or does fall within the meaning of 'special educational provision'. What I think clear is that measures taken by a local education authority which are subject to appeal before the SENT under section 326 must be correctly related to the child's learning difficulties. Economic problems faced by the child's parents, where for example different and perhaps more spacious living accommodation would in an ideal world be suitable for the family because of the child's physical disabilities, are not ordinarily within the remit of the SENT. Nor are difficulties associated with the parent's disabilities, where the effect is that the child is, in physical terms, more difficult to look after. Problems of this kind, in my judgment, will generally fall to be dealt with not under the 1996 Act, but (so far as they may be met by public provision) under social welfare measures made in other statutes and delegated legislation. However, while that is, in my judgment, the general position, I should say that I certainly accept that there is no hard edge. As a matter of common sense and ordinary human experience conditions in the home are almost always bound to have some effect, for better or worse, on a child's learning capacity and educational chances. That is a general fact of family life; but for present purposes it must be distinguished from circumstances, which I acknowledge it is clearly possible to envisage, where some kinds of day to day domestic problems may directly relate to the child's learning difficulties. Such a direct relation must in my judgment be shown in order to involve such problems in the tribunal's jurisdiction under section 326.

This exegesis, helpful as it is, poses a further question in the present case: are the therapies which S needs directly related to his learning difficulties? This, once again, must be principally a matter of judgment first for the LEA and then for the SENT. If it is contested as a question of law, it is to the statute that the court must turn for the answer.

...

I prefer Mr Gordon's approach to the meaning of 'special educational provision' in Part IV of the Act. Whether a form of help needed by the child falls within this description is a question primarily for the LEA and secondarily for the SENT's expert judgment. If, but only if, the SENT has gone wrong in law will the High Court overset its judgment.

...

The tribunal's conclusion that physiotherapy, occupational therapy and speech therapy were all measures which related directly to S's learning difficulties, and therefore amounted to a special educational provision, was a conclusion properly open to it, provided that it is not read as meaning that these therapies were exclusively educational. What mattered was that in the tribunal's judgment the therapeutic input listed in part 3 could not be delivered by the combination of R School and P Home consistently with S's other needs, but could be so delivered by C School. In brief, S's education called for day-long and year-round attention to many of his physical needs.

In *R v Hereford and Worcester County Council, ex p P* [1992] 2 FCR 732, McCullough J held that the LEA was under an obligation to provide non-stressful transport to a five-year-old boy with Down's syndrome. He stated that it forms part of the non-educational provision for the child and should be specified in Part 6 of the statement of special educational needs.

In *R v Lambeth London Borough Council, ex p M* (1995) 94 LGR 122, the court held that the provision of a lift at a mainstream primary school to enable a disabled pupil to use the science room and library on the first floor could not be regarded as a provision for an educational need. If a lift was necessary, it was necessary to assist the pupil's mobility and not as a special educational provision.

- *Would M now have a claim under the Disability Discrimination Act 1995?*

PLACEMENT

The type of school that is appropriate for the child should be specified in Part 4 of the statement. The name of a particular school may be included.

Education Act 1996, Sch 27, para 3(3)

Choice of school

3(1) Every local education authority shall make arrangements for enabling [*Wales*] a parent on whom a copy of a proposed statement has been served under paragraph 2 [*England*] [a parent—
(a) on whom a copy of a proposed statement has been served under paragraph 2,
(b) on whom a copy of a proposed amended statement has been served under paragraph 2A, or
(c) on whom an amendment notice has been served under paragraph 2A which contains a proposed amendment about—
   (i)   the type or name of a school or institution, or
   (ii) the provision made for the child concerned under arrangements made under section 319,

to be specified in the statement,]

to express a preference as to [the maintained school] at which he wishes education to be provided for his child and to give reasons for his preference.

   ...

(3) Where a local education authority make a statement in a case where the parent of the child concerned has expressed a preference in pursuance of such arrangements as to the school at which he wishes education to be provided for his child, they shall specify the name of that school in the statement unless—
(a) the school is unsuitable to the child's age, ability or aptitude or to his special educational needs, or
(b) the attendance of the child at the school would be incompatible with the provision of efficient education for the children with whom he would be educated or the efficient use of resources.

   ...

Note that from 1 January 2002, different provisions apply to England and Wales. The provisions that operate in Wales were those that formerly applied in England.

Two issues have been of particular concern to parents and have resulted in much litigation. First, the extent to which the parent's wishes should be taken into account;

and second whether an LEA must name a school. An incidental issue relates to the payment of fees where an independent school is named.

(1) Parental wishes

R v Surrey County Council Education Committee, ex p H (1984) 83 LGR 219 at p 235:

> There is no question of Parliament having placed the local authority under an obligation to provide a child with the best possible education. There is no duty on the authority to provide such a Utopian system or to educate him or her to his or her maximum potential.

This was reiterated by Sedley J in *R v Cheshire County Council, ex p C* [1998] ELR 66 at 78 where he stated:

> ... there is nothing in the statutory scheme which calls upon the local education authority to specify the optimum available provision and much in its general duty of financial husbandry to entitle it to choose the least expensive of the appropriate options.

In *Surrey County Council v P and P* [1997] ELR 516 Kay J stated:

> Once a conclusion had been reached that each of the two alternatives would be appropriate to the special education needs of a child, the parents' choice would prevail unless either of the exceptions set out in Sch 10 [now Sch 27], para 3(3) applied. Where it is necessary to consider whether they apply, then it seems contrary to the Act to weigh at that stage advantages to be gained by the child in considering whether the child's attendance at the school would be incompatible with the provision of efficient education for the other children with whom he would be educated or incompatible with the efficient use of resources.
> ...
> If the situation was that one alternative would result in significant additional expenditure, then provided both schools were appropriate for the child's special educational needs, the local authority would be entitled to justify sending the child to a school other than that of the parents' choice. To hold otherwise would, in my judgment, be to oblige the local education authority to make the best possible education available and as Latham J pointed out ... in *S v Special Educational Needs Tribunal and the City of Westminster* 'Parliament has imposed an obligation to meet the needs of the child and no more'.

C v Buckinghamshire County Council and SENT [1999] ELR 179

[N, who was born on 17 June 1982, was seriously dyslexic and had special educational needs.]

Sedley LJ: The tribunal noted the wish of Mr and Mrs C that N should remain at Z School, an independent special needs school, where he now was. It considered this proposal against that of the authority, which believed that N's needs would be better addressed in the specialist unit for children with specific learning difficulties at Y School, a maintained secondary school. The tribunal formed the clear view that a residential placement such as Z School provided was not necessarily the best thing for N, and that his needs could be met at Y School, where (they concluded) his development and future progress made it appropriate to place him. No cost or resource factors entered into this decision: the tribunal was told that because of the special support N would need at Y School the cost implications were much the same whichever school was chosen.

...

For a child with special educational needs the statutory scheme is very different. A series of quite onerous obligations comes to rest upon the local education authority, calling for a series of difficult decisions which are plainly intended by Parliament to be geared so far as practicable to the child's individual needs. The parents' voice is heard in this process if anything more clearly than in the ordinary school selection process; but where Sch 27, para 3 does not make parental choice determinative, it is because the child's needs or the efficient use of resources point elsewhere. If the difference between the parents and the local education authority cannot be resolved by negotiation, the tribunal is there to resolve it. It is likewise required by the Act to follow a process of inquiry and reasoning directed to meeting the child's needs, which both values and limits parental choice. In such a process, the reasons for the parental choice are of the first importance; the bare fact of parental choice, which in the nature of things is simply a function of their reasons, is logically of only marginal significance. What mattered in the present case, for example, was that the parents considered that the achievement of functional literacy was more important for N than preparation for college, and that he was not ready for education in a mainstream school. All of this the tribunal considered.

...

I see no basis in the statute for requiring a tribunal which finds that two schools are adequate but that one is markedly more suitable than the other to the child's special needs to ignore the difference and abdicate its judgment in favour of the parents'. To do so, since a s 9 choice may lawfully include an independent school, would be to extend the mandatory range of parental choice beyond that to which it is explicitly limited by Sch 27, para 3(1).

...

Thorpe LJ: That said, it is clear from s 324(4)(a) of the Education Act 1996 that the LEA has a duty to ensure that a child with special educational needs is placed at a school that is 'appropriate'. It is not enough for the school to be merely adequate. To determine if the school is appropriate, an assessment must be made both of what it offers and what the child needs. Unless what the school offers matches what the child needs, it is unlikely to be appropriate. The assessment of the child's needs necessarily imports elements of a welfare judgment. If there are two schools offering facilities and standards that exceed the test of adequacy, then I would hope that ordinarily speaking the better would be judged appropriate, assuming no mismatch between specific facilities and specific needs. Parental preference obviously has a part to play in the assessment of what is appropriate. In a case where there appears to be parity of cost and parity of facilities, parental preference may be the decisive factor. But it would be wrong to elevate parental preference to the height that Mr Bowen appeared to contend for in his submissions. A bare preference might be ill-informed or capricious. In practice, parental preference may mean a fair opportunity to the parents to contend by evidence and argument for one school in preference to another. Therefore, preferences must be reasoned to enable the parent to demonstrate that they rest on a sound foundation of accurate information and wise judgment.

See also the Court of Appeal's comments on parental preference in *L v Worcestershire County Council and Hughes* [2000] ELR 674 (above).

In *B v Harrow London Borough Council* [2000] ELR 109 the House of Lords held that, in determining whether the education of a child with a statement of special educational needs at a school in a neighbouring authority preferred by the parents was incompatible with the efficient use of resources (Education Act 1996, Sch 27, para 3(3)(b)), the LEA responsible for assessing the child's needs should only take into account its own resources. (See also *Oxfordshire County Council v B* (unreported, 2001), CA.)

(2) The LEA is not under an absolute duty to name a school
The Court of Appeal heard the following three cases together, which were primarily concerned with whether an LEA or SENT were required to name a particular school in Part 4 of the child's statement.

Richardson v Solihull Metropolitan Borough Council and SENT [1998] ELR 319

Beldam LJ: The question common to all three appeals [ie the appeal and the two immediately following] is whether, and in what circumstances, the tribunal is obliged to order a local education authority to specify the name of the school as part of the special educational provision to be made for a child who has special educational needs in a statement of those needs pursuant to s 324(1) of the 1996 Act.

...

On 1 October 1996 Mrs Richardson appealed against the statement disagreeing with the description of B's educational needs, the proposed special educational provision and contending that the authority were under a duty to name the Boston Higashi School in part 4. Before the tribunal the authority did not put forward a particular school or produce any evidence as to the suitability or availability of any other school.

White v London Borough of Ealing and SENT [1998] ELR 319

Beldam LJ: Mrs White was dissatisfied with the statements of special educational needs prepared by Ealing Borough Council (the authority) for her twin sons SW and DW. Both boys suffer from learning difficulties associated with autism. ... The tribunal concluded that neither Bradstow nor Higashi was appropriate, though it was of opinion that DW and SW required residential placements in order to develop their education and that it was appropriate for the authority to be fully responsible for funding the placements.

...

I would reject the submission that 'special educational provision' in s 324 by necessary implication includes the naming of a particular school in every case. 'Special educational provision' is defined in s 312(4):

...

Whilst this definition is clearly wide enough to include the naming of a particular school, it is not implicit that a school must be named. It is also clear from s 319 that an authority may make special educational provision in other ways than in a school.
Further it seems to me that the words in s 324(4)(b):

> ... which they consider would be appropriate for the child and should be specified in the statement,

require the authority only to specify the name of a school if it considers the school appropriate and that it should be specified. The authority thus has a discretion whether to name a school or not. Section 324(5) requires the authority to arrange that the special educational provision specified in the statement is made for the child unless the child's parent has made suitable arrangements and it is implicit in s 324(5)(b) that there may be cases in which the name of a maintained, grant-maintained or grant-maintained special school is not specified in the statement.

As to the position on appeal to the tribunal, I share the judge's view that it is inconceivable that Parliament would have required the tribunal to order the authority to name a particular school if it had not made it obligatory for the authority to do so.

Hereford and Worcestershire County Council v Lane [1998] ELR 319

Peter Gibson LJ: The primary questions raised in these appeals relate to the duties imposed on a local education authority (LEA) and a Special Educational Needs Tribunal (SENT) respectively in respect of the naming of a school in the statement of special educational needs of a child for whom special educational provision is to be made. First, is there an obligation on the LEA in the case of every such child to name a school, as contended for by the appellant parents in the *Richardson* and *White* cases? Secondly, is there an obligation on the SENT to which an appeal is made in a case where a school is not named by the LEA, or the school so named is rejected, to order the amendment of the statement by requiring the naming of a school, as those appellant parents also contend? Thirdly, where the school named by the LEA is considered by the SENT to be inappropriate but the school named by the parent is capable of meeting the child's educational needs, is the SENT obliged to order the amendment of the statement by naming the latter school, as is contended for by the respondent parent in the *Lane* case?

In my judgment it is therefore apparent from the statutory language that there is no absolute duty on the LEA in every case to name a school. I do not doubt that in most cases the circumstances would be such that the LEA, having specified the type of school which it considers appropriate, if it considers a particular school appropriate for a child will also consider that the school should be specified in the statement. As Miss Booth QC for the Richardson and the Lane parents rightly points out, the Code of Practice, to which regard should be had (s 313(2) and (3)), contemplates that there will be a school named in part 4 of the statement. But in accordance with the governing words of s 324(4), it is a matter for the judgment of the LEA whether that should be done in a particular case. The LEA will bear in mind that if a school is not named in the statement that in itself is a ground of appeal. But the very fact that it is expressly contemplated in s 326(1) and (4) that there may be cases where no school is named in the statement tends to provide support for the view that there is no absolute duty to name a school.

...

The fact that the LEA is not under an absolute duty to name a school in every case is a strong pointer to there being no duty on the SENT to require the LEA to name the school. To my mind the obvious intention of Parliament must be taken to be that the decision whether or not the SENT should require the LEA to name a school should be left to the judgment of the SENT applying the relevant criteria.

(3) It follows from the conclusion which I have reached on the second question that the SENT is not obliged to order the amendment of the statement by naming the school named by the parent even if that is capable of meeting the child's educational needs and the school named by the LEA is found by the SENT not to be appropriate. It must exercise its own judgment, and have regard to such matters as the duty on the LEA to avoid unreasonable expenditure and to use resources efficiently. It defies common sense that even though the school named by the parent is a considerably more expensive residential school and even though the SENT regards that school as providing far more than is needed, the SENT has no choice but to require the naming of the school of the parent's choice.

In *P v Swansea City and County* (2000) Times, 1 December, Elias J held that a Pupil Referral Unit could be named in a statement, although it was likely to be a relatively rare occurence.

(3) Payment of fees

In many of these cases parents want an independent school or non-maintained special school to be named in the statement. The school need not be in the UK (see above). If it is so named the LEA will be required to pay the school fees, including where necessary the cost of board and lodging (s 348 of the EA 1996).

In *R v Hackney London Borough, ex p GC* [1996] ELR 142, CA, the parents wished their child to attend an orthodox fee-paying Jewish school, which the LEA considered suitable for him provided that the services of a special needs assistant, for which they were willing to pay, were made available. The court held that the naming of the particular school in the statement could not, in the circumstances, be elevated into an undertaking to pay all the fees at the school.

(4) Special schools

Since 1980 there has been a decrease in the number of children attending special schools because of the increasing emphasis on integrating children with special educational needs into mainstream schools. Where the LEA decides that it is not appropriate for a child with special educational needs to be educated in a mainstream school the child will be educated in a special school. Most children attending a special school have a statement of special educational needs. A 'special school' is one which is specially organised to make special educational provision for pupils with special educational needs and is approved as such by the Secretary of State (s 337 of the EA 1996). The Secretary of State may also approve independent schools for 'statemented' children (s 347 of the EA 1996).

Therefore, children with special educational needs may attend mainstream schools, maintained special schools, non-maintained special schools or independent schools.

Review, amendment and reassessment

Parents can ask that the formal assessment be repeated for their 'statemented' child so long as six months have elapsed since the last assessment. The LEA should comply with the request if it concludes that it is necessary to make an assessment. If the LEA does not comply with the request then the parent can appeal to SENT. In any event the statement should be reviewed by the LEA every 12 months (s 328 of the EA 1996).

The Special Education Needs and Disability Act 2001 (s 10 and Sch 1) has amended Sch 27 of the EA 1996 and gives parents additional rights where the LEA is proposing to amend their child's statement.

7.   APPEALS AND REVIEWS

The Special Educational Needs Tribunal (SENT) was established by the Education Act 1993 and started hearing cases in September 1994. The number of appeals has more than doubled since its inception. SENT is based in London, but hearings are held around the country as and when required.

The constitution, powers and procedure of SENT are contained in the Education Act 1996 (ss 333-336) and in the Special Educational Needs Tribunal Regulations 2000, SI 2001/600. Its jurisdiction has been extended by SENDA 2001 to include most disability discrimination claims against schools, and it will be renamed the Special Educational Needs and Disability Tribunal (SENDIST).

The Education Bill 2001/02 provides for a separate tribunal in Wales from September 2002, which will be known as the Special Educational Needs Tribunal for Wales and will hear both SEN and disability discrimination.

The president has overall responsibility for the Tribunal's operation. Each tribunal has three members. The chairman is legally qualified and is assisted by two lay members who have knowledge or experience of either children with SEN or local government. The Tribunal is supervised by the Council on Tribunals.

Appeals

The right to appeal is granted to the parent rather than the child (*S v SENT and the City of Westminster* [1995] 1 WLR 1627). 'Parent' includes any person who has 'parental responsibility' under the Children Act 1989, and includes a foster parent (*Fairpo v Humberside County Council* [1997] 1 All ER 183).

The parent may appeal in the following situations.
–   where the LEA refuses a parent's request to carry out a formal assessment of their child (s 329 of the EA 1996)
–   where the LEA refuses the school's request to carry out a formal assessment of their child (s 329A(8) of the EA 1996)
–   where the LEA after making an assessment decides not to make a statement under s 324 (s 325 of the EA 1996)
–   where the parent disagrees with the contents of the statement eg the description of the child's SEN, the special education provision specified, or the fact that no school is named (s 326 of the EA 1996).
–   where the LEA refuses to reassess the child's educational needs more than six months after the last review (s 328 of the EA 1996)
–   where the LEA refuses to change the school named in the statement more than one year after the statement was made (s 326 of the EA 1996)
–   where the LEA reassess the child's educational needs but decides not to amend the statement (s 326 of the EA 1996)
–   where the LEA ceases to maintain a statement (Sch 27, para 11 to the EA 1996).
Where the LEA decides to cease to maintain a statement, the LEA is required to continue to maintain the statement until the outcome of any appeal is heard (Sch 27, para 11(5) of the EA 1996 inserted by SENDA 2001, s 6).

The following table shows the outcome of appeals according to type of appeal.

SENT Annual Report 1999/2000

Outcome of appeals

The following table shows the outcome of appeals decided during last year. I comment separately below on the outcome of appeals against the contents of a child's statement.

Appeals not involving contents of statements	Decisions issued in 1999/00					Decisions issued in 1998/99				
	Upheld*		Dismissed#		Total	Upheld*		Dismissed#		Total
Refusal to assess	185	63%	110	37	295	212	64%	118	36%	330
Refusal to statement	80	61%	52	39%	132	112	72%	43	28%	155
Refusal to re-assess	12	57%	9	43%	21	14	78%	4	22%	18
Cease to maintain	21	68%	10	32%	31	20	63%	12	38%	32
Totals	298	62%	181	38%	479	358	67%	177	33%	535
Contents of statement										
Parts 2 and/or 3, not 4	150	93%	12	7%	162	147	89%	18	11%	165
Parts 2, 3 and 4	373	93%	26	7%	399	296	91%	28	9%	324
Part 4 only	89	71%	37	29%	126	106	62%	65	38%	171
Refusal to change school named	19	70%	8	30%	27	12	55%	10	45%	22
Failure to name a school	2	67%	1	33%	3	2	67%	1	33%	3
Totals	633	88%	84	12%	717	563	82%	122	18%	685
Total decisions issued	931	78%	265	22%	1196	921	75%	299	25%	1220

*   Total upheld appeals includes those cases remitted to the LEA in the refusal to statement category

\#   Total dismissed appeals includes strike outs

Appeals against the contents of statements

A high proportion of the appeals against the contents of statements has consistently been recorded as upheld, and the trend is upward. Excluding those which relate exclusively to placement, ie appeals against the contents of Part 4 only, 93.2% were upheld last year, 90.5% in the previous year and 67.3% in the year before that. The impression given by these figures can be misleading.

The possible outcomes of this type of appeal are set out in s 326(3) of the EA 1996. The Tribunal can dismiss the appeal, order the authority to amend it or, which is rare, order the authority to cease to maintain the statement. Our statistics reflect these possibilities, which means that if the Tribunal orders any amendment at all the appeal has been upheld.

Powers of SENT

Education Act 1996, s 325

(3) On an appeal under this section, the Tribunal may—
(a) dismiss the appeal,
(b) order the local education authority to make and maintain such a statement, or
(c) remit the case to the authority for them to reconsider whether, having regard to any observations made by the Tribunal, it is necessary for the authority to determine the special educational provision which any learning difficulty the child may have calls for.

The Special Educational Needs Tribunal has a limited jurisdiction. Where the issue is a question of maladministration, for example delay by the LEA, a parent should complain to the Local Government Ombudsman (see chapter 8). A parent has no formal means of redress in certain circumstances, for example about the quality of the provision made by the LEA to meet their child's needs, or in relation to non-educational provision.

Appeal to the High Court

Both the parent and the LEA have the right to appeal on a point of law from SENT to the High Court. The Court of Appeal has stated that a challenge to a SENT decision should be by way of appeal rather than by judicial review (*R v SENT, ex p South Glamorgan County Council* [1996] ELR 326).

Review

The Special Educational Needs Tribunal can review its own decisions under the Special Educational Needs Tribunal Regulations 2001, SI 2001/600. Regulation 37:

(1) A party may apply to the Secretary of the Tribunal for the decision of the tribunal to be reviewed on the grounds that—
(a) its decision was wrongly made as a result of an error on the part of the tribunal staff;
(b) a party, who was entitled to be heard at a hearing but failed to appear or to be represented, had good and sufficient reason for failing to appear;
(c) there was an obvious error in the decision; or
(d) the interests of justice require.

8.   THE FUTURE OF SENT

The establishment of SENT in 1994 was a major improvement for parents on the local authority committees (similar to admission and exclusion appeal committees) which had previously heard such appeals. In a major piece of research Professor Neville Harris assessed the strengths and weaknesses of SENT.

Access to Justice

Chapter II, 'Conclusion'

... Overall, the SENT is making an important contribution to enabling many more parents and (although only indirectly, as we have seen) their children than before to secure access to justice in respect of disputes over SEN issues. The tribunal membership offers an appropriate blend of specialist knowledge and experience and legal skills. The SENT's independence, enhanced by operating on a national basis under a President, is a considerable strength, as is the tribunal's general openness of approach — exemplified by the President's publication of Digests of Decisions of the tribunal. The President and his staff have taken a number of steps to improve the operation of the tribunal and to develop both the skills and knowledge of panel members through training programmes. They have also taken very seriously their mission of providing an accessible, 'user-friendly' system, although the formality of some of the procedural arrangements and documentation which they have employed have undermined their own efforts at times, whilst also tending to emphasise that, in a basically adversarial situation, where impartiality is essential, and where the issues are often complex, a degree of impersonality and judicial detachment is necessary, even if off-putting to some.

...

Overall, the research confirms the benefits of representation for parents at tribunal hearings. Nevertheless, the effectiveness of such representation could be improved, and the continuing dialogue on this subject between the President and voluntary organisations is likely to be very useful.

There are two groups whose access to the tribunal seems to be limited. Ethnic minorities appear to be seriously under-represented among appellants (and also among the tribunal membership, as noted in Chapter 4). This might well reflect a general reluctance on the part of some ethnic minorities to utilise legal processes, and is a matter which the President ought to investigate, if he is not doing so already, through discussions with relevant bodies, including the Commission for Racial Equality. The other group has no direct access to the appeal system at all — children. The arguments relating to the fact that children are not parties to appeals (including appeals from the SENT to the High Court), nor are likely to be called as witnesses or asked for their views, were discussed at various points throughout the book. It was surprising, during the observations of hearings, to find that the child was in attendance in so few cases. At the very least, the tribunal ought to take greater account of the recommendation of the Code of Practice that the views of children are important and should be considered in the light of their age and understanding. Indeed, the ascertainment of those views ought to become a standard feature of SENT procedure. If the views were presented in writing, however, there would be doubts about whether they truly were the child's own. It might be necessary, therefore, for those views to be recorded by or in the presence of the 'named person', but it would be even better if there was a person acting in an equivalent role to that of the guardian ad litem in Children Act 1989 proceedings who could represent the child's interests independently, which does not happen at present.

...

Some LEAs believe that the new appeal system results in decisions which, while of benefit to the individual children concerned, place an undue financial burden on the LEA and may skew its allocation of resources by diverting a disproportionate amount to the education of children for whom there have been successful appeals, leaving less for special educational provision as a whole. There is, however, no good evidence that tribunals are acting other than fairly within the range of their powers and the statutory framework.

The 2001 Regulations (SI 2001/600) give the child who is the subject of the appeal the right to attend the hearing, and the LEA is required to ascertain the views of the child on the issues raised by the appeal.

In 1999 the DfEE announced that it intended to conduct a review of SENT, and in August 2000 a report on the first stage of the review was published.

Quinquennial Review of the Special Educational Needs Tribunal (August 2000)

Executive Summary

Introduction

1 This report sets out the findings from the first stage of the quinquennial review of the Special Educational Needs Tribunal (SENT) carried out between the end of 1999 and early 2000. Its main focus is to examine the case for the continued existence of the SENT and how its functions can be best fulfilled. It will be followed by Stage 2 of the review, which will examine a number of issues identified in this Stage 1 report, and analyse the adequacy of the SENT's financial and management systems to support its key objectives.

2 The Review Team concluded that the evidence pointed overall to the following main conclusions and recommendations.

Main conclusions and recommendations

(i)   There is a clear need for a formal system for resolving special educational needs (SEN) disputes between parents and local education authorities (LEAs). Both parents and LEAs welcomed a formal mechanism. Most respondents to the review questionnaire thought the SENT was the appropriate body to deliver the function. Those who disagreed did not offer an alternative but expressed a general desire to see greater use of conciliation arrangements.

(ii)   There is clear support for the interests of the child being a key factor in determining outcomes of the SENT and recognition of their achievements in focusing on the needs of the child in complex appeal cases. However, concern was expressed, largely by LEAs, that the SENT paid little attention to factors such as local SEN policies and priorities, LEA funding/resource constraints and difficulties in securing specialist help from other statutory bodies.

(iii) Although several comments were made on the time taken to resolve appeals, this time has reduced each year since the SENT was established. Respondents generally commented that the SENT was an improvement on the previous appeals system which involved a very lengthy appeals process.

(iv)   There was no evidence to suggest the SENT would not be needed in future. The general view is that its business will continue in the way it has to date, as its remit becomes well known.

(v)   There is no obvious case for changing the status of the SENT particularly in relation to its judicial functions which statute dictates must remain within the control of government. However, it is **recommended** that consideration is given in Stage 2 to whether the non-judicial administrative functions of the SENT are suitable for contracting out on efficiency grounds.

(vi) The government's decision to take steps to extend the remit of the SENT to encompass rights of redress in relation to disability discrimination in schools was noted. This will present a significant challenge for the SENT and its operational consequences will have to be kept under review.

(vii) The SENT was generally considered to be effective by respondents. Performance information from annual reports provide evidence of this showing year on year improvements in the time taken to deal with appeals while the number of appeals registered and decisions issued has risen steadily. Although the judicial cost of making an appeal has increased, this reflects factors such as increases in member expenses and increased accommodation costs in central London. The cost of administering the SENT has gone down.

(viii) Parents and voluntary sector representatives expressed concern that there was an imbalance of expertise and access to information between the parties. It is **recommended** that the SENT produce further guidance on evidence to be presented and ensure it is clear what facilities are available to parents whose first language is not English in order to help them access the Tribunal process. In addition, the Department should continue to support the role of Independent Parental Supporters and encourage Parent Partnership Services to target their services in schools.

(ix) A number of respondents to the consultation questionnaire expressed concern that panel decisions were inconsistent. While there was no firm evidence to support this, it is **recommended** that research into potential inconsistencies in panel decisions and the need for enhanced training and guidance to avoid this, be considered in Stage 2 of the review.

(x) The opportunity for early dialogue and conciliation between parties was recognised as beneficial in resolving SEN disputes and for contributing to the greater efficiency of the SENT. It is **recommended** that Stage 2 of the review should consider whether the Tribunal's remit should be extended to include a role in conciliation.

(xi) The review highlighted the difficulties that can arise when SENT decisions are not implemented. Although there was some support for the SENT having a role in the implementation of decisions this was more in terms of a progress-noting role rather than an enforcement role. No other tribunals have an enforcement role and there seems no good reason for the SENT to be an exception to this. It is however **recommended** that the Department explore ways to monitor implementation and explore the impact on LEAs that implementing decisions might have, particularly in relation to funding. In addition, Stage 2 of the Review should consider whether tribunals should take more account of LEA constraints when reaching their decisions.

The jurisdiction of SENT has been extended by the Special Educational Needs and Disability Act 2001 (SENDA 2001) to include disability discrimination claims against schools and LEAs. Note also that from January 2002 LEAs are required to provide a mediation service for parents (EA 1996, s 332B).

The Leggatt Review of Tribunals reported in 2001 (Tribunals for Users, One System, One Service). The report recommended the establishment of an Education and Regulatory tribunal within a unified Tribunals Service. This new tribunal would include SENT and its successor SENDIST.

However, this rights-based approach which focuses on individuals has some disadvantages.

Ann Blair 'Rights, duties and resources: the case of special educational needs' 12(3) Education and the Law 177 (2000) at 189–91

Conclusion: rethinking rights, duties and resources

Welfare rights theory of the 1970s and 1980s concentrated principally on the question of whether rules or discretion are better suited to determining need. In the case of the Social Fund we arrived at a position of accepting a discretion to refuse to meet acknowledged need. To some extent this is the Professional Treatment model; professionals work usually with finite resources and insofar as they are required to match their workloads to resources they will classify their caseload and prioritise within it, perhaps without acknowledging that some need will be unmet because it is not serious enough to attract scarce resources rather than because it is not genuine. In *Barry* it was accepted that, in community care, assessment of need can be consciously tailored to fit the resources available to meet it even where the legislation contains no explicit authority for this approach; a very different view to that taken in SEN (Palmer & Sunkin, 1998).

The system for meeting SEN has avoided some of the problems that have beset other systems for meeting need. This shows that the fulfilment of rights is well served by the separation of the professional judgement from the holder of the purse strings and through the support of an appeal system where a tribunal has the power to substitute an assessment of need with its own view of the merits (Harris, 1997; Simmons, 1998). Nevertheless rights-based systems do make it very difficult if not impossible to contain costs. Where resources are limited, an explicit method of balancing needs against resources through prioritisation or through alternative systems of provision may be required. We also have to face the fact that rights do seem to be pursued more effectively by middle-class claimants and that, without proper safeguards, rights can be used to subvert the very purposes that the system was set up for in the first place with the net effect of the shifting of resources out of mainstream and into special schools, or enabling articulate parents to use the child's specific learning difficulty to result in the naming of a preferred school that they might not have been able to gain a place at otherwise. If we accept that we cannot solve all of these problems with a system of rights then the challenge will be to ensure that LEAs have the resources available to them that allow them to make balanced choices and that there are mechanisms for redress built in to provide remedies where schools and LEAs fail to deliver. As we have seen, a halfway-house proposal for some forms of SEN may offer one possible answer to these seemingly intractable problems, but it will be important to build in safeguards to deal with the difficulty of ensuring that weakening the hold of individual rights does not mean that we are persuaded to accept levels of provision which are inadequate to meet genuine need.

Can welfare rights analysis help? While Mashaw accepted that in practice decision-making systems contain elements of each of his models, what we have seen develop since the inception of SEN is not so much a system with elements of others, but a Professional Treatment model with a Bureaucratic Rationality model grafted on to deal with the problems arising out of new funding structures in education and a Moral Judgement model grafted on for parents disappointed by the outcome of assessment, where professional discretion can be tested according to whether it has delivered their children's rights correctly. There are inherent problems in all of Mashaw's models; he himself noted that it is not logical to criticise a system for failing to meet objectives which are alien to it; a more useful question is whether a system is well adapted to meeting the values identified as important. The need now is to clarify exactly what values we are trying to accommodate and to continue to hybridise where this enables us to negotiate the difficult task of balancing all of these conflicting interests.

• *What values have been identified as important in special educational needs legislation?*

9.   YOUNG ADULTS WITH SPECIAL NEEDS

A 'child' with special needs includes any person under the age of 19 so long as they are a registered pupil at a school (s 312(5) of the EA 1996). Where a child aged 14 attends school at the first review of the statement after the child has normally started Year 10, the head teacher must obtain written advice about various matters including, for example, details of the child's progress and any transition plan. The head teacher must call a meeting which is chaired by the LEA, and the LEA must prepare a transition plan. The LEA must follow a similar procedure where the child does not attend school: Education (Special Educational Needs) (England) (Consolidation) Regulations 2001, SI 2001/3455.

The SEN Code of Practice (2001) describes in some detail the nature and purpose of the annual reviews which should occur once the pupil is in Year 10.

The LEA's duty to maintain a statement does not cease when the child reaches the age of 16. However, in some LEAs the policy is for pupils with special educational needs to be educated in further education colleges rather than in schools. In this situation the young person is no longer a 'child registered as a pupil at a school' and the young person and their parents no longer enjoy the rights belonging to such a 'child'. The LEA may also attempt to cease to maintain the statement. The legal position of the LEA and the young person has been considered in a number of cases.

R v Dorset County Council and Further Education Funding Council, ex p Goddard [1995] ELR 109

Auld J: Mark Goddard, who is now 16 (born 3 August 1978) and lives with his parents in Dorset, has severe speech and language problems. Since about 1985 the Dorset County Council (Dorset), as the appropriate local education authority, has maintained a statement of his special educational needs under s 7(1) of the Education Act 1981, and has arranged special educational provision for him as specified in that statement as required by s 7(2) of that Act.

The most recent statement was made on 29 October 1992, when he was 14 and attending Moor House School, in Oxted, Surrey, an independent special residential school for children up to the age of 16.

...

Mark continued to attend Moor House School until the end of the summer term 1994, that is until just before his sixteenth birthday on 3 August 1994. Since then Dorset has declined to make any further arrangements for Mark's education, maintaining that now he is over compulsory school age, it is no longer responsible for him and that the responsibility, if any, is that of the Further Education Funding Council (the FEFC). More precisely, Dorset maintains that its statement of Mark's special educational needs, because of the way in which it was worded, applied only so long as he was of compulsory school age and thus that its — Dorset's — obligation to arrange the special educational provision specified in it came to an end on his sixteenth birthday.

...

Mark left Moor House School at the end of the 1994 summer term. Dorset has continued to refuse to make any provision for him since he reached the age of 16, and he has not since attended school of any sort.

The first and most important question on this application is whether a statement of special educational needs in respect of a pupil under the age of 16 lapses when he reaches that age, and with it a local education authority's responsibility to make provision for such needs, where either:

(1)   the statement does not in terms specifically provide for any change in provision that reaching that age may necessitate; or

(2)   the statement is so drawn as to specify the special educational provision only up to the pupil's sixteenth birthday regardless of his continuing special educational needs.

If a local education authority can shed responsibility simply by not amending statements to reflect the necessary consequences of transition from pre- to post-16 education, or by careful drafting of them so as to confine them to pre-16 education, the potential prejudice to 16 to 18-year-olds with special educational needs is great. Once a pupil loses the protection of the statutory regime of the Education Acts, in particular the rights to make representations and of appeal, he will not find it replicated in the 1992 Act when seeking alternative provision from the FEFC.

....

In summary, a local education authority cannot divest itself of responsibility for a pupil's schooling when he reaches 16 by wrongfully failing to specify it, either by silence or express exclusion, in his statement and by refusing to provide it when he reaches 16 so that he cannot then satisfy the condition of the authority's continuing responsibility under s 4(2)(a) of the 1981 Act, namely by being a registered pupil at a school appropriate to his needs.

...

I express some scepticism about Dorset's decision in June 1994 that Mark, on reaching the age of 16, would no longer require the statemented provision. It seems to me to have been driven by considerations of money rather than reason. In particular, it appears to be inconsistent with the March 1994 review report as supplemented by the principal of Moor House School in his letter to Dorset of 12 May 1994, with Mrs Goddard's report of 27 April 1994 and with Dorset's apparent initial acceptance of the review report as requiring continuation of the specified provision at St Catherine's School. Also, and putting Dorset's case at its best in this respect, it seems to have resulted from scant investigation by it of, and unpromising indications from, Yeovil College as to whether it could effectively meet Mark's needs. ...

Dorset has the primary responsibility for Mark. It had at the commencement of these proceedings, and has, a continuing duty to maintain his statement and to arrange the special educational provision specified in it. That means that unless or until Dorset amends the statement or ceases to maintain it, subject in either case to Mr and Mrs Goddard's right of appeal, Dorset is bound to secure for him the provision specified in it at a school which it considers appropriate for him. Such responsibility as might fall upon the FEFC as a result of its consideration would thus be secondary to that of Dorset.

[The Learning and Skills Council replaced FEFC in 2001 (see p 377, below).]

However, *ex p Goddard* was distinguished in the following case.

R v Oxfordshire County Council, ex p B [1997] ELR 90

Butler-Sloss LJ: This is an appeal from the refusal of Brook J on 21 November 1995 to grant an application for judicial review in respect of B (the applicant) by his mother and next friend. The applicant was 18 on 12 July 1996 having been born on 12 July 1978. He has the misfortune to suffer from autism which causes him to have severe learning difficulties. In a revised statement of special educational needs made by the education authority (the county council) in the summer of 1992 his range of difficulties and particular needs were set out in detail. Among his problems was an inability to communicate by normal speech and a limited ability to use sign language.

The county council has adopted a policy whereby its special schools take pupils with learning difficulties up to and not beyond the age of 16. This policy was set out in para 21 of its Policy Statement for Pupils with Special Education Needs of September 1993. At 16 pupils move on to a college of further education.

P attended a special school (AB School) between September 1983 and July 1994. AB School is approved by the Secretary of State to take children from 2 to 16. In the past, exceptionally, a few children have remained at the school beyond the statutory school-leaving age.

Until April 1993 the county council was responsible for schools and colleges of further education within its area both for management and funding the cost of children with special educational needs at either institution. From April 1993 the new Further Education Funding Council (FEFC) under the provisions of the Further and High Education Act 1992 took over responsibility for the education of those over 16 with learning difficulties.

...

The decision to send the applicant to a college of further education was communicated to the mother by letter dated 3 August 1994. In the letter the chief education officer informed the mother of the offer of a place at a college (CD College) and that, as a result of that place being available, the council intended to cease to maintain the applicant's statement of special needs from 31 August 1994. That decision is the subject of the application for judicial review.

...

There are a number of important differences in the facts of the Dorset case and the present appeal. Most important, in my view, is that the policy in Dorset was to educate those with special educational needs in the school system to 18 and thus to continue to maintain a statement in respect of those children registered with them. That policy is in contrast to the policy of the county council on this appeal which is to educate their special needs children in school to 16 and thereafter at college, a genuine policy applied long before the introduction of the FEFC responsibility for colleges of further education. The criticisms levelled at the Dorset County Council as the LEA cannot apply to the policy of this county council which was not in any sense a sham.

...

Upon the child leaving school whether without further education or to go on to college, the child will no longer be registered at a school maintained by them and they will no longer be responsible for the child.

In *S v Essex County Council and SENT* [2000] ELR 718 the High Court allowed a parent's appeal against the decision of SENT that the parent no longer had a right of appeal against a decision to cease to maintain a statement once the pupil reached the age of 16 years and was no longer on the roll of the secondary school he had attended before his compulsory education ended.

S v Essex County Council and SENT [2000] ELR 718

Turner J: ...

(41) The effect of the local education authority's position in the present case is thus: if the definition of 'child' in s 312(5) is conclusive in the applicant never acquired an enforceable right of appeal to the Tribunal. The question thus is: whether, in the context in which the

applicant found herself, the LEA's notice of intention to cease to maintain the statement given, as it was, after JWS had ceased to be a pupil at the Kingswode Hoe school, effectively deprived her of her statutory right of appeal to the Tribunal? That does not provide the full answer to the question since s 579 may yet come into play.

(42) In the circumstances I have described, the question is: whether or not the context, as I have described it to be, requires that the word 'child' be given some other meaning than the narrow definition in s 312(5) or that contained in s 579 itself? Noting, as I have, that the definition in s 312(5) is inclusive rather than exclusive, I am driven to conclude that the context of the present case required some other definition to be given to the word 'child' than that contained either in s 312 or s 579. Any other result would have to be rejected as being so unreasonable that Parliament and the relevant Secretary of State cannot have intended the result for which the LEA contended and the Tribunal decided.

(43) 'Child', in the circumstances of the present case, must mean a child who was the subject of a statement of the special educational needs at the time when the local education authority decided to give notice to determine to cease maintaining the statement. My judgment is accordingly.

This situation should not arise again now that SENDA 20001, s 6 has come into force which provides that LEAs may not cease to maintain a statement where an appeal is being made against the decision to cease to maintain it (see above).

Until 2001 the Further Education Funding Council (FEFC) had a general duty to 16- to 18-year-olds (Further and Higher Education Act (FHEA) 1992, s 2), and a qualified duty to 16- to 24-year-olds with learning difficulties (s 4 of the FHEA 1992). Where a statemented young person left school and went into further (or higher) education then he was less well protected because the FHEA 1992 did not have the same assessment, review and appeal procedures as the EA 1996. In addition to the legislative provisions FEFC published circular 97/01 on students with learning difficulties and/or disabilities.

In *R v FEFC, ex p Parkinson, R v Bradford Metropolitan District Council, ex p Parkinson* [1997] ELR 204, the High Court stated that the duty to make provision for a person over school leaving age with learning difficulties rested with FEFC, but that FEFC was not under a duty to secure the education.

Steven Hocking 'Further education, learning difficulties and the law' 9(1) Education and the Law 13 (1997) at 21–2

The facts of the case were simple and tragic. The applicant was a very severely disabled 20-year-old man. In addition to serious physical disability his communication skills were extremely limited. He could not speak and did not appear to understand speech and in general his ability to communicate with others was very severely limited. It did however appear that this ability was growing and there was no way of knowing to what extent it might develop. The applicant's parents wanted him to attend a Mencap college in Wales, and required assistance with the fees of some £30,000 per annum.

　　...
　　In the event the court found that neither the LEA nor the FEFC were under a duty to secure the education [.]

The case ... revealed an unsatisfactory lacuna in the law; in that education for those very severely disabled appears to be the statutory responsibility of neither LEAs nor the FEFC. The case also illustrates the confusion caused by the division of the responsibilities between FEFCs and LEAs.

The Learning and Skills Council

The Further Education Funding Council has now been replaced by the Learning and Skills Council which has the following powers in relation to England. The National Council for Education and Training for Wales has similar powers (Learning and Skills Act (LSA) 2000, s 41).

Learning and Skills Act 2000, s 13

(1) In discharging its functions under sections 2, 3, 5(1)(a) to (d) and (g) and 8 the Council must have regard—
(a)   to the needs of persons with learning difficulties, and
(b)   in particular, to any report of an assessment conducted under section 140.

(2) If the Council is satisfied that it cannot secure the provision of facilities for education or training which are sufficient in quantity and adequate in quality for a person with a learning difficulty who is over compulsory school age but who has not attained the age of 19 unless it also secures the provision of boarding accommodation for him, the Council must secure the provision of boarding accommodation for him.

(3) If the Council is satisfied that it cannot secure the provision of reasonable facilities for education or training for a person with a learning difficulty who has attained the age of 19 but not the age of 25 unless it also secures the provision of boarding accommodation for him, the Council must secure the provision of boarding accommodation for him.

(4) If the Council is satisfied that it cannot secure the provision of reasonable facilities for education or training for a person with a learning difficulty who has attained the age of 25 unless it also secures the provision of boarding accommodation for him, the Council may secure the provision of boarding accommodation for him.

(5) A person has a learning difficulty if—
(a)   he has a significantly greater difficulty in learning than the majority of persons of his age, or
(b)   he has a disability which either prevents or hinders him from making use of facilities of a kind generally provided by institutions providing post-16 education or training.

(6) But a person is not to be taken to have a learning difficulty solely because the language (or form of language) in which he is or will be taught is different from a language (or form of language) which has at any time been spoken in his home.

Section 2 of the LSA 2000 is concerned with education and training for persons aged 16 to 19, whereas s 3 is concerned with education and training for persons over 19; and s 5 deals with the provision of financial resources. (See chapter 2.)

- *Compare the age range covered by the LSA 2000 with that of the FHEA 1992.*

Assessment

The LSA 2000 also provides for an assessment of young persons with learning difficulties.

Learning and Skills Act 2000, s 140

(1) Subsection (2) applies if—
(a) a local education authority maintains a statement of special educational needs for a person under section 324 of the Education Act 1996, and
(b) the Secretary of State believes that the person will leave school at the end of his last year of compulsory schooling to receive post-16 education or training (within the meaning of Part I of this Act) or higher education (within the meaning of the Education Reform Act 1988).

(2) The Secretary of State must arrange for an assessment of the person to be conducted at some time during the person's last year of compulsory schooling.

(3) The Secretary of State may at any time arrange for an assessment to be conducted of a person—
(a) who is in his last year of compulsory schooling or who is over compulsory school age but has not attained the age of 25,
(b) who appears to the Secretary of State to have a learning difficulty (within the meaning of section 13), and
(c) who is receiving, or in the Secretary of State's opinion is likely to receive, post-16 education or training (within the meaning of Part I of this Act) or higher education (within the meaning of the Education Reform Act 1988).

(4) For the purposes of this section an assessment of a person is an assessment resulting in a written report of—
(a) his educational and training needs, and
(b) the provision required to meet them.

(5) A local education authority must send a copy of a statement maintained by it under section 324 of the Education Act 1996 to the Secretary of State on his request.

- *What is the difference between the obligations in subss (2) and (3)?*

- *Who is responsible for arranging the assessment? How does this differ from the provisions relating to the assessment of a 'child' under 16?*

Where the Learning and Skills Council provides money to an institution it has the power to impose conditions which may include requiring the college to make the provisions specified in a report of an assessment conducted under s 140 (LSA 2000, s 6(3)(f)).

The Qualifications and Curriculum Authority when carrying out its functions under the Education Act 1997, is required to have regard to the needs of any person with special learning needs. Note that there is no upper age limit in s 26(6)(b) of the EA 1997.

Education Act 1997, s 26

...

(6) In this section 'persons with special learning needs' means—
(a)   children with special educational needs (as defined in section 312 of the Education Act 1996); or
(b)   persons (other than children as so defined) who—
    (i)   have a significantly greater difficulty in learning than the majority of persons of their age, or
    (ii)   have a disability which either prevents or hinders them from making use of educational facilities of a kind generally provided for persons of their age.

• *Would the applicant in ex p Parkinson (see above) be in any better position under the Learning and Skills Act 2000?*

10.   DISABLED PUPILS AND YOUNG PERSONS

Some pupils with statements of special educational needs are also likely to have rights under legislation aimed at assisting disabled persons or preventing discrimination against them.

'Disabled persons'

When a child with a statement reaches the age of 14, at any subsequent annual review or reassessment of the child's educational needs the LEA shall ask the local authority whether or not the child is a disabled person within the Disabled Persons (Services, Consultation and Representation) Act 1986 (s 5).

A 'disabled person' is a person aged 18 or over who is blind, deaf or dumb, or who suffers from a mental disorder, or who is substantially and permanently handicapped by illness, injury, or congenital deformity or other prescribed disability (s 29(1) of the National Assistance Act 1948 as amended).

Where a disabled student is in full-time education, either at school or at a further or higher education institution, there is an obligation on respectively the LEA or the governing body to provide the local authority with certain information including, for example, the date when it is anticipated that the student will cease to receive full-time education. The local authority is then obliged to carry out an assessment of the welfare needs of the disabled person.

Guidance is provided in DES circular 2/88 to local authorities (Disabled Persons (Services, Consultation and Representation) Act 1986 implementation of ss 5 and 6). (See also the definition of disabled person under the Disability Discrimination Act 1995, p 323, above.)

11.   DISABILITY DISCRIMINATION ACT 1995

The Disability Discrimination Act (DDA) 1995 initially placed very limited responsibilities on schools and LEAs as well as FE and HE institutions. Schools were required to include certain information in the annual reports, while LEAs, FE colleges and universities were required to publish disability statements. The obligation to publish disability statements has been removed by SENDA 2001 (s 34). Educational institutions are also subject to the employment provisions of the DDA 1995.

The Special Educational Needs and Disability Act 2001 has extended the core provisions of the DDA 1995 to educational institutions. The main provisions require schools and LEAs as well as further and higher education institutions:
−   not to discriminate against disabled pupils (see definitions, p 323, above)
−   to make reasonable adjustments to increase the accessibility of schools and colleges for disabled pupils and students.

New rights are given to improve access to further, higher and adult education. These rights will be supported by a Code of Practice prepared by the Disability Rights Commission. These provisions are likely to come into force in September 2002.

The requirements until 2002

Schools

Education Act 1996, s 317

...

(6) The annual report for [each community, foundation or voluntary school] shall also include a report containing information as to—
(a)   the arrangements for the admission of disabled pupils;
(b)   the steps taken to prevent disabled pupils from being treated less favourably than other pupils; and
(c)   the facilities provided to assist access to the school by disabled pupils;

and for this purpose 'disabled pupils' means pupils who are disabled persons for the purposes of the Disability Discrimination Act 1995.

LEAs

Education Act 1996, s 528

(1) Every local education authority shall publish disability statements at such intervals as may be prescribed.

(2) In subsection (1) 'disability statement' means a statement containing information of a prescribed description about the provision of facilities for further education made by the local education authority in respect of persons who are disabled persons for the purposes of the Disability Discrimination Act 1995.

Detailed requirements are contained in regulations, for example, the Education (Disability Statements for Local Education Authorities)(England) Regulations 1997, SI 1997/1625. Advice on these provisions can be found in:
– DfEE Circular 12/97 (guidance on disability statements for local education authorities)
– DfEE Circular 20/99 (what the Disability Discrimination Act (DDA) 1995 means for schools and LEAs).

Further and higher education

The Disability Discrimination Act 1995, ss 29 and 30 amended existing legislation and in effect required the governing bodies of:
– FE colleges
– sixth form colleges
– universities
– other higher education institutions
to publish disability statements.

In addition the various funding agencies (eg HEFC, LSC) are required to have regard to the requirements of disabled persons. The Learning and Skills Council has the power to impose conditions on colleges to which it grants money.

Learning and Skills Act 2000, s 6

...

(4) The conditions may—
(a) relate to the provision made (or to be made) with respect to disabled persons by a person providing or proposing to provide education or training;
(b) require a person providing education or training to publish at specified intervals statements containing information of a specified description about the facilities for education or training provided by him with respect to disabled persons.

Disabled persons are persons who are disabled for the purposes of the Disability Discrimination Act 1995 (LSA 2000, s 6(6)).

Special Educational Needs and Disability Act 2001

The Act contains some provisions which are common to all sectors of education, such as the definition of discrimination. There is a considerable difference in the way in which the legislation will be enforced for pupils as compared with students at FE colleges and universities. In particular compensation will not be payable to pupils who are discriminated against because of their disability.

The Act inserts new sections into the DDA 1995. There is an emphasis on forward planning and informal dispute resolution, so that litigation only arises as a last resort.

Schools and LEAs

Each LEA must prepare an accessibility strategy, and the governing body of every school (including independent and non-maintained special schools) must prepare an accessibility plan for its school. Plans and strategies must be:
–   in writing
–   implemented, and
–   kept under review.

Disability Discrimination Act 1995, s 28D

...

(2) An accessibility strategy is a strategy for, over a prescribed period—
(a)   increasing the extent to which disabled pupils can participate in the school's curriculums;
(b)   improving the physical environment of the schools for the purpose of increasing the extent to which disabled pupils are able to take advantage of education and associated services provided or offered by the schools; and
(c)   improving the delivery to disabled pupils—
   (i)   within a reasonable time, and
   (ii)   in ways which are determined after taking account of their disabilities and any preferences expressed by them or their parents,
   of information which is provided in writing for pupils who are not disabled.

...

(9) An accessibility plan is a plan for, over a prescribed period—
(a)   increasing the extent to which disabled pupils can participate in the school's curriculum;
(b)   improving the physical environment of the school for the purpose of increasing the extent to which disabled pupils are able to take advantage of education and associated services provided or offered by the school; and
(c)   improving the delivery to disabled pupils—

(i)   within a reasonable time, and
(ii) in ways which are determined after taking account of their disabilities and any preferences expressed by them or their parents,

of information which is provided in writing for pupils who are not disabled.

...

CONCILIATION

The Disability Rights Commission has the power to arrange for the establishment of conciliation services to resolve disputes involving allegations of unlawful discrimination made by pupils or students. This may prove to be of great importance in practice to pupils and students.

Disability Discrimination Act 1995, s 31B

(1) The Disability Rights Commission may make arrangements with any other person for the provision of conciliation services by, or by persons appointed by, that person in connection with disputes.

...

(8) 'Conciliation services' means advice and assistance provided to the parties to a dispute, by a conciliator, with a view to promoting its settlement otherwise than through a court, tribunal or other body.

...

The responsible bodies

SCHOOLS

Disability Discrimination Act 1995, s 28A

(1) It is unlawful for the body responsible for a school to discriminate against a disabled person—
(a)   in the arrangements it makes for determining admission to the school as a pupil;
(b)   in the terms on which it offers to admit him to the school as a pupil; or
(c)   by refusing or deliberately omitting to accept an application for his admission to the school as a pupil.

(2) It is unlawful for the body responsible for a school to discriminate against a disabled pupil in the education or associated services provided for, or offered to, pupils at the school by that body.

...

(4) It is unlawful for the body responsible for a school to discriminate against a disabled pupil by excluding him from the school, whether permanently or temporarily.

...

(6) In the case of an act which constitutes discrimination by virtue of section 55, this section also applies to discrimination against a person who is not disabled.

Normally the LEA will be liable for any disability discrimination by a school, but in certain circumstances the governing body will be the 'responsible body'. For example, the governing body of a voluntary aided school is responsible for admissions and will be liable for any disability discrimination arising in the exercise of that function. In the case of an independent school the proprietor of the school is the responsible person (Sch 4A, para 1 of the DDA 1995).

Section 55 of the DDA 1995 makes it unlawful to victimise a person who may be involved in a claim relating to the DDA.

FURTHER AND HIGHER EDUCATION

An almost identical provision applies to FE colleges, sixth form colleges, and universities (s 28R of the DDA 1995). The governing body will normally be the 'responsible body' (Sch 4B, DDA 1995).

LEAs

Each LEA is also under a residual duty not to discriminate against pupils or potential pupils (s 28F of the DDA 1995); and LEAs and schools which provide further education or training facilities are also under a duty not to discriminate (ss 28U and 28R of and Sch 4C to the DDA 1995).

Meaning of discrimination

Discrimination is defined in s 28B(1) and s 28C(1) of the DDA 1995. These definitions are similar to those contained in the employment part of the DDA 1995. Employment law cases should be considered when interpreting these provisions.

Disability Discrimination Act 1995, s 28B

(1) For the purposes of section 28A, a responsible body discriminates against a disabled person if—

(a)   for a reason which relates to his disability, it treats him less favourably than it treats or would treat others to whom that reason does not or would not apply; and

(b)   it cannot show that the treatment in question is justified.

(2) For the purposes of section 28A, a responsible body also discriminates against a disabled person if—

(a)   it fails, to his detriment, to comply with section 28C; and

(b)   it cannot show that its failure to comply is justified.

(3) In relation to a failure to take a particular step, a responsible body does not discriminate against a person if it shows—

(a)   that, at the time in question, it did not know and could not reasonably have been expected to know, that he was disabled, and

(b)   that its failure to take the step was attributable to that lack of knowledge.

(4) The taking of a particular step by a responsible body in relation to a person does not amount to less favourable treatment if it shows that at the time in question it did not know, and could not reasonably have been expected to know, that he was disabled.

(5) Subsections (6) to (8) apply in determining whether, for the purposes of this section—

(a)   less favourable treatment of a person, or

(b)   failure to comply with section 28C,

is justified.

(6) Less favourable treatment of a person is justified if it is the result of a permitted form of selection.

(7) Otherwise, less favourable treatment, or a failure to comply with section 28C, is justified only if the reason for it is both material to the circumstances of the particular case and substantial.

(8) If, in a case falling within subsection (1)—

(a)   the responsible body is under a duty imposed by section 28C in relation to the disabled person, but

(b)   it fails without justification to comply with that duty,

its treatment of that person cannot be justified under subsection (7) unless that treatment would have been justified even if it had complied with that duty.

- *Will a selective secondary school which does not offer a place to a pupil with dyslexia, who has failed the English paper which forms part of the selection process, be acting in breach of the DDA 1995?*

Similar provisions are contained for FE and HE institutions in s 28S of the DDA 1995. However, it should be noted that student services are included and that the justification defence is wider.

Disability Discrimination Act 1995, s 28S(6), (7)

(6) Less favourable treatment of a person is justified if it is necessary in order to maintain—

(a)   academic standards; or

(b)   standards of any other prescribed kind.

(7) Less favourable treatment is also justified if—
(a)   it is of a prescribed kind;
(b)   it occurs in prescribed circumstances; or
(c)   it is of a prescribed kind and it occurs in prescribed circumstances.

Disabled pupils and students must not be substantially disadvantaged

Disability Discrimination Act 1995, s 28C

(1) The responsible body for a school must take such steps as it is reasonable for it to have to take to ensure that—
(a)   in relation to the arrangements it makes for determining the admission of pupils to the school, disabled persons are not placed at a substantial disadvantage in comparison with persons who are not disabled; and
(b)   in relation to education and associated services provided for, or offered to, pupils at the school by it, disabled pupils are not placed at a substantial disadvantage in comparison with pupils who are not disabled.

(2) That does not require the responsible body to—
(a)   remove or alter a physical feature (for example, one arising from the design or construction of the school premises or the location of resources); or
(b)   provide auxiliary aids or services.

...

(4) In considering whether it is reasonable for it to have to take a particular step in order to comply with its duty under subsection (1), a responsible body must have regard to any relevant provisions of a code of practice issued under section 53A.

...

(8) This section imposes duties only for the purpose of determining whether a responsible body has discriminated against a disabled person; and accordingly a breach of any such duty is not actionable as such.

A similar provision applies to further and higher education institutions (s 28T of the DDA 1995).

Parents, pupils and students may make a 'confidentiality request' to the LEA (or the governing body) asking that the nature or the extent of their disability be treated as confidential. This may arise, for example, where a pupil or student is HIV positive. In such a case the duty on the LEA (or the governing body) to take a particular step may be constrained by the need to maintain confidentiality.

In addition FE and HE institutions may be required to make alterations to premises which they lease (s 28W of the DDA 1995).

Remedies

In England and Wales parents can appeal to the Special Educational Needs and Disability Tribunal (SENDIST) on the grounds that their child has been unlawfully discriminated against by the LEA (or the governing body) or by their employees or agents.

Disability Discrimination Act 1995, s 28 I(3), (4)

(3) If the Tribunal considers that a claim under subsection (1) is well founded—
(a)   it may declare that A has been unlawfully discriminated against; and
(b)   if it does so, it may make such order as it considers reasonable in all the circumstances of the case.

(4) The power conferred by subsection (3)(b)—
(a)   may, in particular, be exercised with a view to obviating or reducing the adverse effect on the person concerned of any matter to which the claim relates; but
(b)   does not include power to order the payment of any sum by way of compensation.

The Tribunal has no power to award compensation for breach of the disability provisions. The Tribunal can declare that the pupil has been unlawfully discriminated against and make an appropriate order which would, for example, obviate or reduce the adverse effect of the discrimination. This may of course result in expenditure by the LEA or governing body. Such an order could include providing additional tuition to enable a child to catch up or relocating a library to the ground floor, so long as no physical alterations to the school premises are required.

Any claim should be brought within six months of the act complained of (DDA 1995, Sch 3, Part 3).

It is likely that where appropriate a discrimination appeal could be heard as part of a SEN appeal.

There are exceptions where SENDIST will not have jurisdiction. These relate to admission and exclusion appeals (ss 28K and 28L of the DDA 1995). Where these appeals raises issues of disability discrimination the matter is to be resolved by the independent appeal panels which normally hear such appeals. It is surprising that such panels, which are comprised of lay volunteers, should be expected to grapple with complex issues of discrimination law.

DISABLED STUDENTS

Students are entitled to bring disability discrimination claims in the county court and may be awarded damages. The claim should be brought within six months of the act complained of, and there is likely to be a limit to the amount of damages that may be awarded for injury to feelings (DDA 1995, Sch 3, Part 4).

Disability Discrimination Act 1995, s 28V

(1) A claim by a person—
(a)   that a responsible body has discriminated against him in a way which is unlawful under this Chapter,

(b) that a responsible body is by virtue of section 57 or 58 to be treated as having discriminated against him in such a way, or

(c) that a person is by virtue of section 57 to be treated as having discriminated against him in such a way,

may be made the subject of civil proceedings in the same way as any other claim in tort ...

(2) For the avoidance of doubt it is hereby declared that damages in respect of discrimination in a way which is unlawful under this Chapter may include compensation for injury to feelings whether or not they include compensation under any other head.

(3) Proceedings in England and Wales may be brought only in a county court.

...

(5) The remedies available in such proceedings are those which are available in the High Court ...

In addition FE and HE institutions may be required to make reasonable adjustments to physical features of their premises occupied under a lease (s 28W of the DDA 1995).

12.   TORTIOUS LIABILITY OF LEA FOR FAILURE TO DIAGNOSE AND/OR REMEDY CHILD'S SPECIAL EDUCATIONAL NEEDS

The law does not provide compesation for parents or their children where, for example, an LEA is in breach of its statutory duties under the education legislation. A claim for compensation in the form of an award of damages may, however, fall within the tort of negligence. Such a claim is normally brought as a last resort and may indicate that the existing procedures failed to provide for the child's educational needs.

There have been two important House of Lords decisions on this topic. However, it is worth noting that except for *Phelps* (see below) the decisions were on preliminary issues rather than appeals following a full trial. The *Christmas* case subsequently went to full trial.

The claims have primarily been concerned with first whether LEAs owe a direct common law duty of care in performing their functions under the Education Acts; and secondly whether LEAs may be vicariously liable under the tort of negligence for the failure of educational psychologists and teachers employed by them to diagnose and alleviate a pupil's special educational needs.

***X (Minors) v Bedfordshire County Council, M (A Minor) v Newham London Borough Council, E (A Minor) v Dorset County Council, Christmas v Hampshire County Council, Keating v Bromley London Borough* [1995] 2 AC 733**

Lord Browne-Wilkinson: My Lords, in each of these five appeals the plaintiffs by their statements of claim allege they have been injured by public authorities in the carrying out of functions imposed upon them by statute. The defendants have applied to strike out the claims on the grounds that they disclose no cause of action. In the first group of appeals (the *Bedfordshire* case and *Newham* case) the allegations are that public authorities negligently carried out, or failed to carry out, statutory duties imposed on them for the purpose of protecting children from child abuse. In the second group (the *Dorset* case, the *Hampshire* case and the *Bromley* case) the plaintiffs allege that the local authorities failed to carry out duties imposed upon them as education authorities by the Education Acts 1944 to 1981 in relation to children with special educational needs.

...

General approach

Introductory—PUBLIC LAW AND PRIVATE LAW

The question is whether, if Parliament has imposed a statutory duty on an authority to carry out a particular function, a plaintiff who has suffered damage in consequence of the authority's performance or non-performance of that function has a right of action in damages against the authority. It is important to distinguish such actions to recover damages, based on a private law cause of action, from actions in public law to enforce the due performance of statutory duties, now brought by way of judicial review. The breach of a public law by itself gives rise to no claim for damages.

...

Private law claims for damages can be classified into four different categories, viz: (A) actions for breach of statutory duty simpliciter (ie irrespective of carelessness); (B) actions based solely on the careless performance of a statutory duty in the absence of any other common law right of action; (C) actions based on a common law duty of care arising either from the imposition of the statutory duty or from the performance of it; (D) misfeasance in public office, ie the failure to exercise, or the exercise of, statutory powers either with the intention to injure the plaintiff or in the knowledge that the conduct is unlawful.

Category (D) is not in issue in this case.

...

In my judgment the correct view is that in order to found a cause of action flowing from the careless exercise of statutory powers or duties, the plaintiff has to show that the circumstances are such as to raise a duty of care at common law. The mere assertion of the careless exercise of a statutory power or duty is not sufficient.

...

Co-existence of statutory duty and common law duty of care

It is clear that a common law duty of care may arise in the performance of statutory functions. But a broad distinction has to be drawn between: (a) cases in which it is alleged that the authority owes a duty of care in the manner in which it exercises a statutory discretion; (b) cases in which a duty of care is alleged to arise from the manner in which the statutory duty has been implemented in practice.

An example of (a) in the educational field would be a decision whether or not to exercise a statutory discretion to close a school, being a decision which necessarily involves the exercise of a discretion. An example of (b) would be the actual running of a school pursuant to the statutory duties. In such latter case a common law duty to take reasonable care for the physical safety of the pupils will arise. The fact that the school is being run pursuant to a statutory duty is not necessarily incompatible with a common law duty of care arising from the proximate relationship between a school and the pupils it has agreed to accept. The distinction is between (a) taking care in exercising a statutory discretion whether or not to do an act and (b) having decided to do that act, taking care in the manner in which you do it.

...

Direct liability and vicarious liability

In certain of the appeals before the House, the local authorities are alleged to be under a direct duty of care to the plaintiff not only in relation to the exercise of a statutory discretion but also in relation to the operational way in which they performed that duty.

This allegation of a direct duty of care owed by the authority to the plaintiff is to be contrasted with those claims which are based on the vicarious liability of the local authority for the negligence of its servants, ie for the breach of a duty of care owed by the servant to the plaintiff, the authority itself not being under any relevant duty of care to the plaintiff.

...

This distinction between direct and vicarious liability can be important since the authority may not be under a direct duty of care at all or the extent of the duty of care owed directly by the authority to the plaintiff may well differ from that owed by a professional to a patient. However, it is important not to lose sight of the fact that, even in the absence of a claim based on vicarious liability, an authority under a direct duty of care to the plaintiff will be liable for the negligent acts or omissions of its servant which constitute a breach of that direct duty. The authority can only act through its servants.

...

The Education Cases

The legislation

Each of these three cases is brought against the local education authority alleging failures in their performance of their statutory duties under the Education Acts, in particular in relation to children with special educational needs. The relevant statutory provisions are to be found in the Education Acts 1944 and 1981 and regulations made thereunder.

...

The Dorset case

The facts

The plaintiff in this case attended Milton Abbas First School, a state primary school maintained by the appellant, the defendant authority. It is common ground that the plaintiff had specific learning difficulties causing him difficulties with literacy and numeracy, often called dyslexia.

...

Common law duty of care — direct

...

In my judgment, as in the child abuse cases, the courts should hesitate long before imposing a common law duty of care in the exercise of discretionary powers or duties conferred by Parliament for social welfare purposes. The aim of the Act of 1981 was to provide, for the benefit of society as a whole, an administrative machinery to help one disadvantaged section of society. The statute provides its own detailed machinery for securing that the statutory purpose is performed. If, despite the complex machinery for consultation and appeals contained in the Act, the scheme fails to provide the benefit intended that is a matter more appropriately remedied by way of the Ombudsman looking into the administrative failure than by way of litigation.

For these reasons I reach the conclusion that an education authority owes no common law duty of care in the exercise of the powers and discretions relating to children with special educational needs specifically conferred on them by the Act of 1981.

I turn them to the other duty of care which, it is alleged, the defendant authority owes directly to the plaintiff. There the position is wholly different. The claim is based on the fact that the authority is offering a service (psychological advice) to the public. True it is that, in the absence of a statutory power or duty, the authority could not offer such a service. But once the decision is taken to offer such a service, a statutory body is in general in the same position as any private individual or organisation holding itself out as offering such a service. By opening its doors to others to take advantage of the service offered, it comes under a duty of care to those using the service to exercise care in its conduct. The position is directly analogous with a hospital conducted, formerly by a local authority now by a health authority, in exercise of statutory powers. In such a case the authority running the hospital is under a duty to those whom it admits to exercise reasonable care in the way it runs it: see *Gold v Essex County Council* [1942] 2 KB 293.

For these reasons, I can see no ground on which it can be said at this stage that the defendant authority, in providing a psychology service, could not have come under a duty of care to the plaintiff who, through his parents, took advantage of that service.

...

Common law duty of care — vicarious

The claim is that the educational psychologists and other members of the staff of the defendant authority owed a duty to use reasonable professional skill and care in the assessment and determination of the plaintiff's educational needs. It is further alleged that the plaintiff's parents relied on the advice of such professionals. The defendant authority is vicariously liable for any breach of such duties by their employees.

Again, I can see no ground for striking out this claim at least in relation to the educational psychologists. Psychologists hold themselves out as having special skills and they are, in my judgment, like any other professional bound both to possess such skills and to exercise them carefully. Of course, the test in *Bolam v Friern Hospital Management Committee* [1957] 1 WLR 582 will apply to them, ie they are only bound to exercise the ordinary skill of a competent psychologist and if they can show that they acted in accordance with the accepted views of some reputable psychologist at the relevant time they will have discharged the duty of care, even if other psychologists would have adopted a different view. In the context of advice on the treatment of dyslexia, a subject on which views have changed over the years, this may be an important factor.

...

My conclusion therefore in the *Dorset* case is that the defendant authority is under no liability at common law for the negligent exercise of the statutory discretions conferred on them by the Education Acts 1944 to 1981, but could be liable, both directly and vicariously, for negligence in the operation of the pyschology service and negligent advice given by its officers.

The Hampshire case

The facts

Between 1978 and 1984 the plaintiff attended Binsted Church of England School, a primary school maintained by the defendant authority. At Binsted School the plaintiff manifested severe behavioural problems and learning difficulties, especially learning to read. His symptoms were consistent with the learning difficulty known as dyslexia. His parents expressed their concern to the headmaster and members of the teaching staff on numerous occasions and asked for advice and further investigation into the plaintiff's condition. The headmaster told the plaintiff's parents that the plaintiff did not have any special learning difficulty.

Eventually, in about June 1984, the headmaster referred the plaintiff to the Mid-Hampshire Teachers' Centre (an advisory service run by the defendant authority) for an assessment of the plaintiff's learning difficulties. The headmaster reported to the plaintiff's parents that 'the advisory teacher felt that [the plaintiff] had no serious handicaps, but that it was mainly a question of a good deal of regular practice.' The plaintiff's parents acted on this advice.

...

[T]he plaintiff claims that the defendant authority is vicariously liable for the negligence of the headmaster of Binsted School and the county advisory service. It is alleged that the headmaster was negligent in failing to refer the plaintiff either for formal assessment of his special educational needs or to an educational psychologist experienced in the field. The plaintiff alleges against the advisory service that it was negligent between June–July 1984 and 1985 in failing to ascertain that the plaintiff had a specific learning difficulty, failing to assess the nature of his learning difficulty, failing to diagnose dyslexia and failing to refer the plaintiff or advise his parents to refer him to an educational psychologist.

The statement of claim claims that as a result the plaintiff suffered injury because, if he had been correctly diagnosed and appropriate remedial treatment instituted, his behavioural problems would have been ameliorated. As a result the plaintiff had been disadvantaged in realising his potential and his vocational opportunities and prospects significantly restricted.

...

In this case, unlike the other educational cases, the plaintiff's claim is based solely on an allegation that the defendant authority is vicariously liable, for the breaches of a duty of care owed by its employees, the headmaster and the members of the advisory service. The duty of care in no sense arises from the statutory machinery laid down by the Act of 1981; the negligence complained of has nothing to do with the Act of 1981; no complaint is made as to the statement made in January 1989 nor as there any allegation of any other failure to operate the statutory regime. The claim is a pure common law claim based on a duty of care owed by a headmaster and educational advisory to a pupil.

...

In my judgment a school which accepts a pupil assumes responsibility not only for his physical well being but also for his educational needs. The education of the pupil is the very purpose for which the child goes to the school. The head teacher, being responsible for the school, himself comes under a duty of care to exercise the reasonable skills of a headmaster in relation to such educational needs. If it comes to the attention of the headmaster that a pupil is under-performing, he does owe a duty to take such steps as a reasonable teacher would consider appropriate to try to deal with such under-performance. To hold that, in such circumstances, the head teacher could properly ignore the matter and make no attempt to deal with it would fly in the face, not only of society's expectations of what a school will provide, but also of the fine traditions of the teaching profession itself. If such head teacher gives advice to the parents, then in my judgment he must exercise the skills and care of a reasonable teacher in giving such advice.

Similarly, in the case of the advisory teacher brought in to advise on the educational needs of a specific pupil, if he knows that his advice will be communicated to the pupil's parents he must foresee that they will rely on such advice. Therefore in giving that advice he owes a duty to the child to exercise the skill and care of a reasonable advisory teacher.

Once it is established that a head teacher or advisory teacher is under some duty of care to the pupil in relation to his educational well being, it is impossible to strike out the claim in this case. But I must again emphasise that the failure to strike out the claim does not indicate any view as to the likelihood of success in the action. The head teacher and the advisory teacher were only bound to exercise the skill and care of a reasonable head teacher and advisory teacher.

...

The Bromley case

The facts

The plaintiff was born on 24 May 1971 and has at all times resided in the area for which the Bromley London Borough Council is the local education authority.

...

Breach of statutory duty simpliciter (Category (A))

There are two aspects to the plaintiff's case: (1) the failure by the authority to provide him with any schooling at all between June 1977 and May 1979 and from September 1985 to November 1986; (2) the provision by the authority of inappropriate education (ie at special schools rather than at an ordinary school) resulting from failures to carry out proper assessment procedures.

The claim in relation to the failure to provide any schooling is based on an alleged breach of section 8 of the Act of 1944.

...

Therefore, as Sir Thomas Bingham MR has demonstrated, there is no long line of authority supporting the existence of a statutory right of action for damages for breach of section 8 of the Act of 1944 and in my judgment no such right exists.

The second aspect of the plaintiff's claim (damages for failure to provide appropriate schooling) depends upon alleged breaches of the duties imposed by sections 8(2)(c), 33 and 34 of the Act of 1944 and of sections 4, 5 and 7 of the Act of 1981.

Although, for present purposes, I am prepared to assume that the plaintiff, as a child having special educational needs, was a member of a class for whose protection the statutory provisions were enacted, I can find nothing in either set of statutory provisions which demonstrates a parliamentary intention to give that class a statutory right of action for damages.

...

Common law duty of care — direct

The particulars which are given of the alleged negligence in effect allege nothing more than that the defendants failed to take proper care in relation to the assessment of the plaintiff's disability in making the decision to educate him in special schools. At no stage does the pleading identify what was done, by whom or the respects in which it was negligent so to act.

From this pleading it appears that the only duty of care and the only breaches of such duty alleged relate to the manner in which the defendant authority exercised the statutory discretions conferred on it by the Education Acts 1944 to 1981. I have already expressed the view in dealing with the *Dorset* case, that there is no common law duty of care in relation to the exercise of such statutory discretions. Therefore in my judgment the only claim alleging a direct liability at common law should be struck out.

Common law duty of care — vicarious

...

I think it is right to assume that, at trial, the plaintiff will be able to allege and prove that one or more professionals employed by the defendant authority came into a relationship with the plaintiff which gave rise to a normal professional duty of care. On that assumption, for the reasons given in relation to the *Hampshire* case, I agree with the Court of Appeal that the claim should not be struck out since, in law, such duty of care is capable of existing.

- *Did Lord Browne-Wilkinson consider that an LEA could (a) be liable in damages for breach of a statutory duty imposed by the education legislation, or (b) be directly rather than vicariously liable at common law?*

- *On what ground was each LEA potentially liable in the Dorset case, the Hampshire case, and the Bromley case?*

The decision of the House of Lords established that in principle an LEA owes a common law duty of care to pupils for negligent advice given by its employees or for failure to exercise reasonable care. Once it had been established that the LEA could be vicariously liable for the negligence of its employees, the case of *Christmas v Hampshire County Council* went to trial. The case illustrates some of the difficulties in bringing such claims, such as obtaining evidence and establishing a causal link.

Christmas v Hampshire County Council [1998] ELR I

Ian Kennedy J: This is an action brought by Mark John Christmas against Hampshire County Council claiming damages for injury, loss and damage as result of the defendants, their servants or agents at Binsted Church of England School and the Mid-Hampshire Teachers' Centre. The action centres upon the alleged failure to detect and address the plaintiff's dyslexia. The Teachers' Centre is the title given to the defendant council's advisory teacher service.

This action has earlier been to the House of Lords on the question of the defendant council's duty to the plaintiff. The existence of a duty of care in respect of the matters relevant to this action is no longer in question. Breach of duty and damage remained to be decided.

When the action was opened I suggested that the complications concerning both the issues of breach and that of the quantum of damage were such that it would be better to defer the latter until liability had been established. My suggestion met no opposition, and hence this action has proceeded as a split trial.

...

The plaintiff's ambition is to be a charge nurse, but that career as well as substantial promotion in his present field is effectively denied him by his difficulties in reading, writing and spelling. These difficulties, his case is, could and would have been avoided, or substantially reduced, had his dyslexia or specific learning difficulty been recognised and addressed by the staff at Binsted or by those in the council's advisory teacher service.

...

It is certainly the case that whatever was done was ineffective, or at best not very effective, but I cannot reason back from that that the attention he had received was necessarily substandard. More House does not appear to have been any more successful, rather the plaintiff fell further behind his peers, and More House was, or claimed to be, a specialist school.

...

It is necessarily extremely difficult at this or any similar remove in time to identify exactly what was done towards helping any pupil with a specific learning difficulty. The teaching profession is not one which commits a great deal to paper (particularly at the primary level), and I would not want to be thought to be implying that education generally would be improved if it did. The records ordinarily kept by a school are usually quite limited, rarely will they go beyond the termly reports, any correspondence that there may have been. The teacher's mark book is generally his or her own property, and may well not be kept by the school.

The material upon which I must make my decision is thus limited. Those teachers whose evidence I have heard have impressed me as thoughtful and able, and I instance Mrs Beyfus, Mrs Burgess and Mr Nelson. In the case of Mr Head the contemporaneous material belies the impression of a man merely seeing out time. Mrs Stevens has died: her successor cannot now be identified. It is all too easy to find negligence against those not present to answer for their actions. Unless there is evidence to point towards some failure on their part I cannot think it is right to assume that they were at fault. It is not every problem that can be resolved, even if statistically the great majority can be ameliorated or overcome.

...

If I conclude that the defendant council's advisory teachers failed the plaintiff, it must, on the evidence that I have heard, follow that More House in its turn failed him. While it is perfectly possible that a series of teachers and schools missed what was, at this time, a fairly well-known difficulty, the improbability of that explanation increases with each opportunity for a review.

I have already referred to the difficulty of examining actions and inactions at such a remove. I have to be persuaded on the balance of probabilities that there was a want of reasonable care on the part of the servants of the defendant council's advisory teacher service. In the event I am not, and this limb of the plaintiff's case also fails.

In 2000 a group of educational negligence appeals was allowed by the House of Lords. The *Phelps* case is particularly important because the case had gone to trial, whereas the other appeals were concerned with preliminary issues.

Phelps v Hillingdon London Borough Council [2000] ELR 499

Lord Slynn of Hadley: My Lords, the appeals in these four cases were heard together. They all raise questions as to the liability of a local education authority for what is said to have been a failure, either by the local authority or by employees for whom the local authority was vicariously liable, in the provision of appropriate educational services for children at school.

Three cases are concerned with children who were dyslexic; the fourth was a child suffering from Duchenne Muscular Dystrophy. In one case (*Phelps*) there has been a trial. The plaintiff succeeded before the judge, but failed in the Court of Appeal. In two others, there was an application to strike out the statement of claim under Rules of the Supreme Court 1965, Ord 18, r 19 as being an abuse of the process of the court, or as disclosing no cause of action — in one of those (*G*) the judge struck out the statement of claim but the Court of Appeal reinstated it: in the other (*Jarvis*) the judge did not strike out the claim in negligence, the Court of Appeal struck it out. In the fourth case (*Anderton*) the question was whether pre-action discovery should be ordered on the basis that the intended claim was for 'personal injuries to a person'. The master and the judge held that it was and ordered discovery; the Court of Appeal held that it was not and refused the order.

In this area of the law, as Auld LJ said in his valuable analysis in the Court of Appeal in *G*, 'The law is on the move and much remains uncertain'. These cases were accordingly heard together so that your Lordships could reconsider the principles to be followed and the House has had the benefit of very able arguments on behalf of all parties.

...

Pamela Helen Phelps

Pamela was born on 30 December 1973 and, as is now known, since birth has been dyslexic. Dyslexia is normally a congenital condition defined by the World Federation of Neurology (1958) as 'a disorder manifested by difficulty in learning to read despite conventional instruction, adequate intelligence and socio-cultural opportunities. It is dependent upon fundamental cognitive disabilities which are frequently of constitutional origin'. It is agreed that at all material times methods of psychological assessment have been in use which provided guidance as to whether a person might be dyslexic and that the techniques for mitigating the effects of dyslexia by a multi-sensory and structured approach were known. It is, however, accepted that the extent to which the effects of dyslexia can be ameliorated varies widely.

...

Garland J (*Phelps v London Borough of Hillingdon* [1998] ELR 38), after a careful review of the evidence and the submissions, held that Miss Melling [an educational psychologist] owed a duty of care to Pamela on the basis that her findings, recommendations and advice would be acted upon by the plaintiff through her parents, none the less so because her advice was also relied on by Hillingdon and the school. Hillingdon was vicariously liable for breaches of that duty by Miss Melling. She was in breach, first, when she failed in October 1985 to diagnose that Pamela was dyslexic. ... She was in breach, second, when she did not revise her opinion when Pamela 'made so little progress despite special needs teaching'.

He held, however, that although a school may owe a duty of care to an under-performing pupil the teachers here relied on Miss Melling and kept Pamela's case under review through the care committee. To have expected the school to have required Miss Melling or someone else to take a fresh look at Pamela would be to impose too high a duty when the school was being advised by Miss Melling as part of the defendants' Educational Psychology

Service, by Mrs Roberts, the Special Needs Advisory Teacher and itself providing special needs teaching by suitably qualified staff in accordance with the scheme and provisions of the 1981 Act ... He awarded special damages for tuition fees incurred and likely to be incurred and for future loss of earnings together with general damages of £12,500, making a total award of £44,056.50 plus interest.

In the present case, although the duties were intended to benefit a particular group, mainly children with special educational needs, the Act is essentially providing a general structure for all local education authorities in respect of all children who fall within its provision. The general nature of the duties imposed on local authorities in the context of a national system of education and the remedies available by way of appeal and judicial review indicate that Parliament did not intend to create a statutory remedy by way of damages. Much of the Act is concerned with conferring discretionary powers or administrative duties in an area of social welfare where normally damages have not been awarded when there has been a failure to perform a statutory duty.

...

Taking all these factors into account, it does not seem to me that it can be said that Parliament intended that there should be a remedy by way of damages for breach of statutory duty in respect of the matters complained of here.

The common law

It does not follow that the local authority can never be liable in common-law negligence for damage resulting from acts done in the course of the performance of a statutory duty by the authority or by its servants or agents. ...

In Pamela's case ... the question to be determined is whether the damage relied on is foreseeable and proximate and whether it is just and reasonable to recognise a duty of care (*Caparo Industries plc v Dickman and Others* [1990] 2 AC 605, at pp 617–618). If a duty of care would exist where advice was given other than pursuant to the exercise of statutory powers, such duty of care is not excluded because the advice is given pursuant to the exercise of statutory powers. This is particularly important where other remedies laid down by the statute (eg an appeals review procedure) do not in themselves provide sufficient redress for loss which has already been caused.

Where, as in Pamela's case, a person is employed by a local education authority to carry out professional services as part of the fulfilment of the authority's statutory duty, it has to be asked whether there is any overriding reason in principle why (a) that person should not owe a duty of care (the first question) and (b) why, if the duty of care is broken by that person, the authority as employer or principal should not be vicariously liable (the second question).

...

The result of a failure by an educational psychologist to take care may be that the child suffers emotional or psychological harm, perhaps even physical harm. There can be no doubt that if foreseeability and causation are established, psychological injury may constitute damage for the purpose of the common law. But so in my view can a failure to diagnose a congenital condition and to take appropriate action as a result of which failure a child's level of achievement is reduced, which leads to loss of employment and wages. Questions as to causation and as to the quantum of damage, particularly if actions are brought long after the event, may be very difficult, but there is no reason in principle to rule out such claims.

...

I do not think that in this case it is any answer to the claim that a duty of care existed that others had been involved in psychological advice at an earlier stage, or that she was said to be part of the multidisciplinary team, including the teaching staff. At Mellow Lane, she was the professional person brought in to this case and her role, difficult though it was, was pivotal. I see no reason why in this situation she did not have a duty of care to Pamela. Her relationship with the child and what she was doing created the necessary nexus and duty. The judge was both entitled and right to find that she owed a duty of care. He was equally entitled and might hold that, if she was in breach of her duty, Hillingdon was vicariously liable.

Lord Slynn went on to hold that the judge was entitled on the evidence to find that there had been a breach of the duty of care which caused the damage claimed, and confirmed the award of damages.

...

Direct liability

I do not rule out the possibility of a direct claim in all situations where the local authority is exercising its powers. If it exercises its discretion by deciding to set up a particular scheme pursuant to a policy which it has lawfully adopted, there is no, or at least there is unlikely to be any, common-law duty of care. If, however, it then, for example, appoints to carry out the duties in regard to children with special educational needs a psychologist or other professionals who at the outset transparently are neither qualified nor competent to carry out the duties, the position is different. That may be an unlikely scenario, but if it happens, I do not see why as a matter of principle a claim at common law in negligence should never be possible.

...

G

David, who was born on 27 June 1984, suffers from Duchenne Muscular Dystrophy which involves progressive muscle wasting. He was provided with a statement of special needs which emphasised the need for him to have access to a computer and to be trained in its use. ... He claims that negligently and in breach of duty to him, Bromley failed to provide a proper education and, in particular, computer technology and suitable training to enable him to communicate and to cope educationally and socially. As a result he suffered damage in the form of a lack of educational progress, social deprivation and psychiatric injury consisting of clinical depression.

...

The issues broadly are whether teachers owe a duty at common law to exercise reasonable skill and care and to exercise the reasonable skills of their calling in providing education for their pupils in relation to their needs, and to take reasonable care for their health and safety, including the monitoring of their needs and performance. If there is such a duty, what is its nature? Is the existence of such a duty at any rate arguable? The second issue is whether in the light of Art 6 of the European Convention for the Protection of Human Rights and Fundamental Freedoms 1950 and the Human Rights Act 1998 it is right to strike out the action before trial. The third issue is whether G can claim for psychiatric damage or economic loss if there was a negligent failure to provide him with teaching at an appropriate standard.

...

[His Lordship refused to strike out the claim by G.]

Jarvis

The issues raised on the strike-out are ... whether a claim that there has been a failure to diagnose and ameliorate any specific learning difficulty is a 'personal injury' claim or is a claim for pure economic loss; whether there can be a claim in damages when there is no recognisable psychiatric condition as described in the nervous shock cases; and whether the strike-out procedure violates Art 6(1) of the European Convention for the Protection of Human Rights and Fundamental Freedoms 1950.

The essence of the claim is that Marcus should have been put in a special unit expert in teaching dyslexic children and that to put him in schools for children with moderate learning difficulties was wrong; such a decision led to a deterioration of his behaviour which resulted in his being in prison for robbery. The question is whether Hampshire is directly liable or vicariously liable for the acts of the education psychologist or the education officers for the advice and decisions which were given and made.

...

Anderton

She suffered severe speech and language problems and was eventually diagnosed as being severely dyslexic ... She alleges that here [at the local state secondary school] she was bullied and she developed psychological problems due to the failure to make suitable educational provision for her. As a result of the treatment at both schools, she suffers from psychological problems.

...

The questions raised are in summary (i) whether the effect of failing to diagnose and deal with dyslexia is 'personal injury'; (ii) whether the effects of such failure sound in damages where there is no recognisable psychiatric condition; ...

The Court of Appeal held that the evidence fell far short of establishing that the applicant suffered any psychiatric injury and that:

> Even if dyslexia can be regarded as an impairment of the applicant's mental condition, it is not caused by the potential defendant. It is a congenital and constitutional condition. Failure to diagnose it does not exacerbate the condition. (*Anderton v Clwyd County Council and Another* [1999] ELR 1, at p 3).

The Court of Appeal therefore held that failure to mitigate or ameliorate the consequences of the condition could not be an injury.

...

The broad definition of injury in s 35(5) makes it clear that the power under s 33(2) is not limited to physical injury, the sense in which as a matter of ordinary speech the word might be understood. Having regard to the purpose of the provision it would in any event, in my view, be wrong to adopt an over-legalistic view of what are 'personal injuries to a person'. For the reasons given in my opinion in *Phelps*, psychological damage and a failure to diagnose a congenital condition and to take appropriate action as a result of which a child's level of achievement is reduced (which leads to loss of employment and wages) may constitute damage for the purpose of a claim.

- *Is dyslexia a personal injury?*

- *What is the limitation period applicable to a claim based on failure to diagnose dyslexia?*

- *Is the common law duty of care owed to all pupils or only those with SEN?*

- *When, if at all, will the LEA be directly liable where there has been a failure to diagnose dyslexia?*

The educational negligence cases are a major development both within the tort of negligence but also because of their impact on the legal relationship between the provider of public services and the recipient or consumer of those services.

Jonathan Greenwold 'Lawyer in the classroom' 12(4) Education and the Law 245 (2000) at 252–5

Analysis: why the law has evolved towards wider LEA liability

In *Phelps*, the House of Lords removed LEAs from the virtually all-encompassing immunity which had been built up around public bodies. But why did the Law Lords create an entirely new area of liability by giving pupils a remedy in damages against educationally negligent LEAs? The key to this change lies in their accepting the way that the Thatcher, Major and Blair governments have arguable promoted a 'managed' market for education within the public sector (see Harris, 1993, 1998; Bainham, 1998; Whitty & Menter, 1989). These reforms encouraged the courts to expand consumer rights to the recipients of public services.

   ...

The Lords refused to give LEAs immunity from tortuous actions simply because of their status as public bodies. With the new climate of consumerism, liability is so much easier to establish because it has extended consumer rights into the public sector. Adjudicating the question of liability is now simply a question of applying the basic principles of duty of care, breach of duty, standard of care, proximity and whether damage has been suffered or not. The policy considerations which made liability neither fair, just nor reasonable, are no longer relevant. Now the House of Lords was able to fit LEAs into its traditional fault-based paradigm of corrective justice liability (Williams, 1984).

[P]ublic bodies largely operate within the terms of positive duties and powers. LEAs, for example, work to give pupils the positive benefit of an education. In the courts' eyes claimants fighting public bodies must therefore have seemed to be asking the court to grant damages when the defendant had not inflicted any negative harm but had merely failed to confer a positive benefit. Such claims failed because there was no 'fault'.

In addition, outside this strict corrective justice approach, these were strong 'policy' reasons why the wider, proactive nature of a public body's duties made it important to *constrain* liability. The fact that public bodies have a positive role to play in society was seen to merit their protection, rather than opening them up to wider liability. Judges seemed to feel that the pro-active nature of public bodies' statutory duties and discretions should not open them up to wider claims than those faced by private bodies. Rather, they were prepared to sacrifice the claims of the few individuals harmed by public bodies for the sake of the benefits these bodies conferred on the general community.

However, this wall of immunity is now crumbling as LEAs have come to be seen as quasi-private, semi-commercialised institutions. The new climate emphasises freedom of choice and individual autonomy along the lines of the corrective justice 'exchange model' of social relations. It places schools and pupils and/or parents in a quasi-contractual relationship. It encourages the view that schools are the suppliers of a product (education) which children, and their parents, consume. This commercial relationship brings education back into the model of corrective justice liability, laying certain obligations on schools, which, if broken, must be recompensed.

It was in this vein that the House of Lords treated the defendant LEAs far more like any other professional organisation rather than a branch of local government. For example, in 1995 Lord Browne-Wilkinson had emphasised that there must be 'no potential conflict of duty between ... the professional [educator] being under a duty of care to the claimant and the discharge by the authority of its statutory duties'. He did so because he saw the LEA as a public body. Foremost in his mind, therefore, were its statutory duties. This year, in *Phelps*, Lord Clyde argued that liability would not 'add burdens and distractions to the already intensive life of teachers'.

There was a crucial change of emphasis here. In 2000, the judges treated the matter as one between teachers, who just happen to be employed by a professional body, and pupils. In 1995, the fact that these teachers were employed by a public body was by far the most important factor in the judgment.

...

In this way, claimants have the upper hand because the House of Lords now treats education, not as a public service, but as a product being supplied by a commercial enterprise to a customer. The matter was seen as essentially one of professional negligence. The statutory context *encourages* litigation rather than mitigating against liability.

The legal revolution initiated by these cases will rumble on. The emphasis on the quality of educational provision brings with it the increased likelihood of claims by parents and pupils where they are exposed to failing teachers, schools or LEAs.

Laura Berman and others 'Educational negligence' 13(1) Education and the Law 51 (2001) at 65–6

It seems very probable that the Lords will be asked to address further issues arising out of their decisions in *X* and *Phelps* on issues such as limitation and quantum. The arrival of contingency fees and the abandonment of the availability of public funding in personal injury cases have added extra urgency to the question as to how these actions should be classed.

13. HUMAN RIGHTS

A number of cases have been brought under the European Convention on Human Rights (ECHR) by the parents of children with special educational needs. The claims were mainly concerned with the decision-making process which existed before SENT was established by the Education Act 1993. None of the claims was considered admissible by the European Commission which acted as a filter before the reorganisation of the ECHR institutions.

In *Simpson v UK* 64 DR 188 (1989) Application No 14688/89 the applicant, who was born in 1973, suffered from dyslexia and had a statement of special educational needs under which the LEA agreed to pay for the applicant to attend a private fee-paying special school. The applicant's family then moved into a different LEA which reviewed the statement and proposed that the applicant should attend a mainstream comprehensive school with 1400 pupils, which had an Individual Learning Department. The applicant's mother unsuccessfully appealed to the local appeal committee and the Secretary of State, which were the appeal routes then available. The applicant applied unsuccessfully to the European Human Rights Commission which declared the application inadmissible.

Simpson v UK 64 DR 188 (1989) Application No 14688/89

...

As regards the applicant's personal complaint of a denial of his right to education under Article 2 of Protocol No 1 (P1–2), the Commission observes that Article 2 of Protocol No 1 (P1–2) is not an absolute right which requires Contracting Parties to subsidise private education of a particular type or level. In principle, it guarantees access to public educational facilities which have been created at a given time and the possibility of drawing benefit from the education received. This right 'by its very nature calls for regulation by the State, regulation which may vary in time and place according to the needs and resources of the community and of individuals', as long as the substance of the right to education is preserved (ECourt HR, Belgian Linguistic judgment, 23 July 1968, Series A no 6, pp 30–31, paras 3–5).

The Commission notes that the United Kingdom Government provides special education for disabled children either in normal mainstream schools with special departments, or in specialised segregated institutions. In keeping with current educational trends s 2 of the Education Act 1981 provides that children with special educational needs should be educated in an ordinary school with normal children of their own age if that is compatible with the special education which the former require, the provision of efficient education for other children at the school and the efficient use of resources. The Commission recognises that there must be a wide measure of discretion left to the appropriate authorities as to how to make the best use possible of the resources available to them in the interests of disabled children generally. While these authorities must place weight on parents' and pupils' views, it cannot be said that the first sentence of Article 2 of Protocol No 1 (P1–2) requires the placing of a dyslexic child in a private specialised school, with the fees paid by the State, when a place is available in an ordinary State school which has special teaching facilities for disabled children.

As regards the facts of the present case, the Commission notes that the applicant's behavioural problems in a State school arose at a time when his disabilities had not been diagnosed or treated. His dyslexia has now been identified and would be treated in the special department of the comprehensive school proposed by the education authorities. It is not the Commission's task to assess the standard of the special facilities provided by this State school. It is clear however, that the applicant's progress at the school would be monitored and his needs kept under review by the education authorities. In these circumstances, the Commission concludes that the applicant is not denied his right to education and that the present case does not disclose any appearance of a violation of Article 2, first sentence, of Protocol No 1 (P1–2). It follows that this aspect of the application is manifestly ill-founded within the meaning of Article 27 para 2 (Art 27–2) of the Convention.

Although the existing ECHR case law is not encouraging, there is some potential for claims to be brought by children with special educational needs or disabled pupils under the Human Rights Act 1998.

Jonathan Black-Branch 'Equality, non-discrimination and the right to special education; from international law to the Human Rights Act' [2000] EHRLR 297

The Commission's remit is to examine breaches of human rights and is thus reluctant to serve as a court of last resort in relation to professional negligence as in the case of *S P.* Once the Commission was satisfied that the child in question had access to education, and indeed in this case had been tested by the education authority's psychologist, there was little reason for them to weigh issues of effectiveness. The Commission is an international tribunal seeking to ensure basic standards of rights recognition. Prima facie there was no denial of the right to education and they were thus satisfied.

Under the Human Rights Act, however, domestic courts are likely to examine the right to an effective education, and not simply whether the applicant has access to educational institutions. Theirs will be a more stringent task of weighing the options. Indeed, as public bodies, courts will be compelled to hear such cases even if in the end they do not amount to breaches of the rights, per se.

The Scope of Education

In addition, Article 2 of the First Protocol serves to broaden the scope of the right to education in the United Kingdom. Specifically, the second phrase of the article provides that the State must respect 'the right of parents to ensure such education and teaching in conformity with their ... philosophical convictions' as it relates to 'the exercise of any functions which it assumes in relation to education and to teaching'. Although, at first glance, this clause might seem more likely to encompass belief systems that are more spiritual in nature, the Court of Human Rights has set a broader test than merely spiritual or religious beliefs. Thus, it could be argued that providing one type, or method, of education to one's child does indeed conflict with a parent's philosophical convictions. Specifically, there is a major division of informed opinion as to how special education students should be educated. On the one hand, there are those who advocate segregating special needs students from the mainstream/regular group so they can receive individualised attention in a separate environment. On the other hand, there are those who believe in integrating them into regular settings (mainstreaming) where they can receive special assistance within this normal environment.

...

According to the test set out in *Campbell and Cosans* [v *United Kingdom*, 4 EHRR 293], two important precedents are set for parents with special needs students. First, the second sentence of Article 2 applies to 'all' aspects and functions of education, including administrative decision-making relating to the formulation and financing of special educational programmes, and indeed curriculum and pedagogy. No aspect is to be precluded from scrutiny under this provision. Secondly, a parent's views on a particular type of special educational programme seems likely to fall within the scope of a philosophical conviction and accordingly must be respected. Parental convictions regarding instruction, delivery and administration of special educational programmes should hold the necessary degree of cogency, seriousness, cohesion and importance so as to warrant a violation of their rights, or at least judicial scrutiny thereof. Although the *Campbell and Cosans* case was different in that it questioned the use of corporal punishment, which admittedly is quite different from issues of special education, per se, the case nevertheless establishes the principle that parents should have a degree of participation in determining what is appropriate concerning their child's education.

...

Local authorities may well be compelled to limit expenditures in other areas of spending in order to guarantee education to *all* students. Expensive school equipment, class trips and so forth may have to be reconsidered if finite resources are allocated to embellish the needs of the mainstream group at the expense of those with more basic educational needs, ie special needs students. Failing that, the local education authority could be perceived as discriminatory, advantaging one group of students over another.

Further, the Government reservation itself refers to 'the avoidance of unreasonable public expenditure'. The question is whether requiring education authorities to provide education for *all* its citizens is considered 'unreasonable'. This author would argue that aspiring to educate *all* students, regardless of ability or disability, is not unreasonable. And, therefore, increasing public expenditure to accommodate basic needs of exceptional children does not constitute an 'unreasonable public expenditure'. It should not be left to the goodwill of authorities. Education is the cornerstone of an egalitarian society where *all* citizens should have an equal opportunity to achieve their full individual potential without undue privilege, preferential treatment or discrimination.

Discrimination and Equal Treatment

As described above, Article 14 seeks to prohibit against discrimination, providing a number of grounds relating thereto. Amongst the grounds listed it does not expressly list mental disability, physical disability or behavioural afflictions as proscriptive grounds of discrimination. In order to argue this provision in special education cases, the first task would be to establish that the student in question falls within the intended category of the prohibition. That said, Article 14 is considered an 'open-ended' clause which is not exhaustive in its scope. It seems that other grounds such as mental or physical disability may well be included under its guise. It would seem that this is not a very high hurdle to clear. Most other national human rights instruments prohibit against discrimination on these same grounds and whilst non-binding on UK courts, their precedents are likely to be highly persuasive in establishing mental and physical disability as grounds under the prohibition. The Canadian Charter of Rights and Freedoms, for example, expressly lists 'mental or physical disability' as a ground in its equal rights clause. 'Every individual is equal before and under the law and has the right to the equal protection and equal benefit of the law without discrimination and, in particular, without discrimination based on ... mental or physical disability'. Similarly, the South African Bill of Rights states that 'Everyone is equal before the law and has the right to equal protection and benefit of the law. ... The state may not unfairly discriminate directly or indirectly against anyone on one or more grounds, including ... disability ...' It is likely that disability would fall within the categories intended under the Convention.

Conclusion

The institution of the Human Rights Act 1998 invariably opens the way for many challenges relating to special education. The right to an 'effective' education and the right to non-discrimination is to be protected under domestic law where local courts will be both empowered and indeed compelled to hear alleged violations thereof. As a result, local education authorities will increasingly come under scrutiny in relation to issues of curriculum and pedagogy, services and facilities, equipment and accessibility. Courts will invariably come under increased pressure to hear such cases and indeed to weigh the merits of such arguments in some depth. Predicting how they will rule on such issues remains speculative. They are likely to be decided based on the facts of the particular case and the individual circumstances surrounding the issues in dispute.

That said, there are a number of steps which local education authorities can take towards eliminating potential disputes. First, they should take care to insure the accurate and proper identification of special needs students. Secondly, they should design individualised programmes of instruction which are appropriate to the specific needs of the student identified. And thirdly, they should insure the effective delivery and monitoring of such programmes. Not only would this assist to eliminate, or at least defuse, costly legal disputes, but it would assist to establish educational programmes that promote a more inclusive society whereby all students are eligible to achieve their full academic potential as full participants in an otherwise equal society.

Chapter 6

The school curriculum

1. INTRODUCTION

There is no legal definition of curriculum. The *Shorter Oxford English Dictionary* defines it as including: 'a regular course of study as at a school'. The school curriculum has only become subject to detailed legal regulation in the last two decades. Prior to that time there was little central regulation of, let alone legislation on, the curriculum. In 1986 the Education (No 2) Act (E (No 2) A) 1986 gave the LEA, the police, the local community, governors and teachers the right to be consulted on a school's curriculum. The Education Reform Act (ERA) 1988 introduced central control over the curriculum with the introduction of a National Curriculum for England and Wales. The current legislation is found in the Education Act (EA) 1996 and the School Standards and Framework Act (SSFA) 1998, together with numerous regulations which are supplemented by circulars. The Education Bill 2001/02 provides for a separate curriculum for England and Wales, and re-enacts the majority of the provisions in the Education Act 1996.

These legislative provisions only apply to state primary and secondary schools, and are concerned mainly with the years of compulsory schooling, that is 5 to 16 years of age. They do not apply to nursery schools or to nursery classes in primary schools. A non-statutory foundation stage applies to children receiving nursery education. The Education Bill 2001/02 provides that the foundation stage will form part of the National Curriculum, and will therfore be governed by legislation. Independent schools are not subject to these legal requirements nor are parents who teach their children at home.

Legislative regulation of the curriculum is the norm in the European Union. England and Wales was one of the exceptions. In some countries the written constitution sets out such rights, which are enforceable in varying degrees by the courts. For example, in the United States of America the First Amendment to the Constitution provides that:

> Congress shall make no law respecting an establishment of religion, or prohibiting the
> free exercise thereof; or abridging the freedom of speech or of the press; ...

These two clauses, known respectively as the establishment clause and the freedom of speech clause, have been the subject of a considerable amount of litigation involving schools (see below).

In Germany there are State Administrative Courts which have jurisdiction to hear educational litigation including curriculum disputes; and in Japan, Austria, Belgium and Switzerland the courts may examine the constitutionality of education law.

In Japan the government was held to have acted unconstitutionally when it censored the contents of history and geography textbooks, although it was entitled to have a system of certification. This issue came before the Japanese Supreme Court again in 1997 when it ruled that the Japanese Education Ministry had acted illegally in censoring a history textbook. This was the latest in a series of cases brought by Professor Saburo Ienaga. He started his action in 1965 after the Education Ministry ordered him to omit or amend certain passages in his book *New History of Japan*, including those which described the activities of a Japanese germ warfare unit. However, the court did not rule on his central claim which was that state censorship of textbooks is in breach of the Japanese constitution.

The United Kingdom does not have a written constitution or a system of administrative courts, unlike Germany or France. Litigation on the curriculum has been minimal. The majority of disputes are resolved at local level or by the Secretary of State. However, art 2 of protocol 1 of the European Human Rights Convention 1950, which has been incorporated into domestic law by the Human Rights Act 1998, may provide a remedy for parents concerned about aspects of the school curriculum. The most contentious areas are likely to be sex and religious education (see below).

2.   THE BASIC CURRICULUM

The two key terms in the current legislation are the 'basic curriculum' and the 'National Curriculum'. The main statutory provisions relating to the curriculum are to be found in EA 1996, Pt V, which superseded ERA 1988 and came into force on 1 November 1996.

The 'basic curriculum' is more broadly defined than the National Curriculum which comes within its definition. The Secretary of State, LEAs, school governing bodies and head teachers are under a general duty to exercise their functions with a view to ensuring that the school curriculum for maintained schools is balanced and broadly based.

Education Act 1996, s 351

(1) The curriculum for a school satisfies the requirements of this section if it is a balanced and broadly based curriculum which—

(a)   promotes the spiritual, moral, cultural, mental and physical development of pupils at the school and of society, and

(b) prepares pupils at the school for the opportunities, responsibilities and experiences of adult life.

...

Education Act 1996, s 352

(1) The curriculum for every maintained school shall comprise a basic curriculum which includes—
(a) provision for religious education for all registered pupils at the school (in accordance with such of the provisions of [Sch 19 to the School Standards and Framework Act 1998] as apply in relation to the school),
(b) a curriculum for all registered pupils at the school of compulsory school age (known as 'the National Curriculum') which meets the requirements of s 353,
(c) in the case of a secondary school, provision for sex education for all registered pupils at the school, and
(d) in the case of a special school, provision for sex education for all registered pupils at the school who are provided with secondary education.

(2) Subsection (1)(a) does not apply in the case of a maintained special school (provision as to religious education in special schools being made by regulations under s 342(6)).

(3) In this Act 'sex education' includes education about—
(a) Acquired Immune Deficiency Syndrome and Human Immunodeficiency Virus, and
(b) any other sexually transmitted disease.

The Education Bill 2001/02 re-enacts s 352 and provides that the National Curriculum will apply to children who have attained the age of three rather than five to reflect the incorporation of the foundation stage within the National Curriculum. In addition, the Secretary of State will be granted new powers including the power to vary the content of the curriculum. For example, the Secretary of State could require 14-16-year-olds to undertake community services. LEAs, governing bodies and head teachers have legal responsibilities in relation to ensuring that:
(a) the National Curriculum is implemented (s 400 of the EA 1996);
(b) the statutory requirements concerning collective worship and religious education (see below) are complied with;
(c) political indoctrination is forbidden (s 406 of the EA 1996);
(d) a balanced treatment of political issues is secured (s 403 of the EA 1996);
(e) any sex education complies with statutory requirements (see below);
(f) careers education and guidance are provided (see below).
Parents are entitled to be provided with information by the school or the LEA about the curriculum offered in their child's school. The information includes the following.

Education Act 1996, s 408(2)

(2)...
(a) the curriculum for maintained schools,

(b)   the educational provision made by the school for pupils at the school and any syllabuses to be followed by those pupils,

(c)   the educational achievements of pupils at the school (including the results of any assessments of those pupils, whether under this Part or otherwise, for the purpose of ascertaining those achievements), and

(d)   the educational achievements of [such classes or descriptions of pupils] as may be prescribed (including results of the kind mentioned in paragraph (c)).

Section 409 of the EA 1996 provides for regulations to be made to implement this principle. Where the information is not forthcoming a complaint can be made to the LEA (EA 1996, s 409; see below).

The Qualifications and Curriculum Authority (QCA)

The QCA came into operation on 1 October, 1997 and has a general duty to advance and promote quality and coherence in education and training in England. It has limited duties in relation to Wales and Northern Ireland (ss 21, 22 of the EA 1997). There is a separate Qualifications, Curriculum and Assessment Authority for Wales.

The QCA oversees the curriculum, assessment and qualifications from pre-school to higher vocational levels. The Chairman and the members of the Commission are appointed by the Secretary of State.

The QCA has two main areas of responsibility. The first is in relation to curriculum and assessment; the second covers external vocational and academic qualifications where the main legal responsibility rests on the Secretary of State.

Curriculum and assessment

The QCA publishes materials on and information about the school curriculum as well as being responsible for the assessment arrangements and keeping the curriculum under review.

Education Act 1997, s 23

(1) The Qualifications and Curriculum Authority shall have the functions set out in subsection (2) with respect to pupils of compulsory school age at maintained schools in England.

(2) The functions are—

(a)   to keep under review all aspects of the curriculum for such schools and all aspects of school examinations and assessment;

(b)   to advise the Secretary of State on such matters concerned with the curriculum for such schools or with school examinations and assessment as he may refer to them or as they may see fit;

(c)   to advise the Secretary of State on, and if so requested by him assist him to carry out, programmes of research and development for purposes connected with the curriculum for such schools or with school examinations and assessment;

(d) to publish and disseminate, and assist in the publication and dissemination of, information relating to the curriculum for such schools or to school examinations and assessment;

(e) to make arrangements with appropriate bodies for auditing the quality of assessments made in pursuance of assessment arrangements; and

(f) so far as relevant to such schools, the functions conferred by section 24(2)(h) and (i).

(3) The Authority shall have, in relation to England, the function of developing learning goals and related materials for children who are under compulsory school age.

(4) The Authority shall have, in relation to England, the following functions in connection with baseline assessment schemes (within the meaning of Chapter I of Part IV), namely—

(a) if designated by the Secretary of State for the purpose, any function of a designated body under that Chapter; and

(b) any other function which may be conferred on the Authority by the Secretary of State.

....

External vocational and academic qualifications

Such qualifications are defined in the Learning and Skills Act (LSA) 2000 as follows.

Learning and Skills Act 2000, s 96

...

(6) A qualification is awarded by an outside person if it is awarded by a person other than—

(a) the school or institution or employer, or

(b) a member of the staff of the school or institution or employer.

(7) A qualification is authenticated by an outside person if it is awarded by the school or institution or employer and is authenticated by a person other than—

(a) the school or institution or employer, or

(b) a member of the staff of the school or institution or employer.

The following courses are specifically excluded from this definition (LSA 2000, s 96(5)):

(a) a course for the further training of teachers or youth and community workers;

(b) a postgraduate course (including a higher degree course);

(c) a first degree course;

(d) a course for the Diploma of Higher Education;

(e) a course for the Certificate in Education.

ROLE OF THE QCA

The QCA is responsible for reviewing external qualifications, advising the Secretary of State and developing criteria for the accreditation of such qualifications. The powers of the QCA have been extended by LSA 2000, s 103 so that, for example, literacy and numeracy tests may be developed for adults.

Education Act 1997, s 24

(1) The Qualifications and Curriculum Authority shall have, in relation to England, the functions set out in subsection (2) with respect to external qualifications.

(2) The functions are—

(a)   to keep under review all aspects of such qualifications;

(b)   to advise the Secretary of State on such matters concerned with such qualifications as he may refer to them or as they may see fit;

(c)   to advise the Secretary of State on, and if so requested by him assist him to carry out, programmes of research and development for purposes connected with such qualifications;

(d)   to provide support and advice to persons providing courses leading to such qualifications with a view to establishing and maintaining high standards in the provision of such courses;

(e)   to publish and disseminate, and assist in the publication and dissemination of, information relating to such qualifications;

(f)   to develop and publish criteria for the accreditation of such qualifications;

(g)   to accredit, where they meet such criteria, any such qualifications submitted for accreditation;

(gg) to make arrangements (whether or not with others) for the development, setting or administration of tests or tasks which fall to be undertaken with a view to obtaining such qualifications and which fall within a prescribed description.

In most cases the QCA's functions do not apply to qualifications awarded by universities or other higher education institutions. National Vocational Qualifications (NVQs) do come within this section. The QCA can withdraw accreditation from an awarding body, and has done so in the case of, for example, the Road Transport Industry Training Board Services Ltd.

ROLE OF THE SECRETARY OF STATE

The power of the Secretary of State to regulate certain publicly-funded and school courses (for pupils of compulsory school age) leading to an external qualification has been amended by the Learning and Skills Act 2000. The provisions now vary according to whether the pupils or students taking the course are aged under or over 19 years. The LEA and the governing bodies of schools are responsible for ensuring that only approved courses are offered. Courses may be approved by the Secretary of State, by the Learning and Skills Council, by LEAs or by any other body designated by the Secretary of State (LSA 2000, ss 98, 99, 100). The provisions do not apply to informal courses which do not lead to a qualification.

Under 19 years

Learning and Skills Act 2000, s 96

(1) This section applies to a course of education or training—
(a)   which is provided (or proposed to be provided) by or on behalf of a school or institution or employer,
(b)   which leads to an external qualification, and
(c)   which is provided (or proposed to be provided) for pupils who are of compulsory school age or for pupils who are above that age but have not attained the age of 19.

(2) Unless the external qualification is approved under section 98 or 99, the course must not be—
(a)   funded by an authorised body (as defined in section 100), or
(b)   provided by or on behalf of a maintained school.

...

19 years or over

Learning and Skills Act 2000, s 97

(1) This section applies if an institution or employer—
(a)   receives financial resources from an authorised body (as defined in section 100), and
(b)   provides for persons who have attained the age of 19 a course of education or training which leads to an external qualification.

(2) The authorised body must carry out its functions with a view to securing that, unless the external qualification is approved under section 98 or 99, the institution or employer does not make a payment which—
(a)   is a payment in respect of the qualification,
(b)   is made to the outside person who awards or authenticates the qualification, and
(c)   can reasonably be said to consist of or come from the financial resources received from the authorised body (or those resources and others).

...

This is less restrictive than s 96. It requires the Learning and Skills Council, the NCETW (National Council of Education and Training for Wales) and LEAs (authorised bodies) to ensure that public money is only used to pay for approved external qualifications.

The powers of the QCA

The QCA has a general duty to advise the Secretary of State on matters connected with the provision of education and training in England (s 25 of the EA 1997), and is required to have regard to certain matters when carrying out its functions.

Education Act 1997, s 26

(1) In carrying out their functions under this Part the Qualifications and Curriculum Authority shall—

(a)   comply with any directions given by the Secretary of State; and

(b)   act in accordance with any plans approved by him; and

(c)   so far as relevant, have regard to—

(i)   the requirements of section 351 of the Education Act 1996 (general duties in respect of curriculum),

(ii)   the requirements of industry, commerce, finance and the professions regarding education and training (including required standards of practical competence), and

(iii) the requirements of persons with special learning needs.

(2) In carrying out those functions the Authority shall in addition have regard to information supplied to them by Her Majesty's Chief Inspector of Schools in England or by any body designated by the Secretary of State for the purposes of this section.

....

- *How, if at all, may the exercise of the powers in s 26(1)(c) be challenged, and by whom?*

3.   THE NATIONAL CURRICULUM

The National Curriculum was established by the Education Reform Act 1988. The power to establish and revise a National Curriculum is vested in the Secretary of State. The detailed provisions are contained in orders, which are published as a statutory instrument.

Education Act 1996, s 356

(1) The Secretary of State shall so exercise the powers conferred by subsection (2) as to—

(a)   establish a complete National Curriculum as soon as is reasonably practicable (taking first the core subjects and then the other foundation subjects), and

(b)   revise the National Curriculum whenever he considers it necessary or expedient to do so.

(2) The Secretary of State may by order specify in relation to each of the foundation subjects—

(a)   such attainment targets,

(b)   such programmes of study, and

(c)   such assessment arrangements,

as he considers appropriate for that subject.

(3) An order made under subsection (2) may not require—

(a)   the allocation of any particular period or periods of time during any key stage to the

(b) the making in school timetables of provision of any particular kind for the periods to be allocated to such teaching during any such stage.

Note the limitations on the Secretary of State's powers contained in sub-s (3).

The Education Bill 2001/02 re-enacts s 356 to include the foundation stage.

The Secretary of State must follow specified procedures when proposing to alter certain aspects of the National Curriculum (EA 1996, s 368). For example, the Secretary of State must refer the proposals to the QCA, which must consult with various bodies such as associations representing LEAs, governing bodies and teachers. The Education Bill 2001/02 re-enacts this provision in relation to England.

The role of the school and the LEA

The day-to-day responsibility for implementing the National Curriculum rests on the head teacher with overall responsibility resting on the governing body and the LEA.

Education Act 1996, s 357

(1) In relation to any maintained school and any school year—
(a)   the local education authority and the governing body shall exercise their functions with a view to securing, and
(b)   the head teacher shall secure,

that the National Curriculum as subsisting at the beginning of that year is implemented.

...

The Education Bill 2001/02 re-enacts EA 1996, s 357 and extends the duty to all providers of the foundation stage who are receiving early years education funding from the government.

Content

The National Curriculum has been revised several times since it was established under the Education Reform Act 1988. The current version was introduced in September 2000. The curriculum is divided into four stages (EA 1996, s 355):

Key Stage 1:   Years 1 and 2 (ages 6 to 7)

Key Stage 2:   Years 3 to 6 (ages 8 to 11)

Key Stage 3:   Years 7 to 9 (ages 12 to 14)

Key Stage 4:   Years 10 and 11 (ages 15 and 16)

The Education Bill 2001/02 adds the foundation stage to the National Curriculum for England. The foundation stage applies to children aged 3-5 years. The Bill also sets out the content and structure of the foundation stage in England. Different provisions apply to the incorporation of the foundation stage in the National Curriculum for Wales.

For each stage and for each subject there are:

– attainment targets
– programmes of study
– assessment arrangements (see EA 1996, s 356(2) above).

Education Act 1996, s 353

The National Curriculum shall comprise the core and other foundation subjects and specify in relation to each of them—
(a) the knowledge, skills and understanding which pupils of different abilities and maturities are expected to have by the end of each key stage (referred to in this Part as 'attainment targets'),
(b) the matters, skills and processes which are required to be taught to pupils of different abilities and maturities during each key stage (referred to in this Part as 'programmes of study'), and
(c) the arrangements for assessing pupils in respect of each key stage for the purpose of ascertaining what they have achieved in relation to the attainment targets for that stage (referred to in this Part as 'assessment arrangements').

The content of the National Curriculum is found in the programmes of study and attainment targets.

The National Curriculum is composed of core and foundation subjects (EA 1996, s 354). The legislation sets out minimum rather than maximum requirements. Section 354 was amended by the Foundation Subject (Amendment)(England) Order 2000, SI 2000/1146 and the Foundation Subject (Amendment)(Wales) Order 2000, SI 2000/1882.

The Education Bill 2001/02 re-enacts EA 1996, ss 353 and 354 but separates out the requirements for each stage, including the foundation stage, so that in future the requirements for a particular stage may be amended more easily than under the existing legislation.

Core subjects:	Mathematics
	English
	Science

Foundation subjects:	Technology		
	Physical Education	}	first three key stages
	History		
	Geography		
	Art and design		
	Music		

Modern foreign language	3rd and 4th key stage
Citizenship	3rd and 4th key stage from 2002

In practice the detailed content of each subject is contained in a National Curriculum document which is referred to in the relevant order. The primary legislation only addresses the specific content of the curriculum in relation to one aspect of science, as follows.

- *Are team games compulsory at Key Stage 4 in England?*

Education Act 1996, s 356(9)

(9) The Secretary of State shall, in exercising his power under subsection (2), ensure that the subject of science does not include—
(a) Acquired Immune Deficiency Syndrome and Human Immunodeficiency Virus,
(b) any other sexually transmitted disease, or
(c) aspects of human sexual behaviour, other than biological aspects.

- *Does this mean that pupils cannot be taught these topics in school? In which part of the curriculum and at what age should pupils study these topics?*

The core and foundation subjects are implemented by numerous orders, eg Education (National Curriculum) (Attainment Targets and Programmes of Study in History) (England) 2000, SI 2000/1606. A 'modern foreign language' in England is one specified in an order published by the Secretary of State, whereas in Wales the order must be passed by the National Assembly for Wales.

- *Find out which languages have been specified by order in either England or Wales.*

In Wales in Welsh-speaking schools, Welsh is also a core subject, whereas in non-Welsh speaking schools, it is a foundation subject.

Education Act 1996, s 354(8)

(8) For the purposes of this section a school is Welsh-speaking if more than one half of the following subjects are taught (wholly or partly) in Welsh—
(a) religious education, and
(b) the subjects other than English and Welsh which are foundation subjects in relation to pupils at the school.

In all Welsh schools 'art' is a foundation subject rather than 'art and design'; there is no requirement to study a modern foreign language at Key Stage 4; and citizenship is not a foundation subject at any stage.

4.   ASSESSMENT ARRANGEMENTS

The head teacher is responsible for implementing the National Curriculum which includes making arrangements for assessing pupils at the end of each key stage. 'Assessing' may involve examining and testing. The statutory orders can require the governing body, the head teacher, and the LEA to be responsible for aspects of the assessment arrangements (EA 1996, s 356(5), (6)).

The imposition of national testing was resisted by some teaching unions. The question of whether the statutory responsibility for implementing the assessment arrangements rests on the head teacher or on all teachers was raised in *Wandsworth London Borough Council v NASUWT* [1994] ELR 170.

Wandsworth London Borough Council v NASUWT [1994] ELR 170

NASUWT balloted teachers who were members of the Union. The ballot paper itself in para 5 posed this question:

> In order to protest against the excessive workload and unreasonable imposition made upon teachers, as a consequence of National Curriculum assessment and testing, are you willing to take action, short of strike action?

88 per cent of voters voted in favour of a boycott [of testing and assessment procedures].
...
Before the judge the case for the council was put forward in two ways:

(a) on the basis that the union could not rely on the protection afforded by s 219 of the 1992 Act [Trade Union and Labour Relations (Consolidation) Act] because the dispute was not a trade dispute within the meaning of s 244;

(b) on the basis that the members of the union were under a statutory duty to implement the National Curriculum and in particular to carry out the assessment of pupils in certain core subjects at key stage 3.

The judge rejected the council's case on both bases. In this court, however, the council do not seek to revive the argument that the members of the union are under a statutory duty to implement the National Curriculum. The only question for decision therefore is whether there is a trade dispute within the meaning of s 244 of the 1992 Act.

It is for the union to establish that they are protected from liability in tort by the provisions of the 1992 Act. By s 219 it is provided:

> An act done by a person in contemplation or furtherance of a trade dispute is not actionable in tort on the ground only—
>
> (a) that it induces another person to break a contract or interferes or induces another person to interfere with its performance ...

It is accepted on behalf of the union that their members who are schoolteachers are contractually obliged to carry out assessments and tests in accordance with the National Curriculum. It is further accepted that unless protected by s 219 the union is liable in tort by inducing its members to break their contracts of employment by the instructions it gave in relation to the boycott of certain parts of the test.
...

> In our judgment the dispute does mainly relate to the terms and conditions of employment of the union's members and is a trade dispute within the meaning of s 244 of

the 1992 Act. We consider that the judge reached the correct decision on these facts and we would dismiss the appeal.

• *Were the teachers potentially in breach of any legal duty?*

Baseline assessment

The Education Act 1997, s 16 introduced the concept of baseline assessment for children entering primary school. The purpose of baseline assessment is to identify problems at an early stage and to measure a pupil's progress through school.

White Paper *Excellence in Schools* (Cm 3681, 1997)

Assessment when starting school

12 Assessment of our youngest pupils when they start school is an essential first step on the way to improving basic skills in literacy and numeracy. A nationwide approach, building on the best of current practice, will be introduced from September 1997. It will show the value the school is adding and help teachers to:
• identify and plan activities to meet the needs of each and every pupil, in some cases providing early warning of special educational needs; and
• check the rate of pupils' progress as they learn.

The head teacher can decide that a particular pupil need not be assessed because, for example, such an assessment has already been carried out at another school (s 17 of the EA 1997).

The governing body of each maintained primary school is required to adopt a baseline assessment scheme, which has been accredited by the QCA. Each LEA must select an accredited baseline assessment scheme which they consider suitable to be adopted by the governing body, but the governing body does not have to use the scheme approved by its LEA. However, the Secretary of State has the power to impose a scheme on 'each maintained primary school', in which case there will be no choice as to which scheme can be adopted (s 16(6) of the EA 1996).

The governing body, the LEA where relevant, and the head teacher are under a duty to ensure that the pupils are assessed in accordance with the scheme, and to send the results of any assessments to the QCA.

The provisions contained in the Education Act 1997 (ss 15–18) are supplemented by regulations (Education (Baseline Assessment)(England) Regulations 1998, SI 1998/ 1551), and explained in DfEE circular 6/98 (Baseline Assessment of Pupils Starting Primary School).

The Education Bill 2001/02 removes the statutory requirement on schools to carry out a baseline assessment. Instead, schools will be required to complete a foundation stage profile for each pupil at the end of the foundation stage, which is normally the end of the reception year when the pupil is aged 5.

Assessment at Key Stages 1-3

Pupils are assessed in the three core subjects, mathematics, English, and science at the end of each of the three key stages. Statutory assessment materials are produced by the QCA. In addition to sitting the tests, each pupil's progress is formally assessed by their teachers. Pupils are assessed as working at a particular level.

Key stage	National test/teacher assessment	Typical level
1	7 years	2
2	11 years	4
3	14 years	5/6

The assessment arrangements vary according to the key stage and are contained in statutory orders, for example, the Education (National Curriculum)(Key Stage 1 Assessment Arrangements)(England) Order 1999, SI 1999/1236 as amended by SI 1999/2187 and SI 2000/1242.

An LEA is required to verify or monitor assessments at all three key stages. In addition at Key Stage 3 the pupil's papers are marked by an external agency.

Assessment at Key Stage 4

At this stage most pupils prepare for external qualifications such as GCSEs or NVQs. Pupils should only follow approved courses (see above) leading to such qualifications. Governing bodies should inform parents whether or not their child will be entered for a particular examination. Parents should not be charged for their child's examination entry (see below) where it is the first attempt.

Education Act 1996, s 402

(1) Subject to subsections (2) and (3), the governing body of a maintained school shall secure that each registered pupil at the school is entered, at such time as they consider appropriate, for each prescribed public examination for which he is being prepared at the school at the time in question in each syllabus for that examination for which he is being so prepared.

(2) The governing body are not required to secure that a pupil is entered for any examination, or for an examination in any syllabus for that examination, if either—
(a)   they consider that there are educational reasons in the case of that particular pupil for not entering him for that examination or (as the case may be) for not entering him for that examination in that syllabus, or

(b) the parent of the pupil requests in writing that the pupil should not be entered for that examination or (as the case may be) for that examination in that syllabus;

but this subsection does not apply to an examination which is part of the assessment arrangements for the fourth key stage and applies in the case of that pupil.

(3) The governing body are not required to secure that a pupil is entered for any examination in any syllabus for that examination if they have secured his entry for another prescribed public examination in a corresponding syllabus.

* *May the parent of a 15-year-old pupil refuse to let their child take a GCSE examination in (a) French or (b) religious education?*

Exemption from the National Curriculum

Exemption from the national curriculum is possible in certain circumstances. The exemption may apply to an individual pupil or it may apply to a particular school, or there may be a general disapplication. There are four main types of exemption set out in EA 1996, ss 362-367. These sections are re-enacted in the Education Bill 2001/02.

(1) Pupils with statements of special educational needs (see chapter 5)

Education Act 1996, s 364

The special educational provision for any pupil specified in a statement under section 324 of his special educational needs may include provision—
(a) excluding the application of the National Curriculum, or
(b) applying the National Curriculum with such modifications as may be specified in the statement.

Although a statement may provide that the pupil should not follow any or some of the National Curriculum, there is a presumption that such pupils should follow the National Curriculum unless it is expressly disapplied. In *R v Kingston upon Thames Council and Hunter* [1997] ELR 223 the court was required to decide whether the placement of a pupil (L) at a pupil referral unit (Four Oaks) which did not offer the full National Curriculum was 'appropriate', bearing in mind that Part 3 of the pupil's statement required her to have access to the full National Curriculum.

R v Kingston upon Thames Council and Hunter [1997] ELR 223

McCullough J: In February 1995 she [L] started to attend part-time at an annexe of Four Oaks known as Q2. Q2 makes specialist provision for children in need of intensive support. While there she was given individual tuition. Her work was set by Coombe [Girls' School]; this was in English, maths, science, history and geography. She made good progress and on 29 November 1995 moved into Four Oaks itself. She has been there ever since. The tribunal was told that she had continued to progress very well. At the time of the tribunal hearing L was attending Four Oaks 21 hours a week and was at key stage 3 and due to start key stage 4, and her GCSE course, in September 1996.

The authority's view was that it would be best if she were gradually reintegrated with mainstream education, and their plan for L was to bring this about in stages with L being taught the subjects which are not taught at Four Oaks in a mainstream school, this arrangement being increased step by step, subject by subject.

...

Mrs R submitted to the tribunal that Four Oaks was inappropriate because it could not offer the full National Curriculum and it was unrealistic to suggest that L was ever likely to be integrated back into a mainstream school. Nor did it provide L with art, except to a limited degree, nor music or drama. She said it would be appropriate for L to attend Queen's Park. This was a small mixed school taking pupils with specific learning difficulties between the ages of 8 and 16, where the full National Curriculum was taught and where L could also take art, music and drama in the same place.

...

A good deal of the argument was about whether L would ever again be able to cope with a mainstream school. The tribunal held that, with gradual reintegration, she would, and on this basis the tribunal regarded L's placement at Four Oaks as appropriate. Their attention would not appear to have been focused on the point on which I think this appeal turns, namely the authority's decision, when formulating part 3, not to use its powers under s 18 of the 1988 Act to modify or exclude, on a temporary basis, part of the National Curriculum. The critical question of how, in the light of the sentence 'No disapplication of the National Curriculum', Four Oaks could be appropriate for L in the period before her emotional stability permitted her to attend classes at a mainstream school to be taught the balance of the National Curriculum was never addressed.

In a case where the powers under s 18 of the 1988 Act are not used, I see nothing in principle unlawful in specifying in part 4 of a statement a PRU in which the full National Curriculum is not taught, provided that arrangements are made for the subjects which are not taught in the school itself to be taken at another school, but, as is accepted by the authority, such arrangements could not at the material time be made for L because of her emotional and behavioural problems. I hold that Four Oaks is not in law an appropriate placement for L because she cannot be taught the entire National Curriculum there and because her emotional condition precludes her, for a time at least — and that is enough — from being taught the balance in a mainstream school. Part 4 must therefore be quashed and Mrs R's appeal reconsidered by a differently constituted tribunal.

(2) Temporary exceptions for individual pupils

The head teacher of any maintained school may direct that all or part of the National Curriculum should not apply to a particular pupil for a specified period.

Education Act 1996, s 365

(1) Regulations may enable the head teacher of a maintained school, in such cases or circumstances and subject to such conditions as may be prescribed, to direct in respect of a registered pupil at the school that, for such period as may be specified in the direction (the 'operative period' of the direction), the National Curriculum—

(a) shall not apply, or
(b) shall apply with such modifications as may be specified in the direction.

(2) The conditions prescribed by the regulations shall, in particular, limit the operative period that may be specified in a direction to a maximum period specified in the regulations.

(3) Any maximum period specified (whether in relation to directions given under the regulations or in relation to directions given under the regulations in circumstances specified in the regulations) shall be either—
(a) a fixed period not exceeding six months, or
(b) a period determinable (in such manner as may be specified in the regulations) not later than six months from its beginning.

There are two types of directions: general and special. A general direction is normally regarded as a short-term measure where, for example, a pupil is unwell but is likely to be able to follow the National Curriculum in six months time or less. A special direction would apply where the head teacher considers that a pupil with special educational needs should undergo a statutory assessment, and during the assessment period the pupil should not follow any or part of the National Curriculum. The maximum period normally permissible under the regulations is 12 (special directions) or 18 (general directions) months.

The detailed legislation is contained in regulations (Education (National Curriculum) (Temporary Exceptions for Individual Pupils) (England) Regulations 2000, SI 2000/ 2121; (Wales) 1999, SI 1999/1815) which are supplemented by guidance (DES Circular 15/89 (Education Reform Act 1988: Temporary Exceptions from the National Curriculum); DfEE Guidance 0084/2000 (Guidance: Disapplication of the National Curriculum)).

Parents have the right to request the head teacher to give, vary or revoke a direction.

Education (National Curriculum) (Temporary Exceptions for Individual Pupils) (England) Regulations 2000, SI 2000/2121, reg 12

(1) Subject to paragraphs (2) and (3), a parent of a registered pupil may at any time request the head teacher to give a direction (or a further direction), or to revoke or vary a direction currently in force.

(2) Such a request may be made orally or in writing and shall include the reasons for which it is made.

(3) The head teacher shall not be obliged to entertain a request to revoke or vary a direction currently in force more than once during each of—
(a) the operative period of that direction; and
(b) the operative period of any further direction or directions given under regulation 9 or 10.

There is a right of appeal to the governing body against the head teacher's decision.

Education Act 1996, s 367

...

(2) On such an appeal, the governing body may—
(a)   confirm the head teacher's action, or
(b)   direct the head teacher to take such action authorised by the regulations as they consider appropriate in the circumstances.

(3) The head teacher shall comply with any directions of the governing body given under subsection (2)(b).

(4) The governing body shall notify the appellant and the head teacher in writing of their decision on such an appeal.

Where the parent is dissatisfied with the decision of the governing body he or she may invoke the complaints procedure established under EA 1996, s 409 (see below).

- *Compare these rights with the parental right to withdraw the child from religious and sex education.*

In addition head teachers have been given the power to modify or disapply the National Curriculum for certain pupils at Key Stage 4 (see (4) below).

(3) Temporary exception for a particular school

The Secretary of State has the power to waive or modify the National Curriculum in a particular school so that development work or experiments may be carried out. This power may be used in an Education Action Zone (EAZ) (see chapter 2).

Education Act 1996, s 362

(1) For the purpose of enabling development work or experiments to be carried out, the Secretary of State may direct in respect of a particular maintained school that, for such period as may be specified in the direction, the National Curriculum—
(a)   shall not apply, or
(b)   shall apply with such modifications as may be specified in the direction.

(2) A direction under subsection (1) may apply either generally or in such cases as may be specified in the direction.

(3) In the case of a community, voluntary controlled or community special school, a direction shall not be given under subsection (1) except on an application—
(a)   by the governing body with the agreement of the local education authority,
(b)   by the local education authority with the agreement of the governing body, or
(c)   by the appropriate curriculum authority with the agreement of both the local education authority and the governing body.

(4) In the case of a foundation, voluntary aided or foundation special school, a direction shall not be given under subsection (I) except on an application by the governing body or by the appropriate curriculum authority with the agreement of the governing body.

- *Who may ask the Secretary of State to make a direction, and whose agreement must be obtained before such a request can be made?*

(4) General power to disapply the National Curriculum

The Secretary of State also has a general power to make regulations which permit the waiver or modification of the National Curriculum (EA 1996, s 363). This power has been used sparingly and mainly in relation to the teaching of Welsh and technical changes. Examples of such regulations include the Education (National Curriculum) (Exceptions) (Wales) Regulations 1995, SI 1995/1574 and the Education (National Curriculum) (Exceptions) Regulations 1996, SI 1996/2083.

Some pupils at Key Stage 4 (the last two years of compulsory schooling) are able to undertake extended work experience which has been arranged by the LEA or the governing body of the school (EA 1996, s 560 as amended by s 112 of the SSFA 1998). The power under s 363 of the EA 1996 has been used to make regulations relating to disapplication of the National Curriculum for such pupils. Detailed provisions are found in the Education (National Curriculum) (Exceptions at Key Stage 4) (England) Regulations 2000, SI 2000/1140. Guidance is contained in DfEE 0084/2000 (Guidance: Disapplication of the National Curriculum). One of the aims of this legislation is to reduce the rate of truancy among pupils of this age group who have become disenchanted with education.

Education (National Curriculum) (Exceptions at Key Stage 4) (England) Regulations 2000, SI 2000/1140, reg 6

In these Regulations an extended work-related learning programme is a programme which—
(a)   offers pupils experience of the working environment and working practices;
(b)   provides pupils with the opportunity to develop literacy, numeracy and key skills through such experience;
(c)   is designed to complement the education being provided to pupils through the remainder of the curriculum which they are studying at school;
(d)   contributes, so far as is practicable, towards approved qualifications, whether vocational or not; and
(e)   cannot be provided alongside the full National Curriculum at Key Stage 4.

In addition, from 1 August 2000 the National Curriculum for pupils at Key Stage 4 may be disapplied for three types of pupil. These are pupils who are taking part in an extended work-related learning programme, or who demonstrate strenghts in a particular curriculum area, or who are making significantly less progress than other pupils. In the case of the first category of pupil the head teacher may decide that a particular pupil need not study up to two of the following subjects: modern foreign language; design and technology, or science. In the case of the other two categories of pupil the head teacher may decide that the pupil need not study a modern foreign language and/or design and technology. Schools have also been given greater flexibility in the choice of science, design and technology, and modern foreign language courses offered to pupils at Key Stage 4 (reg 12).

The head teacher has the power to decide whether to modify or disapply the National Curriculum. Unlike the case for temporary exceptions parents do not have a right of appeal to the governing body against the head teacher's decision.

SI 2000/1140, reg 7

(1) The provisions of the National Curriculum specified in this regulation shall not apply to a pupil in the following circumstances—
(a)   the pupil is participating in an extended work-related learning programme; or
(b)   the pupil has, in the opinion of the head teacher, demonstrated strengths in a particular curriculum area and is emphasising that curriculum area; or
(c)   the pupil is, in the opinion of the head teacher, making significantly less progress than other pupils of his age group and is consolidating his learning and progress across the curriculum.

(2) The head teacher may determine in the case of a pupil to whom paragraph 1(a) applies that the provisions of the National Curriculum regarding one or two of the following subjects should not apply to him:
(a)   modern foreign language;
(b)   design and technology;
(c)   science.

(3) The head teacher may determine in the case of a pupil to whom paragraph 1(b) or (c) applies that the requirements of the National Curriculum regarding one or both of the following subjects should not apply to him:
(a)   modern foreign language;
(b)   design and technology.

(4) In no circumstances shall these Regulations permit a pupil to have more than two of the subjects referred to in paragraph (2) disapplied in relation to him.

The Regulations require, for example, that before a decision to disapply the National Curriculum is made, the head teacher ensures that a careers interview has taken place with the pupil concerned, that a curriculum plan has been agreed with the pupil and his or her parents, and that the modified curriculum will be monitored (reg 8).

The Education Bill 2001/02 extends the power of the LSC to fund education or training provided for 14-16-year-olds at a FE college or at an employer's premises.

5.   CHARGING

One of the fundamental principles underpinning public sector education is that it should be free. The main area of contention relates to the provision of free school transport from home to school and back. The legislation is supplemented by guidance in DFE Circular 2/94 (Local Management of Schools), for example, paras 147-51.

This principle means that, with some exceptions, maintained schools cannot charge for admission (EA 1996, s 450).

Education Act 1996, s 450

(1) No charge shall be made in respect of admission to a maintained school.

(2) Subsection (1) does not apply to the admission of any person to any maintained school for the purpose of—
(a)   part-time education suitable to the requirements of persons of any age over compulsory school age;
(b)   full-time education suitable to the requirements of persons who have attained the age of 19; or
(c)   teacher training.

Nor can schools normally charge for education provided at school during school hours (EA 1996, s 451). The most important exception in practice relates to music tuition. Where the education is provided outside school hours a charge can be levied unless it falls within the statutory exceptions.

Education Act 1996, s 451

(1) ... this section applies in relation to education provided at any maintained school for a registered pupil at the school.

(2) Where the education is provided for the pupil during school hours no charge shall be made in respect of it.

(3) Subsection (2) does not apply in relation to tuition in playing a musical instrument where the tuition is provided either individually or to a group of not more than four pupils, unless the tuition is—
(a)   required as part of a syllabus for a prescribed public examination which is a syllabus for which the pupil is being prepared at the school, or
(b)   provided in pursuance of a duty imposed by section 357(1) (implementation of National Curriculum) or section 69 of the School Standards and Framework Act 1998 (duty to secure due provision of religious education).

(4) Where the education is provided for the pupil outside school hours no charge shall be made in respect of it if it is—

    (a) required as part of a syllabus for a prescribed public examination which is a syllabus for which the pupil is being prepared at the school, or

    (b) provided in pursuance of a duty imposed by section 357(1) or section 69 of the School Standards and Framework Act 1998.

No charge should be levied, for example, for:

–   education not at the school or outside school hours relating to the National Curriculum or religious education

–   prescribed public examination entrance fees (EA 1996, s 453)

–   materials, books and equipment eg safety goggles (EA 1996, s 454)

–   transport incidental to free education, eg between the school premises and the swimming pool where lessons are held.

Education outside school hours

Charges can be levied if 50 per cent or more of an educational activity, including travelling time, falls outside school hours.

Education Act 1996, s 452

(1) Where a period allowed for any educational activity at a maintained school falls partly during school hours and partly outside school hours, then—

    (a) if 50 per cent or more of the time occupied by that period together with any connected school travelling time falls during school hours, so much of the education provided during that period as is provided outside school hours shall be treated for the purposes of section 451 as provided during school hours, and

    (b) in any other case, so much of the education provided during that period as is provided during school hours shall be treated for those purposes as provided outside school hours.

(2) In subsection (1) 'connected school travelling time' means time spent during school hours by the pupils taking part in the educational activity concerned in getting to or from the place where the activity takes place.

(3) Where any education provided at a maintained school is provided on a residential trip, then—

    (a) if the number of school sessions taken up by the trip is equal to or greater than 50 per cent of the number of half days spent on the trip, any education provided on the trip which is provided outside school hours shall be treated for the purposes of section 451 as provided during school hours, and

    (b) in any other case, any education provided on the trip which is provided during school hours shall be treated for those purposes as provided outside school hours.

(4) In this section 'half day' means any period of 12 hours ending with noon or midnight on any day.

(5) For the purposes of subsection (3)—

(a) where 50 per cent or more of a half day is spent on a residential trip, the whole of that half day shall be treated as spent on the trip, and

(b) a school session on any day on which such a session takes place at the school concerned shall be treated as taken up by a residential trip if the time spent on the trip occupies 50 per cent or more of the time allowed for that session at the school.

(6) Nothing in section 451 shall be read as prohibiting the making of a charge in respect of board and lodging provided for a registered pupil at a maintained school on a residential trip.

Optional extras

In addition to charges being permitted for board and lodging on a residential trip, charges may also be made for additional education or transport costs, and for sitting additional public examinations.

Education Act 1996, s 455

(1) Subject to subsection (2), a charge may be made in respect of—

(a) education provided for a registered pupil at a maintained school other than education in respect of which, by virtue of section 451, no charge may be made,

(b) the entry of a registered pupil at a maintained school for a public examination in any syllabus for that examination otherwise than in circumstances in which, by virtue of section 453(1), no charge may be made,

(c) transport provided for a registered pupil at a maintained school other than transport in respect of which, by virtue of section 454(3) or 509(2), no charge may be made, and

(d) board and lodging provided for a registered pupil at a maintained school on a residential trip.

(2) A charge may not be made—

(a) by virtue of subsection (1)(a) in respect of the provision for a pupil of education,

(b) by virtue of subsection (1)(b) in respect of the entry of a pupil for an examination in any syllabus for that examination, or

(c) by virtue of subsection (1)(c) in respect of the provision for a pupil of transport,

unless the education is provided, the pupil is entered for the examination in that syllabus, or the transport is provided, by agreement with the pupil's parent.

(3) Any education, examination entry or transport in respect of which a charge may be made by virtue of subsection (1) is referred to in this Chapter as an 'optional extra'.

These are described as 'regulated charges' (EA 1996, s 456). They are not to exceed the actual cost of making the provision and are to be paid by the pupil's parent. The cost is fixed by the governing body or the LEA depending upon which body pays the overall cost. There are detailed provisions relating to what costs can be regarded as 'regulated charges'.

Education Act 1996, s 456

...

(4) Without prejudice to the generality of subsection (3), the cost of the provision of an optional extra includes costs, or an appropriate proportion of the costs—

(a)   incurred in respect of the provision of any materials, books, instruments or other equipment used for the purposes of or in connection with the provision of the optional extra, or

(b)   attributable to the provision of non-teaching staff for any purpose connected with the provision of the optional extra, or

(c)   attributable to the provision of teaching staff engaged under contracts for services for the purpose of providing it.

(5) Subject to subsection (6), the cost of the provision of an optional extra shall not be taken to include any costs attributable to the provision of teaching staff other than staff engaged as mentioned in subsection (4)(c).

(6) Where the optional extra in question consists of tuition in playing a musical instrument, the cost of its provision shall include costs, or an appropriate proportion of the costs, attributable to the provision of teaching staff employed for the purpose of providing the tuition.

However, charges can only be made if the governing body and the LEA have a charges and remissions policy, which must be kept under review (s 457 of the EA 1996; Education (School Sessions and Charges and Remissions Policies) (Information) (England) Regulations 1999, SI 1999/2255). The policy should be made available to parents and staff. It should, for example, provide for the remission of board and lodging charges for parents on low incomes.

Education Act 1996, s 457

...

(4) A remissions policy shall provide for complete remission of any charges otherwise payable in respect of board and lodging provided for a pupil on a residential trip if—

(a)   the education provided on the trip is education in respect of which, by virtue of section 451, no charge may be made, and

(b)   the pupil's parents are in receipt of—
       (i)   income support,
       (ii)   family credit,
       (iii) an income-based jobseeker's allowance (payable under the Jobseekers Act 1995), or
       (iv)   disability working allowance,

in respect of any period wholly or partly comprised in the time spent on the trip.

The Education Bill 2001/02 amends EA 1996, s 357 to bring it into line with changes in social security benefits.

- *Year 10 pupils studying geography at Hillbank Community School are expected to go on a geography field trip to Norfolk. The trip lasts three days. The plan is that the pupils should leave at 6.00 p m on Thursday evening and return at 6.00 p m on Sunday evening. The journey from school to Norfolk takes three hours each way. Can the school charge each pupil's parent for all or part of the field trip?*

  What difference would it make, if any, if the field trip started on Wednesday and returned on Saturday?

  Would it make any difference if the purpose of the visit was to enable members of the school orchestra to attend a residential music workshop?

Voluntary contributions

Governing bodies and LEAs are permitted to request or invite voluntary contributions for the benefit of the school or school activities. However, such requests are required to emphasise the voluntary nature of any contribution.

Education Act 1996, s 460(2)

(2) Any request or invitation made by or on behalf of such a body or authority for contributions for the benefit of a school or school activities shall not be regarded for the purposes of subsection (1) as a request or invitation for voluntary contributions unless it is clear from the terms in which it is made—

(a) that there is no obligation to make any contribution, and

(b) that registered pupils at the school will not be treated differently according to whether or not their parents have made any contribution in response to the request or invitation.

- *Does a request, which states that if insufficient parents agree to make the payment the activity will be unable to proceed, satisfy the requirements of this section?*

Free school transport

The LEA may be obliged to provide suitable transport arrangements between home and school where, for example, the school is not within walking distance of the child's home. The statutory provisions on transport also apply to students attending certain sixth form and FE colleges (EA 1996, s 509(1)(b), (c) and (d)) and new provisions were introduced by SSFA 1998, s 124 for children receiving nursery education otherwise than at school (EA 1996, s 509A). The Education Bill 2001/02 provides that LEAs should have a co-ordinating role in the provisions of transport for sixth form and FE students aged 16-19.

In addition to the legislation guidance is contained in DFE Circular Letter 21 January 1994 (school transport).

Education Act 1996, s 509

(1) A local education authority shall make such arrangements for the provision of transport and otherwise as they consider necessary, or as the Secretary of State may direct, for the purpose of facilitating the attendance of persons receiving education—
(a)   at schools, …

(2) Any transport provided in pursuance of arrangements under subsection (1) shall be provided free of charge.

…

(4) In considering whether or not they are required by subsection (1) to make arrangements in relation to a particular person, a local education authority shall have regard (amongst other things)—
(a)   to the age of the person and the nature of the route, or alternative routes, which he could reasonably be expected to take; and
(b)   to any wish of his parent for him to be provided with education at a school or institution in which the religious education provided is that of the religion or denomination to which his parent adheres.

Where the LEA does not provide free school transport this may provide a defence for a parent who is prosecuted under EA 1996, s 444 for failing to ensure that their child regularly attends school (see chapter 3).

Education Act 1996, s 444

(4) The child shall not be taken to have failed to attend regularly at the school if the parent proves—
(a)   that the school at which the child is a registered pupil is not within walking distance of the child's home, and
(b)   that no suitable arrangements have been made by the local education authority … for any of the following—
    (i)   his transport to and from the school,
    (ii)   boarding accommodation for him at or near the school, or
    (iii) enabling him to become a registered pupil at a school nearer to his home.

(5) In subsection (4) 'walking distance'—
(a)   in relation to a child who is under the age of eight, means 3.218688 kilometres (two miles), and
(b)   in relation to a child who has attained the age of eight, means 4.828032 kilometres (three miles),

in each case measured by the nearest available route.

The definition of 'walking distance' is derived from the Education Act 1944 and reflects a time when many children walked or cycled to school, there were far fewer cars on the road, and there was less concern about assaults on children and young people.

The meaning of 'suitable arrangements' and 'nearest available route' has been discussed in a number of cases.

• Should 'nearest available route' mean as the crow flies, or by the most direct walking route, or the most direct driving route, or by the safest route?

'Suitable arrangements'

R v Kent County Council, ex p C [1998] ELR 108

[NB: This case was concerned with the duty under EA 1944, s 55(1), the precursor to EA 1996, s 509.]

McCullough J: Rosalind Corby (R), who is 12, lives in Chiddingstone Hoth near Edenbridge in Kent; she is in her second year at Tonbridge Girls' Grammar School (TGGS), which is a grant-maintained (GM) school. After she had been selected for the school but before she transferred to it the local education authority (LEA), which is the Kent County Council (KCC), told her that they would not provide transport for her between home and school free of charge. The reason the KCC gave for this was that TGGS was not the nearest school which would have been suitable for R. Her father appealed to the KCC's Case Subcommittee of the Education Committee, but was told in a letter of 16 February 1996 that his appeal had failed. Through her father and next friend she now applies for judicial review of this decision.

...

In *R v Rochdale Metropolitan Borough Council ex p Schemet* [1992] 91 LGR 425, Roch J held that arrangements for enabling a child to become a registered pupil at a school nearer to his home would not be suitable unless the school itself were suitable for the particular pupil (see p 442). In his judgment he noted that Rose J had expressed a contrary view in *R v East Sussex County Council ex p D* (1991) 15 March (unreported). The view of Roch J was, however, endorsed by Staughton LJ in *R v Essex County Council ex p C* [1993] 93 LGR 10, who said (at p 14):

> The county council ... say that under s 39(2)(c) it is the arrangements that have to be suitable, not the school nearer home. That argument ... does not appeal to me. Arrangements for unsuitable transport, or unsuitable boarding accommodation, or an unsuitable school nearer home, are in my judgment unsuitable arrangements. I cannot elaborate the point further than that.

In the same case I take Steyn LJ to have shared this view. He said (at 17):

> Moreover in my view s 39(2)(c) of the Education Act 1944 (as amended) contemplates that a [LEA] is entitled to make arrangements for a child registered at one school to become a registered pupil at another suitable school nearer her home.

R v Dyfed County Council ex p S was decided at first instance by May J. The issue in the case was whether the county council was lawful in refusing to provide free transport under s 55 to the three children of an English-speaking family who had moved to Wales. The children attended a school circa 10 miles from home. They could have attended a school nearer home, but their parents preferred the further school because it was more English-speaking and less Welsh-speaking than the nearer one. The county council refused to provide free transport to the further school, basing their decision on the view that the nearer school would have been suitable for the children.

...

I have not found it easy ... to know what meaning the Court of Appeal was saying should be given to the words 'suitable arrangements ... for enabling him to become a registered pupil at a school nearer to his home'.

...

I think it right to follow *R v Dyfed County Council ex p S* only so far as the decision binds this court. I take the case to have decided that the objective suitability of the nearer school was not a matter for the court to determine. Either that was all it decided, or, additionally, which I think more likely, it decided that the relevant question was whether the authority's view that the nearer school was suitable had been shown to have been reached unlawfully ... In my judgment: (1) a LEA cannot properly refuse to provide free transport on the basis that there is a nearer school which a child could attend unless it is of the view that the nearer school would be a suitable school for that child to attend, and (2) when considering a challenge to a local authority's refusal to provide free transport, if the refusal was based on the authority's view that there was a nearer suitable school, the function of the court is to see whether it has been shown that the authority's view about that school's suitability was lawfully reached, which in most cases will require no more than a consideration of the rationality of its conclusion. This accords with the approach of Staughton LJ, Roch J and May J, and I infer that Steyn LJ agreed with it. It agrees with the view of the Secretary of State as expressed in the circular, which, I note, he has not modified despite the decision in *R v Dyfed County Council ex p S*. This is Circular No 1 of 1994, headed 'School Transport'.

...

Kent County Council's free transport to school policy

Kent County Council operate a variety of different schemes of education. West Kent is one of five areas in the county. Within West Kent there are four different schemes of education, one of each of four sub-areas, as I shall call them. Two of these are material to this case. In the larger and more populous sub-area, which includes Sevenoaks, Tonbridge and Tunbridge Wells, there are grammar schools and high schools and a system of assessment (ie selection) at the age of 11. In the smaller and less populous sub-area, which includes Edenbridge, there are only wide-ability schools, ie schools which cater for all children of secondary school age. Chiddingstone Hoth is in the Edenbridge sub-area.

When the parent of a child approaching secondary school age in West Kent is considering whether to enter his child for selection for a grammar school (or whether he would prefer the child, regardless of his ability, to go on to a wide-ability school) he is sent a variety of documents which contain information about the secondary schools in the area. These include information about the county council's transport to school policy, in relation to which the parent is told that if his child lives more than 3 miles from what the county council calls the 'nearest appropriate school' he can claim travel assistance to that school, but not otherwise.

...

The Eden Valley School caters for children of all abilities, including those able enough to attend a grammar school. For that reason, in KCC's view, it is a suitable school for R. As I have said earlier in this judgment, the function of the court is to see whether it has been shown that this view was unlawfully reached. In my judgment that has not been shown. As Circular No 1 of 1994 advised, and as s 36 implicitly required, the LEA's view took account of R's ability and aptitude. Even looking at the matter objectively, which is not the court's function, the fact that she had been selected for a grammar school could not make the Eden Valley School unsuitable for her. If the parent of a very bright child in Chiddingstone decided, for whatever reason (perhaps because he disapproved of selection or did not want to separate her from her friends) not to enter his child for PESE, no one could reasonably tell him that the Eden Valley School was not a suitable school for her. If the Eden Valley School is suitable for a child it cannot become unsuitable simply because she passes an examination which shows that she is also suitable for a grammar school.

In *R (on the application of J) v Vale of Glamorgan County Council* [2001] EWCA Civ 593, [2001] ELR 758, the Court of Appeal rejected the parents' argument that the LEA should pay the transport costs to enable their son to attend a particular secondary school that had an appropriate racial mix. The LEA decided that a local secondary school within walking distance of their home was a suitable school for him, even though pupils who had bullied their son at a primary school, because of his racial background, would also be attending the school. Schiemann LJ stressed that the LEA is only required under EA 1996, s 509(1) to make such arrangements 'as they consider necessary'. In *R v Carmarthenshire County Council, ex p White* [2001] ELR 172, a mother moved her child to a new primary school because her daughter had been bullied at her former school. The LEA refused to pay the transport costs to the new school because the former school was her local school and there was an anti-bullying policy in operation at the school. The court held that the LEA's decision was not unlawful.

'Nearest available route'

Essex County Council v Rogers [1987] AC 66

Lord Ackner: This appeal is concerned with the 'walking distance' from Shirley's home to her school and in particular whether 'the nearest available route' exceeded three miles, she being in the older age group referred to in s 39(5) quoted above. The dispute arises in the following circumstances.

The facts

The distance from Shirley's home to the school by the shortest route is 2.94 miles. That route involves crossing Copford Plains by an isolated and partly unmade track which is entirely unlighted. In winter this route is one of considerable danger for a young girl who would have to walk over Copford Plains in darkness. Copford Plains are also extremely difficult to cross in winter and may be passable on foot in the morning but impassable by the evening. There is an alternative route by metalled roads but this is 3.2 miles in length. The respondents quite reasonably regarded by the Copford Plains route as unsuitable for use by Shirley, if unaccompanied. Thus, since as stated above, the appellants were only prepared to make the school bus available on payment of the concessionary fare, which the respondents were not willing to pay, Shirley stayed away from school during the period 13 December 1983 until 17 April 1984.

...

The availability of the route cannot be determined by the mere study of a map. That it must be reasonably practicable for a child to walk along it to school does not, to my mind, admit of any argument. Of course, it must be free from obstructions or obstacles which would make its use impracticable. Dangers inherent in a particular route are factors that must be taken into account when considering its availability. A route which involved crossing a river by means of a footbridge would, other things being equal, qualify as an available route. However, if as a result, for example, of recent severe flooding, the bridge became unstable and unsafe to use, that route would cease to be available.

The short issue in this appeal is whether 'availability' is to be measured by what is reasonable for an *unaccompanied child* to use?

Mr Lightman submits that once the child is of sufficient age to go out on a street alone, then if the route is not reasonably safe for the child to walk along it unaccompanied the route is not 'available'. Quite apart from the fact that there are no words in the section to support such a submission, the test suggested is hopelessly vague. What sort of street is one to have in mind, what sort of traffic is it to carry, what time of day, indeed what weather or season is to be assumed etc etc? Further, is the test an objective test applicable to all children of a given age or is it to be applied subjectively to the particular child whose parents have raised the issue? The complete impracticability of such a test in itself persuades me that it was never in the contemplation of Parliament.

In my judgment a route to be 'available' within the meaning of s 39(5) must be a route along which a child accompanied as necessary can walk and walk with reasonable safety to school. It does not fail to qualify as 'available' because of dangers which would arise if the child is unaccompanied.

Devon County Council v George [1989] AC 573

Lord Keith of Kinkel: My Lords, this appeal concerns an application for judicial review of the decision of a local education authority not to provide free transport to and from school for a nine-year-old boy named Christopher ('the applicant').

The facts at the material time were that the applicant's family included his stepfather, his mother, a twelve-year-old brother and a four-year-old sister. The applicant and his brother were registered pupils at Bradford School, Holsworthy, Devon. The family home lay 2.8 miles by road from that school. The route between them was rural, being unlit and having no footpath and used to some extent by tractors, milk tankers and cattle wagons. The applicant's mother was a housewife whose activities included looking after the four-year-old sister. His stepfather was unemployed, and the family subsisted on welfare benefits. The elder brother suffered from asthma and for that reason was provided with free transport to and from school by Devon County Council ('the council') as local education authority.

...

Before the applicant attained the age of eight years the council provided him with free transport to and from school, because the distance between home and school exceeded two miles.

...

After the applicant attained the age of eight years the council refused to provide him with free transport to and from school.

...

Turning to the actual decision of the school transport panel, it is apparent that it took into account the applicant's age and the nature of route he would be expected to take, in particular its length. The senior assistant education officer Mr Grigg had inspected the route and his description of it was contained in an affidavit before the panel. The panel considered whether for safety reasons a child walking the route should be accompanied, taking the view that this was so, and whether it was reasonably practicable for the applicant to be accompanied. The panel was not satisfied that this would not be reasonably practicable. There was material upon which the panel might properly have concluded affirmatively that it was in fact reasonably practicable for the boy to be accompanied, in respect that his stepfather had stated in an affidavit that he was unemployed and available for the purpose.

...

It was argued for the applicant that the matter of the accompaniment of a child was relevant only to the question of the availability of a route under s 39(5) of the Act of 1944, and that a local education authority was not entitled to take into account in making a decision under s 55(1) even the possibility of a child being accompanied. So if a route, however short, was unsafe for an unaccompanied child, then the local education authority was obliged to provide free transport. This argument must be rejected. By virtue of s 39 of the Act the parent of a child is under a legal duty to bring about the attendance of the child at a school where he is a registered pupil, and, subject to the statutory excuses, is guilty of an offence if he or she fails to do so. There are various things which a parent may have to do to bring about the child's attendance at school, such as seeing that he gets up in the morning and sets out in reasonable time. In the case of an unwilling child it may be necessary for the parent to take the child to school in order to bring about his attendance. In general, the parent must do those things which are reasonably practicable to be done and which an ordinary prudent parent would do. This may include accompanying the child in situations where it would be unsafe for the child to go to school unaccompanied. In a case where the child lived 100 yards from school but the route involved crossing a busy trunk road, and the parent, although available to do so, refused to accompany the child and refused to allow him to go to school on the ground that it would be dangerous, there can be no doubt that the parent would be guilty of an offence ... It must follow, I think, that Parliament contemplated that in appropriate circumstances, a child would be accompanied to school. So a local authority is fully entitled, when making a decision under s 55(1), to take into account whether or not there are any circumstances which prevent its being reasonably practicable for the child to be accompanied to school over a route which would fall to be treated as not available to an unaccompanied child. That is one of the questions which the panel asked itself in the present case, and which it answered by expressing itself as not satisfied that there were any such circumstances.

R v Essex County Council, ex p EB [1997] ELR 327

McCullough J: What is sought here is leave to challenge a decision reached by the Essex County Council on 10 October 1996 not to make available to the applicant free transport to the school she has been attending since last September. Only one route between home and school calls for consideration. Although it is just under 3 miles long and thus less than the statutory 'walking distance', there is an issue between the parties as to whether children can walk along it with reasonable safety when accompanied. The applicant's father, who is her next friend in these proceedings, and the parents of more than 100 other children who live nearby, take the view that the route is not safe and that transport should be provided under s 55(1) of the Education Act 1944. The headteacher supports this point of view. There is evidence that an inspector of police in the Essex Constabulary does so too.

...

I see nothing in the volume of correspondence, or in the number of children involved, which makes this court the more suitable forum for the resolution of the central question in this case.

I take the three points in turn: first, that the decision that the route was safe for an accompanied child was manifestly ridiculous. This court could of course hold that the decision was *Wednesbury* unreasonable, but that is all. It is not for the court to judge safety. The court would not go to the route and look at it for itself. The Secretary of State, on the other hand, through his officials, could do exactly that and, if need be, on different occasions. He is in a far better position to assess safety by watching the traffic, considering visibility, taking account of the width, and perhaps the absence of verges and so on — all matters more suitable for decision by the Secretary of State.

...

In my judgment, looking at the matter overall, the issue is one pre-eminently suitable for decision after complaint to the Secretary of State other than by application to this court. I do not believe that this court would provide a speedier decision than would the Secretary of State.

...

The availability of the means of making complaint under the Educational Act is the reason why this application for leave to move for judicial review is refused.

The newspaper stories on this case (eg The Times, 4 February 1997) indicated that the applicant was an 11-year-old girl who would have to walk just under three miles to school using the nearest available route. This route included walking along a path across fields at the back of the school, crossing an 'A' road, walking along an unlit road with no footpath and a 60 mph speed limit.

In addition an LEA has the discretion to pay all or part of the travelling expenses of a pupil who is not entitled under s 509(1) to free school transport. This power is rarely exercised.

Education Act 1996, s 509(3)

(3) A local education authority may pay the whole or any part, as they think fit, of the reasonable travelling expenses of any person receiving education—
(a)   at a school, or
(b)   at any such institution as is mentioned in subsection (1),

for whose transport no arrangements are made under that subsection.

R v East Sussex County Council, ex p D CO/1408/90

Rose J: The applicant was an 11-year-old schoolboy. The respondent local education authority dismissed the applicant's appeal to grant him a place at a co-educational school and confirmed his allocation to a boys only school. The applicant was later granted a place at a co-educational school 12 miles from his home. The school transport panel refused to grant free travel or transport assistance for his journey to that school. The applicant applied for judicial review of both decisions.

...

The transport challenge

The question to be asked, if a child cannot be offered a place at a school of his or her choice because of oversubscription but instead is offered a place at an alternative school, and if the parents turn that offer down and select a school outside the area, is whether it is the duty of the respondent to pay for travel? The 'suitability' which had to be considered under the provisions of s 39(2)(c) of the Education Act 1944 related to the arrangements for transport enabling attendance at a school. It was not possible to read the word 'suitability' in that section as embracing consideration of suitability of the proffered and/or alternative schools. Section 6 of the Education Act 1980 had not changed the practice which prevailed under the 1944 Act. If Parliament wished free transport to be provided for those children who have to travel long distances in order to enable them to attend the school in accordance with their parent's preferences, Parliament must say so; but it had not yet said so.

6.   RELIGION IN SCHOOLS

Religion has a place in the curriculum of all maintained schools in two ways. The first is that religious education is part of the basic curriculum; and the second is that an act of collective worship should take place each day. However, a child can be excused from attending religious worship and religious education classes at the parent's request. Pupils attending a special school are expected to receive the same provision, and their parents also have a right to withdraw them from such provision (SSFA 1998, s 70(7)).

The statutory provisions are supplemented by guidance (DFE Circular 1/94 (Religious Education and Collective Worship); Non-Statutory Guidance on RE, QCA February 2000).

The nature of the religious provision will depend upon the category of school. The School Standards and Framework Act 1998 introduced the concept of schools with a 'religious character'. There are three categories of school in this context.

School Standards and Framework Act 1998, s 69

...

(2) Schedule 19 has effect for determining the provision for religious education which is required by section 352(1)(a) of that Act to be included in the basic curriculum of schools within each of the following categories, namely—
(a)   community schools and foundation and voluntary schools which do not have a religious character,
(b)   foundation and voluntary controlled schools which have a religious character, and
(c)   voluntary aided schools which have a religious character.

(3) For the purposes of this Part a foundation or voluntary school has a religious character if it is designated as a school having such a character by an order made by the Secretary of State.

(4) An order under subsection (3) shall state, in relation to each school designated by the order, the religion or religious denomination in accordance with whose tenets religious education is, or may be, required to be provided at the school in accordance with Schedule 19 (or, as the case may be, each such religion or religious denomination).

The Secretary of State designates a school as having a religious character. The order states the religion or religious denomination to which the school adheres. See, for example, the Designation of Schools having a Religious Character (England) Order 1999, SI 1999/2432.

• *Which category of school will never have a 'religious character'?*

Most voluntary aided schools will have a religious character as will many voluntary controlled and some foundation schools. Attendance at a place of worship, such as church or Sunday school should not be a condition of attending a school with a religious character.

Education Act 1996, s 398

It shall not be required, as a condition of—
(a)   a pupil attending a maintained school, or
(b)   a person attending such a school to receive further education or teacher training,

that he must attend or abstain from attending a Sunday school or a place of religious worship.

This does not mean that when offering places at such a school preference cannot be given to pupils or families who attend a particular church or other place of worship (see chapter 3). It may also be lawful to offer places at a non-denominational school to non-churchgoers in preference to churchgoers.

R v Lancashire County Council, ex p Foster [1995] 1 FCR 212

Lord Justice Kennedy: This is an application for judicial review of a decision of Lancashire County Council's education officer in a letter, dated 1 March 1994, refusing a boy, aged 10, who was a Roman Catholic and who had attended a Roman Catholic primary school, a place in September 1994 in Highfield School, and offering him a place in St Mary's High School, Blackpool. Although the challenge is in the form of a challenge to an individual decision in relation to a particular child, it is in reality a challenge to an important part of the policy of the Lancashire County Council, which becomes effective whenever more parents wish to send children to a particular non-denominational school than it can accommodate. In other words, it is over-subscribed.

. . .

Lancashire County Council has an unusually high number of Roman Catholic and Church of England voluntary aided schools. There are 22 Roman Catholic schools and six Church of England schools out of a total of 99 schools, and 20 per cent of the children attend the Roman Catholic secondary schools.

. . .

That provision enables the governing bodies of Roman Catholic schools to agree with the local education authority a limit of the non-Roman Catholic children who may be admitted, and many such agreements have been made between governing bodies and Lancashire County Council. Some of the agreements provide that no children who are not Roman Catholic shall be admitted; others provide for the admission of a small percentage of the non-Catholic children. In the case of St Mary's High School the percentage is 10 per cent.

. . .

[O]n 16 November 1993, the boy's parents completed the form which expressed their preference as follows: (1) Highfield, (2) St Bede's, (3) St Mary's. At the head of the form there appear these words:

Before completing this form parents are strongly advised to read the booklet 'Secondary School Admissions 1994'.

Paragraph 14, headed 'If my child goes to a Roman Catholic primary school, may I express a preference for a county or voluntary controlled high schools?' reads:

Yes. However, you should be aware that where there are more applicants for a school than the places available, the policy of the county council is to allocate places to Roman Catholic children attending Roman Catholic primary schools only after other applications have been met.

That paragraph sets out the policy which is at the heart of this case

...

The education committee had to decide whether to change their policy. In the event they decided to adhere to their policy, and in a letter dated 29 October 1993 the Department for Education was so informed. Part of that letter reads:

If a significant number of Roman Catholic pupils were to take up places in country [sic] [now community] or controlled schools in an area, then non-Catholic pupils could find that there were no places available for them in the locality. This would lead to considerable parental discontent, inconvenience for pupils, additional expenditure for the authority in home-to-school transfer costs and pressure to provide additional accommodation without adequate capital resources to respond.

Standing in isolation and without explanation a policy which allocates places to Roman Catholic children attending a Roman Catholic primary school only after other applications have been met sounds discriminatory and unsustainable, but when set out in the context, as it exists in this local education authority's area, it seems to me to be impossible for this court to say that it is so unreasonable that the court should interfere. Put very simply, the situation is that a large number of children have to be accommodated in a finite number of secondary schools which fall into two groups: the county high schools and the Roman Catholic schools. Because of arrangements made between the Roman Catholic Diocesan authorities and the local education authority pursuant to the 1980 Act, very few non-Catholic children can be accommodated in Roman Catholic schools even if they wanted to go there.

If too many Roman Catholic children from the Roman Catholic primary schools express a preference to go to county schools and those preferences are considered in the same way as all other preferences, then the local authority will be left with a number of children who cannot be given places, as they should be, in the areas in which they live, so the local education authority has formulated its policy and after carefully considering the advice of the Department for Education, has decided to adhere to it. It may be that for those who have to formulate the policy the arguments are, as the Roman Catholic and Diocesan authorities observed, finely balanced, but we are not entrusted with that task.

Accordingly, in my judgment, this application fails and should be dismissed.

Religious education

Religious education forms one strand of the basic curriculum for all maintained schools.

Education Act 1996, s 352(1)(a)

(1) The curriculum for every maintained school shall comprise a basic curriculum which includes—
(a)   provision for religious education for all registered pupils at the school (in accordance with such of the provisions of [Schedule 19 to the School Standards and Framework Act 1998] as apply in relation to the school),

The head teacher has the main responsibility for ensuring that religious education is taught in the school. However, the LEA and the governing body also have subsidiary legal duties.

School Standards and Framework Act 1998, s 69

(1) Subject to section 71, in relation to any community, foundation or voluntary school—
(a)   the local education authority and the governing body shall exercise their functions with a view to securing, and
(b)   the head teacher shall secure,

that religious education is given in accordance with the provision for such education included in the school's basic curriculum by virtue of section 352(1)(a) of the Education Act 1996.

Schedule 19 sets out the requirements for the content of the religious education curriculum, which will vary according to the category of school.

Community schools and foundation and voluntary schools without a religious character

School Standards and Framework Act 1998, Sch 19, para 2

...

(2) Subject to sub-paragraph (4), the required provision for religious education in the case of pupils at the school is provision for religious education in accordance with an agreed syllabus adopted for the school or for those pupils.

...

(5) No agreed syllabus shall provide for religious education to be given to pupils at a school to which this paragraph applies by means of any catechism or formulary which is distinctive of a particular religious denomination (but this is not to be taken as prohibiting provision in such a syllabus for the study of such catechisms or formularies).

An 'agreed syllabus' is defined in the Education Act 1996.

Education Act 1996, s 375

...

(2) In this Act 'agreed syllabus' means a syllabus of religious education—
(a)   prepared before the commencement of this Act in accordance with Schedule 5 to the Education Act 1944 or after commencement in accordance with Schedule 31, and
(b)   adopted by a local education authority under that Schedule,

whether it is for use in all the schools maintained by them or for use in particular such schools or in relation to any particular class or description of pupils in such schools.

(3) Every agreed syllabus shall reflect the fact that the religious traditions in Great Britain are in the main Christian whilst taking account of the teaching and practices of the other principal religions represented in Great Britain.

...

In 1994 the School Curriculum and Assessment Authority (SCAA), whose role has now been taken over by the QCA, drew up two model syllabuses for religious education. Each LEA has a SACRE (Standing Advisory Council on Religious Education), and should adopt an 'agreed syllabus'.

Schedule 19(2) (5) of the SSFA 1998 combined with s 375(3) of the EA 1996 clearly indicate that in schools which do not have a 'religious character' the religious education syllabus, whilst being mainly Christian, should not be denominational and should consider other principal world religions.

Where parents of pupils attending such a school want their children to receive religious education in accordance with a particular religion or religious denomination, the LEA may be required to provide facilities at the school for such education. However, the cost of doing so should not be borne by the school or the LEA (SSFA 1998, Sch 19(3)).

Foundation and voluntary controlled schools with a religious character

School Standards and Framework Act 1998, Sch 19, para 3

...

(2) Subject to sub-paragraph (4), the required provision for religious education in the case of pupils at the school is provision for religious education—
(a)   in accordance with any arrangements made under sub-paragraph (3), or
(b)   subject to any such arrangements, in accordance with an agreed syllabus adopted for the school or for those pupils.

(3) Where the parents of any pupils at the school request that they may receive religious education—
(a)   in accordance with any provisions of the trust deed relating to the school, or
(b)   where provision for that purpose is not made by such a deed, in accordance with the tenets of the religion or religious denomination specified in relation to the school under section 69(4),

the foundation governors shall (unless they are satisfied that because of any special circumstances it would be unreasonable to do so) make arrangements for securing that such religious education is given to those pupils in the school during not more than two periods in each week.

...

In the case of such schools the religious education syllabus may either be drawn up in accordance with the school's trust deed or be the 'agreed syllabus' adopted by the LEA.

Voluntary aided schools with a religious character

School Standards and Framework Act 1998, Sch 19, para 4

...

(2) The required provision for religious education in the case of pupils at the school is provision for religious education—
(a)   in accordance with any provisions of the trust deed relating to the school, or
(b)   where provision for that purpose is not made by such a deed, in accordance with the tenets of the religion or religious denomination specified in relation to the school under section 69(4), or
(c)   in accordance with any arrangements made under sub-paragraph (3).

(3) Where the parents of any pupils at the school—
(a)   desire them to receive religious education in accordance with any agreed syllabus adopted by the local education authority, and
(b)   cannot with reasonable convenience cause those pupils to attend a school at which that syllabus is in use,

the governing body shall (unless they are satisfied that because of any special circumstances it would be unreasonable to do so) make arrangements for religious education in accordance with that syllabus to be given to those pupils in the school.

Where parents of pupils attending such a school want their children to receive religious education in accordance with the LEA's 'agreed syllabus', the governing body of the school may be required to make arrangements for such education to be provided at the school (SSFA 1998, Sch 19, para 4(3)).

Schools 'with a religious character' are permitted to teach a particular religious denomination, such as Roman Catholicism, or a particular religion, for example Judaism, in the religious education classes.

• *Is there a statutory limit on the number of school periods which may be devoted to religious education in a school with a religious character?*

Compliance with the statutory requirements

An analysis of SACRE reports by SCAA indicated that there was generally better provision of religious education at Key Stage 1 than 2, and that provision at Key Stage 4 was often inadequate.

Analysis of SACRE Reports 1997 (SCAA)

1. Religious education

...

1.2 The provision and quality of RE

On the basis of the summaries of Ofsted findings and local surveys, SACREs reported the findings below.

PRIMARY SCHOOLS

In general, standards were at least satisfactory and they were frequently good, though there were few LEAs where individual schools did not give some cause for concern. Where comparisons were made with former years, the positive influence of a new agreed syllabus was often noted as a significant factor in raising standards. Although there was considerable variation in the results of inspections reported from the different LEAs, making any broad generalisations difficult, it would appear that there was often better provision at Key Stage 1 than at Key Stage 2. At this latter key stage there were more reports of inadequate time for RE, with lack of challenge and continuity inhibiting pupils' learning.

...

SECONDARY SCHOOLS

There was evidence of satisfactory provision at Key Stage 3 in terms of curriculum time, specialist staffing and, to a lesser extent, resources. This meant that at this key stage standards were generally sound or better, with many examples of very good practice. But whereas most schools made adequate provision at Key Stage 3, few did so at Key Stage 4 or in the sixth form.

In 2001 the QCA reported that there was an upward trend in both the provision and standards of religious education across Key Stages 1 to 4. There continued to be some inadequacies, for example patchy provision for all pupils at Key Stage 4 (*Religious education and collective worship, An analysis of 2000 SACRE Reports* (QCA/01/779)).

Collective worship

All pupils at a maintained school shall on each school day take part in an act of collective worship.

School Standards and Framework Act 1998, s 70

(1) Subject to section 71, each pupil in attendance at a community, foundation or voluntary school shall on each school day take part in an act of collective worship.

(2) Subject to section 71, in relation to any community, foundation or voluntary school—
(a)   the local education authority and the governing body shall exercise their functions with a view to securing, and
(b)   the head teacher shall secure,

that subsection (1) is complied with.

(3) Schedule 20 makes further provision with respect to the collective worship required by this section, including provision relating to—
(a)   the arrangements which are to be made in connection with such worship, and
(b)   the nature of such worship.

Section 71 is concerned with a parent's right to withdraw his or her child from religious education classes and collective worship (see below). The arrangements for collective worship are set out in Sch 20.

School Standards and Framework Act 1998, Sch 20, para 2

...

(1) This paragraph applies to any community, foundation or voluntary school.

(2) The arrangements for the required collective worship may, in respect of each school day, provide for a single act of worship for all pupils or for separate acts of worship for pupils in different age groups or in different school groups.

(3) For the purposes of sub-paragraph (2) a 'school group' is any group in which pupils are taught or take part in other school activities.

(4) Subject to sub-paragraph (6), the arrangements for the required collective worship shall be made—
(a)   if the school is a community school or a foundation school which does not have a religious character, by the head teacher after consulting the governing body;
(b)   if the school is a foundation school which has a religious character or a voluntary school, by the governing body after consulting the head teacher.

(5) Subject to sub-paragraph (6), the required collective worship shall take place on the school premises.

(6) If the governing body of a community, foundation or voluntary school are of the opinion that it is desirable that any act of collective worship in the school required by section 70 should, on a special occasion, take place elsewhere than on the school premises, they may, after consultation with the head teacher, make such arrangements for that purpose as they think appropriate.

(7) The powers of a governing body under sub-paragraph (6) shall not be exercised so as to derogate from the rule that the required collective worship must normally take place on the school premises.

- *Should the whole school take part in a single act of collective worship? May the act of collective worship normally take place in, for example, a church or a mosque?*

The nature of the act of collective worship varies according to the category of maintained school. Note that there are only two categories of school in relation to collective worship whereas there are three categories in relation to the provision of religious education.

Community schools and foundation schools without a religious character

School Standards and Framework Act 1998, Sch 20, para 3

...

(2) Subject to paragraph 4, the required collective worship shall be wholly or mainly of a broadly Christian character.

(3) For the purposes of sub-paragraph (2), collective worship is of a broadly Christian character if it reflects the broad traditions of Christian belief without being distinctive of any particular Christian denomination.

(4) Not every act of collective worship in the school required by section 70 need comply with sub-paragraph (2) provided that, taking any school term as a whole, most such acts which take place in the school do comply with that sub-paragraph.

(5) Subject to sub-paragraphs (2) and (4)—
(a) the extent to which (if at all) any acts of collective worship required by section 70 which do not comply with sub-paragraph (2) take place in the school,
(b) the extent to which any act of collective worship in the school which complies with sub-paragraph (2) reflects the broad traditions of Christian belief, and
(c) the ways in which those traditions are reflected in any such act of collective worship,

shall be such as may be appropriate having regard to any relevant considerations relating to the pupils concerned which fall to be taken into account in accordance with sub-paragraph (6).

(6) Those considerations are—
(a) any circumstances relating to the family backgrounds of the pupils which are relevant for determining the character of the collective worship which is appropriate in their case, and
(b) their ages and aptitudes.

(4) In this paragraph references to acts of collective worship in the school include such acts which by virtue of paragraph 2(6) take place otherwise than on the school premises.

Paragraph 3(2) and (3) stress that the act of collective worship should be 'wholly or mainly of a broadly Christian character', but paragraph 3(4) indicates that this need not be the case on every day of each term. Paragraph 3(5) and (6) set out the factors which should be taken into account by the head teacher in deciding upon the nature of the act of collective worship.

- *In a Bradford primary school, which is a community school, 80 per cent of the pupils are from Moslem families. Advise the head teacher as to the legal requirements on the arrangements and content of the act of collective worship in this school.*

The head teacher may ask the SACRE to make a determination that paragraph 3(2) and (3) should not apply to a particular class or to the school as a whole (Sch 20, para 4).

The meaning of 'wholly or mainly of a broadly Christian character' is remarkably elastic, as can be seen from the following case.

R v Secretary of State for Education, ex p R and D [1994] ELR 495 at 501

McCullogh J: The Secretary of State's conclusion can, in essence, be restated as follows: it is necessary for most of the acts of collective worship to 'contain some elements which can be related specifically to the traditions of Christian belief, and which accord some special status to the persons of Jesus Christ'.
...
In my judgment, the Secretary of State was unarguably right in his view that the Act permitted some non-Christian elements in the collective worship so long as these did not deprive it of its broadly Christian character, and that this character would not be lost by the inclusion of elements common to Christianity and to one or more other religions.

That being so, he was entitled to conclude (as it is plain that he did) that children of other faiths could participate in acts of worship which mainly reflected the broad traditions of Christian belief.

This case highlights the problems associated with the legislation on collective worship in schools. The Christian worship provisions are in stark contrast to a multi-cultural educational policy.

A Bradney 'Christian worship?' (1996) 8(2) Education and Law 127 at 128–34

Many teachers have only reluctantly accepted the religious worship provisions of the 1988 Act. 'It is clear that from 1988 onwards many secondary school have been trying to introduce daily collective worship where none existed before'. Yet it is also true that analyses of the reports from HMIs and SACREs have consistently suggested that significant numbers of schools are failing to meet the legal requirements for collective worship because of 'the absence of any religious content'. The interpretation of the phrase 'broadly Christian character' has been inventive and imaginative with, for example, '[m]any schools ... [beginning] to explore silence as one medium for collective worship'. In this context McCullough J's loose and liberal interpretation of the legislation is likely to receive widespread assent. Those who wish to continue multi-faith worship will see sustenance for their position in some parts of the judgment. Whether the judgment is coherent is, however, another matter.

The intention of Parliament

McCullough J's interpretation explicitly rests on the foundation that the approach he adopts reflects the intention of Parliament. If this is true, traditional constitutional theory would argue that whether his approach is coherent or desirable is not to the point; his approach is simply the law as Parliament passed it.

...

The passages from *Hansard* ... suggest three different positions being taken by those generally in support of the Bill. First, there was the Government position that religious worship is desirable in schools but that the law extant at the time of the Bill was broadly appropriate. Secondly, there was the position taken by Baroness Cox and her supporters which held that what schools needed was worship which was explicitly Christian. Thirdly, there was the view that worship in school is necessary and that worship in schools had fallen below the desirable standard but that any adjustments had to be made in the conscious knowledge of the changing nature of spiritual life in Great Britain.

...

A detailed reading of the legislative passage of the Christian worship provisions in the 1988 Act supports the arguments of those ... who reject all notions of legislative intent. In doing so it reveals the foundational weakness of McCullough J's arguments for his interpretation of the provisions. Notwithstanding McCullough J's contentions about what 'Parliament contemplated' and 'the clear intention of Parliament', the debates recorded in *Hansard* do not compel any particular reading of the Christian worship provisions. To argue, as McCullough J does,

> that Parliament contemplated that pupils who did not come from Christian families should be able to take part in the daily act of collective worship

is, if that argument results in the continuance of multi-faith worship, to favour the expressed preferences of some members of the legislature over those of others.

The meanings of Christian worship

The interpretation of the Christian worship clauses in *R and D* cannot be justified on the basis that that interpretation is the intention of Parliament because there is clearly no single intention of Parliament in this respect. The first question to be asked about *R and D* therefore becomes not, is its interpretation of the Christian worship provisions correct, but, rather, is that interpretation within the range of interpretations which can legitimately be drawn from the appropriate sources? The debates in *Hansard* do not command any particular reading of the Christian worship provisions. The words of the statute upon their face are opaque. The choice of an interpretation must, therefore, be ideological: that is to say any reading selected must in part be chosen because of policy preferences. That is not to say that every reading is acceptable or that all readings have equal validity. Although the debates about the Act and words of the statute itself do not compel any interpretation they do forbid some. The words are open-textured and the debate contradictory. However, if the words of the statute communicate at all there must be some limit to what they might mean; were it otherwise the words would merely be noise. Equally, *Hansard* hints at many meanings but not at all meanings.

The interpretation of the Christian worship sections approved by McCullough J conceives of a possibility of worship where all those from monotheistic faith backgrounds can meaningfully take part in a form of worship which is still broadly Christian, according the special status that Christians do to Jesus Christ. The interpretation values the collectivity of worship as much as its Christianity though the fact of the Christianity is retained. Meaningful worship involving those from different faith backgrounds must be possible McCullough J argues because the worship demanded by the statute must, according to s 7(2), cross different Christian denominations. However, just as the foundational justification, the intention of Parliament, that McCullough J gives for his interpretation fails, so this second argument fails. Ecumenical worship and multi-faith worship are different things. The possibility of worship involving different Christian denominations can rest on the assertion of a core Christian identity which continues even whilst there are doctrinal differences about non-core matters. Worship can then address this core, be meaningful and yet involve different denominations. By analogy multi-faith worship would have to look for a core of matters common to all religions and address those. This core could not include the special status accorded to Jesus Christ by Christians since it is that status which best distinguishes Christianity from other monotheistic religions. Hamilton's description of this approach to multi-faith worship as 'naïve' is accurate. Moreover, as Cox has noted of collective worship

> Those who take part in it will find it full satisfying only if they have a shared belief in God, some agreement as to what that God is like and what demands that deity makes of them.

It is difficult to see that mere agreement about the existence of just one God satisfies these conditions; that such worship would be worship in the normal sense of the word. McCullough J's interpretation fails not because the policy preferences it reflects are unacceptable but because it is incapable of coherent application in practice. A core of religious sentiments common to monotheistic religions cannot include the Christian's special regard for Jesus Christ and collective worship of the kind found in ecumenical worship cannot be found in multi-faith worship.

Bradney argues that the judge's interpretation of the legislation fails 'not because the policy preferences it reflects are unacceptable but because it is incapable of coherent application in practice'. Bradney considers that the legislation fudged the central issue and that if the matter were litigated in the future, the court would logically have to choose between a predominantly multi-cultural and multi-religious approach to collective worship or a predominantly Christian approach.

Hamilton and Watt further argue that the collective worship provisions are in breach of domestic discrimination law.

C Hamilton and R Watt 'Discrimination Education: Collective Worship in schools' (1996) 8(1) Child and Family Law Quarterly 28

The changes to the collective worship requirements brought about by the Education Reform Act 1988, and the Secretary of State's interpretation of these provisions in the *Ruscoe* case, raise two issues. The first of these is whether the UK is complying with its positive duty under the various international instruments to provide religious freedom to its citizens. Under the current jurisprudence of the European Court of Human Rights, the UK is unlikely to be found in violation of its obligations. However, it is not providing equal treatment to all its children. The second issue is whether the UK is fulfilling its negative obligations under the international treaties — does it ensure that there is no discrimination against its non-Christian citizens?

...

It could be argued that the provisions of the Education Reform Act 1988 are not intended to have a discriminatory purpose, and that non-Christian children may withdraw from such worship, or provide their own at their own cost. However, the fact that non-Christians must pay for their own religious education and worship while Christians are provided with theirs free is of itself discriminatory. The provisions of free religious education undoubtedly benefit one group as against another, but this may be regarded as an easily remediable discrimination. The State has only to make funding available to support non-Christian religious education.

There is a strong argument to be made for the view that unequal provision for members of different religions is unlawful under current UK law. First, it is clear from the House of Lords in *R v Birmingham City Council ex p Equal Opportunities Commission* [1989] IRLR 173, that the lesser provision of places for girls in selective schools, when compared with boys, is discrimination on the grounds of sex contrary to s 1(1)(a) of the Sex Discrimination Act 1975. The fact that some would not consider a grammar school place to be an advantage does not affect the discriminatory nature of the decision to allocate resources preferentially. The mere fact that more males than females have a greater opportunity to secure what they, or their parents, might consider a benefit is sufficient. Similarly, it could be argued that the lack of opportunity for certain groups of children to take part in acts of collective worship deemed acceptable by their religion would amount to discrimination. This point could be supported on the authority of *Mandla*. If it is discrimination to deny a boy the right to wear a turban and to leave his hair uncut for religious reasons, it could well be argued that it is discrimination to deny a Muslim child the right to pray according to religious requirements when providing this to his Christian classmate.

...

[T]he emphasis upon Christian worship seems to be discriminatory. There seem to be a number of possible resolutions to the problem. One possible resolution might be to allow each faith group to have its own form of religious worship every day. The problem with such an approach is that it is divisive for the school body. Children belonging to minority religions, possibly unpopular religions represented by very small numbers in a school, will once again face the problem of declaring themselves as different from the majority of children and probably the majority of teachers.

A second alternative is to review the need for collective worship in schools. If the aim of collective worship is to bring about solidarity between pupils in a school and to promote a common ethos and shared values, this aim is unlikely to be achieved through worship 'wholly or mainly of a broadly Christian character' in a multi-cultural society. If the aim is rather to encourage spiritual and moral development, this can be achieved without the specific introduction of Christianity. Non-denominational forms of worship and reading could be substituted.

A third alternative would be to remove collective worship from schools altogether, a decision made by the USA in the eighteenth century.

Foundation schools with a religious character and voluntary schools

School Standards and Framework Act 1998, Sch 20, para 5

In the case of a foundation school which has a religious character or a voluntary school, the required collective worship shall be—
(a) in accordance with any provisions of the trust deed relating to the school, or
(b) where—

> (i)   provision for that purpose is not made by such a deed, and
> (ii)   the school has a religious character,

in accordance with the tenets and practices of the religion or religious denomination specified in relation to the school under section 69(4).

An analysis of SACRE reports by SCAA indicated that a majority of secondary schools did not comply with the collective worship requirement.

Analysis of SACRE Reports 1997 SCAA

2.   Collective worship

2.1 Monitoring

Most SACREs reported considering the provision of collective worship in their schools as revealed by Ofsted inspections or by their own surveys. Some 23 gave sufficient detail for comparisons to be made, though even here firm figures were not easy to arrive at. In more than one case it was stated that several Ofsted reports did not say to what extent the statutory requirement for daily collective worship was being met. Nevertheless, the general picture is very much a repetition of previous years.

Nearly all primary schools provide daily acts of collective worship for their pupils; some SACREs reported 100 per cent compliance, others at least 80 to 90 per cent.

In secondary schools, on the other hand, 80 per cent or more were regularly failing to comply, and in some authorities none of the secondary schools inspected did comply.

In several cases, secondary schools were said to be having difficulty in finding staff willing to conduct acts of collective worship.

Some schools attempted to provide collective worship in form groups, but a significant number of teachers felt uncomfortable about participating and exercised their right to be exempted.

Where collective worship of a good quality was observed, it contributed significantly to the school's ethos and to the spiritual, moral, social and cultural development of the pupils.

One report singled out the fact that only in a minority of primary schools were there frequent, planned opportunities for pupils to reflect on their own lives and the lives of others, whilst many secondary schools do not utilise the opportunities provided by assemblies to deepen pupils' spiritual awareness and understanding. There were, however, examples of acts of worship which set a contemplative and spiritual tone to the start of the school day.

In 2001, the QCA reported that the requirement for collective worship to be held every day in secondary schools continued to exercise SACREs. Some schools have a short 'thought for the day' (*Religious education and collective worship, An analysis of 2000 SACRE Reports* (QCA/01/779)).

Right to withdraw pupils

Parents have the right to withdraw their child from religious education classes and from collective worship. The number of withdrawals appear to be extremely small

(Religious education and collective worship, An analysis of 2000 SACRE Reports (QCA/01/779)).

School Standards and Framework Act 1998, s 71

(1) If the parent of a pupil at a community, foundation or voluntary school requests that he may be wholly or partly excused—
(a)   from receiving religious education given in the school in accordance with the school's basic curriculum,
(b)   from attendance at religious worship in the school, or
(c)   both from receiving such education and from such attendance,

the pupil shall be so excused until the request is withdrawn.

...

(3) Where in accordance with subsection (1) a pupil has been wholly or partly excused from receiving religious education or from attendance at religious worship and the local education authority are satisfied—
(a)   that the parent of the pupil desires him to receive religious education of a kind which is not provided in the school during the periods of time during which he is so excused,
(b)   that the pupil cannot with reasonable convenience be sent to another community, foundation or voluntary school where religious education of the kind desired by the parent is provided, and
(c)   that arrangements have been made for him to receive religious education of that kind during school hours elsewhere,

the pupil may be withdrawn from the school during such periods of time as are reasonably necessary for the purpose of enabling him to receive religious education in accordance with the arrangements.

(4) A pupil may not be withdrawn from school under subsection (3) unless the local education authority are satisfied that the arrangements there mentioned are such as will not interfere with the attendance of the pupil at school on any day except at the beginning or end of a school session (or, if there is only one, the school session) on that day.

...

A parent is not required to give reasons for his or her decision. The pupil may be withdrawn from school during the time allocated to religious education to receive religious education approved by the parent elsewhere. Where religious education is integrated into other parts of the curriculum the right to withdraw may be difficult to exercise in practice.

R v Secretary of State for Education, ex p Ruscoe (R & D in title) [1994] ELR 495 at 505

McCullough J: [T]he Secretary of State has, as the law requires, recognised that if a child is excused religious worship and/or religious education, the duty to provide his secular education is unaffected. In any event, there is no evidence that the curriculum now in place would result in any interference with a pupil's secular education were he to be excused from attending religious education.

Family breakdown may result in disputes between parents over their child's religious education as occurred in the following case.

Re T and M (Minors) [1995] ELR 1

Judge Ryland: In this case I am concerned with at least two matters, two applications, that concern two children. The first and eldest boy is TM (T), who was born on 13 October 1983, and the younger boy is MM (M), who was born on 5 April 1985.

...

The father applies for an order that the two boys reside with him, and also for either a specific issue order or a prohibited steps order, prohibiting the mother from removing them from the religious education classes at their school — the collective religion classes — which I understand take place mainly in assembly in the morning.

Both boys attend a school that is extremely local to both of the parties and that is called St James's. That school is apparently a Church of England school and the reason why both boys went there was because a local Roman Catholic school had no places available for either of these boys at the relevant time. That brings into play starkly the situation with regard to the religion of these boys.

It is common ground that both the mother and the father, in comparatively recent times, had been members of the Roman Catholic Church. However, in 1992, the mother converted, to become a follower of the Islamic religion and she is now a staunch and sincere member of that religion.

...

[T]hese children have been treated by both their parents, and by the school authorities, as being Christians of the Roman Catholic denomination, although, as I say, the school is a Church of England school.

After her conversion the mother was unhappy about the situation whereby these two boys received religious instruction in the Church of England school, and in accordance with her statutory right she notified the head-teacher of her desire to have those two boys withdrawn from collective education classes and the assembly. She told me that what happened was that she wrote a letter to the head-teacher indicating that that was her wish, the head-teacher then wrote back to both parents, and she showed ('she' being the mother) the father that letter. The father, she said, declined to go to the school to sort out the question as to whether or not these children should be withdrawn from their collective religion classes, so the mother went along alone, with the consequence that the children were withdrawn from those classes for a period of time.

Subsequently the father caused the children to be returned to those classes, and the mother complains about that, because she says that that was done without her co-operation and, indeed, without her being asked her views on that particular issue.

Up until this morning, when I heard the evidence of an expert on the faith of Islam and the way of life of Islam, which I think are very much coincidental, Mr Min, I think it was the mother's view — which she now recognises to be erroneous — that the children could not continue to go to Christian religious classes, or where the Christian religion was taught, and also attend teachings in the Islamic faith. Her expert said to me in evidence this morning that that, in the special circumstances of this case, would not be a matter that Islam would rule against, and indeed that it would not be a matter outside the generally accepted norm, that children of that age, of that sex and in those circumstances, where the father is of a different religion from the mother, would permit the children to go to religious education in a religion that is different from Islam. He said that Islam would regard it as being, perhaps, beneficial to the children, that they should get a broad grounding in comparative religions besides the Islamic religion, because the principle that he told me about was that children, both boys and girls (and I am, of course, concerned with boys in this case) when they attain the age of responsibility, which is some time after puberty, can decide on their own account which religion they wish to follow. He made it very clear to me that it was a cardinal principle that Islam would not force anyone to become beholden to a religion which that person, being of sufficient intelligence and age, has chosen not to follow.

...

It is agreed between the counsel for each side that the mother has a right to remove these children from their religious education under statute. It is also agreed, as I understand it, that the court can, as a matter of law, make orders in respect of that. Whether or not I should make an order is a matter which I have to determine. It seems to me that I have again to approach that question in this way. First of all, I have to ask myself: *would it be in the interests of these children for the mother to be able to exercise her statutory right, unilaterally without consulting either the court or the father?* And secondly: *is she likely to take that step?* It seems to me that, for the reasons that I have already given in this judgment, it would not be in the interests of these children for the mother to remove them from their collective religious teaching at the school which they are attending. The consequences of doing that are documented in the schoolteachers' reports on these children and I am satisfied that that action on the part of the mother in removing the children from that religious education had, at least, a contribution to the harmful effects upon each of these boys; it is so documented.

I therefore have drawn the clear conclusion that it would not be in the interests of the boys for the mother to be able to remove them from that education because I think that would have a very destabilising effect upon the boys, and I think it would have the effect of making them feel, yet again, that they were being treated differently from their fellow-pupils.

I am proposing to say that the mother should be forbidden, until further order, to instruct the school to withdraw these children from the religious education that is given there[.]

Should religion form part of the basic curriculum?

Why are religious education and collective worship part of the basic curriculum?

The answer is mainly historical. The Church of England is the established church in England. The monarch is the Defender of the Faith, that is the faith as practised by members of the Church of England.

Religion has had a major impact on the history of the United Kingdom, and the state has been closely linked to the Church of England since its establishment in the sixteenth century. King Henry VIII initiated the Protestant Reformation by severing the English church from the Catholic church in Rome. The tension between the Protestant and Catholic churches continued into the seventeenth century and erupted into disputes between the monarch and Parliament over the power and religion of the monarch, which continued into the eighteenth century until the collapse of the second Jacobite rebellion in 1745. In the seventeenth century restrictions were placed on the civil rights of Roman Catholics, Jews, and non-conformists which lasted until the nineteenth century. In Ireland the dispute with Great Britain now over the future of Northern Ireland is ostensibly linked to the religious divide between Protestants and Roman Catholics.

Against this backcloth the English Parliament in 1870 adopted the principle that most maintained schools should be non-denominational, whilst permitting the continued existence and creation of church and other religious schools. The emphasis on Christianity was introduced by the Education Reform Act 1988. The approach in England and Wales can be compared with that in Northern Ireland where the great majority of schools are denominational being either Protestant or Catholic, and in the United States of America where no religious teaching is permitted in publicly funded schools.

(For the position in France, see Bell 'Religious Education in Secular Schools: a French Solution' (1990) 2(3) Education and the Law 121 which discusses, in particular, the wearing of the chador by Muslim pupils.)

Should religious education and collective worship form part of the basic curriculum?

The answer to this question is not to be found in the law. However, the human rights and comparative legal context is worth examining.

European Convention on Human Rights 1950, Art 9 and Protocol 1

Article 9

1. Everyone has the right to freedom of thought, conscience, and religion; this right includes freedom to change his religion or belief, and freedom, either alone or in community with others and in public or private, to manifest his religion or belief, in worship, teaching, practice and observance.

2. Freedom to manifest one's religion or beliefs shall be subject only to such limitations as are prescribed by law and are necessary in a democratic society in the interests of public safety, for the protection of public order, health or morals, or the protection of the rights and freedoms of others.

Protocol 1

...

Article 2

No person shall be denied the right to education. In the exercise of any functions which it assumes in relation to education and teaching, the state shall respect the right of parents to ensure such education and teaching in conformity with their own religious and philosophical convictions.

Whereas the right to freedom of religion is that of the child, the right to ensure education in accordance with religious convictions is given to the parent.

Valsamis v Greece **[1998] ELR 430**

(6) The three applicants are Jehovah's Witnesses. Elias and Maria Valsamis are the parents of Victoria, who was born in 1980 and is currently a pupil in the last 3 years of State secondary education at a school in Melissia, Athens. According to them, pacifism is a fundamental tenet of their religion and forbids any conduct or practice associated with war or violence, even indirectly. It is for this reason that Jehovah's Witnesses refuse to carry out their military service or to take part in any events with military overtones.

(7) On 20 September 1992 Mr and Mrs Valsamis submitted a written declaration in order that their daughter Victoria, who was then 12 and in the first 3 years of secondary education at a school in Melissia, should be exempted from attending school religious-education lessons, Orthodox Mass and any other event that was contrary to her religious beliefs, including national-holiday celebrations and public processions.

(8) Victoria was exempted from attendance at religious-education lessons and Orthodox Mass. In October 1992, however, she, in common with the other pupils at her school, was asked to take part in the celebration of the National Day on 28 October, when the outbreak of war between Greece and Fascist Italy on 28 October 1940 is commemorated with school and military parades.

...

(9) Victoria informed the headmaster that her religious beliefs forbade her joining in the commemoration of a war by taking part, in front of the civil, Church and military authorities, in a school parade that would follow an official Mass and would be held on the same day as a military parade. According to the applicants, the school authorities refused to accept her statement. In the government's opinion, it was imprecise and muddled and did not make clear the religious beliefs in question. At all events, her request to be excused attendance was refused but she nevertheless did not take part in the school's parade.

...

(21) Relying on Art 2 of Protocol No 1 and Arts 3, 9 and 13 of the Convention, the applicants complained of the penalty of one day's suspension from school that was imposed on the pupil Victoria, who had refused to take part in the school parade on 28 October 1992, a national day in Greece. Since, owing to their religious beliefs, Mr and Mrs Valsamis were opposed to any event with military overtones, they had sought an exemption for their daughter, but in vain. They relied on the Commission's opinion in the case of *Arrowsmith v the United Kingdom* (application no 7050/75, Decisions and Reports no 19, p 5(69)), according to which pacifism as a philosophy fell within the ambit of the right to freedom of thought and conscience, and the attitude of pacifism could thus be seen as a belief protected by Art 9(1). They therefore claimed recognition of their pacifism under the head of religious beliefs, since all Jehovah's Witnesses were bound to practise pacifism in daily life.

...

(31) While it is not for the Court to rule on the Greek State's decisions as regards the setting and planning of the school curriculum, it is surprised that pupils can be required on pain of suspension from school — even if only for a day — to parade outside the school precincts on a holiday. Nevertheless, it can discern nothing, either in the purpose of the parade or in the arrangements for it, which could offend the applicants' pacifist convictions to an extent prohibited by the second sentence of Art 2 of Protocol No 1.

Such commemorations of national events serve, in their way, both pacifist objectives and the public interest. The presence of military representatives at some of the parades which take place in Greece on the day in question does not in itself alter the nature of the parades.

Furthermore, the obligation on the pupil does not deprive her parents of their right 'to enlighten and advise their child, to exercise with regard to their child natural parental functions as educators, or to guide their children on a path in line with the parents' own religious or philosophical convictions' ....

(32) It is not for the Court to rule on the expediency of other educational methods which, in the applicants' view, would be better suited to the aim of perpetuating historical memory among the younger generation. It notes, however, that the penalty of suspension, which cannot be regarded as an exclusively educational measure and may have some psychological impact on the pupil on whom it is imposed, is nevertheless of limited duration and does not require the exclusion of the pupil from the school premises (Art 28(3) of Decree no 104/1979) ...

(33) In conclusion, there has not been a breach of Art 2 of Protocol No 1.

...

(37) The Court notes at the outset that Miss Valsamis was exempted from religious education and the Orthodox Mass, as she had requested on the grounds of her own religious beliefs. It has already held, in paras (31)–(33) above, that the obligation to take part in the school parade was not such as to offend her parents' religious convictions. The impugned measure therefore did not amount to an interference with her right to freedom of religion either (see, in particular, the *Johnston and Others v Ireland* judgment of 18 December 1986, Series A no 112, p 27, § 63).

(38) There has consequently not been a breach of Art 9 of the Convention.

...

(49) Like the Commission, the Court thus finds, having regard to all the circumstances of the case, that the applicants did not have an effective remedy before a national authority in order to raise the complaints they later submitted at Strasbourg. There has consequently been a breach of Art 13 of the Convention ...

Northern Ireland

L Lundy 'Law, Policy and Practice in Northern Ireland' SLS Legal Publications (NI)

Comparison with England and Wales

5.55 The provisions on religious education in Northern Ireland are very similar to those in England and Wales in that all schools are required to provide religious education and daily collective worship. However, Northern Ireland does not have any bodies equivalent to the Standing Advisory Councils on Religious Education (SACREs). Each LEA must have a SACRE whose membership includes representatives of the Church of England as well as the other principal religious traditions in the area. The SACREs agree the core syllabus for their area and consider applications from schools which want exemption from the requirements in relation to Christian worship. In Northern Ireland, the core curriculum for religious education was agreed by the four main churches. Moreover, because of the relatively small number of non-Christian residents, there is no provision for schools to be granted exception from the collective worship provisions. However, the major different between the two jurisdictions lies not so much in the content of the legislation as in the response to the equivalent provision. In England and Wales the religious education provisions have proved controversial. Particular criticisms have surrounded the emphasis on Christianity when many schools have a majority of pupils who are non-Christians. In contrast, in Northern Ireland, schools and parents are generally supportive of the importance of an integral Christian education. This can be explained to some extent by the fact that Northern Ireland is not an ethnically diverse society. However, it is also a further indication of the status of the churches in Northern Ireland society. Northern Ireland has an extremely large number of people affiliated to the main Christian traditions and it is unsurprising that the community is generally supportive of integral religious education.

The United States

First Amendment to the US Constitution 1776: freedom of establishment

Congress shall make no law respecting an establishment of religion, or prohibiting the free exercise thereof.

This has been regularly invoked in disputes relating to religion in schools.

Wallace v Jaffree, 472 US 38 (1985)

Justice Stevens delivered the opinion of the Court. At an early stage of this litigation, the constitutionality of three Alabama statutes was questioned: (1) § 16–1–20, enacted in 1978, which authorised a 1-minute period of silence in all public schools 'for meditation';[1] (2) § 16–1–20.1, enacted in 1981, which authorised a period of silence 'for meditation or voluntary prayer';[2] and (3) § 16–1–20.2, enacted in 1982, which authorised teachers to lead 'willing students' in a prescribed prayer to 'Almighty God ... the Creator and Supreme Judge of the world.'[3]

...

[2]Alabama Code § 16–1–20.1 (Supp 1984) provides:

'At the commencement of the first class of each day in all grades in all public schools the teacher in charge of the room in which each class is held may announce that a period of silence not to exceed one minute in duration shall be observed for meditation or voluntary prayer, and during any such period no other activities shall be engaged in.'

...

The Court of Appeals agreed with the District Court's initial interpretation of the purpose of both § 16–1–20.1 and § 16–1–20.2, and held them both unconstitutional. We have already affirmed the Court of Appeals' holding with respect to § 16–1–20.2. Moreover, appellees have not questioned the holding that § 16–1–20 is valid. Thus, the narrow question for decision is whether § 16–1–20.1, which authorises a period of silence for 'meditation or voluntary prayer', is a law respecting the establishment of religion within the meaning of the First Amendment.

Appellee Ishmael Jaffree is a resident of Mobile County, Alabama. On May 28, 1982, he filed a complaint on behalf of three of his minor children; two of them were second-grade students and the third was then in kindergarten. The complaint named members of the Mobile County School Board, various school officials, and the minor plaintiffs' three teachers as defendants. The complaint alleged that the appellees brought the action 'seeking principally a declaratory judgment and an injunction restraining the Defendants and each of them from maintaining or allowing the maintenance of regular religious prayer services or other forms of religious observances in the Mobile County Public Schools in violation of the First Amendment as made applicable to states by the Fourteenth Amendment to the United States Constitution.' The complaint further alleged that two of the children had been subjected to various acts of religious indoctrination 'from the beginning of the school year in September, 1981'; that the defendant teachers had 'on a daily basis' led their classes in saying certain prayers in unison; that the minor children were exposed to ostracism from their peer group class members if they did not participate; and that Ishmael Jaffree had repeatedly but unsuccessfully requested that the devotional services be stopped.

...

Just as the right to speak and the right to refrain from speaking are complementary components of a broader concept of individual freedom of mind, so also the individual's freedom to choose his own creed is the counterpart of his right to refrain from accepting the creed established by the majority. At one time it was thought that this right merely proscribed the preference of one Christian sect over another, but would not require equal respect for the conscience of the infidel, the atheist, or the adherent of a non-Christian faith such as Islam or Judaism. But when the underlying principle has been examined in the crucible of litigation, the Court has unambiguously concluded that the individual freedom of conscience protected by the First Amendment embraces the right to select any religious faith or none at all. This conclusion derives support not only from the interest in respecting the individual's freedom of conscience, but also from the conviction that religious beliefs worthy of respect are the product of free and voluntary choice by the faithful, and from recognition of the fact that the political interest in forestalling intolerance extends beyond intolerance among Christian sects — or even intolerance among 'religions' — to encompass intolerance of the disbeliever and the uncertain.

...

The legislature enacted § 16–1–20.1, despite the existence of § 16–1–20 for the sole purpose of expressing the State's endorsement of prayer activities for one minute at the beginning of each schoolday. The addition of 'or voluntary prayer' indicates that the State intended to characterise prayer as a favoured practice. Such an endorsement is not consistent with the established principle that the government must pursue a course of complete neutrality toward religion.

The importance of that principle does not permit us to treat this as an inconsequential case involving nothing more than a few words of symbolic speech on behalf of the political majority. For whenever the State itself speaks on a religious subject, one of the questions that we must ask is 'whether the government intends to convey a message of endorsement or disapproval of religion'. The well-supported concurrent findings of the District Court and the Court of Appeals — that § 16–1–20.1 was intended to convey a message of state approval of prayer activities in the public schools — make it unnecessary, and indeed inappropriate, to evaluate the practical significance of the addition of the words 'or voluntary prayer' to the statute. Keeping in mind, as we must, 'both the fundamental place held by the Establishment Clause in our constitutional scheme and the myriad, subtle ways in which Establishment Clause values can be eroded', we conclude that § 16–1–20.1 violates the First Amendment.

Chief Justice Burger, dissenting. Some who trouble to read the opinions in these cases will find it ironic — perhaps even bizarre — that on the very day we heard arguments in the cases, the Court's session opened with an invocation for Divine protection. Across the park a few hundred yards away, the House of Representatives and the Senate regularly open each session with a prayer. These legislative prayers are not just one minute in duration, but are extended, thoughtful invocations and prayers for Divine guidance. They are given, as they have been since 1789, by clergy appointed as official chaplains and paid from the Treasury of the United States. Congress has also provided chapels in the Capitol, at public expense, where Members and others may pause for prayer, meditation — or a moment of silence.

Inevitably some wag is bound to say that the Court's holding today reflects a belief that the historic practice of the Congress and this Court is justified because members of the Judiciary and Congress are more in need of Divine guidance than are schoolchildren. Still others will say that all this controversy is 'much ado about nothing', since no power on earth — including this Court and Congress — can stop any teacher from opening the schoolday with a moment of silence for pupils to meditate, to plan their day — or to pray if they voluntarily elect to do so.

I make several points about today's curious holding.

(a)   It makes no sense to say that Alabama has 'endorsed prayer' by merely enacting a new statute 'to specify expressly that voluntary prayer is one of the authorized activities during a moment of silence', ... To suggest that a moment-of-silence statute that includes the word 'prayer' unconstitutionally endorses religion, while one that simply provides for a moment of silence does not, manifests not neutrality but hostility toward religion. For decades our opinions have stated that hostility toward any religion or toward all religions is as much forbidden by the Constitution as is an official establishment of religion. The Alabama Legislature has no more 'endorsed' religion than a state or the Congress does when it provides for legislative chaplains, or than this Court does when it opens each session with an invocation to God.

...

(d)   The notion that the Alabama statute is a step toward creating an established church borders on, if it does not trespass into, the ridiculous. The statute does not remotely threaten religious liberty; it affirmatively furthers the values of religious freedom and tolerance that the Establishment Clause was designed to protect. Without pressuring those who do not wish to pray, the statute simply creates an opportunity to think, to plan, or to pray if one wishes — as Congress does by providing chaplains and chapels. It accommodates the purely private, voluntary religious choices of the individual pupils who wish to pray while at the same time creating a time for nonreligious reflection for those who do not choose to pray. The statute also provides a meaningful opportunity for schoolchildren to appreciate the absolute constitutional right of each individual to worship and believe as the individual wishes. The statute 'endorses' only the view that the religious observances of others should be tolerated and, where possible, accommodated. If the government may not accommodate religious needs when it does so in a wholly neutral and noncoercive manner, the 'benevolent neutrality' that we have long considered the correct constitutional standard will quickly translate into the 'callous indifference' that the Court has consistently held the Establishment Clause does not require.

The robust dissenting judgment by Chief Justice Burger indicated the potential for future litigation.

CJ Russo and RD Mawdsley 'An update on the conflicting First Amendment Jurisprudence of the US Supreme Court' (2000) 12(3) Education and the Law 195

Near the end of its 1999–2000 term, the United States Supreme Court, in a pair of unrelated cases involving the Establishment Clause of the First Amendment to the

Constitution, revealed its polarization involving Church–State relations. In *Sante Fe Independent School District v Doe (Santa Fe)*, the Court affirmed that a board policy permitting student-led prayers prior to the start of high school football games violated the Establishment Clause. Subsequently, in *Mitchell v Helms (Helms)*, with the majority and dissent basically changing sides, the Court held that a federal statute that permits states to lend educational materials and equipment to public and religiously affiliated non-public schools did not contravene the Establishment Clause.

Supreme Court majority decision

The Supreme Court reviewed the limited question of the football prayer policy. A divided Court, in a six to three vote, affirmed that the policy was unconstitutional. Writing for the majority, Justice Stevens found that just as in *Lee*, prayer at a school-sponsored event, whether a football game or a graduation ceremony, violated the Establishment Clause. However, in *Sante Fe*, Justice Stevens relied on the endorsement test rather than the psychological coercion test enunciated in *Lee*. Put another way, Justice Stevens reviewed the status of prayer from the perspective of whether its being permitted at football games was an impermissible governmental approval or endorsement rather than as a form of psychological coercion which subjected fans to values and/or beliefs other than their own. In vitiating the prayer policy, Justice Stevens rejected the district's three main arguments. First, he disagreed with the district's position that the policy furthered the free speech rights of students. Second, he disagreed with the district's stance that the policy was neutral on its face. Third, Justice Stevens rebuffed the district's defence that a legal challenge was premature since prayer had not been offered at a football game under the policy.

Supreme Court dissent

Chief Justice Rehnquist's dissent began by declaring that Justice Stevens' opinion 'bristles with hostility to all things religious in public life'. What Chief Justice Rehnquist apparently considered most disturbing was, since policy was never implemented, Justice Stevens' refusal to defer to the district's purposes as other than religious and dismissing them as a sham.

Chief Justice Rehnquist viewed the issue in *Sante Fe* as student, not government, speech where, unlike *Lee's* having a prayer delivered by a rabbi under the direction of a school official, the policy allowed prayer to be selected or created by a pupil. As Chief Justice Rehnquist asserted, if the student had been selected on wholly secular criteria such a public-speaking skills or social popularity, he or she could have delivered a religious message that would probably have passed constitutional muster.

Reflections

Sante Fe Independent School District v Doe and *Mitchell v Helms*, although addressing different issues in the wide range of Church–State relations, evidenced an internal consistency as the dissenters in *Sante Fe* who would have permitted prayer, in turn, favoured aid in *Helms* while the justices who struck down the prayer policy largely opposed Chapter 2 aid to students who attended religious schools. In viewing *Helms* and *Sante Fe* synoptically, it is fascinating to observe the split among the Supreme Court justices. At present, the justices fit into three fairly consistent categories as accommodationists who would permit state aid to students in religious schools and prayer in public schools, separationists who would oppose both of these, and the moderate, or swing, votes. The three accommodationists are Chief Justice Rehnquist and Justices Scalia and Thomas. At the other end of the bench, Justices Stevens, Souter, Ginsberg, and Bryer are the separationists. The two moderates, Justices O'Connor and Kennedy, tip the Court's balance by joining the accommodationists or separationists.

Of the two cases, Helms appears to be more far-reaching than Sante Fe for two reasons. First, Helms is likely to have a greater impact than Sante Fe not only because estimates are that more than 1 million children in the United States benefit from Chapter 2 but also since it may open the door to other forms of governmental aid, such as vouchers.

The second reason why Helms appears to be of greater significance is that Sante Fe essentially follows an almost unbroken 40-year line of Supreme Court cases prohibiting prayer in public schools that began with Engel v Vitalie. Conversely, Helms continues to expand the boundaries of permissible state aid to religious schools in striking down cases to the contrary.

In addition to claims under the First Amendment's establishment clause, there have been claims under the freedom of speech clause.

First Amendment to the US Constitution 1776: freedom of speech

Congress shall make no law respecting an establishment of religion, or prohibiting the free exercise thereof; or abridging the freedom of speech....

Lamb's Chapel v Center Morches Union Free School District, 508 US 384 (1993)

Justice White delivered the opinion of the Court. New York Educ. Law § 414 (McKinney 1988 and Supp 1993) authorises local school boards to adopt reasonable regulations for the use of school property for 10 specified purposes when the property is not in use for school purposes. Among the permitted uses is the holding of 'social, civic and recreational meetings and entertainments, and other uses pertaining to the welfare of the community; but such meetings, entertainment and uses shall be non-exclusive and shall be open to the general public.' § 414(c). The list of permitted uses does not include meetings for religious purposes, and a New York appellate court in Trietley v Board of Ed of Buffalo, 409 NYS 2d 912, 915 (App Div 1978), ruled that local boards could not allow student bible clubs to meet on school property because '[r]eligious purposes are not included in the enumerated purposes for which a school may be used under section 414.'

...

[T]he Board of Center Moriches Union Free School District (District) has issued rules and regulations with respect to the use of school property when not in use for school purposes.

...

Rule 7 ... provides that '[t]he school premises shall not be used by any group for religious purposes.' App to Pet for Cert 57a.

The issue in this case is whether, against this background of state law, it violates the Free Speech Clause of the First Amendment, made applicable to the States by the Fourteenth Amendment, to deny a church access to school premises to exhibit for public viewing and for assertedly religious purposes, a film series dealing with family and child-rearing issues faced by parents today.

Petitioners (Church) are Lamb's Chapel, an evangelical church in the community of Center Moriches, and its pastor John Steigerwald. Twice the Church applied to the District for permission to use school facilities to show a six-part film series containing lectures by Doctor James Dobson. A brochure provided on request of the District identified Dr Dobson as a licensed psychologist, former associate clinical professor of paediatrics at the University of Southern California, best-selling author and radio commentator. The brochure stated that the film series would discuss Dr Dobson's views on the undermining influences of the media that could only be counterbalanced by returning to traditional, Christian family values instilled at an early stage. The brochure went on to describe the contents of each of the six parts of the series. The District denied the first application, saying that '[t]his film does appear to be church related and therefore your request must be refused.' App 84. The second application for permission to use school premises for showing the film series, which described it as a 'Family oriented movie — from a Christian perspective,' id, at 91, was denied using identical language.

...

The Court of Appeals appeared to recognise that the total ban on using District property for religious purposes could survive First Amendment challenge only if excluding this category of speech was reasonable and viewpoint neutral. The court's conclusion in this case was that Rule 7 met this test. We cannot agree with this holding, for Rule 7 was unconstitutionally applied in this case.

The Court of Appeals thought that the application of Rule 7 in this case was viewpoint neutral because it had been, and would be, applied in the same way to all uses of school property for religious purposes. That all religions and all uses for religious purposes are treated alike under Rule 7, however, does not answer the critical question whether it discriminates on the basis of viewpoint to permit school property to be used for the presentation of all views about family issues and child rearing except those dealing with the subject matter from a religious standpoint.

There is no suggestion from the courts below or from the District or the State that a lecture or film about child rearing and family values would not be a use for social or civic purposes otherwise permitted by Rule 10. That subject matter is not one that the District has placed off limits to any and all speakers. Nor is there any indication in the record before us that the application to exhibit the particular film series involved here was, or would have been, denied for any reason other than the fact that the presentation would have been from a religious perspective. In our view, denial on that basis was plainly invalid under our holding in *Cornelius*, ... at 806, that

> [a]lthough a speaker may be excluded from a non-public forum if he wishes to address a topic not encompassed within the purpose of the forum ... or if he is not a member of the class of speakers for whose especial benefit the forum was created ..., the government violates the First Amendment when it denies access to a speaker solely to suppress the point of view he espouses on an otherwise includible subject.

The film series involved here no doubt dealt with a subject otherwise permissible under Rule 10, and its exhibition was denied solely because the series dealt with the subject from a religious standpoint.

The US Supreme Court held that the board had violated the freedom of speech clause. The church was discriminated against by the board. If the board permitted the church to use its property, this would not amount to advancing religion and would not be in breach of the establishment clause.

Canada

In Canada, whose population like that of the USA predominantly comprises immigrants from many different countries, the law prohibits discrimination on the grounds of religion. This applies to pupils and students, and has implications for English law once the EU anti-discrimination directive comes into force. The directive will outlaw various forms of discrimination including religious discrimination.

A Khan 'Canadian education authorities' duty to make reasonable accommodation for religious belief' (1997) 9(4) Education and the Law, 307

The Canadian Charter of Rights and Freedoms stipulates equal treatment, thus proscribing discrimination inter alia on racial and religious grounds. The Charter also guarantees to everyone 'the fundamental freedom' of 'freedom of conscience and religion'. One of the outcomes is the imposition of the duty on employers, educational authorities and others of reasonable accommodation of a minority's sincere beliefs based on religion or conscience. This duty, which provides enforceable legal rights for employees and users of education, has become an important factor in the formation and implementation of educational policies and practices. This is in contrast with British law, where no such constitutional duty exists.

Wearing of religious manifestations

In cases where serious disadvantage (perceived serious by the majority) is suffered, accommodation of religious beliefs is most likely provided. But in the case of beliefs which are not perceived by the majority of the population or even the courts as serious — for example dress codes (turban, hijab or head-scarf) that a teacher or a pupil insists on observing in school, or the insistence that the physical education or swimming classes be held separately for boys and girls, or wearing of a kirpan (knife) as a religious symbol during school hours — problems can arise if the school principal or education authorities show inflexibility. So far as can be judged from the reported cases in higher courts in this respect — or lack of them, principals and education authorities have been flexible and have endeavoured to be accommodating, so that compromises, in association with the parents' involvement, can be made. Major problems are likely to arise when parents demand alteration of school curriculum or removal of certain texts or parts of books to reflect the religious beliefs of a certain group or individual. The issue of dress code for women can be problematic, because certain parents believe that their daughters should wear a head-dress in school, whereas others might see this as a symbol of women's 'oppression'. It is submitted that as this causes no harm to any one, except to the feelings of some extremely sensitive people, the parents' or pupils' wishes to wear a hijab (or turban) should be respected. It is a very small accommodation to make, where no one else is directly affected — being discomfited is surely not a valid ground for denying this freedom of religious belief.

Sincerely held belief

On the one hand, intention to discriminate is not a prerequisite to finding discrimination, on the other the complainant, whose freedom of religion is not accommodated, is required to sincerely and genuinely believe in his or her faith, and not merely to use it as a cloak for demanding favours. As elaborated by the Supreme Court of Canada, when a (wo)man complains of discrimination by failure of accommodation, the question is, 'At what point in the profession of his faith and the observance of its rules does he go beyond the mere exercise of his rights and seek to enforce upon others conformance with his beliefs?'

Another difficulty is that the believer may believe in a tenet or rule which to others may appear to be weird or offensive, e g smoking of hashish/ganja on the school premises, although in this example the difficulty is resolved because the act of smoking is illegal. But there can be instances of other 'weird' rules. The question, in a different context, has been asked by a British academic: 'Should the law protect all religions, howsoever weird and potentially harmful to the community ...?' It is submitted that the answer depends on the impugned rule itself and the individual who is answering it. Therefore, the courts' task, as has been realised by the Canadian and British courts, is not an easy one, which may explain why so many safeguards have been introduced in the duty to accommodate.

- *Should predominantly Christian religious education and collective worship prevail in non-denominational schools in a multi-cultural society?*

Hamilton and Watt argue that religious freedom, which is protected by the European Convention on Human Rights (see above), should be broadly interpreted.

C Hamilton and B Watt 'A discriminating education — collective worship in schools' (1996) 8(1) Child and Family Law Quarterly 28 at 32

Religious freedom and tolerance

There has, as yet, been little discussion in UK or European Court jurisprudence of the meaning of religious freedom. A narrow interpretation of religious freedom or 'tolerance' as it is sometimes referred to, would guarantee to all people the right to practise their religion and manifest their religious beliefs without State interference. The stronger and wider conception of religious freedom would require the State to treat all religions equally, by providing adherents of each religion with the necessary facilities and opportunities to live a religious life in accordance with their own sensibilities. From this principle would follow the policy that there could be no discrimination against members of minority religions and no favourable treatment of the members of a majority religion.

...

The best practical conception of religious freedom seems to require more than people merely refraining from repressing that which they dislike and are able to suppress, but to grant others the space in which to practise their own ways. Susan Mendus refers to this as 'the positive interpretation of toleration' and notes that 'it requires assisting, aiding and fostering'. The argument in this article is that religious toleration requires this latter positive interpretation. The question then becomes whether in England, State maintained schools can achieve such 'assisting, aiding and fostering' in the shadow of an established church.

- *Consider whether the statutory requirements on religious education and collective worship comply with the provisions of the Human Righs Act 1998.*

7.   SEX AND RELATIONSHIP EDUCATION

Sex education has been compulsory for pupils at secondary school since 1994, subject to their parents having the right to withdraw them from the classes. Sex and Relationship Education is perceived by the DfEE as being linked to the Science Curriculum and to the PSHE and Citizenship framework.

Education Act 1996, s 352(1)(c)

(1) The curriculum for every maintained school shall comprise a basic curriculum which includes—

...

(c)   in the case of a secondary school, provision for sex education for all registered pupils at the school, ...

In England the responsibility for providing appropriate sex education rests primarily upon the governing body and the head teacher. The role of the English LEA has been restricted by the Learning and Skills Act 2000 (s 351(6), (7) of the EA 1996 as amended by LSA 2000).

Education Act 1996, s 403

(1) The ... governing body and head teacher shall take such steps as are reasonably practicable to secure that where sex education is given to any registered pupils at a maintained school, it is given in such a manner as to encourage those pupils to have due regard to moral considerations and the value of family life.

(1A) The Secretary of State must issue guidance designed to secure that when sex education is given to registered pupils at maintained schools—
(a)   they learn the nature of marriage and its importance for family life and the bringing up of children, and
(b)   they are protected from teaching and materials which are inappropriate having regard to the age and the religious and cultural background of the pupils concerned.

(1B) In discharging their functions under subsection (1) governing bodies and head teachers must have regard to the Secretary of State's guidance.

(1C) Guidance under subsection (1A) must include guidance about any material which may be produced by NHS bodies for use for the purposes of sex education in schools.

(1D) The Secretary of State may at any time revise his guidance under subsection (1A).

...

In Wales, the LEA also has responsibilities under s 403(1) of EA 1996, but the guidance referred to in s 403(1A) does not automatically apply to Wales. The current statutory guidance is DfEE Guidance 00116/2000 (Sex and Relationship Education).

Statements of policy

All maintained schools are required to have a written sex education policy.

Education Act 1996, s 404(1)

(1) The governing body of a maintained school shall—
(a) make, and keep up to date, a separate written statement of their policy with regard to the provision of sex education, and
(b) make copies of the statement available for inspection (at all reasonable times) by parents of registered pupils at the school and provide a copy of the statement free of charge to any such parent who asks for one.

In England the statement of policy must explain that a parent has the right to withdraw their child from sex education classes.

Although primary schools are not legally required to provide sex education classes for their pupils the DfEE guidance encourages them to do so.

DfEE Guidance 00116/2000 (Sex and Relationship Education) paras 1.12–1.16

1.12 The Department recommends that all primary schools should have a sex and relationship education programme tailored to the age and the physical and emotional maturity of the children. It should ensure that both boys and girls know about puberty and how a baby is born – as set out in Key Stages 1 and 2 of the National Science Curriculum. Section 3 gives further information on what should be taught at these stages and how this should be rooted in the PSHE framework.

1.13 All children, including those who develop earlier than the average, need to know about puberty before they experience the onset of physical changes. In the early primary school years, education about relationships needs to focus on friendship, bullying and the building of self-esteem.

1.14 Meeting these objectives will require a graduated, age-appropriate programme of sex and relationship education. Teaching methods need to take account of the developmental differences of children and the potential for discussion on a one-to-one basis or in small groups. Schools should set a framework for establishing what is appropriate and inappropriate in a whole-class setting. Teachers may require support and training in answering questions that are better not dealt with in front of a whole class.

1.15 It is important that the transition year before moving to secondary schools supports pupils' ongoing emotional and physical development effectively. As well as consulting parents more generally about the school's overall policy, primary schools should consult with parents before the transition year about the detailed content of what will be taught. This process should include offering parents support in talking to their children about sex and relationship education and how to link this with what is being taught in school.

1.16 Schools should have clear parameters on what children will be taught in the transition year before moving to secondary school. This should include:

- changes in the body related to puberty, such as periods and voice breaking:
- when these changes are likely to happen and what issues may cause young people anxiety and how they can deal with these; and
- how a baby is conceived and born.

Content

Section 403 of the EA 1996 was amended by the Learning and Skills Act 2000, s 148(4). The legislation specifically refers to 'moral considerations and the value of family life', together with the nature and importance of marriage. The age as well as the religious and cultural background of the pupils should also be taken into account.

In addition the DfEE recommends (DfEE Guidance 00116/2000) that sex education should include those subjects expressly excluded from the Science part of the National Curriculum (s 356(9) of the EA 1996). The subjects are:

- Acquired Immune Deficiency Syndrome and Human Immunodeficiency Virus,
- any other sexually transmitted disease, or
- aspects of human sexual behaviour, other than biological aspects.

The government attempted unsuccessfully in 2000/2001 to repeal 'Clause 28'(s 2A(1) of the Local Government Act 1986) which prohibits the promotion of homosexuality by local authorities. The DfEE guidance states that there should be no direct promotion of sexual orientation (para 1.30).

Under age sex

Pupils under 16 may seek contraceptive advice from teachers or other members of the school staff. Sexual intercourse is unlawful for such pupils and where such advice is given the member of staff risks being prosecuted. The liability of health professionals in this context was considered in the following case.

Gillick v West Norfolk and Wisbech Area Health Authority [1985] 3 All ER 402

Lord Fraser of Tullybelton. My Lords, the main question in this appeal is whether a doctor can lawfully prescribe contraception for a girl under 16 years of age without the consent of her parents. The second appellant, the Department of Health and Social Security (the DHSS), maintains that a doctor can do so. The respondent, Mrs Gillick, maintains that he cannot.

...

In December 1980 the DHSS issued guidance on family planning services for young people, which was a revised version of earlier guidance on the same subject, and which stated, or implied, that, at least in certain cases which were described as 'exceptional', a doctor could lawfully prescribe contraception for a girl under 16 without her parents' consent. Mrs Gillick, who is the mother of five daughters under the age of 16, objected to the guidance and she instituted the proceedings which have led to this appeal, and in which she claims a declaration against both appellants that the advice given in the guidance was unlawful.

...

Three strands of argument are raised by the appeal. These are: (1) whether a girl under the age of 16 has the legal capacity to give valid consent to contraceptive advice and treatment including medical examination; (2) whether giving such advice and treatment to a girl under 16 without her parents' consent infringes the parents' rights and (3) whether a doctor who gives such advice or treatment to a girl under 16 without her parents' consent incurs criminal liability.

...

It seems to me verging on the absurd to suggest that a girl or a boy aged 15 could not effectively consent, for example, to have a medical examination of some trivial injury to his body or even to have a broken arm set. Of course the consent of the parents should normally be asked, but they may not be immediately available. Provided the patient, whether a boy or a girl, is capable of understanding what is proposed, and of expressing his or her own wishes, I see no good reason for holding that he or she lacks the capacity to express them validly and effectively and to authorise the medical man to make the examination or give the treatment which he advises.

...

I conclude that there is no statutory provision which compels me to hold that a girl under the age of 16 lacks the legal capacity to consent to contraceptive advice, examination and treatment provided that she has sufficient understanding and intelligence to know what they involve.

...

It is, in my view, contrary to the ordinary experience of mankind, at least in Western Europe in the present century, to say that a child or a young person remains in fact under the complete control of his parents until he attains the definite age of majority, now 18 in the United Kingdom, and that on attaining that age he suddenly acquires independence. In practice most wise parents relax their control gradually as the child develops and encourage him or her to become increasingly independent. Moreover, the degree of parental control actually exercised over a particular child does in practice vary considerably according to his understanding and intelligence and it would, in my opinion, be unrealistic for the courts not to recognise these facts. Social customs change, and the law ought to, and does in fact, have regard to such changes when they are of major importance.

...

[T]here will be some cases, where the girl refuses either to tell the parents herself or to permit the doctor to do so and in such cases the doctor will, in my opinion, be justified in proceeding without the parents' consent or even knowledge provided he is satisfied on the following matters: (1) that the girl (although under 16 years of age) will understand his advice; (2) that he cannot persuade her to inform her parents or to allow him to inform the parents that she is seeking contraceptive advice; (3) that she is very likely to begin or to continue having sexual intercourse with or without contraceptive treatment; (4) that unless she receives contraceptive advice or treatment her physical or mental health or both are likely to suffer; (5) that her best interests require him to give her contraceptive advice, treatment or both without the parental consent.

...

The submission was made to Woolf J on behalf of Mrs Gillick that a doctor who provided contraceptive advice and treatment to a girl under 16 without her parents' authority would be committing an offence under s 28 of the Sexual Offences Act 1956 by aiding and abetting the commission of unlawful sexual intercourse. When the case reached the Court of Appeal counsel on both sides conceded that whether a doctor who followed the guidelines would be committing an offence or not would depend on the circumstances. It would depend on the doctor's intentions; this appeal is concerned with doctors who honestly intend to act in the best interests of the girl, and I think it is unlikely that a doctor who gives contraceptive advice or treatment with that intention would commit an offence under s 28. It must be remembered that a girl under 16 who has sexual intercourse does not thereby commit an offence herself, although her partner does: see the Sexual Offences Act 1956, ss 5 and 6. In any event, even if the doctor would be committing an offence, the fact that he had acted with the parents' consent would not exculpate him as Woolf J pointed out ([1984] 1 All ER 365 at 373, [1984] QB 581 at 595).

...

I would hold that as a matter of law the parental right to determine whether or not their minor child below the age of 16 will have medical treatment terminates if and when the child achieves a sufficient understanding and intelligence to enable him or her to understand fully what is proposed. It will be a question of fact whether a child seeking advice has sufficient understanding of what is involved to give a consent valid in law. Until the child achieves the capacity to consent, the parental right to make the decision continues save only in exceptional circumstances. Emergency, parental neglect, abandonment of the child or inability to find the parent are examples of exceptional situations justifying the doctor proceeding to treat the child without parental knowledge and consent; but there will arise, no doubt, other exceptional situations in which it will be reasonable for the doctor to proceed without the parent's consent.

When applying these conclusions to contraceptive advice and treatment it has to be borne in mind that there is much that has to be understood by a girl under the age of 16 if she is to have legal capacity to consent to such treatment. It is not enough that she should understand the nature of the advice which is being given: she must also have a sufficient maturity to understand what is involved. There are moral and family questions, especially her relationship with her parents; long-term problems associated with the emotional impact of pregnancy and its termination; and there are the risks to health of sexual intercourse at her age, risks which contraception may diminish but cannot eliminate. It follows that a doctor will have to satisfy himself that she is able to appraise these factors before he can safely proceed on the basis that she has at law capacity to consent to contraceptive treatment. And it further follows that ordinarily the proper course will be for him, as the guidance lays down, first to seek to persuade the girl to bring her parents into consultation, and, if she refuses, not to prescribe contraceptive treatment unless he is satisfied that her circumstances are such that he ought to proceed without parental knowledge and consent.

- *What is the test which should be used to determine whether a girl below the age of 16 can legally consent to be prescribed contraceptives?*

The DfEE guidance states:

DfEE Guidance 00116/2000 (Sex and Relationship Education) paras 2.9–2.13, 7.9, 7.11

Contraception

2.9 In England in 1998 there were over 100,000 conceptions to teenagers, of which over 8,000 were to girls under 16. This is clearly totally unacceptable. Not only are there obvious risks to health, but this also leads to greater dependence, undermining potential achievement in education and in further employment, placing greater stress on the young person and their family, and denying choices available to others. This puts at risk the broader development of pupils mentioned in paragraph 2 of the introduction. It is therefore appropriate for secondary schools to provide education about contraception.

2.10 Knowledge of the different types of contraception, and of access to, and availability of contraception is a major part of the Government's strategy to reduce teenage pregnancy. Effective sex and relationship education in secondary schools has an important role to play in achieving this.

2.11 Trained staff in secondary schools should be able to give young people full information about different types of contraception, including emergency contraception and their effectiveness. Pupils may wish to raise further issues with staff arising from discussion in the classroom. Trained teachers can also give pupils — individually and as a class — additional information and guidance on where they can obtain confidential advice, counselling and, where necessary, treatment.

2.12 This should be made clear in the school's sex and relationship education policy. Section 7 also refers to the role of health professionals in the school.

2.13 In addition to what is put in place in a school's sex and relationship education policy to inform and counsel young people on sex and relationships, there will be rare occasions when a primary school teacher is directly approached by a child who is sexually active or contemplating sexual activity. This will always raise child protection issues and sensitive handling will be needed to ensure that a proper balance is struck between the need to observe the law and the need for sensitive counselling and treatment including protection from disclosure to inappropriate adults. Section 7 contains a fuller account of the procedures for handling such cases.

7.9 In such cases there should be a pathway for dealing with the situation:
- the teacher should approach the designated member of staff (this could be the sex and relationship education teacher, or other member of staff with pastoral responsibility or on-site health professional);
- the designated member of staff should make sensitive arrangements, in discussion with the child, to ensure that parents or carers are informed; and
- the designated member of staff should address child protection issues and ensure that help is provided for the child and family.

7.11 Nonetheless, there may be cases where a teacher learns from an under 16-year-old that they are having, or contemplating having, sexual intercourse. In these circumstances, schools ought to be in a position to take steps to ensure that:
- wherever possible, the young person is persuaded to talk to their parent or carer;
- any child protection issues are addressed; and
- that the child has been adequately counselled and informed about contraception, including precise information about where young people can access contraception and advice services.

- *Is a teacher or a school nurse likely to be regarded by the courts in the same way as a doctor who provides contraceptive advice to a 'Gillick competent' pupil?*

Right to withdraw pupil from sex education

Parents have the right to withdraw their children from some or all of the sex education classes.

Education Act 1996, s 405

If the parent of any pupil in attendance at a maintained school requests that he may be wholly or partly excused from receiving sex education at the school, the pupil shall, except so far as such education is comprised in the National Curriculum, be so excused accordingly until the request is withdrawn.

However, parents may not withdraw their child from other aspects of the curriculum which they find unacceptable. For example, members of certain Christian sects may be opposed to their children being taught about the theory of evolution in Science because they accept the Book of Genesis in the Bible which states that Adam and Eve were the first humans.

Arguably, requiring children of such parents to be taught about the theory of evolution as part of the National Curriculum is in breach of Article 2 of protocol 1 of the ECHR (see above). This is because the Education Act 1996 does not respect a parent's right to ensure that such teaching is in conformity with his or her religious convictions. However, the following case indicates that such an argument is unlikely to be successful.

Kjeldsen, Busk Madsen and Pedersen v Denmark (1976) 1 EHRR 711

The Facts

14. The applicants, who are parents of Danish nationality, reside in Denmark, Mr Viking Kjeldsen, a galvaniser, and his wife Annemarie, a schoolteacher, live in Varde; Mr Arne Busk Madsen, a clergyman, and his wife Inger, a schoolteacher, come from Åbenrå; Mr Hans Pedersen, who is a clergyman, and Mrs Ellen Pedersen have their home in Ålborg.

All three couples, having children of school age, object to integrated, and hence compulsory, sex education as introduced into State primary schools in Denmark by Act No 235 of 27 May 1970, amending the State Schools Act (*Lov om aendring af lov om folkeskolen*, hereinafter referred to as 'the 1970 Act').

    ...

21. In 1968, after a thorough examination of the problem, the above-mentioned committee, which was composed of doctors, educationalists, lawyers, theologians and government experts, submitted a report (No 484) entitled 'Sex Education in State Schools' (*Seksualundervisning i Folkeskolen m v, Betaenkning Nr 484*). Modelling itself on the system that had been in force in Sweden for some years, the committee recommended in its report that sex education be integrated into compulsory subjects on the curriculum of State schools.

    ...

[T]he setting and planning of the curriculum fall in principle within the competence of the Contracting States. This mainly involves questions of expediency on which it is not for the Court to rule and whose solution may legitimately vary according to the country and the era. In particular, the second sentence of Article 2 of the Protocol does not prevent States from imparting through teaching or education information or knowledge of a directly or indirectly religious or philosophical kind. It does not even permit parents to object to the integration of such teaching or education in the school curriculum, for otherwise all institutionalised teaching would run the risk of proving impracticable. In fact, it seems very difficult for many subjects taught at school not to have, to a greater or lesser extent, some philosophical complexion or implications. The same is true of religious affinities if one remembers the existence of religions forming a very broad dogmatic and moral entity which has or may have answers to every question of a philosophical, cosmological or moral nature.

The second sentence of Article 2 implies on the other hand that the State, in fulfilling the functions assumed by it in regard to education and teaching, must take care that information or knowledge included in the curriculum is conveyed in an objective, critical and pluralistic manner. The State is forbidden to pursue an aim of indoctrination that might be considered as not respecting parents' religious and philosophical convictions. That is the limit that must not be exceeded.

Such an interpretation is consistent at one and the same time with the first sentence of Article 2 of the Protocol, with Articles 8 to 10 of the Convention and with the general spirit of the Convention itself, an instrument designed to maintain and promote the ideals and values of a democratic society. ...

54. In order to examine the disputed legislation under Article 2 of the Protocol, interpreted as above, one must, while avoiding any evaluation of the legislation's expediency, have regard to the material situation that it sought and still seeks to meet.

The Danish legislator, who did not neglect to obtain beforehand the advice of qualified experts, clearly took as his starting point the known fact that in Denmark children nowadays discover without difficulty and from several quarters the information that interests them on sexual life. The instruction on the subject given in State schools is aimed less at instilling knowledge they do not have or cannot acquire by other means than at giving them such knowledge more correctly, precisely, objectively and scientifically. The instruction, as provided for and organised by the contested legislation, is principally intended to give pupils better information: this emerges from, inter alia, the preface to the 'Guide' of April 1971.

Even when circumscribed in this way, such instruction clearly cannot exclude on the part of teachers certain assessments capable of encroaching on the religious or philosophical sphere; for what are involved are matters where appraisals of fact easily lead on to value-judgments. The minority of the Commission rightly emphasised this. The Executive Orders and Circulars of 8 June 1971 and 15 June 1972, the 'Guide' of April 1971 and the other material before the Court plainly show that the Danish State, by providing children in good time with explanations it considers useful, is attempting to warn them against phenomena it views as disturbing, for example, the excessive frequency of births out of wedlock, induced abortions and venereal diseases. The public authorities wish to enable pupils, when the time comes, 'to take care of themselves and show consideration for others in that respect', 'not ... [to] land themselves or others in difficulties solely on account of lack of knowledge'.

These considerations are indeed of a moral order, but they are very general in character and do not entail overstepping the bounds of what a democratic State may regard as the public interest. Examination of the legislation in dispute establishes in fact that it in no way amounts to an attempt at indoctrination aimed at advocating a specific kind of sexual behaviour. It does not make a point of exalting sex or inciting pupils to indulge precociously in practices that are dangerous for their stability, health or future or that many parents consider reprehensible. Further, it does not affect the right of parents to enlighten and advise their children, to exercise with regard to their children natural parental functions as educators, or to guide their children on a path in line with the parents' own religious or philosophical convictions.

Certainly, abuses can occur as to the manner in which the provisions in force are applied by a given school or teacher and the competent authorities have a duty to take the utmost care to see to it that parents' religious and philosophical convictions are not disregarded at this level by carelessness, lack of judgment or misplaced proselytism. However, it follows from the Commission's decisions on the admissibility of the applications that the Court is not at present seised of a problem of this kind.

The Court consequently reaches the conclusion that the disputed legislation in itself in no way offends the applicants' religious and philosophical convictions to the extent forbidden by the second sentence of Article 2 of the Protocol, interpreted in the light of its first sentence and of the whole of the Convention.

- *In what 'manner' did the Court consider that information and knowledge included in the curriculum should be conveyed in order to comply with the second sentence of Article 2?*

8.   CAREERS EDUCATION AND GUIDANCE

The Education Act 1997 established a new statutory framework which outlines the roles and responsibilities of the various organisations concerned with the provision of careers education and guidance. Schools and FE colleges are expected to enter into a Partnership Agreement with a provider of careers services.

The aim of the new statutory framework is to raise pupils' and students' aspirations, as well as enabling them to make better informed decisions about their career path. This is seen as likely to increase their motivation and their likelihood of success. A more skilled and motivated workforce is also of social and economic benefit to the country as a whole.

Careers education

Schools are under a duty to provide pupils in Years 9-11 (ie 14 to 16-year-olds) with a programme of careers education. This was introduced in 1998 and applies to maintained schools and special schools as well as pupil referral units and city technology colleges. It does not apply to independent schools or FE colleges.

The duty rests with the governing body and the head teacher in the case of maintained schools; with the proprietors of the school and the head teacher in the case of city technology colleges and city colleges for the technology of the arts; and in the case of a pupil referral unit with the LEA and the teacher in charge of the unit.

Education Act 1997, s 43

(1) All registered pupils at a school to which this section applies must be provided, during the relevant phase of their education, with a programme of careers education.

(2) This section applies to—
(a)   community, foundation and voluntary schools;
(b)   ...
(c)   community or foundation special schools (other than those established in hospitals);

(d) city technology colleges, city colleges for the technology of the arts and city academies; and

(e) pupil referral units.

(3) It is the duty of each of the following to secure that subsection (1) is complied with, namely—

(a) in the case of a school falling within subsection (2)(a) to (c), the governing body of the school and its head teacher,

(b) in the case of a school falling within subsection (2)(d), the proprietors of the school and its head teacher, and

(c) in the case of a pupil referral unit, the local education authority maintaining the unit and the teacher in charge of it.

Guidance is provided in DfEE Circular 5/98 (Careers Education in Schools: Provision for Years 9-11). For example the following advice is given to schools.

8. When reviewing your provision of careers education, you should examine the following:
- Is the careers education and guidance policy written down, and has it been reviewed recently?
- How effectively are the aims and contributions of the school and careers service covered in the Partnership Agreement?
- Is there a development plan for careers education, and how does this feed into the whole school development plan?
- Who is the lead teacher on careers education? Is their role clearly specified/contained in a job description? Have they had recognised training?
- How is careers education timetabled/integrated across the curriculum?
- What materials (including new technology) are in use and available for delivering careers education?
- How are careers education learning outcomes defined, monitored, assessed and recorded?
- What opportunities are available for staff development? Is this available to all teachers involved in careers education and guidance?
- Who in the senior management team is responsible for overall management of the careers education programme?
- How is careers education monitored, reviewed and evaluated? Evaluation will be easier where you have developed clearly defined outcomes for careers education.

Duty on schools and FE institutions to co-operate with careers advisers

Since 1994 LEAs have been able to contract out the provision of careers advice to the Careers Service, which is a national network of individual organisations which work under contract to the Secretary of State for Education and Employment. Careers advisers are therefore no longer employed by a LEA, but by a private organisation. Section 44 of the EA 1997 gives such advisers the right to contact, and meet pupils individually or in groups on the premises of a school or an FE college.

Where a careers adviser has responsibilities for pupils and students attending a school (other than a pupil referral unit), an FE college or a sixth form college, then the adviser is entitled to request in writing and be given the name and address of every pupil or student in the equivalent of Year 9 or above, together with any other relevant information that it possesses. However, parents (or pupils aged 18 and above) may refuse to permit that information to be given, and may refuse to be interviewed.

Education Act 1997, s 44

(1) Where a careers adviser has responsibilities in relation to persons attending an educational institution to which this section applies, he shall on request be provided with—

(a) the name and address of every relevant pupil or student at the institution; and

(b) any information in the institution's possession about any such pupil or student which the careers adviser needs in order to be able to provide him with advice and guidance on decisions about his career or with other information relevant to such decisions.

...

(3) Paragraph (a) or (as the case may be) paragraph (b) of subsection (1) does not, however, apply to any pupil or student to the extent that—

(a) (where he is under the age of 18) a parent of his, or

(b) (where he has attained that age) he himself,

has indicated that any information falling within that paragraph should not be provided to the careers adviser.

The institutions subject to this duty differ from those subject to the s 43 duty. The duty under s 44 applies to FE colleges, but not to pupil referral units. The governing body (or proprietor of the school) and the head teacher is responsible for ensuring that the school or FE college complies with these requirements.

Guidance is provided in DfEE Circular 5/97 (Careers Education and Guidance in Schools: Effective Partnerships with Careers Services), and DfEE Circular 6/97 (Careers Education and Guidance in Further Education Colleges).

Provision of careers information

The governing body (or proprietors) of the school or FE college, and the head teacher or principal are under a duty to ensure that careers information is available for their pupils or students. In order to discharge their duty they must seek assistance from outside bodies, such as Connexions, which provide careers services to LEAs.

Education Act 1997, s 45

(1) Persons attending an educational institution to which this section applies must be provided with access to both—

(a)   guidance materials, and

(b)   a wide range of up-to-date reference materials,

relating to careers education and career opportunities.

...

This section does not apply to primary schools or to pupil referral units, but nor is it limited to pupils in Years 9-11.

A comparison of the two circulars on the provision of careers libraries illustrates the approaches considered suitable for the pupils or students.

DfEE Circular 5/97 (Careers Education and Guidance in Schools: Effective Partnerships with Careers Services)

3.9 Section 45 of the Act means that, where practicable, schools should provide their pupils with suitable information through a careers' library, which should be:

(a)   a dedicated area, with suitable space for materials and for the number of pupils and their needs;

(b)   a location within the school which pupils can visit easily;

(c)   open at all reasonable times (for example, break times, lunch and possibly before or after school on given days): the times to be published;

(d)   regularly maintained: the material kept up-to-date and well-structured, enabling pupils to find material themselves and with advice available.

3.10 Where it is not possible for a school to provide a careers' library as described here, the school should work with the careers service to provide the next best form of provision which satisfies pupils' information needs. This might be something other than a dedicated space in the school, such as a mobile display or use of facilities outside the school. The term 'careers' library' is used here for convenience, but refers to whatever form the provision takes.

3.11 There are benefits to pupils in having access to careers information before Year 9. Secondary schools may therefore wish to allow all pupils to use the careers' library.

3.12 Careers services also have to provide material that it is possible for people with learning difficulties or sensory impairments to use and understand. Each school, in drawing up its Partnership Agreement with the careers service, should identify and elaborate the needs of its pupils and agree how information can be most helpfully presented to take account of those needs.

DfEE Circular 6/97 (Careers Education and Guidance in Further Education Colleges)

Careers Library(ies). The college should provide a dedicated area where careers materials and resources can be housed. In a multi-site college there may be several libraries or resource centres throughout the college. A careers library should be:

—   attractive and welcoming;

—   in a position within the college where it is readily accessible to students;

—   appropriate, in terms of its space and materials, to the number of students studying at the college and their needs;

— open at all reasonable times, during the day and (say) 2 evenings per week;
— maintained and staffed according to its use, e g by appropriately qualified librarians or appropriate staff;
— able to be used as much as possible by students themselves with appropriate support.

Further guidance on careers libraries is at Annex 4.

9. RELIGIOUS AND PHILOSOPHICAL VALUES IN THE SCHOOL CURRICULUM

The content of the school curriculum can be contentious, not only in relation to its specific content, but also because it reflects political, moral and social values, which may not be acceptable to all groups in society. There has been considerable debate over, for example, the content of the history syllabus, although it is the areas of religious education and sex education that have proved most contentious (see above).

The Human Rights Act 1998 incorporates Article 2 of Protocol 1 to the ECHR which provides that:

> the state shall respect the right of parents to ensure such education and teaching in conformity with their own religious and philosophical convictions.

The European Court of Human Rights has considered what is meant by 'convictions' in a number of cases, including *Campbell and Cosans v United Kingdom* (1982) 4 EHRR 293, and *Valsamis v Greece* [1998] ELR 430.

Valsamis v Greece **[1998] ELR 430**

The term 'belief' ('convictions') appears in Art 9 in the context of the right to freedom of thought, conscience and religion. The concept of 'religious and philosophical convictions' appears in Art 2 of Protocol No 1. When applying that provision, the Court has held that in its ordinary meaning 'convictions', taken on its own, is not synonymous with the words 'opinions' and 'ideas'. It denotes views that attain a certain level of cogency, seriousness, cohesion and importance (see the *Campbell and Cosans v the United Kingdom* judgment of 25 February 1982, Series A no 48, p 16, § 36).

(26) As the Court observed in its judgment of 25 May 1993 in the *Kokkinakis v Greece* case (Series A no 260-A, p 18, § 36), Jehovah's Witnesses enjoy both the status of a 'known religion' and the advantages flowing from that as regards observance. Mr and Mrs Valsamis were accordingly entitled to rely on the right to respect for their religious convictions within the meaning of this provision. It remains to be ascertained whether the State failed to discharge its obligations to respect those convictions in the applicants' case.

(27) The Court reiterates that Art 2 of Protocol No 1 enjoins the State to respect parents' convictions, be they religious or philosophical, throughout the entire State education programme (see the *Kjeldsen, Busk Madsen and Pedersen v Denmark* judgment cited above, p 25, § 51). That duty is broad in its extent as it applies not only to the content of education and the manner of its provision but also to the performance of all the 'functions' assumed by the State. The verb 'respect' means more than 'acknowledge' or 'take into account'. In addition to a primarily negative undertaking, it implies some positive obligation on the

part of the State (see the *Campbell and Cosans v the United Kingdom* judgment cited above, p 17, § 37).

The Court has also held that 'although individual interests must on occasion be subordinated to those of a group, democracy does not simply mean that the views of a majority must always prevail: a balance must be achieved which ensures the fair and proper treatment of minorities and avoids any abuse of a dominant position' (*Young, James and Webster v the United Kingdom* judgment of 13 August 1981, Series A no 44, p 25, § 63).

(28) However, 'the setting and planning of the curriculum fall in principle within the competence of the Contracting States. This mainly involves questions of expediency on which it is not for the Court to rule and whose solution may legitimately vary according to the country and the era' (see the *Kjeldsen, Busk Madsen and Pedersen v Denmark* judgment cited above, p 26, § 53). Given that discretion, the Court has held that the second sentence of Art 2 forbids the State 'to pursue an aim of indoctrination that might be regarded as not respecting parents' religious and philosophical convictions. That is the limit that must not be exceeded'.

- *Some Muslim parents may have strongly held religious and cultural views that their daughter should attend a single-sex rather than a mixed sex secondary school. If a place at such a school is not available in the LEA area would the LEA be in breach of the Human Rights Act 1998?*

Under existing domestic law parents do not have the right to insist that their daughter (or son) should attend a single-sex school (see *R v Governors of the Buss Foundation Camden School for Girls, ex p Lukasiewicz* [1991] COD 98).

Whereas the ECHR protects the subjective religious and philosophical convictions of parents, the UK legislation has adopted, in the context of political views, an objective approach which is concerned with ensuring pupils are given information on a range of views. The Education Act 1996 provides that a school should offer a balanced and broadly based curriculum (s 351).

The legislation provides that political indoctrination is forbidden and that there should be a balanced treatment of political issues. However although political issues should be dealt with in an even-handed manner, this approach is not adopted in relation to religion, sex education, or other areas of philosophical debate.

Education Act 1996, s 406

(1) The local education authority, governing body and head teacher shall forbid—
(a) the pursuit of partisan political activities by any of those registered pupils at a maintained school who are junior pupils, and
(b) the promotion of partisan political views in the teaching of any subject in the school.

(2) In the case of activities which take place otherwise than on the school premises, subsection (1)(a) applies only where arrangements for junior pupils to take part in the activities are made by—
(a) any member of the school's staff (in his capacity as such), or
(b) anyone acting on behalf of the school or of a member of the school's staff (in his capacity as such).

...

'Senior' pupils are permitted to pursue 'partisan political' activities both on and off school premises. Mock general elections in secondary schools would not fall foul of this provision. The key requirement is that teachers should not promote 'partisan political views'.

- *Define a 'partisan political view'. What amounts to 'promotion' of such a view? Should a Science course based on the theory of evolution be forbidden?*

Education Act 1996, s 407

(1) The local education authority, governing body and head teacher shall take such steps as are reasonably practicable to secure that where political issues are brought to the attention of pupils while they are—
(a)   in attendance at a maintained school, or
(b)   taking part in extra-curricular activities which are provided or organised for registered pupils at the school by or on behalf of the school,

they are offered a balanced presentation of opposing views.

- *May a parent's philosophical convictions prevail over sections 406 and 407?*

10.   COMPLAINTS ABOUT THE CURRICULUM

In 1988 LEAs were required to set up a procedure for dealing with curriculum complaints, which should be approved by the Secretary of State. The current provisions are now in the Education Act 1996 as amended by the SSFA 1998.

Education Act 1996, s 409

(1) A local education authority shall, with the approval of the Secretary of State and after consultation with governing bodies of foundation and voluntary aided schools, make arrangements for the consideration and disposal of any complaint to which subsection (2) applies.

(2) This subsection applies to any complaint which is to the effect that the authority, or the governing body of [any community, foundation or voluntary school maintained by the authority or any community or foundation special school] so maintained which is not established in a hospital—
(a)   have acted or are proposing to act unreasonably in relation to the exercise of a power conferred on them by or under a relevant enactment, or
(b)   have acted or are proposing to act unreasonably in relation to the performance of, or have failed to discharge, a duty imposed on them by or under a relevant enactment.

(3) In subsection (2) 'relevant enactment' means—

(a)   any provision which by virtue of section 408(4) is a relevant provision of this Part for the purposes of section 408(1), and

(b)   any other enactment (whether contained in this Part or otherwise) so far as relating to the curriculum for, or religious worship in, maintained schools....

(4) The Secretary of State shall not entertain under section 496 (power to prevent unreasonable exercise of functions) or 497 (powers where a local education authority or governing body fail to discharge their duties) any complaint to which subsection (2) applies, unless a complaint concerning the same matter has been made and disposed of in accordance with arrangements made under subsection (1).

The essence of the complaint should be that the LEA or a school's governing body has acted unreasonably in exercising its statutory powers in relation to:
–   the basic curriculum
–   the National Curriculum
–   religious education
–   collective worship
–   SACREs
–   external qualifications or syllabuses
–   the provision of curriculum information.

The complaints procedure should be used before the Secretary of State will consider exercising his default powers (EA 1996, ss 496 and 497; see chapter 8). Most LEAs have designated the local SACRE as the body responsible for considering formal complaints against the religious education curriculum and collective worship provision in schools. Guidance is contained in DES Circular 1/89 (Education Reform Act 1988: Local Arrangements for the Consideration of Complaints), and DFE Circular 1/94 (Religious Education and Collective Worship).

DES Circular 1/89 (Education Reform Act 1988: Local Arrangements for the Consideration of Complaints)

4. The Secretary of State expects that any concerns expressed by parents and others about the school curriculum and related matters will continue to be considered and, so far as possible, dealt with in *informal* discussion with teachers and head teachers in the first instance. It is not the intention that all such expressions of concern should be considered as 'complaints' and dealt with under the approved arrangements. However, there will be cases where such concerns cannot be resolved informally, and will fall to be considered as *formal* complaints under the arrangements to be made under Section [409]. The purpose of such arrangements is to offer parents and others a readily accessible and clearly understood *local* route through which to pursue any complaint about the school curriculum and related matters.

5. The Secretary of State believes that it is right for such formal complaints also to be dealt with in the first instance by those with direct responsibility for the matters involved, so long as the procedures adopted secure that full and fair consideration is given to the views of the complainant and that there is opportunity for complaints to be considered beyond that, if necessary, by responsible persons who have not been directly involved in the issues complained about.

6. It is therefore intended that the local arrangements should ensure that a complaint is fully considered and can be pursued through the various relevant tiers of local responsibility. Normally, the first stage of the procedure for handling of complaints will be informal discussion with staff at the school.

...

10. ... Complaints about the education provided for pupils are to be considered as complaints about the exercise of the governing body's responsibilities in respect of the school curriculum....

19. As indicated in paragraph 4 above, there is no intention of inhibiting the number of complaints which can be disposed of informally. The proposed arrangements are intended to require a formal statement of local procedures for the consideration of complaints, rather than the creation of any new administrative or appeals machinery. The resources which authorities will need to allocate to the consideration of complaints will depend both on the number of complaints which fail to be disposed of informally and the nature of their formal arrangements.

This complaints procedure is potentially wide-ranging, but there is little evidence on the extent to which it is used. Perhaps, virtually all complaints are resolved informally, or perhaps this procedure is not widely known about or used.

DFE Circular 1/94 develops DES Circular 1/89 in the context of the religious curriculum.

DFE Circular 1/94 (Religious Education and Collective Worship)

Local Complaints Procedure

134. Concerns expressed by parents and others about the school curriculum and related matters, including RE and collective worship, will normally be considered and, so far as is possible, dealt with in informal discussion with teachers and head teachers in the first instance. There will, however, be cases where such concerns cannot be resolved informally, and will fall to be considered as formal complaints.

135. Under the 1988 Act each... .maintained school has a local complaints procedure for the consideration of any formal complaint. The purpose of the procedure is to offer parents and others a readily accessible and clearly understood local route through which to pursue any complaint about the school curriculum, including RE and collective worship, and related matters, such as the establishment of a SACRE or review of an agreed syllabus. Full details for LEAs are set out in Circular 1/89...

136. Each LEA must have a contact officer to advise on the arrangements which apply to...maintained schools. LEAs should publicise their arrangements widely and some LEAs have produced leaflets explaining how to make a complaint. In addition, a full copy of the local complaints procedure should be available in each school...and the school prospectus must include a reference to it.

137. The stages of the procedure are generally as follows:

Complaint About LEA-Maintained School's Duties	...	Complaint About LEA's Duties
LEA contact officer	...	LEA contact officer
Consideration by	...	governing body
Consideration by LEA	...	Consideration by LEA

138. The complaints procedure of an LEA should fully acknowledge the rights of the governing bodies of voluntary...schools in respect of their responsibility for RE and religious worship.

139. Concern has been expressed that the current arrangements for handling complaints may inhibit parents and others in resolving satisfactorily their concerns about this aspect of school provision. LEAs and grant-maintained schools should ensure that:
*   local arrangements are straightforward and not daunting to those who wish to make a complaint; and
*   decisions are reached as quickly as is consistent with the proper consideration of the complaint.

A complainant may make a complaint through a third party and be accompanied by that party when representations are made at each stage.

Bearing in mind that there is no other formal complaints procedure currently available to parents, it is surprising that this procedure appears to be rarely used. The following case highlights some of the defects in the procedure, in particular the length of time taken to deal with the mother's complaint.

R v Secretary of State for Education, ex p R and D [1994] ELR 495

Summary of facts

In December 1989 the mothers of two boys formally complained about the collective worship and religious education provided at their sons' county primary school. The complaints were considered first by the governing body of the primary school, which dismissed them in July 1990. In August 1990 the two mothers appealed to the LEA, which in November 1990 appointed a senior inspector (equal opportunities) to investigate and report on the complaints. This was completed in July 1991 and the complaints board of the LEA dismissed the appeal in September 1991. In October 1991 the two mothers made their complaints to the Secretary of State, who dismissed them in June 1992. The two mothers applied for leave to apply for judicial review of the Secretary of State's decision. The court hearing took place on 26 February 1993 more than three years after they made their formal complaint.

McCullough J held: Mr Knox makes a further challenge to the Secretary of State's conclusion on the second complaint. This is based on the fact that, whereas religious education alone was the subject of one lesson a week, there were five other lessons during which religious education was taught in conjunction with other subjects: variously, art, geography, history, maths, English, science and design/technology. This 'integrated' approach would mean, as the head teacher said in her statement, that it would be very difficult for a child to avoid seeing or hearing things which related to topics that had been covered in the religious education lesson from which he had been excused. Further, in response to the parents' requests for their children not to be exposed to 'non-Christian religions and traditions', Mr Hainsworth had said in a letter of 19 November 1987, that he did not see how any school which worked with an integrated curriculum would be able to satisfy the applicants' requests in a way that did not involve fundamental implications for their secular education.

In the light of this material, Mr Knox submits that the Secretary of State could not reasonably have said that the evidence suggested that should a request to be excused from religious education be received and arrangements made for withdrawal from it, pupils would still have the opportunity to participate fully in the secular curriculum.

Whatever be the merits of this challenge, it could avail the applicants nothing were it to succeed. Their children left the school in October/November 1987. They are by now too old to return. The Secretary of State could not give any direction under ss 68 or 99 of the 1944 Act which would be of any use to them. Whatever the opinions expressed in 1987, the Secretary of State has, as the law requires, recognised that if a child is excused religious worship and/or religious education, the duty to provide his secular education is unaffected. In any event, there is no evidence that the curriculum now in place would result in any interference with a pupil's secular education were he to be excused from attending religious education.

For these various reasons, the application for leave to move for judicial review is refused.

CHAPTER 7

The quality of educational provision

The quality of educational provision has increasingly dominated the political agenda since the late 1980s. This reflects twin concerns. A child should have the right to an education of a reasonable standard; and publicly funded education should provide value for money.

Until the introduction of the National Curriculum at the end of the 1980s there was considerable variation in the quality and content of the education provided in different schools. This was perceived as being inequitable because children were not being provided with equality of opportunity. This change in attitude was in part a consequence of the changes in public perception towards the provision of education and the role of the teachers. Parents came to regard themselves as consumers of educational services, who have 'consumer rights' (see chapter 1). Furthermore the teaching profession lost some of the respect accorded to 'school masters' and 'school mistresses', and parents were prepared to challenge their professional judgment.

At the same time as the introduction of the National Curriculum, LEAs lost their financial dominance over schools. Increasing financial delegation (see chapter 2) meant that the responsibility for educational provision rested primarily on the governing body.

These concerns led to the introduction of the national curriculum, target setting, inspections, and the publication of information including school reports and league tables, which have informed and empowered parents and pupils. They have also led to Education Action Zones (EAZs), City Technology Colleges (CTCs) and specialist schools in an attempt to raise standards.

These changes have affected further and higher education to a lesser extent. The quality and content of HE courses was determined mainly by the institutions, although that was influenced in part by the requirements of professional bodies. The Council for National Academic Awards (CNAA), which had validated polytechnic degrees, was abolished once polytechnics were entitled to award their own degrees. However, students began to be perceived as 'consumers' of educational services.

In the context of further and higher education, further education institutions and polytechnics became independent institutions with their own budgets and were no longer under any local authority control. However, central government was anxious to ensure that educational institutions were accountable for the public investment they received, and monitoring of performance, inspections and audits became the norm for all institutions, including the 'old' universities.

Nevertheless, education 'consumers' in practice have limited means of redress where the availability or quality of the educational services provided are deficient (see chapter 8). For example, where there is a shortage of school places parents have few effective rights against the LEA (see chapter 3).

Where the quality of special educational needs provision is poor, pupils may be able to bring an action in negligence (see chapter 5), but the evidential and legal difficulties are considerable. In principle schools, as well as FE and HE institutions, owe a duty of care to all pupils and students in relation to the quality of education provided, and a claim for damages is possible. FE and HE institutions may also be liable to a student for breach of an express or implied term of the contract relating to the quality of education. However, such claims are in their infancy.

1.   MAINTAINED SCHOOLS

The Labour government placed great emphasis on raising standards in schools. In the past intervention occurred only after the school or the LEA has been identified as failing. Now the aim is to identify problems at an earlier stage where, for example, schools do not meet their targets (see below). The Secretary of State can set up EAZs (see chapter 2) where educational provision is poor in a particular area, and LEAs can intervene in schools which are causing concern (see below). In addition LEAs are also inspected.

The Labour government, which was elected in May 1997, built upon the foundations laid by the previous Conservative governments between 1979 and 1997. Within two months of being elected the Labour government published an education White Paper which identified the quality of educational provision in schools as being a key problem.

White Paper *Excellence in Schools* (Cm 3681, July 1997)

9 The problem with our education system is easily stated. Excellence at the top is not matched by high standards for the majority of children. We have some first-class schools and our best students compare with the best in the world. But by comparison with other industrialised countries, achievement by the average student is just not good enough.
...

Raising standards: our top priority

I All the evidence indicates that standards rise fastest where schools themselves take responsibility for their own improvement. But schools need the right balance of pressure and support from central and local government. Because the education service has been poorly co-ordinated in recent years, we have not achieved that balance. The support from central and local agencies has been patchy and inconsistent. Schools have had plenty of pressure, but not always of a kind which raised standards. There has been an excessive concentration on the structure and organisation of schools at the expense of improving teaching, learning and leadership.

2 We need to improve the combination of pressure and support which central and local government apply to schools to stimulate constant improvement and tackle underperformance. There is already regular high quality external inspection by OFSTED of schools. To complement this, schools must have annual plans for improving their performance which are focused on better teaching and learning, and are based on the results they are already achieving. The way they set plans should follow best practice and be approved by the LEA. LEAs' work in raising standards will itself be improved through pressure and support from the DfEE, spearheaded by the new Standards and Effectiveness Unit. OFSTED inspection of LEAs will complement this.

Measuring performance to raise standards

3 One of the most powerful underlying reasons for low performance in our schools has been low expectations which have allowed poor quality teaching to continue unchallenged. Too many teachers, parents and pupils have come to accept a ceiling on achievement which is far below what is possible.

4 Schools often fail to stretch the most able; and they have not been good at identifying and pushing the modest or poor performers, or those with special educational needs. In some cases the excuse has been that 'you cannot expect high achievement from children in a run-down area like this'. Even more often, schools in comfortable circumstances have complacently accepted average performance when they should be aiming for excellence. ...

Excellence for everyone

1 If we are to prepare successfully for the 21st century, we shall have to do more than just improve literacy and numeracy skills. In the past, there was a wide range of low-skill jobs; this is no longer the case. Equally, high-skilled work in some areas was obtained through apprenticeships that allowed individuals to mature and develop skills whilst at work, once their formal schooling had finished. Again, this has substantially disappeared and has therefore cut off a key route to those who gained from it and whose wider educational achievement was thereby enhanced. The demands of the future will require that everyone succeeds in secondary education. We are not going back to the days of the 11-plus; but neither are we prepared to stand still and defend the failings of across-the-board mixed ability teaching. That debate is sterile and provides no solutions. We intend to modernise comprehensive education to create inclusive schooling which provides a broad, flexible and motivating education that recognises the different talents of all children and delivers excellence for everyone.

In February 2001 the Labour government published a Green Paper before the June general election and a White Paper followed in Sepember 2001 (*Schools Achieving Success*, Cm 5230). The White Paper set out the government's view of its achievements since 1997, and its proposals for the future, which focus on the 'transformation' of secondary education.

White Paper *Schools Achieving Success* (Cm 5230, September 2001)

2.22 The evidence shows that secondary schools are moving forwards. There has been a steady improvement in the achievement of 16-year-olds. Between 1996 and 2000 the percentage of pupils achieving 5 or more good GCSEs (or equivalent) increased by almost 5 percentage points to 49.2 per cent in 2000. There are now far fewer unsatisfactory lessons. In 1995/96 OFSTED deemed 16 per cent of lessons in secondary schools to be unsatisfactory or poor. By 2000 this had been reduced to 6 per cent.

2.23 As with primary schools, LEAs, heads, teachers and governors are better at dealing with schools that run into difficulty—the number of secondary schools in special measures has fallen from 90 at the end of the 1997/98 academic year to 65 at the end of 2000/01. Turning a school round is one of the greatest challenges facing those who work in schools and many have risen to it magnificently—100 schools have been turned round. But we still need to do more to make sure that they sustain their improvement and to identify and support schools in danger of slipping into special measures.

...

2.33 The next phase of reform must focus on the transformation of secondary education. There is much to be done to build on the stronger foundations now provided at primary level, to reduce the wide disparities in performance and make sure that every secondary school offers its pupils the challenge, support and inspiration they deserve. We cannot accept, and we know that teachers do not accept, that less should be expected of some pupils or that some are destined to fail. The challenge of radical modernisation of our comprehensive schools is the challenge of meeting the needs of each and every child.

2.34 The selective system failed to meet the needs of all children and the talents of many were not recognised. Comprehensive schools overcame the ill effects of rigid selection and have done a great deal to improve opportunity. But within comprehensive schools, too often the needs of individual pupils go unmet.

2.35 All schools must deliver high minimum standards and constantly push up the ceiling on aspiration, ambition and achievement. In transforming standards for 11 to 14-year-olds we want to establish a springboard for meeting individual talents and aspirations at 14 to 19 in a way that has never been achieved before. We want greater choice between worthwhile options at 14, a significant increase in young people's participation in worthwhile learning and training beyond 16 and increased participation in higher education.

The Education Bill 2001/02 gives legislative effect to the proposals in the White Paper. In particular, the Bill provides for additional powers of intervention in schools and LEAs causing concern, as well as changes to the school curriculum.

The role of the governing body

Governing bodies are responsible for the management and conduct of a school (see chapter 2), and in particular for the standard of educational provision.

School Standards and Framework Act 1998, s 38

...

(2) The governing body shall conduct the school with a view to promoting high standards of educational achievement at the school.

The standard of educational provision in schools is regulated by statute in three ways:
- target-setting
- performance monitoring
- inspection.

Target-setting

Governing bodies are required to set annual school performance and school attendance targets.

School performance targets

In May 1997 the government announced national targets in literacy and numeracy. This was followed by the White Paper, *Excellence in Schools* (Cm 3681, July 1997) which sets out the rationale for school targets as well as the role played by the LEA and OFSTED.

White Paper *Excellence in Schools* (Cm 3681, July 1997)

Setting school targets

12 From September 1998, each school will be required to have challenging targets for improvement. If schools are to take their targets seriously, it is important that they should take direct responsibility for them. Governing bodies as part of their startegic role set out in Chapter 7 should take time to consider all the available information and discuss in detail their school's targets, together with proposals from the headteacher on the necessary improvement plans to achieve them.

13 School targets should be based on:
- benchmark information on the performance of similar schools, at national and local level;
- information on the rate of progress needed to achieve national targets; and
- the most recent inspection evidence.

The Secretary of State has the power to make regulations which would require governing bodies of maintained schools to sccurc that annual targets are set in respect of the performance of pupils. In the case of pupils of compulsory school age the targets would be public examination or National Curriculum assessments. For other pupils the targets would be public examinations or attaining other external qualifications.

Education Act 1997, s 19

(1) The Secretary of State may by regulations make such provision as the Secretary of State considers appropriate for requiring the governing bodies of maintained schools to secure that annual targets are set in respect of the performance of pupils—

(a)   in public examinations or in assessments for the purposes of the National Curriculum, in the case of pupils of compulsory school age; or

(b)   in public examinations or in connection with the attainment of other external qualifications, in the case of pupils of any age over that age.

(2) Regulations under this section may require—

(a)   such targets, and

(b)   the past performance of pupils in the particular examinations or assessments, or in connection with the attainment of the particular qualifications, to which such targets relate,

to be published in such manner as is specified in the regulations…

The Education (School Performance Targets) (England) Regulations 1998, SI 1998/1532 came into force on 1 September 1998. They are supplemented by DfEE Circular 11/98 Target-Setting in Schools).

The regulations originally required targets to be set for pupils completing Key Stage 2 (reg 3), that is at the end of the last year of primary school, and for pupils completing Key Stage 4, that is at the end of the last year of compulsory education when GCSEs are taken (reg 4).

In 2001 target-setting was introduced for pupils completing Key Stage 3 (reg 3A), that is at the end of the third year of secondary school (Year 9); and for pupils with special educational needs who would not otherwise be set a target (reg 4A). The statutory requirements are detailed and precise as can be seen from the following extract from the 1998 Regulations (as amended).

Education (School Performance Targets) (England) Regulations 1998, SI 1998/1532, as amended by SI 2001/827

Targets for pupils aged 15

4 (1) This regulation applies to every school where education is provided which is suitable to the requirements of pupils who have attained the age of 15.

(2) The governing body of a school to which this regulation applies shall, by no later than 31st December in every school year, set the targets specified in paragraph (3) in connection with the performance of the relevant group of pupils aged 15 in GCSE examinations or vocational qualifications.

(3) The targets referred to in paragraph (2) are—

(a) the percentage of the relevant group of pupils aged 15 to achieve, by the end of the following school year, grades A* to C in five or more subjects in GCSE examinations;

(b) the percentage of the relevant group of pupils aged 15 to achieve, by the end of the following school year, grades A* to G in one or more subjects in GCSE examinations; and

(c) the average point score for the school to be achieved by the relevant group of pupils aged 15 by the end of the following school year in GCSE and vocational qualifications.

(4) In paragraph (3)(a) and (b), references to pupils achieving particular grades in GCSE examinations shall be construed for the purposes of those provisions so as to include references to pupils achieving corresponding awards in an equivalent number of vocational qualifications.

(5) Schedule 1 shall have effect for determining for the purposes only of this regulation and regulation 6—

(a) questions as to—

   (i)   which vocational qualification award corresponds to which GCSE examination grade, and

   (ii) the equivalency between GCSE examination results and vocational qualifications; and

(b) the calculation of the average point score for the school in relation to pupils' achievements in GCSE examinations and vocational qualifications.

(6) In this regulation, 'the relevant group of pupils aged 15', in relation to—

(a) a school, and

(b) any school year during which the governing body have a duty to set the targets specified in paragraph (3),

means all persons who, in the following school year, the governing body anticipate—

   (i)   will be registered pupils at the school on the third Thursday in January, and

   (ii) will have attained the age of 15 during the period of twelve months ending on the 31st August immediately preceding that day.

Targets for groups of pupils with special educational needs

4A (1) This regulation applies where a target set by the governing body for a group of pupils under regulation 3, 3A or 4 is zero.

(2) Where this regulation applies and subject to paragraph (3), the governing body shall, within the time limits in those regulations, set additional appropriate targets for the performance of that group of pupils in appropriate public examinations or in appropriate assessments for the purposes of the National Curriculum.

(3) The governing body of a school to which regulation 3A applies shall not be required to set targets under this regulation in the 2000–01 school year.

Schools may choose to set other performance targets, for example in relation to pupils with high ability, but they are not legally required to do so (DfEE Circular 11/98, paras 15 and 16).

The normal procedure in the case of a primary (or middle) school, for example, is as follows. In the autumn term the governing body sets targets for pupils who are in Year

5, who will take the Key Stage 2 assessment in the summer term eighteen months later, at the end of Year 6. Governing bodies are required to estimate the percentage of pupils they expect to achieve level 4 or above in the National Curriculum tests in English and mathematics. This is the same measure as that used for the national literacy and numeracy targets set for 2002.

The governing body should, in addition to setting targets, review the targets set the previous year and assess what more should be done to ensure that those targets are met. A performance target may not be changed once it has been set.

The governing body should take into account the targets contained in the LEA's Education Development Plan together with the national comparative performance information published each year. Local Education Authorities should advise and support the governing bodies as well as agreeing to the performance targets set by them. The LEA can ask a governing body to revise its targets if it considers that they are unrealistically high or if they are not sufficiently challenging.

School attendance targets

Although the 1997 White Paper (Cm 3681) stated that the government wished to improve school attendance there was no statutory requirement on governing bodies to set attendance targets until 1999. In 1998 Parliament conferred on the Secretary of State the power to make regulations requiring governing bodies to set attendance targets for their schools with the aim of reducing truancy as well as unauthorised absences condoned by parents.

School Standards and Framework Act 1998, s 63

(1) Regulations may make provision for and in connection with—
(a)   requiring, or
(b)   enabling the Secretary of State to require,

governing bodies of maintained schools to secure that annual targets are set for reducing the level of unauthorised absences on the part of relevant day pupils at their schools.

(2) Regulations under this section may, in particular, make provision—
(a)   for the Secretary of State to impose such a requirement on the governing body of a maintained school where—
   (i)   the specified condition is for the time being satisfied in relation to the school, and
   (ii)   he considers it appropriate to impose the requirement;
(b)   for such a requirement to be imposed by the Secretary of State in such manner, and for such period, as may be specified in or determined in accordance with the regulations;
(c)   for the Secretary of State, where he considers it appropriate to do so, to exempt the governing body of a maintained school, in relation to any school year, from a requirement imposed by virtue of subsection (1)(a) or (b).

(3) For the purposes of subsection (2)(a)(i) the specified condition is for the time being satisfied in relation to a maintained school if in the previous school year the level of unauthorised absences on the part of relevant day pupils at the school (as determined in accordance with the regulations) exceeded such level as may for that year be specified in or determined in accordance with the regulations...

The requirement may only be imposed if certain conditions are satisfied, and the Secretary of School has the power to exempt a school. The conditions which must be satisfied are spelt out in the regulations. Once an attendance target has been set it may not be altered without the approval of the Secretary of State.

Education (School Attendance Targets) (England) Regulations 1999, SI 1999/397

Duty to set school attendance targets

3 (1) Where the Secretary of State gives notice to the governing body of a school under regulation 4, that body shall secure that a target is set for the school in accordance with the following provisions of this regulation in respect of each of the three school years immediately following the notice year.

(2) The target to be set in respect of each school year concerned is the level (expressed as a percentage) to which the unauthorised absence rate on the part of relevant day pupils at the school is to be reduced in that year.

(3) The governing body shall secure that the targets referred to in paragraph (1) are set by no later than three months after the date on which notice is given under regulation 4.

(4) Immediately after they have set targets pursuant to this regulation, the governing body shall give notice in writing to the Secretary of State setting out details of those targets and the school year to which each of them relates...

Notice by the Secretary of State

4 (1) The notice referred to in regulation 3(1) is a notice in writing given by the Secretary of State to the governing body of a school—
(a)   informing them of the matters referred to in paragraph (2)(a) and (b) below, and
(b)   requiring them to set an attendance target for the school in respect of each of the three school years immediately following the end of the notice year.

(2) The Secretary of State may give such a notice to the governing body of a school only where—
(a)   it appears to him that regulation 5 applies to that school in respect of each of the two school years immediately preceding the notice year; and
(b)   he considers that it is appropriate to require the governing body to set an attendance target for each of the three school years immediately following the notice year.

(3) The Secretary of State may give notice under this Regulation in any school year beginning with the 1998–99 school year; but he may not do so later than four months preceding the beginning of the first school year in respect of which an attendance target is to be set.

Condition precedent

5 (1) This regulation applies to a school in respect of any school year where the school's unauthorised absence rate for that year exceeds the national average for that year by at least 3 percentage points.

(2) For the purposes of this regulation 'the national average', in relation to a school year, means—
   (a) in relation to a primary school, other than a special school, the aggregated unauthorised absence rate in that year for every such school in England divided by the total number of such schools in England;
   (b) in relation to a secondary school, other than a special school, the aggregated unauthorised absence rate in that year for every such school in England divided by the total number of such schools in England; and
   (c) in relation to a special school, the aggregated unauthorised absence rate in that year for every maintained special school in England divided by the total number of maintained special schools in England.

The Code of Practice on LEA-School Relations (England), 2001 provides guidance in Annex 1.

- *When may the Secretary of State require a governing body to set attendance targets? How long does the requirement last?*

Performance monitoring

A major innovation during the last fifteen years from a parent's perspective has been the increase in the amount of written information available about school performance and about their child's progress. Although league tables are criticised as providing crude information which does not reflect social and economic factors that affect the performance of pupils and the school, some information is better than no information, which was often the position before the introduction of these requirements.

Governors are also required to publish annual reports (SSFA 1998, s 42), and to provide pupil reports to parents, as well as ensuring that the school maintains pupil records.

School performance

The Education Act 1996 (ss 537–541) places a statutory obligation on various bodies to provide information to the Secretary of State or to other institutions. Parents have no right to information under these provisions, but the aim of s 537 (as amended by SSFA 1998, s 140, Sch 30, para 152) in part is to assist parents in 'choosing' a school for their child. Note that parents have no right to 'choose' a school for their child, merely a right to 'express a preference' (see chapter 3).

The Secretary of State has the power to require schools, including independent schools, but not nursery schools, to provide him or her with the information specified in regulations. The Secretary of State may publish the information, but individual pupils should not be identifiable.

Education Act 1996, s 537

(1) The Secretary of State may by regulations make provision requiring—
(a)   the governing body of every school which is—
    (i)   maintained by a local education authority, or
    (ii) a special school which is not maintained by such an authority, and
(b)   the proprietor of every independent school,

to provide such information about the school as may be prescribed.

(2) For the purposes of this section information about the continuing education of pupils leaving a school, or the employment or training taken up by such pupils on leaving, is to be treated as information about the school.

(3) Where the Secretary of State exercises his power to make regulations under this section he shall do so with a view to making available information which is likely to—
(a)   assist parents in choosing schools for their children;
(b)   increase public awareness of the quality of the education provided by the schools concerned and of the educational standards achieved in those schools; or
(c)   assist in assessing the degree of efficiency with which the financial resources of those schools are managed...

(5) No information provided in accordance with regulations under this section shall name any pupil to whom it relates.

In *R v Secretary of State for Education and Employment, ex p Governing Body of West Horndon County Primary School and the National Association of Head Teachers* [1997] ELR 350 the court was asked to consider the legality of a decision made by the Secretary of State under the Education (Schools) Act 1992, s 16, which was the predecessor to s 537. The case illustrates some of the debates surrounding the publication of school league tables.

R v Secretary of State for Education and Employment, ex p the Governing Body of West Horndon County Primary School and the National Association of Head Teachers [1997] ELR 350

Harrison J: This is an application by the Governing Body of West Hornden County Primary School and by the National Association of Head Teachers seeking leave to apply for judicial review of a decision of the Secretary of State for Education and Employment which was made in October 1996 to publish in March 1997 the first primary school performance tables for maintained schools in a form laid down in circular 15/96.

The applicants' case, put shortly, is that the manner in which the information in the tables is to be presented is *Wednesbury* unreasonable or perverse, and that it would frustrate rather than fulfil the intentions of Parliament. The complaint concerning the tables is made in two respects: first, the treatment of what was described initially as a special unit, but which was subsequently described as a special class for children with special educational needs; and, secondly, the treatment of children who, due to absence or disapplication, did not take part in the tests. Children who are disapplied are those to whom the national curriculum does not apply by virtue of certain sections of the Education Reform Act 1988.

...

The position is that the Secretary of State proposes to exclude special schools, for administrative simplicity, on this first occasion of the publication of performance tables; but she proposes to consider that afresh thereafter. However, there will be included in the tables the special classes or special units. The applicants are concerned that the inclusion of pupils in special classes, whose results are likely to be lower than those in the mainstream, will give an unfair and misleading impression of the school's performance, particularly where, as in the case of West Horndon County Primary School, the classes are small and, more particularly, where children with special educational needs form a significant proportion of the total number of pupils within the year group. In the particular case of the first applicant, I was informed that there are some 23 statemented pupils within the school, which is approximately 19 per cent of the total of the school, whereas the national average would be 2 per cent. One can therefore understand the concerns that have been expressed. The Secretary of State does, however, propose to include the total number of pupils with special educational needs at a school in the published tables in the contextual data. Nevertheless, as I have said, one can understand the concern of the applicants relating to that aspect of the matter.

The second area of concern relates to absent or disapplied pupils. The concern here is that the figures in the published tables will not give the numbers of those who took the test because the test results will be related to the total of eligible pupils, which would in itself include those who were absent or disapplied. Thus, says Miss Booth, the effect would be to treat those pupils who are absent or disapplied as failures. That again is a matter of concern, because on the face of it the inclusion of those who are absent or disapplied will make the results sound poorer than they in fact are. In the case of the first applicant, out of the relevant class of 17 pupils, four were absent for varying reasons and did not take the test.

...

It is important to bear in mind at the outset, in considering those submissions, that the principle of the publication of performance tables, although a matter of controversy in some quarters, is not a principle at issue in these proceedings. The only issue in these proceedings relates to those two areas of criticism of the presentation of the information in the tables. My starting-point, therefore, must be s 16 of the 1992 Act, the relevant provisions of which I have already read.

It is clear that s 16 gives the Secretary of State a wide discretion as to the form and manner in which the information in the performance tables is to be published. This court could only interfere with the exercise of that discretion if it could be shown by the applicants that the Secretary of State has acted unreasonably in the legal sense—that is to say, that no reasonable Secretary of State could have decided that the tables should be presented in the manner set out in Circular 15/96—or otherwise has acted perversely. That is a high threshold for the applicants to satisfy. Of course, as this is a leave application, they only have to show that that threshold has arguably been satisfied.

In my judgment, the applicants have not shown that the Secretary of State has arguably acted unreasonably or perversely. Given the principle of the publication of the performance tables, there is inevitably considerable scope for argument as to what should or should not be included in the tables and how it should be presented. That is a matter for the Secretary of State, subject to the unreasonable/perversity criteria. I can well understand that there may be aspects of the tables which are considered by some to be unsatisfactory. Two such matters have been raised by the applicants in this case. I have no doubt at all that their objections are genuinely held, and I fully understand why they feel as they do. However, this is a far cry from being an arguable case on unreasonable/perversity grounds.

I bear in mind first of all that the Secretary of State took into account the objections raised by the applicants on the consultation exercise and, indeed, amended her proposals as a result of those objections. She has to form an overall judgment, having regard to a very wide number of considerations. It has been pointed out that the published tables are only one of the sources of information that are available. I have already mentioned the publication by the first applicants of details relating to their school which excludes the matters which they complain are now to be included in the published tables. So far as the inclusion of the absent or disapplied pupils is concerned, the inclusion of the percentage of them as well as the percentage of eligible pupils achieving level 4 and above will provide a clear indication of the proportion of the class that were absent or disapplied in relation to each of the three core subjects separately, as well as providing the same percentage information relating to the teacher assessments in those subjects. Although it is right to say that the number of pupils taking the tests is not actually given, the level of information which will thereby be provided, although not as complete as many would require and with the shortcomings that have been mentioned, cannot, in my judgment, reasonably be argued to be perverse or outwith the purposes of the legislation.

...

As Mr Elvin correctly submitted, if special classes were excluded from the tables, it would result in a situation in which some pupils with special educational needs would not be included in the tables—namely those in special classes—and other pupils with special educational needs would be included within the tables because they are within the mainstream classes.

It is clear from the documents to which I have been referred that the Secretary of State would wish, as a matter of policy, to seek to achieve uniformity, whereas the applicants' proposal on this aspect would lead, in the words of Mr Elvin, to discrimination between pupils with special educational needs within a school. It is right to say that the Secretary of State is proposing to exclude special schools, which in itself would appear to run contrary to the uniformity approach; but that is, as I have mentioned, for reasons of administrative simplicity and it will not necessarily continue in the future.

Having regard to the matters to which I have referred, it is clear to me that the Secretary of State was faced with a difficult decision. She took into account the point that had been raised by the applicants and decided to deal with it in the way which I have described, namely by including the total number of pupils with special educational needs in the school in the performance tables. That in itself may be argued, as it is argued by the applicants, as being not a perfect answer to the problem. I sympathise again with the point that is raised by the applicants on that aspect. But it is a matter for the Secretary of State, and she has applied her mind to it and has reached a decision which, in my view, cannot be reasonably argued to be perverse or outwith the intentions of the statute.

Detailed provisions are contained in Education (School Performance Information) (England) Regulations 1999, SI 1999/1178 as amended by SI 1999/2158 and SI 1999/2387.

The governing body of a maintained school is required to provide the Secretary of State with specific information concerning the performance of the school in the National Curriculum assessments at the end of Key Stages 1, 2 and 3 as well as in public examinations taken by pupils aged 15 to 18 years. The governing body must also provide the National Data Collection Agency and the external marking agency with information relating to second and third key stage assessments. The head teacher of every maintained school is required to provide the governing body with this information. The period for which the information is requested is normally referred to as the 'reporting school year'. This means the school year immediately preceding the school year in which information provided to the Secretary of State is to be published by him.

Advice is contained in various circulars, for example, DfEE Circular 7/97: Publication of Information about Secondary Schools in Performance Tables in 1997; Circular 14/97; Publication of 1996 Key Stage 2 National Curriculum Assessment Results in Primary School Performance Tables; Circular 7/98; School Prospectuses in Primary Schools—1998/99 onwards; Circular 8/98, School Prospectuses in Secondary Schools).

Individual pupils' performance

In relation to school performance targets the Secretary of State is given the power to make regulations requiring governing bodies and independent schools to provide to the Secretary of State individual performance information relating to past and present pupils. The sections provides that the information may be given to prescribed persons including 'information collators'.

Education Act 1996, s 537A

(1) Regulations may make provision requiring—
(a)   the governing body of every school which is—
    (i)   maintained by a local education authority, or
    (ii)   a special school which is not maintained by such an authority, and
(b)   the proprietor of every independent school,

to provide to the relevant person such individual pupil information as may be prescribed.

(2) In subsection (1) 'the relevant person' means one or more of the following—
(a)   the Secretary of State, and
(b)   any prescribed person...

(7) No information received under or by virtue of this section shall be published in any form which includes the name of the pupil or pupils to whom it relates....

(9) In this section—
'individual pupil information' means information relating to and identifying individual pupils or former pupils at any school within subsection (1), whether obtained under subsection (1) or otherwise;
'information collator' means any body which, for the purposes of or in connection with the functions of the Secretary of State relating to education, is responsible for collating or checking information relating to pupils.

•   *Can individual performance information be published in any form which includes the name of the pupil to whom it relates?*

Regulations made under this section include:

- Education (Individual Pupil Information) (Prescribed Persons) Regulations 1999, SI 1999/903
- Education (Information About Individual Pupils) (England) Regulations 2000, SI 2000/3370.

The following extract from the regulations illustrates the type of information collected.

Education (Information About Individual Pupils) (England) Regulations 2000, SI 2000/3370

Provision of information by schools maintained by local education authorities to their local education authorities

4.   Within fourteen days of receiving a request from the local education authority by which a school is maintained, the governing body of that school shall provide to the authority such of the information referred to in the Schedule to these Regulations as is so requested.

SCHEDULE
PROVISION OF INFORMATION ABOUT INDIVIDUAL PUPILS

Regulation 4

PART I
ALL PUPILS

1 In respect of each pupil on the school's Register on the date specified in the request for information the following information.

2 (1) The pupil's—
(a)   gender;
(b)   date of birth;
(c)   current unique pupil number, and, where the school has held a previous unique pupil number for that pupil, the previous number;
(d)   surname, and where the pupil has a former surname which is known to the governing body, that former surname;
(e)   first name, or if more than one, each first name;
(f)   ethnic group;
(g)   date of admission to the school; and
(h)   first language.

(2) The postcode of the home where the pupil normally resides.

3 Whether the pupil is a day or boarding pupil at the school.

4 Whether, pursuant to section 512(3) and (3A) [Subsection (3A) was inserted by the School Standards and Framework Act 1998, …s 115(4) with effect from 6 December 1999] of the 1996 Act, the pupil has applied and been found to be eligible for free school meals.

5 Where the pupil has special educational needs, which stage of the five stage scale

referred to in 'The Code of Practice on the Identification and Assessment of Special Educational Needs' *[ISBN 085522 444 4. The Code of Practice, originally issued under the Education Act 1993 (c 35), continues to have effect by virtue of the 1996 Act, Sch 39, para 1]* issued, and from time to time revised, under section 313 of the 1996 Act applies to him.

6 In the case of a school which provides primary education—
(a)   whether the pupil is receiving nursery education in a nursery class at the school; and
(b)   where the pupil is under compulsory school age, whether he is part-time, and, for the purposes of this paragraph, 'part-time' means that the pupil is attending fewer than ten school sessions in any week during which the school meets.

7 In the case of a school which provides secondary education and where the pupil is aged 16 or over on 31st August preceding the date on which the request for information is made—
(a)   the number, if any, of GCSE subjects the pupil is studying;
(b)   the number, if any, of GCE 'A' level examination subjects (excluding the subject entitled 'general studies') the pupil is studying;
(c)   the number, if any, of GCE 'AS' examination subjects the pupil is studying;
(d)   whether the pupil is studying a post advanced level course;
(e)   the level of any GNVQ for which the pupil is studying;
(f)   the level of any GNVQ precursor for which the pupil is studying;
(g)   the level of any NVQ for which the pupil is studying; and
(h)   whether the pupil is studying a course other than any of the kind referred to above.

8 In the case of a special school that is not a special school established in a hospital whether the pupil boards at the school for seven or less nights per week.

9 In the case of a special school, including a special school established in a hospital—
(a)   whether the pupil is a registered pupil at one school or more than one school; and
(b)   where the pupil is registered as a pupil at more than one school, the school that the pupil attends for the majority of his time.

• *Why do you think this information is being collated? Are there any human rights implications?*

Pupil records and reports

Maintained schools, other than nursery schools, are required to provide parents with a written report at least once a year. Regulations set out what must be contained in the report.

The regulations also require that a school should keep a 'curricular record' as well as an 'educational record' for each pupil. Parents have the right to see their child's school records, which may be important when a child is trying to change schools or where a parent wishes to appeal against a decision to permanently exclude their child.

Pupils have the right to access personal information under the Data Protection Act 1998 (see eg Sch 11).

Schools are required to transfer the records when a child changes school, and provide a school leaver's report to pupils who leave the school at the end of their compulsory schooling.

Education (Pupil Information) (England) Regulations 2000, SI 2000/297

Interpretation

2 (1)   ...
'curricular record' means a formal record of a pupil's academic achievements, his other skills and abilities and his progress in school; ...

Meaning of educational record

3 (1) In these Regulations 'educational record' means any record of information which—
(a)   is processed by or on behalf of the governing body of, or a teacher at, any school specified in paragraph (2);
(b)   relates to any person who is or has been a pupil at the school; and
(c)   originated from or was supplied by or on behalf of any of the persons specified in paragraph (3),

other than information which is processed by a teacher solely for the teacher's own use.

(2) The schools referred to in paragraph (1)(a) are—
(a)   a school maintained by a local education authority; and
(b)   a special school which is not so maintained.

(3) The persons referred to in paragraph (1)(c) are—
(a)   an employee of the local education authority which maintains the school;
(b)   in the case of—
      (i)   a voluntary aided, foundation or foundation special school; or
      (ii)   a special school which is not maintained by a local education authority,
      a teacher or other employee at the school (including an educational psychologist engaged by the governing body under a contract for services);
(c)   the pupil to whom the record relates; and
(d)   a parent of that pupil.

Duties of head teacher—curricular records

4 The head teacher of every school maintained by a local education authority, except a nursery school, and of every special school not so maintained, shall keep a curricular record, updated at least once a year, in respect of every registered pupil at the school.

Duties of head teacher—educational records

5 (1) Upon receiving a written request by a parent for disclosure of a pupil's educational record, the head teacher of a school maintained by a local education authority, except a nursery school, and of a special school not so maintained, shall, within fifteen school days, make it available for inspection, free of charge, to the parent.

(2) Upon receiving a written request by a parent for a copy of a pupil's educational record, the head teacher shall, within fifteen school days, give the parent a copy of it on payment of such fee (not exceeding the cost of supply), if any, as the governing body may prescribe.

(3) In every case where the pupil is under consideration for admission to another school (including an independent school) or to an institution of further or higher education, the head teacher shall transfer the pupil's curricular record to the responsible person, free of charge, if that person so requests, within fifteen school days of receiving the request. The record supplied shall not include the results of any assessment of the pupil's achievements.

(4) When complying with a request for disclosure or a copy of a pupil's educational record under this regulation, a head teacher shall not disclose any documents which are subject to any order under section 30(2) of the Data Protection Act 1998.

Head teacher's report to parents and adult pupils

6 (1) The head teacher of every maintained school shall each school year make available in writing to the persons specified in paragraph (2) a report containing the information specified in paragraphs (4) to (6).

(2) The persons are—
(a)   in the case of pupils registered at the school aged 18 or over at the time a report is sent and who are not proposing to leave school by the end of the school year to which the report relates, each such pupil and, if the head teacher considers there to be special circumstances which make it appropriate, the parent of each such pupil,
(b)   subject to paragraph (3), in the case of all other pupils registered at the school, the parent of each such pupil;

(3) Paragraph 2(b) does not apply to any pupil registered at the school who has ceased to be of compulsory school age and who is proposing to leave school or who has left the school (and in respect of whom the information in regulation 9 is to be made available to the pupil concerned).

(4) The report shall contain the information about the educational achievements of the pupil to whom or to whose parent the report is sent and the other information relating to him specified—
(a)   as respects pupils in the final year of the first, second, third or fourth key stage, in Part 1 of Schedule 1;
(b)   as respects pupils in any other year of a key stage, in Part 2 of Schedule 1;
(c)   as respects pupils who have been entered for GCE 'A' level or GCE 'AS' examinations or IB or who have obtained a vocational qualification, in Part 3 of Schedule 1; and
(d)   as respects all other pupils, in Part 4 of Schedule 1.

(5) In the case of pupils registered at the school in the final year of the first, second or third key stage there shall be included in the report the information relating to the educational achievements of all other pupils in that key stage registered at the school whose achievements were assessed at the same time as the pupil's achievements, and the other information relating to such pupils, specified in Schedule 2.

(6) In the case of pupils registered at the school in the final year of the first, second or third key stage there shall be included in the report the information specified in paragraph 1, 2 or 3, as the case may be, of Schedule 3 relating to the educational achievements of all pupils at schools in England who were in the final year of that key stage in the preceding school year and whose achievements were assessed in that preceding school year...

- *What is the difference between a 'curricular record' and an 'educational record'?*

- *Does a parent have the right to see their child's curricular record and educational record?*

- *Does a parent have to pay for a copy of their child's (a) educational record and (b) school report?*

Guidance on the regulations is provided in, for example:
- DfEE Circular 1/97 (Reports on Pupils' Achievements in Primary Schools in 1996/97)
- DfEE Circular 17/99 (Reports on Pupils achievements at Key Stage 4 and beyond)
- DfEE Guidance 15/2000 (Pupil Records and Reports).

School inspections

Although there have been school inspectors for more than a century, OFSTED (Office for Standards in Education) has a much higher profile than its predecessor Her Majesty's Inspectorate. This is in part due to its increased powers, and the remit to inspect all schools within a specified period.

OFSTED is a non-ministerial government department headed by the Chief Inspector of Schools for England. There is also a Chief Inspector of Schools for Wales. OFSTED was established by the Education (Schools) Act 1992, as amended by Part V of the Education Act 1993. The current legislation is to be found in the School Inspections Act (SIA) 1996, as amended, together with regulations (Education (School Inspection) Regulations 1997, SI 1997/1966, as amended).

Governing bodies of voluntary and foundation schools with a religious character are responsible for arranging the inspection of denominational education and collective worship (ss 10(8), 23 of the SIA 1996).

In addition, LEAs have the power to carry out, at full cost, a school inspection service for schools in their area (s 24 of the SIA 1996), as well as the power to inspect maintained schools for specific purposes (s 25 of the SIA 1996).

School inspection is a central plank in the government's strategy of improving school standards, with OFSTED having a key role.

OFSTED's role

White Paper *Excellence in Schools* (Cm 3681, July 1997)

OFSTED's role

31 Both external inspection of schools and LEAs by OFSTED, and schools' own improvement planning, are essential and indeed complementary parts of the improvement process.

32 We are firmly committed to regular inspection of all schools by OFSTED. It contributes to public accountability and to the improvement of the education service through the comparative data which is then made available. The first cycle of inspections is nearing completion, and has yielded a vast database of information vital to our understanding of the performance of schools. It has also improved performance by clearly identifying strengths and weaknesses. It can give particularly sharp messages at the two extremes: identifying excellent schools from which important lessons can be learned, and also those which are failing to deliver an acceptable standard of education and require urgent attention. But it must also act as a spur to the majority of schools which, while not failing, can still make significant improvements.

The functions and powers of OFSTED are vested in the Chief Inspector who has general duties; a duty to comply with certain requests made by the Secretary of State; and specific duties. Under SIA 1996, s 2(6) the Chief Inspector is required to 'have regard to such aspects of government policy as the Secretary of State may direct'. His duties also extend to teacher training provision, and he is also required to publish an annual report.

School Inspections Act 1996, s 2

(1) The Chief Inspector for England shall have the general duty of keeping the Secretary of State informed about—
(a)   the quality of the education provided by schools in England;
(b)   the educational standards achieved in those schools;
(c)   whether the financial resources made available to those schools are managed efficiently; and
(d)   the spiritual, moral, social and cultural development of pupils at those schools.

(2) When asked to do so by the Secretary of State, the Chief Inspector for England shall—
(a)   give advice to the Secretary of State on such matters as may be specified in the Secretary of State's request;
(b)   inspect and report on such school, or class of school, in England as may be so specified.

(3) The Chief Inspector for England shall, in addition, have the following specific duties—
(a)   establishing and maintaining the register mentioned in section 7(1);
(b)   giving guidance to inspectors registered in that register, and such other persons as he considers appropriate, in connection with inspections of schools in England under section 10 and the making of reports of such inspections;
(c)   keeping under review the system of inspecting schools under that section (so far as it relates to schools in England) and, in particular, the standard of such inspections and of the reports made by registered inspectors;
(d)   keeping under review the extent to which any requirement imposed by or under this Act, or any other enactment, on any registered inspector, local education authority, proprietor of a school or governing body in relation to inspections of schools in England is complied with;
(e)   promoting efficiency in the conduct and reporting of inspections of schools in England by encouraging competition in the provision of services by registered inspectors.

(4) The Chief Inspector for England may at any time give advice to the Secretary of State on any matter connected with schools, or a particular school, in England.

(5) The Chief Inspector for England shall have such other functions in connection with schools in England, including functions with respect to the training of teachers for such schools, as may be assigned to him by the Secretary of State.

(6) In exercising his functions the Chief Inspector for England shall have regard to such aspects of government policy as the Secretary of State may direct....

THE INSPECTORS

There are two kinds of inspection. The more usual is carried out by registered inspectors under SIA 1996, s 10 (see below). The power to arrange school inspections by Her Majesty's Inspectors, who are members of the Inspectorate, is contained in s 3 of the SIA 1996. The HMIs are regarded as more senior than registered inspectors and usually carry out inspections where specific problems have been identified. Inspectors have a right of entry to premises and access to documents backed up by criminal sanctions.

School Inspections Act 1996, s 3

(1) The Chief Inspector for England may cause any school in England to be inspected by one or more of Her Majesty's Inspectors of Schools in England (in this section referred to as 'Inspectors').

(2) Where an inspection of a school in England is being conducted by a registered inspector under section 10 of this Act, the Chief Inspector for England may arrange for that inspection to be monitored by one or more Inspectors.

(3) Any Inspector inspecting a school, or monitoring an inspection, under this section shall have at all reasonable times—
(a)   a right of entry to the premises of the school; and
(b)   a right to inspect, and take copies of, any records kept by the school, and any other documents containing information relating to the school, which he considers relevant to the discharge of his functions.

(4) It shall be an offence wilfully to obstruct any Inspector in the exercise of any of his functions under this section.

(5) A person guilty of an offence under subsection (4) shall be liable on summary conviction to a fine not exceeding level 4 on the standard scale.

THE REGISTERED INSPECTORS

These inspectors are registered by the Chief Inspector, who can also withdraw a registration, or make it conditional. There is a right of appeal to an independent tribunal, the Registered Inspectors of Schools Appeal Tribunal.

School Inspections Act 1996, s 7

...

(3) The Chief Inspector shall not register a person under this section unless, having regard to any conditions that he proposes to impose under subsection (5)(c), it appears to him that that person—

(a)   is a fit and proper person for discharging the functions of a registered inspector; and

(b)   will be capable of conducting inspections under this Part competently and effectively

[and no person shall be so registered if he falls within a category of persons prescribed for the purposes of this subsection].

When a particular school is to be inspected, the Chief Inspector, after consultation with the governing body and/or the LEA, invites tenders from at least two registered inspectors. The inspectors are assisted by a team of 'fit and proper' persons, who will be capable of assisting in the inspection competently and effectively, and who have completed an approved course of training.

School Inspections Act 1998, Sch 3

3...

(2) It shall be the duty of the registered inspector to ensure that—

(a)   at least one member of the inspection team is a person—

   (i)   without personal experience in the management of any school or the provision of education in any school (otherwise than as a governor or in any other voluntary capacity); and

   (ii)   whose primary function on the team is not that of providing financial or business expertise; and

(b)   no member of the inspection team falls within a category of person prescribed for the purposes of this sub-paragraph.

(3) Otherwise, the composition of the inspection team shall be determined by the registered inspector, subject to his complying with any condition imposed under section 7(5)(c)...

(5) It shall be the duty of the registered inspector to ensure that no person takes any part in an inspection if he has, or has at any time had, any connection with—

(a)   the school in question,

(b)   any person who is employed at the school,

(c)   any person who is a member of the school's governing body, or

(d)   the proprietor of the school,

of a kind which might reasonably be taken to raise doubts about his ability to act impartially in relation to that school.

THE INSPECTION

The main provision relating to inspections by registered inspectors is s 10 of the SIA 1996, which sets out the purpose of the inspection.

School Inspections Act 1996, s 10

(1) It shall be the duty of the Chief Inspector for England to secure that every school in England to which this section applies is inspected, at such intervals as may be prescribed, by an inspector registered under section 7(1)...

(5) It shall be the general duty of any registered inspector conducting an inspection under this section to report on—
(a)   the quality of the education provided by the school;
(b)   the educational standards achieved in the school;
(c)   whether the financial resources made available to the school are managed efficiently; and
(d)   the spiritual, moral, social and cultural development of pupils at the school...

All maintained schools (including nursery schools and special schools), as well as city technology colleges, city colleges for the technology of the arts, city academies, and non-maintained special schools and independent schools approved for children with SEN, are to be inspected. The powers of OFSTED have been extended to 16-19 provision in schools, sixth-form colleges and FE colleges (s 60 of the LSA 2000).

An inspection should normally take place once every six years (see reg 4 of the Education (School Inspection) Regulations 1997, SI 1997/1966). Parents must be notified that an inspection is to take place and be given the opportunity to have a meeting with the inspector.

School Inspections Act 1996, Sch 3

6 Where an inspection is arranged, the appropriate authority for the school concerned shall—
(a)   take such steps as are reasonably practicable to notify—
(i)   the parents of registered pupils at the school, and
(ii)   such other persons as may be prescribed,
of the time when the inspection is to take place; and
(b)   arrange a meeting, in accordance with such provisions as may be prescribed, between the inspector conducting the inspection and those parents of registered pupils at the school who wish to attend.

Normally, a registered inspector should carry out the inspection and make a report within a three-month period (SIA 1996, s 15). This time limit does not apply to an inspection undertaken by a member of the Inspectorate.

Guidance on inspections is provided in DFE circular 7/93 (Inspecting schools: a guide to the inspection provisions of the Education (Schools) Act 1992 in England).

Where it is not reasonably practicable for a registered inspector to undertake a s 10 inspection, the Chief Inspector may arrange for one of HM Inspectors to do so (s 12 of the SIA 1996).

THE REPORT

The inspector is required to produce a written report and a summary of the report (s 13(1) of the SIA 1996). The carrying out of the inspection and the making of the report should not normally exceed seven weeks (two weeks for the inspection and five weeks for writing the report). In Wales an additional two weeks is allowed where necessary for translation of the report into Welsh or English.

The report is sent to the governing body and copies of the summary are available to parents (ss 16, 20 of the SIA 1996). Parents are entitled to a copy of the full copy on request. All inspection reports may be published (s 42A of the SIA 1996).

The requirements vary slightly where the school has a religious character or is an independent school.

SCHOOLS AT RISK

Additional procedures apply where an inspector considers that 'special measures' are required.

School Inspections Act 1996, s 13(9)

For the purposes of this Act special measures are required to be taken in relation to a school if the school is failing or likely to fail to give its pupils an acceptable standard of education.

The procedures vary according to the type of school (s 11 of the SIA 1996). Sections 13-15 of the SIA 1996 apply to most school inspections; SIA 1996, ss 16-19 apply to categories of maintained schools, and SIA 1996, ss 20-22 apply to other schools.

For example where a registered inspector considers in his report that the school requires special measures the following procedures apply.

School Inspections Act 1996, s 13

...

(2) Where the inspector is of the opinion that special measures are required to be taken in relation to the school he shall submit a draft of the report of the inspection to the Chief Inspector.

(3) If the Chief Inspector so requests, an inspector who has submitted a draft under subsection (2) shall provide the Chief Inspector with such further information as the Chief Inspector may specify.

(4) The Chief Inspector shall inform an inspector who has submitted a draft under subsection (2) whether he agrees or disagrees with the inspector's opinion.

(5) Where—
(a)   the Chief Inspector informs the inspector that he disagrees with the inspector's opinion, but
(b)   the inspector remains of the opinion that special measures are required to be taken in relation to the school,

the inspector may not make a report stating that opinion unless the terms in which he makes the report are substantially the same (except as to the statement required by subsection (7)(b)) as the draft or as a subsequent draft submitted to the Chief Inspector under this subsection.

(6) Where a subsequent draft is submitted under subsection (5), the Chief Inspector shall inform the inspector whether he agrees or disagrees with the inspector's opinion.

(7) A report made by a registered inspector who is of the opinion that special measures are required to be taken in relation to the school shall—
(a)   state his opinion, and
(b)   state whether the Chief Inspector agrees or disagrees with his opinion...

Where a member of the Inspectorate considers that special measures are required he or she is not required to submit a draft of their report to the Chief Inspector (s 14 of the SIA 1996). However, both types of inspector are required to state their opinion in the report.

Reports stating that a school requires special measures are sent to the governing body and in certain cases to the Secretary of State, as well as to the Chief Inspector, the head teacher, the LEA and, in the case of foundation and non-maintained schools, certain other bodies (ss 16, 20 of the SIA 1996). The Education Bill 2001/02 provides that the Chief Inspector must notify the Secretary of State where an inspector has concluded that a school has serious weaknesses or requires special measures, in order that earlier intervention by the Secretary of State or the LEA is possible.

The appropriate authority, normally the governing body, is required to prepare an action plan (SIA 1996, ss 17, 21).

School Inspections Act 1996, s 17(1)

...the appropriate authority shall prepare and distribute a written statement of the action which they propose to take in the light of the report and the period within which they propose to take it.

Detailed requirements relating to the action plan are contained in reg 8 of the Education (School Inspection) Regulations 1997, SI 1997/1966.

The governing body is required to prepare an action plan in response to a report by a registered inspector, and send it to the Chief Inspector. Where the report is made by a member of the Inspectorate, an action plan is required only where the Inspector considers that 'specials measures' need to be taken (see below). The action plan is to be made public and parents are to receive copies.

Education (School Inspection) Regulations 1997, SI 1997/1966

8 (1) For the purposes of sections 17(2)(a) and 21(2)(a) of the 1996 Act there is prescribed, as the period within which the appropriate authority are to prepare an action plan, the period of forty working days from the date on which they receive the report...

(3) Where an action plan has been prepared by the appropriate authority they shall send copies of it ... as follows—
(a) in all cases, to all persons employed at the school;
(b) in the case of a secondary school, to the Learning and Skills Council for the area in which the school is situated; and
(c) in the case of a special school not being maintained by a local education authority, or an independent school approved by the Secretary of State under section 347(1) of the Education Act 1996, to a further education funding council or any local education authority, if that body are paying fees in respect of the provision of education to any person at the school....

The Education (School Inspection) Regulations 1997, SI 1997/1966 also set out detailed requirements and time limits, as does SI 1998/1866 for Wales.

The LEA is required to prepare a written statement of any action they propose to take in the light of the inspector's report (SIA 1996, s 18), that is their own ation plan.

There is provision for the monitoring of special measures and for further inspections (ss 19, 22 of the SIA 1996).

The governing body of at least one school has challenged the Inspectors' report by way of judicial review. Crown Woods School in Eltham, south-east London was originally inspected in January 1999 and was subject to a follow-up inspection by Her Majesty's Inspectors in April 2000. The Inspectors decided that the school should go on special measures although they only spent two days at the school and concentrated on year 9 lessons. The governors initiated judicial review proceedings. The day before the hearing of the case in December 2000 OFSTED agreed that:

...the judgment made by Her Majesty's Inspectors in April 2000 to place Crown Woods in Special Measures should be quashed. It acknowledges that procedural flaws leading to the section 3 inspection of Crown Woods last spring rendered the judgement unsafe. (OFSTED News Release 2000-75, 15 December 2000)

The procedural flaws included:
* failing to inform the governing body of its concerns when it became aware of the scale of the weaknesses following the original inspection
* failing to assess the quality of the school's action plan and
* failing to inform the governing body of its concerns when the inspectors carried out the further inspection in April 2000.

The role of the LEA

Local education authorities have duties and powers in relation to the quality of education in local maintained schools. The following provision was inserted into the Education Act 1996 by the School Standards and Framework Act 1998, s 5.

Education Act 1996, s 13A

(1) A local education authority shall ensure that their functions relating to the provision of education to which this section applies are (so far as they are capable of being so exercised) exercised by the authority with a view to promoting high standards.

(2) This section applies to education for—
(a)   persons of compulsory school age (whether at school or otherwise); and
(b)   persons of any age above or below that age who are registered as pupils at schools maintained by the authority;

and in subsection (1) 'functions' means functions of whatever nature'.

- *Is this a target duty?*

- *Would a parent be able to (a) complain to the Secretary of State, (b) apply for judicial review, or (c) bring a claim for damages where the LEA failed to promote high standards?*

The LEA is also required under the Education Act 1996, s 13(1) to secure that 'efficient primary and secondary education are available to meet the needs of the population of their area'. In *R (on the application of Rhodes) v Kingston upon Hull City Council* [2001] ELR 230 parents applied for a declaration that the LEA was in breach of this provision because of the poor quality of secondary education in Hull. The parents cited evidence in the June 1999 OFSTED report on Hull LEA, which indicated that the LEA was the worst performing LEA in England at GCSE. The parents also relied on the Chief Inspector's Annual Report for 1998-99, which specifically referred to Hull LEA's 'difficult legacy', as well as a June 2000 draft consultation paper which described Hull as 'a well run LEA with low performing schools'. The parents' application for judicial review was refused because their complaint had already been considered and rejected by the Secretary of State (see chapter 8). The judge commented on the appropriateness of the application in these circumstances.

R (on the application of Rhodes) v Kingston upon Hull City Council [2001] ELR 230

Goldring J:

(49) First, on the facts, it is in my view hopeless. I cannot see, given the OFSTED reports, how it can be said that the local education authority was in breach of its statutory duty.

Moreover, while not the basis of my decision, the fact that no application has been made to quash the Secretary of State's decision on the basis that it was unreasonable or irrational seems to me significant. How could a reasonable or rational Secretary of State not intervene when a local education authority is in breach of its statutory duty under s 13(1)?

(50) Second, Parliament has committed to the local education authority the decision as to what constitutes an efficient education. That is a matter of opinion and degree: R v East Sussex County Council, ex p Tandy [1998] AC 714. The court would be ill equipped to resolve it. Moreover, it would in my view be too simplistic simply to say; the OFSTED figures are clear. They speak for themselves. That is an end to it. Regard has to be had, among other things, to the locality, its problems and the context in which the alleged breach of duty is suggested. This in my view is not a case of illegality or misfeasance in the Meade sense.

(51) Third, judicial review is a discretionary remedy. While there plainly are cases in which the seeking of a declaration by judicial review is appropriate, this in my view is not one of them.

Education development plans

All LEAs are required to produce an education development plan for their area with this aim in view, after consulting local schools and other interested parties.

School Standards and Framework Act 1998, s 6

(1) Every local education authority shall prepare an education development plan for their area, and shall prepare further such plans at such intervals as may be determined by or in accordance with regulations.

(2) An education development plan shall consist of—
(a)   a statement of proposals, which sets out proposals by the authority for developing their provision of education for children in their area, whether by—
   (i)   raising the standards of education provided for such children (whether at schools maintained by the authority or otherwise than at school), or
   (ii)   improving the performance of such schools,
   or otherwise; and
(b)   annexes to that statement...

(6) In preparing an education development plan the authority shall have regard, in particular, to the education of children (within the meaning of subsection (2)) who have special educational needs.

The education development plan will set out performance targets, which schools are also expected to set, based on national and local benchmarks (see school performance targets above).

Further details are contained in the Education Development Plans (England) Regulations 1999, SI 1999/138; and the Education Development Plans (Wales) Regulations 1999, SI 1999/1439. Guidance is provided in the English (2001) and Welsh (1999) Codes of Practice on LEA-School Relations.

Intervention in schools causing concern

The School Standards and Framework Act 1998 has given LEAs similar powers to those previously available under the School Inspections Act 1996. The Secretary of State also has powers to intervene (see below). The Education Bill 2001/02 proposes amendments to the existing legislation in order to encourage earlier intervention in schools causing concern. In addition the Bill extends the existing powers of the Secretary of State in relation to schools in 'special measures' to schools with 'serious weaknesses'. The Secretary of State will, for example, be able to appoint governors, replace the governing body with an 'interim executive board' or direct closure of the school.

An LEA may intervene where a school has been subject to a formal warning, or has serious weaknesses, or requires special measures.

School Standards and Framework Act 1998, s 14

(1) If at any time section 15 applies to a maintained school by virtue of any of the following provisions of that section, namely—
(a)   subsection (1) (school subject to formal warning),
(b)   subsection (4) (school with serious weaknesses), or
(c)   subsection (6) (school requiring special measures),

the provisions mentioned in subsection (2) below (which confer powers of intervention on local education authorities) shall also apply to the school at that time unless excluded by subsection (3) below (intervention by Secretary of State).

(2) Those provisions are—
(a)   section 16 (power to appoint additional governors); and
(b)   section 17 (power to suspend right to delegated budget).

(3) Those provisions shall not apply to a school to which section 15 applies by virtue of subsection (6) of that section (school requiring special measures) if, in connection with the same report falling within paragraph (a) of that subsection—
(a)   the Secretary of State has exercised in relation to the school his power under section 18 (power to appoint additional governors) and any additional governors appointed in the exercise of that power remain in office; or
(b)   he has exercised in relation to the school his power under section 19 (power to direct closure of school)...

What powers of intervention does the LEA have?

Powers of intervention may be exercised in three circumstances which are set out in SSFA 1998, s 15(1), (4), (6).

School Standards and Framework Act 1998, s 15

(1) This section applies to a maintained school by virtue of this subsection if—
(a)   the local education authority have—
    (i)   given the governing body a warning notice in accordance with subsection (2), and
    (ii) given the head teacher of the school a copy of the notice at the same time as the notice was given to the governing body;
(b)   the governing body have failed to comply, or secure compliance, with the notice to the authority's satisfaction within the compliance period; and
(c)   the authority have given reasonable notice in writing to the governing body that they propose to exercise their powers under either or both of sections 16 and 17 (whether or not the notice is combined with a notice under section 62(3)(c)).

(2) A local education authority may give a warning notice to the governing body of a maintained school where—
(a)   the authority are satisfied—
    (i)   that the standards of performance of pupils at the school are unacceptably low and are likely to remain so unless the authority exercise their powers under either or both of sections 16 and 17, or
    (ii) that there has been a serious breakdown in the way the school is managed or governed which is prejudicing, or likely to prejudice, such standards of performance, or
    (iii) that the safety of pupils or staff of the school is threatened (whether by a breakdown of discipline or otherwise); and
(b)   the authority have previously informed the governing body and the head teacher of the matters on which that conclusion is based; and
(c)   those matters have not been remedied to the authority's satisfaction within a reasonable period...

(4) This section applies to a maintained school by virtue of this subsection if—
(a)   a report of an inspection of the school has been made under Part I of the School Inspections Act 1996 in which the person making it stated that in his opinion the school had serious weaknesses; and
(b)   where any subsequent report of an inspection of the school has been made under Part I of that Act, that opinion has not been superseded by the person making the report stating that in his opinion—
    (i)   the school no longer has serious weaknesses, or
    (ii) special measures are required to be taken in relation to the school.

(5) For the purposes of subsection (4) a school has serious weaknesses if, although giving its pupils in general an acceptable standard of education, it has significant weaknesses in one or more areas of its activities.

(6) This section applies to a maintained school by virtue of this subsection if—
(a)   a report of an inspection of the school has been made under Part I of the School Inspections Act 1996 in which the person making it stated that in his opinion special measures were required to be taken in relation to the school;
(b)   either that person was a member of the Inspectorate or the report stated that the Chief Inspector agreed with his opinion; and
(c)   where any subsequent report of an inspection of the school has been made under Part I of that Act, the person making it did not state that in his opinion special measures were not required to be taken in relation to the school.

- *On what grounds may an LEA issue a 'warning notice'?*

- *What is meant by 'serious weaknesses'?*

DfEE Circular 6/99 (Schools Causing Concern), and the Code of Practice on LEA-School Relations (England) 2001 gives guidance on these matters.

The Education Bill 2001/02 proposes to amend SSFA 1998, s 15 so that intervention can occur earlier once a school has been identified as having serious weaknesses as well as when requiring special measures.

The role of the Secretary of State

Currently, the Secretary of State rarely intervenes in the management or conduct of an individual school. Nevertheless, the Secretary of State has recently acquired additional powers to intervene at a local level (Education Act 1996, s 497A) (see chapter 1).

The Secretary of State has reserve powers to ensure that:
- LEAs are properly performing their functions, including the duty under s 13A of the Education Act 1996 to promote high standards (see above), and
- governing bodies and LEAs are acting reasonably and are not in default (ss 496, 497 of the EA 1996) (see chapter 8).

Education Action Zones

The Secretary of State has the power to establish Education Action Zones (EAZs) in areas with severe education problems (see chapter 2). The aim of an EAZ is to improve standards within a group of schools in deprived areas.

School Standards and Framework Act 1998, s10(1)

If the Secretary of State considers that it is expedient to do so with a view to improving standards in the provision of education at any particular maintained schools, he may by order provide for those schools to constitute collectively an education action zone for the purposes of this Chapter.

Each EAZ has an Education Action Forum one of whose functions relates to the improvement of standards.

School Standards and Framework Act 1998, s 12(1)

An Education Action Forum shall have as its main object the improvement of standards in the provision of education at each of the participating schools.

Intervention in schools causing concern

Where a school requires special measures (see above), the Secretary of State has the power to appoint additional governors (s 18 of the SSFA 1998), and to direct closure of the school (s 19 of the SSFA 1998).

The power of the Secretary of State to establish an education association was removed by the SSFA 1998. Previously, where the inspector's report stated that a county or voluntary school required special measures, the Secretary of State could establish an education association (s 218 of the EA 1993, s 31 of the SIA 1996) which would take over the running of the school from the LEA. In effect the school was treated as if it were a grant-maintained school. Once the school had been transferred to an education association it could not revert to LEA control. It either became grant-maintained or was closed (see e g Hackney Downs School: *R v Secretary of State for Education and Employment, ex p Morris* [1996] ELR 198).

Are educational standards in schools improving?
The government clearly considers that the measures put in place during the 1990s have raised standards.

White Paper *Schools achieving success* (Cm 5230, September 2001)

Chapter 2 Reform in progress

...

2.2 Real progress has been made in the priorities we identified in 1997: the early years, literacy and numeracy in primary schools and modernising the teaching profession. All 4-year-olds have a free place in early education. In primary schools, children are in smaller classes and are more literate and numerate than ever before. The percentage of pupils achieving 5 or more good GCSEs has risen by 5 percentage points since 1996 to 49.2 per cent in 2000. Teachers are sharing good practice more effectively. We have put in place strategies for continuing professional development and for supporting school leaders.

2.3 The system as a whole is more accountable—to pupils, to parents and to the wider community—and we know much more about the relative performance of schools. The ambition to raise standards in schools is widely shared. Perhaps more than in any other part of the public service, heads, governors and teachers accept accountability for performance. Clear targets have better evidence available to enable them to evaluate their performance and are increasingly ready to challenge themselves to improve.

...

2.26 Critically, too, achievement gaps are much more pronounced at secondary level.
*   Only 44 per cent of boys achieved 5 or more GCSE grades A*—C at GCSE in 2000 compared to over 54 per cent of girls.
*   There is a very wide variation in performance between children who have parents with a manual occupation and those who come from a non-manual background.
*   There is also a wide variation in achievement between ethnic groups.
...

2.27 The picture is even starker when we compare individual schools. Though nationally 49.2 per cent of the pupils achieve 5 GCSEs at grades A*—C there are 480 schools (around 15 per cent of all secondary schools) where 25 per cent or fewer of their pupils achieve this level. And there are still 41 schools currently at or below 10 per cent. Many of these face extremely challenging circumstances, and teachers and pupils are working very hard indeed against the odds. But the reality is nevertheless that tens of thousands of pupils are not getting the opportunity to achieve their potential.

2.   LOCAL EDUCATION AUTHORITIES

The importance of LEAs has diminished in the past decade (see chapter 1). Nevertheless, they remain legally responsible for most of the legal duties and powers relating to the provision of primary and secondary education. All LEAs are subject to the overriding control of the Secretary of State who can intervene where they act unreasonably or are in default (ss 496, 497, 497A of the EA 1996). However, until the Education Act 1997 the Secretary of State had no right to inspect LEAs, even where they were perceived as 'failing'.

Inspection of LEAs

The right to inspect LEAs was introduced by the Education Act 1997. The inspections are carried out by OFSTED. The Chief Inspector of Schools has the power to arrange for the inspection of any LEA. In addition the Secretary of State can request the Chief Inspector to arrange such an inspection (s 38(1) of the EA 1997). The ambit and purpose of such an inspection is set out in the legislation.

Education Act 1997, s 38

...

(2) An inspection of a local education authority under this section shall consist of a review of the way in which the authority are performing any function of theirs (of whatever nature) which relates to the provision of education—
(a)   for persons of compulsory school age (whether at school or otherwise), or
(b)   for persons of any age above or below that age who are registered as pupils at schools maintained by the authority.

(3) A request by the Secretary of State under this section may relate to one or more local education authorities, and shall specify both—
(a)   the local education authority or authorities concerned, and
(b)   the function of theirs to which the inspection is to relate.

(4) Before making any such request the Secretary of State shall consult the Chief Inspector as to the matters to be specified in the request in accordance with subsection (3).

The inspection can only review those functions of the LEA which are concerned with the provision of education for persons of compulsory school age or for registered pupils at LEA maintained schools. The Audit Commission may be asked to assist with any inspection (s 41 of the EA 1997).

The inspector is required to produce a written report, copies of which are sent to the LEA and to the Secretary of State. The LEA is then required to produce an action plan which sets out in writing the action they propose to take in light of the report and the period within which they propose to take it. The LEA must publish the report and the action plan (s 39 of the EA 1997).

Where an inspection report considers that there are significant weaknesses in the work of the LEA there is likely to be a further inspection. For example, in the case of Hackney LEA in London, there were inspections in 1997, 1999 and 2000. The first two inspections revealed that there were significant weaknesses and the Secretary of State directed (under s 497A of the EA 1996) the Director of Education for Hackney to enter into a contract with a private company which would take over responsibility for the school improvement and ethnic minority support services. After the third inspection in the autumn of 2000 OFSTED remained seriously concerned about the work of the LEA and considered that the government should remove the provision of education in Hackney from the local authority.

By January 2001 18 LEAs had seen some level of intervention by the Secretary of State. The intervention normally results in 'outsourcing' or privatisation of some of the services provide by the LEA.

The Secretary of State has the power to intervene and issue directions where she is satisfied that a local education authority is failing to perform 'to an adequate standard' any function relating to the education of 5-16-year-olds as well as the education of pupils aged 16-18 (EA 1996, s 497A: see also chapter 1). The Secretary of State may direct the LEA to use a third party, including a private contractor, to perform the function.

Education Act 1996, s 497A

...

(3) The Secretary of State may under this subsection direct an officer of the authority to secure that that function is performed in such a way as to achieve such objectives as are specified in the direction.

(4) The Secretary of State may under this subsection give an officer of the authority such directions as the Secretary of State thinks expedient for the purpose of securing that the function—
(a) is performed, on behalf of the authority and at their expense, by such person as is specified in the direction, and
(b) is so performed in such a way as to achieve such objectives as are so specified;

and such directions may require that any contract or other arrangement made by the authority with that person contains such terms and conditions as may be so specified.

...

3.   FURTHER EDUCATION

All LEAs are under a duty to review the quality of education provided in FE institutions maintained by them (s 55(4) of the LSA 2000).

Learning and Skills Act 2000, s 55

(4) In relation to any local education authority institution maintained or assisted by them, a local education authority—

(a)   shall keep under review the quality of education provided, the educational standards achieved and whether the financial resources made available are managed efficiently, and

(b)   may cause an inspection to be made by persons authorised by them.

The Further Education Funding Council was under a duty to assess the quality of education in further education institutions through Quality Assessment Committees (s 9 of the FHEA 1992). The council has been abolished and replaced by the Learning and Skills Council (LSC) (LSA 2000).

Learning and Skills Act 2000, s 9

(1) The Council may develop schemes for the assessment of the performance of persons in providing post-16 education and training.

(2) The Council may take the assessments into account in deciding how to exercise its powers under section 5.

The Explanatory Notes to the LSA 2000 state:

In section 9 the LSC is given the power to assess the quality of the provision it funds, and take judgements about quality into account in deciding which providers it will continue to fund. This will form part of the LSC's quality improvement strategy. The intention is that the LSC secures value for money and that learners are offered provision of a high quality. Findings from the two inspectorates, OFSTED and [Adult Learning Inspectorate], may inform these judgments, but their input will not provide regular, comprehensive information on all providers. Therefore, it is intended that the LSC will take steps to investigate on its own behalf the quality of the provision it funds, through for example, visiting providers, putting arrangements in place for investigating complaints and acting on those which are well-founded. It will also have clear published performance indicators and benchmarks against which to measure quality of provision. The LSC may also draw up a list of accredited provision which meets certain quality thresholds, and cease to fund provision which does not.

Inspection regime

The Learning and Skills Act 2000 has introduced new and extended powers of inspection, although the explanatory note (above) indicates that the LSC is likely to carry out its own investigations as well. The emphasis of the new regime is not just on the quality of educational provision but also on whether it is good value for money.

There are two inspectorates for further education. The first is the Adult Learning Inspectorate (ALI), which inspects work-based and adult education provision in England (s 52 of the LSA 2000). The ALI will be responsible for all 16-19 training provision, and for post-19 education and training outside higher education. There is a Chief Inspector for Adult Learning.

The new inspection regime started operating in April 2001. All FE, sixth-form and tertiary colleges providing education for 16-18 year olds are to be inspected by OFSTED, jointly with the ALI, over a four-year period from September 2001.

Adult Learning Inspectorate

Learning and Skills Act 2000, s 53(1)

The Inspectorate's remit is—
(a) further education for persons aged 19 or over which is wholly or partly funded by the Learning and Skills Council for England;
(b) training for persons aged 16 or over so far as it takes place wholly or partly at the premises of an employer and is wholly or partly funded by the Council;
(c) further education funded by a local education authority in England for persons aged 19 or over;
(d) training for persons aged 16 or over which is funded by the Secretary of State under section 2 of the Employment and Training Act 1973;
(e) such other education or training as may be prescribed by regulations made by the Secretary of State.

In addition the Inspectorate must keep the Secretary of State informed about quality issues, and carry out investigations when asked to do so.

Learning and Skills Act 2000, s 54

(1) The Inspectorate must keep the Secretary of State informed about—
(a) the quality of the education and training within its remit;
(b) the standards achieved by those receiving that education and training; and
(c) whether the financial resources made available to those providing that education and training are managed efficiently and used in a way which provides value for money...

(3) When asked to do so by the Secretary of State, the Chief Inspector of Adult Learning must conduct inspections of such education or training, or such class of education or training, within the Inspectorate's remit, at such intervals, as the Secretary of State may specify.

Office for Standards in Education

The second inspectorate is OFSTED, which must inspect all institutions within the further education sector other than those providing education or training which falls wholly within the remit of the ALI. Inspections are to be conducted at such intervals as may be specified by the Secretary of State (s 62 of the LSA 2000).

The powers of OFSTED in relation to schools have been extended to include FE provision for pupils aged 16 or younger (see chapter 6, Key Stage 4), FE provision for 16 to 19-year-olds in schools and sixth-form colleges as well as FE colleges (s 60, LSA 2000). In Wales the Chief Inspector of Schools' powers have also been extended, and will include the inspection of all post-16 education and training provision. There is also the possibility of joint inspections by OFSTED and the ALI under the control of OFSTED.

Learning and Skills Act 2000, s 60(1)

The following kinds of education and training are brought within the remit of Her Majesty's Chief Inspector of Schools in England by this Chapter—
(a)   secondary education provided in institutions which are in England and within the further education sector;
(b)   further education provided in the further education sector which is suitable to the requirements of those aged 16 or over but under 19 and funded wholly or partly by the Learning and Skills Council for England;
(c)   further education provided by local education authorities in England for persons aged under 19;
(d)   such other education or training (which may, in particular, include training of or for teachers or lecturers) as may be prescribed by regulations made by the Secretary of State.

Common provisions

The ALI and OFSTED (England) must devise a common set of principles which will be known as the Common Inspection Framework (s 69(1) of the LSA 2000).

Both Chief Inspectors are required to produce written reports, which should be published. The institutions inspected are expected to produce in response an action plan, but the requirement may be waived (ss 58, 64 of the LSA 2000). Area inspections (s 65 of the LSA 2000) and joint inspections are permissible (s 71 of the LSA 2000).

The Chief Inspectors are expressly required to address the adequacy of the provision in their written reports. However, while quality is expressly referred to in s 55(2)(a) of the LSA 2000 which applies to reports written by the Chief Inspector of Adult Learning, it is not included in s 62(4)(a) of the LSA 2000 which applies to the report written by the Chief Inspector of Schools.

Learning and Skills Act 2000, s 55(2)(a)

The report—
(a)   must state whether the Chief Inspector considers the education or training inspected to be of a quality adequate to meet the reasonable needs of those receiving it ...

Learning and Skills Act 2000, s 62(4)(a)

The report—
(a) must state whether the Chief Inspector considers the education or training inspected to be adequate to meet the reasonable needs of those receiving it ...

4. HIGHER EDUCATION

The Secretary of State may make grants to each of the Higher Education Funding Councils for England and Wales of such amounts and subject to such terms and conditions as he may determine. However, the Secretary of State cannot impose terms or conditions on individual universities, nor may such terms and conditions be framed by reference to particular courses of study or programmes of research (including the contents of such courses or programmes and the manner in which they are taught, supervised or assessed) or to the criteria for the selection and appointment of academic staff and for the admission of students (s 68 of the FHEA 1992). This is in part to protect academic freedom.

The Secretary of State can give general directions to the Councils (s 81 of the FHEA 1992).

The Councils administer the funds available from the government for higher education and have the power to make grants, loans or other payment to universities 'subject in each case to such terms and conditions as the council think fit' (s 65(3) of the FHEA 1992). This discretion is drafted in broad terms and appears to allow grants to be tied to improvements in the quality of educational provision or research.

The Higher Education Funding Councils are under a duty to assess the quality of education in higher education institutions through Quality Assessment Committees.

Further and Higher Education Act 1992, s 70

(1) Each council shall—
(a) secure that provision is made for assessing the quality of education provided in institutions for whose activities they provide, or are considering providing, financial support ... and
(b) establish a committee, to be known as the 'Quality Assessment Committee', with the function of giving them advice on the discharge of their duty under paragraph (a) above and such other functions as may be conferred on the committee by the council.

(2) The majority of the members of the committee—
(a) shall be persons falling within subsection (3) below, and
(b) shall not be members of the council.

(3) Persons fall within this subsection if they appear to the council to have experience of, and to have shown capacity in, the provision of higher education in institutions within the higher education sector and, in appointing such persons, the council shall have regard to

the desirability of their being currently engaged in the provision of higher education or in carrying responsibility for such provision.

There are two main ways in which the educational provision at higher education institutions is monitored:
- Research Assessment Exercise
- Teaching assessments by the Quality Assurance Agency.

The Research Assessment Exercise (RAE) is a paper evaluation based on published criteria of the research output of subject areas, such as law.

The latest RAE in 2001 resulted in a general improvement in research ratings, but there was insufficient money available to reward all university departments correspondingly, and the current approach to the RAE is being reviewed.

The teaching assessments involve visits to universities to look at both the teaching of particular subjects and the management of the institution. The procedure was criticised for the methods used to assess quality, as well as for being bureaucratic, costly and time-consuming. In 2001 new 'lighter touch' assessment procedures were announced in response to this criticism.

OFSTED inspections

In addition OFSTED may inspect teacher training courses provided by universities or other higher education institutions.

Education Act 1994, s 18A

(1) The Chief Inspector may inspect and report on—
(a)   any initial training of teachers, or of specialist teaching assistants, for schools, or
(b)   any in-service training of such teachers or assistants,

which is provided by a relevant institution.

...

(4) The Chief Inspector may—
(a)   make such reports of inspections carried out by him under this section as he considers appropriate, and
(b)   arrange for any such report to be published in such manner as he considers appropriate,
       ...

(3) The Chief Inspector may at any time give advice to—
(a)   the Secretary of State,
(b)   a funding agency,
(c)   the General Teaching Council for England, or
(d)   the General Teaching Council for Wales,

on any matter connected with training falling within subsection (1)(a) or (b).

The main funding agency is the Teacher Training Agency (TTA) which allocates funds to and accredits institutions providing teacher training. In *R (on the application of University of Exeter) v Teacher Training Agency* [2001] All ER (D) 81 the TTA decide to commence withdrawal of the accreditation from the university and to reduce the university's student allocation for primary school level teacher training courses by 50 per cent. The TTA's decision was made as a result of an OFSTED inspection which rated the university's provision for undergraduate teacher training as inadequate. The university was phasing out its undergraduate provision, in any case, and planned to concentrate on postgraduate provision. However, because of the approach adopted by the TTA the number of postgraduate places were also reduced as a consequence of the OFSTED report. The High Court held that the approach was not unreasonable and that the TTA had not fettered its discretion.

R (on the application of University of Exeter) v Teacher Training Agency [2001] All ER (D) 81

Sullivan J: In the absence of a particularly egregious error, it would not normally be appropriate for an applicant to seek judicial review of a decision to commence withdrawal of accreditation procedures, as the application would be premature. Withdrawal procedures did not result in withdrawal without a further opportunity for the institution to remedy the identified shortcomings, and there was accordingly scope for any errors of law to be corrected, with the institution suffering no damage other than loss of pride and the need to implement a recovery plan ...The agency had no[t] failed to follow its own procedures; it was clear that the university's position was given detailed consideration... On the facts, the agency had not wrongly fettered its discretion, nor had it denied the university a fair chance to make representations in all the circumstances of the case.

5.   COMMON LAW LIABILITY

The logical conclusion of the view that pupils and parents as well as students are consumers of educational services, is that they should have similar right to consumers who, for example, use the National Health Service. In particular, may pupils and students bring a claim in the tort of negligence where the quality of educational provision is below a reasonable standard?

Where a consumer buys services from the private sector, for example, electricity supplies or delivery services, their rights are regulated mainly by the contract, together with relevant statutory provisions such as the Unfair Contract Terms Act 1977 or the Unfair Terms in Consumer Contracts Regulations 1999, SI 1999/2083. In an educational context, the law of contract is unlikely to be relevant to pupils attending maintained schools. It is relevant to pupils attending independent schools and to many students attending FE and HE institutions.

6.   TORT OF NEGLIGENCE

Schools, FE and HE institutions owe a duty of care in relation to, for example, the safety of the premises, and may be vicariously liable for the negligence of their employees (see chapter 2). An area of particular interest, in the light of the House of Lords decision in *Phelps v London Borough of Hillingdon* [2000] ELR 499 (see chapter 5), is whether teachers (and by implication lecturers in FE and HE institutions) owe all their pupils (and students) a duty of care in relation to the quality of education provided.

In *Gower v London Borough of Bromley* [1999] ELR 356 (heard by the House of Lords as part of the *Phelps* appeal) the Court of Appeal (Auld LJ) considered whether teachers owe their pupils a duty of care in relation to the quality of the education they provided. He considered that in the light of the decisions of the House of Lords in *X (Minors) v Bedfordshire County Council* [1995] ELR 404, and *Barrett v Enfield London Borough Council* [1999] 3 All ER 193 certain propositions had been established.

Gower v London Borough of Bromley [1999] ELR 356

Auld LJ: (2) A headteacher and teachers have a duty to exercise the reasonable skills of their calling in teaching and otherwise responding to the educational needs of their pupils. Those responsible for teachers in breach of that duty may be vicariously liable for it. The Court of Appeal and the House of Lords so ruled in the *Hampshire* case in *X (Minors)* in which the House held to be justiciable an action against an education authority for vicarious liability for the negligence of a headteacher in failing to refer a pupil for assessment of his special educational needs. Lord Browne-Wilkinson, with whom all their Lordships agreed, said at pp 766 and 451 respectively:

> ...a school which accepts a pupil assumes responsibility not only for his physical well being but also for his educational needs. The education of the pupil is the very purpose for which the child goes to the school. The head teacher, being responsible for the school, himself comes under a duty of care to exercise the reasonable skills of a head teacher in relation to such educational needs. If it comes to the attention of the head teacher that a pupil is under-performing, he does owe a duty to take such reasonable steps as a reasonable teacher would consider appropriate to try to deal with such under-performance.

Whilst those remarks were principally directed, on the facts of that case, to the duty of a head teacher or a teaching adviser to exercise skill and care in advising on a pupil's educational needs, they are, in my view, equally capable of applying in an appropriate case to a head teacher's and his teaching staff's duty to teach and otherwise meet the educational needs of pupils in their charge. It is plain from the House of Lords' treatment of the matter in *Barrett v Enfield London Borough Council*, in particular that of Lord Slynn, that they regarded Lord Browne-Wilkinson's reasoning in *X (Minors)* as generally applicable to 'operational' negligence of teachers and others in the exercise of their professional responsibilities to children in their charge.

That a duty of care is owed to all pupils was accepted in principle by Lord Nicholls and Lord Clyde in *Phelps v London Borough of Hillingdon* [2000] ELR 499.

Phelps v London Borough of Hillingdon [2000] ELR 499

Lord Nicholls of Birkenhead: My third illustration raises a particularly controversial issue. It cannot be that a teacher owes a duty of care only to children with special educational needs. The law would be in an extraordinary state if, in carrying out their teaching responsibilities, teachers owed duties to some of their pupils but not others. So the question which arises, and cannot be shirked, is whether teachers owe duties of care to all their pupils in respect of the way they discharge their teaching responsibilities. This question has far-reaching implications. Different legal systems have given different answers to this question.

I can see no escape from the conclusion that teachers do, indeed, owe such duties. The principal objection raised to this conclusion is the spectre of a rash of 'gold digging' actions brought on behalf of under-achieving children by discontented parents, perhaps years after the events complained of. If teachers are liable, education authorities will be vicariously liable, since the negligent acts or omissions were committed in the course of the teachers' employment. So, it is said, the limited resources of education authorities and the time of teaching staff will be diverted away from teaching and into defending unmeritorious legal claims. Further, schools will have to prepare and keep full records, lest they be unable to rebut negligence allegations, brought out of the blue years later. For one or more of these reasons, the overall standard of education given to children is likely to suffer if a legal duty of care were held to exist.

I am not persuaded by these fears. I do not think they provide sufficient reason for treating work in the classroom as territory which the courts must never enter. 'Never' is an unattractive absolute in this context. This would bar a claim, however obvious it was that something had gone badly wrong, and however serious the consequences for the particular child. If a teacher carelessly teaches the wrong syllabus for an external examination, and provable financial loss follows, why should there be no liability? Denial of the existence of a cause of action is seldom, if ever, the appropriate response to fear of its abuse. Rather, the courts, with their enhanced powers of case-management, must seek to evolve means of weeding out obviously hopeless claims as expeditiously as is consistent with the court having a sufficiently full factual picture of all the circumstances of the case.

This is not to open the door to claims based on poor quality of teaching. It is one thing for the law to provide a remedy in damages when there is manifest incompetence or negligence comprising specific, identifiable mistakes. It would be an altogether different matter to countenance claims of a more general nature, to the effect that the child did not receive an adequate education at the school, or that a particular teacher failed to teach properly. Proof of under-performance by a child is not by itself evidence of negligent teaching. There are many, many reasons for under-performance. A child's ability to learn from what he is taught is much affected by a host of factors which are personal to him and over which a school has no control. Emotional stress and the home environment are two examples. Even within a school, there are many reasons other than professional negligence. Some teachers are better at communicating and stimulating interest than others, but that is a far cry from negligence. Classroom teaching involves a personal relationship between teacher and pupil. One child may respond positively to the personality of a particular teacher, another may not. A style of teaching which suits one child, or most children in a class, may not be as effective with another child, and so on. The list of factors could continue. Suffice to say, the existence of a duty of care owed by teachers to their pupils should not be regarded as furnishing a basis on which generalised 'educational malpractice' claims can be mounted.

...

Lord Clyde: In the present case I am not persuaded that there are sufficient grounds to exclude these claims even on grounds of public policy alone. It does not seem to me that there is any wider interest of the law which would require that no remedy in damages be available. I am not persuaded that the recognition of a liability upon employees of the education authority for damages for negligence in education would lead to a flood of claims, or even vexatious claims, which would overwhelm the school authorities, nor that it would add burdens and distractions to the already intensive life of teachers. Nor should it inspire some peculiarly defensive attitude in the performance of their professional responsibilities. On the contrary it may have the healthy effect of securing that high standards are sought and secured. If it is thought that there would only be a few claims and for that reason the duty should not be recognised, the answer must be that if there are only a few claims there is the less reason to refuse to allow them to be entertained. As regards the need for this remedy, even if there are alternative procedures by which some form of redress might be obtained, such as resort to judicial review, or to an ombudsman, or the adoption of such statutory procedures as are open to parents, which might achieve some correction of the situation for the future, it may only be through a claim for damages at common law that compensation for the damage done to the child may be secured for the past as well as the future.

Any fear of a flood of claims may be countered by the consideration that in order to get off the ground the claimant must be able to demonstrate that the standard of care fell short of that set by the *Bolam v Friern Hospital Management Committee* [1957] 1 WLR 582 test. That is deliberately and properly a high standard in recognition of the difficult nature of some decisions which those to whom the test applies require to make and of the room for genuine differences of view on the propriety of one course of action as against another. In the field of educational matters there may well exist distinct but respectable opinions upon matters of method and practice, and it may be difficult to substantiate a case of fault against the background of a variety of professional practices. In cases of a failure to diagnose a particular disability from which a child may be suffering there may well be considerable difficulties in the making of the diagnosis which may render proof of negligence hazardous.

Not only may there be difficulties in establishing negligence in relation to the making of professional judgments in particular circumstances or the exercise of a professional choice in particular cases, but there may well be practical difficulties in the adequacy of records or of recollection about the details regarding the educational progress and achievements of a particular child which may be highly relevant to the claim which is brought. But that there may be such difficulty is no reason for excluding deserving cases. There may also be severe difficulty in establishing a causal connection between the alleged negligence and the alleged loss and in the assessment of any damages. But these possible difficulties should not be allowed to stand in the way of the presentation of a proper claim, nor should justice be altogether denied on the ground that a claim is of a complex nature. That any claims which are made may require a large number of witnesses, a consideration which weighed with the Court of Appeal, and involve considerable time and cost, are again practical considerations which should not be allowed to justify a total exclusion of an otherwise legitimate claim. While I recognise that the general view in the jurisprudence of the USA is adverse to the admission of a liability upon teachers for negligence upon general grounds of policy, I am not persuaded that a corresponding view should be taken in this country.

...

- *What are the arguments for and against the common law recognising that teachers owe their pupils a duty of care in respect of the way they discharge their teaching responsibilities?*

- *Would consistent poor quality teaching over a period of two years amount to a breach of a duty of care?*

- *Why do the existing procedures not provide an adequate remedy in Lord Clyde's opinion?*

Educational malpractice in the USA

In *Phelps* in the Court of Appeal, Stuart-Smith LJ considered US case law on 'educational malpractice'. Civil actions for damages have been brought in the US since the 1970s.

Phelps v London Borough of Hillingdon [1998] ELR 587

Stuart-Smith LJ: There are a number of decisions in the US courts where claims for 'educational malpractice' have been struck out both against the public education authority and its individual servants. These cases were not cited to the House of Lords in *X (Minors)*. In addition to the reasons given by Lord Browne-Wilkinson, other considerations have weighed with the US courts. In *Peter W v San Francisco Unified School District* (1976) 60 Cal App 3d 867 a claim based both on direct and vicarious liability for failure to detect the plaintiff's reading disabilities, the Californian Court of Appeal said that 'classroom methodology affords no readily acceptable standards of care or cause or injury' (at p 860); 'there are a host of factors which affect the pupil subjectively from outside the formal teaching process, and beyond the control of its ministers. They may be physical, neurological, emotional, cultural, environmental; they may be present, but not perceived, recognised but not identified' (p 861).

In *Donoghue v Copiague Union* (1978) 407 NYS 2d 874, the Supreme Court, Appellate Division, New York, adopted similar reasoning. In addition the court said at p 880 that the educational enactments:

> ...merely require the creation of a system of free common schools. Their purpose is to confer the benefits of a free education upon what would otherwise be an uneducated public. They were not intended to protect against the 'injury' of ignorance, for every individual is born lacking knowledge, education and experience. For this reason the failure of educational achievement cannot be characterized as an 'injury' within the meaning of tort law.

Similar reasoning was adopted by the Court of Appeals of New York in *Hoffman v Board of Education of New York* (1979) 49 NY 2d 119. A claim against an educational psychologist was struck out: see also *Hunter v Board of Education* (1982) 439A 2d 582. The Court of Appeals in Maryland struck out a claim against the education board, headmaster, a teacher and employee of the board who performed a diagnostic test. Similar decisions are to be found in *Suriano v Hyde Park* (1994) 611 NYS 2d 20, Supreme Court Appellate Division, New York, and in Canada in *Gould v Regina (East) School Division* (1997) WWR 117, Saskatchewan Court of Queen's Bench, where the court followed the US authorities.

...

I find the reasoning of the US courts, which have extended the immunity in educational malpractice suits to cover the individual servants or agents of the education authority, persuasive, though I think in our jurisdiction we should reach the same result by holding that there is no assumption of responsibility giving rise to a duty of care in the mere performance by the servant or agent of his or her duty to the LEA, even though this will inevitably involve a direct relationship with the child who is the subject under consideration and the parents are inevitably told what is the outcome of the advice and decisions made by the LEA or school.

Stuart-Smith LJ's view that English law should not recognise that a duty of care arises between a servant or agent of the LEA and a pupil was rejected by the House of Lords.

The following article is concerned with the American law of remedies for misdiagnosis or misplacement of pupils with special educational needs, but some of the points made are of wider application and provide an interesting comparison.

Robert E Rains 'A primer on special education law in the United States—Part 3: remedies for misdiagnosis or misplacement of special education students' (1998) 10(4) Education and the Law 205

The American cases can be roughly divided into our categories: (1) cases brought in state courts under common law theories of negligence and/or misrepresentation; (2) cases brought under federal law in which parents of special education students have sought reimbursement for payment for private school tuition where the local education agency has offered their children placements in the public school setting which the parents deem to be inappropriate; (3) cases in which students have sought 'compensatory education' past the normal age for termination of educational services to make up for alleged failures of the public school system to provide them with a meaningful education as guaranteed by state and federal law; and (4) cases brought under the federal special education statute and related laws seeking damages for alleged violations of rights guaranteed under those laws.

The 'educational malpractice' lawsuits

Starting in the 1970s, civil actions for damages have been brought in a number of states alleging what has come to be known as 'educational malpractice'. All of these cases have either involved students who in today's terminology would be considered to have disabilities or who allegedly were wrongly placed in special education classes. (The cases should not be confused with traditional tort actions in which students or their parents have sued for damages because a child was physically injured or even killed on school grounds or during a school-related activity.) With one significant exception, which will be noted below, the courts have not been receptive to such a cause of action. The first such case to be reported was *Peter W v San Francisco Unified School District*.

...

The court readily acknowledged the 'truism' that the public authorities who are duty-bound to educate are also bound to do it with 'care'. However, this does not answer the question of whether there is 'duty' in the legalistic sense which sustains liability for negligence in its breach.

The judicial recognition of such a duty ... is initially to be dictated or precluded by considerations of public policy. On occasions when the [California] Supreme Court has opened or sanctioned new areas of tort liability, it has noted that the wrongs and injuries involved were both comprehensible and assessable within the existing judicial framework ... This is simply not true of wrongful conduct and injuries allegedly involved in educational malfeasance. Unlike the activity of the highway or the marketplace, classroom methodology affords no readily acceptable standards of care, or cause, or injury. The science of pedagogy itself is fraught with different and conflicting theories of how or what a child should be taught, and any layman might—and commonly does—have his own emphatic views on this subject. The 'injury' claimed here is plaintiff's inability to read and write. Substantial professional authority attests that the achievement of literacy in the schools, or its failure, are (sic) influenced by a host of factors which affect the pupil subjectively, from outside the formal teaching process, and beyond the control of its ministers. They may be physical, neurological, emotional, cultural, environmental; they may be present but not perceived, recognized but not identified.

The court concluded that in this situation there could be no conceivable 'workability of a rule of care' against which a school district's alleged conduct could be measured, no reasonable degree of certainty that plaintiff suffered injury within the meaning of the law of negligence, and no such perceptible 'connection between the defendant's conduct and the injury suffered'.

Moreover the court noted strong public policy reasons to deny such a cause of action.

To hold public schools to an actionable duty of care in the discharge of their academic functions, would expose them to tort claims—real or imagined—of disaffected students and parents in countless numbers. They are already beset by social and financial problems which have gone to major litigation, but for which no permanent solution has yet appeared. The ultimate consequences, in terms of public time and money, would burden them—and society—beyond calculation.

Thus the court of appeals upheld dismissal of all of the causes of action arising out of SFUSD's alleged 'educational malfeasance'.

Although such claims have been rejected as a matter of policy in the USA, claims in the tort of negligence are possible in the UK. The decision of the House of Lords in *Phelps* is of fundamental importance. Their Lordships recognised that a pupil has a right to claim damages where the standard of education provided falls below an acceptable level. Although in practice it may be difficult to establish negligence in relation to an individual pupil, a picture of an unacceptably low quality of educational provision at a particular school may be built up by use of published information. In particular, the quality mechanisms discussed in this chapter provide independent information on the relative and comparative quality of individual schools. League tables (SAT results, GCSE and A Level results), together with OFSTED reports on the school and the LEA are valuable sources of information.

- *Do you consider that pupils should be able to sue teachers (and their employers) in negligence for poor quality teaching?*

- *What would such pupils have to establish in order to be successful? (See chapter 5)*

Further and higher education

Similarly lecturers at FE and HE institutions are likely to owe their students a duty of care in tort, as well as in contract (see below). Claims in negligence have usually related to the assessment rather than the teaching process, and have not been successful in the past (see e g *Thorne v University of London* [1966] 2 QB 237), but the decision in *Phelps* may change the nature of the claim, and thus increase the likelihood of success.

Again the USA already has experience of such claims.

David Palfreyman 'The HEI-student legal relationship, with special reference to the USA experience' (1999) 11(1) Education and the Law 5

US experience: tort liability

A potential source of tort liability, albeit a generally unsuccessful one for plaintiffs, is the doctrine of 'educational malpractice'. As Kaplin and Lee note:

> Although they often sympathise with students who claim that they have not learned what they should have learnt, or that they, their Professors, were negligent in teaching or supervising them, Courts have been reluctant to create a cause of action for educational malpractice ... [In one case the] Judge disagreed, ruling that the student was ultimately responsible for his academic success.

US Experience: conclusion

So, some comfort for UK HE from the fact that US HE is not as beleaguered by student writs (or at least not by successful ones!) as might be expected, given the popularist understanding of the way that the law works in the USA and given that the US HE system is far further down the road of paying customers/consumerism than yet here in the UK.

7.   BREACH OF CONTRACT

A parent with a child at a publicly funded school is unlikely to be able to bring a claim for breach of contract because there is generally no contract between the parents and the school. Where a child attends an independent fee-paying school there is a contract between the parents and the school, and that is likely to be the basis for a legal claim based on the poor quality of education provided rather than the tort of negligence.

The courts have accepted that there is a contract between a student and his or her university when the student enrols (see chapter 8). Similarly a contract may also exist between a student and the FE institution. A student should in principle be able to sue his or her university for breach of an express or implied term in the contract that the educational services provided should be of a reasonable standard (see eg *Butterworths Education Law Manual*, Division D, chapter 1: Students – Terms of the enrolment contract, Anne Ruff).

In practice, a student may have difficulty in proving that the education provided was not of a reasonable standard, unless there have been adversely critical reports on a particular module or programme by either external examiners or the QAA (see above). The institution is likely to exclude its liability for some breaches of contract, possibly including negligent performance of the contract. To be valid, such clauses will have to satisfy the requirements of the Unfair Contract Terms Act 1977 and the Unfair Terms in Consumer Contracts Regulations 1999, SI 1999/2083.

However, one advantage of a claim for breach of contract rather than in the tort of negligence is that a claim for pure economic loss is possible. Thus a claim for loss of earnings as a consequence of having to repeat a semester, or obtaining a lower class of degree than otherwise anticipated could be brought in a contract claim, but not in a negligence claim unless the loss was consequent on physical or psychological injury.

CHAPTER 8

Complaints procedures

The need for effective complaints procedures has become apparent in the last two decades with the growth of 'parent power'. Parents are now perceived as the education 'consumer' by central government (see chapter 1), whereas traditionally the relationship between LEAs, schools and teachers was at the heart of public sector education.

This development has been mirrored in higher, and to a lesser extent further, education where students can also be perceived as consumers of educational services.

The phrase 'complaints procedures' encompasses a range of procedures whereby a parent or a student has the right to ask that a decision or a policy should be reconsidered or reviewed by a third party. The 'right to education' is not regarded as a civil right under the Human Rights Act 1998 (see chapter 1), and the current provisions have been developed according to domestic UK law principles.

The complaints procedures available continue to reflect the public law nature of education law. Nevertheless the law of contract and the law of tort also have a role. For example, the law of contract is relevant to the relationship between students and further and higher institutions, and the tort of negligence is relevant to the quality of educational provision (see chapters 5 and 7).

Formal complaints procedures provide a means of redress for parents and students. However, they are limited in scope and parents or students do resort to the courts normally using the judicial review procedure. There is no general complaints procedure available against LEAs or schools, although the SSFA 1998 introduced one in principle for schools.

Some of the complaints procedures available deal with specific complaints, and have been considered in the relevant chapter. These include:

- independent appeal panels (school admissions and school exclusions)
- special educational needs tribunal
- curriculum complaints.

There are four general procedures, one or more of which may enable a parent to challenge a decision or a policy which affects their child. However, the first procedure is not yet in operation. The procedures are:

- general complaints procedure for parents
- complaints to the Secretary of State
- complaints to the Local Government Ombudsman
- judicial review.

In the case of students each institution will have its own internal complaints procedures. In addition 'old' universities normally have an independent person, known as the Visitor, who can adjudicate upon disputes between the student and the university.

The Human Rights Act 1998 has been considered in the context of school admission and exclusion procedures (see chapters 3 and 4), as well as religious and sex education (see chapter 6). The Act is unlikely at present to add anything to the procedures discussed in this chapter in relation to schools. Similarly, in the context of further and higher education, the Human Rights Act is unlikely to have a direct impact (see below) although it may lead to the introduction of an independent element into the complaints procedures for 'new' universities.

This chapter is concerned with procedures available to parents, pupils and students. In addition there are grievance, disciplinary and whistle-blowing procedures available to employees of educational institutions which are outside the scope of this book.

1.   MAINTAINED SCHOOLS

Parents may wish to raise a wide range of issues with the school ranging from the quality of the teaching provision, to the school policy on, for example, the wearing of jewellery, or timetabling arrangements. Normally, such an issue would initially be raised with the head teacher, but ultimately it is the governing body which is responsible for the management of the school. Where the governing body acts unlawfully a complaint may be made to the Secretary of State or challenged by way of judicial review. A complaint to the Local Government Ombudsman is only possible where the governing body is the admissions authority.

Parents may also wish to complain about the way in which the LEA has dealt with its statutory responsibilities. There is no statutory requirement on LEAs to have their own general complaints procedure. Formal complaints about 'maladministration' by the LEA may be made to the Local Government Ombudsman. Where the LEA acts unlawfully a complaint may be made to the Secretary of State or the action may be challenged by way of judicial review.

The governing body

In addition to the curriculum complaints procedure (see chapter 6) governing bodies of all maintained schools will be required to set up a general complaints procedure for parents. This procedure will not replace existing procedures.

This is a new requirement, but the necessary regulations were not introduced. The DfEE reportedly had difficulty in reaching a consensus with LEAs, schools and parents organisations over the detailed content of the regulations.

School Standards and Framework Act 1998, s 39

(1) The governing body of a maintained school shall in accordance with regulations—

(a)   establish procedures for dealing with all complaints relating to the school other than those falling to be dealt with in accordance with any procedures required to be established in relation to the school by virtue of any other statutory provision; and

(b)   publicise the procedures so established.

...

The Education Bill 2001/02 re-enacts s 39, but removes the requirement for regulations to be implemented. Instead guidance will be published on the principles which should underpin such a procedure.

Although no formal complaints procedure currently exists the governing body may consider complaints by parents, but there is no requirement to do so and no procedure in place setting out, for example, a timetable for responding to any complaint.

In 1999 the Local Government Ombudsmen recommended that they should be able to investigate complaints against the actions of governors (see below). However, although this may help parents dissatisfied with the response of a governing body, a local complaints machinery is preferable. The curriculum complaints procedures could provide a model, so long as time limits were imposed to ensure that complaints were speedily resolved.

The Secretary of State

The advantage of making a complaint to the Secretary of State is that the department is familiar with the current law and practice and may be able to resolve the matter informally and quickly. Where a formal investigation is carried out it may take at least six months for the matter to be resolved (see for example, *R v Secretary of State for Education, ex p R and D* [1994] ELR 495, chapter 6).

Complaints may be made to the Secretary of State by, for example, parents or governors or MPs, inviting the Secretary of State to find that:

(1)   the LEA or the governing body:
    (a)   has acted unreasonably; or
    (b)   or is in default;

(2)   the LEA has failed to perform certain functions.

The Secretary of State does not have to receive a complaint in order to exercise these powers. Where the Secretary of State makes such a finding, the Secretary of State has the power to give directions to the LEA or governing body. These powers were previously found in s 68 of the EA 1944 and s 219 of the ERA 1988 (which replaced s 99 of the EA 1944). The exercise of these powers may be challenged in the courts by way of judicial review.

Disputes between a governing body and its LEA, as well as disputes between two or more LEAs may be referred to the Secretary of State to resolve (s 495 of the EA 1996). One of the earliest House of Lords decisions on education legislation related to an earlier version of this section. In *Board of Education v Rice* [1911] AC 179, the House of Lords stated that the Board of Education (the equivalent of the DfES) must act fairly when reaching its decision.

Board of Education v Rice [1911] AC 179 at 182

Lord Loreburn LC: In the present instance, as in many others, what comes for determination is sometimes a matter to be settled by discretion, involving no law. It will, I suppose, usually be of an administrative kind; but sometimes it will involve matter of law as well as matter of fact, or even depend upon matter of law alone. In such cases the Board of Education will have to ascertain the law and also to ascertain the facts. I need not add that in doing either they must act in good faith and fairly listen to both sides, for that is a duty lying upon every one who decides anything. But I do not think they are bound to treat such a question as though it were a trial. They have no power to administer an oath, and need not examine witnesses. They can obtain information in any way they think best, always giving a fair opportunity to those who are parties in the controversy for correcting or contradicting any relevant statement prejudicial to their view.

'act unreasonably'

Education Act 1996, s 496

(1) If the Secretary of State is satisfied (either on a complaint by any person or otherwise) that a body to which this section applies have acted or are proposing to act unreasonably with respect to the exercise of any power conferred or the performance of any duty imposed by or under this Act, he may give such directions as to the exercise of the power or the performance of the duty as appear to him to be expedient (and may do so despite any enactment which makes the exercise of the power or the performance of the duty contingent upon the opinion of the body).

(2) The bodies to which this section applies are—
(a)   any local education authority, and
(b)   the governing body of any community, foundation or voluntary school or any community or foundation special school.

The Secretary of State has similar powers in relation to careers education provided by city technology colleges and city colleges for the technology of the arts (EA 1997, s 43(4)). Guidance is provided in, for example, the Code of Practice on LEA-School Relations.

The relationship between the Secretary of State's exercise of this power and the power of the court to review the Secretary of State's decision has been considered in a number of cases, including *Cumings v Birkenhead Corpn* [1972] Ch 12; *Herring v Templeman* [1973] 2 All ER 581, and *Secretary of State for Education and Science v Tameside Metropolitan Borough Council* [1977] AC 1014.

In *Cumings v Birkenhead Corpn* [1972] Ch 12 a parent applied to the court for a declaration that the LEA had acted in breach of their statutory duties and unlawfully. The LEA had sent a letter to parents of children about to apply for secondary school places which stated 'that children attending Roman Catholic primary schools would "normally" be expected to attend Roman Catholic secondary schools', and that 'In the long term, maintained county secondary comprehensive schools may only have sufficient accommodation for pupils from county and Church of England primary schools'(see chapter 3).

One of the issues before the Court of Appeal was whether the parent should have made a complaint to the Secretary of State rather than apply to the court for a declaration.

Cumings v Birkenhead Corpn [1972] Ch 12

Lord Denning MR: It is well settled that, when a public authority is given an administrative discretion, it must exercise its discretion fairly. It must be guided by relevant considerations and not by irrelevant considerations. Such is established by *Padfield v Minister of Agriculture, Fisheries and Food* [1968] AC 997; cf *Breen v Amalgamated Engineering Union* [1971] 2 WLR 742, 749.

Stopping there, however, I would have thought that, in case of a wrong exercise of their discretion, the only remedy is that given by statute. If the education authority fail to discharge a duty which is imposed upon them by the Act, a remedy is given by section 99 of the Act of 1944. If the education authority are acting or proposing to act unreasonably in regard to the execution of their duties, then again a remedy is given by section 68 of the Act. In either case the person aggrieved can apply to the Minister.

...

So here, if this education authority were to allocate boys to particular schools according to the colour of their hair or, for that matter, the colour of their skin, it would be so unreasonable, so capricious, so irrelevant to any proper system of education that it would be ultra vires altogether, and this court would strike it down at once. But, if there were valid educational reasons for a policy, as, for instance, in an area where immigrant children were backward in the English tongue and needed special teaching, then it would be perfectly right to allocate those in need to special schools where they would be given extra facilities for learning English. In short, if the policy is one which could reasonably be upheld for good educational reasons it is valid. But if it is so unreasonable that no reasonable authority could entertain it, it is invalid: see the judgment of Lord Green MR in *Associated Provincial Picture Houses Ltd v Wednesbury Corporation* [1948] 1 KB 223, 228–9. Applying those considerations in the present case, it is quite impossible to suggest that the education authority have gone outside their powers. They have laid down a policy and given good reasons for it. They have said:

> We have not enough room for all comers: so for the time being, those who come up from the Roman Catholic primary schools should go into the Roman Catholic secondary schools, where there is ample room: and not go into the non-Roman Catholic secondary schools where there is not enough room.

That is a sound administrative policy decision to which no objection can be taken, especially when it is realised that in exceptional cases the authority are ready to reconsider the position of any particular pupils.

In my opinion, there is no ground for saying that the education authority have acted beyond their powers. If they have done anything wrong at all—I do not suggest that they have—it is not a matter which comes within the jurisdiction of these courts. If complaint is to be made, it should be made to the Minister, and not to us.

- *Does a parent have a remedy under this section where the parent considers that there has been a wrongful exercise of discretion by the LEA or by the governing body?*

- *When should a parent (a) complain to the Secretary of State; and (b) apply for judicial review?*

One of the most politically contentious cases in education law arose out of the government's policy introduced in the 1970s that comprehensive schools should replace grammar and secondary modern schools. This policy had to be implemented by LEAs which were required to submit proposals to the Secretary of State. In March 1975 the then Labour-controlled LEA of Tameside submitted proposals which were approved by the Secretary of State. Comprehensive education was to be introduced in Tameside in September 1976. In May 1976 the Conservative party took control of the LEA after the local government elections, and the LEA decided to keep five grammar schools. The Secretary of State considered that the LEA was acting unreasonably and issued a formal direction under s 68 of the EA 1944 that the 1975 scheme should be implemented. The LEA refused to accept the direction and the Secretary of State applied to the court for an order of mandamus.

Secretary of State for Education and Science v Tameside Metropolitan Borough Council [1977] AC 1014

Lord Wilberforce: This section does not say what the consequences of the giving of directions are to be, but I accept, for the purposes of the appeal, that the consequences are to impose on the authority a statutory duty to comply with them which can be enforced by an order of mandamus.

Analysis of the section brings out three cardinal points.

(1) The matters with which the section is concerned are primarily matters of educational administration. The action which the Secretary of State is entitled to stop is unreasonable action with respect to the exercise of a power or the performance of a duty—the power and the duty of the authority are presupposed and cannot be interfered with. Local education authorities are entitled under the Act to have a policy, and this section does not enable the Secretary of State to require them to abandon or reverse a policy just because the Secretary of State disagrees with it. Specifically, the Secretary of State cannot use power under this section to impose a general policy of comprehensive education upon a local education authority which does not agree with the policy. He cannot direct them to bring in a scheme for total comprehensive education in their area, and if they have done so he cannot direct them to implement it. If he tries to use a direction under section 68 for this purpose, his direction would be clearly invalid. A direction under section 68 must be

justified on the ground of unreasonable action in doing what the Act the local authority is entitled to do, and under the Act it has a freedom of choice. I do not think that there is any controversy upon these propositions.

The critical question in this case, and it is not an easy one, is whether, on a matter which appears to be one of educational administration, namely whether the change of course proposed by the council in May 1976 would lead to educational chaos or undue disruption, the Secretary of State's judgment can be challenged.

(2) The section is framed in a 'subjective' form—if the Secretary of State is 'satisfied'. This form of section is quite well known, and at first sight might seem to exclude judicial review. Sections in this form may, no doubt, exclude judicial review on what is or has become a matter of pure judgment. But I do not think that they go further than that. If a judgment requires, before it can be made, the existence of some facts, then, although the evaluation of those facts is for the Secretary of State alone, the court must inquire whether those facts exist, and have been taken into account, whether the judgment has been made upon a proper self-direction as to those facts, whether the judgment has not been made upon other facts which ought not to have been taken into account. If these requirements are not met, then the exercise of judgment, however bona fide it may be, becomes capable of challenge: see *Secretary of State for Employment v ASLEF (No 2)* [1972] 2 QB 455, per Lord Denning MR, at p 493.

(3) The section has to be considered within the structure of the Act. In many statutes a minister or other authority is given a discretionary power and in these cases the court's power to review any exercise of the discretion, though still real, is limited. In these cases it is said that the courts cannot substitute their opinion for that of the minister: they can interfere on such grounds as that the minister has acted right outside his powers or outside the purpose of the Act, or unfairly, or upon an incorrect basis of fact. But there is no universal rule as to the principles on which the exercise of a discretion may be reviewed: each statute or type of statute must be individually looked at. This Act, of 1944, is quite different from those which simply create a ministerial discretion. The Secretary of State, under section 68, is not merely exercising a discretion: he is reviewing the action of another public body which itself has discretionary powers and duties. He, by contrast with the courts in the normal case, may substitute his opinion for that of the authority: this is what the section allows, but he must take account of what the authority, under the statute, is entitled to do. The authority—this is vital—is itself elected, and is given specific powers as to the kind of schools it wants in its area. Therefore two situations may arise. One is that there may be a difference of policy between the Secretary of State (under Parliament) and the local authority: the section gives no power to the Secretary of State to make his policy prevail. The other is that, owing to the democratic process involving periodic elections, abrupt reversals of policy may take place, particularly where there are only two parties and the winner takes all. Any reversal of policy if at all substantial must cause some administrative disruption—this was true of the 1975 proposals as of those of the respondents. So the mere possibility, or probability, of disruption cannot be a ground for issuing a direction to abandon the policy. What the Secretary of State is entitled, by a direction if necessary, to ensure is that such disruptions are not 'unreasonable', ie, greater than a body, elected to carry out a new programme, with which the Secretary of State may disagree, ought to impose upon those for whom it is responsible. After all, those who voted for the new programme, involving a change of course, must also be taken to have accepted some degree of disruption in implementing it.

The ultimate question in this case, in my opinion, is whether the Secretary of State has given sufficient, or any, weight to this particular factor in the exercise of his judgment.

• *May the Secretary of State substitute his or her opinion for that of the LEA? Was the Secretary of State permitted to do so in the Tameside case?*

The Secretary of State's power may also be exercised where, for example, the governing body of a teacher training college acted unreasonably. Where the governing body acts *ultra vires* or in breach of the rules of natural justice the complainant may also apply to the court for a remedy (see below *Herring v Templeman* [1973] 2 All ER 581).

'in default'

Education Act 1996, s 497

(1) If the Secretary of State is satisfied (either on a complaint by any person interested or otherwise) that a body to which this section applies have failed to discharge any duty imposed on them by or for the purposes of this Act, he may make an order—
(a)   declaring the body to be in default in respect of that duty, and
(b)   giving such directions for the purpose of enforcing the performance of the duty as appear to him to be expedient.

(2) The bodies to which this section applies are—
(a)   any local education authority, and
(b)   the governing body of any community, foundation or voluntary school or any community or foundation special school.

(3) Any directions given under subsection (1)(b) shall be enforceable, on an application made on behalf of the Secretary of State, by an order of mandamus.

Note that there are two stages in the process namely (a) declaring; and (b) directing. The Secretary of State does not have to issue directions having made a declaration.

• *Could the Secretary of State make a direction without also making a declaration?*

Generally the court will not be prepared to hear an application for judicial review unless a complaint has first been made to the Secretary of State. In *Meade v London Borough of Haringey* [1979] 2 All ER 1016, however, the Court of Appeal considered that where an LEA was in default as a consequence of a decision taken ultra vires or by an act of malfeasance, a parent need not first complain to the Secretary of State before making an application for judicial review.

In *Meade* (see chapter 3) parents challenged the decision of the LEA to close its schools as a consequence of a strike by school caretakers and other ancillary staff. The parents asked the Secretary of State to issue a formal direction on the ground that the LEA was in default of its statutory duty to make schools available for full-time education. The Secretary of State refused to direct the LEA because in her opinion the LEA was not in breach of its statutory duty. After the schools had been closed for four weeks the claimant, a parent, applied for a mandatory injunction.

Meade v London Borough of Haringey [1979] 2 All ER 1016

Denning LJ:

The law

The point of law which arises is this: if the local education authority have failed to perform their duty (to keep open the schools), have the parents any remedy in the courts of law? There is a remedy given by the statute itself. It is to complain to the Secretary of State under s 99 of the [EA] 1994. But that remedy has proved to be of no use to the parents. Can they now come to the courts? This depends on the true construction of the statute.
...

   Now although that section [s 99(1) of the EA 1944] does give a remedy, by complaint to a Minister, it does not exclude any other remedy. To my mind it leaves open all the established remedies which the law provides in cases where a public authority fails to perform its statutory duty either by the act of commission or omission. Thus when a local education authority were put by the statute under a duty to secure that school premises were up to prescribed standards, and they failed in that duty by letting them fall into disrepair, as a result of which a child was injured, it was held that there was a remedy by action in the courts for any person who was particularly damaged by the breach: see *Ching v Surrey County Council* and *Reffell v Surrey County Council*. Again, when a local education authority were under a duty to provide education free of charge and then they sought to exclude some children from that benefit, the parents were held entitled to sue for damages and, if need be, injunction: see *Gateshead Union v Durham County Council* [1918] 1 Ch 146 at 167, where Scrutton LJ said:

   A parent is a person specially injured by any unauthorised exclusion of his child from the free education to which he is entitled, and therefore a person entitled to sue for such a breach of statutory obligation.

Once again, where the local education authority were under a duty to 'maintain' existing schools, or conversely a duty not to 'cease to maintain' them, and they broke that duty in a fundamental respect, by changing the character of the school from a senior school to an infants' school, or from a boys' school into a girls' school, it was held that the parents of the children affected could come to the courts for an injunction so as to ensure that the duty was performed: see *Wilford v West Riding of Yorkshire County Council* and *Bradbury v London Borough of Enfield*.

   So reviewing all the cases afresh, they seem to me to bear out the principle which I stated in *Cumings v Birkenhead Corpn* [1971] 2 All ER 881 at 884 ... that the local education authority are liable when:

   they are acting beyond their powers, or, in Latin, ultra vires. If that were the case, then this court would interfere. The courts will always interfere if a Minister or [local authority] or any other body is acting beyond the powers conferred on it by law.

That view was accepted by Brightman J in *Herring v Templeman*. Conversely, when the local education authority is acting within its powers, there is no recourse to the courts: see *Watt v Kesteven County Council* [1955] 1 All ER 473 ...; *Smith v Inner London Education Authority*.

In *R v Inner London Education Authority, ex p Ali and Murshid* (1990) 2 Admin LR 822, ILEA failed to provide sufficient places for primary school children in the Tower Hamlets area of London. The applicants had complained to the Secretary of State who refused to issue a direction because the LEA was taking reasonable steps to remedy the situation. The applicants applied to the court on the ground that the LEA was in breach of its statutory duty. The preliminary question was whether the court had jurisdiction bearing in mind that the Secretary of State had decided that there were no grounds to issue a direction.

R v Inner London Education Authority, ex p Ali and Murshid (1990) 2 Admin LR 822

Woolf LJ:

The Jurisdiction Question

Subject to any binding authority, I would not accept that the language of the default powers contained in s 68 and s 99 of the [EA 1944] indicate that Parliament intended the jurisdiction of the courts to be ousted from considering the issues which can be considered by the Secretary of State under those sections. The general approach to the suggestion that the court's jurisdiction has been ousted was indicated by Lord Symonds in *Pyx Granite Co Ltd v Ministry of Housing and Local Government* [1960] AC 260, 286:

> It is a principle not by any means to be whittled down that the subject's recourse to Her Majesty's courts for the determination of his rights is not to be excluded except by clear words. That is ... a 'fundamental rule' from which I would not for my part sanction any departure.

The existence of the default powers in the [EA] 1944 ... are fully explained by the responsibilities which the Secretary of State has under s 1 and the fact that he can only fulfil those responsibilities if he is able to control the activities of a local education authority which do not accord with the Act. In other words, the purpose of the machinery which is contained in s 68 and s 99 is to enable the Secretary of State to give directions to the local education authority when his duties require him to take action against a local education authority. Until the power to give directions has been exercised by the Secretary of State, it would be difficult, if not impossible, in practice in most such situations for the court to intervene at the behest of the Secretary of State. The duties placed on the local education authority are so broad as not to be readily susceptible to enforcement by an injunction or by an order of mandamus unless they can be linked to directions.

...

In this case, therefore, the fact that the applicant appropriately made an application to the Secretary of State under s 99 does not deprive the court of jurisdiction but, on the contrary, its relevance is confined to the question of discretion, to which I must now finally turn.

The Discretion Question

...

However, I am satisfied in this case that there would be no prospect of the court granting any relief. I say that because, first of all, the respondent education authority will cease to exist in approximately three to four weeks, so any relief could only be of very limited effect.

In addition, this is a case where what is complained of is inactivity on behalf of the education authority. In such circumstances, on an application for judicial review as in ordinary civil proceedings, the court is in difficulty in providing mandatory relief on the ordinary case, as I have explained. Merely to order a public body to perform its statutory duty does not add anything to that duty. Furthermore, in this case it is clear that a declaration would not assist. To declare that the public body should perform its duty does not add to or clarify the public body's obligations where, as here, that body accepts obligations. At this stage it is possible to say that there are not in this case any specific steps which will be able to be identified which it can be said that the public body is not taking which it should take. The only purpose of continuing the proceedings would be to ascertain whether or not the authority was culpable in reaching the present unsatisfactory situation. Inquests of that sort are not the purpose of judicial review.

In coming to this conclusion, I derive support from the decision of the Secretary of State not to intervene. He is usually in a better position than the courts to assess whether intervention would be constructive and, while not bound in any way by his decision, the courts will have regard to his decision in deciding how to exercise their discretion.

Note that under s 496 of the EA 1996 the Secretary of State can review the exercise of powers as well as duties whereas under s 497 of the EA 1996 the Secretary of State may only review the exercise of duties.

Lord Justice Woolf described the duty on the LEA as a 'target duty' as opposed to an 'absolute duty'. This term was illuminated by Sedley J in *R v Islington London Borough Council, ex p Rixon* [1997] ELR 66, although the case was concerned with different statutory provisions.

R v Islington London Borough Council, ex p Rixon **[1997] ELR 66**

Sedley J:

The law

Some of the relevant legislation contains what are known as 'target duties'. This is a phrase coined by Woolf LJ in *R v Inner London Education Authority, ex p Ali* [1990] 2 Admin LR 822 at 828, in relation to the duty created by s 8 of the Education Act 1944 for every local education authority to secure that there are in their area schools sufficient in number, character and equipment to afford education to pupils of all ages, abilities and aptitudes. The metaphor recognises that the statute requires the relevant public authority to aim to make the prescribed provision but does not regard failure to achieve it without more as a breach.

...

One of the features of a target duty is that it is ordinarily accompanied by default powers vested in the Secretary of State, to which in general the courts defer save where a true question of law arises ...

• *What is the difference between a target duty, a duty and a power?*

In *R v Brent London Borough Council, ex p F* [1999] ELR 32 Tucker J summarised the authorities on when the court should decline jurisdiction where the Education Act 1996, s 497 procedure was available.

R v Brent London Borough Council, ex p F [1999] ELR 32

Tucker J: It is impossible, it seems to me, for a court to make an intelligent evaluation of these matters or to conduct a balancing exercise between the interests of F and other interested parents on the one hand, and the difficulties confronting the local education authority on the other. I entirely agree with Mr Hyams for the respondent that the issues are really educational ones. The best person to resolve them is the Secretary of State himself. Fortunately, as I would expect, there is provision in the Act which enables him to do so and which, in my opinion, affords the best solution to the problem presented by this case.

...

I am fortified by the judgments and observations of other judges in this respect. It is also, to my mind, highly relevant that the Secretary of State himself does not oppose the local education authority's proposals, but indeed supports them. The judgments to which I refer, are as follows: first the judgment of Woolf J, as he then was, in *R v Secretary of State for Education and Science, ex p Chance* (1982) 26 July. That case is unreported but the judgment is referred to by Brooke J, as he then was, in *R v Secretary of State, ex p Prior* [1994] ELR 231, the passage in the judgment of Woolf J being cited at pp 246–7. Here the judge is referring to a previous Act:

> Sections 99 [now s 497 of the EA 1996] and 68 [now s 496 of the EA 1996] are designed to give a person in the position of Mrs Chance a remedy through the office of the Secretary of State. If the Secretary of State exercises his functions properly under those sections, as I am sure he normally does, then that should have the beneficial effect of avoiding the courts getting involved in education matters, which they are much less well equipped to deal with than the Secretary of State.

I respectfully and entirely agree with those observations. These are not matters with which the court can or should grapple.

The second judgment is also that of Woolf LJ, which by this time he had become, in the case of *R v Inner London Education Authority, ex p Ali and Another* [1990] 2 Admin LR 822. The passage in the judgment to which I have been referred is at p 837. The learned Lord Justice says this:

> ...I derive support from the decision of the Secretary of State not to intervene. He is usually in a better position than the courts to assess whether intervention would be constructive, and while not bound in any way by his decision, the courts will have regard to his decision in deciding how to exercise their discretion.

That goes to the other aspect of the matter to which I have referred.

The final judgment in this context on which I rely is that of Harrison J in the case of *R v Secretary of State for Education and Employment and the Governors of Southlands Community Comprehensive School, ex p W* [1998] ELR 413. The passage I refer to is at pp 422–3 where the judge says:

> I am not bound by the Secretary of State's decision even though it was a lawful one. It is nevertheless a highly relevant consideration as to whether I should grant relief as a matter of discretion.

'failed to perform certain functions'

The School Standards and Framework Act 1998 gave the Secretary of State a new power to issue directions to secure the proper performance of the LEA's functions.

The reason for this new power is explained in the White Paper *Excellence in Schools* (Cm 3681, July 1997).

White Paper *Excellence in Schools* (Cm 3681, July 1997)

42 The DfEE, finally, has a role as guarantor of last resort: to deal with the failing schools where LEAs have not dealt with them satisfactorily, and to deal with failing LEAs. The SEU [Standards and Effectiveness Unit] will take the Departmental lead in this work. The fresh start for failing schools that are not recovering was described in paragraphs 29–30. Where it appears that an LEA is failing, the Secretary of State may direct OFSTED to undertake an immediate inspection. If that inspection confirms the failings, it may be necessary for the Secretary of State to intervene, either by directing LEA officers or by enabling others to perform some functions until the LEA has demonstrated its capacity to resume its full responsibilities. The principle of zero tolerance will be adhered to unflinchingly. The government is determined that children should get the good education they deserve.

Education Act 1996, s 497A

(1) This section applies to a local education authority's functions (of whatever nature) which relate to the provision of education—
(a)   for persons of compulsory school age (whether at school or otherwise), or
(b)   for persons of any age above or below that age who are registered as pupils at schools maintained by the authority.

(2) If the Secretary of State is satisfied (either on a complaint by any person interested or otherwise) that a local education authority are failing in any respect to perform any function to which this section applies to an adequate standard (or at all), he may exercise his powers under subsection (3) or (4).

(3) The Secretary of State may under this subsection direct an officer of the authority to secure that that function is performed in such a way as to achieve such objectives as are specified in the direction.

(4) The Secretary of State may under this subsection give an officer of the authority such directions as the Secretary of State thinks expedient for the purpose of securing that the function—
(a)   is performed, on behalf of the authority and at their expense, by such person as is specified in the direction, and
(b)   is so performed in such a way as to achieve such objectives as are so specified;

and such directions may require that any contract or other arrangement made by the authority with that person contains such terms and conditions as may be so specified.

...

(7) Any direction given under subsection (3) or (4) shall be enforceable, on an application made on behalf of the Secretary of State, by an order of mandamus.

This section gives the Secretary of State a wide-ranging power in relation to those functions exercised by the LEA in relation to pupils registered at a school maintained by the LEA (see chapter 1). The possible contents of any direction are spelt out more explicitly in this provision than in ss 496 and 497 of the EA 1996. The Secretary of State has the power to issue a direction, which may specify the way in which and by whom the functions are to be undertaken in order to achieve the objectives specified by the Secretary of State. Where a person is authorised by the Secretary of State to perform some of the LEA's functions they are also given certain powers to assist them do so (s 497B of the EA 1996). These include

- a right of entry to the premises of the authority
- a right to inspect, and take copies of, any records or other documents kept by the authority
- a right to have access to, and inspect and check the operation of, any computer and any associated apparatus or material which is or has been in use in connection with the records or other documents in question.

The LEA and the governing body are required to give such a person reasonable assistance.

Local Government Ombudsmen

The formal title of the Ombudsman is Commissioner for Local Administration. There are three Local Government Ombudsmen for England covering respectively: Greater London; central and southern England including East Anglia; and the West Midlands and the north of England. They are authorised to investigate complaints of maladministration, to consider whether the maladministration caused injustice, and to recommend a remedy.

As the extracts from their reports demonstrate, the Local Government Ombudsmen (LGO) provide an invaluable means of redress for parents. The LGO are familiar with local government bureaucracy, they carry out the investigation at no cost to parents, are able to recommend improvements to existing procedures, and may be able to obtain compensation for the parents. However, they are only able to carry out a limited number of investigations each year.

Jurisdiction

Their jurisdiction derives from the Local Government Act 1974.

Local Government Act 1974, s 26(1)

Subject to the provisions of this Part of this Act where a written complaint is made by or on behalf of a member of the public who claims to have sustained injustice in consequence of maladministration in connection with action taken by or on behalf of an authority to which this Part of this Act applies, being action taken in the exercise of administrative functions of that authority, a Local Commissioner may investigate that complaint.

'Maladministration' is not defined in the legislation, but 29 types of maladministration are listed in the Local Government Ombudsman Annual Report 1999/2000 (Appendix 3(d)). These include:

- Unreasonable delay in taking action
- Failure to provide adequate information, explanation or advice
- Making misleading or inaccurate statements
- Failure to comply with legal requirements
- Failure to take relevant considerations into account in making a decision
- Failure to follow relevant codes of practice without justifiable reasons not to do so
- Failure to inform customers of their rights of appeal against adverse decisions
- Failure to ensure impartial operation of an appeal body
- Unfair discrimination
- Failure to give reasons for an adverse decision.

In the educational context the Local Government Ombudsman (LGO) may investigate complaints against:

- LEAs
- governing bodies (admission matters only)
- admission and exclusion appeal panels
- school organisation committees (Local Government Act 1974, s 25).

The Ombudsmen have recommended that their jurisdiction should be extended to include any complaint against the governing body of a publicly funded school. Were this recommendation to be implemented it would remove the need to implement s 39 of the SSFA 1998 (see 'The governing body' above).

Local Government Ombudsman Annual Report 1999/2000, Appendix 4, at 45

5 Jurisdiction

5.1 The School Standards and Framework Act 1998 brought within the Ombudsmen's jurisdiction from 1 April 1999 the actions of all admission authorities in respect of their admission functions (but not exclusions). The Commission can see no sufficient reason why the other actions of governors of all publicly funded schools should not be brought within the Ombudsmen's jurisdiction.

5.2 Paragraph 5(2) of Sch 5 of the Education Act 1974 excludes from the Ombudsmen's jurisdiction 'any action concerning' internal matters in schools such as the giving of instruction. The Commission proposes that the words 'any action concerning' should be deleted, because they might leave the Ombudsmen open to challenge in the investigation of certain complaints. For example, when investigating a complaint the Ombudsmen may need to consider whether the actual provision being made by a school complies with a child's statement of special educational needs. This might be argued to be about action concerning the giving of instruction. Similarly, the investigation by the Ombudsmen of exclusion appeals (by education appeal panels which are within jurisdiction) might be argued to be action concerning discipline in a school. It is important to remove any scope for argument about this.

The Local Government Act 1974, s 26(6) and Sch 5 sets out matters that the LGO may not investigate.

Local Government Act 1974, s 26(6)

A Local Commissioner shall not conduct an investigation under this Part of this Act in respect of any of the following matters, that is to say—

(a) any action in respect of which the person aggrieved has or had a right of appeal, reference or review to or before a tribunal constituted by or under any enactment;

(b) any action in respect of which the person aggrieved has or had a right of appeal to a Minister of the Crown [or the National Assembly for Wales]; or

(c) any action in respect of which the person aggrieved has or had a remedy by way of proceedings in any court of law:

Provided that a Local Commissioner may conduct an investigation notwithstanding the existence of such a right or remedy if satisfied that in the particular circumstances it is not reasonable to expect the person aggrieved to resort or have resorted to it.

In *R v Comr for Local Administration, ex p Croydon London Borough Council* [1989] 1 All ER 1033 the court considered the approach which should be adopted by the LGO when deciding whether or not they had jurisdiction to investigate a complaint. The local authority challenged the decision of the Ombudsman to investigate a complaint by parents into the way an education appeal committee dealt with their admission appeal, arguing that any challenge should be by way of judicial review (see chapter 3).

R v Comr for Local Administration, ex p Croydon London Borough Council [1989] 1 All ER 1033

Woolf LJ: In my view, when s 26(6) is looked at as a whole it is reasonably clear that what is being dealt with is a situation where if the complaint was justified the person concerned might be entitled to obtain some form of remedy in respect of the subject matter of the complaint if he had commenced proceedings within the appropriate time limits. The commissioner is not concerned to consider whether in fact the proceedings would succeed. He merely has to be satisfied that the court of law is an appropriate forum for investigating the subject matter of the complaint.

The other important feature to observe with regard to s 26(6) is that it is not clear from its language whether it is only a threshold requirement or whether it applies at any stage of an investigation. Counsel for the commissioner submits that it only applies at the stage when the commissioner is deciding whether or not to conduct an investigation and once he has embarked on an investigation it has no application. On balance I agree that s 26(6) is directed to the threshold requirement. However, I do not regard this as being significant, because the commissioner has a continuing discretion not to continue, and to discontinue an investigation. Therefore, even if s 26(6) does not expressly deal with the subsequent stages after the commencement of an investigation, in exercising his discretion under s 26(10) whether to discontinue an investigation the commissioner should approach the matter very much in the same way as he would if s 26(6) did apply. If it becomes apparent during the course of an investigation that the issues being investigated are appropriate to be resolved in a court of law, then giving effect to the general intent of s 26, the commissioner is required to consider whether, notwithstanding this, it is appropriate to continue with the investigation broadly on the lines indicated in the proviso to s 26(6). When performing this exercise the extent to which the investigation has proceeded is a relevant consideration for the commissioner to take into account in deciding whether or not to discontinue the investigation.

Section 26(6) makes it clear that where there is a remedy in the sense which I have indicated, inter alia, in a court of law, the courts do not have the sole jurisdiction and the commissioner may still intervene. On the other hand the general tenor of s 26(6) is that, if there is a tribunal (whether it be an appeal tribunal, a minister of the Crown or a court of law) which is specifically designed to deal with the issue, that is the body to whom the complainant should normally resort.

I suggest this approach is particularly important in the case of issues which are capable of being resolved on judicial review. Parliament, by s 31(6) of the Supreme Court Act 1981 and by the Rules of the Supreme Court, made it clear that in respect of applications for judicial review there should be protection for public bodies and if, as in this case, the commissioner is going to recommend the very same relief as could be provided on judicial review he should take into account before doing so the fact that his jurisdiction is not subject to the same safeguards.

The commissioner should also have well in mind, even when the holder of the office is a distinguished lawyer as is the case here, that his expertise is not the same as that of a court of law. Issues whether an administrative tribunal has properly understood the relevant law and the legal obligations which it is under when conducting an inquiry are more appropriate for resolution by the High Court than by a commissioner, however eminent.

On the facts of this case, having regard to his evidence, I am not prepared to find that the commissioner should have appreciated at the outset that the investigation was one in relation to which the complainant had a remedy by way of judicial review. However, in the course of the investigation it should have been appreciated that the complainant had had such a remedy, particularly bearing in mind the nature of the conclusions to which the commissioner came.

In *R v Comr for Local Administration, ex p H* [1999] ELR 314 the applicant challenged the ombudsman's refusal to investigate the applicant's complaint on the ground that the applicant had a legal remedy. The challenge was unsuccessful and the Court of Appeal refused leave to appeal. Unfortunately, the facts are not clear from the report. It is possible that the applicant sought compensation from the Ombudsman because the applicant would have difficulty, either legally or financially, in bringing a successful claim for damages for negligence or breach of statutory duty.

R v Comr for Local Administration, ex p H [1999] ELR 314

Simon Brown LJ: The position in a nutshell is that the Staffordshire County Council failed to provide the applicant with the education that he should have had from September 1994 to January 1997. That the education authority were guilty of maladministration in that regard may be assumed, although it was not formally established in the judicial review proceedings brought by the applicant in September 1996, proceedings which were made the subject of a consent order in the applicant's favour on 16 December 1996.

It is the applicant's case, however, that whereas judicial review can enforce present and future rights (as undoubtedly this particular judicial review challenge did), it cannot remedy past errors and, more particularly, it could not compensate the applicant in damages for his past loss of education. That it is which the applicant now seeks to achieve by his complaint to the Ombudsman. If the Ombudsman were to report that injustice had been caused to the applicant as a person aggrieved and recommended compensation, then the local authority could make such compensatory payment under s 31(3) of the Local Government Act 1974.

...

I do not accept that the judicial review proceedings go to a different grievance from the complaint sought to be investigated. In my judgment, they both relate to one and the same grievance, namely maladministration by the education authority in denying the applicant the education to which he was, let it be supposed, entitled. It was a continuing grievance and judicial review was necessary to end it. The present question is whether the applicant may seek from the Ombudsman compensation for it. That by virtue of s 26(6)(c) ordinarily he cannot do if judicial review is properly to be regarded as a remedy. I have no doubt that within the true construction of the legislation judicial review is indeed 'a remedy by way of proceedings'. It is a remedy in the sense that it enables the person aggrieved to ventilate in a court of law the matter of which he complains and to have his complaint determined and the maladministration, if such it was, ended.

At the heart of the legislation is Parliament's evident wish that the Ombudsman should investigate complaints of maladministration only if no more suitable means of investigation, for example by way of court proceedings, exist. The possibility of compensation is merely ancillary to that. To my mind it would turn the legislation on its head to suggest that wherever maladministration is established in judicial review proceedings, or indeed otherwise, then compensation should flow by way of a subsequent complaint to the Ombudsman.

This judgment indicates that complainants would be advised to complain to the Ombudsman rather than apply for judicial review whenever they have suffered injustice as a consequence of maladministration.

- *Do you agree with Simon Brown LJ's reasoning?*

- *Are all forms of maladministration judicially reviewable?*

- *Are all decisions which have been judicially reviewed examples of maladministration?*

Schedule 5 to the Local Government Act 1974 sets out specific educational matters which are outside the jurisdiction of the Ombudsmen.

Local Government Act 1974, Sch 5, para 5

Matters not subject to investigation

...

(2) Any action concerning—
(a)   the giving of instruction, whether secular or religious, or
(b)   conduct, curriculum, internal organisation, management or discipline, whether—
      (i) in any school maintained by the authority, or
      (ii) in any college of education or establishment of further education maintained by the authority.

Note that the LGO is excluded from investigating any action concerning discipline, but is permitted to investigate independent exclusion appeal panels.

Education complaints

In 2000/01 education complaints accounted for 7.8 per cent of the 19,179 complaints received (Annual Report 2000/01). The complaints relate to the following matters.

Local Government Ombudsman Annual Report 2000/2001, Appendix 3(a)

Subject of complaints received 2000/01

	Mr Osmotherly	Mr White	Mrs Thomas	Totals
Education:				
Special educational needs	42	87	73	**202**
Admissions	177	321	410	**908**
Exclusions	8	20	17	**45**
Education grants	10	23	20	**53**
Education transport	6	45	25	**76**
Other	77	58	73	**208**
Total education	**320**	**554**	**618**	**1,492**

Not all the complaints will be investigated. Some will be outside the Ombudsman's jurisdiction, and in others a local settlement will be reached. In 2000/01 a local settlement was reached in 244 out of 1,253 education complaints which were accepted as not being premature or outside the Ombudsmen's jurisdiction. As can be seen a relatively small proportion of education complaints are investigated: a total of 48 in 2000/01.

Local Government Ombudsman Annual Report 2000/2001, Appendix 3(c)

Subject of investigation reports 2000/01

	Mr Osmotherly	Mr White	Mrs Thomas	Totals
Education:				
Special educational needs	2	2	9	**13**
Admissions	4	2	21	**27**
Exclusions	-	1	1	**2**
Education grants	-	1	-	**1**
Education transport	1	-	4	**5**
Total education	**7**	**6**	**35**	**48**

Admissions, special educational needs, and exclusions give rise to the majority of education investigations. The following extracts from investigation reports illustrate the types of issues that give rise to a complaint together with the remedies provided. Note that in the first case the parents also complained to the Secretary of State. The last extract is particularly interesting as it deals with bullying and school transport (see also chapter 4).

SCHOOL ADMISSIONS

The first two extracts relate to complaints against voluntary aided schools. The governing body is the admissions authority for these schools and for foundation schools (see chapter 3), and there appear to be a disproportionate number of complaints against governing body admission authorities. As they are composed mainly of volunteers they are perhaps less familiar with the procedures to be followed than LEAs.

Report on an Investigation into Complaint No 99/A/01723 against the Governing Body of Finchley Catholic High School, 30 January 2001

'Mr and Mrs Fox' (not their real names) complained that the Appeal Committee of Finchley Catholic High School (FCHS) did not properly consider their appeal against the Governing Body's decision not to offer their son, 'Joseph', a place at FCHS from September 1999.

The published admission criteria for FCHS said that the Governors would give priority to parents who made FCHS their first choice but that: 'Boys applying from areas outside the Borough of Barnet would not be penalised for applying to other schools'.

Mr and Mrs Fox live outside Barnet. They applied for a place at FCHS. They also applied for a place at two schools in Enfield (neither offered Joseph a place). Joseph also sat the entrance exam for a selective school in Hertfordshire.

The Governors of FCHS did not offer Joseph a place: he was not regarded as a first choice applicant because he had taken the exam for the selective school. Mr and Mrs Fox appealed against the decision. FCHS, acting on behalf of the Governors, sent the Appeal Committee a version of the admission criteria which omitted the sentence which said that boys applying for FCHS from outside Barnet would not be penalised for applying to other schools. So the Appeal Committee was not aware of the provision. But Mr and Mrs Fox referred to it at the appeal hearing; and the Appeal Committee had a copy of a letter from the London Borough of Barnet which said that, under the published admission criteria, account should not have been taken of the application to the selective school. The Appeal Committee did not seek clarification of what Mr and Mrs Fox and Barnet Council had said about the admission criteria. The Appeal Committee rejected the appeal.

Mr and Mrs Fox then obtained a place for Joseph at a private Roman Catholic secondary school in Hertfordshire. He was admitted to it in September 1999. At that time, the fees were £1,900 a term, including the cost of transport between the school and North London. Mr and Mrs Fox also complained to the Secretary of State for Education and Employment about the Governing Body's decision. The Secretary of State was not satisfied that the Governing Body had applied the admission criteria correctly and considered that, if it had done so, Joseph would have had priority for admission. In February 2000, the Secretary of State directed FCHS to admit Joseph. But Mr and Mrs Fox did not take up the place.

The Ombudsman found that there was the following maladministration:

(a) the School, acting on the Governors' behalf, did not send the Appeal Committee the full published admission criteria;

(b) the Appeal Committee invited the head teacher to present, in the absence of the appellants, the detailed case that further admissions would prejudice the provision of efficient education or the efficient use of resources;

(c) the Appeal Committee did not seek clarification of what Barnet Council and Mr and Mrs Fox had said about the admission criteria;

(d) the Appeal Committee did not ensure that records were kept of the reasons for its decisions;

(e) the decision letter sent to Mr and Mrs Fox did not contain an adequate explanation of the decision on their appeal.

The Ombudsman found that the maladministration mentioned in (a) and (c) above caused injustice. He says that, but for that maladministration, Joseph would probably have had a place at FCHS from September 1999; and Mr and Mrs Fox would have been spared the time, trouble and anxiety they were caused. He understood why Joseph's parents decided not to take up the place at FCHS in February 2000 but says this was not a necessary consequence of the maladministration. He recommended the Governing Body to pay Mr and Mrs Fox £2,250.

Report on an Investigation into Complaint No 00/B/03593 against St Clement Danes School, 24 May 2001

Report Summary

EDUCATION ADMISSIONS

Mr A complains that the school did not provide grounds for refusing his son Brian a place under one of the admissions criteria and that this affected the way in which he prepared for the appeal. The Ombudsman found this failure to be maladministration.

During the investigation it became clear that there were inaccuracies in the way in which the school had measured distances from home to school which led to the admission of two pupils under this criterion who lived further away than Brian. The Ombudsman found this error also to be maladministration.

FINDING

Maladministration causing injustice.

RECOMMENDED REMEDY

The school should:

•   offer a place to the complainant's son

•   review its admission procedures

•   pay the complainant £250 to compensate him for his time and trouble in bringing this complaint.

The following extract deals with a complaint against an independent appeal panel set up by an LEA.

Report on an Investigation into Complaint No 99/B/4658 against Northamptonshire County Council, 24 July 2000

Introduction

1. Mr and Mrs Adelaide complain that there was a failing by a school admission appeal panel in that it upheld an appeal for their daughter, Kathy, to attend Broken Hill School, but made that decision conditional upon Mr and Mrs Adelaide providing evidence that they had exchanged contracts for a home in the school's catchment area.

...

28. I am in no doubt that the appeal panel attached a condition to its decision. Does it have the power to do so? In my view, the Code of Practice is clear that panels should seek corroborative evidence where necessary and make their decisions on the strength of it. There is no provision to make a decision conditional on the provision of evidence the panel does not see. The Council has been unable to provide any evidence to support the view that an appeal panel can do so, and the DfEE says panels do not have such a power. I conclude that the appeal panel exceeded its powers in attaching a condition to its decision. That was maladministration. It caused injustice to the complainants who feel that the panel's decision is fatally flawed; and they have been put to considerable time and trouble in trying to persuade the Council they were right.

29. How should that injustice be remedied? I agree with the Council that the appeal panel's decision should be treated as void. I welcome its suggestion that the appeal should be reheard by a new panel. In addition, I believe the Council should recognise their time and trouble in pursuing this matter.

30. Finally, this complaint has raised an issue of some public interest in exposing that it is clearly wrong for appeal panels to attach conditions to their decisions. That is a lesson that is important for this Council, and possibly others, to learn.

FINDING

31. For the reasons in paragraph 28, I find maladministration by the Council causing injustice. To remedy the injustice I recommend that the Council:
(a)   makes a payment of £250 to the complainants;
(b)   convenes a new appeal hearing with a different panel; and
(c)   ensures the maladministration I have identified does not recur.

- *Bearing in mind the judgment of Woolf LJ in R v Comr for Local Administration, ex p Croydon London Borough Council [1989] 1 All ER 1033 (see above), when should a complaint about an admission appeal panel should be investigated by the Ombudsman rather than be challenged by way of judicial review?*

SCHOOL EXCLUSIONS

As indicated above the Ombudsmen have jurisdiction over the independent appeal panels, but not over the procedures followed by the head teacher or the discipline committee of the governing body (see chapter 4).

The first extract relates to a complaint by a pupil's mother that the independent appeal committee failed to consider properly an appeal against her son's permanent exclusion from his secondary school. In particular, the remedy in paragraph 85 and the Ombudsman's comments on training in paragraph 86 are worth noting.

Report on an Investigation into Complaint No 99/C/2819 against the Appeal Committee of St Christopher's Church of England High School, 31 May 2000

CONCLUSION

77. The original date given for the appeal had to be changed because a member of the committee forgot about it. The second date was marginally outside the normal time guidelines. Mrs Lee had prepared for the appeal on one day only to find out when she arrived that it had been cancelled. Such appeals are difficult for all the parties involved and although it was reconvened quickly there will be added stress caused to Robert and his family which I see as injustice resulting from maladministration.

78. There is no dispute over the grounds on which Robert was excluded. Up until the meeting on 11 March it was clear that the school was willing to allow Robert to return. The job of the Appeal Committee was therefore to examine whether exclusion was a reasonable response to a single incident of name calling and the repeating of allegations against a member of staff after the school had concluded that they were unfounded.

79. Two of the members of the Appeal Committee consider that Robert's actions on 11 March were sufficiently serious to warrant the exclusion. The third member, who had more experience of exclusion appeals, regards this view as unreasonable and inconsistent with other exclusion decisions in which he has been involved.

80. Robert was clearly distressed by the separation of his parents and following a series of incidents at school which upset Robert, his previous excellent record changed to one of poor attendance and lateness. Only six weeks after the first incident the head teacher excluded him permanently. At least part of the head teacher's decision appears to have rested on the actions of Mrs Lee rather than her son.

81. I note in particular that at the meeting at which Robert was excluded, the only reference given to a possible sanction for his behaviour was to a suspension if he refused to apologise. Robert apologised. Robert was never given any indication at this meeting that his conduct may result in a permanent exclusion. It is also to be noted that Robert repeated the allegations against the teacher only when asked to do so to provide an explanation for why he did not wish to return to school.

82. Government guidance is clear that exclusion should be used only as the ultimate sanction for serious misbehaviour. I do not accept that the Committee had sufficient regard to this advice in reaching the view that Robert's actions constituted sufficiently serious misbehaviour to warrant exclusion. I consider therefore that the decision to uphold the exclusion was affected by maladministration. In my opinion the conduct was not sufficiently serious to justify exclusion when there was no previous history of misbehaviour and no attempt had been made to try alternative ways of dealing with the situation such as a suspension for a fixed period. I do not accept that any Appeal Committee could reasonably conclude that exclusion was appropriate in these circumstances.

83. I have however seen no evidence to support Mrs Lee's allegation that the head teacher's reference to his position as a JP or the teacher's vulnerable position were matters which were considered by the Committee. I also do not consider his reference to Robert's record to have been unduly prejudicial and I am satisfied that Mrs Lee was aware in advance that this information would be raised by the school. I do not therefore uphold these aspects of the complaint.

84. I also do not uphold the complaint that the Committee failed to let Mrs Lee fully present her case or to challenge other evidence heard. The hearing was extremely long and, from the notes I have seen, repetitive. The Committee should be commended for the time they allowed to all the parties to air their cases. The Committee was fully aware of all the incidents and I do not agree that examination of the magnet would have added anything to their understanding.

85. I consider it would be a waste of everyone's time to rehear the appeal when Mrs Lee has no intention of returning Robert to the school. To remedy the injustice caused by the Committee's decision it should ensure that all school records held on Robert include a copy of this report and its conclusions.

86. The school should also look at training provision for its Appeal Committee members to ensure that they are fully aware of guidance relating to exclusions.

The following extract is concerned with the permanent exclusion of a pupil from a grant maintained school. It is worth noting that the Ombudsman recommended that the governing body should pay compensation to the parents, although strictly speaking the Ombudsman has no jurisdiction in relation to the governing body. Grant-maintained status has been abolished, but governing bodies of foundation and voluntary aided schools are in a similar position.

Report on an Investigation into Complaint No 99/B/00959 against the Appeal Committee of Chalfonts Community College, 6 September 2000

Report Summary

SUBJECT

An Appeal Committee was convened to consider a parents' appeal against permanent exclusion of their son, for allegedly being in possession of illegal drugs. It relied too heavily on hearsay evidence and incorrect information given by the school which it failed to check, allowed its discretion to be fettered by an unequivocal school policy on drugs, and failed to communicate its decision and the reasons for it within the proper time scale. It also failed to take the opportunity to put right these errors, by relying on further information from the school which could not be substantiated and by continuing to fetter its discretion when it was made aware of the correct facts.

FINDING

Maladministration causing injustice.

The School Governing Body should pay the complainants the sum of £750 in recognition of the injustice suffered by them and their son.

SPECIAL EDUCATIONAL NEEDS

Parents of pupils with SEN frequently face considerable delays when trying to ensure that the LEA follows the correct procedures. Even when their child has a statement parents have no way of ensuring that the LEA provides the support specified in the statement (see chapter 5). In 2000/2001 the number of reports on SEN complaints appears to have increased as a proportion of the total number of education reports.

The following extracts illustrate some of the problems faced by parents and LEAs including lack of resources, delay in the statutory assessment process, delay in issuing a statement of special educational needs, delay in providing speech therapy, and failure to implement a decision of the Special Educational Needs Tribunal.

LEA's lack of resources

Report on an Investigation into Complaint No 99/C/1864 against Manchester City Council, 31 May 2000

Report Summary

EDUCATION—SPECIAL EDUCATIONAL NEEDS

The complainant alleged that the Council refused to assess his daughter's special educational needs in 1995 and that he was not advised that he could request an assessment. He said that throughout his daughter's school career the Council had refused to recognise Melanie's special needs or to provide for those needs until forced to do so.

The Ombudsman found that the Council had refused to assess his daughter's special needs in 1995, 1996 and 1998 when requested by her schools to do so. The Council gave as its reasons a lack of resources when it was unlawful to take resources into account when making an assessment of special educational need. She found that the Council had not informed the complainant of his right to request an assessment and his daughter had been assessed in 1998 only after the complainant had taken legal advice. The Ombudsman found that the council did not routinely provide such information for parents until the Council had itself decided that a statutory assessment was necessary.

A senior educational psychologist had stated that the Council did not employ enough educational psychologists to enable the Council to fulfil its statutory responsibilities. The Council denied this, despite its refusal to assess the complainant's daughter on three occasions during the period 1995–1998 on the ground that it had insufficient resources, and has now recruited three more educational psychologists.

The Ombudsman's investigation revealed that, according to officers, the Council had operated a blanket policy that all children assessed as having moderate learning difficulties were sent to special school. The Council denied this. The Ombudsman pointed out that operating such a blanket policy would be fettering its discretion, which would be unlawful. The complainant's daughter's statement initially named a special school but was revised, following the lodging of an appeal, to name the school she was attending.

The Ombudsman was concerned that the Council had decided not to assess the complainant's daughter in 1998 because it said it had not received evidence from the school when the school said it had sent in the evidence before the statutory six-week deadline. She questioned why the Council had not contacted the school to check where its evidence was before making a decision not to assess on the basis of the evidence it had.

The Ombudsman accepted that the school had provided additional help for the complainant's daughter and that she had received an inclusive education in a very good school. However, the Ombudsman considered that, had the child been assessed in 1995, her needs would have been met differently and that her attainment and confidence would have been enhanced.

The Ombudsman accepted that the Council had set up a Parent Partnership Service and an SEN caseworker service, and had provided more resources for special educational needs. However, she recommended that:

(1) the Council should produce guidance for schools, supported by centrally produced materials for early and regular dissemination to parents, on the rights and responsibilities of parents as partners in the special education system;

(2) the Council should ensure that it either employed sufficient educational psychologists to meet its legal responsibilities or that it should 'buy in' resources from elsewhere to meet any shortfall;

(3) the Council should ensure that it took all relevant circumstances into account, disregarded irrelevant issues, and did not fetter its discretion, when considering what provision would be most appropriate for children with moderate learning disabilities.

The Council accepted the Ombudsman's findings and agreed to take the actions listed above. It agreed in addition to pay £1,500 to the complainant, being the difference between the level of special help required by the complainant's daughter and the help that she had received. The Ombudsman commended the Council for its positive response to her report.

FINDING

LOCAL SETTLEMENT.

Delay in assessment process

Report on an Investigation into Complaint Nos 99/B/04029 and 00/B/17234 against South Gloucestershire Council and the former Avon County Council, 15 March 2001

Report Summary

SUBJECT

The complainants alleged unreasonable delay by the former Avon County Council and the South Gloucestershire Council in assessing the special educational needs of their son,

Martin, and a lack of Council help in dealing with school staff who, they believed, had not supported their family or resolved problems of bullying. The investigation concerned Martin's time at secondary school.

...

43. Oak Tree Primary School notified the former Council and Festival School in 1995 that Martin was at Stage 3 of the special educational needs register. On transfer to Festival School, Martin had been receiving support from the former Council's educational psychology service for some seven years. Despite this, there is no evidence that the Council educational psychologist monitored his progress in his first year at Festival School. Given the long history of involvement in Martin's education, I consider this failure by the former Council to be maladministration. Had the maladministration not occurred, I believe it likely that intervention by the educational psychology service would have led to Festival School conducting a review of his special educational needs, preparing an individual education plan, and liaising with Mr and Mrs Smith to discuss his special educational needs during the academic year 1995/1996.

44. The maladministration of the former Council was continued after the new Council became responsible for Martin's education in April 1996. The failure of the Council's educational psychology service to continue supporting Martin from that time, given his previous history, was maladministration.

45. There was a golden opportunity to put things right when Martin's consultant psychiatrist wrote to the Council educational psychologist in October 1997 asking for an assessment. I find it extraordinary that he was told that Festival School had not identified Martin as having any specific special educational needs despite Festival School and the former Council having been informed by Oak Tree School two years before that he was at Stage 3 of the Register. The Council's failure properly to investigate and acknowledge Martin's status in October 1997 was maladministration. Had the Council done its job properly at this stage it should have been clear that Martin's special educational needs might well not have been fully addressed since his transfer to Festival School and that the best way to address them was to carry out the assessment the psychiatrist recommended. And had that happened, it seems to me that the Statement eventually issued in September 1998 could in fact have been issued some six months earlier than it was.

46. What injustice has the maladministration I have identified caused Martin and Mr and Mrs Smith? The Council and Festival School both say that what was in the Statement had been delivered from January 1998. But on balance I conclude that Martin suffered some educational disadvantage from not having an individual education plan in place between September 1995 and May 1998; and from having the publication of his Statement of Special Educational Needs delayed from March to September 1998. An individual education plan and a Statement would have set down what was considered appropriate support, after consultation with Mr and Mrs Smith, and with the Council's educational psychologist. I find it difficult to believe that the support thus properly stipulated would have been entirely provided for without such mechanisms being in place. It is not unreasonable to assume that, with all the support in place that an individual education plan and Statement might have secured him, Martin might well have gained in self-esteem and so have had a less difficult time at Festival School. Mr and Mrs Smith have also suffered some disappointment and frustration from knowing that the Council and Festival School were not doing all they should have done to safeguard Martin's educational opportunities; they were also put to some time and trouble in pursuing their complaint with the Council and with me. I accept they might have done more themselves to keep the authorities on their toes. But I believe the primary responsibility here lay with the former Council and the Council which failed to discharge their obligations to Martin.

47. For the reasons given in paragraph 43 I find maladministration by the former Avon County Council. For the reasons given in paragraphs 44 and 45 I find maladministration by the Council. The maladministration I have identified has caused the injustice identified in paragraph 46. Given that the liabilities of the former County Council have now passed to South Gloucestershire Council, it falls to that Council to consider and act upon any recommendation I make. To remedy the injustice I have identified, I recommend that the Council:

1.   makes Martin an ex gratia payment of £1500;
2.   makes Mr and Mrs Smith an ex gratia payment of £500 and;
3.   reviews its policies and procedures to satisfy itself that it is effectively discharging its duties under the Code of Practice on the Identification and Assessment of Special Educational Needs.

Delay in issuing a statement

Report on an Investigation into Complaint No 99/C/4255 against Sheffield City Council, 14 December 2000

Introduction

1. Mr Taylor complains that there was unreasonable delay by the Council in issuing a final Statement of Special Educational Needs for his son Richard in August 1999 and that the Council failed to provide Richard with suitable education from December 1998 to November 1999.

2. For legal reasons, the names used in this report are not the real names of the people and schools concerned.

3. An officer from the Commission has spoken to Mr Taylor, examined the Council's files and interviewed a Council officer.

4. The Council and Mr Taylor have had the opportunity to comment on a draft of this report.

Legal and Administrative Background

5. Councils, like Sheffield City Council, which are local authorities are required to identify those children in their area with special educational needs for whom they are responsible. Where the Council is of the opinion that a child has or probably has special educational needs it must make an assessment of the child's needs.

6. In carrying out this assessment the Council also has to have regard to a Code of Practice issued by the Department for Education and Employment.

7. There are timescales laid down for the assessment and production of a Statement of Special Educational Needs and these are summarised in the Code of Practice. In total it should take 26 weeks from a parental request to a final Statement. From proposed Statement to final Statement should take eight weeks.

...

33. In October 1998 the Council purported to issue a revised Statement but did not follow the Code of Practice. It apparently failed to set out its proposals in advance or to make clear that such a Statement could be appealed. Mr Taylor had grounds on which he would have wished to appeal the choice of school. Whilst certainty is not possible there is at least the chance that an appeal at that time would have been upheld. I welcome the fact that the Council has now changed its practices to ensure that revised statements do contain details of rights of appeal.

34. Mr Taylor is wrong to say that the Council expected him to guarantee Richard's good behaviour. What it did was quite reasonably to ask Richard to co-operate.

35. A point was then reached when it was clear that Richard was not willing to go to the PRS or to Highfields. Whatever the rights and wrongs of that the Council seems not to have considered properly what to do. The reasons for not taking action against Mr Taylor are confusing and indicate a neglect of its duty to Richard who is the one to suffer if education is not provided. Richard received no education from 17 December 1998 until 6 November 1999.

36. Mr Taylor continued to anticipate some home tuition whilst awaiting a place at Ashbridge. I do not criticise the Council for not providing home tuition but its position was not made clear to Mr Taylor or to his solicitors who were, by then, involved. I note some potential confusion in the use of the term 'home tuition'.

37. The above failures constitute maladministration.

38. In August a properly revised statement was issued (albeit 10 months after it was requested). If Mr Taylor was unhappy at the provision specified he could have appealed it but has not done so. Given the right of appeal it is not for me to criticise the Council for naming Ashbridge or failing to consider other schools. Mr Taylor's decision to make his own provision is not a situation which I can blame on the Council.

39. In short there has been some maladministration by the Council and I believe that this has led in part at least to a lost opportunity of education for Richard. It will also have caused understandable frustration, anxiety and confusion for Mr Taylor. To remedy that injustice the Council should pay Mr Taylor £500 to be used to benefit Richard's education and £250 to account for the other matters referred to above.

Delay in providing speech therapy

Report on an Investigation into Complaint No 00A09964 against Royal Borough of Kensington and Chelsea, 26 June 2001

Investigation

(A) BACKGROUND

11. In March 1999 the Council issued a Statement of Special Educational Needs in respect of Sally, who at that time was nine years old. The Statement identified 'a history of slow development in all areas, most significantly with speech and language development'. Testing

by an educational psychologist had shown her to be significantly behind her peers in educational attainment.

12. The Statement specified various forms of educational provision, including half a day a week support from an individual support teacher and 10 hours a week 'primary helper' time. This was provided by the Council. However, the educational provision section of the Statement also said that Sally 'should be offered speech and language therapy'. By the end of 2000, when Mr Fowler and Ms Owen complained to me, Sally had still not been offered any speech therapy.

Conclusion

30. I understand the difficulties the Council has had when speech therapy was not forthcoming from the health authority. However, I do not agree with Officer A that there is any ambiguity in the legal position or in government advice. On the contrary, it seems to me to be quite clear that where this service is not forthcoming from the health authority there is an absolute duty on the Council to provide what is specified in the Statement.

31. I appreciate that the department concerned was in some disarray at the time, and seems to have had inadequate resources to purchase sufficient independent provision. However, two years to make the necessary arrangements is simply too long unless every reasonable effort had been made to discharge the Council's legal duty.

32. I am not persuaded that this was the case here. The last attempt to identify independent therapists through the Royal College had taken place some time previously. The Association of Speech and Language Therapists in Independent Practice was not contacted. The Council's view that this would not have produced a solution is at best speculative. Its apparent assumption from the position of hindsight that those therapists previously contacted by the Council and found to be fully occupied would still be so does not seem to me to be consistent with a real effort to explore every possible avenue. The use of a waiting list for the Council's existing resources does not appear to me to discharge adequately the Council's legal duty. If necessary extra resources should be found.

33. In my view, therefore, there was unreasonable delay amounting to maladministration in this case. I now turn to the question of the injustice which flows from that maladministration.

34. Here I am in some difficulty. The expert advice from Ms Cole makes it clear that it is impossible to quantify the effects of the delay. Nor is it possible to assess the extent to which the Council's commitment to the funding of any necessary therapy in the future will rectify any damage.

35. That is not to say, however, that it is safe to assume that there has been no damage or that any damage is negligible. If the provision is sufficiently necessary to merit inclusion in the Statement, its absence for a prolonged period is likely to cause some harm. I do not, however, think that I can safely conclude that Sally has lost the opportunity of mainstream education as a result. However, I do consider that there is sufficient evidence to suggest that her social development has been adversely affected.

36. I also take the view that the complainants' anxieties about Sally's welfare have been unnecessarily compounded by the Council's failure to respond appropriately to their enquiries.

Recommendation

37. I recommend that the Council should pay Mr Fowler and Ms Owen the sum of £2000.

Whilst I hope that they will use the greater part of this amount for some purpose of direct benefit to Sally, it is also intended to reflect their own time and trouble in pursuing this complaint. In considering my recommendation the Council may wish to take into account the savings which will have been made through the delay in arranging provision.

Failure to implement a decision of SENT

Report on an Investigation into Complaint No 00/C/05614 against Stockport Metropolitan BC, 15 January 2001

Report Summary

SPECIAL EDUCATIONAL NEEDS

The Council failed to make the full educational provision specified in a Statement of Special Educational Needs. The Statement (following a successful appeal to the Special Educational Needs Tribunal) specified a particular programme (Lovaas) to deal with the child's autism.

The Local Government Ombudsman found that the full provision as specified in the Statement had not been provided but that this was not a consequence of maladministration. She identified genuine difficulties in creating and retaining a team of specialists willing to carry out these specific responsibilities. Nor did she see any other cause for criticism, recognising that the Council could not devote disproportionate resources to this (or any other) particular child.

The Local Government Ombudsman decided to issue a report in order to highlight the difficulties that a local education authority can face in implementing the decision of a Special Needs Tribunal.

FINDING

No maladministration.

The limited nature of the remedies for pupils with special educational needs was recognised by Mrs PA Thomas, one of the three Ombudsmen.

Local Government Ombudsman Annual Report 1999/2000, chapter 3

Parents of children with special educational needs also evoke sympathy, as do councils with a duty to provide support for them but with inadequate funds to do so. I have been concerned at unacceptable delays by councils in meeting urgent needs after recognising them. In one report issued last year I found that a council had taken over two years to issue a final statement of a child's special educational needs. In another case a child with a statement was excluded from school but no alternative found for 18 months, during which time no home tuition was provided. Such times slip by quickly for the council officer sitting behind an overburdened desk, but for any child, let alone one with special needs, the delay can have lasting impact.

Remedies

In general the remedies I seek for complainants are designed to put them back into the position where they should have been had the maladministration not occurred. That is not always possible.

SCHOOL TRANSPORT

This report is of interest bearing in mind that where bullying occurs parents may want their child to move to a different school which is further away from home and may ask the LEA to provide free transport (see chapters 4 and 6).

Report on an Investigation into Complaint No 98/C/5219 against Leeds City Council, 5 October 2000

Report Summary

EDUCATION TRANSPORT

Following incidents of bullying and an injury to her child, the complainant transferred him to another school. The Council, having received a request from the parent for the cost of transport to the new school carried out consultations and rejected the request. The parent provided medical information some of which the Council mistakenly believed was out of date. In reviewing the request the Council introduced a new factor which was not discussed with the parent but led to a further rejection of the request. The Ombudsman found that the Council had not properly reviewed the request.

FINDING

Maladministration causing injustice.

RECOMMENDED REMEDY

The Ombudsman recommended that the Council reconsider its decision on the basis of the full information.

Once the Ombudsman has carried out an investigation there are a variety of possible outcomes.

Local Government Ombudsman Annual Report 2000/2001, p 25, Table 5

TABLE 5: ANALYSIS OF OUTCOME OF COMPLAINTS 2000/01

	Number of complaints	Percentage of total (excluding premature complaints and those outside jurisdiction)
Local settlements (without report)	3,727	31.8%
Local settlement report	60	0.5%
Maladministration causing injustice (issued report)	158	1.4%
Maladministration, no injustice (issued report)	14	0.1%
No maladministration (issued report)	29	0.2%
No maladministration (without report)	4,963	42.4%
Ombudsman's discretion not to pursue complaint	2,760	23.6%
Premature complaints	4,333	
Outside jurisdiction	2,176	
Total	**18,220**	

In *R v Comr for Local Administration, ex p S* [1999] ELR 102 the mother of a 17-year-old boy who suffered from autism applied for judicial review of the Ombudsman's decision that there had been maladministration by a local authority but that she had suffered no injustice.

R v Comr for Local Administration, ex p S [1999] ELR 102

Collins J: The complaints made by the applicant concern the manner in which the council's education authority had dealt with the educational needs of her son, who was born on 22 April 1981. He suffers, as has now been discovered, from Asperger's syndrome, which is a form of autism. This manifested itself initially when he was a primary school.

...

[T]he court will, in cases such as this, be very careful not to interfere unless it is clear that a *Wednesbury* ground has been established. It is not right to go through the decision with a fine tooth comb and to try to find errors, particularly if they are errors of fact. It is only if there is a clear error of law, and that error is one which may have affected the conclusions which were reached, that it would be proper for the court to interfere. If a particular conclusion was fairly open to the Commissioner on the facts found, then this court has no jurisdiction to interfere with that decision.

So far as injustice is concerned, it is clearly not enough that the applicant feels that she has been unfairly treated and so has suffered an injustice. The law permits the Commissioner to find maladministration without injustice. Therefore, it is a trite observation to say that it must follow that the mere finding of maladministration cannot mean that there must be injustice as well. It seems to me that it must be established that there is some prejudice to the applicant before a finding of injustice can properly be made. That prejudice may be no more than the loss of an opportunity (which may be the position here) and certainly it is not required that any particular damage be established. Indeed it is quite plain that the word 'injustice' was used with a view to indicating something wider than is covered by the concept of damage, and also perhaps to avoid the need to delve into questions of causation which might otherwise arise in certain cases.

In the circumstances of this case, the real concern is that J was not diagnosed as suffering from the form of autism sufficiently early. It was accepted by the Commissioner that the council, although it delayed, was not sitting back doing nothing. It was making efforts to find the right solution for J. Those efforts were hampered by the lack of a proper diagnosis as to what was causing the problems which led to the need for special educational provision. Until the cause of his problems was identified, it was obviously not easy, indeed perhaps impossible, to find the right solution. Unfortunately, as I have already indicated, by the time the diagnosis was made it was too late to place J in at least one otherwise appropriate school, and the problems remained which it is said should not have remained.

The Commissioner has found that there was no injustice because the maladministration did not make, and could not have made, any difference to the time at which the diagnosis was made. Thus it could not have made any difference to the steps taken to provide for J's special educational needs. If he was entitled to reach that conclusion then in my judgment he was entitled to find that there was no injustice.

- *What amounts to 'injustice' according to Collins J?*

Judicial review

Judicial review is available to challenge, for example, policy decisions of the Secretary of State, an LEA or a governing body, as well as decisions on individual cases made by the Secretary of State, LEAs, governing bodies, independent appeal committees, school adjudicators, and Local Government Ombudsmen.

The grounds on which a decision may be challenged by judicial review include:
- *Wednesbury* unreasonableness
- taking into account irrelevant considerations
- failing to take into account relevant considerations
- failing to consult interested parties
- procedural impropriety.

Leave of the court is required in order to apply for judicial review of a decision, and the leave application should normally be brought within three months of the decision. The following remedies are available in judicial review proceedings:
- quashing order (certiorari)
- mandatory order (mandamus)
- prohibitory order (prohibition)
- injunction
- declaration.

Compensation is not awarded unless it is linked to an action for breach of contract or a claim in tort or restitution.

Examples of decisions being challenged by way of judicial review can be found in most chapters. Until the Special Educational Needs Tribunal was established in 1994, challenges to LEA decisions on special educational needs provision were brought using the judicial review procedure.

However, where there is an alternative means of redress, for example, an appeal to SENT or a complaint to the Secretary of State or to the Local Government Ombudsman (see above), judicial review is not normally available.

Nevertheless, in *R (on the application of K) v Governors of W School and West Sussex County Council* [2001] ELR 311 the court granted the application for judicial review of the governors' decision to exclude K permanently even though his parents had not appealed to the independent appeal panel. The court stressed the special circumstances of the case which justified the granting of the application.

Reasons and grounds for decision

Normally, it is easier to challenge the legality of a decision where reasons are given, because the giving of reasons is more likely to expose any unfairness or irrationality than the bald decision itself. There is no general statutory obligation on public bodies to give reasons for their decisions. However, certain statutes require reasons or grounds for a decision to be given. In addition, the Tribunals and Inquiries Act 1992, s10(1) provides that most tribunals should give a written or oral statement of the reasons for a particular decision where requested to do so.

School admission appeal panels (see also chapter 3, and chapter 4 on decisions made by exclusion appeal panels) are required by statute to provide 'grounds' rather than 'reasons' for their decision. The following cases consider what this means in practice.

R v Lancashire County Council, ex p M [1995] ELR 136

Macpherson J: There is absolutely nothing wrong with a local authority having a standard form letter which can be modified if required. The question, however, is whether in this particular case the decision letter was adequate. I use that word because, as Miss Caws points out, the statute requires that grounds shall be given for the decision which is made and it does not for example anywhere state that detailed reasons must be given. There is a distinction between grounds and detailed reasons. I accept Miss Caws' submission in respect of this letter which is to the effect that broad grounds must be set out rather than what may be termed detailed reasons.

In *R v Birmingham City Council Education Appeals Committee, ex p B* [1999] ELR 305 Scott Baker J agreed in principle with Macpherson J, but reached a different decision on the facts.

R v Birmingham City Council Education Appeals Committee, ex p B [1999]ELR 305

Scott Baker J: If Macpherson J was there saying that a standard letter without more is sufficient, I respectfully disagree. But I do not think that that is what the judge was saying. He certainly referred to a standard form of letter but he added these important words, 'which can be modified if required'. Of course, there may be many run-of-the-mill cases which can be dealt with by a letter in very much standard form. But it is in my judgment important that an appellant, and in particular an unsuccessful appellant, knows, broadly, why his appeal has been unsuccessful and manifestly that is not the case with regard to this letter and this appellant. The letter tells him absolutely nothing about why his appeal was unsuccessful and does nothing more than make ritual incantation of the two-stage process that is applicable for deciding these appeals.

The crucial question in this case was as to whether the applicant was living. Nothing is said in the letter as to the appeal committee's finding about that.

...

From the material that I have seen there is at the very least a risk that the tribunal embarked on this hearing in such a way as to cause an injustice to this applicant. The letter of 1 May 1998 was deficient in failing to give grounds for the decision as it should have done under Sch 33, para 14.

R v South Gloucestershire Appeals Committee, ex p C [2000] ELR 220

Dyson J: I do not believe that the decision in R v Birmingham City Council Education Appeals Committee, ex p B lays down any general principle save perhaps to say that a minimum requirement of the grounds of a decision is that they explain broadly the basis of the decision. I respectfully agree with what Macpherson J said in R v Lancashire County Council, ex p M [1995] ELR 136: the statute requires broad grounds rather than detailed reasons. What is required will depend on the issues that have been raised on the appeal. In a complex case the grounds may well have to be more elaborate than in a simple one. Where however there is no dispute as to the primary facts, I do not consider that the grounds are required to make findings about those facts.

The Special Educational Needs Tribunal, on the other hand, is under a statutory duty to give reasons for its decision, although the decision is permitted to be in a summary form.

In *S v Special Educational Needs Tribunal and the City of Westminster* [1996] ELR 102 Latham J explained what is required from a statement of reasons in summary form (applied in *H v Kent County Council and the Special Educational Needs Tribunal* [2000] ELR 660).

S v Special Educational Needs Tribunal and the City of Westminster [1996] ELR 102

Latham J: It seems to me, therefore, that a balance has to be struck between giving effect to the clear intention of Parliament that the requirement of reasons is to be met by a short form document, and proper concern that the right of appeal under s 11 of the Tribunals and Inquiries Act 1992 would be emasculated if the document did not at least enable the aggrieved party to identify the basis of the decision with sufficient clarity to be able to determine whether or not the tribunal had gone wrong in law. That, in essence, is the concern underlying the principle enunciated by Megaw J in Re Poyser and Mills' Arbitration (above).

I consider that the balance is properly struck by requiring that the statement of the reasons should deal, but in short form, with the substantial issues raised in order that the parties can understand why the decision has been reached. I consider that the present case is an admirable example of exactly how matters should be dealt with. There is a short form conclusion as to what evidence has been accepted and what evidence has been rejected, with a short form reason for that conclusion. It may not always be possible to identify the precise reason for accepting the evidence of one witness as opposed to another, and in those cases there may have to be the simple assertion of the Tribunal's preference.

Review rather than appeal

Judicial review is not the same as a right of appeal. In judicial review proceedings, the court is concerned with the procedures followed in reaching a decision as opposed to the merits of the decision itself.

R v Comr for Local Administration, ex p S [1999] ELR 102

Collins J: It is clear, and for very understandable reasons, that Mrs Vale took the view that the council should have done more than it did. The Commissioner has, by his finding of maladministration, accepted that there is force in that complaint. However, it is plain from the report that the council was aware of the problem and was doing its best, although its best was, in all the circumstances, not as good as it ought to have been. The Commissioner himself, when one reads the report as a whole, plainly had the important considerations and the rival contentions well in mind.

It seems to me that although I have identified that one error of law, none the less the Commissioner was entitled to take the view that even if the council had acted as they should have done and had pursued the matter in an appropriate and proper fashion, the likelihood would have been that there would have been no difference in the way that J's case was dealt with; more importantly that it would not have affected the manner in which attempts were made to find the best solution for J. It will perhaps be clear, from what I have said that, if this had been an appeal rather than a judicial review, I might well have reached a conclusion which was different to that reached by the Commissioner. But, as I have indicated at the outset, this is not an appeal, this is a judicial review and I do not find it possible to say that the conclusions in relation to injustice were conclusions which were not permissible as a matter of law.

Independent and non-maintained schools

Judicial review is not available to challenge the decisions of a private body. This includes decisions of the head teacher or the governing body of an independent school (*R v Fernhill Manor School, ex p A* [1993] 1 FLR 620; and *R v Incorporated Froebel Institute, ex p L* [1999] ELR 488), and a non-maintained residential school catering for pupils with special educational needs (*R v Muntham House School, ex p R* [2000] ELR 287).

However, judicial review is available to challenge the decision of a city technology college (CTC) and is likely to be available to challenge decisions of city academies.

R v Governors of Haberdashers' Aske's Hatcham College Trust, ex p T [1995] ELR 350

Dyson J: In order to resolve this issue, it is necessary to examine the nature and status of CTCs. They owe their existence to s 15 of the 1988 [Education Reform] Act. No CTC can be established unless the Secretary of State makes an agreement with the person undertaking to establish, maintain and carry on a school having the characteristics specified in s 105(2) of the 1988 Act. Moreover, CTCs are wholly or partly publicly funded. It is a condition of such funding that no charge shall be made in respect of admissions to the school, and subject to any exceptions specified in the agreement, in respect of education provided at the school. In a nutshell, therefore, CTCs are publicly funded non-fee paying urban schools for pupils drawn wholly or mainly from the areas in which the schools are situated, whose curriculum is broad but with an emphasis on science and technology. Both the existence of CTCs and their essential characteristics derive from the exercise by government of a statutory power. On the face of it, CTCs would seem to be public law bodies and their decisions as to admissions, amenable to judicial review.

2.   FURTHER EDUCATION INSTITUTIONS

Further education colleges, sixth-form colleges and tertiary colleges come within the definition of an FE institution (see chapter 2). Such institutions are statutory corporations. They are required to have a constitution, known as the instrument of government, and articles of government (s 20 of the FHEA 1992). Schedule 4 to the FHEA 1992 sets out what should be contained in these documents, and is supplemented by regulations.

Further and Higher Education Act 1992, Sch 4

1. References in this Schedule to an instrument are to an instrument of government or articles of government.

10. An instrument shall make provision about the procedures of the corporation and of the institution.

11. An instrument shall provide—
(a)   for the appointment, promotion, suspension and dismissal of staff, and
(b)   for the admission, suspension and expulsion of students.

12. An instrument may make provision authorising the corporation to make rules or byelaws for the government and conduct of the institution, including in particular rules or byelaws about the conduct of students, staff or both.

The Education (Government of Further Education Corporations) (Former Further Education Colleges) Regulations 1992, SI 1992/1963, Sch 2

3(3) Subject to the provisions of these Articles, to the overall responsibility of the Corporation and to the responsibilities of the Principal; the Academic Board shall be responsible for advising the Principal on the standards, planning, co-ordination, development and oversight of the academic work of the institution, including arrangements for the admission, assessment and examination of students and the procedures for the expulsion of students for academic reasons.

14. After consultation with the staff the Corporation shall make rules specifying procedures according to which staff may seek redress of any grievances relating to their employment.

15(2) The Corporation, after consultation with the Academic Board and representatives of the students, shall make rules with respect to the conduct of students, including procedures for suspension and expulsion.

15(3) In exercise of their responsibilities under article 3(3), the Academic Board, after consultation with the Corporation and representatives of the students, shall advise the Principal on procedures for the expulsion of a student for an unsatisfactory standard of work or other academic reason.

Similar provisions apply to sixth form colleges (see the Education (Government of Further Education Corporations) (Former Sixth Form Colleges) Regulations 1992, SI 1992/1957, Sch 2, paras 3(2)(f), 13, 14(2)).

Although the legislation expressly requires a grievance procedure for staff complaints there is no such requirement for student complaints. However, a college has the power to set up such a procedure if it wishes.

There is no right to complain to the Secretary of State that a college is acting unreasonably or is in default, and the Secretary of State has no power to issue directions to a college. The Secretary of State may, however, issue directions to the funding council (s 25 of the LSA 2000) on the ground that the council is acting unreasonably.

Neither the Local Government Ombudsmen nor the Parliamentary Ombudsman may investigate complaints against FE institutions.

The decisions and actions of an FE institution are potentially subject to judicial review or claims for breach of contract in the same way as are new universities (see below) because both types of institution are statutory corporations. Complaints by students arising out of FE course provision, assessment, or disciplinary action have rarely, if at all, resulted in litigation. University students by comparison appear to be more litigious.

3. UNIVERSITIES

Universities and other higher education institutions may have three or more different internal procedures to deal with complaints brought by students or staff. Procedures are likely to exist to resolve:
- assessment appeals
- breaches of rules of conduct
- grievance procedures
- allegations of discrimination.

The form of the procedures will vary according to whether the institution is a statutory corporation, for example a 'new' university, or a chartered corporation, for example an 'old' university. There may also be complaints by applicants whose application is unsuccessful.

In addition to complaints against their institution, students may also wish to complain about the administration of any financial assistance provided by LEAs.

'New' universities

The new universities are statutory corporations and have the power to establish procedures for the admission, suspension and expulsion of students, and to make rules or byelaws in relation to, for example, the conduct of students and staff.

Education Reform Act 1988, s 125

(1) Any institution conducted by a higher education corporation shall be conducted in accordance with articles of government, to be made by the corporation with the approval of the Secretary of State.

...

(3) The articles of government shall also make provision with respect to the procedure for meetings of the board of governors, of the academic board and of committees of the corporation and the procedure in relation to the appointment of members of the corporation (including in either case quorum and proxies), and may make provision with respect to—

(a)   procedures for the appointment, promotion, suspension and dismissal of staff;
(b)   procedures for the admission, suspension and expulsion of students; ...

(4) The articles of government also make provision authorising the board of governors to make rules or byelaws for the government and conduct of the institution, including in particular rules or byelaws with respect to—

(a)   the conduct of students and staff or either of them; and
(b)   any such procedures as are mentioned in subsection (3)(a) or (b) above.

The decisions and actions of these universities may be challenged by way of judicial review when they are exercising their public law functions. In the context of challenges by students judicial review is the normal remedy, although there are some cases where students have claimed breach of contract. There are two advantages of bringing a claim in contract or tort as opposed to applying for judicial review. The first is that the limitation periods are longer, and the second is that an award of damages may be made to a successful claimant.

'Old' universities

The visitor

These universities were normally established by royal charter. One of the characteristics of the majority of these universities is that disputes, if not resolved internally, are referred to an external adjudicator known as 'the visitor'. Not all 'old' universities have a visitor. For example, Oxford and Cambridge colleges have a visitor, but the universities do not. Some universities have the power to appoint a visitor but did not do so (see, for example, *R v Aston University Senate, ex p Roffey* [1969] 2 QB 538). Some colleges which are not universities have visitors (see, for example, *Herring v Templeman* [1973] 2 All ER 581, *R v Honourable Society of the Middle Temple, ex p Bullock* [1996] ELR 349).

The origins of the visitor lie deep in medieval charity law. The visitor is often the holder of a particular office, for example, the Crown, the Lord Chancellor, or the Archbishop of Canterbury.

DJ Farrington, *The Law of Higher Education* (2nd edn, 1998) p 216

2.202 One area in which the chartered universities of England, Wales and Northern Ireland differ from the rest of the system is the existence of the visitorial jurisdiction—a true 'Alsatia in England' i e where the common law does not run and where the ordinary courts have no jurisdiction. A 'Visitation' has a distinct medieval, ecclesiastical, ring to it, variously described as 'a ghost clanking its chains' or 'an archaic functionary redolent of monarchical paternalism in an isolated, unworldly community of scholars.' The power of the Visitor to determine affairs relating to an eleemosynary (charitable) or ecclesiastical corporation is a direct descendant of the founder's right to determine matters relating to his or her own 'endowment' (interpreted in practice to mean the act of incorporation, since when, for example, a university is created by charter, no money actually changes hands) and, originally, to ensure that it did not veer from its statutes. The jurisdiction survived the general reorganisation of courts etc, effected by the Judicature Act 1873 as was swiftly recognised by the courts in 1878 in *R v Hertford College Oxford*.

...

Origin of the office of Visitor

2.203 John Bridge says that 'the visitor appears to have been an ecclesiastical institution for the purpose of supervising the government of the church and the correction of offences at both diocesan and parochial level' although both the characteristics and the basis of authority of a lay visitor and a bishop seem rather different and the basis of authority quite different. As explained by Hold CJ in *Philips v Bury* the visitorial power 'ariseth from the property which the founder had in the lands assigned to support the charity'. A bishop is a steward but not an owner of property. Both Roman law and the common law furnished analogies and in view of the medieval conception of a municipality, the authority of the common courts to pass upon the reasonableness of municipal customs and byelaws was so like the authority of the episcopal visitor with regard to the regulations and byelaws of a college or religious foundation that as Roscoe Pound said 'there is no wonder the two things became confused'. After the Reformation it was settled that ecclesiastical corporations were subject to visitation by the bishop and lay charitable corporations to visitations by the founder and his heirs unless otherwise provided by the founder. The visitor's role was to ensure the maintenance of good government in corporations and to secure their adherence to the purposes of their institution. Every private corporation had a visitor but other corporations were subject to the visitorial authority of the king, exercisable through his courts and ordinarily exercised by mandamus and by information in the nature of *quo warranto* in the King's Bench.

The jurisdiction of the visitor included the power to resolve disputes between members of the University, that is staff or students, and the University. In 1988 a body called the University Commissioners was established to ensure that these universities established procedures for dealing with complaints made against staff and by staff concerning dismissal and other grievances (s 202 of the ERA 1988). So the visitor no longer had exclusive jurisdiction in employment disputes with members of the academic staff (s 206 of the ERA 1988).

The visitor continues to have exclusive jurisdiction to hear disputes between students and the university, but does not have the power to award compensation (*Casson v University of Aston in Birmingham* [1983] 1 All ER 88).

However, the courts are prepared to review decisions of the visitor where the decision is based on an error of law. In *R v Lord President of the Privy Council, ex p Page* [1993] AC 682 their Lordships expressed differing views as to when the courts could intervene. The case concerned the redundancy of a university lecturer. The House of Lords held by a majority that the visitor's decision was not amenable to judicial review where the decision was made within the visitor's jurisdiction (Lord Browne-Wilkinson, Lord Keith, Lord Griffith).

Lord Browne-Wilkinson (with whom Lord Keith concurred) and Lord Slynn (with whom Lord Mustill concurred) considered that a visitor's jurisdiction was amenable to judicial review where the visitor acted outside his jurisdiction, abused his powers, or acted in breach of the rules of natural justice.

Lord Slynn (and Lord Mustill) went one step further and considered that all decisions by the visitor based on an error of law are reviewable by the courts.

R v Lord President of the Privy Council, ex p Page [1993] AC 682

Lord Griffiths: I do not believe that it would be right to reverse this long line of authority and declare that certiorari should now lie to reverse the decision of a visitor on a question of law. The value of the visitorial jurisdiction is that it is swift, cheap and final. These benefits will be largely dissipated if the visitor's decision can be challenged by way of judicial review.

...

Lord Browne-Wilkinson: It is established that, a university being an eleemosynary charitable foundation, the visitor of the university has exclusive jurisdiction to decide disputes arising under the domestic law of the university. This is because the founder of such a body is entitled to reserve to himself or to a visitor whom he appoints the exclusive right to adjudicate upon the domestic laws which the founder has established for the regulation of his bounty. Even where the contractual rights of an individual (such as his contract of employment with the university) are in issue, if those contractual rights are themselves dependent upon rights arising under the regulating documents of the charity, the visitor has an exclusive jurisdiction over disputes relating to such employment.

Those propositions are all established by the decision of this House in *Thomas v University of Bradford* [1987] AC 795 which held that the courts had no jurisdiction to entertain such disputes which must be decided by the visitor. However, *Thomas's* case was concerned with the question whether the courts and the visitor had concurrent jurisdictions over such disputes. In that context alone it was decided that the visitor's jurisdiction was 'exclusive'. *Thomas's* case does not decide that the visitor's jurisdiction excludes the supervisory jurisdiction of the courts by way of judicial review.

...

Under the modern law, certiorari normally lies to quash a decision for error of law. Therefore, the narrow issue in this case is whether, as Mr Page contends and the courts below have held, certiorari lies against the visitor to quash his decision as being erroneous in point of law notwithstanding that the question of law arises under the domestic law of the university which the visitor has 'exclusive' jurisdiction to decide.

...

The court's inability to determine those matters is not limited to the period pending the visitor's determination but extends so as to prohibit any subsequent review by the court of the correctness of a decision made by the visitor acting within his jurisdiction and in accordance with the rules of natural justice. The inability of the court to intervene is founded on the fact that the applicable law is not the common law of England but a peculiar or domestic law of which the visitor is the sole judge. This special status of a visitor springs from the common law recognising the right of the founder to lay down such a special law subject to adjudication only by a special judge, the visitor.

How then is it contended that the courts have power to review the visitor's decision as to the effect of the domestic law of the university in this case.

...

I accept that the position of the visitor is anomalous, indeed unique. I further accept that where the visitor is, or is advised by, a lawyer the distinction between the peculiar domestic law he applies and the general law is artificial. But I do not regard these factors as justifying sweeping away the law which for so long has regulated the conduct of charitable corporations. There are internal disputes which are resolved by a visitor who is not a lawyer himself and has not taken legal advice. It is not only modern universities which have visitors: there are a substantial number of other long-established educational, ecclesiastical and eleemosynary bodies which have visitors. The advantages of having an informal system which produces a speedy, cheap and final answer to internal disputes has been repeatedly emphasised in the authorities, most recently by this House in *Thomas v University of Bradford* [1987] AC 795; see per Lord Griffiths, at p 825; see also *Patel v University of Bradford Senate* [1978] 1 WLR 1488, 1499–1500. If it were to be held that judicial review for error of law lay against the visitor I fear that, as in the present case, finality would be lost not only in cases raising pure questions of law but also in cases where it would be urged in accordance with the *Wednesbury* principle (*Associated Provincial Picture Houses Ltd v Wednesbury Corporation* [1948] 1 KB 223) that the visitor had failed to take into account relevant matters or taken into account irrelevant matters or had reached an irrational conclusion. Although the visitor's position is anomalous, it provides a valuable machinery for resolving internal disputes which should not be lost.

I have therefore reached the conclusion that judicial review does not lie to impeach the decisions of a visitor taken within his jurisdiction (in the narrow sense) on questions of either fact or law. Judicial review does lie to the visitor in cases where he has acted outside his jurisdiction (in the narrow sense) or abused his powers or acted in breach of the rules of natural justice.

...

Lord Slynn: With deference to the contrary view of the majority of your Lordships, in my opinion if certiorari can go to a particular tribunal it is available on all the grounds which have been judicially recognised. I can see no reasons in principle for limiting the availability of certiorari to a patent excess of power (as where a visitor has decided something which was not within his remit) and excluding review on other grounds recognised by the law. If it is accepted, as I believe it should be accepted, that certiorari goes not only for such an excess or abuse of power but also for a breach of the rules of natural justice there is even less reason in principle for excluding other established grounds. If therefore certiorari is generally available for error of law not involving abuse of power (as on the basis of Lord Diplock's speeches I consider that it is so available) then it should be available also in respect of a decision of a visitor.

I am not persuaded that the jurisdiction of the visitor involves such exceptional considerations that this principle should be departed from and that some grounds be accepted and others held not to be available for the purposes of judicial law.

ROLE OF THE COURT

In *R v University of London Visitor, ex p Vijayatunga* [1989] 2 All ER 843 the Court of Appeal was asked to quash the decision of the visitor. The student had argued unsuccessfully before the visitor that the persons chosen to act as examiners for her PhD thesis were not competent because they were not specialists in her area of study.

R v University of London Visitor, ex p Vijayatunga [1989] 2 All ER 843

Bingham LJ: [T]here is no doubt about the role of this court, which is to confine itself to correction of demonstrated errors of law. We could not properly interfere with any exercise of discretion or judgment by the committee unless of opinion that it was wrong in law.

However, their Lordships did not make the distinction drawn subsequently by Lord Browne-Wilkinson in *ex p Page* between errors of law within and outside the visitor's jurisdiction.

ROLE OF THE VISITOR

In *R v Honourable Society of the Middle Temple, ex p Bullock* [1996] ELR 349, Brooke J was asked to review the decision of the visitor, Tucker J. The applicant was a student who failed two assessments, which formed part of the Bar Vocational Course, and was required to resit them. He argued unsuccessfully that the failures should have been condoned.

R v Honourable Society of the Middle Temple, ex p Bullock [1996] ELR 349

Brooke J: There has been an unusual amount of litigation concerned with visitors to educational foundations in recent years. Its effect can be summarised as follows:

(1) A visitor has a general power to right wrongs and redress grievances within the foundation to which he is appointed (*R v Her Majesty the Queen in Council, ex p Vijayatunga* [1988] QB 322, per Simon Brown J at p 344).

(2) This power gives him an untrammelled jurisdiction to investigate and correct wrongs done in the administration of the internal law of that foundation, which he may exercise in whatever way he considers appropriate (ibid).

(3) In other words, he should investigate the basic facts underlying a grievance to whatever depth he considers appropriate, and he may interfere with any decision he concludes to be wrong (ibid).

(4) In certain contexts there may be considerations which quite properly inhibit him from embarking on a general fact-finding role, because as visitor he lacks the particular experience and expertise which is possessed by those within the foundation on whom the relevant responsibility lies. Examples include:

(a)   the appointment of examiners;

(b)   the decision of examiners on the standard attained by a candidate;

(c)   decisions which depend to a material extent (ie not de minimis) on the exercise of academic or scientific or other technical judgment (R v Her Majesty the Queen in Council, ex p Vijayatunga [1988] QB 322, per Kerr LJ at pp 333–4 and per Simon Brown J at p 344).

(5) In these, and indeed in such other contexts as he may think fall within this general rubric, the visitor may properly limit himself to determining whether there was any reliable evidence on which the foundation could reasonably have taken the decision complained of, and that the decision was taken in good faith and not for any extraneous reason such as bias or other improper motive. Examples include:

(a)   a decision by a foundation that a member of it was guilty of persistent insobriety such as in its opinion to render him or her unfit to remain a member;

(b)   a decision by a foundation that a student failed in its opinion to attain the academic standard required of its students (R v Her Majesty the Queen in Council, ex p Vijayatunga [1990] 2 QB 444, per Bingham LJ at pp 457–8).

All these principles were approved by the majority of the Court of Appeal in R v Her Majesty the Queen in Council, ex p Vijayatunga [1990] 2 QB 444, per Bingham LJ at p 457, and per Lord Donaldson of Lymington MR at p 460) and are binding on me.

Judicial review

Judicial review applications may be brought by a student:

- against a decision made by a new university
- against a decision of a visitor
- against decision of an old university which does not have a visitor.

There is no statutory obligation on these bodies to give reasons for their decision, although in practice they are likely to do so. In *Nash v Chelsea College of Art and Design* (2001) Times, 25 July, the court was asked to consider whether the late reasons, given for the academic committee's decision not to allow her appeal against her grades, could be accepted.

The original decision on her grades had been taken in May 1998. She appealed, alleging that she had been sexually harassed by one of her tutors, and her work was reassessed in February 1999. She appealed against the reassessment decision. The academic committee met in July 1999 and rejected her appeal. She successfully challenged that decision by way of judicial review in May 2000 (*R v Chelsea College of Art and Design, ex p Nash* [2000] ELR 686) on the ground that she was not allowed to submit certain evidence to the committee. The committee was, therefore, required to reconsider her appeal, which it did in June 2000. In a letter dated 30 June the committee rejected her appeal, but reasons for the decision were not provided until 3 October 2000.

Nash v Chelsea College of Art and Design (2001) Times, 25 July

Stanley Burton J: His Lordship said that the following propositions appeared from previous authorities:
(i)   where there was a statutory duty to give reasons as part of notification of the decision, only in exceptional circumstances would the court accept subsequent evidence of the reasons;
(ii) in other cases, such as the present, the court would be cautious about accepting late reasons, and would consider (a) whether the new reasons were consistent with the original reasons; (b) whether it was clear that the new reasons were indeed the original reasons of the whole committee; (c) whether there was a real risk that the later reasons were composed subsequently in order to support the tribunal's decision, or were a retrospective justification of the original decision; (d) the delay before the later reasons were put forward; (e) the circumstances in which the later reasons were put forward.
Reasons put forward after commencement of proceedings were to be treated especially carefully and reasons put forward during correspondence where parties were seeking to elucidate the decision should be approached more tolerantly.
His Lordship said there were two further considerations:
1   The degree of scrutiny and caution to be applied to subsequent reasons depended on the subject matter of the administrative decision in question. Where important human rights were concerned, anxious scrutiny was required; the less important subject matter, the less demanding and the more readier to accept subsequent reasons would the court be.
2   The qualifications and experience of the persons involved would be borne in mind. Comprehensiveness and clarity could not be demanded from occasional non-lawyer tribunal chairmen and members as much as it could from lawyers and those who regularly sat on administrative tribunals.
Having considered all those factors, his Lordship said that the October 30 decision letter would be accepted as containing reasons for the decision which were sufficient and lawful.
In terms of seriousness of the subject matter, the case was at the lower end of the spectrum. The matters in issue would have had only a marginal effect on the claimant's degree and at most a marginal effect if any on her career.

The majority of judicial review applications brought by students have related to assessment issues. The grounds for the application are normally based on the wrongful exercise of a discretion, or not acting fairly. Most applications are unsuccessful. The increase in the number of applications, particularly from students at new universities without a visitor, together with the Human Rights Act 1998 coming into effect has raised the issue of whether an independent complaints procedure should be available for all students. Following consultation in 2001 Universities UK, the body representing university vice-chancellors and principals, is seeking legislation on a new national independent review mechanism for hearing student complaints.

An application for judicial review should be seen as a last resort. Alternatively a claim for breach of contract may be brought where appropriate (see below).

Clark v University of Lincolnshire and Humberside [2000] ELR 345

Lord Woolf MR: Grievances against universities are preferably resolved within the grievance procedure which universities have today. If they cannot be resolved in that way, where there is a visitor, they then have (except in exceptional circumstances) to be resolved by the visitor. The courts will not usually intervene.

While the courts will intervene where there is no visitor, normally this should happen after the student has made use of the domestic procedures for resolving the dispute. If it is not possible to resolve the dispute internally, and there is no visitor, then the courts may have no alternative but to become involved. If they do so, the preferable procedure would usually be by way of judicial review. If, on the other hand, the proceedings are based on the contract between the student and the university then they do not have to be brought by way of judicial review.

Academic judgment

The first point to note is that normally the internal rules of a university will provide that there can be no appeal against an academic decision so long as the correct procedures have been followed in reaching that decision. In other words where a student has been awarded a fail grade, that grade cannot be challenged on the ground that the student considers that the work merited a pass grade. However, where the student could show that the marking procedures were not followed, for example the work was not sent to an external examiner, an appeal is likely to be available. Similarly the courts will not interfere in matters of academic judgment.

R v University of London Visitor, ex p Vijayatunga [1989] 2 All ER 843

Mann LJ: The issue in this case was whether the examiners appointed by the university to examine the applicant's thesis were competent so to do.

This seems to me wholly a matter of academic judgment in which this court should not interfere.

Mann LJ's statements were approved by Buxton LJ in *R v Cranfield University Senate, ex p Bashir* [1999] ELR 317. A similar view was expressed by Simon Brown LJ in *R v University of Portsmouth, ex p Lakareber* [1999] ELR 135.

R v University of Portsmouth, ex p Lakareber [1999] ELR 135

Simon Brown LJ: Only the clearest and most obvious unfairness or departure from the university's own regulations would justify an attempt by judicial review to impugn an academic decision of this character. It is important to recognise that what would have to be attacked here would be not the original marking of the resits or the original decision requiring the applicant to pass two outstanding units before proceeding to the third year of her course, but rather the decision by the appeal body. If, as here, the academic registrar and the independent member of academic council, having considered the student's detailed written appeal and listened to her for over an hour, conclude that there is frankly nothing in her grievance, this court will not readily hold such a decision to be erroneous in point of law.

In most cases the courts are not prepared to look behind the 'academic veil'. In *R v Leeds Metropolitan University, ex p Manders* [1998] ELR 502 Collins J gave an illustration of when marks could be reviewed on appeal.

R v Leeds Metropolitan University, ex p Manders [1998] ELR 502

Collins J: [I]t is to be noted, that a review of academic results, that is to say a review of exam results, is only permitted on grounds which are set out in the relevant regulations. These specifically do not include any question of academic judgment. Of course, if it is said that there has been bias and a deliberate marking down, that is not a question of academic judgment, but is a specific matter which a student, as I see it, will be clearly entitled to raise on any review.

The Court of Appeal in *R (on the application of Persaud) v University of Cambridge* [2001] EWCA 534, [2001] ELR 480 stated that as a general rule a student would not be able to challenge an academic judgment on the grounds of unfairness. However, where the procedure followed in reaching that decision failed to measure up to the standard of fairness the decision may be open to challenge in the courts. In this case the court allowed the student's appeal on the ground that the Board of Graduate Studies had on the facts not acted fairly towards her because of the defects in the process.

R (on the application of Persaud) v University of Cambridge [2001] EWCA 534, [2001] ELR 480

Chadwick LJ: [37] The question for the court is whether, in that context, the Board acted fairly towards the appellant when making its decision in January 1999 to reject her application for reinstatement as a graduate student. In my view that question must be answered in the negative. There are, to my mind, three factors which compel that answer.

[38] First, the question whether or not the appellant had met Dr Gondhalekar's requirements as to attendance at the Rutherford Appleton Laboratory was an issue of fact. She had provided a detailed account of her attendance at the laboratory. If the Board were minded to reject that account as factually inaccurate, then fairness required that they had to put that possibility to her so that she could meet it. If they accepted the account as factually accurate, then fairness required that they had to put to her the criticism that her attendance did not meet Dr Gondhalekar's reasonable requirements, specifying what those requirements were.

[39] Secondly, the July 1998 decision that the appellant had made no sufficient progress in her research, based as it was on Dr Gondhalekar's report, had to be revisited once the appellant had alleged (as she did in her letter of 23 September 1998) that Dr Gondhalekar had not read the material she had sought to put before him.

...

[T]he question is whether, in the very special circumstances of this case, fairness required that the appellant should have the opportunity to raise any concern that she might have as to qualities of impartiality and expertise which were so obviously necessary in the person by whom her work was to be judged. In my view fairness did require that.

[40] Thirdly, the senior academic appears to have put in question a matter of which the appellant had never been given warning; that is to say whether her research subject had potential to merit the award of a PhD degree. It must have been accepted that her research had such potential when she was admitted to the Register of Graduate Students in 1993; it must have been thought that it still had such potential when she was allowed to continue following the October 1997 decision; and there is nothing to suggest that the potential value of her research had been called in question by Dr Gondhalekar's report. In those circumstances fairness required that she be warned that the decision to refuse her application for reinstatement was to be taken on the basis of this new, unfavourable, appraisal by an unnamed senior academic. Further, for the reasons that I have already given, fairness required that, in this context also, she be given the opportunity to raise any concerns that she might have as to the impartiality and expertise of her academic judge.

...

[41] I would accept that there is no principle of fairness which requires, as a general rule, that a person should be entitled to challenge, or make representations with a view to changing, a purely academic judgment on his or her work or potential. But each case must be examined on its own facts. On a true analysis, this case is not, as it seems to me, a challenge to academic judgment; it is a challenge to the process by which it was determined that the appellant should not be reinstated to the Register of Graduate Students because the course of research for which she had been admitted had ceased to be viable. I am satisfied that that process failed to measure up to the standard of fairness required of the university.

Assessment appeals

The majority of complaints by students relate to assessment decisions. The grounds for challenging such decisions include: breach of the rules of natural justice, failure to take into account relevant considerations such as mitigating circumstances, and irrationality.

NATURAL JUSTICE

The following cases are examples of where there has been an allegation by students that there has been a breach of the rules of natural justice. In *R v Aston University Senate, ex p Roffey* [1969] 2 QB 538 the university had the power to appoint a visitor but had not in fact done so.

R v Aston University Senate, ex p Roffey [1969] 2 QB 538

Donaldson J: Derek Anthony Roffey and Michael Bruce Pantridge were student members of the University of Aston in Birmingham, reading for the degree of Bachelor of Science with honours in behavioural sciences. In June 1967, at the end of the first year of the course, both passed the examinations in the three major subjects, consisting respectively of the elements of psychology, sociology and economics. In addition Mr Pantridge passed in the subsidiary subject of statistics. Unfortunately he failed to achieve a pass mark in the other subsidiary subject of social and economic history. Mr Roffey failed to pass in either subsidiary subject. In September 1967, both Mr Pantridge and Mr Roffey, together with other students who had experienced similar failures, were re-examined in the subjects in which they had been unsuccessful, but again they failed to achieve pass marks.

Thereafter, on or about September 20, 1967, Mr Pantridge and Mr Roffey received letters from their course tutor asking them to withdraw from the behavioural science course and by implication from student membership of the university. Following protests by Mr Pantridge, Mr Roffey, Mr Michael Griffin (the president of the guild of students of the university) and Mr Pantridge's father, this decision was reviewed by the board of examiners, the board of the faculty of social science, and the senate and the council of the university and in the end was affirmed.

Mr Pantridge and Mr Roffey now apply to this court for orders of certiorari to bring up and quash the relevant decision that they be asked to withdraw from the course, and of mandamus requiring the university, by the appropriate body, to determine in accordance with law whether they should be allowed to resit the whole of the examinations which they took in June 1967, or whether they should be asked to withdraw from the course.

The grounds of these applications are broadly that those responsible for the decision to refuse to allow them to continue with their studies and those who reviewed and affirmed the initial decision failed to observe the requirements of natural justice in that they failed to afford the applicants any, or any adequate, opportunity of being heard.

...

I can understand it being argued on the regulations that regard was to be had primarily and possibly exclusively to the examination results and performances in non-examinable subjects. However, the examiners themselves did not adopt this approach, as I think rightly, and they considered a wide range of extraneous factors, some of which by their very nature, for example personal and family problems, might only have been known to the students themselves. In such circumstances and with so much at stake, common fairness to the students, which is all that natural justice is, and the desire of the examiners to exercise their discretion upon the most solid basis, alike demanded that before a final decision was reached the students should be given an opportunity to be heard either orally or in writing, in person or by their representatives as might be most appropriate. It was, in my judgment, the examiners' duty and the students' right that such audience be given. It was not given and there was a breach of the rules of natural justice.

Although the court held that there had been a breach of the rules of natural justice the court declined to give the applicants a remedy. In the case of Mr Roffey this was because he did not wish to resume his studies at Aston, and in the case of Mr Pantridge because he had delayed too long before applying to the court for a remedy.

However, in *Herring v Templeman* [1973] 2 All ER 581, the court was not prepared to intervene because the college had a visitor who had exclusive jurisdiction to hear the student's complaint.

Herring v Templeman [1973] 2 All ER 581

Brightman J: The plaintiff seeks a declaration that a resolution of the governing body passed on 31 January 1972 was ultra vires and therefore null and void. The resolution that is challenged is one which unanimously accepted a recommendation of the academic board of the college that the plaintiff be required to withdraw from the college on academic grounds.

...

It appears from the statement of claim and the documents referred to therein that the college is a teacher-training college originally set up pursuant to charitable trusts declared by the Central Board of Finance of the Church of England by a trust deed dated 5 April 1961. The governing body of the college were given certain powers to vary the terms of the trust deed, as also was the visitor. These powers were exercised. The college is currently governed by what is called a revised trust deed, signed on 9 July 1968 signed by the chairman of the governing body.

Clause 2 of the revised trust deed provides that the college and its endowments (of which the Central Board of Finance is custodian trustee) shall be administered by the governing body as the administering trustees thereof. Clause 3 appoints the Archbishop of Canterbury to be the visitor of the college.

...

[I]n the trust deed one finds cl 24 which is of prime importance, and I will read it in full:

The Principal shall have power to recommend the dismissal of a student from the College. Every such recommendation shall require to be confirmed by resolution of the Governing Body after considering such representations in writing or in person as the student may wish to make except that in emergency the Chairman or in his absence the Vice-Chairman shall have power to act on behalf of the Governing Body and shall report his action to the next meeting of the Governing Body. Every such dismissal, after confirmation by the Governing Body or by the Chairman or Vice-Chairman acting on behalf of the Governing Body, shall at once be reported to the Secretary of State for Education and Science. The Principal, for any reason he may judge adequate, shall have power to suspend any student from his studies in the College and to exclude him from the premises of the College. The Principal shall at once report any such suspension or exclusion to the Chairman or in his absence the Vice-Chairman of the Governing Body.

...

It is common ground that the plaintiff was not accorded a hearing by the academic board itself before the board recommended his dismissal. He was, however, offered a sort of ex gratia hearing before a committee of the academic board by way of informal appeal, but this was not acceptable to him.

The matter came before the governing body on 31 January 1972. The proceedings of the governing body are the subject-matter of lengthy minutes, which counsel agreed that I should read; their accuracy was not challenged. There were present the chairman of the governing body and 11 other members. The plaintiff appeared before the governing body, as also did his solicitor who acted in part as his spokesman. The governing body spelt out its duties as follows, according to the minutes (minute 535(e)):

...the Governing Body must make a decision either to accept the recommendation of the Academic Board or to reject it. It was not the business of the Governing Body to interfere with the Academic Board's assessment of [the plaintiff's] academic and professional competence, but an opportunity must be given to [the plaintiff] to offer reasons why he should be allowed to complete his course.

The governing body had before it one document only, namely, the report of the academic board to which I have already referred. The plaintiff had been given a copy of this report prior to the meeting. In answering questions from the governing body, the plaintiff said that he found it difficult to make a case because the academic board had not told him why he was unfit to be a teacher. There is then this passage in the minutes, recorded as an answer by the plaintiff to a question put to him:

the final teaching practice assessment as an examination result was not being contested, but [the plaintiff] should have been warned he was in danger of failing and given an opportunity to make representations.

...

In the action with which I am concerned, the plaintiff's case is that he did not have a hearing before the academic board, that he did not have a fair hearing before the governing body and that the procedure of his dismissal was defective. In my judgment, these are essentially matters which touch the internal affairs or government of the college and are therefore matters confined by law to the exclusive province of the visitor. The dismissal of a student teacher for failing, in the opinion of those charged with the task of forming an opinion, to match up to the standard required of a teacher is the inevitable duty of an educational establishment which holds examinations and passes out students whom it considers fit to be teachers. The training of a student teacher and the assessment of his competence is the main and indeed the only object of a teacher-training college. The construction of the regulations of the college and the carrying into effect of those regulations in relation to persons who subject themselves to those regulations are, in my view, matters which the decided authorities have committed to the exclusive jurisdiction of the visitor.

In *R v Cambridge University, ex p Beg* [1999] ELR 404 the applicant was informed by the university in July 1996 that an allegation of plagiarism had been made against him. The university's internal procedures were followed and the matter came before the court of discipline, which confirmed the decision. The student appealed to the Septemviri (seven 'men'). The student argued that the essay containing the plagiarism was not the essay that he had submitted. Before the court he argued that there had been a breach of the rules of natural justice and the European Convention on Human Rights.

R v Cambridge University, ex p Beg [1999] ELR 404

Sullivan J: This is a challenge to a decision of the Septemviri of the University of Cambridge, dated 12 May 1997, which confirmed a penalty imposed upon the applicant by the university's court of discipline. The penalty was that the applicant was disqualified from admission to the degree of Master of Philosophy in Finance. The notification of the reasoned decision of the Septemviri is dated 22 May 1997.

In summary, the applicant contends that the determination was in breach of the principles of natural justice and that the penalty imposed upon him was disproportionate to the alleged offence.

By way of background the applicant was studying for the award of the degree of Master of Philosophy in Finance. The university declined to award him the degree because of an allegation of plagiarism by him in the submission of his independent essay. The essay represented 25 per cent of the marks for the degree. The university's allegation was that the applicant knowingly put forward as his own work material in his 'independent essay' without due acknowledgement that the passages came from the work of other individuals.

...

At the hearing before the Septemviri the applicant contended that the essay on which he had been marked had been submitted in his name by his supervisor, Mr K, a Fellow of Pembroke College. Mr K had, according to the applicant, maliciously substituted the essay for the essay which the applicant had submitted. It will be observed that this contention had not been advanced before the court of discipline.

On 12 May 1997 the university informed the applicant's solicitors in writing of the Septemviri's decision, namely that the appeal be dismissed. Full reasons were provided on 22 May 1997.

...

On behalf of the applicant Mr Diamond has advanced two contentions: first, that there has been a breach of natural justice because the applicant has been denied a fair trial and, secondly, the penalty imposed was disproportionate. In support of the first contention Mr

Diamond submits that whilst there was no breach of the procedures prescribed by the university's statutes, the procedure adopted denied the applicant a fair trial in that justice was not seen to be done because the chair of the Septemviri and the university advocate were both members of the university's department of law. The university, he submitted, is a small village. Members of the law department and, indeed, other departments are bound to mix, both socially and professionally. They are linked by ties of employment and there is a hierarchy within the law department.

Mr Diamond does not suggest any lack of integrity or any conscious bias on the part of Professor Hepple or, indeed, Dr Forsythe, but he submits that there should be a clear demarcation between the prosecutor and the tribunal. Here, he submits, there is the appearance of a too cosy relationship between the prosecution and the tribunal and so there is—to use the words of Simon Brown LJ in *R v Inner West London Coroner, ex p Dallaglio and Another* [1994] 4 All ER 139, at p 152:

...a real danger that the decision-maker was unconsciously biased.

Here, submits Mr Diamond, there was a real danger that the Septemviri would unfairly, albeit unconsciously, regard the applicant's allegations against Mr K with disfavour.

Mr Diamond referred to Art 6 of the European Convention for the Protection of Human Rights and Fundamental Freedoms, the right to a fair trial, and submitted that I should apply the common-law principles relating to natural justice in such a way as to be consistent with the requirements of Art 6. In that context he pointed to the decision of the European Court of Human Rights in *Belilos v Switzerland* (1988) 10 EHRR 466 that the applicant in that case could legitimately have doubts as to the independence and organisational impartiality of a Swiss Police Board which exercised judicial functions: see para 67 of that decision.

He also referred to the report of the Commission in *McGonnell v United Kingdom* European Commission of Human Rights, Appn No 28488/95, Report of 20 October 1998, to the effect that the Royal Court of Guernsey is not an independent and impartial tribunal. He emphasises the fact that there was no suggestion of any actual bias by any member of the Royal Court and no reason to doubt the bailiff's impartiality in that case. What the Commission considered to be important was 'the appearance of independence'.

In the present case he submits that appearance was lacking because of the connections between the university advocate and the chairman of the Septemviri.

...

Turning to Mr Diamond's first contention, for present purposes I do not see any distinction between the right to a fair trial under the rules of natural justice at common law and the right to a fair trial under Art 6 of the Convention which will be directly conferred when the Human Rights Act 1998 is brought into force in due course.

I find Mr Diamond's first submission unconvincing, whether the question is considered in terms of the appearance of independence or in terms of a real danger of unconscious bias on the part of the Septemviri. As a starting-point, academic members of the university are particularly well-qualified to decide whether or not plagiarism has taken place and, if it has, what is its significance in academic terms.

The issue as between the applicant and Mr K arose for the first time without any prior notice before the Septemviri. The applicant made no complaint as to the composition of the tribunal. So far as student membership is concerned, not only did he make no complaint before that tribunal but he had not sought the presence of student members when that opportunity was available to him before the court of discipline.

Mr Diamond's primary submission ignores the clear distinction between the role of the advocate and the parties to proceedings. I could well understand the applicant feeling uneasy if he had been criticising the conduct of a member of the law department and the chairman of the Septemviri was the head of that department. In such circumstances Professor Hepple might well have stood down and decided to ask a lawyer from outside the department to chair the tribunal, but that is not this case. Mr K was Director of Studies in Economics at Pembroke College and a non-university teacher within the faculty of economics.

I have set out the composition of the Septemviri on this occasion. None of the members was from Pembroke College, nor were they connected with the faculty of economics. All are very distinguished academics. In the 'village' atmosphere of the university I see no reason why such very senior 'villagers' should be unconsciously biased against a student member of the university as opposed to a lecturer at the university; all are members of the same village community.

...

It is not in the least unusual for a judge to know socially and/or professionally the advocates who appear before him. Whilst he would not dream of sitting as a judge in any action in which they were parties, much less in any proceedings where their credibility might be in issue, he would feel no embarrassment whatsoever in entertaining and then rejecting their submissions advanced as advocates. Whilst the distinction between the advocate and his client might be blurred in the minds of some laymen, it would be clear to any lawyer, and certainly to so distinguished a lawyer as Professor Hepple.

...

For all of these reasons I am satisfied that on the facts there has been no breach of natural justice here in that there is no real danger that the Septemviri were unconsciously biased against the applicant because the university advocate was a member of the department of law, nor does that factor give rise to the appearance of any lack of independence or any lack of impartiality. It follows that this application for judicial review must be dismissed.

• *Do you agree with Sullivan J's view that the position of the chairman of the Septemviri in relation to the student and the lecturer was the same position as a judge hearing a case presented by a barrister whom he knows?*

FAILURE TO TAKE INTO ACCOUNT RELEVANT CONSIDERATIONS

This ground will normally be relied upon where the university is alleged to have failed to take into account or given sufficient weight to mitigating circumstances, as occurred in *R v Manchester Metropolitan University, ex p Nolan* [1994] ELR 380.

R v Manchester Metropolitan University, ex p Nolan [1994] ELR 380 (see ch 1 for the facts)

Sedley J:

(c) Did the board take into consideration all the factors it should have done?
In approaching its task, however, the board had limited material. The academic registrar in para 15 of his second affidavit says:

> I have no doubt having attended the meeting in person that the board was aware of the mitigating circumstances. They were referred to in discussion the board was aware of the applicant's previous achievements and certainly approached its decision on the basis that he was of excellent character. It was fully aware and certainly accepted that he was under stress at the time of the examination. As against this however the board had to deal with infraction of an important regulation governing a professional examination.

If there had been a full oral hearing before the board it would have been up to the applicant to present what material he wished to them, but he had no right to attend and was entirely dependent on what was placed before the board in his absence. It emerges from the evidence—as I have found—that this did not include some important statements in mitigation. In the absence of the recommendation as to penalty which the disciplinary committee should have made and of the disciplinary committee's own minutes and (inevitably) of the applicant himself, this lacuna was certainly significant and may well have been crucial. I am unable to accept Mr Richardson's submission that everything material was substantially known to the board.

I am reinforced in this by three further factors. First, this was the same body as had taken the ultra vires decision on 9 July 1992. While, on good advice, it had rescinded that decision and started again, it behove the board to be doubly cautious in what it then did. Secondly, anticipating for a moment the next head of argument, it was on any view a surprising decision that was reached, suggesting that something material in the applicant's favour may well have been overlooked. Thirdly, I am not convinced that the mere presence of the applicant's personal tutor Miss Deehan affords an assurance that the powerful mitigation which she is minuted as having advanced for him on 25 June 1992 was repeated at the board meeting on 22 September 1992. In the applicant's absence and in the absence of any evidence of what role she played at the latter meeting it would not be right to infer that her voice was heard, or as clearly heard, in the applicant's favour as it had been before the disciplinary committee.

I would therefore hold that there was a material failure on the part of the board of examiners on 22 September 1992 to take into account matters which it was incumbent on them to take into account, namely the full evidence in mitigation which had been placed before and accepted by the disciplinary committee. Such a failure will ordinarily vitiate the material proceedings and nullify the decision.

In *R v South Bank University, ex p Coggeran* [2001] ELR 42 the Court of Appeal confirmed that the university's examination board should reconsider its decision to request the applicant to withdraw from her course and should fully take into account her mitigating circumstances before reaching a new decision. Similarly, in *R (on the applicaton of Burgess) v South Bank University* [2001] ELR 300 the High Court granted a student's application for judicial review. The court considered that the panel, which screened assessment appeals, had acted unfairly because it had failed to take into account the student's mitigating circumstances when deciding that the appeal should not go before the full appeals panel.

IRRATIONALITY

This is more difficult for a student to establish. In neither of the following cases was the student successful. In *R v University of Humberside, ex p Cousens* [1995] CLY 1947, CA a postgraduate student applied for judicial review of the decision of the examining board on a number of grounds, including irrationality. The student had failed a first semester examination, and was not permitted to proceed to the next semester. The board had refused to exercise its discretion in his favour and condone the fail grade. The court held that it was not irrational to ask a student to submit coursework to demonstrate that he was fit to continue with the course.

In *R v University of Central England, ex p Iqbal Sandhu* [1999] ELR 121 the student was awarded a pass degree. He claimed that he should have been awarded an honours degree because the mark for his dissertation should have been take into account. The mark was not taken into account because the dissertation was submitted late because of problems printing the dissertation. The judge found that the student was given permission to submit the dissertation late and that the examination board would then decide whether or not to award the mark. The student appealed unsuccessfully to the Pro-Vice-Chancellor.

R v University of Central England, ex p Iqbal Sandhu [1999] ELR 121

Owen J: The applicant wrote an appeal letter to the Pro-Vice-Chancellor and there were other written representations made to him as well. He in his turn notified the applicant of his decision to reject the appeal in a letter to the solicitors. He had no jurisdiction to examine on the merits and it is conceded that his decision is not a free-standing decision; it follows on the other two. If decision 1 and decision 2 are right then no criticism can be made of the Pro-Vice-Chancellor. If decision 1 and 2 are wrong, then no doubt the Pro-Vice-Chancellor's actions and decision are of no avail, but nobody suggests that he did not do what was proper when he came to his conclusion.

...

As I have indicated, it seems to me that the proper conclusion is that he was told that he could put in his dissertation, that he could put in his explanation and that, of necessity, the matter would then be considered by the examination board. They could have said: 'We will accept this explanation'. As is abundantly clear they considered whether they should do that or not. But in the end they were entitled to find, and certainly it was not in any way unreasonable for them to find, as they did in fact find. In my judgment here there was material upon which they could find that there was no valid extension in accordance with the rules and in those circumstances I reject this argument.

...

The third matter which is raised is that the effect of awarding no marks for the dissertation and therefore making the award of an honours degree impossible was disproportionate given that the dissertation was only one working day late and there is a reference then to undergraduate assessment regulations now in force, those having been copied at p 379 onwards. What has happened is that in order that there should be a uniformity in the various schools of the university, new regulations had been prepared and under those regulations, merely because you are out of time does not necessarily mean that you get no marks, indeed that will not be what in fact has happened, what would happen and what happens under the new regulations is that a proportion of marks is awarded but not the whole, necessarily, given that there is no excuse. And so it is said that that at the very least it is bad luck on this applicant and so it may be, but again one has to see what the position was for the examination board. They had all the facts which were put before them including the applicant's explanation and they decided in accordance with the rules which were then the rules that they would have to award no marks. It cannot be said that those rules were *Wednesbury* unreasonable or that they were irrational; it cannot be said that it is unreasonable or irrational to say that you must have your work submitted on time, particularly not when of course there is a discretion which is available for the board to consider any extenuating circumstances and if they think there is good reason they can allow the dissertation in effect to be marked and marks to be given although out of time. Here the examination board were not prepared to do that and they were entitled, in my judgment, to come to that decision. It is certainly not accepted by the university that the original rules were unfair or unreasonable in any way and indeed at one stage it was pointed out that, particularly in a business studies course, there is a merit in demanding that the students should do their work and arrange their work so that they are able to comply with the requirements of the university. That again is a factor, as it seems to me, which it is right for me to state, although it does not go a great way in making me come to the conclusion which I do, which is that this error which is alleged is not an error at all and certainly not an error in law.

The student applied without success for leave to appeal to the Court of Appeal (*Iqbal Sandhu v University of Central England* [1999] ELR 419).

• *Does this case illustrate any limitations in the judicial review process in the context of student appeals?*

The student does not appear to have had a right of appeal in the sense of a rehearing of the examination board's decision.

Grievance procedures

Sometimes a student will use the grievance procedure to complain about an individual lecturer as well as bringing an appeal against the decision of the assessment or examination board. One issue is whether the two complaints should be investigated concurrently or consecutively; and if consecutively which should be investigated first. This issue was addressed in *R v Leeds Metropolitan University, ex p Manders* [1998] ELR 502.

R v Leeds Metropolitan University, ex p Manders [1998] ELR 502

Collins J: The applicant, Mr Steven Manders, was in 1996 reaching the end of his university degree course at the Leeds Metropolitan University in which he was seeking an LLB. It seems that two factors, according to him, affected the way in which he was able to sit his exams. First of all, he fell ill. Unfortunately at no relevant stage did he indicate to the university the precise nature of that illness. It now transpires that, according to a doctor's note which is in the papers, he was suffering from what is described as chronic fatigue syndrome. Secondly, he had unfortunately fallen out with one of his tutors, Mr Cousins, who was also responsible, it seems, for marking at least one of the papers which he took, namely employment law.

He was granted a pass degree. His work in the years leading up to his finals, he says, suggested that he ought to have achieved a lower second and at worse, one would imagine, a third and thus have received an honours degree.

...

What Mr Manders did was to follow the regulations, which I am bound to say are not as clear as they ought to be, but which in this respect, at least, indicate that there is a separate student grievance procedure from a request for review of a decision of a board of examiners. However, it is perfectly clear that matters which are properly the subject of a student grievance procedure could impact upon a review of a decision of a board of examiners.

...

The complaint is made that by the university's own regulations where there is a student grievance, which is running in tandem, as it were, with an academic complaint, the academic complaint should not be disposed of until the grievance has been decided upon. One can see the force of that if the grievance could impact upon the academic review. The point is taken that the regulations, if read strictly and carefully, only provide that that should be the case if the student grievance is in existence before the academic review claim.

Mr Engleman submits that the regulations do not, in fact, produce that result but that, in any event, if one looks here at the form of the academic review one sees that it specifically refers to the grievance and, at the very least, the review body ought to have asked Mr Manders in what way he said the grievance impacted upon the review. They ought to have made inquiries, or they ought to have had regard to the grievance. Once they were aware, after the first stage of 29 July 1996, of the existence of the grievance they ought to have deferred the consideration of the second stage, that is to say the review of the original decision, until the grievance had been disposed of.

Student conduct and discipline

Students may be asked to withdraw from the university because of their conduct. Where they are on courses leading to professional qualifications they may be asked to withdraw because they are not considered suitable candidates for members of the profession. In *Glynn v Keele University* [1971] 1 WLR 487 the Vice-Chancellor in accordance with s 6 of the university statutes fined a student and excluded him from living on the university's campus for one academic year. The student was able to continue with his course.

Glynn v Keele University [1971] 1 WLR 487

Pennycuick V-C: In this action the plaintiff is Mr Simon Vincent Glynn, who is a last-year undergraduate at the University of Keele. The first defendant is the University of Keele itself; the second defendant is Mr William Alexander Campbell Stewart, who is the vice-chancellor of that university. I have before me a notice of motion whereby the plaintiff seeks an injunction restraining the defendants from excluding him from residence on the campus of the university for the remainder of the current academic year.

The present action, including the motion, arises from an incident on 19 June, 1970; on that day a number of undergraduates of the university were standing or sitting naked on the campus of the university, and that incident gave rise to a great deal of trouble, as one would expect. There is no formal admission by the plaintiff that he was one of the undergraduates concerned; there is, however, evidence of identification, and there is nowhere in his affidavits or in the speeches of his counsel, Mr Sedley, any real suggestion that he was not one of the naked undergraduates on that occasion. I must plainly proceed to deal with this motion on the footing that he was in fact involved in this incident; in other words, no issue of identification is raised.

...

The question is whether, when the vice-chancellor takes a decision under s 6, he is acting in a quasi-judicial capacity, and if that question is answered in the affirmative, whether there has been some failure of the requirements of natural justice in the present case. The two questions as to what constitutes a quasi-judicial capacity, and the duty to comply with the requirements of natural justice, are very closely inter-related.

...

The context of educational societies involves a special factor which is not present in other contexts, namely the relation of tutor and pupil; that is to say the society is charged with the upbringing and supervision of the pupil under tuition, be the society a university or college, or a school. Where this relationship exists it is quite plain that on the one hand in certain circumstances the body or individual acting on behalf of the society must be regarded as acting in a quasi-judicial capacity—expulsion from the society is the obvious example. On the other hand, there is a wide range of circumstances in which the body or individual is concerned to impose penalties by way of domestic discipline. In these circumstances it seems to me that the body or individual is not acting in a quasi-judicial capacity at all but in a magisterial capacity, ie, in the bringing and supervision of the members of the society.

...

The vice-chancellor has under the provisions which I have read no power of expulsion. That power is vested in the council alone. On the other hand, the powers which he has under s 6 are of an extremely far-reaching character. He may under para 4 in s 6 suspend any student from any class or classes, and may exclude any student from any part of the university or its precincts. Those powers, although they do not amount to expulsion, amount in terms to suspension, and also amount in substance to something very like expulsion. If a student is excluded from the university it is hard to see how he can carry on his studies at the university.

I have found considerable difficulty in making up my mind as to which side of the line those powers fall. When the vice-chancellor exercises those powers should he be regarded as acting in a quasi-judicial capacity, or should he be regarded as acting merely in a magisterial capacity?

On the best consideration I can give it—but let me say at once it is by no means the end of the matter—I have come to the conclusion that those powers are so fundamental to the position of a student in the university that the vice-chancellor must be considered as acting in a quasi-judicial capacity when he exercises them; I do not think it would be right to treat those powers as merely matters of internal discipline.

Having reached that conclusion, I must next decide whether in exercising his powers in the present case the vice-chancellor complied with the requirements of natural justice. I regret that I must answer that question without hesitation in the negative. It seems to me that once one accepts that the vice-chancellor was acting in a quasi-judicial capacity, he was clearly bound to give the plaintiff an opportunity of being heard before he reached his decision on the infliction of a penalty, and if so what penalty. In fact he did not do so.

However, his Lordship declined to exercise his jurisdiction and grant an injunction (see 'exercise of discretion' below). In the following case the judge was prepared to grant the student's application on the ground that she had not received a fair hearing.

R v Board of Governors of Sheffield Hallam University, ex p R [1995] ELR 267

Sedley J: [H]er first year (the academic year 1991/92) had been a troubled and unhappy one in her relations with other students. On the academic side, however, which included teaching practice, it had evidently been a successful year. The problem of the first year spilled over into the second, when the applicant found herself giving evidence at a disciplinary proceeding against fellow students one of whom, she said, had persuaded her to try LSD on one occasion, with the result that she had thereafter been harassed. In the early part of 1993 she had the distressing experience of giving evidence against her fellow-students at a disciplinary hearing, following which they suffered minor penalties which did not interrupt their education, while the applicant's behaviour led to inquiries which ultimately culminated in her expulsion.

...

The university's procedures stated that 'Documented evidence of adequate prior warning and advice to students who might be in danger of being recommended for expulsion will always be required and any extenuating circumstances must have been taken into account'. It is not disputed by Mr Gill that failure to adhere to the professional standards specified for training purposes is capable of including behaviour indicative of unfitness to become a teacher, nor that, unexplained, the applicant's behaviour might well be so construed. But he contends that what followed had three fatal flaws: there was no documented evidence of adequate prior warning to the applicant, notwithstanding that she was in danger of being recommended for expulsion, so that the chair of the academic board had no power under the rules to cause a committee of the academic board to be convened to consider expulsion;
...

[S]he was in my judgment entitled to a clear statement not only of what she ought to do but, linked with it, of the possible consequences of her not doing it. The letter from the principal and vice-chancellor dated 29 May 1993, which was handed to the applicant on 7 June 1993, does not in my judgment contain any such warning. It rightly and fairly says:

> Anxieties about your health and well-being shall remain unresolved whilst you refuse to provide us with the evidence we have requested.

But the final paragraph of the letter does no more than warn that Mr Stoddart 'will have no option other than to deem you unfit to pursue your professional studies and to exclude you from the university' if it should turn out that the applicant had been simply lying to staff and students. There is nothing else in the correspondence capable of amounting to an adequate warning, and no evidence of any oral warning of the kind required.

In *Herring v Templeman* (see above) a student unsuccessfully challenged his dismissal from a teacher training course on the ground that he did not have a fair hearing. The academic board of the college decided that the student had shown himself on training practice to be unfit to practise as a teacher.

- *Would the student in Herring v Templeman be more likely to succeed if his application came before the courts now?*

In *R (on the application of M) v University of West of England* [2001] ELR 458, the applicant was a student on a professional social work course. The university removed her from the course on the ground that she was unsuitable for the profession. The decision was made because a local authority social services department, who had been involved with the student on a personal basis, expressed grave concern about her suitability. The student was, therefore, unlikely to obtain a placement which was part of the course. The Court of Appeal held that the university was entitled under its regulations to reach the decision it took, which was lawfully made.

Exercise of discretion

Judicial review is a discretionary remedy. This means that even where the decision has been made in breach of the rules of natural justice or relevant considerations have not been taken into account the court may still refuse to grant the applicant a remedy. Reasons given for refusing to grant a remedy include:

- delay in bringing the application
- internal procedures should be used
- the decision was the proper one in any case
- no practical purpose would be served.

In *R v Aston University Senate, ex p Roffey* [1969] 2 QB 538 (see above) the court found that there was a breach of rules of natural justice but refused to exercise its discretion and award a remedy because of the delay in seeking relief.

In *Glynn v Keele University* [1971] 1 WLR 487 the judge refused to grant an injunction for the following reasons:

Glynn v Keele University [1971] 1 WLR 487 at 496

Pennycuick V-C: I have, again after considerable hesitation, reached the conclusion that in this case I ought to exercise my discretion by not granting an injunction. I recognise that this particular discretion should be very sparingly exercised in that sense where there has been some failure in natural justice. On the other hand, it certainly should be exercised in that sense in an appropriate case, and I think this is such a case. There is no question of fact involved, as I have already said. I must plainly proceed on the footing that the plaintiff was one of the individuals concerned. There is no doubt that the offence was one of a kind which merited a severe penalty according to any standards current even today. I have no doubt that the sentence of exclusion of residence in the campus was a proper penalty in respect of that offence. Nor has the plaintiff in his evidence put forward any specific justification for what he did. So the position would have been that if the vice-chancellor had accorded him a hearing before making his decision, all that he, or anyone on his behalf, could have done would have been to put forward some plea by way of mitigation. I do not disregard the importance of such a plea in an appropriate case, but I do not think the mere fact he was deprived of throwing himself on the mercy of the vice-chancellor in that way is sufficient to justify setting aside a decision which was intrinsically a perfectly proper one.

However, in *R v Board of Governors of Sheffield Hallam University, ex p R* [1995] ELR 267. Sedley J, who had been Mr Glynn's counsel, was prepared to grant the application.

R v Board of Governors of Sheffield Hallam University, ex p R [1995] ELR 267

Sedley J: I do not accept, however, that the present case lies parallel in principle with the case of *Glynn v Keele University*. There it was not possible to show the court that, given the accepted facts, a hearing could have made any significant difference to the outcome. In the present case I have held that the entire purpose of the warning which should have been but was not given was to bring home to the applicant the risk she now faced and what she might yet do to meet it. If I had been persuaded that she was so manifestly and permanently unfit to teach that no warning could have done any good, I would have acceded to Mr Bean's earlier submission that this was a special case in which no warning was adequate warning. My reasons for not doing so, which I have given, must mean that it would be a denial of justice to decline instead to grant the applicant the relief which is otherwise her due on the basis of my own appraisal of her chances. To do so would be, precisely, to substitute the court for the university as the decision-making body.

In *R v Leeds Metropolitan University, ex p Manders* [1998] ELR 502 one ground on which relief was refused was the delay by the student in challenging the review board decision. The student should not have waited until after his grievance claim was rejected by the university.

However, in *R v Liverpool John Moores University, ex p Hayes* [1998] ELR 261 the judge stated that the student should follow the internal appeal process.

R v Liverpool John Moores University, ex p Hayes [1998] ELR 261

Collins J: While I understand and to some small extent sympathise with the applicant's loss of faith in the School, she must realise that, if she wants an honours degree, she can only obtain it through the university, which is constrained to act in accordance with its regulations and must not award a degree unless satisfied that the applicant has achieved a proper academic standard or would, but for mitigating circumstances, have achieved such a standard. She has submitted that she cannot appeal since the decision whether or not to grant a degree is one of academic judgment. That is incorrect since she is seeking to show through the appeal that the PAB/MAB failed to take into account various matters which affected her ability to do herself justice. What effect these matters, if established, would have on her marks is of course a matter of academic judgment, but their existence is not.

Breach of contract

During the past thirty years students have relied on the public law remedies provided by the judicial review procedure. In recent years students have started to bring their claims in the law of contract. The main advantages for doing so are that there is a longer limitation period and damages are available. The claim is normally based on breach of an express or implied term of the contract, which may include negligent performance of the contract and misrepresentation. The case law, in particular *Clark v University of Lincoln and Humberside* [2000] ELR 345, illustrates the long-running debate over when it is appropriate to use private law remedies in public law situations and vice versa.

In the past such claims were likely to be struck out. In *Casson v University of Aston in Birmingham* [1983] 1 All ER 88 the report deals with a decision of the visitor, but refers to an action for breach of contract in the county court being struck out. The visitor, the Lord Chancellor, made the following observations on a possible claim for breach of contract.

Casson v University of Aston in Birmingham [1983] 1 All ER 88

Lord Hailsham: 6. Both petitions arise out of similar facts. The undergraduate prospectus issued by the University for the year 1981–82 listed a course entitled Human Communication, and both petitioners applied for admission to the university for the purpose of taking this course. Both applications were accepted by the university, in the case of the petitioner O'Brien unconditionally, in the case of the petitioner Casson on conditions which, in the event, were fulfilled. The acceptance took the form of an offer of a place for the purpose of studying the course on Human Communication which in each case was accepted by the petitioners.

7. In the events which happened the university found itself unable to mount the course (described by the university as 'the BSc Behavioural Science Course on which you have been offered a place'), but in each case offered the petitioners a place in the university to take a choice of alternative courses. In each case the petitioner concerned accepted this offer and was in fact admitted to the university to study a course referred to as Human Psychology.

8. In October 1981 both petitioners appeared to have sued the university in the Birmingham County Court for damages for breach of contract arising out of the above matters. In the event it appears that the proceedings were struck out by the registrar, and that on appeal on 16 February 1982 his Honour Judge Toyn upheld the decision of the registrar, but gave leave to appeal to the Court of Appeal. This does not appear to have been pursued. I have not available to me a complete record of the proceedings in the Birmingham County Court, but I have read what purports to be a copy of the judgment declining jurisdiction, on the ground that the matters arising are properly within the exclusive jurisdiction of the visitor. The essence of the judgment as recorded is confirmed by the letter of 3 June 1982 above referred to from the petitioners' solicitors. Having read it with interest and care I do not feel bound to say more than that, in so far as it is inconsistent with what follows, I respectfully disagree with it. I do not regard myself as bound by the decision.

…

10. The two petitions are each founded on an alleged contract between the respective petitioners before they became members of the university [and the university] to provide instruction in accordance with the terms of the original prospectus. The existence of this contract is denied by the university.

…

12. Assuming in favour of the petitioners (but without deciding) that prior to their admission to the university there was a contractual relationship between the petitioners and the university, any 'late and wrongful retraction' (on which the only claim for substantive relief is based) took place prior to the admission of the petitioners to the university and either sounds in contract or in nothing. I refer also to the proposition in Dr Smith's article (with which I also agree) that '…the visitor has no jurisdiction over contracts made between the body, or member of the body of which he is visitor, and a stranger who is outside the foundation' (cf 97 LQR 610 at 637 and passim). The matters complained of in both petitions, if they give rise to complaints at all, occurred at a moment of time when the petitioners were wholly 'outside the foundation of the University', and therefore strangers to it.

The first question is at what point is there a contractual relationship between a student and his or her university. In *Moran v University College Salford (No 2)* [1994] ELR 187 the court was concerned with an applicant rather than an enrolled student. The applicant was made an unconditional offer of a place on a physiotherapy course which he accepted. As a consequence his application did not go into clearing. He also gave notice to his landlord and his employer. Shortly after doing so he contacted the college to check certain details and was told that he had not been offered a place and that none was available to him. There had been an administrative error. The applicant applied for a mandatory injunction which would order the college to give him a place on the course.

Moran v University College Salford (No 2) [1994] ELR 187

Glidewell LJ: The unconditional offer apparently made by UCS of a place for Mr Moran on the physiotherapy course was on the face of it intended to create a legal relationship between the parties, and appeared to be an offer capable of acceptance. When Mr Moran accepted it, at the latest when he notified UCS of his acceptance on 8 July 1993, there is a strong case for saying that an agreement was reached under which UCS agreed to offer him a place if he sought to enrol on the due date. However, Mr Moran would not have been bound to enrol or to pay fees until he did enrol. Under the specific terms of the PCAS 'statement of decisions' leaflet, he was entitled to withdraw completely from the scheme, and to give up any place he was holding, up to 30 September 1993. If he had enrolled, he would then have been bound by a further separate contract to pay fees. I therefore conclude that there is a strong case for saying that there was a binding agreement under which UCS committed itself to accept Mr Moran for the physiotherapy course.

...

Alternatively, it was argued that the detriment Mr Moran suffered by giving up his job and his flat amounted to consideration. However these were not directly related to the agreement, though they arose indirectly out of it. It is thus not surprising that the deputy judge rejected these submissions.

Before us, a more sophisticated submission was advanced. It was that by accepting the unconditional offer, Mr Moran finished his dealings with PCAS, and in particular ceased to be eligible to seek an alternative place through clearing. Thus he gave up the chance, however small, which entry into clearing would offer. That was a detriment which provided consideration for the agreement.

Mr Smouha, in reply, argued that Mr Moran could have sought to rejoin clearing when he spoke to Mr Simpson on 16 August 1993 and was told that there was no place for him. But in my view this is not so. At that stage he was not told the reason why there was no place, and he only learned the correct reason when he received the letter from Mr Kemp of 3 September 1993. By then it was too late—the clearing was almost, if not quite, concluded. In any case, in my view this would go to mitigation rather than destroy this element as consideration.

I therefore conclude that there is a strong and clear case, on which Mr Moran has a good chance of success, that in late June/early July 1993 the parties reached a binding agreement, for good consideration, that UCS would accept Mr Moran for the degree course in physiotherapy commencing in September/October 1993.

...

I must decide whether an interlocutory mandatory injunction should be granted. Clearly this is a matter for our discretion.

On the one side, on the evidence, Mr Moran was clearly misled into believing that there was a place on the course available to him. As a result, he abandoned his chance (which may not have been great) of obtaining another offer at the clearing stage, he gave up his job (though he has succeeded in retaining it temporarily), and he gave notice of his intention to leave his flat. If in the end he succeeds in this action, he will at least be entitled to some damages. Lord Campbell argues that damages will be so difficult to quantify or prove that this remedy will be useless. I am not wholly persuaded by this argument; I can see no reason why Mr Moran should have greater difficulty in proving his damages than do many other plaintiffs.

On the other side, if UCS were bound by an agreement to make available to Mr Moran a place on the course, that agreement arose out of a simple clerical error by a member of its staff. That error in legal phraseology was a mistake which was unilateral, and thus does not vitiate the agreement. Nevertheless it is very relevant to the question, is it just to compel UCS to provide a place on the course?

...

Taking all these matters into account, I am clearly of the view that it would be wrong to grant a mandatory order at this interlocutory stage. Indeed, in my judgment the grant of such an order might very well create injustice. It is for these reasons that I concluded that the appeal should be dismissed.

There should be no reason in principle why a student should not recover damages from a university for breach of contract, and in practice most UK universities appear to settle such a claim.

Martin Davis 'Students, Academic Institutions and Contracts—a ticking time bomb' (2001) 13(1) Education and the Law 9

Direct authority in the United Kingdom on damages in student/university disputes is limited. However, in *Orphanos v Queen Mary College*, Lord Fraser stated:

A claim for damages would be made on the basis that Mr Orphanos has suffered damage to the extent to which he has been overcharged for the first year's fees, namely £1,320, perhaps with the addition of a further sum for loss of interest on that sum, or for the cost of borrowing it. I shall assume, without deciding, that a *claim for damages* could properly be mounted on that basis.

Also, in *Moran v University College Salford* Glidewell LJ stated:

If in the end [Mr Moran] succeeds in this action, he will at least be entitled to some damages. Lord Campbell argues that damages will be so difficult to quantify or prove that this remedy will be useless. I am not wholly persuaded by this argument. I can see no reason why Mr Moran should have greater difficulty in proving his damages than do many other Plaintiffs.

Moreover, the case law in the United States and Canada is both significant and instructive. For example in *McBeth v Governors of Dalhousie College and University* the claimant, a university student brought an action against the university for damages for breach of contract consisting of failure to schedule a supplementary examination after he had missed the regular examination through illness. It was conceded by the university that this had constituted a breach of contract, and it was found by the courts that the breach had adversely affected the claimant's opportunity for employment and his creditworthiness with leading institutions(!).

Special damages (principally linked to student loans) of $4,647.75 and general damages of $1,688.00 were awarded. The latter figure appeared to include some compensation for the general 'difficulties' which the breach had caused the claimant, although not damages for distress or disappointment per se. At no stage did the court indicate that it was doing anything other than applying standard contract principles. In *Universite Laval v Carriere* the claimant was awarded $10,351.93 after a 'mix-up' by the university had led her to believe that a place on a nursing technician course was available to her (whereas her application had been refused). As a result she had resigned from a part-time job, had left for Quebec to find a place to live and had withdrawn her other applications. Rothman JA stated (at p 507):

[the mistake of the university] meant that the applicant was delayed by one year in commencing her professional career [and]…during the first year of her earning career … she would have … earned … $13,709.06 from which we must subtract the total of $3,349.13 which she earned elsewhere during the same year, thus leaving a remainder of $10,351.93 again, without considering the minimal incidental expense of moving to Quebec.

It seems clear that whatever the dearth of domestic case law, universities in practice will settle out of court, often for substantial amounts to avoid litigation. For example in the THES of 23 October 1999 (at p 5) it was reported that a settlement had been reached between Nottingham University and a Romanian research student Manuella Antoniu, at a figure of £35,000. Ms Antoniu had been accepted onto a multi-disciplinary programme in architectural and critical studies to support the PhD she had commenced at the University. She had argued that there was no framework for co-ordination between relevant departments and that (in effect) the University had admitted her onto the PhD 'under false pretences' as he PhD was dependent upon a programme which the University could not provide.

Therefore, a student enters into at least two contracts with their university. The first is when they accept the offer of a place, and the second is when they enrol on the course.

A breach of contract may arise, for example, where a module listed is not available, where the quality of the educational or other provision is below a reasonable standard, or where the university does not follow its own rules when deciding that a student should be withdrawn from a module or a programme.

In *M v London Guildhall University* [1998] ELR 149 a student brought an action based on negligence, breach of contract and misrepresentation. The case was originally brought in the county court and was struck out. The student brought another claim in the High Court on similar grounds. The Court of Appeal dismissed the student's appeal against the High Court judge's decision to strike out the case on the ground that the proceedings were an abuse of process.

M v London Guildhall University [1998] ELR 149

Auld LJ: Mr M then instituted proceedings in the High Court (these proceedings) in much the same terms, alleging negligence, breach of contract and, I think, misrepresentation by the university in its failure to award him an honours degree. He does not appear to have sought to make use of the domestic procedure provided by the university for the challenge of decisions of boards of its examiners.

The university applied to strike out his cause of action, again on the authority of *Thorne v University of London* on the principle adumbrated in that case that the High Court will not act as a court of appeal from university examiners. It also urged the court to rule that the claim was an abuse of process, having regard to the striking out of the almost identical claim in the Mayor's and City of London Court. Deputy Judge Mawrey took the view that the case was governed by the authority of *Thorne v University of London* and that the court had no jurisdiction to consider an issue which was essentially one between Mr M and the examiners at the university. He also took the view that the proceedings were an abuse of process, having regard to the previous striking out of the almost identical proceedings.

...

In my view, this application is not arguable. We are bound by *Thorne v University of London*. The university has a provision to determine disputes of this sort, and that provision and those administering it are the proper vehicles for that determination, not the High Court. In addition, this action is a clear abuse of process, having regard to the earlier dismissal of the matter in the Mayor's and City of London Court.

Since 1998 two things have happened which have arguably affected the way in which the courts perceive contractual claims by students against their university. The first is that many undergraduate students are required to contribute towards their tuition fees, and the second is the introduction of the Civil Procedure Rules 1998.

Although overseas and postgraduate students have often paid their own fees, it was only in 1998 that means-testing was introduced for undergraduate tuition fees. This made the commercial and contractual nature of the relationship between undergraduate and university explicit. The changes in the civil procedure rules have also altered the approach of the courts to abuse of process and the distinction between the remedies in public law and private law actions. The second point is explained fully by Lord Woolf, whose report led to the changes in the rules, in the following case.

In *Clark v University of Lincoln and Humberside* [2000] ELR 345 the Court of Appeal was asked to consider whether a claim against a university by a student for breach of contract was justiciable. The parties reached an agreement after the court heard their arguments but before the court gave judgment. Nevertheless, the court considered that the point was sufficiently important for it to give a reasoned judgment.

Clark v University of Lincoln and Humberside **[2000] ELR 345 at 347F**

Sedley LJ:

History

The appellant was a student at the respondent university between 1992 and 1995, reading for a first degree in humanities. For her final examination she had to submit a paper by 14 April 1995. She chose to do a presentation and academic write-up on *A Streetcar Named Desire*, and she worked on these using her father's computer. She made the mistake many of us make once, and once only: she failed to make a backup copy of her work. On the last day before the deadline all her stored data were lost from the hard disk. All the appellant was able to put in were some notes copied from a Methuen commentary.

The university's Board of Examiners failed her for plagiarism. The appellant says that she had in fact explained the reason for her poor submission to her tutor so that the examiners could be informed; but in the event the Academic Appeals Board accepted that she had not set out to deceive and referred the paper back for remarking. The Board of Examiners marked it 0.

...

Under the respondent's Student Regulations this gave the appellant one more attempt to obtain her degree. But reg 6.5.4 says:

A candidate who satisfies the examiners for the award of a classified degree at the second attempt shall not normally be awarded a degree classification higher than a Third Class.

The appellant resat her finals and was awarded a third class degree, which is not good enough for the further career options which she wanted and still wants to pursue. In mid-1998 (the exact date is in dispute) she issued the present proceedings in the Halifax County Court.

...

ULH is simply a statutory corporation with the ordinary attributes of legal personality and a capacity to enter into contracts within its powers.

The arrangement between a fee-paying student and ULH is such a contract: see *Herring v Templeman* [1973] 3 All ER 569, at pp 584–5. Like many other contracts, it contains its own binding procedures for dispute resolution, principally in the form of the Student Regulations. Unlike other contracts, however, disputes suitable for adjudication under its procedures may be unsuitable for adjudication in the courts. This is because there are issues of academic or pastoral judgment which the university is equipped to consider in breadth and in depth, but on which any judgment of the courts would be jejune and inappropriate. This is not a consideration peculiar to academic matters: religious or aesthetic questions, for example, may also fall into this class. It is a class which undoubtedly includes, in my view, such questions as what mark or class a student ought to be awarded or whether an aegrotat is justified. It has been clear, at least since *Hines v Birkbeck College* [1986] Ch 524 (approved in *Thomas v University of Bradford*), that this distinction has no bearing ob the availability of recourse to the courts in an institution which has a visitor. But where, as with ULH, there is none, the decision of the New Zealand Court of Appeal in *Norrie v Senate of the University of Auckland* [1984] 1 NZLR 129 and the remarks of Hoffmann J in *Hines v Birkbeck College* at pp 542–3 open the way to the distinction as a sensible allocation of issues capable and not capable of being decided by the courts. It would follow, I think, that the issues which the courts remitted with obvious relief to visitors in such cases as *Thomson v University of London* (1864) 33 LJ Ch 625 (which concerned the award of a gold medal), *Thorne v University of London* [1966] 2 QB 237 and *Patel v University of Bradford Senate; Same v Edwards* [1978] 1 WLR 1488 (both of which concerned the plaintiff's academic competence) would still not be susceptible of adjudication as contractual issues in cases involving higher education corporations.

It is on this ground, rather than on the ground of non-justiciability of the entire relationship between student and university, that the judge was in my view right to strike out the case as then pleaded. The allegations now pleaded by way of amendment are, however, not in this class. While capable, like most contractual disputes, of domestic resolution, they are allegations of breaches of contractual rules on which, in the absence of a visitor, the courts are well able to adjudicate.

...

To permit what is in substance a public law challenge to be brought as of right up to six years later if the relationship happens also to be contractual will in many cases circumvent the valuable provision of RSC Ord 53, r 4(1)—which, though currently due to be replaced by a new Civil Procedure Rule, is unlikely to be significantly modified—that applications for leave must be made promptly and in any event within three months of when the grounds arose, unless time is enlarged by agreement or by the court. Until the introduction of the Civil Procedure Rules 1998 this was a dilemma which could be solved only by forbidding the use of the contractual route—a solution which, as *Roy v Kensington, Chelsea and Westminster Family Practitioners Committee* demonstrated, could not justly be made universal. But as Lord Woolf MR explains in his judgment, the Civil Procedure Rules 1998 now enable the court to prevent the unfair exploitation of the longer limitation period for civil suits without resorting to a rigid exclusionary rule capable of doing equal and opposite injustice. Just as on a judicial review application the court may enlarge time if justice so requires, in a civil suit it may now intervene, notwithstanding the currency of the limitation period, if the entirety of circumstances—including of course the availability of judicial review—demonstrates that the court's processes are being misused, or if it is clear that because of the lapse of time or other circumstances no worthwhile relief can be expected.

The present case is, however, not one in which I would consider it right to strike out or stay the action on this ground.

...

Lord Woolf MR: One of Lord Diplock's reasons which he gave in *O'Reilly v Mackman* for his concern about an ordinary civil action being commenced against public bodies when the more appropriate procedure is under Ord 53 was the fact that in ordinary civil proceedings the claimant could defer commencing the proceedings until the last day of the limitation period. This compares unfavourably with the requirement, that subject to the court's discretion to extend time, under Ord 53 proceedings have to be commenced promptly and in any event within three months. If a student could bypass this requirement to bring proceedings promptly by issuing civil proceedings based on a contract, this could have a very adverse affect on administration of universities.

This is a matter of considerable importance in relation to litigation by dissatisfied students against universities. Grievances against universities are preferably resolved within the grievance procedure which universities have today. If they cannot be resolved in that way, where there is a visitor, they then have (except in exceptional circumstances) to be resolved by the visitor. The courts will not usually intervene.

While the courts will intervene where there is no visitor, normally this should happen after the student has made use of the domestic procedures for resolving the dispute. If it is not possible to resolve the dispute internally, and there is no visitor, then the courts may have no alternative but to become involved. If they do so, the preferable procedure would usually be by way of judicial review. If, on the other hand, the proceedings are based on the contract between the student and the university then they do not have to be brought by way of judicial review.

...

Where a student has, as here, a claim in contract, the court will not strike out a claim which could more appropriately be made under Ord 53 solely because of the procedure which has been adopted. It may however do so, if it comes to the conclusion that in all the circumstances, including the delay in initiating the proceedings, there has been an abuse of the process of the court under the Civil Procedure Rules 1998. The same approach will be adopted on an application under Part 24.

The emphasis can therefore be said to have changed since *O'Reilly v Mackman*. What is likely to be important when proceedings are not brought by a student against a new university under Ord 53, will not be whether the right procedure has been adopted but whether the protection provided by Ord 53 has been flouted in circumstances which are inconsistent with the proceedings being able to be conducted justly in accordance with the general principles contained in Part 1. Those principles are now central to determining what is due process. A visitor is not required to entertain a complaint when there has been undue delay and a court in the absence of a visitor should exercise its jurisdiction in a similar way. The courts are far from being the ideal forum in which to resolve the great majority of disputes between a student and his or her university. The courts should be vigilant to ensure their procedures are not misused. The courts must be equally vigilant to discourage summary applications which have no real prospect of success.

- *What difference, if any, would it have made were the university in this case an old university with a visitor?*

The implications of there being a contractual relationship between students and their university is considerable. Students will have rights not only under common law principles but also under statutory consumer law provisions relating to unfair contract terms and the supply of goods and services (see M Davis 'Students, Academic Institutions and Contracts – a ticking time bomb' (2001) 13(1) Education and the Law 9 which contains a comprehensive examination of the implications of there being a contractual relationship between students and their university).

Nevertheless it is arguable that such disputes are not and should not be normally resolved in the courts.

Martin Davis 'Students, Academic Institutions and Contracts—a ticking time bomb' (2001) 13(1) Education and the Law 9

Much of the above might suggest an academic atmosphere poisoned by litigation and lawyers. However, despite the rather doom-laden title of the article, this is far from the case. Disputes with the potential to go the full distance through the courts are still relatively unusual and most of these tend to be settled out of court. However, anyone involved in higher education over (say) the last fifteen years or more will have noticed the steady change in student attitudes and expectations. Not least because of their increased personal financial stake in their own education, students increasingly expect to have rights and the means of redress if things go awry with their course of study. For universities and colleges the challenge is clear; to respond positively to this change by way of improved documentation and student charters, transparent internal appeal and mediation procedures and (not least) more realistic claims as to what will be provided on courses, or to mount rearguard actions testing step by step through the courts the willingness of the latter to apply standard contractual principles to disputes between their students and themselves. It seems evident that the former approach is much to be preferred, not least because the latter is (as this article attempts to indicate) ultimately doomed to expensive failure.

The Human Rights Act 1998

The two provisions of the ECHR most relevant to students are Article 6 and Article 2 of Protocol 1 (see also chapter 1). However, they may in practice be of little assistance because of the way the European and UK courts have interpreted the provisions.

First, education is not perceived as a 'civil' right. However, if the right breached is considered to be a contractual right as opposed to the right to education there would be a requirement to comply with Article 6.1. Secondly, it is not certain that Protocol 1 applies to further and higher education.

ARTICLE 6.1

Lalu Hanuman v United Kingdom **[2000] ELR 685**

The Court has examined the above application from which it appears that the applicant complains under Art 6 of the European Convention for the Protection of Human Rights and Fundamental Freedoms 1950 about the fairness of an appeal initiated before the Academic Appeals Committee of the University of East Anglia and about the fairness of the rejection, without reasons, of his application to the visitor. However, these proceedings do not involve the determination of a civil right or of a criminal charge against him within the meaning of Art 6 of the Convention. It follows that the application is incompatible ratione materiae with the provisions of the Convention, within the meaning of Art 35.3 of the Convention, and must be rejected, in accordance with Art 35.4.

Accordingly, the Court *declares* the application inadmissible.

In *R v Cambridge University, ex p Beg* [1999] ELR 404 (see above) Sullivan J considered that there was no distinction between the right to a fair trial under the rules of natural justice at common law and the right to a fair trial under Article 6.

Despite the case law being unpromising some academics consider that Article 6 will be able to provide redress for students.

T Kaye 'Academic judgment, the university visitor and the Human Rights Act 1998' (1999) 11(3) Education and the Law 165

Article 6 and the visitor

A highly significant effect of the incorporation of Article 6(1) of the Convention into domestic law is likely to be its impact on the role of the visitor within chartered [higher education institutions]. Lord Griffiths in *Thomas v University of Bradford* appears to have viewed the role of the visitor through somewhat rose-tinted spectacles. In that case he proclaimed 'the advantage of cheapness, lack of formality and flexibility in the visitorial appeal procedure which is not bound by the intimidating and formalised procedures of the courts of law'. The current reality with many visitorial hearings could hardly be more different. In many cases an application for leave for judicial review is considerably cheaper, quicker and no more formal than the visitorial procedure—and a hearing can be obtained almost as a matter of course if the parties desire one, whilst the visitor often seems inclined to follow his own lights irrespective of the wishes of the parties involved.

Indeed, when judged according to this test laid down by Article 6(1) of the Convention, the determination of disputes by a university visitor simply does not pass muster. Hearings are frequently delayed for long periods until such time as the visitor is available: in such cases they will fall foul of Article 6 by reason of unreasonable delay. Indeed, visitors sometimes choose not to hold a hearing at all. This too would be a clear breach of Article 6 (1) unless the student voluntarily agreed to waive his or her right to a hearing. Moreover, visitorial hearings rarely allow for each party to question the other's evidence in any systematic manner: they are simply conducted according to procedures decided upon by the visitor. Such procedures may not pass the criterion of being 'fair' according to the jurisprudence of the European Court of Human Rights on Article 6. Indeed, there may even be doubts as to whether the visitor is a truly 'independent and impartial tribunal' within the meaning of Article 6 since not only is he appointed under the higher education institution's charter by the university's founder (or the Queen), the visitor may then himself appoint someone else to deputise for him in fulfilling that role. This is certainly not the manner in which impartial tribunals are normally expected to be set up: some sort of legislative framework or constitutional structure identifying the tribunal's personnel would seem much more appropriate.

Furthermore, Article 6 requires that hearings should be held in public unless:

> ... in the interests of morals, public order or national security in a democratic society, where the interests of juveniles or the protection of the private life of the parties so require, or to the extent strictly necessary in the opinion of the court in special circumstances where publicity would prejudice the interests of justice.

Yet cases heard by a visitor have never been held in public, and it is difficult to see how any of the permitted exceptions could apply. University students nowadays are almost all adults; academic judgements will rarely (if ever) impinge on a student's private life; and questions of morals, public order or national security would seem to be similarly irrelevant. In *Le Compte, Van Leuven and De Meyere v Belgium*, for example, the ECHR struck down a decision to discipline several doctors by the Belgian equivalent of the British Medical Association on the grounds that neither the disciplinary hearing nor the judgment had been held or delivered in public. Only if the student concerned agreed to waive the requirement for a public hearing could it then take place in private and still satisfy Article 6(1). Moreover, a subsequent public hearing on an application for judicial review will not cure this defect since a judicial review hearing would be unable to 'take cognisance of the merits of cases' so that numerous issues arising in disputes concerning 'civil rights and obligations' would fall outside its jurisdiction.

Since s 6 of the Human Rights Act 1988 will make it unlawful for higher education institutions to act in a way which is incompatible with Article 6 of the Convention, it is therefore clear that universities will not be able to rely on the settling of disputes before the visitor in order to satisfy their legal obligations under the Act. Indeed, since hearings before a visitor will not pass muster under Article 6 if they continue in their present form, it is possible that students could effectively bypass the visitorial stage altogether. This is because in *Golder v UK* the ECHR held that Article 6(1):

> ... is not applicable solely to proceedings which are already in progress: it may also be relied on by anyone who considers that an interference with the exercise of one of his (civil) rights is unlawful and complains that he has not had the possibility of submitting his claim to a tribunal meeting the requirements of Article 6(1).

However, the Court has held more recently that the 'right to a court':

> ... does not oblige the Contracting States to submit ... disputes ... over 'civil rights and obligations' to a procedure conducted at each of its stages before 'tribunals' meeting the Article's various requirements. Demands of flexibility and efficiency, which are fully compatible with the protection of human rights, may justify the prior intervention of administration or professional bodies and, *a fortiori*, of judicial bodies which do not satisfy the said requirements in every respect; the legal tradition of many member States of the Council of Europe may be involved in support of such a system.

On this basis, an aggrieved student at a chartered university would be obliged to go through the institution's procedures invoking the jurisdiction of the visitor before s/he could think of taking legal action in the courts unless the university were prepared to waive this requirement.

Article 6 and judicial review

It could, of course, be argued that someone aggrieved at the decision of the visitor could then seek judicial review of the visitor's decision. Judicial review in its present form is not, however, likely to be found to be an adequate way of remedying the defects in the visitorial procedure posed by Article 6. There are two reasons for taking such a view. The first is that, as was explained earlier, the courts have held that the visitor has exclusive jurisdiction over matters of academic judgement so that they will intervene only when the visitor has exceeded his/her jurisdiction or acted contrary to the rules of natural justice. This blanket refusal to intervene will therefore have to be completely abandoned if the courts are to discharge their own obligations under ss 6(1) and (3)(a) of HRA 1998. Visitors will no longer enjoy untrammelled power to adjudicate upon domestic disputes within chartered higher education institutions.

But whilst a preparedness to intervene in domestic university disputes over matters of academic judgement according to the usual rules of judicial review laid down by the House of Lords in *Anisminic Ltd v Foreign Compensation Commission* is undoubtedly a necessity if judicial review is to satisfy the requirements of Article 6(1) of the Convention in this context, it will be insufficient on its own. This is because judicial review is a legal process designed to enquire only into the procedures according to which a decision was taken. It is emphatically not designed as a means of enquiring into the substantive merits of the case: no witnesses are even called to give evidence. Thus it is incapable of acting as an independent forum wherein a student's civil rights and obligations may be fairly determined, as Simon Brown LJ pointed out with some force at the beginning of his judgment in *R v University of Nottingham, ex p K*. For the same reasons judicial review, as currently conducted, will also be unsuitable as a means of resolving disputes arising within statutory higher education institutions. It remains to be seen whether the judicial review procedure will have to be amended to cater for this sort of issue, or whether other legal avenues will have to be pursued by aggrieved students.

ARTICLE 2 OF PROTOCOL 1

In *Sulak v Turkey* (Application No 24515/94) 84-A DR 98 (1996) (see also chapter 1, the Human Rights Act 1998) the Commission held inadmissible an application by a university student that his expulsion from university was in breach of the Convention. The Commission did not rule on whether higher education falls within Article 2.

Sulak v Turkey (Application No 24515/94) 84-A DR 98 (1996)

On 4 September 1991 the applicant sat a foreign languages examination in the Engineering and Architecture Faculty of the University of X where he had been studying.

In a decision dated 27 September 1991, the Administrative Board of the Faculty found that the applicant had copied from another student during the examination of 4 September 1991, which constituted a disciplinary offence in accordance with the Disciplinary Regulations for students attending Higher Education Institutions (Yüksek Ögretim Kurumlara Ögrenci Disiplin Yönetmeligi—'the Disciplinary Regulations'). It observed that the applicant had committed the same disciplinary offence for the third time. The Board decided to expel the applicant from the University in accordance with the provisions of the Disciplinary Regulations.

...

The applicant complains that his expulsion from the university pursuant to a disciplinary measure deprived him of the right to education. He also alleges that under the national regulations, expelled students are prevented from enrolling in another higher education institution to pursue their studies.

...

In the present case the education in question is higher education. However, even assuming that Article 2 of Protocol No 1 (P1-2) is applicable to the present case, the application is in any event manifestly ill-founded for the following reasons....

In the present case, the Commission notes that the applicant had an opportunity to follow his chosen course of study in the University of X. It further notes that the applicant had been disciplined on two occasions for cheating and can have been in no doubt as to the requirement of the rules and regulations of the institution or as to the likely consequences of a further breach of those rules. Consequently, after having been found to have cheated a third time, he was expelled from the University as a disciplinary measure. In addition, the Commission observes that the applicant had an opportunity to challenge the disciplinary measure in question before national courts which found that his expulsion was lawful.

It is true that the applicant submits that under the national regulations, students expelled from higher education institutions are prevented from enrolling in another higher education institution to pursue their studies. However, even assuming that this submission is correct, in the circumstances of the present case, the Commission cannot find that the expulsion

of the applicant injured the substance of the right guaranteed by Article 2 of Protocol No
1 (Pl-2) or amounted to a denial of the applicant's right to education guaranteed by that
Article.

Secretary of State

There are no formal procedures whereby a student or any other interested person may
make a complaint to the Secretary of State. Nevertheless the Secretary of State has the
power to give directions to HEFC, in particular in relation to the provision of financial
support where an institution's financial affairs are being mismanaged (s 81 of the
FHEA 1992).

Local education authorities

Higher education students who wish to have their tuition fees paid by the LEA, or who
are eligible for an award or a grant paid by the LEA, are required to apply to the LEA.
Where the application process or the provision of financial assistance suffers from
'maladministration' the student may make a complaint to the Local Government
Ombudsman (see above).

The following report is an example of an investigation where the Ombudsman
found that there was maladministration causing injustice. The student was a registered
blind person and was entitled to a Disabled Students Allowance. In September 1996 he
requested help from the county council to purchase computer equipment, which would
assist him with his university studies. The Council received a letter from the university
stating that he had everything he needed to complete his course successfully. In
February 1997 the Council rejected his application. Lengthy correspondence and
discussions ensued. From December 1998 until September 1999 the student withdrew
from his course because of depression. The complaint was lodged with the Ombudsman
in August 1999.

Report on an Investigation into Complaint No 99/B/2282 against Wiltshire County Council, 18 May 2000

43. Then the council received the view of John's consultant opthalmic surgeon which
argued forcefully that he needed very special help that he currently did not have. And then
it was told by John that another official of the University had suggested an independent
report by an Access Centre. Quite properly, the council commissioned such a report and
this was received in September 1997. It recommended new equipment and upgrades
costing just over £1,500.

44. Government guidance is the 'LEAs should be prepared to accept such independent
assessments'. Clearly the council must have the discretion to reject an assessment where
it feels it is somehow flawed. But in that case it would need to commission an alternative
independent assessment on which it could feel safe to rely. Even a critique which undermined

the value of the first assessment would not justify the council in doing nothing at all; it would merely justify the production of a second opinion. What happened here? In effect, the council rejected the independent assessment on the basis of the original statement of the University's lecturer. But it was this very statement that the independent assessment had been commissioned to evaluate. It seems to me that the exchange of e-mails between Officer B and her superior reveal a cavalier and uncaring attitude to John's needs as a disabled person. It also shows disgracefully inadequate consideration to the Access Centre report that the council had itself commissioned. I conclude that in these circumstances it was maladministration for the council to reject the recommendations of the Access Centre's report.

45. When the council received further representations from John's parents, the Education Department asked a council computer expert to advise it. I find it extraordinary that, without being asked to see John and assess his needs, Officer C was expected to give a technical view on which officers could rely in reviewing their refusal to accept the results of an independent assessment. The way this review of the council's decision was conducted was also maladministration.

46. The council maintained its position, even in the face of expert evidence from the RNIB, although it moved to the extent of offering to make a contribution to some of the costs of equipment John's parents had by now bought him. That equipment cost nearly £1,700, well within the DSA ceiling; the council offered £670.

47. What injustice has the council's maladministration caused John? It is, I believe, considerable. The distress, depression and dislocation to his studies that John has suffered are clearly evidenced not only by his own views but by staff at the University. It may be that, even with the equipment the Access Centre said he should have had, John's disability could have caused him problems in pursuing his studies. But on balance I conclude that the council's maladministration has contributed avoidably and considerably to the trouble he has had. In addition, his parents have been put to financial expense they should not have had to bear.

Finding

48. For the reasons given in paragraphs 44 and 45 above, I find maladministration by the council causing the injustice described in paragraph 47. To remedy that injustice I recommend that the Council:
1.   apologise to John for the way it has treated him;
2.   review its arrangements for processing applications for Disabled Students' Allowances to ensure that, as far as possible, the maladministration I have identified does not recur;
3.   reimburse the cost of the new equipment his parents purchased with interest at the county court rate;
4.   make John an ex gratia payment of £2,000 for his distress, worry, and frustration, and as some compensation for the break to his studies to which the council's maladministration has contributed.

Reform

As already indicated it is likely that there will be reform of the complaints procedures in universities.

Tim Birtwistle 'Should Multiple Systems for Academic Appeals Remain?
The Role of the Visitor' [2000] Education LJ 135

Reform

Both Dearing and the government recognised the need for a review of the complaints in universities. The unrelated but cumulative changes to the law have resulted in a debate about the nature of the role of the visitor within the new legal framework. The debate also has a policy dimension to it. If there is a single university system, should that system have a single appeals and complaints framework.

The visitors are under pressure operating as they currently do. The pressures are in terms of increasing volume of activity resulting in increasing pressure on time. The visitors do not receive any form of payment for undertaking the role. This is proving to be a burden across the wide and varied spectrum of those who act as visitors, from the Lord Chancellor's Department to the Archbishop of Canterbury. This pressure has some significance in terms of policy, not law.

It would be possible to provide some guidelines for visitors to enable them all at least to have access to a suggestion of good practice in carrying out their duties. This might be in terms of oral hearings, time limits for the process, the giving of written reasons for the decision. At the moment there is no such uniformity of practice let alone uniformity of expertise in dealing with claims, evidence and adjudication skills. Access to the guidelines would bring about greater uniformity if all visitors chose to follow what could only be a voluntary code. However, visitors are already complaining about the burden placed upon them and to follow such guidelines will, for many, merely increase the burden even within the existing volume of complaints reaching the visitor.

Differing forms of modernisation have been suggested. Queen's University Belfast has a board of visitors (four) appointed by the Queen on the advice of the Privy Council for a renewable term of five years and finds that this works well. Isaac proposed a panel of 'HE commissioners' and a set of guidelines to go with this structure. However, the exact nature of the relationship between the commissioners and the visitor or the commissioners and judicial review would still need clarifying. The Nolan Report (*Second Report of the Committee on Standards in Public Life* (1996)), looked at dispute resolution and questioned the absolute validity of the visitor, but rejected a full-time ombudsman. At a recent UCELNET workshop most of the visitors present felt that the system was inherently fair and welcomed the proposed guidelines. At the same meeting student representatives took the view that the system is inherently flawed. The QAA has equally had problems in establishing a common approach even when bringing together the stakeholders in HE. Not only could an agreed process not be arrived at (the idea of an independent external overview not being universally welcomed), but also there remained widely divergent views on whether or not academic judgement can be a ground for appeal.

To modify the current system is one answer. To replace it is another. If a green field site existed and a complaints and appeals process were to be formulated a simple process could be adopted:

Principle >>> Policy >>> Legislation

First, establish what principle should govern the process, from that determine, secondly, a policy to achieve the principle and from that, thirdly, bring about whatever legislation might be needed to give effect to the policy. If that were the case then surely the principle would be equality of treatment for all. The policy would therefore be a single process governing all disputes within a particular category (academic appeals, complaints etc), thus giving equality of treatment to all. The legislation would therefore remove the visitor's powers regarding appeals and complaints. The question remaining would be whether to then leave each university to establish its own process or whether to put into place a new tier of appeal along the lines of the HE commissioners (as proposed by Isaac).

This proposal is legally achievable. It would meet the requirements of all aspects of legislation. It would meet the requirements of Nolan, Dearing and *Higher Education for the 21st Century*. It would leave the courts as the final reference point if this had to be. Any robust and transparent system would not fear the possibility of judicial review. All concerned with the law recognise that having to resort to the lawyers and the courts is not in the best interests of dispute resolution, but in terms of ultimate transparency and impartiality access to the courts is probably required.

Other jurisdictions have reached the conclusion that the visitor acting as the final stage of an appeal process is no longer appropriate. Schedule 1 to the University Legislation (Amendment) Act 1994 in New South Wales has the following section:

Section 14

(1) The Governor is the visitor of the University but has ceremonial functions only.
(2) Accordingly, the visitor has no functions or jurisdiction with respect to the resolution of disputes or any other matter concerning the affairs of the university (other than a matter involving the exercise of ceremonial functions only).

What process has been put in place? This appears to be varied but does include the use of a student academic appeals committee (a sub-committee of the senate) acting as 'the last court of appeal *within* the university' (author's emphasis). Most statutes contain precise information on composition (including student representation), grounds (including some aspects of academic judgement), tight timescale, and the right of the appellant to be accompanied by a friend. Some universities require their equivalent panel to be chaired by a legally qualified person.

It would seem that 'the medieval visitor procedure that forces students to accept the unreasoned judgment of a remote senior legal figure is indefensible and is rightly doomed'.

If the visitor is no longer compatible with the law, nor acceptable to students, then the appeal processes must change. Universities (and their stakeholders) should lobby for this change and then be proactive in putting together, with the lawyers, a fair, workable, speedy system that will be durable, and will, because of its transparent nature, meet the needs of all participants in the process of HE. Problems with any new system will include the possible increased intervention of the lawyers and the courts, allied to this the inevitable fact of a rising set of costs, and a need to ensure compliance with all aspects of the law. The system must be capable of weeding out any vexatious actions at an early stage. The system must be robust but objective and transparent. If it is, then the system will provide, in most cases, a fair outcome to a dispute. All sense of perspective must not be lost. However, the changing nature of the overall legal context and the, surely overriding, need to treat all students equally in this day and age, may require a change as a matter of policy even if the cumulative legal changes do not.

It is becoming apparent that, as in the US, the role of the law will be increasingly visible in the future affairs of universities. This will certainly be at the procedural level and may well also encroach at the academic level. It would seem, like it or not, that 'Lawyers may soon find themselves at the centre of academic disputes'.

• *What form of independent review mechanism would be desirable for new universities?*

Index

Acts of Parliament, 12
Adjudicators, 108, 175-183
    Code of Practice, 177, 183
    objections, and, 176-183
    significant change in character of school,
        and, 179-180
Admission appeals, 225-252
    aims of process, 226
    challenging panel's decision, 250-252
        jurisdiction issue, 251-252
    constitution of panels, 226-228
    decision of panel, 243-245
        notification to parents, 243-245
    infant class size, 239-242
    multiple, 237-239
        comparison of one child's case with
            another, 238-239
        procedures for dealing with, 238
    objectives of process, 226
    permanently excluded pupil, 242
    powers of panels, 229-231
    'prejudice' appeals, 231-237
        extra expenditure, and, 237
        second stage approach, 234-236
        two-stage exercise, 232-233
    role of panel, 228
    statistics, 246-250
    statutory provisions, 225
    who may sit on panel, 226-228
Admissions arrangements, 171-211
    adjudicator, 175-183. *See also* ADJUDICATOR
    Admission Forums, 173-174
    admissions authorities, 171-175
        Code of Practice, 172
        consultation, 172-173
    admissions criteria, 198-210. *See also*
        ADMISSIONS CRITERIA

Admissions arrangements—*contd*
    information, 192-194
        Code of Practice, 193-194
    number of places, 194-198
        infant class size, 195-198
        standard number, 194-195
    selective schools, *See* SELECTIVE SCHOOLS
    variation, 174-175
    withdrawal of offer of place, 210-211
Admissions criteria, 198-210
    catchment areas, 203-205
    Code of Practice, 199-200
    distance between home and school, 200-
        202
    oversubscription, 199-200
    religious affiliation, 206-210
    selection by lottery, 205-206
Adult Learning Inspectorate, 522
After school clubs, 74
Appeals
    admission. *See* ADMISSION APPEALS

Banding
    selection, and, 185-188
Basic curriculum, 408-414
    meaning, 408
    Qualifications and Curriculum Authority,
        410-414
        assessment, 410-411
        external vocational and academic
            qualifications, 411-412
        powers, 413-414
        role, 411-412
    Secretary of State, role of, 412-413
Battery
    corporal punishment, and, 283
Behaviour support plans, 274

Breach of contract
quality of educational practice, and, 533-534
universities, 596-604
Bullying, 264-272
criminal liability, and, 271-272
effect, 267
function of schools, 267-268
liability in negligence, and, 268-271
meaning, 265
nature of, 265-266
non-statutory guidance, 265, 267-268
outside school's premises, 271
statistics, 266
victims, 266

Canada
Religious education. *See* RELIGIOUS EDUCATION
Careers education and guidance, 475-479
careers libraries, 478-479
duty on schools and FE institutions to co-operate with careers advisers, 476-477
duty to provide, 475-476
provision of careers information, 477-479
Catchment areas
admission criteria, and, 203-205
Central government
role of, 5-6
Charging, 427-439
education outside school hours, 428-431
free school transport, 431-439. *See also*
FREE SCHOOL TRANSPORT
music tuition, 427
optional extras, 427-428
voluntary contributions, 431
Chief education officer, 19
Child
meaning, 319
Childcare, 62-64
early years development partnership, 63
legal entitlement, 64
local authorities, 63-64
local education authorities, 62-63
Children Act 1989, 32
Children 'in need', 337-339
meaning, 338
Children unable to attend school through illness, 325-328
Children with disabilities, 323-325
disability, meaning, 323-325
Children's rights, 25-29
approach, 26
child as social actor, 26-27
community mental health approach, 27
participation in legal process, 25-26
Scotland, 28-29
variable competence in children, and, 27

City academy
meaning, 69
City college for the technology of the arts
meaning, 69
City technology college
meaning, 69
Collective worship, 445-452
Christian worship, 449-451
community schools, 447-451
foundation schools with religious character, 451-452
foundation schools without religious character, 447-451
monitoring, 452
Parliament, intention of, 449
reasons, 455-466
right to withdraw pupils, 452-455
voluntary schools, 451-452
Community school
meaning, 68
Complaints procedures, 535-612
further education institutions, 572-573
governing body, 536-537
judicial review, 568-572.*See also* JUDICIAL
REVIEW
Local Government Ombudsmen, 548-568.*See also* Local Government
Ombudsman
maintained schools, 536-572
Secretary of State, 537-548
'act unreasonably', 538-540
complaint by parent, 540-541
discretion, 544-545
'failed to perform certain functions', 546-548
'in default', 542-544
judicial review, and, 540-541
jurisdiction, 544
target duties, 545-546
universities, 573-611. *See also* UNIVERSITIES
Compulsory school age, 65-66
leaving school, 66
starting school, 65-66
Consumer rights, 1
Consumer, role of, 24-29
Consumerism, 6-7
Contraceptive advice, 469-472
Corporal punishment, 277-285
abolition, 278-280
battery, and, 283
human rights, and, 278-283
Courts, role of, 29
Criminal liability
bullying, and, 271-272
Curriculum, 407-485
basic, 408-414. *See also* BASIC CURRICULUM
careers education and guidance, 475-479.

Curriculum—*contd*
  careers education and guidance—*contd*
    See also Careers education and
    guidance
  collective worship, 445-452. *See also*
    COLLECTIVE WORSHIP
  complaints, 481-485
    collective worship, 483-484
    essence of, 482
    local arrangements for consideration,
      482-483
    religious education, 483-484
  European Union, 407-408
  legislative control, 407-408
  meaning, 407
  National. *See* NATIONAL CURRICULUM
  religion. *See* RELIGION
  religious and philosophical values,
    479-481
  sex and relationship education, 467-475.
    See also SEX AND RELATIONSHIP EDUCATION

Detention, 276-277
  false imprisonment, and, 276-277
Disability
  meaning, 323-325
Disability discrimination, 42-43
  meaning, 42
  substantial disadvantage, 43
Disability Discrimination Act 1995, 380-388
  discrimination, meaning, 384-385
  further education, 381-382
  higher education, 381-382
  justification, 385-386
  LEAS, 381
  remedies, 386-388
    disabled pupils, 387
    disabled students, 387-388
  requirements until 2002, 380-382
  responsible bodies, 383-384
    further education, 384
    higher education, 384
    LEAs, 384
    schools, 383-384
  schools, 380
  special educational needs, and, 382-383
Disabled pupil
  meaning, 323
Drugs
  exclusion, and, 294

Education Act 1944 (Butler Act), 3-5
  breakdown in consensus, and, 7-8
  changes since 1980, 5-11
  development of consumerism, and, 6-7
  development of emphasis on rights, and, 8
  making of, 5

Education Act 1944 (Butler Act)—*contd*
  reforms introduced by, 4-5
  scope, 3-4
  sophisticated legal structure, 4
Education action zones (EAZ), 119-120, 517
Education Department
  origin of, 2
Education development plan, 20-21, 514
Education law
  issues comprising, 1
  legal context, 31-36
  legal framework 11-12
  modernising, 15-16
Educational malpractice
  USA, in, 530-532
Educational record
  meaning, 503
Employment law, 31
Equal opportunities, 37-43
European Convention on Human Rights, 44-55. *See also* HUMAN RIGHTS
  application of rights to education, 54-55
  right to education, 44-55
    applicant child or parent, whether, 46-47
    'civil' right, 52
    civil right within Article 6, whether,
      45-47
    consequences, 53-54
    extent, 49-51
    interpretation adopted by court, 49-51
    nature of, 45
    university education, and, 51-55
    whether child has right, 47-49
European Union Law, 32-36
  Community competence in education after
    TEU, 33-34
  competence prior to TEU, 33
  movement of workers, 35-36
  right to education, 34-36
  'worker', meaning, 32
Excellence in Schools (White Paper), 8-10
  policy principles, 9
  quality of provision, 9-10
Exclusions, 285-314
  drugs-related, 294
  governing body, and, 296-300
    discipline committee, 296-300
    procedures, 299-300
  head teacher, role of, 289-296
    appropriateness of exclusion, 290
    fair hearing, 292-293
    identification, 291-292
    power to exclude, 289-290
    Social Inclusion Pupil Support, 294
    use of exclusion, 291

Exclusions—*contd*
  independent appeal pupil, 300-314
    challenging decision, 304
    composition, 301-302
    criminal prosecution pending, 304-305
    evaluation, 312-314
    new evidence after decision reached,
      309-310
    reinstatement, 306-310. *See also*
      REINSTATEMENT
    responsibility of LEA where exclusion
      upheld, 304
    role, 302-304
    statistics, 310-312
    two stages, 303
  need for, 286
  procedure, 295-296
  pupils with special educational needs, 295
  statistics, 287, 288
  welfare or justice, 313-314

False imprisonment
  detention, and, 276-277
Foundation school
  meaning, 68
Free school transport, 431-439
  Kent County Council, 433-435
  'nearest available route', 435-438
  'suitable arrangements', 433-435
  'walking distance,', 432
Further education, 120-132
  board of governors, 124-125
  complaints procedures, 572-573
  corporation, 123-124
  definition, 61
  education maintenance allowance, 131-
    132
  financial support for students, 129
  financing, 127-129
  funding for 16 to 19 year olds, 129-130
  grievance procedures, 573
  institutions, 122
  Learning and Skills Council, 125-132
  meaning, 121-122
  post-compulsory education awards, 131

Governing body, 75-82
  complaints procedures, 536=537
  composition, 76-77
  conduct of school, 77
  ensuring that school attendance targets are
    set, 79
  establishment of complaints procedure,
    77-78
  exclusion, and, 296-300
  functions, 77-82
  holding annual parents' meeting, 78
  legal status, 75-76

Governing body—*contd*
  producing school behaviour and discipline
    policy, 78-79
  producing written annual report, 78
  quality of educational provision, and. *See*
    QUALITY OF EDUCATIONAL PROVISION
  reform, 82
  responsibilities, 77-82
  school discipline, and, 263-264
Grammar schools, 189-191
  ballots, 190-191
  meaning, 69
Guidance, 13-15. *See also* STATUTORY GUIDANCE

Head teacher
  exclusions, and. *See* EXCLUSIONS
  school discipline, and, 264-272
High Court
  Appeal from SENT, 368
Higher education, 132-152. *See also*
    UNIVERSITIES
  definition, 61
  financing of institutions, 139
  freedom of speech, 139-141
  legal status of institutions, 133-138
  litigation, 134-136
  meaning, 132-133
  student finance, 145-152. *See also* STUDENT
    FINANCE
  student unions, 141-145. *See also* STUDENT
    UNIONS
Historical background, 2-3
Holiday activities, 74
Home-school agreements, 255-258
  control of parents, and, 257-258
  meaning, 256
Hospital school
  meaning, 69
Human rights, 1-2
  corporal punishment, and, 278-283
  international law, 55-58
    Iran, 57
    Japan, 57
    Macedonia, 57
    right to education, 55-58
    state violations, 58
  religious and philosophical values, and,
    479-480
  religious education, and, 456-458
  special educational needs, and. *See* SPECIAL
    EDUCATIONAL NEEDS
  universities, and, 604-608
Human Rights Act 1998, 43-58
  effects, 55

Infant class size, 195-198
  appeals, 239-242
  excepted pupils, 197-198

Infant class size—*contd*
  limit on, 196

Judicial review, 568-572
  complaints procedures, and, 568-572
  independent schools, 571-572
  non-maintained schools, 571-572
  reasons and grounds for decision, 569-571
  review rather than appeal, 571
  universities, and. *See* UNIVERSITIES

Learning and Skills Council, 125-132, 377-378
  duties, 126-127
Learning difficulty
  meaning, 318-319, 320
Local education authorities, (LEA)
  central government, and, 21-23
  chief education officer, 19
  contracting out of functions, 23
  D of EE Policy Paper, 23
  duties, 19-23
  education development plan, 20-21
  functions
    Secretary of State, and, 17-18
  meaning, 19
  obligation to consult, 21
  reduction in significance of functions, 22
  role, 19-23
  school organisation, 105-120. *See also* SCHOOL ORGANISATION IN A LOCAL EDUCATION AUTHORITY
Local government
  role of, 5-6
Local Government Ombudsman, 548-568
  analysis of outcome of complaints, 2000/ 01, 567
  delay in issuing statement, 562-563
  delay in providing speech therapy, 563-565
  education complaints, 553-554
  implementing decision of SENT, 565-566
  judicial review, and, 552
  jurisdiction, 548-552
  LEA's lack of resources, 559-560
  maladministration, 548-549
  matters not subject to investigation, 552-553
  refusal to investigate, 551-552
  school admissions, 554-556
  school exclusions, 556-559
  school transport, 566-567
  special educational needs, 559-560
Lottery
  selection by, 205-206

Maintained schools complaints procedures. *See* COMPLAINTS PROCEDURES

Management. *See* MANAGEMENT OF MAINTAINED SCHOOLS
  meaning, 68
  quality of educational provision. *See* QUALITY OF EDUCATIONAL PROVISION
Management of maintained schools, 74-105
  employer, 91-105
    appointment of non-teaching staff, 93
    appointment of teachers, 92-93
    community schools, 91
    community special schools, 91
    foundation schools, 93
    foundation special schools, 93
    negligence, liability in, 97-99
    psychological injury, 103-105
    religious opinions, 95-96
    schools which have religious character, 94-95
    vicarious liability, 99-103
    voluntary aided schools, 93
    voluntary controlled schools, 91
  financial arrangements, 82-91
    delegated budget, 87-88
    individual schools budget, 85
    LEAs financial schemes, 84
    local schools budget, 84-85
    reform of LEA funding, 88-91
    role of LEA, 83-84
    school's budget share, 85-87
  governing body, 75-82. *See also* GOVERNING BODY
Middle school
  meaning, 67
Music tuition
  charge for, 427

National Curriculum, 414-417
  assessment arrangements, 418-426
    key stage 4, 420-421
    key stages, 1-3, 420
  baseline assessment, 419-420
  content, 415-417
  exemptions, 4221-426
    general power to disapply, 425-426
    pupils with statements of special educational needs, 421-422
    temporary exception for particular school. 424-425
    temporary exceptions for individual pupils, 422-424
  LEA, role of, 415
  legislation, 414-415
  school, role of, 415
  Welsh, 417
Natural justice
  university assessment appeals, and, 583-588

Negligence
bullying, and, 268-271
quality of educational provision, and, 527-533
Non-maintained special school
meaning, 69
Northern Ireland
religious education, 458-459
Nursery education, 62-64
early years development partnership, 63
legal entitlement, 64
local authorities, 63-64
local education authorities, 62-63
Nursery school
meaning, 69

OFSTED, 522-523
higher education, and, 525-526
Ombudsman, 31
Organisation of education, 59-152
further education, 120-132
regulation and control, 61
sixth form colleges, 120-132

Parental preference
school admissions, and, 166-171
Parents, 24-25
alternatives to preference, 258-260
duties, 252-258
attendance of child at school, 252-253
defences, 254-255
home-school agreements, and, 255-258
registered pupil, 253-255
right to express preference, 212-224
exceptions, 217-223
pupil permanently excluded from two or more schools, where, 223-224
racial grounds, 212-214
reasons for, 214-217
section 86(3)(A) exception, 217-220
section 86(3)(B) exception, 220-221
section 86(3) (C) exception, 221-223
rights, 24-25
who is, 24-25
Performance monitoring, 496-505
individual pupils, 500-502
league tables, 497-499
pupil records and reports, 502-505
duties of head teacher, 503-504
educational record, meaning, 503
head teacher's report to parents and adult pupils, 504-505
school performance, 496-500
Permanently excluded pupil
admission appeal, 242
Physical force, 277-285
power to restrain pupils, 284-285
Polytechnics, 3. *See also* HIGHER EDUCATION

Primary education
definition, 59-60
Primary school
meaning, 67
Psychological injury
management of maintained schools, and, 103-105

Qualifications and Curriculum Authority, 410-414. *See also* BASIC CURRICULUM
Quality of educational provision, 487-534
breach of contract, 533-534
common law liability, 526-527
educational malpractice in the USA, 530-532
further education, 521-524
Adult Learning Inspectorate, 522
common provisions, 523-524
inspection regime, 521-522
OFSTED, 522-523
governing body, role of, 490-491
higher education, 524-526
OFSTED inspections, 525-526
Labour government, and, 488-490
LEAs, 519-52
education development plans, 514
inspection of, 519-520
intervention in schools causing concern, 515
powers of intervention, 515-516
role of, 513-517
'serious weaknesses', 517
target duty, 513
maintained schools, 488-519
negligence, and, 527-533
further education, 532-533
higher education, 532-533
performance monitoring, 496-505. *See also* PERFORMANCE MONITORING
school attendance targets, 494-496
school inspections, 505-512. *See also* SCHOOL INSPECTIONS
school performance targets, 491-494
Secretary of State, role of, 517-519
education action zones, 517
improvement in standards, whether, 518-519
intervention in schools causing concern, 518
target-setting, 491-496

Race discrimination, 39-42
functions of LEAs, 40-41
religion, and, 41
school admissions, and, 212-214
segregation, 39
student unions, and, 143-144

Registered pupil
truanting, 253-254
Reinstatement, 306-310
meaning, 306-307
refusal of school to comply with direction, 307-309
trade dispute, and, 309
Religion, 439-466
collective worship. *See* COLLECTIVE WORSHIP
statutory provisions, 439-440
Religious affiliation
admissions criteria, and, 206-210
Religious and philosophical values, 479-481
human rights, and, 479-480
'partisan political' activities, 481
Religious education, 441-445
Canada, 465-466
sincerely held belief, 465-466
wearing of religious manifestations, 465
community schools, 442-443
compliance with statutory requirements, 444-445
foundation schools with religious character, 443-444
foundations without religious character, 442-443
human rights, and, 456-458
multi-cultural society, and, 466
Northern Ireland, 458-459
primary schools, 445
reasons for, 455-466
right to withdraw pupils, 452-455
secondary schools, 445
United States, 459-464
first Amendment to US Constitution, 459-464
voluntary aided schools with religious character, 444
voluntary controlled schools with religious character, 443-444
voluntary schools without religious character, 442-443
Restraint of pupils, 284-285

School admissions, 153-260
alternatives to parental preference, 258-260
appeals, 225-252. *See also* ADMISSION APPEALS
arrangements. *See* ADMISSIONS ARRANGEMENTS
duties of LEAs, 154-171
children to be educated in accordance with parental wishes, 158-161
single-sex schools, 160-161
grant-maintained schools, 165-166
non-discrimination, 161-166

School admissions—*contd*
duties of LEAs—*contd*
non-discrimination—*contd*
enforcement, 162-163
parental preference, 166-171
Code of Practice, 170-171
lawfulness of policy, and, 168-170
sufficient schools, 155-158
duties of parents, 252-258. *See also* PARENTS
LEA power to direct, 224
parents, rights of, 212-252. *See also* PARENTS
right to express preference, 212-224. *See also* PARENTS
supply and allocation of school places, 153-154
School attendance orders, 253
School attendance targets, 494-496
condition precedent, 496
duty to set, 495
notice by Secretary of State, 495
School boards, 2-3
School day
duration, 73-74
School discipline, 261-314
bullying. *See* BULLYING
corporal punishment, 277-285. *See also* CORPORAL PUNISHMENT
detention. *See* DETENTION
exclusions. *See* EXCLUSIONS
governing body, 263-264
head teacher, 264-272
improving, 262
LEAs, role of, 273-275
behaviour support plans, 274
duty to prepare plan relating to children with behavioural difficulties, 275
physical force, 277-285. *See also* PHYSICAL FORCE
restraint of pupils, 284-285
teacher, 273
School inspections, 505-512
inspection, 508-509
inspectors, 507
OFSTED, 505-506
registered inspectors, 507-508
report, 510
schools at risk, 510-512
School organisation committees, 106-107
School organisation in a local education authority, 105-120
adjudicators, 108
alteration of schools
mainstream schools maintained by LEAs, 109-114

School organisation in a local education authority—*contd*
  alteration of schools—*contd*
    prescribed alteration, 111-112
  closure of schools, 108-119
  discontinuance of schools, 114-119
    parents 'appropriate persons' to be consulted, whether, 115-116, 118
    publication of proposals, 114-115
    special schools maintained by LEAs, 117
  establishment of schools, 108-119
    consultation, 110-113
      meaning, 112-113
    mainstream schools maintained by LEAs, 109-114
  publication of statutory proposals, 113
    approval, 114
    objections, 113
  rationalisation of school places, 118-119
  reorganisation of schools, 108-119
  school organisation committees, 106-107
  school organisation plans, 107
School performance targets, 491-494
  groups of pupils with special educational needs, 493-494
  pupils aged 15, 492
Selective schools, 184-191
  general restriction on selection by ability and by aptitude, 184
  grammar schools, 189-191. *See also* GRAMMAR SCHOOLS
  selection by ability, 184-188
    banding, 185-188
    pre-existing arrangements, 185
  selection by aptitude for particular subjects, 188-189
School transport
  Free. *See* FREE SCHOOL TRANSPORT
School with a religious character
  meaning, 69
School year
  duration, 73-74
Schools, 64-74
  categories, 68-69
  meaning, 64-65
  pupil referral, 65
  types, 66-73
Schools Achieving Success (White Paper), 10-11
  diversity in schooling, 10-11
  excellence, innovation and diversity, 11
  inclusive faith schools, 11
  modernising education law, 15-16
Schools with a religious character, 70-73
  Australia, 71-73
  DOGS case, 71-72
  United States, 71-73

Scotland
  children's rights, 28-29
Secondary education
  definition, 60
Secondary school
  meaning, 67
Secretary of State, 16-19
  functions of local education authorities, and, 17-18
  relevant policy considerations, and 17
  role, 16-19
Selective school
  meaning, 69
Sex discrimination, 37-39
  'responsible body', 38
  school admissions, and, 161-166
Sex and relationship education, 467-475
  content, 469
  contraceptive advice, 469-472
  right to withdraw pupil from, 472-475
  statements of policy, 468-469
  under age sex, 469-472
Sixth form colleges, 120-132. *See also* FURTHER EDUCATION
Special educational needs, 315-405
  assessment, 346-351
    parent's right to request, 349
    statutory procedure, 351
  children 'in need', 337-339
    resource consideration, 339
  children unable to attend school through illness, 325-328
  children with disabilities, 323-325. *See also* Children with disabilities
  definitions, 318-328
  Disability Discrimination Act 1995, 380-388. *See also* DISABILITY DISCRIMINATION ACT 1995
  disabled persons, 379-380
    young persons, and, 379-380
  district health authorities, and, 335-337
  governing body, role of, 341-345
    provide information to parents, 342-343
    relationship with LEA, 343-345
    secure appropriate provision, 341-342
  human rights, and, 401-405
    discrimination, 404
    education, scope of, 403-404
    equal treatment, 404
  identification, 345-346
  LEA
    compliance with SENT orders, 341
    duty to educate in mainstream education, 328-330
    education otherwise than in mainstream schools, 330-331

Special educational need—*contd*
LEA—*contd*
  mainstream school or special school,
    332-333
  provision of advice, information and
    mediation, 339-341
  resolution of disputes, 740
  role of, 328-341
  view of, 316-317
Learning and Skills Council, 377-378
learning difficulty, 320
local authorities, and, 335-337
meaning, 318
nature of, 319-323
rethinking rights, duties and resources,
  371-372
statement of, 351-365
  amendment, 365
  choice of school, 360-365
    LEA not under absolute duty to
      name school, 363-364
    parental wishes, 361-363
    payment of fees, 365
    special schools, 365
  content, 353-365
  form, 353-365
  meaning of special educational needs,
    356-357
  meaning of special educational
    provision, 356-360
  placement, 360-365
  reassessment, 365
  review, 365
  school's right to request, 350-352
  statutory test, 352
  writing, 354-356
tortious liability of LEA for failure to
  diagnose and/or remedy, 388-401
  causation, 394-395
  Bromley case, 393-394
  co-existence of statutory duty and
    common law duty of care, 389-
    390
  common law, 397-398
  direct liability, 390, 398
  Dorset case, 390-392
  evidence, 394-395
  evolution towards wider liability, 400-
    401
  general approach, 389
  Hampshire case, 392-393
  Phelps case, 396-399
  public and private law, 389
  vicarious liability, 390
whether child must attend school,
  333-335
young adults, 373-379
  assessment, 378-379

Special educational need—*contd*
young adults—*contd*
  Qualifications and Curriculum
    Authority, and, 379
  LEAs, and, 373-374
**Special Educational Needs Tribunal
(SENT), 30, 365-372**
access to justice, and, 369-370
Annual Report 1999/2000, 367
appeals, 365-368
future, 368-372
High Court, appeal to, 368
jurisdiction, 371
powers, 368
quinquennial review, 370-371
reviews, 365-368
Special educational provision
meaning, 319, 320-323
Special school
meaning, 69
Specialist schools
proposal to increase number of, 70
Statutory guidance, 13-15
legal effect, 15
meaning and effect of obligation to act
  under 14-15
Statutory instruments, 13
Student finance, 145-152
discretionary awards, 145-146
fees, 146-147
grants, 146-147
  living costs, for, 152
  postgraduate students, 152
loans. *See* STUDENT LOANS
mandatory awards, 145-146
tuition fees, 147-150
Student loans, 150-152
cancellation, 151-152
Student unions, 141-145
meaning, 141-143
race discrimination, and, 143-144
Students
litigation by, 29

Teacher
school discipline, and, 273
Trade dispute
reinstatement, and, 309
Tribunals, 30-31
Leggatt Review, 30-31
reform proposals, 30-31

United States
Religious education. *See* RELIGIOUS EDUCATION
Universities. *See also* HIGHER EDUCATION
academic judgment, 581-583
assessment appeals, 583-591

Universities—*contd*
  assessment appeals—*contd*
    failure to take into account relevant
        consideration, 588-589
    irrationality, 589-591
    natural justice, 583-588
  breach of contract, 596-604
    relationship between student and
        university, 597-603
  complaints procedures, 573-611
    LEAs, and, 608-609
    reform, 609-611
    Secretary of State, and, 608
  grievance procedures, 591-592
  historical development, 3
  human rights, and, 604-608
    Article 2 of Protocol 1, 607-608
    Article 6, 604-607
  hybrid, legal status of, 138
  judicial review, 579-603
    exercise of discretion, 594-596
    last resort, as, 580
  'new'
    complaints procedures, 574

Universities—*contd*
  'old'
    complaints procedures, 574-579
  student conduct and discipline, 592
  use of title, 136-137
  visitor, 574-579
    origin of office, 575-576
    review of decisions, 575-578
    role, 578-579
    role of court, and, 578

Vicarious liability
  management of maintained schools, and,
      99-103
Voluntary aided school
  meaning, 68
Voluntary controlled school
  meaning, 69
Voluntary school
  meaning, 68

Young adults
  special needs, 373-379

DATE DUE

DEMCO, INC. 38-2931